ECONOMIC AND SOCIAL COMMISSION FOR ASIA AND THE PACIFIC
Bangkok, Thailand

PROCEEDINGS
OF THE
TENTH SESSION
OF THE
COMMITTEE ON NATURAL RESOURCES

WATER RESOURCES SERIES
No. 59

UNITED NATIONS
New York
1985

ST/ESCAP/SER.F/59

UNITED NATIONS PUBLICATION
Sales No. 85.II.F.14
ISBN   92-1-119273-0
ISSN   0082-8130

Price $US 30.00

FOREWORD

This publication is presented in three parts: part one consists of the report of the tenth session of the Committee on Natural Resources of the Economic and Social Commission for Asia and the Pacific (ESCAP), which was held at Bangkok, Thailand, from 25 to 31 October 1983; part two contains the working and technical papers presented by the secretariat; and part three contains information and technical papers submitted by Governments.

Because of limitations of space and budget, it has not been possible to reproduce all the papers in full; some have been summarized or abridged.

The views expressed by individual authors are their own and do not necessarily reflect the views of the United Nations.

In the presentation of data in tables in the text, the use of a dash (—) indicates nil or a negligible amount, and the use of leaders (. . .) indicates that no data were available when the table was being prepared.

National currency equivalents for countries included in the publication

Country	Currency and abbreviation	Unit of currency per United States dollar (period average)		
		1979	1980	1983
Australia	Australian dollar ($A)	0.895	0.885	1.09
China	RMB	–	–	1.99
Iran	Rial	–	–	85.20
Indonesia	Rupiah (Rp)	623.05	627.07	987.0
Japan	Yen (Y)	219.41	232.10	230.5
New Zealand	New Zealand dollar ($NZ)	0.971	0.975	1.53
Philippines	Peso (P)	7.378	7.492	13.97
Sri Lanka	Rupee (SRs)	15.569	16.208	24.38
Thailand	Baht	20.419	20.439	22.96
USSR	Roubles (Rou)			0.75

Note: Conversion given shows market rate/par or central rate taken as monthly average in the market of the country.

CONTENTS

Part One
REPORT OF THE SESSION

		Page
Summary of conclusions and recommendations		3
I.	Organization of the session	5
II.	Review of implementation of the Mar del Plata Action Plan	6
III.	Multidisciplinary and systems approach to integrated river basin development	8
IV.	Assessment and consideration of irrigation efficiency in irrigated areas of the ESCAP region	8
V.	Pollution problems related to the current programmes of low-cost technology applications to water supply and sanitation in the ESCAP region	9
VI.	Activities of ESCAP in the appraisal, development and management of natural resources	10
VII.	Activities of other international bodies in the appraisal, development and management of water resources	12
VIII.	Review of the medium-term plan (1984-1989) and the programme of work and priorities in the appraisal, development and management of Natural Resources (1984-1985): Programme changes	14
IX.	Consideration of the agenda and arrangements for subsequent sessions	16
X.	Other matters — wild life and national parks management in the ESCAP region	17
XI.	Adoption of the report	17

Part Two
WORKING PAPERS PRESENTED BY THE SECRETARIAT

		Page
I.	Review of implementation of the Mar del Plata Action Plan	21
II.	Progress report on the interagency task force on water for Asia and the Pacific	40
III.	Multidisciplinary and systems approach to integrated river basin development	41
IV.	Water as a factor in energy resource development	54
V.	Assessment and consideration of irrigation efficiency in irrigated areas of the ESCAP region	73
VI.	Assessment of irrigation efficiency — note prepared and presented by the United Nations Food and Agriculture Organization (FAO-RAPA)	82
VII.	Pollution problems related to the current programmes of low cost technology applications to water supply and sanitation in the ESCAP region	95
	A. Measures to reduce the cost of rural water supply	95
	B. Measures to reduce the cost of urban waste disposal facilities	112
	C. Water quality management in the ESCAP region	128
	D. Low cost water treatment process and equipment	150
	E. Low cost wastewater treatment process and equipment	163
	F. Low cost technology for water supply and sanitation: Pollution and health problems related to incorrect applications	178

Part Three
COUNTRY INFORMATION PAPERS SUBMITTED BY GOVERNMENT REPRESENTATIVES

Page

I.	Australia	193
II.	People's Republic of China	200
III.	Indonesia	203
IV.	The Islamic Republic of Iran	229
V.	Japan	237
VI.	New Zealand	258
VII.	Philippines	268
VIII.	Sri Lanka	274
IX.	Thailand	280
X.	U.S.S.R.	296

LIST OF TABLES

Page

Table	1.	National water policy and planning in the ESCAP regional countries	27
Table	2.	Water charges in some ESCAP countries	28
Table	3.	National water legislation status in some ESCAP countries	29
Table	4.	Institutional arrangements for co-ordinating water related interests in some ESCAP countries	30
Table	5.	Shared water resources development in some ESCAP countries	31
Table	6.	Observation networks and data collection status in ESCAP countries	32
Table	7.	Data processing and dissemination, areal assessment and co-ordination in some ESCAP countries	33
Table	8.	Main areas of water resources development for agriculture in ESCAP countries	34
Table	9.	Trained manpower and advisory services in support of agricultural water development in some ESCAP countries	35
Table	10.	Manpower situation in water resources development in some ESCAP countries	36
Table	11.	Education and training of manpower in some ESCAP member countries	37
Table	12.	Research and development in water resources in some ESCAP member countries	38
Table	13.	Technical co-operation among developing countries in the ESCAP region	39
Table	14.	Water requirements for some energy conversion and extraction processes in terms of water-energy coefficients	58
Table	15.	Selected countries obtaining most of their electricity from hydropower 1980	59
Table	16.	Estimated hydropower potential, economically exploitable potential and peak loads in developing countries of ESCAP region (1980)	61
Table	17.	Irrigation in Asia Pacific region	90
Table	18.	Cereal production in Asia Pacific regional countries	91
Table	19.	Rice production in Asia Pacific countries	92

Table 20. Average conveyance efficiency in irrigation   93

Table 21. Average farm ditch efficiency in irrigation   93

Table 22. Average distribution efficiency of rotational supply under optimum conditions   93

Table 23. Average application efficiency in irrigation   93

Table 24. Designed and actual efficiency ranges   94

Table 25. Some examples of conveyance loss in irrigation system   94

Table 26. Some examples of distribution losses in irrigation   94

Table 27. Some examples of loss in early stage of irrigation in Muda Project, Malaysia   95

Table 28. Cost data for various sources for water supply   102

Table 29. Financial costs per metre of various pipe materials   108

Table 30. Economic costs per metre of various pipe materials   109

Table 31. Economical life time of bamboo pipes for different methods of protection and different project
locations   109

Table 32. A general comparison of on-site and off-site technologies   122

Table 33. Average annual investment and recurrent cost ($US) per household for sanitation technologies   123

Table 34. Selected input costs and conversion factors for sanitation   124

Table 35. Average annual on-site, collection and treatment costs per household   124

Table 36. Descriptive comparison of urban sanitation technologies for developing countries   127

Table 37. Severity and extent of water quality problems in some ESCAP regional countries   130

Table 38. Major contributors to degradation of water quality in some ESCAP regional countries   131

Table 39. Problems relating to or induced by degradation of water quality in some ESCAP regional countries . . .   132

Table 40. Action being taken for water quality management in some ESCAP regional countries   134

Table 41. Availability and general objectives of national policy for water quality management and its consistency
with national water policy in some ESCAP regional countries   135

Table 42. Legislative and institutional measures to implement national policy and achieve objectives of water
quality management in some ESCAP regional countries   137

Table 43. Technical strategies for implementation of national policy and achievement of objectives of water
quality management in some ESCAP regional countries   138

Table 44. Availability of water quality monitoring systems in some ESCAP regional countries   140

Table 45. Stream-water quality parameters usually monitored in some ESCAP regional countries   141

Table 46. Education, training and research activities to implement national policy and achieve objectives of water
quality management in some ESCAP regional countries   143

Table 47. Economic and financial instruments for implementing national policy and achieving objectives of water
quality management in some ESCAP regional countries   145

Table 48. Types of low cost water treatment for different qualities of groundwater   151

Table 49. Types of low cost water treatment for different qualities of surface water   154

Table 50. Filter media characteristics   157

Table 51. Treatment potential of various processes in removing contaminants from raw water   160

Table 52. Effectiveness of water treatment processes in removing various impurities   162

Table 53. Cost comparison of biological treatment processes   165

Table 54. Performance of wetland processes (percentage removal of contaminants)   168

Table 55. Nutrient removal by water hyacinths   170

Table 56. Performance of physical treatment processes 171

Table 57. Disinfectant options 173

Table 58. Amounts of chlorine required for disinfection of sewage and sewage effluents 173

Table 59. Performance of selected wastewater treatment processes in removing particulate solid materials and organic compounds 175

Table 60. Performance of selected wastewater treatment processes in pathogen removal 176

Table 61. Diseases related to improper use of low cost technologies 179

Table 62. Pollution and health problems related to use of simple, low cost and appropriate technologies in water supply and sanitation 187

Table 63. Summary of recent Australian contributions to water resources development in the ESCAP region ... 199

Table 64. Wells already commissioned and those handed over to the farmers in Indonesia 206

Table 65. Reclaimed and settled swamps in Sumatra and Kalimantan in Indonesia 207

Table 66. Hydrological simulation results of CJC project in Indonesia 218

Table 67. CJC (Indonesia) project optimization model results 221

Table 68. CJC (Indonesia) project scheme designation 222

Table 69. CJC (Indonesia) project scheme characteristics 222

Table 70. CJC (Indonesia) project alternative characteristics 223

Table 71. CJC (Indonesia) project multicriteria analysis comparison of various alternatives 224

Table 72. CJC (Indonesia) project recommended programme alternative features 226

Table 73. Present national land use data of Iran 236

Table 74. Projected land use scheme of Iran 236

Table 74A. Water Resources in Iran 236

Table 75. Precipitation and available water resources in Japan 237

Table 76. Water demand trend in Japan 239

Table 77. Water demand and supply forecast to 1990 in Japan 241

Table 78. Proposed comprehensive measures regarding water supply and demand in Japan 242

Table 79. List of major dams in Japan 244

Table 80. List of dams under construction in 1983 in Japan 244

Table 81. List of economic benefits from completed dams in Japan 245

Table 82. Project work items under reservoir area development scheme in Japan 245

Table 83. Projected arable area versus irrigable area in Japan 247

Table 84. Water demand for agricultural use in Japan 247

Table 85. Industrial water consumption trend in Japan 250

Table 86. Industrial water consumption by sectors (1980) in Japan 251

Table 87. Existing hydropower generating facilities in Japan 252

Table 88. Hydropower generating facilities under construction in 1983 in Japan 253

Table 89. Trend of hydropower generating capacity in total generating capacity in Japan 253

Table 90. Trend of hydroenergy production in total electric energy in Japan 253

Table 91. Share of hydropower energy in primary energy supply in Japan 254

Table 92. Accomplishment rate on water quality criteria in Japan 254

Table 93. Training courses and dispatch of experts on water resources by Japan (1980-1982) 257

Table 94. New Zealand irrigation area coverage 260

Table 95. Medium term investment in water resources development in Sri Lanka 275

Table 96. Proposed new water resources development project in Sri Lanka 277

Table 97. Thailand's irrigated area and other related information, 1981-1982 281

Table 98. Thailand's water resources development summary, 1980-1983 284

Table 99. Water resources development activities by national energy administration of Thailand 284

Table 100. Construction and maintenance of water resources projects undertaken by accelerated rural development office of Thailand 285

Table 101. Rural community development (6 centres) undertaken by accelerated rural development office of Thailand 286

Table 102. Construction of water resources projects for poor villages undertaken by accelerated rural development office of Thailand 286

Table 103. Well drilling data by the Department of Mineral Resources in Thailand 286

Table 104. Groundwater wells drilled by the Public Works Department of Thailand 287

Table 105. Water supply concession in Thailand in 1982 287

Table 106. Hydrological investigation in Thailand in 1983 287

Table 107. Network of hydro-meteorological and hydrological stations in 1976 in Thailand 288

Table 108. Summary of hydro potential in Thailand 289

Table 109. List of hydroelectric projects in Thailand 289

Table 110. Proposed hydroelectric projects to 1993 in Thailand 290

Table 111. Potential international projects involving Thailand 290

Table 112. Existing dams and hydropower plants of Thailand 291

Table 113. Dams and hydropower plants under construction in Thailand in 1983 292

Table 114. Dams, reservoirs and other related projects for government approval in Thailand 293

Table 115. Increase in irrigation area in the republics of Central Asia and Kazakhstan 305

Table 116. Increase in gross agricultural production in the USSR 305

Table 117. Increase in water intake in the republics of Central Asia and Kazakhstan 307

Table 118. Economic development of Uzbekistan 307

Table 119. Effectiveness of the functioning of economy branches connected with WMS in Uzbekistan 308

LIST OF FIGURES

Page

Fig. 1. Stages of a systems approach to integrated river basin development 47

Fig. 2. Energy development in a water resource system 57

Fig. 3. Water consumption in refining and conversion processes 58

Fig. 4. Graphical representation of multiobjective theory 70

Fig. 5. Various irrigation efficiencies of water use 83

Fig. 6. Main irrigation system efficiency and costs of operation and maintenance per hectare 85

Fig. 7. Farm irrigation losses in the field 87

Fig. 8. Schematic diagram of water collection off roof thatch 99

Fig. 9. Extending the rafters to produce an overhanging eave 99

Fig. 10. Using split bamboo guttering with palm thatch 100
Fig. 11. Simple device to separate debris from rain water during collection 100
Fig. 12. Dragon-bone water lift 107
Fig. 13. Cross-section of glass fibre SWS "Camp" filtration unit in sand bed 107
Fig. 14. Stainless steel minifiltration unit buried in a sand bed 107
Fig. 15. Ventilated improved pit latrine 115
Fig. 16. Ventilated improved double pit latrine 116
Fig. 17. Pour-flush units for displaced pits 117
Fig. 18. Pour-flush toilet-septic-tank systems 118
Fig. 19. Evolution of governmental programmes in water quality control 135
Fig. 20. Essential elements of comprehensive national water quality control programme 138
Fig. 21. Multiple-tray aerator 152
Fig. 22. Cascade aerator 152
Fig. 23. Multiple-platform aerator 152
Fig. 24. Rapid filter (open, gravity type) 153
Fig. 25. Rapid filtration of pre-treated water 153
Fig. 26. Horizontal gravel filter 153
Fig. 27. Charcoal water filter 154
Fig. 28. Simplified slow sand filter 155
Fig. 29. Simple slow sand filter 156
Fig. 30. Sketch of a 4-person household slow sand filter 156
Fig. 31. Jempeng stone filter 158
Fig. 32. Influence of time and temperature on survival of selected pathogens in composting 166
Fig. 33. Infant mortality and sanitation coverage in some southwest Asian countries 180
Fig. 34. C.J.C. river basin development project location in Indonesia 213
Fig. 35. C.J.C. project (Indonesia) situation map 214
Fig. 36. Hydraulic network of C.J.C. project in Indonesia 217
Fig. 37. C.J.C. (Indonesia) project optimization model (economic data) 219
Fig. 38. C.J.C. (Indonesia) project recommended alternatives 225
Fig. 38A. Flow diagramme of the System Approach in C.J.C. Project 228
Fig. 39. Major river basin map of Iran 231
Fig. 40. Water management regions and study areas of Iran 233
Fig. 41. Major dams in Iran 234
Fig. 41A. Water cycle in Iran 235
Fig. 42. New Zealand local authority sewage disposal system coverage of total population 262
Fig. 43. New Zealand water and soil conservation administration 265
Fig. 44. Informational composition of the SWC parts in the USSR 297
Fig. 45. Continuation of Fig. 44 298
Fig. 46. Structural pattern of water use in the USSR 300
Fig. 47. The state water Cadastre — Information retrieval system — Water use flow chart used in the USSR 301
Fig. 48. Scheme of WMS influence on the economy of arid zone in the USSR 309

Part One

REPORT OF THE SESSION

Part One
REPORT OF THE SESSION

SUMMARY OF CONCLUSIONS AND RECOMMENDATIONS

The pertinent conclusions and recommendations which the Committee wishes to bring to the attention of the Commission are as follows:

(1) The Committee urged that the international community and the United Nations financing agencies should take urgent and appropriate steps to enable the developing countries to achieve the objectives of the Mar del Plata Action Plan (paragraph 14).

(2) It endorsed, in general, the recommendations in paragraph 16 to facilitate the implementation of the Mar del Plata Action Plan.

(3) It emphasized the need for TCDC activities in water resource management and development on a greater scale and called upon the secretariat to expand its activities in this field (paragraph 19).

(4) It agreed on the importance and necessity of taking into consideration the points in paragraph 24 in the application of multidisciplinary and systems approach to integrated river basin development to achieve maximum benefits.

(5) It recommended that ESCAP should encourage and support exchange of information regarding the experiences and results of the application of the multidisciplinary and systems approach among the countries of the region (paragraph 27).

(6) It considered that a comprehensive approach for the improvement of irrigation efficiency should be adopted and should include engineering, managerial, agricultural, socio-economic and institutional measures (paragraph 32).

(7) It recommended that a methodology should be devised so that irrigation efficiency could be determined on the basis of uniform standards (paragraph 36).

(8) It recommended the strategies in paragraph 43 to overcome pollution and health problems related to low-cost technology applications to water supply and sanitation in the region.

(9) It expressed support for the organization of a seminar on water quality monitoring systems (paragraph 46).

(10) It requested the secretariat to look into the possibility of publishing the proceedings of the ESCAP seminar on water resources development planning organized in the USSR in 1982 (paragraph 53).

(11) It noted that comparatively more attention should be paid on the development of mini-hydroelectricity under the regional programme of action on NRSE on the basis of a time-bound action plan (paragraph 62), and that the ESCAP energy programmes should be undertaken on a priority basis as well as in a more practical and feasible manner (paragraph 63).

(12) It agreed with the following suggestions towards the successful implementation of ESCAP activities in the field of energy:

(a) Strengthening linkages with member countries;

(b) Placing emphasis on least developed countries and rural areas;

(c) Fostering co-operation among developing countries (paragraph 64).

(13) It expressed appreciation of the support extended by UNDP and donor countries, both developed and developing, and strongly urged their continued support towards the implementation of ESCAP's energy programmes (paragraph 65).

(14) It endorsed the activities of the secretariat and its efforts for the preparation of reviews and analyses of mineral resources in the region, compilation of regional special-purpose maps on geology and minerals, programmes for dissemination of experience and technology on the search and exploration of mineral and energy raw materials onshore and offshore (paragraph 68).

(15) It supported the major training activity for 1984 of RMRDC namely the Symposium on the Geology of Tin Deposits to be held in Guangxi, China, in October/November 1984 (paragraph 70).

(16) It strongly appealed to UNDP for continued institutional support in addition to the existing programme support to RMRDC (paragraph 71).

(17) It suggested that efforts should be made to recruit associate experts for the Regional Remote Sensing Programme (paragraph 78).

(18) It urged that the pilot information system for remote sensing, surveying and mapping should be carefully structured in the early stages to ensure its effectiveness and usefulness (paragraph 81).

(19) It expressed the view that the secretariat should provide the countries with more detailed and timely information on the fellowships for remote sensing and in the announcement of programme activities. It also recommended that the fellowship funds be used for advanced training abroad only (paragraph 82).

(20) It also expressed the view that sufficient time should be given to the countries so that they could properly prepare themselves for the meeting for the establishment of the Intergovernmental Consultative Committee on remote sensing. The need to minimize overheads on Committee meetings and to concentrate more on the technical work was also urged (paragraph 85).

(21) It requested that the Information Note compiled by DIESA giving a complete listing of all scheduled activities of the organizations of the United Nations system engaged in water resources, continue to be compiled and also supplied to ESCAP member countries on a regular basis (paragraph 96).

(22) It recommended that more work be carried out on the hydrological aspects of the programme element 2.3 (paragraph 102).

(23) It also recommended that the following activity be added to the programme of work for 1984-1985 as output (ii) (e) under element 2.1, "Study tour to selected irrigation systems in the region (1985) (XB)" (paragraph 104).

(24) It noted that the organization of the meeting of ministers of energy scheduled for 1985 should be considered after the specific issues to be discussed were identified and after views of the member countries were ascertained; and requested that the secretariat place its specific proposals before the Commission at its fortieth session (paragraph 106).

(25) It urged that the programme for meeting the energy requirements of rural areas and programmes for improvement in the efficient use of energy should be given more emphasis (paragraph 110).

(26) It recommended the programme changes listed in paragraph 112.

(27) It endorsed the recommendation by the Committee for Programme and Co-ordination that programme element 1.4 (Energy Conservation and Conversion Policy) of the work programme on science and technology of ESCAP be included under the energy programme (paragraph 113).

(28) It recommended the programme changes listed in paragraph 115.

(29) It also recommended that the following activity be added as output (c) under programme element 1.3 (i) "Seminar on Drilling, Sampling and Borehole Logging (1985) (XB)" (paragraph 116).

(30) It further recommended that ESCAP should concentrate in helping the States in the region to build up their national capabilities for better utilization of marine resources and ensure that overlapping of functions within the agencies of the United Nations system should be minimized if not avoided (paragraph 120).

(31) It reiterated the need for proper communications with the appropriate agencies in remote sensing; expressed its concern of the difficult communication procedure; and requested that copies of invitations should be also sent directly to the appropriate agencies or institutes (paragraph 123).

(32) It suggested that pilot studies on remote sensing, surveying and mapping should include the monitoring of land surface cover and biomas (paragraph 124).

(33) It supported the work programme of the secretariat in the field of remote sensing, surveying and mapping and the idea that participation should be drawn from the ESCAP region on the basis of technical co-operation among developing countries (paragraph 127).

(34) It stressed the importance of evolving the Regional Remote Sensing Programme through workshops/symposia whose themes should be focused to some specific applications and carefully planned and structured to achieve the goals of energizing awareness of remote sensing and also evolving plan of action for joint projects (paragraph 128). In evolving the programmes, maximum co-ordination between the United Nations agencies and minimized overheads on the secretariat's activities were urged. The ESCAP Regional Remote Sensing Programme should accordingly be co-ordinated on its technical elements with the United Nations Outer Space Affairs Division which is following up UNISPACE-82 activities so as to avoid duplication of efforts (paragraph 129).

(35) It recommended the provisional agenda for its eleventh session as detailed in paragraph 131.

(36) It also recommended that the topics listed in paragraph 133 be considered for inclusion in the agenda for the thirteenth session.

I. ORGANIZATION OF THE SESSION

1. The Committee on Natural Resources held its tenth session at Bangkok from 25 to 31 October 1983.

Attendance

2. The session was attended by representatives of the following ESCAP member and associate member countries: Australia, Bangladesh, Brunei, China, Democratic Kampuchea, France, India, Indonesia, Iran, Japan, Lao People's Democratic Republic, Malaysia, Netherlands, New Zealand, Pakistan, Philippines, Republic of Korea, Sri Lanka, Thailand, Union of Soviet Socialist Republics, United Kingdom of Great Britain and Northern Ireland, United States of America and Viet Nam. A representative of Israel also attended in accordance with paragraph 9 of the terms of reference of ESCAP.

3. The following United Nations bodies and specialized agencies were represented: United Nations Department of Technical Co-operation for Development (DTCD), United Nations Department of International Economic and Social Affairs (DIESA), United Nations Industrial Development Organization (UNIDO), United Nations Children's Fund (UNICEF), United Nations Development Programme (UNDP), United Nations Environment Programme (UNEP), International Labour Organisation (ILO), Food and Agriculture Organization of the United Nations (FAO), United Nations Education, Scientific and Cultural Organization (UNESCO) and World Health Organization (WHO). The Interim Committee for Co-ordination of Investigations of the Lower Mekong Basin and the International Commission on Irrigation and Drainage (ICID) were also represented. There were also observers from the Asian Institute of Technology (AIT) and the East-West Centre.

Opening of the session

4. The Executive Secretary of ESCAP opened the session.

5. In his opening statement, the Executive Secretary pinpointed the current major issues concerning natural resources in general. The chief aims of the Committee should be to find approaches that would enable member countries to develop natural resources in ways that were not only economically efficient and sustainable but that also guarded against irreversible damage to the physical environment or shortchanging future generations.

6. Referring to the principal subject of the session which was water, he traced the important role of water in history which illustrated the need to give great attention to water resource development in the region. It was fitting that the Commission continued to give considerable attention to the development of water resources since the region had a number of important rivers systems such as Changjiang, Hwangho, Mekong, Irrawaddy, Brahmaputra, Ganges and Indus that were veritable "sleeping giants" in terms of their vast beneficial potential to the region. Briefly reviewing each of the substantive issues before the session he expressed the hope that the Committee would express its views on each issue and recommend corresponding appropriate measures needed to be taken at the national level as well as at the regional level for the benefit of the member countries.

Election of officers

7. The Committee elected Mr. R. Rangachari (India) as Chairman, Mr. Sunthorn Ruanglek (Thailand) and Mr. Nong Kaiqing (China) as Vice-Chairmen and Mr. R.S. Jayaratne (Sri Lanka) as Rapporteur. It also elected Mr. Mardjono Notodihardjo (Indonesia) as Chairman of the Drafting Committee.

Adoption of the agenda

8. The Meeting adopted the following agenda:

1. Opening of the session

2. Election of officers

3. Adoption of the agenda

4. Review of the implementation of the Mar del Plata Action Plan

5. Multidisciplinary and systems approach to integrated river basin development

6. Assessment and consideration of irrigation efficiency in the irrigated areas of the ESCAP region

7. Pollution problems related to the current programmes of low-cost technology applications to water supply and sanitation in the ESCAP region

8. Activities of ESCAP in the appraisal, development and management of natural resources

   (a) Water resources

   (b) Energy resources

   (c) Mineral resources

   (d) Remote sensing, surveying and mapping

9. Activities of other international bodies in the appraisal, development and management of water resources

10. Review of the medium-term plan, 1984-1989, and the programme of work and priorities in the appraisal, development and management of natural resources, 1984-1985: programme changes:

    (a) Water resources

    (b) Energy resources

    (c) Mineral resources

(d) Remote sensing, surveying and mapping

11. Consideration of the agenda and arrangements for subsequent sessions of the Committee

12. Other matters

13. Adoption of the report

II. REVIEW OF THE IMPLEMENTATION OF THE
MAR DEL PLATA ACTION PLAN
(Agenda item 4)

9. The Committee considered documents E/ESCAP/NR.10/11 and E/ESCAP/NR.10/19 prepared by the ESCAP secretariat and some country papers and noted the relevant information provided in document E/C.7/1983/11 which was prepared in the context of the review and appraisal of the International Development Strategy for the Third United Nations Development Decade and submitted to the eighth session of the Committee on Natural Resources of the Economic and Social Council in June 1983. The report was prepared by the Secretary General of the United Nations in close consultation with the regional commissions and specialized agencies through the Intersecretariat Group for Water of the Administrative Committee on Co-ordination (ACC) and presented a broad picture of the current situation of and prospects for water resources development at the national level as a follow-up to the Mar del Plata Action Plan.

10. The representative of DIESA drew the attention of the Committee to resolutions 1981/80 and 1981/81 of 24 July 1981 and 1983/57 of 28 July 1983 of the Economic and Social Council concerning the implementation of the Mar del Plata Action Plan.

11. The Committee noted the information provided on the current status in 22 countries and areas of the region in six broad areas covered by the Mar del Plata Action Plan. Those areas were: (a) policy, planning, legislation and institutional arrangements; (b) assessment of water resources; (c) water resource development and use for agriculture; (d) education, training and public information; (e) research and development; and (f) technical co-operation among developing countries (TCDC).

12. It noted with interest the additional information provided by some representatives in their respective countries concerning the topics covered by the Mar del Plata Action Plan.

13. Some problems mentioned which could be valid for a number of countries were: lack of accountability of water

authorities to governments and communities, environmental damage, increased competition for limited financial resources, lack of trained manpower and inadequate information. Suggested solutions to those problems were: improved planning, better institutional arrangements, co-ordinated land and water management, improved efficiency of water use, substitution of water use, improved data collection, improvement of water quality and proper catchment controls.

14. The Committee noted that the Mar del Plata Action Plan envisaged multidimensional activities and called for investment of huge resources which was beyond the capacity of many developing countries and particularly the least developed countries. The situation therefore called for massive transfer of resources and technology. The Committee urged that the international community and the United Nations financing agencies should take urgent and appropriate steps to enable the developing countries to achieve the objectives of the Action Plan. In that connection, the representative of Australia informed the Committee that his Government would be prepared to consider favourably requests for assistance from the ESCAP secretariat for that purpose subject to budgetary constraints and in the light of other commitments in the region.

15. Some delegations noted that limiting and eliminating the arms race under the conditions of peace and security and partial diversion of funds therefrom could be a source of additional funds for development of natural resources in the ESCAP region. Some delegations, however, regretted that matter had been introduced as it was outside the mandate of the Committee and was irrelevant in the context of the subject under discussion.

16. The Committee endorsed, in general, the following recommendations:

    (a) Countries without a national water policy and a master plan for water resources development should give serious consideration to formulating the first and preparing the second;

(b) Governments should make continuous efforts to make the beneficiaries share more of the costs of water projects in order to improve financial viability and ensure the efficient operation and proper maintenance of the projects;

(c) Countries still lacking national legislation regulating the ownership of or the right to use water and the protection of water quality should consider framing such legislation compatible with modern management and planning principles.

(d) Where no mechanism exists for co-ordinating all water interests at the national level, the countries concerned should consider setting up arrangements to ensure real co-ordination among all bodies responsible for the investigation, development and management of water resources;

(e) The development of shared water resources in the region is an area in which more efforts are required to be exerted by all concerned, particularly in the establishment of joint programmes and institutions necessary for the co-ordinated development of such resources;

(f) In a number of Asian countries and Pacific island countries the observation networks of water resource data need improvement which should be carried out as soon as possible;

(g) In view of the large demand for trained manpower at various levels in the field of water resource development, it was recommended that the establishment of the Regional Network for Training in Water Resources Development which was part of the work programme of the ESCAP secretariat be implemented as soon as possible to enhance the training capacities and capabilities of the countries' institutions participating in the network;

(h) More resources, both national and external, should be provided to support water research;

(i) The ESCAP secretariat should implement as early as possible the preparation of a roster of water specialists available for TCDC as envisaged in its 1984-1985 work programme.

17. Several representatives expressed the view that as the beneficiaries of water projects in developing countries were very poor, they would be unable to share fully in the project costs and that for many years, the sharing would continue to be on a limited basis. It was pointed out, however, that if project costs were not shared by the

beneficiaries, the operation and maintenance of the projects would likely be inadequate owing to lack of funds.

18. The Committee noted the seriousness and the delicate problems of shared water resource development. Noting that the Indo-Bangladesh Joint Rivers Commission between Bangladesh and India was endeavouring to resolve the various issues and that some progress had been achieved, it emphasized that it was most essential to reach a tangible and acceptable solution in the near future.

19. The Committee emphasized the need for TCDC activities in water resource management and development to be undertaken on a greater scale and called upon the secretariat to expand its activities in that regard.

20. A suggestion was made that a more quantitative approach be adopted in monitoring the progress of the Mar del Plata Action Plan. A major difficulty in that regard was the non-availability at the time of adoption of the Mar del Plata Action Plan of data which could be used as a baseline reference for quantitative monitoring on a country basis. The Committee noted that compliance with that suggestion could be facilitated if all member countries provided the water resource statistics requested annually by the secretariat for publication in the ESCAP *Statistical Yearbook.*

21. Regional member countries concerned were furnished advance copies of a comprehensive questionnaire on the progress and prospects of the Mar del Plata Action Plan. The information to be obtained by means of the questionnaire would be used for both regional and global reviews. The global review would be carried out in 1985 by the Committee on Natural Resources of the Economic and Social Council and would include the mid-period review of the International Drinking Water Supply and Sanitation Decade.

22. The Committee also noted the progress report on the work of the Interagency Task Froce on Water for Asia and the Pacific. The Task Force had been established by ESCAP in response to a recommendation of the Committee at its fourth session to assist co-operation and, as appropriate, joint action among participating bodies in support of national programmes for investigation, development and management of water. It noted that the Task Force had identified two projects on which joint efforts could be concentrated. They were: (a) the establishment of a regional network for training in water resource development; and (b) the accelerated manufacture of hand pumps for rural water supply.

III. MULTIDISCIPLINARY AND SYSTEMS APPROACH TO INTEGRATED RIVER BASIN DEVELOPMENT
(Agenda item 5)

23. The Committee had before it documents E/ESCAP/NR.10/1 and E/ESCAP/NR.10/3 and some country papers.

24. The Committee endorsed the contents of those documents in general. It agreed that the application of the multidisciplinary and systems approach would be beneficial and stressed that the importance and necessity of taking the following points into consideration in order that maximum benefits could be achieved: setting up of an overall river basin authority or other similar body (with the participation of other sectors of development) as an advisory body to the decision-maker; the availability of sufficient and reliable data, and the time constraint that might result from lack of such data; the requirement to test the models as to their suitability for the country concerned or the problem under consideration; the question of priority between water and other sectors in planning; the constraints generated by the lack of adequately trained personnel for systems analysis that underlined the urgent need to provide such training; and the need to provide continuity of expertise particularly when external experts were engaged.

25. The Committee pointed out that developing countries often required immediate action to complete development projects and might not be able to afford the resulting delay and cost if the multidisciplinary and systems approach were applied in view of the considerable data and time required for that purpose. It was pointed out that hasty development might prove to be costly in the long run.

26. Countries which had applied the multidisciplinary and systems approach expressed the view that an essential requirement was the establishment of river basin authorities which had the very important role of directing and co-ordinating all the work to be carried out. The desirability was expressed of involving decision-makers in the very process of system-oriented studies.

27. The Committee also noted that a number of countries in the region had been using a multidisciplinary and systems approach to planning with some success and recommended that ESCAP encourage and support the exchange of information regarding the experiences and results of the application of such techniques among the countries of the region.

28. The Committee noted with interest the activities of ICID in systems analysis as applied to irrigation and also in water as a factor in energy resource development.

IV. ASSESSMENT AND CONSIDERATION OF IRRIGATION EFFICIENCY IN THE IRRIGATED AREAS OF THE ESCAP REGION
(Agenda item 6)

29. The Committee had before it a note by the ESCAP secretariat E/ESCAP/NR.10/2, an information note prepared by FAO and some country papers.

30. The Committee noted that improvement of irrigation efficiency in the irrigated areas of the region was necessary in order to maximize agricultural production from limited land and water resources. It could also have additional benefits in the reduction of water-logging and salinity problems.

31. It was noted that irrigation efficiency in the region was affected to a large extent by engineering and managerial problems, agricultural factors and the socio-economic and institutional setting.

32. For that reason, the Committee considered that a comprehensive approach for the improvement of irrigation efficiency should be adopted and should include engi-neering, managerial, agricultural, socio-economic and institutional measures. Some of the measures that could contribute to the improvement of irrigation efficiency in the region were: proper operation and maintenance of irrigation systems; provision of suitable incentives to farmers to participate and assume responsibility in the operation and maintenance of irrigation systems; lining of canals in porous soils; close supervision and adequate control of water distribution; improvement of the availability, adequacy and reliability of hydrologic data; use of high-yielding varieties of crops compatible with irrigation; provision of adequate agricultural extension services; promotion of proper land levelling and shaping; establishment of a co-ordination body for better co-operation between agricultural and irrigation personnel at all levels; introduction of effective agrarian reforms; establishment and enforcement of appropriate water legislation and rules and regulations governing the use of irrigation water;

devising and imposing a practical and equitable system of water pricing; expansion of various training programmes in irrigation and water management; establishment of pilot water management projects to serve as demonstration models; and undertaking applied research aimed at improving irrigation efficiency.

33. The Committee considered that document E/ESCAP/NR.10/2 with its comprehensive coverage of the subject could provide useful guide-lines to staff engaged in the improvement of irrigation efficiency.

34. The Committee noted the information provided by some countries on the basis of their national experience concerning irrigation efficiencies, loss rates, causes of water losses and the measures on which they placed emphasis to minimize water losses. The measures included: the need to initiate and maintain a dialogue between engineering and agricultural staff; organization of farmers' associations; provision of complete engineering facilities, improved operation and maintenance; full utilization including conjunctive use of ground and surface waters; rotation system of water delivery; and effective water pricing policy.

35. The social aspects were considered to be quite important. Progressive land reform could greatly assist in improving irrigation efficiency. That could be achieved with the organization of a group of owner operators in place of absentee landowners. It was pointed out that owing to very small landholdings, farm ditches could not often be provided as owners were reluctant to give up their land for the purpose.

36. In conclusion, the Committee recommended that a methodology should be devised so that irrigation efficiency could be determined on the basis of uniform standards.

37. In that connection, the Committee noted that ICID was carrying out an assessment of irrigation efficiency in the irrigated areas of the ESCAP region through its various working groups organized to examine the various aspects of irrigation efficiency.

38. The Committee in noting the proposal contained in the note by FAO on the collection, compilation and analysis of irrigation efficiencies of irrigation projects in the region with the objective of identifying those requiring improvement regretted that the note was distributed too late to be properly studied and discussed.

V. POLLUTION PROBLEMS RELATED TO THE CURRENT PROGRAMMES OF LOW-COST TECHNOLOGY APPLICATIONS TO WATER SUPPLY AND SANITATION IN THE ESCAP REGION

(Agenda item 7)

39. The Committee noted the information contained in documents E/ESCAP/NR.10/4 and 5, E/ESCAP/NR.10/7, E/ESCAP/NR.10/10 and E/ESCAP/NR.10/14 prepared by the ESCAP secretariat, E/ESCAP/NR.10/15 prepared by the World Health Organization (WHO) and some country papers.

40. Like any technology, low-cost technology for water supply and sanitation could be applied successfully to achieve the basic health objectives only if great care and attention were paid to the potential pollution and health hazards attendant upon the incorrect application of the technology. Being simple, and generally implemented on an individual basis, low-cost facilities were apt to be poorly conceived, constructed and maintained.

41. In most cases, the pollution effects and health problems in low-cost technology applications in water supply and sanitation were due to faulty conception and application of the technology and lack of public appreciation for proper usage which resulted in contamination at the source of water supply, contamination in pumping, piping, manual transport and storage in the home, pollution of surface and ground water by sewage, and food contamination through

fly and mosquito breeding in accumulated water and rodent infestation.

42. Those problems were potential sources of infections leading to a large number of diseases which were waterborne and water-related as well as others resulting from soil pollution and food contamination. Thus, the health benefits which should have resulted from large investments in water supply and sanitation were not realized.

43. The strategies recommended to overcome such pollution and health problems included, among others, highlighting and disseminating information regarding pollution and health hazards arising from faulty design and incorrect application of low-cost technologies and preventive measures necessary to forestall such hazards, systematic monitoring and evaluation of the systems to assess the performance and utilization of the facilities by the community and initiating training programmes for the staff involved in implementation at all levels, as well as educational programmes for the public to achieve social acceptance and proper operation and maintenance of the system. Further, in order to reach rural people better the water supply and sanitation programmes could benefit from

closer co-operation with the primary health care programmes in the countries.

44. The Committee listened with interest to some countries' national experiences in low-cost technology applications to water supply and sanitation and noted that community participation (involving for example the donation of free labour and free land by some prospective beneficiaries) was an important feature of their successful experiences.

45. The Committee considered that the use of bucket latrines and the use of ultraviolet radiation could not be

considered appropriate low-cost technologies. The former which involved the manual handling of night soil was degrading to human dignity while the latter was only of academic interest.

46. The Committee expressed support for the organization of a seminar on water quality monitoring systems by the secretariat because of its importance to water quality management, noting the often quite different requirements in monitoring water quality as compared with water quantity.

VI. ACTIVITIES OF ESCAP IN THE APPRAISAL, DEVELOPMENT AND MANAGEMENT OF NATURAL RESOURCES
(Agenda item 8)

47. The Committee reviewed the activities of the secretariat in the field of natural resources as reported in documents E/ESCAP/NR.10/6, E/ESCAP/MR.10/12, and E/ESCAP/NR.10/16 and 17.

48. The Committee expressed its strong support to the publication of the newsletters *Confluence (Water Resources Newsletter), Energy News* and *Remote Sensing Newsletter* which served as effective media for the exchange of information and knowledge in their respective disciplines and contributed to the important role of information dissemination by the secretariat. It therefore called upon ESCAP member countries to provide on a regular basis relevant information to the secretariat.

A. WATER RESOURCES

49. The Committee noted the activities of the secretariat in the development of water resources as described in document E/ESCAP/NR.10/6.

50. The Committee was informed that in response to the recommendation of the Meeting on Water Resources Development in the South Pacific, held at Suva from 14 to 19 March 1983, ESCAP was in the process of carrying out consultations with DTCD, UNESCO and WMO concerning the organization of an interdisciplinary mission to examine the water problems of the countries which had requested the services of such a mission and to recommend appropriate solutions.

51. With the technical and financial assistance of the Government of Japan, the Roving Mission on the Improvement of Systems for Typhoon and Flood Damage Data Collection was organized. It visited Hong Kong, Malaysia, the Philippines, Thailand and Viet Nam during the period 5 September to 6 October 1983. In addition to rendering

advisory services, it conducted a one-day seminar on the subject for each member of the Typhoon Committee which it visited.

52. The Committee was also informed that in response to the Commission's directive that the secretariat should look into the possibility of establishing in the South Pacific a programme similar to that of the Typhoon Committee, a survey mission was being mounted with the financial assistance of the Government of New Zealand from October to December 1983 by ESCAP, WMO and the Office of the United Nations Disaster Relief Co-ordinator (UNDRO) to determine the need for, as well as the possible structure of, a regional body which the countries concerned might wish to establish.

53. The Committee requested the secretariat to look into the possibility of publishing the proceedings of the ESCAP Seminar on Water Resources Development Planning organized in the USSR in 1982 in accordance with the recommendation of the Seminar.

54. The hope was expressed that developed countries would continue to provide support to the subprogramme.

B. ENERGY RESOURCES

55. The Committee considered document E/ESCAP/NR.10/17, which reported activities regarding energy resources.

56. The Committee expressed appreciation of the efforts made by the secretariat in the implementation of three regional energy programmes, namely the Regional Energy Development Programme (REDP), the Pacific Energy Development Programme (PEDP) and the Regional Programme of Action on New and Renewable Sources of

Energy, as well as of projects under ESCAP's regular programme.

57. With regard to new and renewable sources of energy (NRSE), the Committee was informed of the financial support extended by the Government of Japan for the establishment of an information network on biomass, solar and wind energy.

58. The Committee noted that although the lack of reliable data was one of the obstacles for strengthening national capabilities in energy policy formulation, the lack of skilled and experienced manpower in some countries was a more important factor than information constraints.

59. One representative expressed the view that the stress on NRSE in the secretariat's activities was overstated and that relatively high priority should be accorded to conventional sources of energy, such as coal, oil, natural gas, nuclear and hydropower.

60. One representative observed that "energy conservation" as used in the secretariat's paper took the narrow view that conservation necessitates a reduction in activity and that it should also include increases in efficiency of energy use which could achieve the same output for less energy input.

61. The Committee also noted the fact that national energy strategies during the energy transition could involve extensive use of imported energy in some countries. That should not be overlooked when the necessity of interfuel substitution in the ESCAP region was considered.

62. The Committee noted that comparatively more attention should be paid on the development of mini-hydro generation of electricity under the regional programme of action on NRSE on the basis of a time-bound action plan.

63. It also noted that the ESCAP energy programmes should be undertaken on a priority basis as well as in a more practical and feasible manner. Such priority had been taken care of in the work programme for 1984-1985.

64. The Committee agreed with the suggestion towards the successful implementation of ESCAP activities expressed in the secretariat's paper, namely:

(a) Strengthening linkages with member countries;

(b) Placing emphasis on least developed countries and rural areas; and

(c) Fostering co-operation among developing countries.

65. The Committee expressed its appreciation of the support extended by UNDP and donor countries, both developed and developing, and strongly urged their con-

tinued support towards the implementation of ESCAP's energy programmes.

C. MINERAL RESOURCES

66. The Committee noted the progress made in the activities of the secretariat regarding geology and mineral resource development as described in document E/ESCAP/NR.10/9 and as reported to it at the session.

67. The Committee agreed that one of the important factors in attaining economic independence, developing a national industrial base and raising the prosperity of people in developing countries of the ESCAP region was the rational development and use of mineral resources with due regard to the sovereignty of those countries over their natural resources.

68. It expressed appreciation of the secretariat's efforts in the preparation of reviews and analyses of mineral resources in the region, the compilation of regional special-purpose maps on geology and minerals, programmes for dissemination of experience and technology on the search and exploration of mineral and energy raw materials onshore and offshore, and it endorsed those activities.

69. The Committee noted that the sixth session of the Governing Council of the Regional Mineral Resources Development Centre (RMRDC), which was also the first meeting of its newly elected members, was held at Manila, Philippines, from 28 September to 3 October 1983, and reviewed staff and mission activities of the Centre, its work programme and financial problems.

70. The Committee supported the major training activity for 1984 of RMRDC namely the Symposium on the Geology of Tin Deposits to be held in Guangxi, China, in October/November 1984.

71. It noted that the RMRDC Governing Council, being fully aware of the financial requirements for institutional support, had strongly appealed to: UNDP for continued support; to all ESCAP countries, especially participating countries, to make new cash contributions or increase contributions; and to donor countries for continued support. In recognition of the great benefits derived by the developing countries from RMRDC's various programmes, and in order not to disrupt the momentum of the progress made by that regional body to which all countries of ESCAP belong, the Committee strongly appealed to UNDP for continued institutional support in addition to the existing programme support.

72. The Committee commended the efforts of the secretariat in keeping the activities of RMRDC going after the termination of support by UNDP of the Co-ordinator's post at the end of 1982 and for making arrangements for

the appointment of a Co-ordinator on an interim basis after the thirty-ninth session of the Commission. It was pleased to be informed that other steps were being taken to resolve the problem of appointment of a Co-ordinator for the Centre on a permanent basis.

73. The Committee noted with interest the more important events concerning the Committee for Co-ordination of Joint Prospecting for Mineral Resources in South Pacific Offshore Areas (CCOP/SOPAC) that had occurred after the preparation of document E/ESCAP/NR/10/12. At it twelfth session in Tonga, in October 1983, CCOP/SOPAC had admitted Tuvalu as a member, agreed to double member Governments' annual cash contributions, initiated action to recruit a suitable national to take up the new post of Director of its technical secretariat, and agreed to hold an extraordinary meeting to discuss, and reach agreement, on its institutional/legal status.

74. The Committee commended the positive efforts of the secretariat in assisting the regional and subregional projects, the Committee for Co-ordination of Joint Prospecting for Mineral Resources in Asian Offshore Areas, CCOP/SOPAC, RMRDC and the South-East Asia Tin Research and Development Centre.

75. The Committee was informed that two *ad hoc* expert working group meetings to consider the feasibility and establishment of a subregional body for Indian Ocean exploration were held at ESCAP headquarters in August 1982 and January 1983. Bangladesh, India, Pakistan and Sri Lanka had taken part in those meetings. The draft terms of reference, programme outlines and other recommendations of the meetings were being examined by the concerned Governments.

D. REMOTE SENSING, SURVEYING AND MAPPING

76. The Committee was informed of the programme of activities of the secretariat with regard to remote sensing, surveying and mapping as reported in document E/ESCAP/NR.10/16.

77. The Committee was advised that the Regional Remote Sensing Programme had started with a budget of $US 1.8

million. The project manager and the remote sensing expert had arrived in March 1983. However, since that time no qualified associate expert had been provided, and two positions were still open.

78. The Committee expressed great disappointment that the positions of associate experts had not been filled and suggested that efforts should be made to recruit personnel to fill them.

79. The project staff, members of Remote Sensing Units of FAO and DTCD which were associate executing agencies, had redesigned the work plan in accordance with the budget and findings of the evaluation missions of the project staff.

80. It was recognized that workshops, seminars and study tours were important vehicles for the exchange of technological information provided that participants were selected from ongoing or recently completed projects within the ESCAP region who could truly share their experience.

81. It was also urged that the pilot information system should be carefully structured in the early stages to ensure its effectiveness and usefulness.

82. The Committee expressed the view that the secretariat should provide the countries with more detailed and timely information on the fellowships and programme activities. It also recommended that the fellowship funds be used for advanced training abroad only.

83. The Committee noted that several developed countries were providing training support and intended to continue their efforts.

84. The Committee expressed concern about the current system of communication which had caused significant delays. Often information had not reached the appropriate agencies.

85. The Committee expressed the view that sufficient time should be given to the countries so that they could properly prepare themselves for the meeting for the establishment of the intergovernmental consultative committee. The need to minimize overheads on committee meetings and to concentrate more on the technical work was also urged.

VII. ACTIVITIES OF OTHER INTERNATIONAL BODIES IN THE APPRAISAL, DEVELOPMENT AND MANAGEMENT OF WATER RESOURCES
(Agenda item 9)

86. The Committee noted the information provided by the representatives of other international bodies concerning the appraisal, development and management of water resources.

87. The attention of the Committee was drawn to the second issue of the semi-annual *Information Note* (August 1983) and its supplement prepared by DIESA in its capacity as the secretariat of the ACC Intersecretariat Group

for Water which had the responsibility for the co-ordination of activities of the members of the United Nations system engaged in water resource development. The Committee noted with interest the contents of the note which included a calendar of meetings, seminars, symposia and conferences and technical co-operation projects, and details concerning reports and studies under preparation or recently issued, *ad hoc* training courses and newsletters of the organizations of the United Nations system.

88. The Department of Technical Co-operation for Development, through its Division of Natural Resources and Energy and its Water Resources Branch, currently executed approximately 85 projects in the field for water, of which over 30 were in the Asian and Pacific region. Water resource projects often involved ground water exploration and development, creation or strengthening of national technical services, establishment of data banks, artificial recharge of aquifers and river basin planning. DTCD had recently published *Ground Water in the Pacific Region* and would soon issue *Ground Water in the Asian Region* under its *Water Series*. Recent publications included those concerning water pricing, water resources planning, rural water supply, international rivers and lakes, and flood damage and prevention in China.

89. The United Nations Children's Fund was involved in the provision of safe drinking water and sanitation facilities in remote areas in various countries and in the promotion of the International Drinking Water Supply and Sanitation Decade activities.

90. The United Nations Environment Programme served as the focal point for environmental action and co-ordination within the United Nations system and for securing the effective co-operation of, and contributions from, the relevant scientific and other professional communities. As an illustration of UNEP's activities, an extract on the water section contained in the System-Wide Medium-Term Environment Programme for 1984-1985 was circulated for the Committee's information.

91. The Food and Agriculture Organization of the United Nations was involved in several activities involving water development and management.

92. The objectives of the activities of UNESCO in water resources in the Asia and the Pacific region were planned to contribute to training of specialized personnel and building up research and training institutions, to increase and disseminate scientific and technical knowledge on water

resources concerning their development and conservation, and to stimulate public awareness on the development and management of water resources.

93. The World Health Organization was involved in the health aspects of water supply and sanitation which included among other things, promotion of activities pertaining to the International Drinking Water Supply and Sanitation Decade, the provision of technical assistance to countries in preparing Decade plans, identifying new projects, and evaluating ongoing and completed projects, and the provision of assistance in exploring external sources of funds, training, institution building and developing appropriate technology.

94. The International Commission on Irrigation and Drainage carried out various activities concerning irrigation, drainage and flood control including the organization of seminars, conferences and study tours and the dissemination of information. ICID had recently published a flood control manual, "Irrigation in the World", and a multi-lingual dictionary of irrigation terminologies. The twelfth Conference of ICID was held in Fort Collins, Colorado, the United States, in May 1984.

95. The Environment and Policy Institute of the East West Centre based in Honolulu, Hawaii, was developing a five-year project which would involve sustained and in-depth studies of selected major water resource problems in Asia by means of case studies and comparative cross-country analyses of water resource problems and management experiences. It organized a workshop in Honolulu in May 1984 on the analysis of management problems associated with river and reservoir sedimentation in Asian countries.

96. Noting the usefulness to the countries of the *Information Note* compiled by DIESA giving a complete listing of all scheduled activities of the organizations of the United Nations system engaged in water resources, the Committee requested that the *Note* continue to be compiled and also supplied to ESCAP member countries on a regular basis.

97. The Interim Committee for Co-ordination of Investigations of the Lower Mekong Basin expressed its support for the Committee's work, and its special interest in the management of shared water resources and river basin development. It brought to the attention of the Committee two recent publications dealing with the assessment of environmental impact of river basin development, available from the Committee.

VIII. REVIEW OF THE MEDIUM-TERM PLAN, 1984-1989, AND THE PROGRAMME OF WORK AND PRIORITIES IN THE APPRAISAL, DEVELOPMENT AND MANAGEMENT OF NATURAL RESOURCES 1984-1985: PROGRAMME CHANGES
(Agenda item 10)

A. MEDIUM-TERM PLAN, 1984-1989

98. The Committee reviewed the ESCAP programmes as it would affect energy and natural resources (minerals, water, cartography and remote sensing) included in the medium-term plan, 1984-1989, as adopted by the United Nations General Assembly at its thirty-seventh session in 1982, as set out in document E/ESCAP/NR.10/20.

99. The Committee did not propose any revision to the programmes of the medium-term plan.

B. PROGRAMME OF WORK AND PRIORITIES, 1984-1985

1. Water resources

100. The Committee reviewed the programme of work and priorities for the rational development, management and utilization of water resources for 1984-1985 as endorsed by the Commission at its thirty-ninth session in 1983, as set out in document E/ESCAP/NR.10/8.

101. One representative reiterated the position of his country concerning its reservation about high priority being accorded to output (iii) (b) under programme element 2.2.

102. The Committee recommended that more work be carried out on the hydrological aspects of the programme element 2.3.

103. The representative of the USSR confirmed in principle its agreement to participate in the proposed regional network for training in water resources development provided that training of specialists from the ESCAP region in the Soviet Union could be financed from the USSR contribution to the United Nations Technical Assistance Fund. Likewise, under the same funding arrangements, the USSR was prepared to host a seminar on the efficient use of water in energy resource development in May 1984 at Volgograd and a study tour on capital investments in water resources development in 1986.

104. The Committee recommended that the following activity be added to the programme of work for 1984-1985 as output (ii) (e) under element 2.1.

"Study tour of selected irrigation systems in the region (1985) (XB)".

2. Energy resources

105. The Committee considered document E/ESCAP/NR.10/18 containing the programme and programme changes of work and priorities in the appraisal, development and management of energy resources for 1984-1985 as endorsed by the Commission at its thirty-ninth session.

106. The Committee noted that the organization of the meeting of ministers of energy scheduled for 1985 should be considered after the specific issues to be discussed were identified and after views of member countries were ascertained. The Committee requested the secretariat to place its specific proposals before the Commission at its fortieth session.

107. The Committee was informed by China that the first training course of small hydropower which was organized by the Regional Research and Training Centre on Small Hydropower had been held in China in May 1983 and that the preparation for the second training course tentatively scheduled for the first quarter of 1984 was well underway and could be carried out as expected because the approval of the project document for the second phase of REDP was expected in the near future.

108. The Committee was informed by the USSR that the USSR was ready to consider the possibilities of arranging the following studies:

(a) Regional study on use of peat as fuel;

(b) Study on socio-economic benefits on rural electrification.

109. One representative expressed the view that relatively lower priority should be placed on new and renewable sources of energy except fuelwood and small-scale hydroelectricity because they were not likely to be economical on short- and medium-term bases.

110. The Committee urged that the programme for meeting the energy requirements of rural areas and programmes for improvement in the efficient use of energy should be given more emphasis.

111. The Committee noted that the mechanism to facilitate the capital flow for the development of NRSE should be established. It also noted that while the technical feasibility of increasing energy supplies from NRSE had been demonstrated, the socio-economic and financial

problems were still to be satisfactorily resolved in most developing countries of the region.

112. The Committee recommended the following programme changes as contained in annex II of the document E/ESCAP/NR.10/18:

    (a) *Addition of the following outputs:*

        1.2(i) (c) One expert group meeting on pricing study (1984) (REDP)

        (d) One forum meeting on energy economy patterns (REDP)

        3.1(ii) (c) Training in coal utilization in industries (1985) (REDP)

        3.2 (i) (c) Expert group meeting on natural gas planning and utilization (1984) (REDP)

    (b) *Deletion of the following outputs:*

        1.3(ii) Study on manpower and training requirements in the field of energy (1985) (REDP)

        2.2(ii) Expert group meeting on biogas (REDP) (1985) (XB)

113. The Committee also endorsed the recommendation by the Committee for Programme and Co-ordination that programme element 1.4 (Energy Conservation and Conversion Policy) of the work programme on science and technology of ESCAP be included under the energy programme.

3. Mineral resources

114. The Committee considered documents E/ESCAP/NR.10/9 and Add.1 which detailed the programme of work and priorities in the exploration, evaluation, rational utilization and management of mineral resources for 1984-1985 as endorsed by the Commission at its thirty-ninth session in 1983 and the proposed revision to be made owing to constraints in regular and extrabudgetary resources.

115. The Committee recommended the following programme changes as contained in document E/ESCAP/NR.10/9/Add.1.

    (a) Deletions of the following:

        1.1 (ii) (f)

        1.3 (i) (c)

        1.4 (ii) (a), (b) and (c);

    (b) Amendments of the following:

        1.3 (i) (a) Reduction in number of missions from 6 to 4

        1.4 (i) Reduction in number of reports from 2 to 1.

116. It also recommended that the following activity be added as output (c) under programme element 1.3 (i) "Seminar on drilling, sampling and borehole logging (1985) (XB)". In that connection, it accepted with appreciation China's offer to host the seminar.

117. The Committee noted with appreciation the offer of the USSR to organize the seminar on exploration and development of coal resources in the region in 1986 instead of 1984.

118. The Committee noted also the statement of the USSR that it would be prepared to organize at a suitable date a seminar on modern methods of mineral prospecting.

119. The USSR also reaffirmed that if the developing countries in the region were interested, it would be prepared to assist in the field of mineral and energy resources research in the offshore areas of Eastern Asia and South Pacific.

120. The Committee recommended that ESCAP should concentrate in helping the States in the region to build up their national capabilities for better utilization of marine resources. In that context it must be ensured that overlapping of functions within the agencies of the United Nations system should be minimized if not avoided.

4. Remote sensing, surveying and mapping

121. The Committee reviewed the programme of activities of the secretariat in remote sensing, surveying and mapping as reported in document E/ESCAP/NR.10/13.

122. The Committee supported the work programme and did not propose any change.

123. It reiterated the need for proper communications with the appropriate agencies and expressed its concern over the difficult communication procedure. It requested that copies of invitations should be also sent directly to the appropriate agencies or institutes.

124. The Committee suggested that pilot studies should include the monitoring of land surface cover and biomass.

125. The Committee noted with appreciation the offer of Indonesia to host two training courses in remote sensing. Those would be: (a) regular course at Gaja Mada University of 12 months for a maximum of six students a year; and

(b) on-the-job training at the National Co-ordination Agency for Surveys and Mapping and at the Centre for Remote Sensing, Ministry of Public Works. Indonesia also offered to host a seminar on remote sensing.

126. The Committee also noted with appreciation the offer of the USSR to host a seminar on the application of remote sensing techniques to the search and exploration of mineral deposits in 1985.

127. The Committee supported the work programme and the idea that participation should be drawn from the ESCAP region on the basis of technical co-operation among developing countries.

128. The Committee underlined the importance of evolving the Regional Remote Sensing Programme through workshops/symposia, the themes of which should be focused on some specific applications and carefully planned and structured so as to achieve the goals of energizing awareness of remote sensing and also evolving a plan of action for joint projects.

129. In evolving the programmes, maximum co-ordination between the United Nations agencies and minimized overheads on the secretariat's activities were urged. The ESCAP Regional Remote Sensing Programme should accordingly be co-ordinated in its technical elements with the United Nations Outer Space Affairs Division, which was following up UNISPACE-82 activities, so as to avoid duplication of efforts.

IX. CONSIDERATION OF THE AGENDA AND ARRANGEMENTS FOR SUBSEQUENT SESSIONS

(Agenda item 11)

A. ELEVENTH SESSION

130. The Committee considered document E/ESCAP/ NR.10/22 containing a suggested provisional agenda for the eleventh session which would deal principally with the subject of energy resource development.

131. It recommended the following provisional agenda for its eleventh session:

1. Opening of the session

2. Eelection of officers

3. Adoption of the agenda

4. Energy for economic and social development

    (a) Current energy situation in the ESCAP region

    (b) Technology for development – strategies for energy sector

5. Acceleration of development of new and renewable sources of energy

6. Prospects of coal and natural gas as alternative sources of energy

7. Future trends of electric power in the ESCAP region

8. Activities of ESCAP in the appraisal, development and management of natural resources

    (a) Energy resources (other than those activities referred to above)

    (b) Mineral resources

    (c) Water resources

    (d) Remote sensing, surveying and mapping

9. Activities of other international bodies in the appraisal, development and management of energy resources.

10. Review of the medium-term plan, 1984-1989, the draft programme of work and priorities in the appraisal, development and management of natural resources: 1986-1987; and programme changes in the 1984-1985 work programme

    (a) Energy resources

    (b) Mineral resources

    (c) Water resources

    (d) Remote sensing, surveying and mapping

11. Consideration of the agenda and arrangements for subsequent sessions of the Committee

12. Other matters

13. Adoption of the report

132. The Committee agreed that item 5 of the provisional agenda should include the development of mini-hydro plants and peat.

B. THIRTEENTH SESSION

133. The Committee recommended that the following topics be considered for inclusion in the agenda for the thirteenth session:

(a) Progress in the implementation of the Mar del Plata Action Plan;

(b) Environmental issues of water resources development in the ESCAP region;

(c) Development of groundwater resources.

C. GENERAL

134. A view was expressed that in view of the general applicability of remote sensing to natural resource development, the subject of remote sensing applications should be included as a separate item in the agenda of all subsequent sessions of the Committee.

X. OTHER MATTERS
(Agenda item 12)

A. WILDLIFE AND NATIONAL PARK MANAGEMENT IN THE ESCAP REGION

135. The Committee had before it document E/ESCAP/NR.10/21 which contained the conclusions and recommendations addressed partly or wholly to ESCAP in the report of the Joint Inspection Unit on the subject. It also had an information note by UNEP on the subject.

136. The Committee agreed that it was a subject which, because of its importance, deserved very careful attention and study by the member countries. Since, however, the delegations had not been able to seek the official views of their respective governments on the subject in view of the very late distribution of document E/ESCAP/NR.10/21, the Committee was neither able to express its views nor reach a decision on the matter.

XI. ADOPTION OF THE REPORT
(Agenda item 13)

137. The Committee adopted the report on its tenth session on 31 October 1983.

Part Two

WORKING PAPERS PRESENTED BY THE SECRETARIAT

Part Two
WORKING PAPERS PRESENTED BY THE SECRETARIAT

I. REVIEW OF IMPLEMENTATION OF THE
MAR DEL PLATA ACTION PLAN
(E/ESCAP/NR10/19)

Introduction

At its seventh session in 1980, the Committee on Natural Resources Plan suggested that the monitoring of the implementation of the Mar del Plata Action should be institutionalized. On 11 January 1983, the secretariat circulated to all member countries a "Questionnaire on progress in the implementation of the Mar del Plata Action Plan: present status of and prospects for water resources development at the national level". As of 31 July 1983, completed questionnaires had been received from 22 members and associate members as follows: (a) Asian subregion — Afghanistan, Brunei, China, Hong Kong, India, Indonesia, Japan, Nepal, Pakistan, Philippines, Republic of Korea, Singapore and Thailand; (b) Pacific subregion — Australia, Fiji, Guam, Kiribati, New Zealand, Samoa, Solomon Islands, Tonga and Vanuatu. This paper is based on an analysis of those returns.[1]

The review covers six broad areas: (a) policy, planning, legislation and institutional arrangements; (b) assessment of water resources; (c) water resources development and use for agriculture; (d) education, training and public information, (e) research and development; and (f) technical co-operation among developing countries.

A. POLICY, PLANNING, LEGISLATION AND INSTITUTIONAL ARRANGEMENTS

1. National water resources policy and planning

The Mar del Plata Action Plan called upon each country to formulate and keep under review a general statement of policy in relation to the use, management and conservation of water as a framework for planning, and recommended some broad guidelines. The Action Plan pointed out that the statement of policy should be conceived and carried out within the framework of interdisciplinary national economic, social and environmental development policies.

---

[1] After the tenth session of the Committee on Natural Resources another completed questionnaire was received from Sri Lanka. This document E/ESCAP/NR.10/19 is revised to incorporate this information.

As shown in table 1, of the 23 respondent countries, 18 countries have a water policy statement. Most countries had specified the role of water resources development and management in the framework of national economic and social development, mainly to increase food production and electric power generation and to improve navigation and this had generally been reflected in their five-year development plans. In India, notwithstanding the fact that there is no formal water policy statement, the development of water resources had been studied on a national basis, and policy guidelines had been issued from time to time by the Central Government to the State Governments.

Ten countries and areas are considering the revision of their water policy statement. China stressed the importance of the protection of water quality and the provision of financial assistance to water projects in poverty-stricken areas. Hong Kong, the Philippines, Thailand, Fiji, Guam, Kiribati, Tonga and Vanuatu stressed the importance of providing adequate and clean water to urban and rural people for domestic use. Countries and areas with a limited supply of fresh water, such as Hong Kong, Guam and Kiribati, underlined the importance of the conservation of water.

In Australia, short-term and long-term goals to be attained by water development and management are comprehensively described in the statement "A national approach to water resources management, 1978", formulated by the Australian Water Resources Council and endorsed by the Commonwealth and State Governments of Australia. It also outlines the specific activities required to implement the policies.

The Government of Japan estimated the total river water demand for 1990 and prepared a development plan to meet this demand. In the Republic of Korea, a comprehensive development plan of river improvement, multipurpose reservoirs and disaster prevention was prepared to meet water demand until the year 2001.

As shown in table 1, 13 countries and areas have a comprehensive master plan for water resources development. Among the 10 which do not have, seven are making efforts to formulate one.

The water pricing practices used to recover investment cost and operating and maintenance costs from direct project beneficiaries in various countries and areas are shown in table 2. Generally the portion of the capital as well as operation and maintenance costs repaid by the beneficiaries of rural water supply and irrigation works were smaller than those paid by the beneficiaries of urban and industrial water supply works. It is noted, however, that even for urban and industrial water supply works only the Philippines and Vanuatu recovered fully the capital cost, while only seven or nine countries fully recovered the operation and maintenance costs.

As for rural water supply and irrigation works, no country recovered the full capital cost while only four to five countries recovered the full operation and maintenance costs.

The willingness to pay by customers of urban water supply depends very much upon the adequacy of water supply and efficiency of the management of the system. In many urban centres of the developing countries the water is supplied intermittently and inadequately [1]. Among the 23 countries and areas listed in table 2, 11 fully meter their major urban water supplies, while in 10 the major urban water supplies are only partly metered. The high percentage of water unaccounted for (about 50 per cent or more in many developing countries) not only reduced the available quantity for the use of the customer, but also increased significantly the unit cost of the water sold.

In Asia, the small holdings and low incomes of farmers are the main causes of the low rates for irrigation water. In two countries (Afghanistan and Thailand) there is generally no charge for irrigation water use. A large part of the costs of large irrigation projects in the countries of the region is currently borne by the governments or the general taxpayer. However, the farmers in small irrigation projects, including pumping irrigation in some countries (Bangladesh, Thailand), are willing to pay a much higher rate for water than those in large projects, as a result of more reliable water supply [1].

Although many countries had made great efforts to allocate a larger part of project costs to direct beneficiaries, the situation wherein governments bore a large part of the costs, particularly for rural water supply and irrigation projects, has not changed much. In many cases the shortage of operation and maintenance funds seriously affects the efficient operation of completed projects.

2. National water legislation

Among the 23 respondents, 15 to 17 have national water legislation regulating the ownership of and/or the right to use water. In six (China, Thailand, Fiji, Guam, Samoa and Tonga), the existing legislation does not regulate the right to use water. There are 16 countries where

legislation regulated the protection of water quality. In countries with a federal type of government, such as Australia and India, each state/territory has its own water legislation.

As shown in table 3, 14 countries or areas are planning or have introduced changes in existing legislation.

Most respondents indicated that regional and local governments are responsible for the administration of water resources. Only in four countries (Pakistan, Fiji, Sri Lanka and Solomon Islands) is this responsibility entirely in the hands of central government.

3. Institutional arrangements

The Action Plan called upon each country to ensure that the development and management of water resources take place in the context of national planning and that there be real co-ordination among all bodies responsible for the investigation, development and management of water resources.

Twelve countries and areas have a central mechanism for co-ordinating all water interests at the national level (see table 4). There are three types of such mechanism: (a) a principal water ministry, such as the Ministry of Irrigation in Afghanistan and India, Ministry of Construction, and Land Agency in Japan, National Water and Soil Conservation Organization in New Zealand and Environmental Protection Agency in Guam; (b) a specifically designated committee or council composed of members from various ministries and agencies, such as the Central River Management Committee in the Republic of Korea, National Water Resources Council in the Philippines, and Water and Energy Commission in Nepal; and (c) national economic development planning board, such as the National Economic and Social Development Board in Thailand. The Australian Water Resources Council is composed of water resources ministers from Commonwealth and State Governments. These bodies have different degrees of involvement and responsibility in the preparation, implementation and evaluation of plans and policies for co-ordinated water development and management. The main function of these organizations is to co-ordinate the preparation of development plans.

In some large countries, river basin organizations were set up for planning and implementation of inter-province water projects, such as the Huanghe River Water Conservancy Commission and Changjiang River Water Conservancy Commission in China and the Narmada Control Authority and Damodar Valley Corporation in India.

Among the 11 countries which do not have a central co-ordinating mechanism, only three planned to establish such a machinery (see table 4).

4. Shared water resources development

With regard to the development of shared water resources, the Action Plan recommended: (a) countries sharing water resources should review existing and available techniques for managing shared water resources and co-operation in the establishment of programmes, machinery and institutions necessary for the co-ordinated development of such resources; (b) national policies should take into consideration the right of each state sharing the resources equitably to utilize such resources; and (c) a concerted and sustained effort is required to strengthen international water law as a means of placing co-operation among states on a firmer basis.

Among the 23 respondents, seven (Afghanistan, China, India, Indonesia, Nepal, Pakistan and Thailand) have shared water resources (see table 5).[2] Six countries have some form of agreement for development of shared water resources with their neighbours. These agreements provide for the setting-up of joint institutional mechanisms. However, three countries (Nepal, India and Thailand) felt that there was a need for the establishment of new or expanded agreements. Talks between India and Nepal were underway for this purpose.

B. ASSESSMENT OF WATER RESOURCES

1. Observation networks and data collection

The establishment of meteorological and hydrological observation networks varied widely among the countries of the region. Greater efforts are needed to establish an adequate network in large countries. As shown in table 6, many countries and areas are collecting adequate and reliable data on meteorology and surface water, while fewer are collecting adequate and reliable data on ground water and water quality.

In the Asian subregion, Afghanistan, China, Nepal and Thailand have indicated the need to improve their networks for all four categories. In this subregion all countries, except India and Pakistan, have inadequate groundwater data. In small countries and areas with dense population, such as Brunei, Singapore and Hong Kong, much attention is being paid to the collection of water quality data.

In the Pacific subregion, Australia, Fiji, Guam and New Zealand are advanced in collecting meteorological and

---

2 Other countries in the region which did not respond to the questionnaire but which have shared water resources are: Bangladesh, Bhutan, Democratic. Kampuchea, Lao People's Democratic Republic, Iran, Malaysia, Papua New Guinea and Viet Nam.

hydrological data. In the Solomon Islands, Tonga and Vanuatu, data are mostly insufficient and much improvement is needed.

It is interesting to note that among the respondents, 19 have a plan for expanding their observation networks.

2. Data processing and dissemination

The processing, storage, retrieval and dissemination of hydrological data had been fully computerized in only three countries and areas — Hong Kong, Japan and Australia. In most countries these activities are only partly computerized. In some less-developed and small island countries in the Pacific, automation has not yet been started (see table 7).

In Fiji and New Zealand, computerization of the processing of hydrological data is in progress.

In 14 of the 23 countries and areas, there is a mechanism for disseminating data to users at regular intervals.

3. Areal assessment of water resources

The areal assessment of water resources requires adequate and reliable hydrological data covering the whole territory or a large part of it. As shown in table 7 about half of the countries and areas reported that their areal assessment of water resources was adequate. In the other half continuous efforts are needed to improve the areal assessment of their water resources. Sixteen have an investigation programme up to 1990-2000. This indicates that only a few countries have not paid much attention to the areal assessment of their water resources.

4. Institutional aspects

In most countries and areas each agency carries out a hydrological survey programme according to its own interests and policies. In three, China, Sri Lanka and the Philippines, co-ordination extended to the possibility of use of the data by other agencies to a great degree. In 12, there is such co-ordination to some degree. It is believed that the co-ordination: in hydrological surveys among various agencies has improved since the Water Conference.

Four countries facing this co-ordination problem have taken steps to establish a new body with comprehensive responsibilities for water resources assessment.

C. WATER RESOURCES DEVELOPMENT AND USE FOR AGRICULTURE

The Action Plan on water for agriculture stressed that the development of efficient new irrigation, the improvement of existing irrigation and the improvement of drainage facilities constituted the core elements for action in respect of the development and use of water for agricultural purposes. Countries were urged to: (a) prepare financial requirements for a phased action programme; (b) assess present and future needs for trained manpower; (c) promote national advisory services; and (d) establish and improve the institutional framework for management, administration and legislative support.

1. Main areas of activity

In most developing countries in Asia, 70 to 85 per cent of the total population lives in rural areas. Livelihood depends mainly on agriculture. To increase productivity and improve living standards, the improvement of water supply for agriculture is of great importance to the mass population. As shown in table 8, except for Brunei, Hong Kong and Singapore the areas of which are small, in most Asian countries almost all aspects of irrigation activity have been receiving emphasis and priority since the Conference. The main activities include the improvement of existing irrigation, expansion of new irrigation, drainage and reclamation and aquaculture in rural areas. In the Pacific subregion, however, the emphasis in most island countries is the provision of a drinking water supply for human settlements. Only a few Pacific island countries have irrigated large areas. Most Asian countries expect that these main fields of activity of water resources development for agriculture will continue to be emphasized in the future.

Among the Asian countries and areas, except for Japan and the Republic of Korea, all have made substantial progress in increasing cereals production since the Conference. According to the statistical information available [2] the ratio of cereals production of 1981 to 1977 is 1.40 in Indonesia, 1.08 in India, 1.20 in Pakistan, 1.10 in the Philippines and 1.47 in Thailand. The yield per hectare of cereals in these countries also increased substantially. This increase reflects the results of the expansion of new irrigation, the improvement of existing irrigation systems and other agricultural improvements. In Japan and the Republic of Korea, both the harvested area and yield declined during the period. A part of the cultivated area was lost to urban growth and factories.

In many developing countries in Asia, such as India, Indonesia, the Philippines and Thailand, irrigation development has received high priority in five-year economic development plans. A very large portion of government capital funds allocated to agriculture sector is devoted to irrigation development. In India's Sixth Plan (1980/81-1984/85), the Government plan to allocate Rs 84,484

million to major and medium irrigation projects and Rs 18,100 million to minor irrigation projects [3]. By comparison, the Plan outlay to agriculture excluding irrigation is only Rs 56,956 million [4]. In Thailand, about 60 per cent of the public investment in agriculture has been for irrigation development [5].

Despite large investments in irrigation, the average yields of cereals in most countries in Asia are still very low, ranging from 1.3 to 2.0 tons per ha as compared with 5 tons per ha in Japan and the Republic of Korea. The deficiencies of existing irrigation systems and the need for their improvement or rehabilitation have gradually been recognized since the Conference. For example, in the Fifth National Economic and Social Development Plan (1982-1986) of Thailand it is pointed out that in 1982 only 1 per cent of the total irrigated area has complete irrigation systems with land consolidation, while 52 per cent of the total irrigated area has complete ditches and dikes. The rest (47 per cent) of the irrigated area has no ditches and dikes, and some projects have even no canals. Capital returns from rehabilitation and improvement of existing systems are generally higher compared with the investment return for new schemes. In Indonesia, from 1979 to 1984 more than 536,000 ha of existing irrigated area planned to be rehabilitated or improved, while about 700,000 ha of new irrigation systems are to be constructed [6].

2. Training of manpower

Among the 14 Asian respondents, ten or eleven countries consider that in order to implement programmes of irrigation development, training of personnel is needed in: (a) professional and technical, (b) research, (c) extension, and (d) basic education areas as shown in table 9.

Since the Conference, many countries in the region have upgraded the design standards of irrigation systems. More qualified professional and technical personnel are therefore required to implement the expanded programmes. For operation and maintenance of existing and new irrigation systems additional technical personnel at various levels would be required. It had been pointed out that inefficient operation and inadequate maintenance of irrigation systems were mainly due to lack of funds and technical personnel [7].

In India, steps have been initiated to train irrigation engineers and other scientists associated with water management problems. The establishment of a national staff training institute has been proposed. States are also being persuaded to start similar training institutes for training their operating-level, junior-level, middle-level and senior-level personnel [7].

3. National advisory services

As shown in table 9, 12 countries and areas in Asian subregion have taken action to promote national advisory services in support of agricultural water development. Most of these services deal with planning and design. Nine to ten countries have taken action to promote national advisory services dealing with construction, operation and maintenance.

In the formulation and implementation of national programmes for agricultural water development, the shortage of financial resources is considered as the main constraint by most countries. The second common constraint is the lack of qualified manpower. Only six countries consider that institutional deficiencies and lack of equipment are constraints.

D. EDUCATION AND TRAINING

1. Comprehensive survey of manpower needs

The Action Plan recommended that countries should make a comprehensive assessment of the requirements of manpower for water development in the professional and sub-professional categories of personnel.

As shown in table 10, 8 of the 23 countries and areas have taken action to carry out a comprehensive survey of manpower needs in the field of water resources development. In the Philippines, the requirements cover various subject areas, such as water resources assessment, planning, project design, construction techniques and procedures, operation and maintenance, environment and flood loss management. In Australia, a working group of the Australian Water Resources Council is reviewing the adequacy of education and training within the water industry, and is expected to recommend action required to meet the changing needs of water development and management, including public education in water conservation, pollution control and cost of water.

While in most Asian countries the manpower situation has either improved or remained essentially the same in terms of available and adequate skills, in many of them the number of middle-level engineers and university educated engineers has increased since the Conference.

In the Pacific subregion, the manpower situation in Samoa, Tonga and Vanuatu has deteriorated. The causes of manpower deterioration are migration to other countries, lack of suitable candidates, and lack of employment opportunities. The manpower situation in other Pacific countries has remained essentially the same.

2. Education and training

The Governments of China, Indonesia, India, Nepal, the Philippines, the Republic of Korea, Singapore, Sri Lanka and Thailand have taken action to set up new institutions or enlarge or improve existing ones for the training and education of skilled workers, technicians and university educated engineers (see table 11). In some countries, training is also provided for research scientists and planners.

In the Pacific subregion, no country, except Fiji, has taken any action to set up new institutions or enlarge existing ones for training and education in water resources. For those small island countries, the constraints faced in increasing education and training activities are the lack of qualified teachers, financial resources and students. Most of these countries consider that external co-operation would help in alleviating some of these constraints.

E. RESEARCH AND DEVELOPMENT

The Action Plan recommended that countries should strengthen existing research institutions, where gaps exist, and establish new ones, wherever necessary, for the specific purpose of conducting water resource research on problems closely related to developmental needs.

As shown in table 12, 11 countries and areas have taken action to establish or strengthen water resource research institutes. Most of these institutes deal with general water resources or specialized topics. In these countries and areas significant progress has been made in the use of local materials and use of labour-intensive methods and standardization of equipment.

In India, the National Institute of Hydrology has been established. In Pakistan, waterlogging and salinity are subjects of specialized research. In Sri Lanka, irrigation and water management are subjects of specialized research. In New Zealand, specialized research topics include systems modelling, low-flow studies, oxygen modelling, eutrophication studies, estuarine mixing and land-use effects on water quality, among others.

In most developing countries, a lack of financial resources and a shortage of qualified manpower are the main constraints to research. The institutional problem is also one of the main constraints in many Asian countries.

F. TECHNICAL CO-OPERATION AMONG DEVELOPING COUNTRIES

The Water Conference was aware that alternate appropriate technologies in the field of water resources had been developed by some developing countries and may be usefully applied by other developing countries. The Action Plan contained specific recommendations for implementation at the national, regional and subregional level. These recommendations, *inter alia,* called for: (1) the establishment of an improved information base; (2) the promotion of research, education and training on an intercountry basis; (3) the exchange of experts and consultancy services; and (4) standardization of engineering services and equipment.

As shown in table 13, a large number of developing countries has made significant progress in technical co-operation among developing countries (TCDC) in the area of information exchange. Five or six countries have made progress in TCDC in relation to technical/economic co-operation projects and exchange of consultant services. In India, a water resources engineering consultant firm has increased its activities since the Conference.

Most countries were interested in TCDC-oriented projects in the following areas: joint ventures, technical/ economic co-operation projects, information exchange, establishment of institutional machinery, exchange of experts and consultant services and standardization of engineering services.

G. CONCLUSIONS AND RECOMMENDATIONS

Based on the above analysis of the questionnaire returns from 23 members and associate members, the following conclusions and recommendations may be made.

(1) Most countries and areas in the region have a water policy statement and have specified the role of water resource development and management in the framework of national economic and social development. Some have been continuously reviewing their policy to cope with the changing situation. Thirteen have a comprehensive master plan for water resources development while seven are making efforts to formulate a master plan.

(2) Countries without a national water policy and a master plan for water resources development should give serious consideration to formulating the first and preparing the second.

(3) Most governments still bear a large part of project costs of rural water supply and irrigation projects. Governments should make continuous efforts to share more of these costs with the beneficiaries in order to improve the financial viability and efficient operation and maintenance of the projects.

(4) Many of the countries and areas have national water legislation regulating the ownership of right to use water and the protection of water quality. Countries still lacking such legislation should consider framing such legislation compatible with modern management and planning principles.

(5) About half of the countries and areas have a central mechanism for co-ordinating all water interests at the national level. In a number of them, co-ordination is achieved through the Ministry of Planning or an inter-ministerial committee. Where no such mechanism exists, the countries concerned should consider setting up arrangements to ensure real co-ordination among all bodies responsible for the investigation, development and management of water resources.

(6) The development of shared water resources in the region is an area in which more efforts are required to be exerted by all concerned, particularly in the establishment of joint programmes and institutions necessary for the co-ordinated development of such resources.

(7) Among the four categories of water resources data — meteorological, surface water, groundwater and water quality — the collection of the last two categories requires more effort on the part of countries of the region. In a number of Asian countries and Pacific island countries the observation networks of all these four categories need improvement which should be carried out as soon as possible.

(8) Various water development projects for agriculture have received high priority in many developing countries in Asia. However, despite large investments in irrigation development the average yield of cereals is still very low. Many more efforts are required to improve or rehabilitate existing irrigation systems for large areas in many developing countries in Asia.

(9) In most Asian countries, the manpower situation in water resource development has remained essentially the same with some slight improvements in some countries. Many governments have taken action to set up new institutions or enlarge existing ones for training and education of skilled workers, technicians, engineers and research scientists. In small Pacific island countries, the manpower situation has deteriorated for various reasons. Except for Fiji, no country has taken any action to set up new training institutions or enlarge existing ones. In view of the large demand for trained manpower at various levels in the field of water resources development, it is recommended that the establishment of the Regional Network for Training in Water Resources Development, which is part of the work programme of ESCAP, be implemented as soon as possible.

(10) Many countries and areas have strengthened their research institutes dealing with general water resources or specialized subjects to cope with their specific problems.

The lack of financial resources and a shortage of qualified manpower are the main constraints in the area of research. It is recommended that more resources, both national and external, be provided to support this activity.

(11) Many developing countries have made significant progress in technical co-operation among developing countries in the area of information exchange. Most of the respondent countries and areas are interested in TCDC-oriented projects. It is recommended that, for a start, ESCAP implement as early as possible the preparation of a roster of water specialists available for TCDC as envisaged in the 1984-1985 work programme of ESCAP.

REFERENCES

(1) Proceedings of the Expert Group Meeting on Water Pricing, *Water Resources Series No. 55,* Bangkok, 1981.

(2) *FAO Production Yearbook,* 1979 and 1981.

(3) Economic Return to Investment in Irrigation in India, *World Bank Staff Working Papers No. 536,* 1982.

(4) *Sixth Five Year Plan, a mid-term appraisal,* Birla Institute of Scientific Research, 1982.

(5) William R. Gasser, *Survey of Irrigation in Eight Asian Nations,* Washington D.C., United States Department of Agriculture, 1981.

(6) *Indonesia Third Five-Year Plan,* 1979-1984.

(7) Report of the expert group meeting on measures to improve the performance of irrigation project (E/ESCAP/NR.8/6), 1981.

Table 1. National water policy and planning in the ESCAP regional countries

| | Availability of a water policy statement | | Revision of water policy | | | | Availability of a comprehensive master plan for WRD | | Are there any efforts to formulate a master plan? | |
| | | | Has taken place | | Under study | | | | | |
	Yes	No	Yes	No	Yes	No	Yes	No	Yes	No
A. Asia										
Afghanistan	x			x		x		x	x	
Brunei	x			x			x			
China	x				x		x			
Hong Kong	x			x	x		x			
Indonesia	x			x		x		x	x	
India		x		x				x	x	
Japan	x			x	x		x			
Korea, Republic of	x		x				x			
Nepal	x							x	x	
Pakistan		x					x			
Philippines	x		x				x			
Singapore	x			x		x	x			
Sri Lanka		x		x		x	x			
Thailand	x			x	x		x			
B. Pacific										
Australia	x		x		x			x		
Fiji	x		x		x		x			
Guam	x			x	x		x			
Kiribati	x				x			x		x
New Zealand		x						x		x
Samoa	x				x			x	x	
Solomon Islands		x						x	x	
Tonga	x		x		x		x			x
Vanuatu	x					x		x	x	

Table 2. Water charges in some ESCAP regional countries

| | Recovery of fixed costs (investment) | | | | | | | | Recovery of operation and maintenance costs | | | | | | | | Extent to which major urban water supplies are metered | | | Is there any charge for irrigation water use | |
| | Urban water supply | | Industrial water supply | | Rural water supply | | Irrigation | | Urban water supply | | Industrial water supply | | Rural water supply | | Irrigation | | | | | | |
	F	P	F	P	F	P	F	P	F	P	F	P	F	P	F	P	F	P	Not at all	Yes	No
A. Asia																					
Afghanistan	x		x		x				x		x		x				x				x
Brunei		x								x							x				
China	x		x		x		x		x		x		x				x			x	
Hong Kong	x		x		x		x		x		x		x				x				
Indonesia	x		x		x		x		x		x		x				x			x	
India																					
Japan	x		x		x		x		x		x		x		x		x			x	
Korea, Republic of	x		x		x		x		x		x		x		x		x			x	
Nepal										x				x	x			x		x	
Pakistan										x		x		x	x			x		x	
Philippines	x			x		x		x		x		x		x	x				x	x	
Singapore		x		x		x		x		x		x		x			x				
Sri Lanka										x		x			x				x	x	
Thailand	x					x		x		x		x		x			x			x	
B. Pacific																					
Australia	x		x		x		x		x		x		x		x		x			x	
Fiji	x		x		x		x		x		x		x		x		x			x	
Guam	x		x		x		x		x		x		x		x		x			x	
Kiribati	x		x		x		x		x		x		x		x				x	x	
New Zealand	x		x		x		x		x		x		x		x				x		
Samoa	x		x		x				x		x		x		x		x				
Solomon Islands	x				x					x			x				x				
Tonga	x		x		x					x		x		x					x		
Vanuatu	x		x						x		x		x				x				x

F – Fully   P – Partly

Table 3. National water legislation in some ESCAP countries

| | Aspects regulated by existing legislation | | | | | | Whether changes in existing legislation have been introduced or planned | | Extent to which the existing legislation provide for central co-ordination of the responsibilities of central government agencies | | Whether regional and local governments hold responsibilities in administration of water resources | |
| | Ownership of water | | Right to use water | | Protection of water quality | | | | | | | |
	Yes	No	Yes	No	Yes	No	Yes	No	All	Some	Yes	No
A. Asia												
Afghanistan	x		x		x			x	x		x	
Brunei	x		x						x		x	
China		x		x		x	x			x	x	
Hong Kong	x		x		x		x		x		x	
Indonesia	x		x		x		x		x		x	
India	x		x		x		x	x		x	x	
Japan	x		x		x					x	x	
Korea, Republic of	x		x		x		x			x	x	
Nepal			x			x		x		x		x
Pakistan	x		x		x		x			x	x	
Philippines	x		x		x			x	x	x		x
Singapore		x	x		x		x	x		x		x
Sri Lanka	x		x			x	x			x		
Thailand		x		x	x							
B. Pacific												
Australia	x		x		x		x			x		x
Fiji		x		x			x			x	x	
Guam		x		x	x		x		x			
Kiribati	x		x		x		x			x	x	
New Zealand	x		x		x		x			x	x	
Samoa		x	x		x		x		x	x		x
Solomon Islands		x		x		x		x				
Tonga	x			x		x	x		x	x	x	
Vanuatu	x		x			x		x	x	x	x	

Table 4. Institutional arrangements for co-ordinating water-related interests in some ESCAP countries

	Existence of a central mechanism for co-ordinating all water interests at the national level		Does the mechanism have responsibility for preparation, implementation and evaluation of plans and policies for water development and management		If there is no co-ordinating machinery how are the water-related interests dealt with?			Plans to establish a co-ordinating machinery at national level	
	Yes	No	Yes	No	Through ministry of planning	Through interministrial committee	By each ministry without consultation	Yes	No
A. Asia									
Afghanistan	x		x		Yes	Yes	Yes		
Brunei		x		x	Yes				
China		x			Yes				x
Hong Kong	x		x						
Indonesia		x	x		Yes			x	
India	x				Yes				
Japan	x		x						
Korea, Republic of	x		x						
Nepal	x		x						
Pakistan		x			Yes				
Philippines	x		x						
Singapore		x			Yes	Yes			x
Sri Lanka		x				Yes		x	
Thailand	x		x				Yes		
B. Pacific									
Australia	x		x						
Fiji		x					Yes		x
Guam	x		x						
Kiribati		x							x
New Zealand	x		x						
Samoa		x					Yes	x	
Solomon Islands		x					Yes		x
Tonga	x		x			Yes			
Vanuatu		x					Yes		x

Table 5. Shared water resources development in some ESCAP countries

	Are there shared water resources?		Existence of agreement with neighbouring countries for development of shared water resources		Whether agreement provides for the setting up of joint institutional mechanisms		Whether there is a need for establishment of new or expanded agreements	
	Yes	No	Yes	No	Yes	No	Yes	No
A. Asia								
Afghanistan	x		x		x			x
Brunei		x						
China	x		x		x			
Hong Kong		x						
Indonesia	x							
India	x		x		x		x	
Japan		x						
Korea, Republic of								
Nepal	x		x		x		x	
Pakistan	x		x		x			
Philippines		x						
Singapore		x						
Sri Lanka		x						
Thailand	x		x		x		x	
B. Pacific								
Australia		x						
Fiji		x						
Guam		x						
Kiribati		x						
New Zealand		x						
Samoa		x						
Solomon Islands		x						
Tonga		x						
Vanuatu		x						

Table 6. Observation networks and data collection in some ESCAP countries

	Time dependent data																Time-independent data[a]				Whether a plan exists for expanding the network	
	Meteorological				Surface water				Ground water				Water quality									
	Adequacy		Reliability		Adequacy		Reliability		Adequacy		Reliability		Adequacy		Reliability		Adequacy		Reliability			
	Suff.	Insuf.	Suff.	Insuf.	Suff.	Insuf.	Suff.	Insuf.	Suff.	Insuf.	Suff.	Insuf.	Suff.	Insuf.	Suff.	Insuf.	Suff.	Insuf.	Suff.	Insuf.	Yes	No
A. Asia																						
Afghanistan		x		x		x				x				x				x			x	
Brunei		x		x		x				x		x		x				x			x	
China	x		x			x			x		x		x		x		x				x	
Hong Kong	x		x		x		x		x			x	x			x					x	
Indonesia	x		x			x		x	x		x		x			x	x				x	
India	x		x		x		x			x	x			x		x	x		x		x	
Japan	x		x		x		x		x		x		x		x		x		x		x	
Korea, Republic of	x		x		x		x			x	x			x	x		x				x	
Nepal		x				x				x		x		x		x		x	x		x	
Pakistan	x		x			x			x					x				x			x	
Philippines	x		x			x				x	x		x		x		x		x			
Singapore	x		x			x				x			x			x		x	x			
Sri Lanka	x		x			x				x				x		x		x	x			
Thailand		x		x		x		x	x		x		x		x		x				x	
B. Pacific																						
Australia	x		x		x		x			x	x		x			x	x			x	x	
Fiji	x		x		x		x		x		x		x			x	x				x	
Guam	x		x		x		x		x			x	x			x					x	
Kiribati	x		x			x				x				x				x			x	
New Zealand	x		x		x		x			x	x		x		x		x				x	
Samoa		x		x		x				x	x		x		x		x		x		x	x
Solomon Islands		x		x		x				x			x		x		x				x	x
Tonga		x		x						x			x			x		x	x			x
Vanuatu		x		x		x				x	x			x		x				x		x

a   Including physiographical, geological, hydrological, boring description and well legs data.

Table 7. Data processing and dissemination, areal assessment and co-ordination in some ESCAP countries

	Extent of automation (computerized of processing, storage, retrieval and dissemination of the data)			Existence of a mechanism for disseminating data to users		Present state of areal water assessment		Existence of a government investigation programme up to 1990-2000		Extent of co-ordination to the possibility of use of the data by others			Establishing a new body with comprehensive responsibility for water assessment
	Fully	Partly	Not at all	Yes	No	Adequate	Inadequate	Yes	No	To a large degree	To some degree	Extent not known	
A. Asia													
Afghanistan			x		x		x	x			x		x
Brunei			x		x			x				x	
China		x		x		x		x		x		x	
Hong Kong	x			x		x		x					
Indonesia		x		x			x		x		x		
India		x		x		x		x			x		
Japan	x			x		x		x			x		
Korea, Republic of		x		x		x		x			x		
Nepal		x		x			x	x			x		x
Pakistan			x	x			x	x			x		
Philippines		x		x			x	x		x			x
Singapore		x		x			x	x					
Sri Lanka			x		x		x		x	x			
Thailand		x		x			x	x			x		
B. Pacific													
Australia	x			x		x		x			x		
Fiji		x		x		x			x		x		
Guam			x	x		x		x			x		
Kiribati		x		x				x					x
New Zealand		x		x		x			x		x		
Samoa			x		x				x		x		x
Solomon Islands			x		x		x		x			x	
Tonga			x			x		x					
Vanuatu			x		x		x		x		x		

Table 8. Main areas of water resources development for agriculture in some ESCAP countries

	Main areas of activity since the Conference						Projected main areas of activity in future					
	Improvement of existing irrigation	New irrigation	Drainage and reclamation	Flood protection	Water supply for human settlement	Aquaculture in rural area	Improvement of existing irrigation	New irrigation	Drainage and reclamation	Flood protection	Water supply for human settlement	Aquaculture in rural area
A. Asia												
Afghanistan	X	X	X	X	X	X	X	X	X	X	X	X
Brunei	X	X			X		X	X			X	
China	X		X	X	X		X	X	X	X	X	
Hong Kong	X	X	X	X	X		X	X		X	X	
Indonesia	X	X	X	X	X	X	X	X	X	X	X	X
India	X	X	X	X	X		X	X	X	X	X	X
Japan		X	X					X	X			
Korea, Republic of	X	X	X	X	X		X	X	X	X	X	
Nepal	X	X	X	X	X		X	X	X	X	X	
Pakistan	X	X	X	X			X	X	X	X		
Philippines	X	X	X	X	X	X	X	X		X		X
Singapore												
Sri Lanka	X	X	X	X	X	X	X	X	X	X	X	X
Thailand	X	X	X		X	X	X	X			X	
B. Pacific												
Australia	X		X	X	X		X		X	X	X	
Fiji					X						X	
Guam	X	X		X	X	X	X	X		X	X	X
Kiribati					X						X	
New Zealand	X	X	X		X		X					
Samoa					X						X	
Solomon Islands					X							
Tonga					X						X	
Vanuatu					X						X	

Table 9. Trained manpower and advisory services in support of agricultural water development in some ESCAP countries

	Need for trained manpower to implement agricultural water development programme				Action taken or planned to promote national advisory services to deal with:					Constraints in formulation and implementation of agricultural water development			
	Professional and technical	Research	Extension	Basic education	Planning	Design	Construction	Operation maintenance	Supplies and equipment	Lack of qualified manpower	Shortage of financial resources	Institutional deficiencies	Lack of equipment
A. Asia													
Afghanistan	x	x	x		x	x	x	x	x	x	x	x	x
Brunei	x	x	x		x	x				x			
China	x	x	x	x	x	x							
Hong Kong	x			x						x	x		
Indonesia	x	x	x	x	x	x	x	x	x	x	x		x
India	x	x	x		x	x	x	x	x		x		x
Japan		x	x	x	x	x	x	x			x		
Korea, Republic of	x				x	x	x				x		
Nepal	x	x	x	x	x	x	x	x		x	x	x	x
Pakistan	x	x			x	x	x	x		x	x	x	
Philippines		x	x	x	x	x	x	x		x	x	x	x
Singapore													
Sri Lanka	x	x	x		x	x	x	x	x	x	x	x	x
Thailand	x		x		x	x	x	x		x	x	x	
B. Pacific													
Australia											x		
Fiji													
Guam											x		
Kiribati													
New Zealand					x	x	x	x	x				
Samoa		x			x						x		
Solomon Islands										x			
Tonga													
Vanuatu													

Table 10. Manpower situation in water resources development in some ESCAP countries

	Comprehensive survey of manpower needs in water resources development		Change of manpower situation since the Conference																Cause of manpower deterioration			
	Action taken	Action planned	Skilled workers			Middle-level engineers			University educated engineers			Research scientists			Administrators and planners			Transfer to other fields	Migration to other countries	Lack of suitable candidates	Lack of funds to employ
			I	D	N	I	D	N	I	D	N	I	D	N	I	D	N				
A. Asia																					
Afghanistan																					
Brunei		x			x		x			x			x		x				x	x	x
China	x			x			x		x								x			x	x
Hong Kong	x		x				x		x			x			x						
Indonesia	x			x		x			x			x			x						
India			x				x		x			x				x					
Japan												x				x					
Korea, Republic of	x		x			x			x			x					x				
Nepal		x			x	x			x				x			x					
Pakistan					x	x							x			x				x	
Philippines	x	x	x				x		x			x			x			x	x	x	x
Singapore				x			x			x			x		x					x	x
Sri Lanka		x		x			x			x			x		x				x	x	x
Thailand				x			x			x			x		x				x		x
B. Pacific																					
Australia	x			x			x		x			x			x						x
Fiji	x			x			x			x					x						x
Guam							x			x			x		x						x
Kiribati			x				x			x			x		x						x
New Zealand							x			x		x			x						
Samoa		x			x																
Solomon Islands		x		x			x		x				x			x		x	x	x	x
Tonga	x	x	x				x			x			x		x					x	x
Vanuatu	x	x			x		x			x			x		x				x	x	x

I – Improved   D – Deteriorated   N – No change

Table 11. Education and training of manpower in some ESCAP countries

	Action		Setting up new institutions or enlarge existing institutions for training and education					Constraints for increasing education & training activities				
	Taken	Planned	Skilled workers	Technicians & middle-level engineers	University educated engineers	Research scientists	Administrators and planners	Lack of qualified teachers	Lack of teaching aids	Limitation of financial resources	Lack of students	Lack of proper curricula
A. Asia												
Afghanistan		x						x	x	x		x
Brunei		x						x				
China	x		x	x	x	x	x					
Hong Kong												
Indonesia	x	x	x	x	x	x	x	x	x	x		
India	x	x	x	x	x	x	x		x	x		
Japan												
Korea, Republic of	x		x	x	x	x		x	x	x		x
Nepal	x	x	x	x	x			x		x	x	
Pakistan												
Philippines	x	x	x	x	x	x	x	x	x	x		x
Singapore	x		x	x	x			x				
Sri Lanka	x		x	x			x	x	x	x	x	x
Thailand			x	x	x		x	x	x	x		
B. Pacific												
Australia												
Fiji			x	x	x			x	x	x	x	x
Guam								x	x	x	x	x
Kiribati										x		
New Zealand												
Samoa									x	x	x	x
Solomon Islands										x	x	
Tonga								x	x	x	x	
Vanuatu								x		x	x	x

Table 12. Research and development in some ESCAP countries

	Establishment or strengthening of water resources research institutes		Subjects of research			Areas of research with significant progress				Constraints in area of research		
	Action taken	Plans made	General natural resources	General water resources	Specialized topic	Use of local materials	Use of labour intensive methods	Interchangeability in servicing and spare parts	Standardization of equipment	Lack of financial resources	Shortage of qualified manpower	Institutional problem
A. Asia												
Afghanistan	x		x	x						x	x	x
Brunei												
China	x										x	
Hong Kong	x	x	x	x		x	x	x	x	x	x	x
Indonesia		x		x	x	x	x	x	x	x	x	x
India	x			x	x	x	x	x				
Japan												
Korea, Republic of						x			x	x		x
Nepal						x	x			x	x	x
Pakistan	x	x			x					x	x	x
Philippines	x				x	x	x		x	x	x	x
Singapore												
Sri Lanka	x				x	x	x		x	x	x	x
Thailand	x			x	x	x	x			x	x	x
B. Pacific												
Australia	x	x		x	x					x	x	x
Fiji										x	x	
Guam												
Kiribati	x								x			
New Zealand	x	x	x	x	x	x	x		x		x	
Samoa	x					x	x	x	x	x	x	
Solomon Islands						x	x		x		x	
Tonga	x	x	x	x	x	x			x	x	x	x
Vanuatu	x									x	x	

Table 13. Technical co-operation among developing countries (TCDC) in ESCAP region

	Areas of significant progress in TCDC in water resources development					Area of government interest towards the promotion of TCDC					
	Joint venture	Technical/ economic co-operation projects	Information exchange	Establishment of institutional machinery	Exchange of consultant services	Joint venture	Technical economic co-operation projects	Information exchange	Establishment of institutional machinery	Exchange of consultant services	Standardization of engineering services
A. Asia											
Afghanistan								x			
Brunei						x	x	x	x	x	x
China								x			
Hong Kong			x						x	x	x
Indonesia			x	x		x	x		x	x	x
India			x	x	x	x	x	x	x	x	
Japan							x	x			
Korea, Republic of							x	x	x	x	
Nepal						x	x	x	x	x	
Pakistan			x				x	x	x	x	
Philippines	x		x				x	x	x		
Singapore		x					x	x			
Sri Lanka	x	x					x	x			
Thailand		x			x	x	x		x		
B. Pacific											
Australia		x	x	x		x				x	
Fiji	x									x	
Guam			x							x	
Kiribati		x				x					
New Zealand			x	x							
Samoa						x			x	x	x
Solomon Islands						x			x	x	
Tonga									x	x	x
Vanuatu									x	x	x

II. PROGRESS REPORT ON THE INTERAGENCY TASK FORCE
ON WATER FOR ASIA AND THE PACIFIC
(E/ESCAP/NR.10/11)

A. ORGANIZATION OF THE TASK FORCE

At its fourth session, in August 1977, the ESCAP Committee on Natural Resources noted that the Mar del Plata Action Plan contained a number of recommendations concerning sectoral development and management of water which should be handled in an integrated manner, nationally and internationally. It also noted that the United Nations was involved in a wide range of water-related activities and that co-ordination of this was essential for efficient use of available personnel and other resources. In discussing the need for co-ordination at the regional level, the Committee recommended that an inter-agency task force on water should be established for the ESCAP region to assist co-operation and, as appropriate, joint action among participating bodies, in support of national programmes for investigation, development and management of water.

In pursuance of this recommendation, ESCAP took the necessary steps to organize an Interagency Task Force on Water for Asia and the Pacific. It invited the Centre for Natural Resources, Energy and Transport, UNIDO, UNICEF, UNDP, UNEP, ILO, FAO, UNESCO, IBRD, WHO and WMO to join the Task Force. At its first session, in September 1978, the Task Force adopted its terms of reference.

B. WORK OF THE TASK FORCE

Since September 1978, the Task Force has held 11 sessions. The principal items discussed by the Task Force since its inception are briefly described below.

1. Co-operative action in support of national water programmes

The Task Force compiled a staff list of its members working in the field of water in the region. It was agreed that any member could approach other members for assistance whenever difficulty was experienced in recruiting experts in certain fields. It was planned to update the list from time to time.

Members exchanged copies of their regional programmes and activities in support of national water programmes and indicated their interest in certain projects or activities of other members as well as inputs which they could contribute to the projects. A uniform format was devised and adopted for the purpose of providing information on projects and activities of members.

This exchange of information among members on 1980-1981 and 1982-1983 regional programmes has been found to be very useful not only in keeping members informed of the ongoing and planned activities of each member but also in minimizing duplication when formulating future work programmes.

Probable areas for co-operation which have been discussed and are still under consideration are a manpower survey for water resources development and correlation of improvement in rural water supply (and sanitation) with a reduction in the incidence of water-borne/related diseases.

2. Regional follow-up to the United Nations water conference

The Task Force summarized the recommendations for international action in the Mar del Plata Action Plan and identified the action being taken at the regional level by its members in order to identify gaps in the implementation of the Plan and to determine what measures should be taken to fill such gaps. It was agreed that proposals for co-operative projects would be drawn up to fill any gaps so identified.

In carrying out this work, the Task Force agreed that most of the recommendations for international action in the Mar del Plata Action Plan were being implemented to a certain extent through some form of activity by one or more of the members. It was, however, difficult to determine, from the information provided, the areal extent, quality and substantive coverage of such activities in order to have a basis for identifying areas or items on which the United Nations system should concentrate more effort.

Two formats were, therefore, devised which, when completed, would provide more information on members' ongoing and planned regional/subregional activities which could be considered as responding to the Mar del Plata Action Plan. Although the formats were adopted by the Task Force, many members found it difficult to complete them and to provide the necessary information.

Nevertheless, the Task Force was able to identify two co-operative projects which were expected to fill serious gaps in the implementation of the Action Plan. These are:

(a) The establishment of a regional network for training in water resources development, which was endorsed by the Commission at its thirty-eighth session in 1982;

(b) The accelerated manufacture of hand pumps for rural water supply, which would contribute considerably to achieving the targets of the International Drinking Water Supply and Sanitation Decade.

The members of the Task Force collaborated in compiling, through their respective country representatives/experts, and providing relevant information on the basis of which ESCAP drafted project proposals for these co-operative projects. The draft proposals were discussed and amended at subsequent sessions of the Task Force to take into account the views of the members.

As agreed by the Task Force, the project proposal for the accelerated manufacture of hand pumps for rural water supply was sent to the Steering Committee for the Decade for submission to potential donors.

As regards the regional network for training, the Task Force discussed and reached agreement on the draft questionnaire to determine country requirements for training. It was planned that, on the basis of country returns and the views of Task Force members as well as the participating institutes, which had been nominated by the countries, the fields of training and the form and structure of the training network could be determined.

C. GENERAL ASSESSMENT

Attendance by members has been quite good. The United Nations Department of Technical Co-operation for Development and WMO, which do not have regional offices, occasionally send representatives who are on mission in the region to the sessions of the Task Force which have always been held in Bangkok. Representation is at the technical level.

In general, co-operation has been satisfactory but not equally uniform owing probably to differences in legislative mandates, organizational structure, programming cycles, degree of decentralization etc.

For example, the South-East Asia Regional Office of WHO appears to be highly decentralized and has been quite co-operative and in 1980 engaged a consultant to prepare a paper for the ESCAP Committee on Natural Resources. Likewise, it readily agreed to prepare one of the main background papers for the tenth session of the Committee. In comparison, its two other regional offices in the ESCAP region have not been as active in the Task Force, since they have not had the opportunity to participate in its deliverations. Some of the members are highly dependent on their headquarters for information and decisions, as a result of which the submission of their inputs are often delayed.

While members are willing to undertake joint projects on a collaborative basis, their actual participation is contingent upon the availability of resources over and above their regular budgets. In this regard, mention must be made of ILO's readiness to commit $US 10,000 of its own resources to participate in missions concerning the establishment of the regional training network.

There is as yet no experience concerning the modalities for undertaking collaborative projects, as the two projects, which have been identified, are still in the preparatory stages.

III. MULTIDISCIPLINARY AND SYSTEMS APPROACH TO INTEGRATED RIVER BASIN DEVELOPMENT
(E/ESCAP/NR. 10/1)

NOTE BY THE SECRETARIAT

The paper advances the view that while the *multidisciplinary and systems approach to integrated river basin development originate in developed* countries in order to cope with problems arising from their existing complicated infrastructures and administrative systems, this approach is also applicable and would be useful to developing countries, particularly in optimizing benefits from integrated river basin development.

In view, however, of the complicated techniques and procedures involved, expertise and data requirements and cost vis-à-vis the current level of staff and financial resources of the countries, the question arises as to whether it would be cost-effective for developing countries to adopt this approach.

The point is made that if the scope of the task were properly selected, the application of a multidisciplinary and systems approach to integrated river basin development by developing countries would be appropriate.

Going into the historical background of this subject, proponents of integrated river basin planning and development took the United States Tennessee Valley Authority system as a model. In the 1950s and 1960s, the United Nations and its specialized agencies advocated and promoted the concept of integrated river basin development. Subsequently, a number of large-scale projects were undertaken by Governments with financial support from a number of financial institutions and donor agencies.

With the completion of these projects and the experience gained from their operations, it was found that a number of problems were encountered with their cost, levels of output and social and environmental aspects. This was not surprising considering the various disciplines involved to satisfy multiple purposes with different priorities and the multiple social, economic and environmental objectives which had to be met.

Clearly there appears to be a need to improve the procedures and techniques used in integrated river basin development. The multidisciplinary and systems approach described in the paper is one such attempt which could be worth considering by those concerned.

Introduction

Properly speaking, this paper ought to contain two separate parts: one in which integrated river basin development is described and in which convincing arguments in favour of it are laid down; and a second one, in which multidisciplinary and systems approach are described and their indispensibility for the above mentioned development is proven.

It would seem, however, that the first part is not really necessary, as its contents would largely coincide with those of a paper produced for the seventh session of the Committee on Natural Resources in 1980: E/ESCAP/NR.7/3, entitled Integrated Optimum Development of the Deltaic and Upland Portions of a River Basin. (Ref.1). More general information on the subject is given in ref. 6 and ref. 7.

Very briefly put, upstream development, if not judicially geared to downstream development, may be harmful to the latter, whilst in case of integration of development, it may be beneficial. Thus, the economy of an entire basin or country, and the welfare of its people may depend on the administration's ability to integrate. The objects of downstream development are, *inter alia,* flood protection, channel preservation, harbour and shipping development, prevention of salt intrusion, as well as soil-improvement, irrigation and drainage for the benefit of agriculture, and the protection of water quality and environment. In the upstream regions, the development may also consist of channel improvement, but is mostly directed towards reservoir-construction for river regulation, flood protection, irrigation and water power. Downstream channel erosion or siltation may result from the upstream development, as well as harm to the environment by upstream waste discharge. In the paper mentioned above, ideas are laid down

to co-ordinate upstream and downstream activities to mutual benefit.

As to the multidisciplinary and systems approaches, there is one difficulty in describing them and arguing in favour of them in a setting of ESCAP countries, or developing countries in general. The approaches originate from developed countries, and have been applied to their type of problems. An effort to provide a link is to be found in ref. 2, where a comparison between the Netherlands and Bangladesh was made. In a developed country, the problems are superimposed on existing complicated infrastructure and existing administrative systems, and one important objective often is to provide governments and the public with clear and comparable policy options to choose from. In a developing country, the objective would rather be to create a kind of "master plan", and to determine in what sequence, depending on the financial possibilities, the contributing projects should be carried out to obtain maximum benefit.

An international aspect is, that in negotiations between countries sharing transboundary water bodies, the methods under consideration may serve to convince partners, that certain projects might be carried out to mutual benefit.

A. TERMINOLOGY

Throughout this paper, a few notions will be used or implied, that call for definition. These notions are *multidisciplinary approach, systems approach* and *integrated river basin development.* As a short-cut definition of these terms is not possible, an effort will be made to describe their meaning as briefly as possible.

1. *Multidisciplinary approach.* Up to only a few decades ago it was customary and possible (although failures or partial successes did occur) for a civil engineering team to design and build a reservoir dam, for electrotechnical engineers to plan a high voltage electricity transport grid, or for agriculturalists to create an effective irrigation and drainage system, to name a few examples.

Modern society has very quickly become so complicated, and in many places population density is so great, that in most cases such largely uni-disciplinary approaches are no longer acceptable: in this respect, there is little difference between developed and developing countries. An example may serve best to clarify this point.

What is needed for designing, planning and constructing a large reservoir is not only civil engineers and geologists to plan a safe dam and a non-leaking reservoir. If the object of the dam is just power production, at least electrotechnical engineering will come in, whilst obviously, physical planners will have to decide, whether the plant is needed in that area, and whether the transport system fits into the general planning of the region; the same applies to the siting of the reservoir itself. The cost-benefit ratio of a reservoir will be better, if it is also used for irrigation purposes: this is where agriculturalists come in, and they will need physical planners as well. Then, of course, there are the demographic experts and sociologists for resettlement of people, experts of nature, landscape and ecology, and of course lawyers and financial experts for the appropriation of the land. Water managers and administrators must not be forgotten, but it will be obvious that this listing cannot be complete and depends on local and regional circumstances.

The object of what was said above is to show that many professions or "disciplines" are necessary to get a project of any size going and keep it that way. Almost always there is a project manager, who can only fulfil his responsibilities with a multidisciplinary team to back him up: this is what is meant by the words "multidisciplinary approach".

2. *Systems approach*. In the fields of science, technology and also of policy the words "model" and "modelling" are very much in fashion. Often they are used in the conjunction "computer model" etc.

This wording covers a variety of notions, and consequently gives rise to a lot of confusion. Some of these computer models have much in common with a type of model that has been used for a long time and still is being used extensively: the so-called physical models, of which hydraulic models are well-known examples. These resemble computer models in that both try to copy a specific part of reality, can do so only by stylizing and schematizing reality. In both cases, therefore, conclusions and predictions pertaining to reality are only valid after calibration and careful scrutiny, using the laws (for physical models these include scale laws) that govern the relations between model and reality.

As to computer models, the resemblance just described only applies to very sophisticated ones. "Models", in common language, however, mean a lot more, and mostly much simpler things. Any formula, complicated or simple, that describes a relation between variables, is sometimes called a "model". The variables may be of a physical nature, but may also pertain to economic, social, psychological or other phenomena. In some cases, a "model" is simply the expression of a way of thinking: e.g. "conflict model" vs. "harmony model". In the following, the word model may be understood in any of these senses.

In modern society, whether in developed or in developing countries, it is, because of the complex interrelationships, no longer possible to formulate government policies without the aid of the instrument called "planning". To state, as an example, the subject under consideration: a policy for integrated river basin development, whether national or regional, will have to be based on sound planning. This planning will pertain to the water *system* of the basin: obviously, therefore, the water courses of a river basin present themselves to one's mind as a system. From the previous remarks on multidisciplinary approach it may be clear that it is also possible, or even highly desirable, to include, in the notion about the water system, many more issues.

In order to obtain a good understanding of such a system it will have to be analyzed. This analysis usually cannot be carried out using "a model", because too substantial a part of reality has to be looked into for any model to be able to cope with it. Many parts of the system, however, will usually be analyzed by using specific models (though other techniques are also available), whilst other models or techniques again are used to link together the various models or their results. All these activities, aimed at analysing and understanding a complicated system, are often indicated by the term "systems-approach". This is a wider notion than "systems analysis", that may be part of it, while on the other hand "policy analysis" may be one of the aims of systems approach.

Policy analysis and systems approach are, therefore, closely related. The aim of policy analysis generally is, to provide political decision makers with a limited number of attractive possible policies, and with a possibility to compare them using a number of previously defined criteria.

3. *Integrated river basin development*. The meaning of this expression was made sufficiently clear in the 1980-paper for the Committee on Natural Resources, mentioned in the introduction (Ref.1). Development of the water-connected resources of a river basin should be carried out using an overall plan for the entire basin, in order to avoid that activities in one part of the basin adversely affect other parts: on the contrary, if well designed, the various parts of the plan may be mutually beneficial. It is not necessary to carry out such a plan as it were "in one stride", because often financial and technical resources are limited. It is desirable, however, that the sequence (or priorities) of the various projects should be part of the overall plan, aiming at the most efficient utilization of the available resources.

Phrased in this way, integration is limited to water development. Obviously, integration has also a bearing on the various aspects of water: surface and groundwater, waterquality and quantity. Water policy, moreover, is connected to other policy areas, such as, *inter alia*, agricultural and environmental policies, power development, transport, industrialization etc.

To take an example, a country, in the course of its development, may have a policy of industrialization, and may even have a "master plan" for this activity. Obviously, such a plan would not be limited to any specific river basin, but would comprise the country, or parts of it. Within a river basin, however, the "water-plan" and the "industry-plan" may interact. It is contended here, that in an integrated river basin plan, the integration should comprise those aspects of other policy areas that may influence the river basin policy, or be influenced by it.

It is hoped, that in this paragraph, the main concepts behind the terms used in the title of this paper, have been sufficiently clarified. In what follows, for simplicity's sake, the words *systems approach* will be used, implying that the approach is multidisciplinary and is applied to integrated river basin development.

B. INDICATION OF CASES REQUIRING SYSTEMS APPROACH

Systems approach may be and has been applied to many problem areas: from city transport systems to space travel planning, from military/strategic build-up to air pollution abatement. The cases and examples put forward in this paper will be limited to the water field, notably to river basin development.

The object of this paragraph is, to convey the feeling, to what type of problems systems approach is applicable. It is difficult, if not impossible, to do this in general terms, because, in fact, there is nothing against applying these techniques to any problem that seems confusing and complicated to those faced with it.

In the following, therefore, three examples will be given that more or less cover the range: a very complicated case, a relatively simple case, and a suggestion of application in a developing country. All three have been described in literature, so here a short characterization may suffice.

1. The PAWN-study, standing for "Policy Analysis of Water Management for the Netherlands", carried out from 1976-1979, through commission of the Dutch Public Works Department, by the Rand Corporation (Santa Monica, Cal. U.S.A.) and the Delft Hydraulics Laboratory, Netherlands, with active co-operation of the Public Works Department itself. Extensive information on this study is to be found in ref. 3, 4 and 5.

At all times, water has played a prominent part in the Netherlands. The country is the estuarine area of the rivers Rhine and Meuse, and has always been threatened by storm surges from the sea and floods from the rivers, as well as by salt intrusion from the sea. In due time, the rivers and a network of water courses, became also a positive factor because of very favourable navigation possibilities. Naturally, ground water as well as surface water, where of acceptable quality, have served the needs of agriculture and human consumption.

Although the Netherlands have always had an abundance of water and have through the centuries developed a very satisfactory water infrastructure, in recent decades the threat of shortage in very essential use-categories has become ever more real. Among the many reasons for this were population growth, industrialization and water pollution, the latter of which has three components: salt from the sea, national waste and heat discharge, and the dramatic deterioration of the Rhine water quality by upstream activities.

Not surprisingly, a host of ideas arose to diminish this threat and, in the process, to protect the environment. The ideas pertained to infrastructural improvements (often very expensive), to better systems of management, to regulation and legislation, and also to economic measures, such as pricing or imposing charges. Putting into practice such ideas might be effective or not, harmful or not, might be in harmony or contradictory, might be mutually harmful or harmful to other interests, or in general beneficial or harmful to, e.g. economy or the environment. It may be imagined that, in a highly developed and complicated society like the Dutch, the formulation of a rational and generally accepted water policy ran into difficulties.

After several efforts it was decided to tackle the problem by systems approach, that took the form of a fullfledged policy analysis. The object was to find, from a practically unlimited number of possible policies, a few effective ones, and to present these to decision makers in such a way, that their impacts on the many sectors and facets of society became clear, explicit and comparable. A "policy" in this context means a certain combination of measures of any kind, necessary to arrive as closely as possible at a solution of the problems.

The notable aspect of this example is, that in a developed society with a highly developed water system, problems arose, that had to be solved by superimposing measures upon a complicate system, taking into account the intricacies of a society that appears almost frozen by its very complexity.

2. The Drenthe study, Drenthe being a relatively sparsely populated province of the Netherlands, with sandy soil and such a land elevation that no problems of sea floods or salt water intrusion are encountered. The study was carried out from 1980 to 1982, and a description can be found in ref. 5 (page 137).

Drenthe having little access to surface water, (this problem, by the way, was subject of a previous study), the objective of the study was to develop a rational ground-water management policy, taking into account trends in water demand, and the various affected interests.

The problem area can easily be described as a system, and therefore the effort to solve the problem falls under the heading "systems approach", whatever may be the differences with the PAWN-study. In fact, this example has been chosen because of these differences, to illustrate the range of policy areas that may call for systems approach. To name a few of these differences:

a. PAWN was nation-wide, the Drenthe study was applied to a limited area (a province);

b. PAWN included many types of soil, levels, hydrological circumstances, degrees of population-density and industrialization, etc.; the Drenthe study pertained to a more or less homogeneous environment;

c. PAWN covered the entire range of water management aspects, in Drenthe only quantitative aspects of ground-water abstraction to meet demands were involved, though the impacts of the policies considered upon landscape and ecology were taken into account;

d. In PAWN, computer models of high sophistication were used, and others that needed the largest computers because of the number of input- and output data required; naturally, also simpler methods of reasoning and analysis were used, but more than once PAWN touched on the limits of knowledge in science, modelling techniques and computer-capacity; in the Drenthe study, much common-sense reasoning and basic analysis methods were used, and the modelling techniques were of a not too complicated nature; computers were also applied, but mainly because of the large amount of data to be processed;

e. The main efforts of PAWN lay in information-gathering and model-building, and many disciplines, authorities and institutes were involved; in this respect, the Drenthe study differed not so much in principle, but in scope.

The implication of the preceding is not, that PAWN is the most highly developed thinkable tool based on systems approach, nor that much simpler analyses than the Drenthe study may not be called systems approach. It is but an effort to indicate the range of problem areas that are suitable to be approached by these techniques.

3. The third example pertains to a developing country: Bangladesh. It does not deal with a study that has been carried out, but with a problem area that has possibilities for systems approach. Suggestions for these possibili-

ties have been given in ref. 2, so considerations here may be brief.

Let it first be assumed, that for Bangladesh a Master Plan for integrated river basin development covering the entire country, is in existence (which, in fact, is not the case). A country like Bangladesh has no use for a study with objectives, comparable to PAWN. However, a river basin plan would be very costly and time consuming to carry out. As resources in money and man-power are scarce in any case, it is of major interest to divide the plan into separate projects, and to find out in what sequence such projects should be carried out to yield an optimum of "value for money", whilst at the same time they should lie on the shortest path towards completion of the master plan.

This sequence (or setting of priorities) may be found by application of systems approach. The considerations and factors determining the sequence may be complicated and numerous, and the "best" sequence may be one that makes the execution of the various projects seem unconnected: this can only be found out by methods of analysis that are not prejudiced by any preconceived ideas of what is the right approach. It may be assumed (although it cannot be proven without previous analysis) that such a study could be carried out by a systems approach of a not too complicated type.

In this respect, the development of the "Master Plan" itself is quite another matter. The difference from PAWN would be, that it would not have to be superimposed upon an already existing highly developed system, meaning that many more degrees of freedom would be available. Nevertheless, it would be fairly complicated, it would demand sophisticated methods of analysis, and would need a national team of experts from many disciplines, probably aided by outside consultancy.

Just like in the Netherlands, the nature of the plan would depend on the degree of co-operation that could be obtained with upstream countries. If various alternatives were developed, it might even help negotiations, as it might prove mutual benefits to certain forms of co-operation.

The article of ref. 2 suggests, that resources for systems approach and the setting up of a multidisciplinary team, might be well spent development aid because it could prevent later losses by wrongly conceived plans and by mismanagement through lack of knowledge of the system (this word being used in its widest sense).

It is hoped that the choice of examples in this paragraph will enhance the reader's ability to recognize problems in the waterfield, occurring in the ESCAP region, as being suitable for analysis by systems approach.

C. SYSTEMS APPROACH: ACTIVITIES
AND PROCEDURES

Obviously it is not possible to give a general recipe on how to go about doing an analysis by systems approach. Some activities and procedures drawn from the PAWN-experience will be summed up in the following, trusting the reader to be able, in cases of less complicated approaches, to identify the parts it is justified to skip.

Any authority, responsible for parts of governmental activities, is constantly faced with the need to formulate policies concerning certain aspects. There are cases, where the policy area under consideration is so complicated, that after several efforts the authority fails in developing a policy, that is satisfactory to itself, the higher or lower authorities or the public. This may be a signal to consider systems approach, though the preceding efforts should never be neglected, because systems approach is generally demanding in time, personnel and money.

If a team is available or can easily be formed, that can be charged with the analysis, there is one problem the less. If not, a consulting firm, inside or outside the country, may be commissioned to do the work. If the type of problem is anticipated to occur only once, the commission can be simple. Should, however, a "continuing story" be expected, it is essential that the commission include the transfer of knowledge, models and techniques developed, so that in future the authority will be able to do such analyses, or at least essential parts of it, without outside help. But even the first time it is essential that the authority has available sufficient expertise to follow, steer and if necessary limit the study.

In complicated cases, the analysis must be preceded by a feasibility study. This should include: a precise problem formulation; reasonable proof that the problem is suitable for systems approach, and that capacity is available to carry it out properly; an estimate of the time, manpower and financial resources required; and a description, obviously not of the answers, but of the type of output to be expected and the form in which it is going to be presented.

If the feasibility study yields satisfactory results, the actual analysis can start, provided the necessary financial and manpower resources have been obtained. A small steering committee will be formed, consisting of those responsible for the study with a few advisers; also the executive multidisciplinary team will be put together, in which experts from the responsible authority and from the executing institute or institutes will take part. The chairman will be the project leader, who will also take part in the steering committee, preferably be its secretary.

First, a description will be given of the types of work that have to be done, after that the system and the various stages into which they will fit, is to be indicated.

1. To improve the water management in a river basin, a large number of simple measures can be thought of. These shall be called "tactics". Tactics may be of a *technical* nature (building things, improving the infrastructure) of a *managerial* nature (operating sluice gates, controlling water levels or discharges), they may consist of *regulations* (laws, rules, licences, restrictions) or be of the *economic* type (pricing, charges etc.).

A primary and essential activity is to try and think of every conceivable tactic that may be part of a final plan or policy.

2. An essential task is to build the necessary computer models or design any kind of analytical technique that appears useful to the analysis. To do this, obviously the system of analysis to be followed must be known: this will be dealt with presently.

Although, as will be stressed again later on, an analysis should be as simple as possible, which means that models may not even be used, on the other hand it is quite possible that many types of models will be needed. Examples are: a basin-wide water-distribution model, if possible including quality parameters; models representing the courses of sectoral activities in society, such as electricity production, shipping, drinking-water production and distribution, agricultural water use, etc; models describing certain processes of a physical, biological or economic nature, such as eutrophication, processes of water and salt being used by plants in the root-zone, transport of sand and silt in rivers and the silting up or scouring of channels; efforts to build optimization models are always attractive, but experience with this specific tool (at least in systems approach in the water field) is as yet not encouraging.

For some models, it will be possible to interconnect them; of others one will have to be content by using their results as inputs to others. Some models are useful in one specific stage of the analysis, others will be needed in more, or even in every stage.

3. It will be necessary to gather information and data to use as inputs to the models or in other analysis techniques. In some cases, such as hydrological or meteorological data, these may be available but will have to be put at the team's disposal and be processed for the purpose of utilization. If they are not available in sufficient quantities, monitoring programmes will have to be carried out during a period, that is adequate to obtain sufficient information by statistical means; in complicated cases, lack of this type of data may cause delay in the investigation.

Other types of information may be gathered by interviews, e.g. on technical processes in industry, of agricultural processes and habits, on sociological background and political structures, on chemical and biological processes in cases of water pollution or water purification, on economic circumstances and relations within regions, within the country or between countries; etc. Typical information and data used in the PAWN study are listed in the Annex.

4. The activities mentioned under a, b and c must all be more or less completed, before the models can be run to provide answers. The activities, as will also be seen later, will run simultaneously, and even during the final stage of running the models, new questions will arise, that make continuation of the other activities necessary.

In the following, the various stages that, together, comprise a systems approach, will be described; the previously described activities are all part of it. For the description, fig. 1 will be used for reference: it is, actually, the PAWN systems diagram, and as such must be regarded as an example only. Other lines of systems approach may be just as valuable or even more so, but a general approach to a description might suffer of an unsatisfactory vagueness. It should be remarked, that PAWN was a *policy* analysis, which is not quite the same as a systems approach. But systems approach was largely used in PAWN, and the whole exercise fits well into the title of this paper. In the figure below, the word "policy" has not been removed to be replaced by, e.g. "Master Plan". For the purpose of this paper it will be assumed, that the "policy" from PAWN and the "Master Plan" this paper is after, are identical notions.

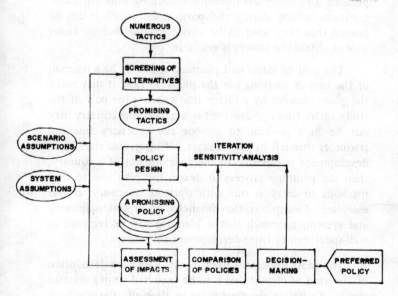

Figure 1. Stages of a systems approach to integrated riverbasin development (Source: PAWN literature)

The primary inputs to the systems approach are represented by the oval "boxes" on top and to the left. The "system assumptions", in fact, describe the system under consideration, with all the elements that are subject to

change or improvement. The "scenario assumptions" also pertain to the system, but they contain those elements that are externally given and not subject to change, such as meteorological conditions or the general hydrological regime of a river.

The "numerous tactics" are those referred to under *a* in the previous part on activities. Most probably the number of those tactics is so vast, that it is not feasible to take all combinations of all tactics into account. Their number must be reduced by a process called "screening": a tactic is accepted or rejected on the basis of a number of criteria, the choice of which lies with the analysts. A few obvious examples will be given.

Since a tactic has an objective, the first criterion, will be the ability of the tactic to meet the objective. A second criterion will be, whether benefits are greater than costs. Another may be whether other interests benefit from a tactic or are harmed by it: in this connection, environment and ecology should not be forgotten, though they can generally not be expressed in monetary terms. The list could be extended, and will depend very much on the circumstances in the river basin under consideration.

Experience shows that there are often more than one or even many tactics that meet the criteria: in those cases only the best is retained, the others are rejected, provided there are no secondary circumstances to retain them. The tactics retained are labelled "promising tactics", and their number ought to be very limited in order to keep further analysis workable.

The next step is "policy design", or in the case under consideration, the design of the desired Master Plan, by combining, in a coherent way, various tactics. It is reasonable to assume, that a *number* of Plans can be designed by choosing different combinations of tactics: several "promising policies" or "promising plans" are obtained in this way. At first sight, it may not be possible to choose the "best Plan" by unprejudiced judgement.

The next stage, therefore, is the "assessment of impacts". The impact of a specific plan on various interests must be investigated. This may be economy, agriculture, shipping, environment, industry, water quality etc. In this connection, it is important to remark that the entire analysis should be carried out in close contact between the analysts, the steering group, and especially the decision makers, who ought to be induced to follow closely the proceedings: it is their primary task to choose the impact categories and they could not do so without being closely connected to every stage in the progress of the study.

After impact assessment, the performance of each plan regarding each impact category must be made visible in such a way that the plans become comparable. There are several techniques to do that: none of them can give an objective picture that provides an easy choice: the responsibility of decision-making is not taken off the politicians' shoulders: what can be done, however, is to remove any doubts as to the consequences of a decision.

The figure virtually ends with the box "decision-making", but from there shows a loop back to policy design. As computer models are always based on simplifying assumptions, and as science and technology are not always able to provide unequivocal relations, the model output may deviate from reality. It is essential, therefore, to test the sensitivity of model results to the variability of the inputs. If sensitivity to an important input is not negligible, the plan will contain certain risk factors, that must also be made clear.

This means, that several iteration loops may be necessary before a well founded choice can be made. If all goes well, in the end a "preferred policy" of final "Master Plan" will be chosen and adopted.

The inpression may have been given, that systems approach is something that runs along well-prepared and systematic lines. In practice, it is unavoidable that all activities and stages run parallel, and mistakes are being made and have to be corrected. A model, designed for a certain stage often proves suitable for another as well (e.g. screening and impact assessment) but has to be adjusted, while runs for the first stage are being made. All this is in the nature of the method of systems approach, but it puts a heavy burden on, and demands great competence, from the management and the project leader.

D. REQUIREMENTS AND OUTPUT

Before a listing is given of the outputs to be expected from a study on the basis of systems approach, some remarks will be made on the requirements for such a study.

It seems to be a rather obvious statement to say that a strong desire to develop a river basin is necessary. The question is: *who* desires it? In all cases, such an idea must live in the people of nation, and must be worded by an authority, representing the people. In other words, the authorities, responsible for the development of water resources, together with those responsible for developing the nation's economy, have to be sure that an ambitious plan will be recognized by the population as being in its own interest: only then its co-operation is ensured. Without such co-operation, the best plan is liable to failure. This difficulty has been experienced in developed countries, and will doubtlessly, also occur in developing countries.

For the multidisciplinary effort involved, the technical capability has to be available, as well as readiness of those involved to work in close co-operation. It is unlikely that these conditions can be met from the outset in a developing country. That this is by no means meant in a disparaging way is illustrated by the fact that these very pre-conditions were not met in the Netherlands at the outset of PAWN: in fact, they developed during the study, as many authorities and institutions found it to be in their own interest to participate in the study. This shows that what may be labelled a requirement on the one hand, may, on the other hand, be part of the output of a systems study.

The preceding observations mean that the capabilities to carry out this type of planning can also be bought, which, in fact, happened in the Netherlands. There are signs, however, that in the ESCAP region, countries will try to *train* multidisciplinary teams beforehand, which may also be a good method, now that some countries and consulting firms have gathered sufficient experience. Obviously, this training will also require the availability of financial resources.

Expertise and money are the most important prerequisites to start and carry out successfully a study based on systems approach. As to money, however, one should be aware of the fact that it is not the cost and complexity of a method that determines its suitability for a certain objective. On the contrary, it is advisable to start a study by simple and straightforward methods, and resort to complicated and computer-intensive modelling only for those questions arising during the project, for which it can be proven that they have to be answered and that no easier way to obtain the answer is available.

The cost of integrated planning will only be a fraction of the cost of carrying out the plans: in fact, it may make the plans cheaper by a factor that exceeds the cost of the study many times. Nevertheless, a developing country may not be in a position to provide the necessary financial resources through its own budget. If integrated river basin development is essential to the development of a country, then the planning process to design the plan and to find methods to carry it out with optimal efficiency, is also essential. This means, that financing of a multidisciplinary and systems approach to the planning can be regarded as well-spent money from development aid sources.

The most important item of this paper is a description of the kind of *output* that is to be expected from a systems study. To define the final stage is, after all, that has been said not too difficult: this may be the adoption of a master plan for integrated river basin development, preferably combined with a priority list (the sequence and timing of operationalisation of the various parts of the plan), as well as a multi-annual plan for the financing of the execution.

The plan itself will consist of various categories. Generally, in the situation of a developing country, the most important item will be the *works* to be carried out to improve the infrastructure. Also it is necessary to know, what methods will be used to influence the *behaviour* of the population in such a way, that they can be expected to utilize the improved situation to the best advantage of themselves and the country. For this, a set of laws, rules and regulations may have to be designed or adopted to the new situation, but also a system of information and education may be of importance. Also economic incentives, like pricing, charges, levies etc. may be expected to be effective. Finally, the *policies* adopted to make the plan work must be made to fit the national policy. In cases, where the river basin covers an entire country or a very substantial part of it, it may be necessary to adopt the national water policy to the requirements of the basin plan.

It has been said that the adoption of the plan is the *final* stage of the operation. From previous chapters it may be gathered, that one of the principal assets of a systems study is, that it results in a *number* of plans to be presented to the decision makers to choose from. The plans will be comparable in that they explicitly show the impacts on various sectors of society and on the various interests that are manifest in a country. What systems approach *cannot* do is, to assign weights to the various impact components: this is essentially a part of the decision-making process. Systems approach will not make this difficult process any easier: it will, however, make explicitly clear the consequences of a decision.

In conclusion, one more remark on the words "final stage" used before: if a plan is finally adopted, financed and carried out, it may take many years to complete. During this period, circumstances will change, objectives may be modified and the progress of the plan itself may throw a different light on previous opinions. It is, therefore, essential that the instruments used and/or developed during the study, as well as the expertise, be in the possession of the responsible authority by the end of the study: this, in fact, has to be an explicitly stated objective and an output of the study. There is hardly any doubt, that the execution of the plan will have to be accompanied by a continuation (admittedly with lower effort) of the study with the methods available.

E. CONCLUSIONS AND RECOMMENDATIONS

1. Conclusions

a.   The desirability of integrated river basin development has been demonstrated in many studies, including a previous ESCAP secretariat paper (ref.1).

b.   Modern societies, developed or developing, are so complex that projects of any size can only be planned and carried out through multidisciplinary approach.

c.   Although multidisciplinary and systems approach originate from developed countries and were primarily geared to their kind of problems, the methods are equally well suited to be applied in developing countries.

d.   In a developing country, the methods would not only serve the designing of a "Master Plan" for integrated river basin development, but may also indicate the most efficient sequence of works and measures to achieve the objectives.

e.   Multidisciplinary and systems methods may prove the advantage of international co-operation to upstream and downstream countries, and so be beneficial to negotiations.

f.   The knowledge and experience needed for multidisciplinary and systems approach may be acquired through "learning by doing" (to be effectuated by close co-operation with an experienced consulting firm), or by training a team in advance.

g.   An essential part of a multidiciplinary and systems approach is the gathering of information. This may involve much time and effort, and the information may vary from hydrological data series to knowledge of the economic situation of an industry, a region, or even of a country.

h.   A development plan for a river basin may consist of a mix of measures (or "tactics") of a technical, managerial, legislative and economic type.

i.   For a developing country, the main feature of an integrated river basin plan will be the *works* to improve the hydrological and economic situation. It may, however, be equally important to influence the behaviour of the people and interest groups, which can be done by legislation and regulation, by information and education, and by economic incentives, like pricing, charges, subventions etc.

j.   The output of planning by multidisciplinary and systems approach will be a (limited) number of promising plans, that are comparable on the basis of previously agreed criteria. As the weighting of these criteria remains subjective, the responsibility of a choice remains with decision makers.

k.   If the quality of the development of a river basin and the efficiency of its planning and execution can be enhanced by multi-disciplinary and systems approach, there is much in favour of financing this approach by resources from development aid.

2. Recommendations

a.   The integration of river basin development should not be limited to water aspects, but should include aspects of all relevant sectors of national policy.

b.   A prerequisite for planning by multidisciplinary and systems approach is, that a country's administrative system contain an authority that is able to bear the responsibility for this work.

c.   For planning by multidisciplinary and systems approach to succeed, hierarchical and organisational structures must not prevent close co-operation under a recognized project leader, between authorities, disciplines and experts.

d.   Before a large scale planning operation is started, it should be ensured that such a plan will be understood and accepted by the population.

e.   Prior to the planning, it is essential that the sources of manpower, expertise and financing be identified.

f.   As multidisciplinary and systems approach may or may not involve complicated computer models and highly sophisticated methods of analysis, the complex approach should only be adopted after the insufficiency of simple methods has been proven.

g.   A complicated study should be preceded by a feasibility study.

h.   The reliability of results should be properly verified, *inter alia,* by sensitivity analyses.

i.   Proper documentation of all models and techniques, as well as of the entire study, is of crucial importance.

j   Though *all* conceivable interests involved in integrated river basin development should be duly taken into account, *special* attention should be given to environmental and ecological aspects: in this way, expensive remedies in later stages may be avoided.

k.   A contract with a consultant to carry out a systems study should include not only extensive reporting, but also the transfer of: knowledge, model documentation and analysis techniques, to a national team of experts and to the responsible authority.

l.   A planning operation may well be followed by others, and the execution of a plan may involve adaptations to changed circumstances. It is, therefore, essential to preserve and keep up-to-date the acquired instruments and data and the capabilities to operate them, and to ensure continuity in the expertise and in the team.

m.   It is essential that decision makers be closely involved in every step of a study by multidisciplinary and systems approach, thus enabling them to influence the course a study takes, and to familiarize themselves with the way of thinking: if this is neglected, the process of decision-making may fail.

n.   If from multidisciplinary and systems approach a preferred water policy for a river basin emerges, care should be taken that this policy be in line with the general policies of the country.

F. REFERENCES

1.   E/ESCAP/NR.7/3 Note by the secretariat: Integrated optimum development of the deltaic and upland portions of a river basin (paper prepared by Prof. ir. A. Volker, Netherlands).

2.   K.P. Blumenthal: The functions of integrated national water planning in the Netherlands and in Bangladesh (Contribution to National Symposium of River Basin Development, Dacca, Bangladesh, December 5-10-1981: appeared in: M. Munir-Uz-Zaman), (editor): River Basin Development, Tycooly International Publishing Ltd, Dublin, Ireland, January 1983, ISBN 0 907567 57 6, ISBN 0 907567 56 8).

3.   Rand Corporation, Santa Monica, C.A. 90406: Policy Analysis of Water Management for the Netherlands, 1981, 1982, prepared for the Netherlands Rijkswaterstaat. N-1500/1-NETH through N-1500/20-NETH, volumes I through XX.

4.   Economic Commission for Europe (UN), Geneva. Seminar 13th-18th October 1980 at Veldhover, Netherlands on "Economic Instruments for the Rational Utilization of Water Resources".   Choice of papers, entitled: "Policy Analysis for the National Water Management of the Netherlands", appeared in:

a.   Commissie voor Hydrologisch Onderzoek TNO, verslagen en mededelingen no. 29a, The Hague, 1982.

b.   Rijkswaterstaat Communications nr. 31, 1982.

Includes:

c.   K.P. Blumenthal: General aspects of the policy analysis for the water management of the Netherlands (PAWN).

d.   G. Baarse and E. van Beek: A methodology to determine consequences of variations in water management for agriculture.

e.   P.K. Koster and F. Langeweg: A cost minimization analysis of the future drinking water supply in the Netherlands.

f.   P.J.A. Baan: Minimum cost allocation to drinking water companies and industries.

g.   J.W. Pulles: Consequences for shipping of water withdrawals from the river Rhine in the Netherlands and the method used in the PAWN study to estimate the final implications.

h.   J.W. Pulles: The relation between water management and power production and the way its consequences are investigated in the PAWN study.

i.   G. Baarse, E. van Beek and J.P.M. Dijkman: A model describing the water distribution in the Netherlands/the screening of water management tactics.

j.   W.A. Dorsman: Screening of pricing and regulation measures for water allocation in the PAWN study.

k.   G. Baarse and E. van Beek: Design of policies for the water management of the Netherlands.

l.   G. Baarse and E. van Beek: Assessing impacts of water management policies.

5.   M.J. Lowing (editor): Optimal Allocation of Water Resources, IAHS Publication No. 135: Proceeding of a symposium held during the First Scientific General Assembly of the International Association of Hydrological Sciences (IAHS) at Exeter, U.K. 19-30 July 1982.

Including:

a.   page 103: K.P. Blumenthal: Overview of the Dutch water management system.

b.   page 113: M.A. Veen and G. Baarse: Policy analysis of water management for the Netherlands (PAWN).

c.   page 123: E. van Beek: Approach of various competitive water users and impact categories in PAWN.

d.   page 137: E. Romijn and M. Tamminga: Allocation of water resources in the eastern part of the Netherlands.

e.   page 155: G. Baarse and G. Miedema: Modelling approach for a regional water management study in a polder area.

f.   M.A. Veen, G. Baarse and E. van Beek: Water resources management: from policy analysis to policy formulation.

6.   Water Resources Series No. 41: Water Resource Planning.

7.   Flood Control Series No. 7: Multiple-purpose River Basin Development, Part I: Manual of River Basin Planning (out of print).

Annex

Description of type of data used in the PAWN-study

Introduction

The PAWN-study makes use of much data. Most of the data is placed in data files that are read into the computer at the start of a model run. The principal model of PAWN is the Distribution Model (DM), which is a computer simulation of the surface water distribution system in the Netherlands. Other models are:

.   DISTAG (District Hydrologic and Agriculture Model)

.   EPRAC (Electric Power Reallocation and Cost Model)

.   IRSM (Industry-Response Model)

.   RIDOM (Drinkingwater Model)

.   Shipping model

.   Sedimentation model

.   Salt intrusion model.

There are submodels, but they can also been used separately. Some data files are used by DM and one or more of the submodels.

A. DISTRIBUTION MODEL

1.   The distribution system infrastructure

The main infrastructure is schematized as a network consisting of nodes and links. The majority of links represents the major rivers and canals of the country. Sometimes they represent open connections between the bodies of water or sluices, locks, and pumps that transport water between the bodies of water.

The majority of the nodes represents locations where the rivers and canals meet, or where there are major bodies of water (so-called storage nodes).

The following data has to be collected:

—   Each link is identified by a number, a name and the nodes that the link connects. The parameters of the link are the *minimum, maximum* and *desired* flow. (for flushing, cooling or locking operations), the *surface area* and the *volume* of the link.

—   The nodes are also identified by number and names. Their parameters are the *area* and the *volume* (for the nodes, with storage), initial *salinity* and heat input at node.

— The agricultural areas (districts) extract or discharge water from the nodes of the network through the district links, according to rules known as "distribution keys". A district distribution key contains up to four triples of parameters, each triple being a node name, *the maximum capacity of the district link* to that node and the fraction of district extractions (or discharges) *assigned to that district link.*

2. *The external supply*

— River discharge by decade

— Precipitation and open water evaporation data from weather stations

— External drainage

— Seepage.

The date concerning the internal supply (small rivers, internal drainage and groundwater) are parts of the DISTAG submodel.

3. *The pollution parameters*

— Salinities of the river discharges by decade

— For the same rivers, monthly concentrations of the following pollutants: Phosphate, BOD, Nitrogen, Chromium

— Decay Rates and Bottom Release Rates at nodes for each Pollutant.

4. *The water demand*

— The water demand calculated in the submodels DISTAG, IRSM and RIDDM

— Some other demands of drinking-water companies and industry, represented by *fixed extractions* at nodes, as far as they don't belong to that input of DISTAG

— Extractions by Belgium, according to a treaty between Belgium and the Netherlands

— Water demands for pollution control purpose, like: flushing in districts, salinity control at salt-fresh locks, flushing of pollutant out of urban nature and recreation areas.

— Water requirements in those links supplying the cooling water for the electrical power plants

— Water demands for lock operation.

Most of the water demands mentioned above are represented in the Distribution Model as desired and minimum flows on link.

5. *Data concerning costs*

. Cost parameters for each technical tactic

. Cost of waterboard plans

. Cost of sprinklers.

B. DISTRICT HYDROLOGIC AND AGRICULTURE MODEL

The Netherlands is divided into 78 districts (hydrologic units). For each district the following data is needed:

— total area

— urban area

— open water area

— open water volume

— flushing minimum

— industrial extractions from and discharges to surface water

— salinity industrial discharges

— initial salinity of surface water

— precipitation (of the nearest weather station)

— open water evaporation (idem).

The 78 districts are divided into 144 subdistricts. Each subdistrict has the same mean groundwater table of many years duration (shallow, middle, deep) and the same soil type (root zone and subsoil). For each subdistrict the following data is needed:

— mean groundwater table (shallow, middle, deep)

— soil type (there are 26 possibilities for the root zone and the subsoil) with for each soiltype: the permeability, the percentage of moisture, the thickness of soil layers, etc.

— functions for infiltration from surface water to the groundwater or drainage and *vice versa*

— intensity and salinity of seepage

— industrial and drinking water extractions (partly calculated by IRSM and RIDDM) from ground- and surface water

— area where surface water supply is possible.

The 144 subdistricts are divided into ca. 1400 "plots", based on two criteria:

— crop type (there are 14 possibilities) with for each crop: the water demand, the financial value and the sensitivity for dryness and salinity

— type of watersprinkling (none, by surface water or by groundwater) with corresponding energy- and labour costs.

C. ELECTRIC POWER REDISTRIBUTION AND COSTS MODEL

The Netherlands is divided into five regions.

Concerning the demand for electricity, data have to be known about:

— the national demand for electricity per hour

— for each region the share of these national demands.

There are 35 power plants with a total of 125 units. Per unit the following data are to be collected

— region in which it is located

— capacity of power production

— maximum waste heat

— mean efficiency

— is there a cooling tower?

— type of fuel with costs

— costs during transportation by grid

— capacity of power grid and transformers.

D. INDUSTRY RESPONSE MODEL

For each type of industry there are functions for the costs in relation to the capacity of groundwater extractions, of recycling cooling water and of surface water extractions.

Further information required:

— number of companies

— the quantity of groundwater extractions

— the quantity of cooling water

— the quantity of recycled water

— the distance to the surface water (to calculate the cost of using it)

— the price of drinking water

— the growing-rate of the type of industry

— the taxes for groundwater use.

E. DRINKING WATER MODEL

— the demand for drinking water per province

— the possibilities of supply (groundwater or surface water)

— capacity of the sources

— capacity of transport infrastructure

— costs of production per source

— costs of transport.

F. SHIPPING MODEL

— number of shipping fleet, shipping routes (seven route groups)

— low water loss functions, developed for each route

— critical depth and critical points

— costs caused by low water.

G. SEDIMENTATION

— function of relation between sand carrying capacity of the river and the sedimentation

— dredging costs.

H. SALT INTRUSION

— function between river discharges and salinity at several points.

IV. WATER AS A FACTOR IN ENERGY RESOURCES DEVELOPMENT
(E/ESCAP/NR.10/3)

Introduction

Water is now emerging as a major factor in the development of energy resources in the region. This is because water is involved in all phases of energy development, that is, both energy extraction and energy conversion. In energy extraction processes, water is needed for mining of fossil fuels and uranium, oil refining and vegetative growth which provides fuelwood and biomass; in energy conversion processes, water is needed to convert heat energy into mechanical energy and then into electrical energy and also as a cooling agent for internal combustion engines and other energy conversion processes that do not need water. Water is also widely used for generating hydro-electric power.

Water and energy resources development are closely interrelated. This relationship is discussed in greater detail in section I. Just as water is involved in many aspects of energy production, energy is also consumed in various aspects of water resources development and management. The development of water and energy resources have a complimentary effect on one another, that is, the development of water resources creates a favourable condition for energy resources development and *vice versa*.

The main objective of the development of these resources is usually to satisfy their demand as an essential input in various national development projects. There are two ways of achieving this: either through increasing the supply by developing these resources or through reducing the demand by proper management to eliminate unnecessary waste and increase the efficiency of their use. In areas characterized by an abundance of undeveloped supplies of these resources, it is enough to concentrate on the development aspects of supply and to leave the demand aspects to the market created by consumers. However, in cases where these two resources have become scarce, it is not sufficient to emphasize the supply aspects alone. Proper management of the demand use of these resources is necessary to achieve sustained economic growth as a result of balanced supply and demand. This is true because whatever amount is saved by conservation and cutting down wastage can be regarded as an extension of supply of these resources. It is also observed that conservation in the use of one resource generally leads to the reduction in the use of the other with very few exceptions. In view of this, various means of reducing water and energy requirements are dealt with in this paper. These means may be considered in planning water and energy resources development and management in the developing countries of the region.

Water itself is also a main source of mechanical as well as electrical energy. For instance, hydropower is obtained by converting the potential energy of water into electrical energy and is regarded as one of the promising renewable energy resources to relieve the energy crisis of the Asian and Pacific region. This region is endowed with a large hydropower potential and only a small percentage of it is being developed at present. Hydropower, at present, is the only renewable form of energy that can be developed extensively in many countries immediately for large-scale generation of electricity without waiting for further technical developments.

The development of hydropower in industrialized and developing countries differs according to the scale and character of energy consumption. In industrialized countries that development is often restricted to large plants to serve growing rapidly loads over large areas. In developing countries, the consumption of electricity is comparatively low and scattered over small areas located very far from one another, and therefore the development of small-scale hydropower is as important as that of large plants. While the role of hydropower will be a substantial one in reducing the demands on non-renewable resources, its exploitation must not be indiscriminate and should take due consideration of its environmental effects, because it is cheaper to take anticipatory remedial measures than to rectify damage after it has occurred.

In their efforts to achieve a targeted rate of growth of hydropower generation many countries are concentrating their activities on the exploration and development of new projects which require huge investments. This is quite justifiable for countries that can seek and obtain necessary funds for such capital intensive projects. However, for less fortunate countries that find it difficult to raise sufficient funds for such activities it may be more practical to look for other less capital-intensive alternatives that can be funded from their own resources. Few countries seem to be aware of or interested in retrofitting existing dams and irrigation canals with electricity-generating equipment, improving the efficiency of their old hydro-electric power plants, adding new units to existing plants and increasing the storage capacity of regulation ponds. In this connection, it should be noted that although such rehabilitation and modernization projects do not have as great an impact on the country's power system as new large-scale projects, they can be managed with available financial resources in most developing countries.

In view of the close relationship between water and energy resources development, an integrated planning approach is necessary in order to provide dynamic economic growth in the region. With this objective in mind, a number of mathematical models have been developed over the past decade to assist in the investigation of various alternatives and obtain optimum results for future water-energy systems. A review of some of these models has been made so that an appropriate model could be selected for possible application in developing countries. These models, particularly the resource allocation models, are useful for allocation of water between various sectors as well as between various energy production facilities within the energy sector. However, these models are mainly concerned with maximizing economic benefits and/or minimizing resource use and do not consider the social aspects such as social preferences and environmental effects. The social aspects of planning are of particular importance when allocating water between competing energy and non-energy uses. This has led to the adoption of a more comprehensive approach which considers the minimization of the detrimental environmental impacts of the projects as one of the main objective functions.

Inclusion of environmental quality as an objective of development recognizes the fact that the welfare of society has other dimensions beside economics, and it makes the planning process more complex than ever before. The task of incorporating the environmental effects within the planning framework is difficult, because it is not possible to express the benefit of supplying domestic water to a society in monetary terms or to assess the damage for not providing a minimum discharge in rivers for pollution control. Such analyses often involve the question of choice or value judgement. The task of water allocation for energy development and other uses is characterized by the same difficulties, a rational solution to which may be made by the application of the multi-objective theory discussed in this paper. This theory was first developed by the United States Water Resources Council in 1973 and was later tested and modified by the Centre for Environmental Studies, University of Melbourne, Australia, for Australian conditions. It should be noted that further modifications may be necessary to adapt this method to varying conditions in individual countries. A simplified version of this multi-objective theory is presented here for the dual-component objective function — economic efficiency and social/environmental quality. Then, the water allocated to the energy sector may be reallocated further among various energy resource developments by using one of the appropriate water-energy models.

A. RELATION BETWEEN WATER AND ENERGY RESOURCES DEVELOPMENT

Water can be either directly or indirectly involved in energy production. Water as an energy producer is found in rainfall-generating agricultural products, water wheels powering mills and lifting up irrigation water, and ocean waves, tides and falling water generating hydroelectric power. An indirect involvement of water in energy production is found in processes, such as mining, reclamation of mined lands, on-site processing, transportation, refining of fuels etc., as well as energy-generating facilities, such as thermal power stations, nuclear power stations, steamers, locomotives, steam-operated compressor stations etc. Similarly, energy is also involved in various water resources development facilities. Examples of energy being consumed in water resources systems may be found in the use of electrical or mechanical energy to operate the gates of dams, waterways, navigation locks etc. and to pump water from lakes, rivers or underground sources.

An approach which is often neglected in water and energy supply fields is demand management. It should be noted that efforts and technologies to decrease water and energy requirements are as important as those for increasing these resources. The water-energy relation is such that better management and use of water resources can lead to reduced energy consumption and *vice versa*. If less water is used for irrigation, industry, cities or pollution control, less energy will be required. Some useful measures that can be taken to reduce water and energy requirements are described below.

Energy-related water use may be divided into two categories: consumptive use and non-consumptive use. The consumptive use of water may be defined as the permanent removal of water from the actively circulating terrestrial system. This may be by incorporation into the product, through return to atmosphere as evapotranspiration, or by placing the water in permanent storage in rocks. This section deals with the consumptive aspects.

1. Measures to reduce water and energy requirements in agriculture

In agriculture, it is well within current technological capability to achieve an annual reduction of 10 to 50 per cent [1] in energy consumed in providing water supplies. Energy requirements for irrigation can be reduced by improving irrigation efficiency, increasing pumping plant efficiency, reducing water application, improved management of electric pumping plants and reuse of irrigation runoff.

According to a research in Nebraska, United States, [1] under certain conditions of soil moisture holding capacity, an irrigation system which can provide about half the evapotranspiration rate is found to be sufficient for maintaining normal crop production. Depending on the crop, soil and climate, a programmed depletion of soil moisture can reduce water application and associated energy requirements for pumping from 20 to 50 per cent. As a result of combining this technology with irrigation scheduling, a maximum saving of energy can be obtained. Irrigation schedules may be designed in such a way that electrically operated irrigation pumping plants are shut down during peak hours of load, thereby reducing maximum daily and overall peaks for a given power supply system.

Installation of reuse systems on irrigated lands having a substantial pumping lift can reduce total power consumption from 10 to 25 per cent or more.[1] Significant energy savings may also be achieved through modernization of present irrigation systems and improved design of new ones. For example, automatic surface irrigation systems can provide greater than 90 per cent water application efficiency with energy savings of 50 per cent or more.[1]

2. Measures to reduce water and energy requirements in industry

Industries use energy to move water through processing systems and to heat and cool water for various purposes. A major manufacturer in the United States (Texas Instruments, Attleboro, Massachusetts) reduced its water consumption by as much as 58 per cent[2] by undertaking two water conservation programmes — one focussed on employee education and the other on curtailing the company's use of production water. For the employee education programme, articles on the need for water conservation were published in the employee newsletter; employee teams responsible for reducing the wastage of water were formed for each manufacturing building; water conservation information kits were sent to each manager; water conservation posters were posted throughout the plant; and a water use chart showing the results of the manufacturer's water management programme was installed in the cafeteria. In reducing the use of production water, the manufacturer first developed a piping system in order to identify those areas or items of machinery where cooling water could be recirculated. After identifying areas suitable for water conservation, a system was designed to recirculate the used water through a cooling tower, which allowed collected heat in the water to be dissipated into the atmosphere. Thus, instead of 100 per cent of cooling water being wasted, the new system cools and circulates 95 per cent of the water.

A significant reduction in the consumptive use of water may be achieved in the field of energy conversion processes, where large amounts of water are used in evaporative cooling processes. For example, wet cooling, which is used in most thermal electric plants, can be substituted by more expensive dry cooling or wet/dry cooling. According to design studies of large combination wet/dry cooling towers by the General Electric Company, United States, in 1976, [3] the capital cost was nearly double that of comparable wet (evaporative) cooling towers. But when the cost of raw water exceeds $US 0.5 per cubic metre, the wet/dry concept has an economic advantage in addition to the fact that it consumes only about one-tenth of the water of a comparable all evaporative system. Thus, the wet/dry cooling method may find important applications where water supply is severely limited. It is to be noted, however, that dry cooling methods consume more energy than wet cooling methods. In geothermal energy production, the requirement for surface water withdrawals can be eliminated by modifying the closed-cycle system in such a way that geothermal fluids are captured and used for cooling rather than recharged.

Consumptive use of water for other purposes, such as for dust control, revegetation at mines, ash disposal and stack gas scrubbers, can also be reduced to modest levels at reasonable cost.

Other major consumptive uses of water include chemical processes which utilize water as a source of hydrogen to raise the hydrogen content of the product stream. In such cases, which include high BTU coal gasification, coal liquefaction, *in situ* oil shale retorting and petroleum refining, the use of water is essential and cannot be reduced.

3. Measures to reduce water and energy requirements in water supply

Energy expended for municipal water use may be excessive for any one of such reasons as inefficient management, suboptimal design, poor operation and land use practices which have led to artificial movement of water over significant horizontal and vertical distances. Energy is required to pump, treat and transport water for cities. Most of the electrical energy used in water treatment and distribution systems is consumed by pumping. Thus, a surface water source is inherently more energy efficient than a ground water supply. Smaller, more compact distribution systems are also more efficient in that booster pumping is usually reduced. Since pumping is the principal consumer, it is evident that plans to reduce the quantities of water used can be effective in easing energy requirements.

Existing technology allows significant reductions in energy consumption when ground water is the source. A factor in achieving reductions is maximizing the efficiency of wells. Use of gravel packs, well screens and aquifer development by jetting can routinely produce wells having an efficiency of 80 per cent or more.[1]

Many energy saving options may also be found in the field of water quality improvement. For a given pollutant, alternative treatment processes usually exist with varying energy requirements. However, it should be noted that the least cost solution may not be the one with minimum energy requirements. One technological approach that contributes to reducing energy consumption in pollution control works is to make use of waste heat sources from facilities such as sewage treatment plants.

Water and energy conservation may also be achieved by bringing about a change in the water-use habits of the people. This may be effected by metering of all residential water supply lines. A number of studies have been made in the United States to compare water consumption before and after installation of water meters. Generally, they indicate an initial reduction in consumption from 15 to 50 per cent.[4] Water use may be classified as required or discretionary. Required water is that needed to sustain life and manufacture goods. Discretionary water would include that for sprinkling lawns, washing cars, filling swimming pools and similar activities. The above study indicated that metering had little effect on required water usage, but has a very significant effect on discretionary water use.

A study undertaken by Clouser and Miller [5] in the United States indicated that the use of modern day water intensive appliances or activities had a great effect on household water consumption and hence on energy consumption. It was observed that an increase in the *per capita* consumption of water was associated with the use of washing machines, dish washers, swimming pools and lawn watering. Therefore, a substantial reduction in water consumption could be obtained by the use of water-saving devices. The estimate on the amount of water that could be saved by using such devices was based on the assumption that the daily *per capita* consumption was 60 gallons, average family size was 2.5 individuals, 40 per cent of water was required for toilet, 37 per cent for bathing and the rest for other uses. A conventional toilet requires an average of about five gallons per flush and a total of 24 gallons per day per capita was allotted to this use. A typical water saving toilet required an average of 3.4 gallons per flush, and therefore a saving of 1.6 gallons per flush could be made by using it. This amounts to reducing the water use by about one-third of 8 gallons *per capita* per day, which means a total saving of 7,300 gallons per year for each family.

Similar savings may be obtained with respect to water use for bathing. A conventional shower head releases water at an average rate of five gallons per minute. If a flow restrictor is installed in it, the water use can be reduced by about 50 per cent, thus a reduction of 10,100 gallons per year for each household. Water-saving devices installed in households represent an alternative method of extending water supplies in communities.

In this connection, governmental action could encourage the consumer to save water. Building codes could

be changed to require water-conserving devices in new construction, such as flow-control shower heads, low-flow toilets, and water-efficient dishwashers and clothes washing machines. Government-enforced labelling of appliances indicating water-use rate and energy consumption or a publication of comparative use rates could help the customer select more efficient appliances.

In addition to the above measures, subsidization of the price of water-saving devices and regulation of water use by appropriate water pricing policies can produce significant water conservation.

Pricing policy plays an important role in the efforts to balance the supply and demand of water and energy. As long as fuel and water are priced artificially low, that is, in cases where users pay less than what it costs, there is no incentive to conserve or make better use of existing supplies. Therefore, the adoption of realistic pricing policies can effectively alter trends of spiraling prices for these scarce resources. Political and social considerations, however, require that the pricing policies effecting conservation of these resources have the least economic and social disruption.

In addition to changes in pricing policy, education, revisions in institutional structures, technological innovations and other conservation actions may be considered as effective tools for achieving more efficient use of water and energy resources.

Water, as mentioned before, is a key input to various kinds of energy resources development. In areas of limited water supply and many competing demands, scarcity of water may become a limiting factor to energy development. The need to overcome such an obstacle would be very urgent when it comes to energy development in areas with abundance of fossil energy supplies.

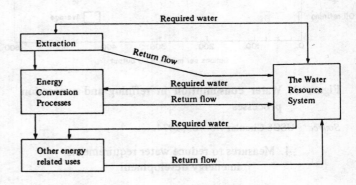

Figure 2. Energy development in a water resource system

Source: Reference 6.

Table 14. Water requirements for some energy conversion and extraction processes in terms of water energy coefficients

Process	Upper limit of energy output		Lower limit of water use	
	per AF of water use (BTU x 10⁹)	Per m³ of water use (J x 10⁹)	per BTU of energy output (AF x 10⁻⁹)	per joule of energy output (m³ x 10⁻⁹)
Oil refining	42.99	36.77	0.023	0.027
Coal mining	1.90×10^{-5}	1.63×10^{-5}	5.230×10^{4}	6.119×10^{4}
Coal slurry	1.25×10^{-6}	1.07×10^{-6}	7.980×10^{5}	9.336×10^{5}
Coal liquefaction	3.26	2.81	0.306	0.358
Coal gasification	2.83	2.42	0.353	0.413
Tar sands	97.86	83.70	0.010	0.012
Electrical generation	1.99	1.70	5.017	5.868
Oil production	106.80	91.34	0.009	0.011
Gas production	195.00	166.78	0.005	0.006
Oil shale	11.60	9.92	0.086	0.101

Note: AF = acre-feet, BTU - British Thermal Units, J = joule, Kg = kilogram, m = metre
Source: Reference 6.

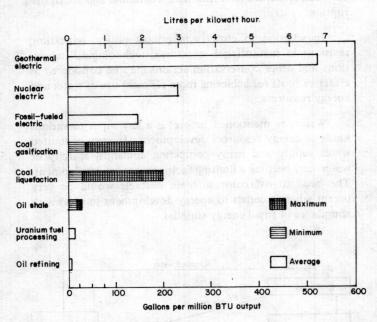

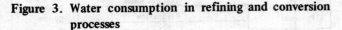

Figure 3. Water consumption in refining and conversion processes

Source: USGS Circular No. 703, 1974.

4. Measures to reduce water requirements in energy development

A diagrammatic presentation of the cycle of water used for energy development in a water resource system is shown in figure 2. It serves as a tool for visualizing and analyzing water-energy relationships in the integrated planning and management of water and energy resources. Generally, the most significant energy-related water consumption is in the refining and conversion processes. Water requirements by some energy conversion and extraction processes are given in table 14 and figure 3. The figures given in table 14 are rather conservative, that is, they indicate lower than average energy output and higher than average water consumption respectively and are based on current energy extraction and conversion technology in the United States. In figure 3, the difference between maximum and minimum values of water consumption indicates possible water savings depending upon the cost and availability of water.

A close relationship between water and energy resource development suggests that any kind of energy development will have a certain environmental impact, particularly on water quality. Potential water quality impacts must therefore be studied and minimized in energy development. In some cases control of thermal pollution may be just as important as control of chemical pollution in order to keep the disruption of fish life to a minimum. However, it is generally accepted that waste water discharges from energy production facilities should not present any unmanageable water quality problems if the necessary environmental regulations are established and effectively enforced.

In general, a reduction of the water requirement in energy resource development and *vice versa* can be achieved by establishing a framework within which both the water and energy resources are to be developed and managed. Such a framework should ensure that the development of water and energy resources not only consider the separate specific need for each resource, but also recognize the combined demands for both.

B. WATER AS A RENEWABLE ENERGY RESOURCE

Exploitation of water power as an energy resource is mainly concerned with the non-consumptive aspects of water use in the sense that water is used only to transform its potential energy into mechanical/electrical energy by the use of turbines and generators and then returned to the water system for further use. Water is the source of one fourth of the world's electricity, according to a study by Worldwater Institute, Washington D.C. [7] However, despite hydropower's prominence as an energy source, most of its potential remains untapped, especially in developing countries of the region. If all the economically available hydropower potential were harnessed, most of the world's electricity needs could be satisfied.

1. Importance and advantages of hydropower

Growing energy demands necessitate the development of new and renewable sources of energy. Hydropower is the only renewable form of energy that can be used extensively in many countries immediately for large-scale generation of electricity as it is not necessary to wait for further technical development. Together with other forms of renewable energy that can be economically exploited it may, therefore, be developed to help fill the energy requirements. Moreover, for many developing countries much of the planning and technology necessary to develop hydropower is available locally and thus need not be imported at high cost from other countries.

Hydropower has good prospects of becoming a cornerstone of a sustainable energy economy in the future because of the following advantages. First, it is inexhaustible and clean — no smoke or wastes. Hydroelectric complexes will be producing energy long after the oil wells have run dry and the coal fields are exhausted. Secondly, it is an almost inflation-proof energy source because only its small operating and maintenance costs are subject to inflation. Thirdly, hydropower resources, unlike fossil fuels, are widely dispersed throughout the world. Asia has more than one fourth of the world's potential hydropower resources; South America, one fifth; and North and Central America, about one sixth.[7]

Fourthly, while the initial capital costs for hydro developments are high, operational and running costs are minimal, as fewer personnel are needed to operate and maintain a hydropower station than in a thermal power plant of equivalent size. Although it may probably take a comparatively longer time to pay for itself, the hydropower plant is worth the front-end costs, because once the pay-

back period passes, the energy is inexpensive and not dependent on any kind of fuel. Estimates show that average capital costs for hydropower in 1985 will be $US 1,750 per KW, coal-fired plants $US 1,100 – $US 1,200 per KW and nuclear plants $US 1,500 per KW.[8] Although under normal circumstances hydropower is more expensive than power from large fossil fuel plants, the rising cost of oil and coal has now made its cost competitive.

Fifthly, hydropower stations have a longer useful life than thermal power stations. Finally, hydropower is unique in that the main development process entails other significant benefits. Dams are seldom constructed only for a single purpose like electricity generation; they also could simultaneously provide irrigation, flood control, better navigation, recreation, wildlife enhancement and low flow regulation.

In view of the above-mentioned advantages of hydropower development, some countries have already begun to exploit their hydropower resources. The share of electricity by hydropower generation in the overall power system in selected countries is presented in table 15.

Table 15. Selected countries obtaining most of their electricity from hydro-power, 1980

Country	Share of electricity from hydro-power (percentage)
Countries of the ESCAP region	
Nepal	91
Sri Lanka	89
New Zealand	75
Afghanistan	72
Burma	70
Pakistan	57
Countries outside the ESCAP region	
Ghana	99
Norway	99
Zambia	99
Mozambique	96
Zaire	95
Brazil	87
Portugal	77
Switzerland	74
Austria	67
Canada	67

Source: United Nations, *World Energy Supplies.*
United Nations, *Electric Power in Asia and the Pacific 1979 and 1980.*

Large dams for hydropower generation have a great impact on the energy situation in a country. For example, the Itiapu Dam between Brazil and Paraguay on the Parana River is designed to generate as much power as 13 large nuclear power plants, making it the largest power complex in the world, [7] and China's planned Three Gorges Dam on the Yaugtze River will be twice this size. Such dams can have a substantial impact on national economies. With power from the Aswan High Dam, for example, Egypt has been able to provide electricity to 99 per cent of its villages. And in north-east Brazil, cheap hydropower is said to have created almost one million new jobs for the people.

In the industrial world, the United States, Europe, Japan and the Soviet Union are said to have many existing non-hydropower dams that have become viable sources of power as a result of rising oil prices. This will most probably hold true in the developing countries as well. Throughout history, the availability of hydropower resources has been central to the location of industries and the relative strength of nations. Since most of the world's untapped hydroelectric potential lies in remote regions, its development may have an impact on the international economic system by altering the location of important energy-intensive industries.

2. Problems associated with hydropower development

In spite of the several advantages which have been put forward in favour of its development, hydropower has certain drawbacks. It is to be noted, however, that these drawbacks are not serious and are, therefore, not unsurmountable. First, most sites that are economically attractive to develop are located far from consumers. This necessitates an investment in transmission facilities and a certain amount of preinvestment in the infrastructural works, which may not be allocated totally to hydropower. This is one of the reasons why rural electrification in developing countries has long been hampered. China[7] has tackled this problem by building small hydro units — some 90,000 since 1968. These are often attached to irrigation ditches and are built by village artisans using local materials and techniques. Such facilities are said to power rural industries, provide electric light and minimize the manual labour in lifting water, sawing wood and grinding grain. There is no reason why a similar strategy cannot be applied in other developing countries.

Secondly, some of the attractive hydropower sites may have a relatively small output to be connected to large national power grids. This drawback is of more relevance to industrialized countries than to the developing countries. In this connection, it is necessary to examine the difference in the roles played by hydropower in meeting energy demands in industrialized countries as compared to developing countries. In industrialized countries, power systems are very large in order to cope with their huge power requirements. Therefore, hydropower cannot provide an overall solution to their energy problems; it can only assume the role of relieving the demand for some nonrenewable energy resources.

Next, considering the size of these power systems, only large generating stations can make a significant contribution to increasing the capacity of power system to serve loads which are growing rapidly over large areas. Thus, the development of hydropower in these countries is often restricted to large plants, usually with capacities over 15 MW, which can fit into their large, complex power systems. Small hydropower plants in the range between 1.5 and 15 MW that can be connected to existing power systems without too much difficulty and may be economically useful in the foreseeable future are also considered for development, but are given a lower priority; whereas very small projects with capacities less than 1.5 MW are assigned the lowest priority.

The situation in developing countries is quite different. The power systems are very small and in some cases even smaller than the capacity of one large generating station in the industrialized countries. The use of electricity is also quite limited in nature and often decentralized because of the existence of isolated rural communities. Thus, all scales of hydropower development — whether large, small or very small — have their own significant economic usefulness in the developing countries.

While large-scale hydro developments may be included in the power system to supply the industrialized urban areas, the smaller ones not suitable for connection to the national grid may be used to supply the respective isolated localities in which they are situated. Moreover, the so-called small and very small categories, as defined according to the standards of industrialized countries, may prove to be large enough to be interconnected to the power system in many developing countries.

Thirdly, hydropower is not a constant power source. In summer and during droughts, output drops, while in the wet season production can be at peak rates. This problem can be solved by regulating the seasonal fluctuation of flow by the use of storage reservoirs and/or scheduling the output of power consuming production facilities, where possible, to correspond with the seasonal fluctuation of power output. In addition, hydropower may be connected to the power system so that energy surplus to the site needs can be sold to the power system during the wet season and system energy can be supplied to the site during low flow periods.

Fourthly, turbines and generators are expensive, particularly for low-head schemes, namely, those with heads of 20 m or less. In most hydro-electric projects, head is the principal factor affecting project economic feasibility. There is almost a direct relationship between head and equipment cost: the higher the head, the lower the cost.

Hence, it is advisable to place emphasis on high head projects first and to deal with the less economical low head projects later.

Another point worthy of mention is that greater economy is usually achieved by developing large-scale projects than small ones. However, quite recently, new technologies in industrialized countries now permit the manufacture in bulk of small-scale turnkey package plants which are sufficiently inexpensive to become comparable with large-scale hydropower developments. These standardized pre-engineered turbines are said to cost only about one half as much as custom-designed turbines.[8]

Fifthly, although hydropower is a clean renewable source of energy, its development has a certain impact on the environment, especially when it involves the construction of large dams. The construction of a large dam carries both opportunities and dangers. Sometimes, the real benefits of agricultural land opened to irrigation and energy generated may not surpass the loss resulting from some valuable land submerged by the dam. In tropical regions, reservoirs may endanger many people by spreading waterborne diseases, and it may also threaten wildlife and rare plant species. Possibly the largest neglected cost of large dams stems from the substantial number of people whose homelands are flooded. For example, the Aswan High Dam in Egypt forced 80,000 people from their homes and the three Gorges Dam in China is expected to displace 2,000,000 people.[7] In contrast to large-scale developments, small scale hydropower developments have a minimal adverse environmental impact.

3. Role of hydropower in the overall energy resources development of the region

With regard to the prospects of hydropower development in the ESCAP region, countries of this region can be divided into three groups depending upon the importance of hydropower to these countries[9]:

(a) Countries where hydropower is not an important energy source (0 to 15 per cent of the total energy generated): the countries in this group are the Cook Islands, Fiji, Kiribati, Hong Kong, Sabah and Sarawak in Malaysia, Mongolia, the Republic of Korea, Singapore, Solomon Islands, Tonga and Tuvalu;

(b) Countries where hydropower is an important energy source (16 to 40 per cent of total energy generated): the countries in this group are Australia, Bangladesh, China, Iran, Japan, Peninsular Malaysia, the Philippines, Samoa and Thailand;

(c) Countries where hydropower is the main energy source (more than 40 per cent of total energy): the countries in this group are Afghanistan, Bhutan, Burma, India, Indonesia, the Lao People's Democratic Republic, Nepal, New Zealand, Pakistan and Sri Lanka.

A current assessment of the hydropower potential in the developing countries of the ESCAP region is presented in table 16. The assessment of estimated potential is based on mean annual discharge and available head corresponding to the technically feasible maximum dam height. The economic potential is the maximum technically feasible potential at which the benefit-cost ratio is greater than or

Table 16. Estimated hydropower potential, economically exploitable potential and peak loads in developing countries of ESCAP region (1980)

	Estimated potential (MW)	Economically exploitable potential (MW)	Peak load (MW)
Afghanistan	5 000.0	2 000.0	220.0
Bangladesh	371.6	148.6	395.0
Bhutan	2 000.0 (1972)	800.0	1.75
Burma	2 000.0 (1969 provisional)	2 000.0	...
China	680 000.0	272 000.0	...
Fiji	300.0	120.0	...
India	100 000.0	40 000.0	...
Indonesia	31 500.0	12 600.0	...
Iran	14 000.0	14 000.0	3 621.0 (1979)
Lao People's Democratic Republic	13 213.0	5 285.2	...
Malaysia:			
Peninsular Malaysia	2 190.0	2 190.0	1 399.0
Sarawak	20 000.0	8 000.0	73.6
Nepal	83 000.0	33 200.0	56.9
Pakistan	20 000 to 30 000	8 000 to 12 000	2 702.9
Papua New Guinea	14 228.6 (1974)	5 691.4	...
Philippines	8 000.0	3 200.0	...
Republic of Korea	2 301.0	1 157.0[a]	5 457.0
Samoa	13.8	5.5	5.8
Solomon Islands	21.0	21.0	...
Sri Lanka	1 540.0	616.0	368.5
Thailand	8 009.1	3 203.6	2 379.5

Source: Based on *Electric Power in Asia and the Pacific* 1979 and 1980, United Nations Sales publication No. E.82.II.F.15.

[a] Potential already exploited.

equal to one. Thus, the estimated potential and economically exploitable potential are the same for Burma, Iran, Peninsular Malaysia and Solomon Islands. The economic potential for the remaining countries is taken as 40 per cent of the estimated potential, which is the approximate average value for the whole region. Hence, the true economic potential for these countries may either be greater than or less than the values indicated.

According to a recent study by the ESCAP secretariat, the total installed capacity of hydropower stations in the developing countries of the region is 40,955 MW, which represents only 4.1 per cent of the estimated potential of 1,007,688 MW in those countries. In view of the large unexploited potential of the developing countries in the region, prospects for their development are very good. For example, Afghanistan, Iran, Nepal, Pakistan, Sri Lanka and Thailand are among the countries whose economically exploitable hydroelectric potential, if developed, can satisfy the present total peak loads (table 16). However, there exists a number of constraints in developing this potential. First, there is a general lack of reliable basic data (long-term stream flow data, topographic maps, geologic data at dam sites etc.); secondly, there is lack of power market at or near the source of supply; thirdly, there is a shortage of financial resources; and fourthly, there is lack of trained personnel.

The first problem may be solved when those developing countries that had not done so take the necessary steps towards formulation and implementation of programmes for hydrological, meteorological and geological investigations as well as for carrying out topographical surveys and mapping at promising hydropower sites.

In order to solve the second problem, it is necessary to find a power market. Since the amount of electricity generated depends on the amount consumed, it is important to secure a market commensurate with the size of development. It is here that subregional and regional co-operation can be of great value in balancing demand and supply conditions through electricity trade. It may be noted from table 16 that in some least developed countries like Nepal and the Lao People's Democratic Republic, there is abundant exploitable hydroelectric potential which cannot be developed because the load centres, apart from being remote from their sources, have a low demand. According to the country statistics on electricity generation and supply for Nepal, electricity trade between India and Nepal has been in existence for many years. It is, therefore, envisioned that similar sub-regional co-operation and/or upgrading as well as the expansion of such co-operation to include all affected neighbouring countries in the region will contribute greatly to the development of hydroelectric resources.

The third problem is common to all the developing countries in the region. Large capital investments associated with hydropower development are a limiting factor in their development. In Asia and the South Pacific, the Asian Development Bank (ADB) is financing such projects. The ADB is an important source of financing for power projects in the region and has accounted for as much as 20 per cent of the foreign exchange requirements of the electricity sector in its borrowing member countries since it began operations. Even if funds are made available from international financing institutions, they may cover only a small portion of the total development requirements.

Another approach to this problem is to emphasize the development of low investment small-scale hydropower, to make wide use of standardized equipment (turbines and generators), to retrofit existing irrigation canals and dams not producing hydropower at present with hydro-generating equipment in order to avoid civil engineering construction cost, to add new units to existing plants, to modernize and upgrade old hydroelectric power-plants using new technology to improve their efficiency and thus increase their output, and to create or increase storage capacities to improve the firm capacity of run-of-river type hydroelectric plants.

The fourth problem — shortage of trained personnel at various levels in developing countries — is one which can be solved by assistance from international organizations. Such assistance may take the form of providing expert services and organizing workshops, training courses, expert group meetings and group study tours to more experienced countries in the field of hydropower planning and development.

C. MODELS FOR PLANNING WATER-ENERGY SYSTEMS

Energy and water systems are economically and physically interlinked and can best be developed if a conjunctive water-energy system planning approach is adopted to minimize development costs and resource use for the region.

Current planning practices for energy resources development usually consist in siting the energy generating facilities based on the energy system economies with some prescreening to ensure water availability. The regional water resource is then developed to meet the regional demands for energy conversion and other purposes. Such planning practices do not ensure minimization of resource use and overall development costs. In order to achieve this objective, various models for planning water-energy systems have been developed recently. A general classification of these models and a brief review of some of them are given below.

1. General classification of models

The purpose of developing mathematical models for water-energy systems is to help investigate various alternatives for future water-energy systems. According to Lall and Mays, [23] these models can be divided under three broad categories as water sector models, energy sector models and composite water-energy models.

Water sector models and energy sector models deal with the development and distribution of either water resources or energy in a region respectively. Water sector models may include specifications for energy requirements, and energy models may include water resources constraints. A composite water-energy model encompasses the issues of water and energy supply and development that affect the major sectors of production and demand for both the water and energy systems.

Each of these three categories may be characterized by either one or a combination of features, which identify them as being regional or regionalized models, optimization or simulation models, single-objective or multi-objective models, static (single period) or dynamic (multi-period) models, facility siting (location) or resource capacity allocation models, etc.

According to Buras, [19] a regional model refers to one portion of a larger geographic entity defined in accordance with some criteria, while a regionalized model represents the interrelationships between the subregions within the larger geographic entity. The distinction between the optimization and simulation models is that optimization models are developed to determine the optimal sites and sizes of power plants, the optimal combinations of energy and water resources developments etc. in order to achieve one or more of such criteria as net economic benefits, maximum net energy output, minimum total annuitized cost or minimum use of resources in order to meet a certain demand for water and energy. Simulation models are those in which natural processes such as fluctuation of annual river discharges or peak loads of electricity are put in the form of mathematical expressions in order to study their future trend. In such models the reliability of the estimates or predictions depends upon the accuracy of these models in representing the natural processes.

The difference between single-objective and multi-objective models is that single-objective models are developed for achieving only one objective, whereas multi-objective models are developed for achieving at least two or more objectives. The difference between static models and dynamic models is that static models are designed for a single planning period, whereas dynamic models are designed for various planning periods.

Facility siting or location models are intended to identify probable locations for future power plants or other water-energy facilities. The allocation models are primarily screening models to identify subregions for large-scale developments and to indicate possible patterns for regional resource development and transportation between competing subregions.

2. Mathematical models for water-energy systems

A brief review of mathematical models for water-energy systems is given below for each of the three categories described in the preceding paragraphs.

(a) Water sector models

A number of water-resource sector allocation models, utilizing various solution techniques, such as linear programming, net-work theory and non-linear programming, have been developed by Aron et al., [13] Hamdan and Meredith, [14] King et al., [15] Reynolds, [16] Texas Department of Water Resources, [17] Young and Pisano [18], etc. for the identification of cost — effective water-distribution strategies.

(b) Energy sector models

(i) Models that do not consider water-resources constraints

A variety of simulation and optimization models for planning electrical systems have been developed by Anderson, [27] Farrar and Woodruff, [28] Gately, [29] Sawey, [30] Thompson et al. [31], etc.

A few models have also been developed to optimize plant siting and distribution for coal gasification, notable among which is a linear programming model developed by Whitlatch, [32] where a mix of gasification plants is considered in the development of a distribution strategy.

Most of the single-objective regional and regionalized energy models developed for energy systems from the points of view of production and economics have been reviewed by Cohen and Costello [26] and Buras. [19] Buras stated that these energy-economy models did not explicitly take account of the availability of water resources for energy-related activities. Then, he explored the feasibility of incorporating water resource constraints into some of the regionalized energy models. The models selected by Buras for the purpose were: the Regional Energy System Optimization Model (RESOM), a multi-regional and inter-industry model developed by Brookhaven National Laboratory; and the Energy Policy Model (EPM), a general equilibrium network model of the energy sector of the United States, economy developed by the Lawrence Livermore Laboratory.

(ii) *Models that consider water-resources constraints*

The models RESOM and EPM, as modified by Buras, incorporate the constraints on regional water supplies for energy development. On the basis of the application of these models, Buras stressed that the integration of water-resources constraints into regionalized energy-economy models was both relevant and feasible, particularly with regard to evaluations of policy alternatives and interactions arising from competing (energy and non-energy sectors) users of the water resources. A review and evaluation of Buras' improved models by Lall and Mays [23] indicated that although these models considered the use of water resources for several energy processes fairly comprehensively, they failed to consider the competition between non-energy and energy users of water.

Other energy sector models that incorporate water constraints are those developed by Morris, [33] Hobbs and Meier, [34] Cohon et al. [35] and Eagles et al. [36] Eagles' single-objective model was designed to help locate coal and nuclear plants to minimize the energy, resource transhipment, and reservoir development costs subject to such constraints as ensuring a specified power plant mix, limiting plant capacities in cells and around bays, meeting power demand, ensuring continuity of power supply, ensuring continuity of coal supply and demand, limiting water consumption and withdrawal by power plants, limiting waste heat rejection, meeting air quality standards and limiting population impact of nuclear power plants. The multi-objective model of Cohon et al. differs from the single-objective model of Eagles et al. in that four objectives are considered: minimizing transmission costs, minimizing fuel transportation costs, minimizing the cost of water storage in reservoirs and minimizing the population impact of nuclear plants.

(c) *Composite water-energy models*

The composite water-energy models are the result of efforts towards achieving a conjunctive water-energy system planning approach. Some models worthy of mention are those developed by Bishop et al., [6] Brill et al., [20] Provenzano [22] and Lall and Mays. [23]

Bishop et al. used a linear programming approach to analyze water resources' interrelations with contemplated energy developments in order to assess the water-energy tradeoffs between developing or not developing various energy extraction and conversion processes at alternative sites. The authors made an approach to the problem of finding optimal combinations of water allocation and energy resource developments from two perspectives: maximizing net energy output within the limits of water and energy resources availability, and minimizing the amount of water necessary to produce the required levels of energy outputs subject to limitations on the water and raw energy resource availability. Constraints on water availabilities, energy production levels, energy source development or extraction rates, and energy extraction-conversion efficiencies were considered. The possible energy developments requiring water inputs included crude oil pumping, coal mining, oil shale mining, coal-fired electric generating plants, coal slurry lines, coal liquefaction and gasification plants and oil refineries.

In the maximization problem, the net energy output, which is the objective function to be maximized, is expressed as the summation of the products of two variables: the water allocated to develop a particular energy source and the corresponding coefficient representing the energy output per unit of water input, minus any losses due to conversion process inefficiencies. The loss in each process is expressed as the product of two variables, the loss coefficient and the energy output of that process, and is usually obtained as the ratio of the energy loss (that is, the difference between energy input and energy output) to the energy output for that process. The above objective function is then maximized so that the total inputs of water and energy resources do not exceed the respective available supplies.

In the minimization problem, the total water input, which is the objective function to be minimized, is expressed as the summation of the products of two variables: the energy extracted or converted from a particular development and the corresponding coefficient representing the gross water requirement per unit of energy output from that process. The above objective function is then minimized so that the total energy output is equal to or greater than the specified regional or national energy requirements, while at the same time observing that the water and energy resources being used do not exceed the specified limits.

The formulation of energy maximization and water minimization problems was put in a matrix form with each column representing a variable in the model structure and each row representing an objective function or a model constraint. The entries in each matrix represented the coefficients of those variables appearing in the constraint equations or objective function. The matrix representation provides a concise summary of the equational structure of the problem. The optimal solution for the problem is then obtained by using a standard mathematical programming computer package.

Examination and comparison of these optimal solutions were said to provide a number of insights into energy-water development relations.

For the energy maximization problem, the optimal solution indicates the levels and combinations of resources that establish an upper limit on development possibilities. Aspects of the problem which can be analyzed by the model are:

(i)   Whether the total available energy in a deposit could be developed or its development would be limited by water availability;

(ii)   Which water sources should be used for development of particular energy deposits or conversion processes.

In areas of limited water supply and many competing demands, the water minimization problem becomes especially important in terms of the efficient use of resources. The optimal solution here can aid in selecting energy developments that will require the least amounts of water while meeting specified energy product needs. Pertinent issues that can be investigated by this model are:

(1)   Which projects and what levels of development are needed to meet specified energy needs;

(2)   Which sources and how much water are required for development.

The comparison of optimal solutions for both the maximization and minimization problems was said to be useful in examining the range of development possibilities and the levels of water and energy resource use for maximum development versus meeting minimum required levels for energy outputs.

An evaluation of the above two Bishop models by Lall and Mays [23] indicated that the results of these models (maximizing energy and minimizing water consumption) were significantly different, which implied that the way in which these models should be used would depend very much on which planning perspective was most relevant. It was pointed out that the models failed to have a truly composite nature in this respect, which is important for the analysis of conjunctive development of the water-energy systems. Besides, the models did not incorporate any considerations for resource development and supply. Lall and Mays suggested that if the costs of the components of the water-energy resource development and allocation systems were considered, the need for two separate models might be obviated. The reason given was that the costs assign priorities or weights to each activity, providing a rational basis for the selection of each activity level. Lall and Mays, however, acknowledged the possibility of efficiently reformulating the Bishop model into a cost minimization model without sacrificing any of the constraints or its attractive adaptability to parametric analyses.

Brill et al. [21] developed a linear programming model aimed at obtaining a cost effective solution to the problem of optimally siting water, electricity and gasification facilities and the subsequent allocation of the resources. The Brill model, similar to the Lall and Mays model, is intended for preliminary screening purposes. It deals with the water resources system, the gas and coal pipeline system and the electrical systems. Subregions or countries are represented as demand and supply points for various commodities, whereby facility capacities of these subregions rather than individual facilities are considered. The decision variables are the amounts of water, coal, electricity and pipeline gas transported from supply to demand subregions, and the electricity and gas generating capacities located at each supply point. The parameters of the model specify the amounts of coal and water resources available for development at the various source points and the demand levels for additional water, pipeline gas, and electricity. The model does not consider those existing facilities that are used at capacity or otherwise committed. Only incremental product demands arising as a result of large-scale resource development are considered. Consequently, only the resources available after meeting existing demands are considered for resource allocation.

The objective function of the Brill model is to minimize the sum of water supply costs and transportation costs for coal, water, electricity and gas. It was assumed that the costs of mining and pretreating coal and the costs of constructing and operating power plants and coal gasification facilities were site-independent. Brill [20] later extended this model to consider alternate cooling strategies, water quality criteria and capacity expansion. Lall and Mays, [23] in their review of Brill's model, pointed out its inability to accommodate nonlinearities in the cost functions, which made it impossible for the model to give true optimal solutions. Gerstle and Marks [37] also pointed out the shortcomings of Brill's model in that it failed to consider the costs of constructing and operating power plants and to consider the benefits. Therefore, it would not be possible to use this model to obtain the mix of products that maximized net benefits, as all demand levels for all products were specified.

Provenzano, [22] working from the linear programming model for power system investment planning presented by Anderson, [27] developed a dynamic (multi-period), multi-plant linear programming model of an energy production system and its associated water supply components. The objective of the model was to minimize the overall capital, operation and transmission costs for electricity and gas production and transmission. The constraints used in the model were peak power guarantee conditions, electric energy supply guarantee conditions, adequate energy transmission and production capacity, multi-period capital stock relationship constraints, limited water availability for energy production and other physical constraints. Decision variables in the model included choice of nuclear, coal-fired, or gas turbine power generating capacity; size, location and sequence of additions of new steam-electric and coal gasification capacity; and the amount and direction of electricity and gas production and transmission. Optimization was carried out over several time periods.

The model selected a minimum-cost set of locations for new energy facilities from a larger set of prescreened feasible areas. Steam-electric power plants that were constructed prior to the base year of analysis were gradually retired over the course of the planning period. Optimum additions of new generating capacity, therefore, included additions required to meet growing demands as well as additions required to replace retired plants.

The model's selection of the optimum size, type, location and sequence of construction of new energy production facilities was influenced by water supply considerations in two ways. First, the size and sequence of new additions to capacity were constrained by water availability from surface water sources such as rivers and reservoirs for energy production at various points within a region. Second, the selection of a location for a new energy production facility was dependent on capital costs, which included associated water procurement and utilization costs, in particular, reservoir construction costs.

Provenzano's model does not consider the ground water source, which in some cases may be cheaper than a surface water source and, hence, it may not always provide an optimal solution. In addition, the author acknowledged that the solution of such a large-scale model could only be regarded as approximate, because it involved many simplifying physical and economic assumptions.

Lall and Mays [23] developed a mathematical programming model for planning of composite regional water-energy systems, which has a non-linear objective function and linear constraints. The model is a static (single planning period) screening model, where the primary concern is the subregional capacities of resource development rather than facility siting.

The objective of the model is to minimize the sum of the amortized capital, operating and distribution costs incurred in meeting future regional energy-related water, gas, coal and power demands. The decision variables in the model include selection of the type, size and location of new power generation and coal conversion capacities, the amount and direction of power and gas production and transmission to various types of users, and the amount and type of water supplied to various classes of users. Solutions to the model can provide information on optimal types and levels of processes, location and expansion of energy production activities and the corresponding water demand and allocation patterns.

In this model, the water-energy system is viewed in a hierarchical framework consisting of three interacting subsystems: the water subsystem, the power generation subsystem and the coal and synthetic natural gas subsystem. The power subsystem is placed at the highest level, the coal-gas subsystem at the next and the water subsystem at the last. The water and coal-gas subsystems are then viewed as constraints to the power subsystem and the water subsystem as a constraint on the coal-gas subsystem. The development of the power subsystem was based on a review of power system investment planning models presented by Anderson. [27] It was assumed that all the power stations in the region were completely interconnected by a power transmission grid.

The model enables the optimization problem to be solved as an integrated problem which considers the economic interactions between the components of different subsystems as well as the individual optimization problem for each subsystem in order to examine the growth patterns of relatively disjunct planning and its effects. In general, this model may be considered as an improvement over current mathematical planning models, namely, independent planning of water and energy systems and linear optimization models for the integrated system.

Matsumoto and Mays [39] developed a mathematical model for the analysis and planning of large scale water-energy systems, in particular the capacity expansion of water, coal, electrical and gas facilities to meet the growing energy demands. According to the authors, the term large-scale refers to cases with thousands of interactions in the water-energy system. The capacity expansion problem of water-energy systems was stated as the following: given the future demands for water, electricity, gas and coal, and the availability of water and coal, to determine the location, timing and size of new facilities to satisfy the demands with minimum cost, which is the sum of operating and capital costs.

The water-energy system is considered as being composed of four subsystems: water, coal, electricity and gas systems, all of which are interrelated. The water system consists of natural rivers, reservoirs, canals and other water-related facilities. Water sources include surface water or natural inflow, ground-water, reservoir water and water import. Water demands include municipal and industrial demand (MID), agricultural demand, low flow augmentation, coal mining, electric power generation and coal gasification. The coal system consists of coal mines and the coal distribution system. Coal can be either produced at coal mines or imported and shipped to a MID coal plant, a coal-fired plant or a coal gasification plant. Electrical systems include power plants such as hydropower, nuclear, coal-fired, oil-fired and gas-fired power plants and power transmission systems. Electric power can be either generated at these plants or imported from neighbouring systems. Gas systems include coal gasification plants and gas pipeline systems. The alternative of gas importation is also considered.

The authors divided the problems related to water-energy systems into three hierarchical levels. The top level was said to be a capacity expansion problem, the second level a production problem and the third or lowest level a distribution problem. A combination of the second and third levels was said to form the operational aspects of the problem, which was referred to by the authors as a lower level. In investigating various alternatives for future water-energy systems, a plan based on a higher level problem was sent to a lower level, which sought an optimum solution for the given plan. The algorithm for this was said to be based on Benders' decomposition. The capacity problem was solved by the dual simplex method for a generally upper bounded type linear programme (LP); the production problem was solved by the dual simplex method for a simply upper bounded type LP; and the distribution problem was solved by the generalized network algorithm.

It will be observed that earlier models are generally single-objective in nature with a very limited capacity to take into consideration certain objective functions and constraints regarding the availability of resources, while the models developed recently are multi-objective in nature, permitting a conjunctive water-energy system planning approach. Some of the latest models are claimed by their authors as being able to provide optimal solutions regarding facility siting as well as resource capacity allocation that meet various important objective functions within the constraints of resource availability. These models, particularly the resource allocation models, are useful for the allocation of water between various sectors as well as between various energy production facilities within the energy sector. However, almost all of these models are developed for maximization of benefits, minimization of costs or use of resources with no consideration for the social preferences of water use, a very important factor that should be considered in water allocation problems, particularly when there is a keen competition between energy and non-energy uses of water. Hence, regarding the problem of water resource allocation, these models may be effective or reliable only when it comes to allocation of water within the energy sector. A major reason determining the importance and necessity of considering the non-monetary social aspect (or the legal aspect derived from it) is that the influence exerted by social values demands equity irrespective of whether or not gains exceed losses in economic terms.

According to Hensala,[25] a truly interdisciplinary planning approach, a systems approach, that places equal emphasis on social, institutional and environmental values is necessary to ensure sustained economic growth. He stressed that comprehensive planning should place more emphasis on the overall costs and gains, and not on a simple economic benefit-cost analysis. Therefore, planning of large-scale energy resource development projects should recognize the complexity of natural systems and assure that gains from development exceeded the costs.

Besides, it was suggested that the dual development of water and energy resources must look beyond the separate specific needs for either and recognize the combined demands for both. Each has to be recognized as a separate entity and proper regard must be given to their interrelationships, as has already been discussed in previous paragraphs. The focus should not be placed only on one with the other as secondary, because both are primary resources. For example, water is still the key to the quality of our environment and the limiting factor in growth and development, while the need for development of energy resources is apparent from recent global economic, social and political changes.

It must be emphasized that wise use of the available water resources can provide adequate water for energy development as well as other needs of society and this can be achieved if planning recognizes the fact that the demand for water will increase not only for use in energy technology but also for other areas and alternative options. Thus, the task of making water available will require more planning than that for energy development, as it must address not only the engineering, economic, social and environmental factors, but also the institutional factors resulting from legal decisions.

In view of the reasons stated above, any method for allocation of water between energy and non-energy uses should necessarily consider the social aspects as one of the major criteria. A water allocation method which considers the social preferences and which is suggested for possible application in developing countries is given in the following section.

D. OPTIMUM ALLOCATION OF WATER FOR ENERGY DEVELOPMENT AND OTHER USES

The consumptive and non-consumptive uses of water for energy development discussed in the previous sections indicated that water was an essential input to energy resources development. Competing demands upon water resources by agriculture and energy production in addition to domestic uses in areas of severely limited availability are an issue of increasing importance worldwide. Therefore, in regions where the water resources have been fully developed and utilized, any large scale energy development is bound to have a substantial impact on the availability of water for other users.

When viewed from a national perspective, most countries seem to have ample water resources for agricultural, industrial (including energy development) and other uses. However, this simplistic view overlooks the spatial and temporal distribution of the resource. Further, with the continuous and rapid increase in population, water requirements for agriculture, industry and domestic use are also increasing. Hence, certain regions of the world have already started facing water shortages, so much so that water is becoming one of the major constraints for further socioeconomic development.

It is true that various water conservation measures provide a means of extending water supplies for different uses, but in many cases the savings are seldom adequate to meet the increasing requirements. The discrepancy between additional water use as a result of large-scale energy development and the savings in water consumption by conservation measures is a measure of the impact of energy development on water resources systems.

The potential impact of water consumption for large-scale energy developments in the future is of particular concern to agricultural interests in many countries. This concern arises from the fact that in the competing uses of water between agriculture and energy development, agriculture will have difficulty in paying the real cost of irrigation water, considering its low value in crop production. The fact is that the value of water for an industrial use including energy development is commonly higher than the value of the same water for agriculture. However, agriculture in developing countries is a deeply entrenched way of life with strong political support for a preferential position with respect to water resources utilization. On the contrary, more efficient use of water requires that low-value uses of water be shifted to high-value uses. This suggests a need for an integrated approach to energy and water resource development. This approach should be based on the objectives of national economic and social development plans.

In areas with limited water supplies and no scope for additional development of them, as economic activity and population expand, a considerable amount of water required for industrial and municipal use may have to be diverted away from irrigation. Earlier literature on water resources management gave much emphasis to the market system that governed water allocations depending on how much the consumers are willing to pay in the purchase of water. Thus, water prices are used as signals to consumers to increase or decrease the consumption of water. Prices are either raised to discourage consumption or lowered to encourage it. Prices set equal to marginal costs are neither punitive nor permissive; they simply reflect the scarcity of water resources. Punitive prices exceed marginal costs and lead to excessive conservation. Permissive prices are those below marginal costs that lead to waste.

For instance, Georgianna and Haynes [38] stated that optimal allocation of water was a function of the pricing scheme where optimality conditions showed that the price of both agricultural products and energy products were functions of water costs and water pollution abatement costs. Therefore, it may be observed that the market system encourages water to be allocated with greater preference to its most valued uses, which evidently has some drawbacks in that if one industry can generate only a comparatively lower net revenue out of using one unit of water than the other, it will not be able to obtain water if the latter needs all of the water supply. This should not be allowed to happen, as, for instance, agricultural uses, although having a lower marginal value product of water when compared to energy uses, should be assured a certain amount (representing the minimum requirement) of water for food production, because food is a basic necessity of life and there is no reliable way of estimating the benefits of self-sufficiency of food. The same reason applies also to assuring the minimum required quantity of water for domestic use and maintaining acceptable environmental conditions.

Leigh, [24] in her paper presented at the conference on water and energy sponsored by the American Society of Civil Engineers (ASCE) in 1982, addressed the economic and legal issues associated with the competition for water between energy and agriculture in connection with the San Marco coal slurry pipeline linking southern Colorado and the city of Houston, Texas, United States. The two important considerations discussed concerned the economic impacts of the proposed water transfer and the role of legal arrangements in influencing the outcome. This case was representative of many instances where legal and economic interests conflict. It was said that the economic aspects were relatively simple, which in this particular case indicated that transferring water from agriculture to energy would yield substantial net economic benefits. However, legal concerns prevented such transfer from taking place.

The legal issue was mainly concerned with the protection of vested water rights, which may be considered as a reflection of social preferences. The legal issue, in this case, resulted from the uncertainty as to whether there was a tributary relationship between the groundwater to be used for coal slurry and the Rio Grande River, because (a) different sets of rules and regulations applied to tributary and nontributary groundwater, (b) if the groundwater in question was connected to other supplies, the protection of water rights must be considered and (c) if the groundwater was tributary to the Rio Grande River, a water right was subject to the Rio Grande interstate compact.

The positions maintained by the two states on this legal issue were that Colorado would agree if the water was credited to the Rio Grande interstate compact as this would relieve some burden on its curtailed rights, while Texas would not agree to crediting water to the compact as this would entail a reduction in its existing water rights. The contrast between economic and legal considerations illustrates the conflict between social values which are often encountered in resource transfer questions. The legal issue could have been resolved if the social preference in either one of the states decided that the substantial net economic benefits gained were worthy of the sacrifice involved in the reduction of water rights for agriculture.

1. Multi-objective theory for water allocation

The optimum allocation of water for energy development and other uses may be achieved by applying the theory of multi-objective planning, which is an extension of the benefit-cost analysis to provide better assessments of non-monetary as well as monetary aspects in the overall evaluation of projects. The principle of multi-objective planning for water resources management was first developed by the United States. Water Resources Council in 1973 [1] and is applied by various state agencies in water planning.

In 1974, evaluation and testing of this principle as to its applicability in the Australian environment was carried out by the Centre for Environmental Studies, University of Melbourne, with the approval of the Australian Water Resources Council. [10] The study was conducted by a team of three experts, O'Brien, Thornley and Atkins, who made some modifications to suit Australian conditions. This modified version, which would need further evaluation and testing as to its applicability to individual local conditions, may be found useful in many parts of the ESCAP region.

It is now widely recognized that economic efficiency criteria alone are not adequate for project evaluation. The multi-objective theory for water allocation is a technique that enables planners to indirectly quantify social preferences in terms of economic values and then maximize the net economic benefits which involve a certain reduction in social quality that can be accepted or tolerated by the people affected. For simplicity and practicality, a brief description of the multi-objective theory will be presented for the particular case dealing with two major objectives: energy development expressed in terms of economic efficiency (the allocation of water resources to maximize energy output) and social quality (the enhancement of food production, environmental, social and aesthetic factors). This basic formulation may be extended to cover several other objectives, if necessary.

In this dual-component objective function, the energy development component is measured in monetary units, while the social quality component is measured in other appropriate units (e.g. volume of water for other uses, i.e. agriculture, domestic use, minimum discharge of water in river for sanitation, navigation etc.). Figure 4 represents the multi-objective theory for two objectives: the national income objective and the objective of improving social quality.

The first part of the multi-objective analysis is the development of a net benefit transformation function. The initial step in constructing this function is the estimation of net discounted national income benefits for various feasible combinations of investments in energy development. Each alternative combination of investment and management opportunities will, in principle, produce both beneficial and adverse effects in terms of each objective. These effects, the multi-objective benefits and costs, can be displayed for the complete range of possible alternatives by the two-dimensional representation shown in figure 4, where net economic development benefits (arising from water-related energy development) are plotted on the vertical axis and net social quality benefits (measured in this example in volume of water for other uses) are plotted on the horizontal axis.

In any problem, there will always be a scatter of points representing attainable net benefit combinations from various investment alternatives. This scatter of points forms the feasible region for the problem. The boundary of this set is called the net benefit transformation function and the points in the feasible set that are of interest' are those on the transformation function in the region where it slopes from northwest to Southeast, that is, between points B and D in figure 4. These points are called the non-inferior alternatives. They dominate all other points in the feasible region because from any such inferior point as C or E one can move in a northeasterly direction and be unambiguously better off (on the mild welfare assumption that more is better than less). In the negatively-sloped region of the transformation function, however, no movement is unambiguously good on this criterion. A choice must be made and a gain in one objective must be traded-off against a loss in the other.

The second part of the multi-objective decision problem is the determination of social preferences for the various investment alternatives. There are well known difficulties in the formation and measurement of social preferences but there are good reasons to conceptualize that reasonably well defined preferences exist for a wide range of social decision problems.

In figure 4, two social indifference curves (W_1 and W_2) are shown, each representing the locus of all points of equal social utility. The social indifference curves represent the society's preference with respect to maintaining the social quality. For the first few cubic metres of water taken away by energy development the social quality will not be affected much and will be acceptable, but further withdrawals may become intolerable to society. If it is assumed, as before, that greater net benefits towards both objectives are better than fewer, W_2 represents a higher utility than W_1.

The aim of the multi-objective design is to achieve the point in the feasible set that will maximize welfare, that is, to reach the highest attainable social indifference curve; this is point A in figure 4. Note that point A will not in general coincide with point B, the point achieved by the traditional approach of maximizing net economic efficiency benefits.

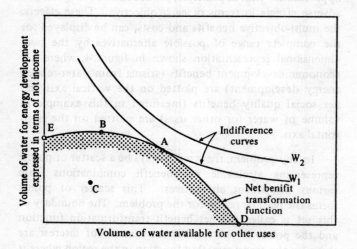

Figure 4. Graphical representation of multi-objective theory

An important aspect of the analysis is the slope of the transformation function at the optimal point A. The extent of this slope (usually termed elasticities) represents the weight placed by society on an additional increment of net benefits for the objective plotted on the horizontal axis in terms of net benefits for the objective plotted on the vertical axis. In the present example, this weight is interpreted as the net income to the economic account that society is willing to sacrifice in order to obtain the marginal amount of water for other uses, that is, the trade-off between economic efficiency and social quality at the optimal level of design. In theory, explicit definition of the value of this trade-off would determine automatically the optimal plan for the system; in practice, such weights or trade-offs usually cannot be specified a priori. This information must be inferred by decision makers from expressions of choice made by the public.

The types of problems encountered in multi-objective analysis will be evident from the preceding description of the approach. The major problems include the careful selection of relevant objectives and the development of appropriate benefit and cost accounts for them, the development of feasible alternatives responsive to alternative weights on objective, and the use of these alternatives to elicit information about preferences from the affected public and from decision makers.

Multi-objective planning enables the planners to move towards a socially acceptable solution while maintaining high economic efficiency or a high benefit-cost ratio. It serves to strike a proper balance between maximizing net economic benefits and satisfying social quality interests. Water use allocation may be carried out in a basin-wide context for optimal solution.

The water allocated to the energy resource development sector according to multi-objective analysis may then be reallocated further among various energy resource developments by using one of the appropriate water-energy models discussed in this section.

E. CONCLUSIONS AND RECOMMENDATIONS

1. Water and energy resources development are interrelated. A similar relationship exists with respect to the conservation aspects of these resources. The tasks of development and conservation of these two resources should be considered together in the planning process, because whatever amount is saved by way of conservation can be regarded as an extension of supply of these resources.

2. Since water and energy issues are inextricably bound, better management and use of developed water resources would reduce energy consumption and *vice versa* as well as minimize detrimental environmental effects. Considerable savings in water consumption may be achieved by improving irrigation efficiency, considering the use of treated industrial and municipal effluents for irrigation where possible, reuse of waste water rather than fresh water by industries in some of their processes and recirculating cooling water in a closed-cycle system, introducing water metering and appropriate prices for water and introducing building codes that require extensive use of water saving devices.

3. Water is not only a major factor in energy resources development but is also a significant renewable energy resource. The hydropower potential in the ESCAP region is very large but the amount exploited is very small. This situation, combined with the scale and character of electricity demand in developing countries and the comparatively

high oil prices, creates a favourable condition for the development of hydropower — both large and small.

4. The development of hydropower usually requires a large capital investment which is often beyond the financial resources of developing countries. Any financial assistance from international institutions, if obtained, can cover only a small portion of large hydroelectric project costs. Therefore, in planning the development of hydropower, it is advisable to give equal emphasis to small-scale projects that involve a comparatively affordable investment and at the same time have comparatively economic efficiency equal to that of large-scale projects. In this connection, consideration of the extensive use of standardized hydro generating equipment and retrofitting of existing dams and irrigation canals with electricity generating equipment are suggested as possible means of reducing investment costs.

5. In the development of hydroelectric projects the possible negative effects they may have on water quality, fisheries, scenic and wild life, historical sites, seismic effects etc., should be taken into consideration and ways should be found of removing them or at least reducing them to levels that can be accepted by the society being effected.

6. A study of recent mathematical models for planning water-energy systems reveals that significant achievements have been made in terms of theoretical concepts and optimization strategies regarding resource allocation and facility siting. However, these models fail to consider adequately the social aspects and therefore cannot provide real optimum solutions with regard to allocation of water between energy and non-energy sectors.

7. Most of the mathematical models discussed in previous sections may be used for allocating water among various energy developments within the allotment apportioned to the energy sector. It should be noted that some of these models are still undergoing testing and evaluation, and therefore further modifications and refinements are expected that will improve the effectiveness of these models.

8. Any attempt to apply the mathematical planning models to developing countries should be preceded by an evaluation of their appropriateness and adaptability, taking account of the local conditions, including technical capabilities and resource persons.

9. Although in general water resources appear to be abundant in many countries of the region, the spatial and temporal distribution of these resources are such that the increasing demand of water for agriculture, industry and domestic use as a result of continuous and rapid increase in population may soon result in water shortages in some areas. In such areas, water supply may become a limiting factor not only for energy development but also for socio-economic development. The optimum allocation of water for energy and other uses will be of paramount importance in finding an effective solution, which may be worked out within the context of multi-objective planning for water resources management. The use of multi-objective analysis for achieving the optimum allocation of water to its users is a sound basis of water resources management but its application will need testing and further improvement to suit diversified economic and social conditions in the developing countries.

10. The interlocking nature of the relationship between water and energy suggests that an integrated multi-disciplinary and systems approach to integrated river basin development is necessary for the planning of energy and water resources systems in order to minimize development costs and optimize benefits for the region. It is recommended that consideration be given by developing countries to the application of the multidisciplinary and systems approach to integrated river basin development for the planning of water-energy systems, taking into account the prevailing physical, economical and social conditions in the ESCAP region.

REFERENCE LIST

1. Viessman Jr., W. and Stork, K.E., "Water and energy crisis", *Water Resources Bulletin,* American Water Resources Association, vol. 10, No. 2, April 1974, pp. 220-228.

2. Levine, P.R., "Industry helps conserve municipal water", *Journal of the American Water Works Association,* March 1982, p. 132.

3. General Electric Company, "Future needs for dry or peak shaved dry/wet cooling and significance to nuclear power plants', *National Technical Information Service,* PB-253-630, 1976.

4. Cornell H., "A consultant looks at future water utility energy problems", *Energy and Water Use Forecasting,* An AWWA Management Resource Book, American Water Works Association, 1980, pp. 21-31.

5. Clouser, R.L. and Miller, W.L., "Household water use: Technological shifts and conservation implications", *Water Resources Bulletin,* American Water Resources Association, vol. 16, No. 3, June 1980, pp. 453-458.

6. Bishop, A.B. et. al., *Water as a factor in energy resources development* (Utah Water Research Laboratory, Utah State University, Logan, Utah, 1975).

7. *American Water Works Association Journal,* August 1981, pp. 40-50.

8. Seitz-Petrash, A., "The new energy boom: small-scale hydropower", *Civil Engineering,* ASCE, April 1980, pp. 66-71.

9. Karkkaineu, S., *Optimization of the Utilization of Electricity Generating Plants* (Finland, Technical Research Centre of Finland Electrical Engineering Laboratory, 1982).

10. O'Brien, W.T. et. al., "Multi-objective planning for water resources management", Australian Water Resources Council Technical Paper No. 27, Canberra, 1977.

11. *Water Power and Dam Construction,* May 1980, pp. 23-25.

12. Hampton, N.F. and Ryan Jr., B.Y., "Water constraints on emerging energy production", *Water Resources Bulletin,* American Water Resources Association, vol. 16, No. 3, June 1980, pp. 508-513.

13. Aron, G., White, E.L. and Coelon, S.P., "Feasibility of interbasin water transfer", *Water Resources Bulletin,* 13 (I), 1972, pp. 267-299.

14. Hamdan, A.S. and Meredith, D.D., "Network analysis of conjunctively operated groundwater-surface water systems", Res. Rep. 74-0076, Water Resources Centre, University of Illinois, Urbana-Champaign, January 1974.

15. King, A.B., Anderson, J.C., Clyde, C.G. and Haggan, D.H., "Development of regional supply functions and a least cost model for allocating water resources in Utah: A parametric Linear programming approach, report", Utah Water Resources Laboratory, Logan, 1972.

16. Reynolds, J.E., "Water allocation models based on an analysis for the Kirsimmee River Basin", Publication 26, *Water Resources Research Centre,* University of Florida, Gainesville, 1973.

17. Texas Department of Water Resources, "Optimal capacity expansion model for surface water resource systems, report", Austin, Texas, 1975.

18. Young, G.K. and Pisano, M.A., "Nonlinear programming applied to regional water resource planning", *Water Resource Research,* 6 (I), 1970, pp. 32-42.

19. Buras, N., "Determining the feasibility of incorporating water resource constraints into energy models", EPRI-EA-1147, Electric Power Research Institute, Palo Alto, California, 1979.

20. Brill, E.D., Velioglu, S.G. and Fuessle, R.W., "Water and energy systems: A planning model", *Journal of Water Resources Planning and Management Division,* American Society of Civil Engineers, 103 (WRI), 1977, pp. 17-32.

21. Brill, E.D., Velioglu, S.G. and Fuessle, R.W., "Mathematical models for use in planning regional water resources and energy systems", Res. Rep. 76-0116, Water Resources Centre, University of Illinois, Urbana-Champaign, November 1976.

22. Provenzano, G., "A linear programming model for assessing the regional impacts of energy development on water resources", Res. Rep. 77-0126, Water Resources Centre, University of Illinois, Urbana-Champaign, July 1977.

23. Lall, U. and Mays, L.W., "Model for planning water-energy systems", *Water Resources Research,* vol. 17, No. 4, August 1981, pp. 853-865.

24. Leigh, M., "Competition for water: energy vs. agriculture", *Proceedings of the Conference on Water and Energy, Technical and Policy Issues,* ed. by Kilpatric, F., et al, ASCE, May-June 1982, pp. 457-462.

25. Hensala, W.E., "A coherent framework for resource development", *Proceedings of the Conference on Water and Energy, Technical and Policy Issues,* ed. by Kilpatric, F., et al, ASCE, May-June 1982, pp. 463-466.

26. Cohen, A.S. and Costello, K.W., *Regional energy modelling: An evaluation of alternative approaches,* Report ANL/AA-1, Argonne National Laboratory, Argonne, Illinois, U.S.A., 1975.

27. Anderson, D., "Models for determining least cost investments in electric supply", *Bell Journal of Economics,* 3 (1), 267-299, 1972.

28. Farrar, D.C. and Woodruff, F., "A model for the determination of optimal electric generating system expansion patterns", *Rep. MIT-EL73-009,* MIT Press, Cambridge, Massachussetts, U.S.A., 1973.

29. Gately, D., *Investment planning for the electric power industry: An integer programming approach,* Report, University of Western Ontario, London, Ontario, Canada, 1970.

30. Sawey, R.M., "Long range planning in electric utility," Ph.D. dissertation, University of Texas, Austin, Texas, U.S.A., 1973.

31. Thompson, R.G. et al., *The cost of electricity: cheap power vs. a clean environment,* Report, Gulf Publishing Co., Houston, Texas, U.S.A., 1977.

32. Whitlatch, E.E., "Coal gasification and water resources development", *Journal of Water Resources Planning and Management Division,* American Society of Civil Engineers, 103 (WR 2), 299-314, 1977.

33. Morris, G.E., An optimization of energy related economic development in the upper Colorado River basin under conditions of water and energy resources scarcity, Ph.D. dissertation, University of Colorado, Boulder, Colorado, U.S.A., 1977.

34. Hobbs, B.F. and Meier, P.M., "An analysis of water resources constraints on power plant siting in the mid-Atlantic states", *Water Resources Bulletin,* 15 (16), pp. 1666-1676, 1979.

35. Cohon, J.L. et al., "Application of a multiobjective facility location model to power plant siting in a six-state region of the U.S.", *Computer Operations Research,* 7(1/2), pp. 107-123, 1980.

36. Eagles, T.W. et al., "Modelling plant location patterns: Applications", EPRI-EA-1375, Electric Power Research Institute, Palo Alto, California, U.S.A., 1980.

37. Gerstle, J.H. and Marks, D.H. "Discussion, water and energy systems: A planning model", *Journal of Water Resources Planning and Management Division,* American Society of Civil Engineers, 104 (WB 1), 1978, pp. 285-286.

38. Georgianna, T. and Haynes, K., "Competition for water resources: coal and agriculture in the Yellowstone Basin", *Economic Geography,* vol. 57, No. 3, July 1981.

39. Matsomoto, J. and Mays, L.W., "A model for planning large-scale water-energy systems", *Proceedings of the Conference on Water and Energy, Technical and Policy Issues,* ed. by Kilpatric, F. et al., ASCE, May-June 1982, pp. 622-627.

V. ASSESSMENT AND CONSIDERATION OF IRRIGATION EFFICIENCY IN THE IRRIGATED AREAS OF THE ESCAP REGION
(E/ESCAP/NR. 10/2)

Introduction

The past two decades have seen an increased awareness of the importance of irrigated agriculture in the ESCAP member countries. Major investments have taken place in the field of irrigation development. Research into water control and management, major crop varieties and cropping patterns has expanded rapidly at the national as well as the international levels.

During the past decade, the shift to the use of modern technology in agriculture has been significant, based mainly on the adoption by cultivators of high-yielding varieties of rice and upland crops. However, most of the existing irrigation systems in the developing countries of the ESCAP region have not been consistent with modern high-yielding agricultural production technology requiring good water control and higher irrigation efficiency; therefore the pace of agricultural modernization has begun to slow down.

Nevertheless, at present, as in the past, the most challenging problem in the region is to assure a stable supply of food to the growing population, and the key role of irrigation development to meet this challenge has been widely recognized.

Irrigation, both intensive and extensive, aims, in general, at maximizing agricultural production. The prospects of the expansion of new irrigated land with up-to-date irriga-

tion systems have become less certain owing to increasing competition for irrigation water and the general scarcity of arable land in the region. Besides, in many cases, economic analyses have shown that, while improvement works require additional capital investments, the returns from improvements to existing irrigation schemes are often higher than expected returns from the same investments in the construction of new sophisticated irrigation systems.

In most agricultural countries of the ESCAP region, an intensive land productivity policy to increase yield per unit area has been adopted. India, Indonesia, Pakistan, the Philippines, Thailand and some other countries, which earlier had pursued an extensive policy of increasing the area of irrigation, have at present also turned to a yield increase policy. The intensive policy of irrigation and drainage in such countries as Japan and the Republic of Korea has brought about a rapid increase in agricultural production.

Thus, the main function of irrigation is to meet the goal of intensification and rationalization in agriculture by contributing to increased land productivity through new agricultural technology, the success of which is dependent upon improved irrigation efficiency, proper engineering water control and use of water by irrigators in conjunction with other managerial, agricultural, socio-economic and institutional inputs. However, despite the considerable efforts which have been made recently to improve agricultural water use, irrigation efficiency in many countries of the region is still very low.

The information available indicates that in many gravity irrigation systems in the region, less than 50 per cent of the water developed at the sources finally reaches the field. Taking into account the low distribution and application efficiency in the farm, overall irrigation efficiency as low as around 30 per cent is common in irrigated areas of the ESCAP region.

A. ASSESSMENT AND CONSIDERATION OF IRRIGATION EFFICIENCY IN THE IRRIGATED AREAS OF THE ESCAP REGION

1. Irrigation efficiency

Irrigation efficiency is normally defined in a physical and economic sense. As the competition for water increases it is more rational to increase physical irrigation efficiency by upgrading irrigation systems and adopting improved methods of controlling, measuring and applying water. However, in many cases there are few socio-economic incentives to improve physical efficiency mainly because of the very low economic value of water.

Socio-economic incentives are a means of motivating farmers to use the available land and water resources, the two most fundamental elements in agricultural production, for maximum returns. Both social and economic incentives, such as land reform programmes, effective water pricing systems, fertilizer subsidies etc., should be used to motivate cultivators to participate actively in the efficient use of water and in the application of modern irrigation techniques and practices.

The term "irrigation efficiency" is used in a variety of senses to describe the performance of irrigation systems and projects. Engineers, agriculturists and economists often have a different notion of what constitutes irrigation efficiency. In agronomy, the term irrigation efficiency is used to express the yield divided by the amount of water consumptively used by the plant during the growing season. Irrgation efficiency from the economic point of view refers to the optimal use of water from the standpoint of the society or the national economy. This involves the internal rate of return, international prices, crop production etc.

This paper examines various physical and non-physical deficiencies and constraints affecting irrigation efficiency in the irrigated areas of the ESCAP region and suggests a number of engineering, managerial, socio-economic and institutional measures to improve it.

2. Physical irrigation efficiency

The concept of considering and assessing the efficiency of water use in an irrigation system as separate operations, elaborated by the International Commission on Irrigation and Drainage, is widely recognized.

The movement of water through an irrigation system can be regarded as three separate operations: conveyance, distribution and field application. The efficiency of each operation is defined as follows:

(a) Conveyance efficiency is the efficiency of canal and conduit networks from the reservoir, river diversion or pumping station to the offtakes of the distributary system;

(b) Distribution efficiency is the efficiency of the water distribution canals and conduits supplying water from the conveyance network to individual fields;

(c) Field application efficiency is by definition the ratio between the quantity of water needed to maintain the soil moisture at the level required for the crop and the quantity of water furnished at the point of delivery to the field. This efficiency is usually called irrigation efficiency at the farm level.

The overall efficiency or "irrigation efficiency" at the project level evaluates the entire operation from the diversion source of water to the rootzone of the crops grown in the irrigated area.

3. Assessment and consideration of irrigation efficiency

The majority of irrigated areas of the ESCAP region are characterized by the methods of simultaneous water distribution and continuous basin irrigation. Rice is the main or the only growing crop.

(a) Conveyance efficiency

The conveyance losses which occur in main, lateral and sublateral canals are often substantial. Thus, the conveyance efficiency heavily depends upon the size of the irrigated area. Increasing canal lengths related to a large irrigated area and the long travel time for water in large open systems cause the conveyance efficiency to decrease. However, as water is usually supplied continuously to the fields at an approximately constant flow, the procedure does not require adjustment of division at inlet structures and does not represent any organizational problem.

For smaller irrigated areas conveyance efficiency decreases mainly because of difficulties encountered by the project management in making the frequent adjustments required in the discharge measuring and regulating structures on the relatively small capacity canals taking into account the fact that, in many cases, small irrigated areas are not managed by an adequate number of operational personnel.

Conveyance efficiency largely depends on the magnitude of the operational losses, which are, in turn, a function of effective management organization. Obviously, there is no efficient water conveyance without well-constructed and maintained irrigation canals and suitable flow-regulating structures.

The other major factors affecting the degree of conveyance losses and consequently the conveyance efficiency are as follows:

(a) Seepage in the canals, which depends on texture of soil, depth of water table, permeability of soil, age of canal and degree of compaction of embankment;

(b) Leakage, which is a function of maintenance of canals and embankments and of maintenance and tightness of gates;

(c) Illegal diversions, the occurrence of which depends on the degree of supervision and patrolling of canals and the co-operation of irrigators.

(b) *Distribution efficiency*

The ultimate goal of an irrigation system or project is to distribute the right quantity of water at the right time over the project area and to the farms within it.

Distribution efficiency is seriously affected by conveyance and farm ditch efficiency. After the irrigation water has been conveyed to the farm inlet, the subsequent stage is the distribution of water to the various farm plots. Farm ditch distribution efficiency largely depends on the skill of famers and is also influenced by seepage losses, the method of water distribution and by the farm size.

Small farms receiving their water at a constant rate and applying it continuously to the field do not have operational difficulties and have a much higher farm ditch distribution efficiency as compared with small farms on a rotational supply. Large farms operating on a rotational distribution basis with adequate skill have a high distribution efficiency.

Farms that have lined ditches or are situated on less permeable soils, like clay, have an above average distribution efficiency.

Good operation and management of an irrigation system by skilled staff is of paramount importance for a high distribution efficiency. The simultaneous distribution method prevails in the region, although rotational distribution is practised in some irrigated areas.

The quality of the communication of the individual farmer with the organization in charge of the diversion and conveyance of the irrigation supply also influences the efficiency of water distribution.

Projects which supply water continuously to farms have a relatively high distribution efficiency mainly because the system does not require frequent adjustment. However, in times of water shortage, rotational distribution should be practised, especially during land soaking and preparation. Water delivery from the farm ditches should also be by rotation. At present, a combination of simultaneous and rotational distribution is being practised in the various irrigated areas of the region.

(c) *Field application efficiency*

Continuous basin irrigation for rice cultivation widely practised in the region has a low application efficiency. This is attributed mainly to the saturation of the soil profile with its consequent percolation losses and also to the fact that the water supply is rarely adjusted with rainfall. It should be noted that a change in some irrigated areas from continuous to rotational basin irrigation did not sharply increase application efficiency because of the farmers' poor skills and operational difficulties.

In general, application efficiency is influenced by the permeability of the soil in relation to the field irrigation method. This correlation is most evident with continuous flooding in paddy cultivation. Hence, the most suitable soils for paddy are clay and silty-clay, for which the application efficiency in the irrigated areas of the ESCAP region equals around 50 per cent.

Intermittent basin irrigation shows a rather high application efficiency for all soils. With this method the application efficiency depends almost entirely on the uniformity of the water depth applied. Proper land levelling can contribute greatly to the improvement of application efficiency.

Field application efficiency can be also improved by minimizing water losses through proper maintenance of paddy dikes, close supervision of the water delivered to the field to avoid overapplication and installation of paddy spillways to control the water depth and to avoid unnecessary drainage.

The overall or project efficiency is the product of the conveyance, distribution and field application efficiencies. Hence, all factors influencing them influence the overall efficiency too.

B. MAJOR DEFICIENCES AND CONSTRAINTS AFFECTING IRRIGATION EFFICIENCY IN THE IRRIGATED AREAS OF THE ESCAP REGION

As stated above, irrigation efficiency is primarily an index of the physical performance of a complete irrigation system or the components of a system. It is affected by many physical factors, such as conveyance, distribution and application losses, evaporation and transporation by non-beneficial vegetation, operational wastes etc. The magnitude of these losses varies widely among irrigation projects because of different physiographic features, water control and conveyance structures, operation and management practices, methods of irrigation, etc.

However, the physical performance of an irrigation system or project is also seriously affected by non-physical factors, such as socio-economic incentives, institutional arrangements, the degree of education and training of farmers and irrigators, the provision of extension services, etc. An integrated approach is needed to assess and consider irrigation efficiency and to identify a set of measures to improve the efficiency of irrigation schemes.

The major problems causing low irrigation efficiency in the irrigated areas of the ESCAP region identified during various seminars and expert group meetings, conducted by ESCAP and other international organizations, can be classified as engineering and managerial, agricultural, socio-economic and institutional.

1. Engineering and managerial problems

The major engineering and managerial deficiencies and constraints causing low irrigation efficiency can be summarized as follows:

(a) Estimates of water availability and water requirements of crops based on inadequate hydrologic data;

(b) Improper hydraulic design of the capacity of different structures (head water intake structure, conveyance and distribution canals and structures etc.), and a resulting incapability to ensure timely and equitable distribution of irrigation water of all parts of the system;

(c) Inefficient or inadequate drainage system or lack of drainage facilities resulting in waterlogging and salinization of irrigated soils;

(d) Lack of proper protection of the irrigated area from floods and salt water intrusion;

(e) Excessive water losses due to leakage, seepage and deep percolation of the irrigation system;

(f) Extensive siltation, erosion and weed infestation of irrigation and drainage canals and ditches;

(g) Inadequate density of irrigation and drainage canals and ditches;

(h) Lack of control and measuring facilities;

(i) Lack of adequate communication equipment for effective operations and maintenance;

(j) Lack of adequate on-farm facilities;

(k) Lack of facilities for conjunctive use of surface and ground water, where necessary.

These shortcomings are mainly attributed to the engineering aspects. The problems of an unefficiently managed and operated irrigation project could be characterized as follows:

(i) Lack of co-ordination among agencies involved in providing essential services required by irrigation projects;

(ii) Lack of co-ordination between agencies concerned and farmers' organizations and individual farmers;

(iii) Lack of co-ordination between the authorities handling engineering and agricultural services;

(iv) Absence of a single agency responsible for the co-ordination of all activities within a project area;

(v) Inadequate assignment of the responsibility between operations and maintenance personnel and farmers;

(vi) Lack of efficient organization capable of carrying out effective operation, maintenance and repair of the system;

(vii) Lack of measurement of water losses in order to identify irrigation system components where remedial measures are required;

(viii) Unscheduled drainage of the fields by farmers leading to waterlogging and salinization of irrigated land;

(ix) Inadequate and uneven water distribution, especially during the dry season irrigation period, resulting in particular in a shortage of water at the tail section;

(x) Wasteful application and illegal diversion of irrigation water by farmers;

(xi) Lack of regular contact and consultations between operations and maintenance personnel and farmers;

(xii) Inadequate feedback on the performance of systems and from farmers etc.

It should be also mentioned that in many irrigation schemes the organizational structure of the irrigated area is not closely related to the framework of the irrigation system from the point of view of the most expedient distribution of all level canals and the most rational water supply and distribution schemes.

2. Agricultural factors

The major agricultural factors detrimental to the efficient use of irrigation water and to the increase of crop yields are:

(a) Absence or irregular land levelling, which is very important because of the continuous submergence method widely used in the irrigated areas of the region;

(b) Inadequate land shaping;

(c) Inefficient cropping pattern;

(d) Inadequate soil management practice;

(e) Poor availability of agricultural inputs, infrastructure, such as farm roads, marketing, credit etc. and incentives to farmers to use modern techniques and practices;

(f) Lack of adequate training for farmers;

(g) Inadequate agricultural research.

Of great importance are the extension services, which include the improved operation of an irrigation system to meet crop requirements, selecting the proper cropping pattern and appropriate seed varieties and sources, selecting and applying correctly fertilizers and pesticides, obtaining institutional credit at reasonable interest rates, etc. Owing to budget constraints, a shortage of trained personnel and other problems, the extension services provided by the governments in the developing countries of the region are usually inadequate. The problems of providing adequate agricultural extension services are as follows:

(i) An inadequate number of extension agents and subject matter specialists;

(ii) A lack of vehicles;

(iii) A lack of technical support from central or provincial departments and research centres;

(iv) Inappropriate methodology of extension and demonstration.

Crop yields under efficient irrigation can be considerably increased with fertilizer application. The major factors affecting the effective use of fertilizers in the region are as follows:

(1) Ineffective control of water;

(2) Poor technical knowledge of the proper fertilizer application;

(3) Accessibility constraints, resulting in inability of farmers to get the proper amount of fertilizers in time;

(4) Economic and financial constraints.

3. Socio-economic and institutional setting

Irrigation efficiency is affected by a number of socio-economic and institutional factors since irrigation is not only a water problem but also involves people and institutions. These factors include appropriate land tenure and water pricing policies, the provision of adequate farm inputs, credit and marketing facilities, a co-ordinated approach to water management at the farm level and the creation of farmer associations.

This group of factors is very important but, at the same time, the most difficult means by which the countries of the region can endeavour to improve irrigation efficiency.

A land reform programme may provide both economic and social incentives, thereby encouraging an increase in agricultural production and more equitable farm income. It usually includes among other agricultural development activities irrigation development and stimulates the efficient use and distribution of irrigation water. A number of countries of the region have instituted agrarian reform measures to break up large land holdings and to improve a poor land tenure system.

An effective water pricing policy is very important for efficient use of irrigation water. In most developing countries of the region the operation and maintenance of the secondary canal systems are the responsibility of the farmers. Very often the insufficient water charges result in poor operation and maintenance of tertiary systems, thereby decreasing irrigation efficiency at the farm level. There are, however, many factors which make it difficult to raise water charges. These include irregularity and unreliability of water supply from irrigation systems, low level of cultural techniques, inadequate supply of farm inputs, credits and other services, small farm holdings, defective tenure systems, great variation of income among and low repayment capacity of farmers, lack of farmer's co-operation and inefficient co-operative organization at the farm level, inadequate government policies and laws dealing with irrigation water charges, and low prices of agricultural products at the farm gate.

To improve irrigation efficiency water-use associations of farmers are being developed in many countries of the region, but confronted by pressure and time constraints of irrigation development and the magnitude of the problem they are not yet cohesive and effective enough. Constraints, such as internal conflicts, waning interest of farmers and deficiency in field staff and funds, are common in the region. Farmers' associations very often serve purposes other than concentration of their efforts on the problems of water distribution, management and maintenance of irrigation systems.

However, there are some good examples. In the Philippines, significant progress has been made in institutional development, using a process which promotes maximum participation of farmers in planning, construction, operation and maintenance of irrigation systems. The process has been tried out in four projects and has been started in 36 other projects. The experience with these projects indicates that to enable farmers to participate, community organizers should be given enough lead time to become integrated with the community and gain the confidence of the farmers and organize the association prior to construction. This requires about 9 to 10 months, depending on prevailing conditions in the projects; engineers should develop flexibility in their attitudes towards farmers and community organizers and should have more understanding of institutional factors and processes; agency policies and procedures which obstruct farmers' participation should be reviewed and amended; engineers and community organizers should work together closely; and technical and organizing activities should be integrated.

While marketing and farm technology services and co-ordination exist in most countries, there is a need for expanding and strengthening these institutions. In many cases, they are not adequate and are not provided on a sustained basis. The various activities within the project area undertaken by different agencies are not properly co-ordinated because of the lack of a unified authority responsible for the area.

An effective co-ordinated approach to water management at the farm level has been introduced in some countries, such as Pakistan and Bangladesh. In Pakistan, a team consisting of specialists on different subjects, relating to water course design and improvement, precision land levelling and improved agricultural practices, has provided advice to the farmers on watercourse command. In Bangladesh, special action programmes have been launched through formation of implementation committees, co-ordinating related agencies, to increase the command area and crop yield through efficient management of irrigation water.

An integrated approach has been adopted in Sri Lanka. Besides irrigation and drainage facilities, social infrastructural facilities are also provided. A village centre which serves 8 to 10 clusters, with 70 to 100 families in each cluster, is provided with a primary school, a co-operative stall, stores, a community hall and a post office. A town centre serving four to five village centres has a central bus stand, a shopping centre, a co-operative headquarters, a bank, a main post office, a telecommunications centre, a gasoline filling station, a police station, a central school, a hospital and other basic facilities.

The establishment of a body with broad powers for water and land development, management, operation and maintenance is a comprehensive measure resorted to in India, which has established Command Area Development Authorities to ensure the proper performance of irrigation projects. The training and visit system adopted is showing good results.

In Viet Nam, irrigation and drainage systems are managed by the State through bodies called "company", "station" and "group". The group is in charge of tertiary canals and is the lowest unit in the hierarchy of state management. In addition, every collective co-operative has its own team which constitutes the grass-root unit for management of irrigation and drainage. The duties of the team include the preparation of a programme for the maintenance and repair of irrigation works and the formulation and implementation of the programme for irrigation and drainage of each field block.

At present, governments increasingly recognize that efficient use of irrigation water is a prerequisite for producing more food and achieving socio-economic targets. Despite traditional socio-economic and institutional patterns and conditions prevailing in the region and posing considerable constraints to changes, important initiatives and measures have been taken recently in a number of developing countries with a view to improving irrigation efficiency in their irrigated areas.

C. MEASURES TO IMPROVE IRRIGATION EFFICIENCY IN IRRIGATED AREAS OF THE ESCAP REGION

1. Engineering and managerial measures

Primary attention should be given to minimizing total water losses, which consist of conveyance, distribution, field application losses, evapotranspiration and percolation. For that purpose consideration should be given to:

(a) Lining of canals constructed on porous soils. Lining porous sections of earth canals where water losses are considerable is a better alternative than, for instance, pumping, as not all the water that seeps from canals can be recovered by pumping due to irretrievable loss through evapotranspiration. However, an economic analysis should be undertaken to determine whether the savings in water by reduction of the seepage rate warrants the expenditure for lining;

(b) Proper maintenance of canals, embankments and farm ditches as well as the proper maintenance of water control and delivery structures to reduce leakage losses;

(c) Eliminating the weeds in the canals and farm ditches to minimize evapotranspiration losses;

(d) Minimizing over-application and illegal diversion losses by means of the co-operation of the irrigators, close supervision on the water distribution and patrolling of canals;

(e) Reducing water losses arising from unscheduled drainage usually practised by farmers during the rainy season and before broadcasting fertilizers. To avoid these losses close co-ordination between farmers and ditchtenders or installation of paddy spillways to control the water depth is necessary.

Irrigation efficiency cannot be improved unless adequate supply, timely delivery and equitable distribution of irrigation water are secured. To ensure these major engineering and managerial principles, the following efforts should be made:

(i) The hydrology of the irrigable area should be reviewed with the objective of reassessing the quantity and quality of available surface and ground water supplies as well as the flood characteristics of the area. On the basis of such a review, the dependable available water supply as well as the size of the area which can be actually irrigated can be determined after taking into account the water requirements of the area. It is possible that adjustments may have to be made in the size of the area to be irrigated as a result of better hydrological analysis and improved estimates of water requirements;

(ii) The hydraulic performance of the irrigation system should also be reviewed to identify those components which act as bottlenecks in the conveyance, distribution, control and delivery of water as a result of inadequate capacity. Such components would have to be redesigned and possibly modified or replaced to increase their hydraulic capacities and performance;

(iii) A review may also be made of the adequacy of the number of water-control and water-delivery structures and where necessary additional structures should be installed to ensure the timely delivery of irrigation water. Care must, however, be taken to determine the effect of such proposed new structures on the performance of the existing ones, particularly those in the lower reaches;

(iv) It would also be useful to review the layout of the distribution network to determine the need for the relocation of any of the conveyance canals to achieve a better and more equitable distribution of irrigation water. At the same time it may be necessary to check whether the principal water control structures at division points are discharging the proper volume of water under their designed operating heads;

(v) There should be adequate provision for drainage in irrigation schemes. This has not always been the case in the irrigated areas in the region. The disposal of excess water in the irrigated area whether from irrigation or other sources is essential not only to provide proper conditions for crop growth but also to prevent water logging and to maintain a proper water-salt balance of the soils. It is also possible that some components of the existing drainage system may have inadequate capacities. These can be observed during periods of heavy rainfall or during the irrigation season. Such components need to be modified or replaced;

(vi) An effective communication system is essential for the efficient operation and maintenance of the system, since contact must be maintained at all times between headquarters and the field. It would, therefore, be necessary for an appropriate communication system to be designed and installed;

(vii) To give operations and maintenance personnel ready access to all parts of the irrigation system for the proper operation, maintenance and repair of its various components, roads should be provided wherever needed. Such roads, which should be designed and constructed so as to support both transport and maintenance equipment, must be regularly maintained and repaired.

One of the most important measures for improving irrigation efficiency in the irrigated areas of the region is the provision by the governments of tertiary, quaternary and terminal facilities at the farm level.

Proper operation and maintenance of an irrigation system are of paramount importance and are different tasks. Operation refers to the allocation of water supplies and involves not only the system's personnel but also farmers. The objective is to maintain irrigation system structures and facilities in good working condition. Maintenance, as a rule, takes place periodically and may not directly involve farmers. The skills required for performing operation and maintenance are also different. These distinctions call for separating operation and maintenance tasks. Nevertheless, co-ordination between the two is necessary and important, and it seems to be generally advantageous to have one single authority responsible for both activities. Operation, as such, can be divided into two phases: the first is the delivery and distribution of water; the second is the use of water distributed to the fields, directly relating to agricultural production e.g. to farmers. They are interdependent and the effectiveness of the second is conditioned by the efficiency of the first.

The important measures which must be carried out to obtain meaningful results are the following:

(1) Introduction of attractive incentives to encourage farmers to participate in the operation and maintenance of irrigation systems;

(2) Assignment to farmers of the responsibility for the operation and maintenance of the farm ditches and on-farm facilities;

(3) Division of the irrigation system into service areas, irrigation sections and units to facilitate operational tasks taking into account such considerations as soil condition, topography and village boundaries;

(4) Measurement of water losses to identify sections where remedial measures are required;

(5) Use of measures to maximize the application of effective rainfall;

(6) In periods of limited water supply, rotational water distribution should be practised to minimize conveyance and distribution losses.

2. Agricultural measures

Certain agricultural measures are necessary components to ensure the improvement of irrigation efficiency. Proper attention should be given to:

(a) The adoption of suitable cropping patterns, including crop rotation, not only to maintain soil fertility but also to enable advantage to be taken of the rainfall pattern of the area as well as to allow better planning in the allocation and distribution of the water supply;

(b) Selection of high-yielding varieties of crops, suitable for irrigation;

(c) Proper application of mineral and organic fertilizers and chemical ameliorants;

(d) Control over changes in the natural condition of the soil in the course of irrigation;

(e) Development of a rational irrigation regime (rate, duration, frequency) based on the prevailing climatic and soil conditions as well as on the type of crop;

(f) Evaluation of the adequacy of agricultural extension services and their effectiveness at the field level in irrigated areas to take necessary steps for improvement;

(g) Proper land levelling and shaping for efficient use of irrigation water;

(h) Close co-operation between agricultural and irrigation personnel at all levels.

Countries should examine and keep under review the requirements of inputs, such as long-term and short-term credit, quality seeds, fertilizers, pesticides, farm implements and machinery for irrigation systems, and take prompt and effective steps to make them available to the farmers on time and at reasonable costs.

3. Socio-economic and institutional measures

The importance of these measures is widely recognized since they involve a number of factors dependent to a large extent on human psychology and behaviour. Special attention should be given to the following measures:

(a) Introduction of effective agrarian reform;

(b) Passage of appropriate water legislation, including regulation of groundwater exploitation;

(c) Promotion of social amenities within the project area, such as schools, hospitals, electricity, drinking water supply and sanitation facilities, post offices etc.;

(d) Provision of a system for policing and enforcement of rules and regulations governing the use of irrigation water;

(e) Devising and imposing an equitable system of water charges which would ensure the provision of funds for the adequate operation, maintenance and repair of irrigation systems and efficient water use and would lead to water conservation;

(f) Ensuring farmers' participation in the operation and maintenance of farm-level facilities by encouraging the organization of farmers' associations and co-operatives.

Farmers should be suitably involved in the planning and implementation of irrigation systems so that a sense of participation is created. The management of irrigation water below the tertiary unit should be undertaken by water-users' associations.

Countries may consider organizing multipurpose farmers' co-operatives as distinct from water-users' associations for making available the necessary agricultural inputs and ancillary facilities.

Strengthening of co-ordination among government agencies involved in providing essential services required by an irrigation project and between these agencies and farmers' organizations as well as individual farmers is of paramount importance. Special attention should be paid to the co-ordination between the authorities handling engineering and agricultural services. Their activities should be organized in such a way that there is a clear division of responsibility and recognition of each agency's field of expertise. Where possible, the creation of a single agency responsible for the co-ordination of all development activities within a project area, regardless of the boundaries of the command area and those of the local civil administration, would be useful.

4. Training and research

The shortage of properly educated and trained personnel in irrigated agriculture is one of the major factors affecting efficient use of irrigation water. The expansion of various training programmes should be further promoted. These programmes should be as comprehensive as possible and may involve:

(a) Local government officials and leaders of farmers on irrigation water management and related modern agricultural practices;

(b) All levels of personnel engaged in operation and maintenance activities;

(c) Farmers, for whom the training programme should be given in a form acceptable and understandable to them;

(d) Establishment of pilot water management projects in representative areas involving a fairly large number of farmers.

Applied research is a prerequisite for effective water use in irrigated agriculture. The priorities of directions for research in the field of irrigated agriculture may include the following research items:

(a) Water losses in the system and economic justification of canal lining;

(b) Operation of the distribution system for even and efficient water supply;

(c) Improvement of irrigation and drainage facilities at different levels;

(d) Local crop water requirements;

(e) Optimization of cropping systems;

(f) Water-soil-plant relationships;

(g) Optimum water input-crop yield relationship;

(h) Drainage methods and systems.

Applied research should also be carried out to identify the relationship between field-water requirements and scheme-water requirements so as to find the bottleneck of low irrigation efficiency as well as a practical method to improve it. Research may also include various water saving measures, particularly in paddy fields, including the restriction of deep percolation, the adoption of intermittent irrigation and the reuse of drainage water.

One of the problem areas which requires intensive research is soil and water conditions for the introduction of diversified agriculture in rice mono-culture irrigated areas.

5. Conclusion

(a) The improvement of irrigation efficiency in the irrigated areas of the ESCAP region, which in a large number of cases is unsatisfactory or disappointing, could play a crucial role in the achievement of self-sufficiency in food production since most of the countries of the region are agriculture-oriented economies. Thus, there is a strong need to undertake nation-wide measures to solve this problem.

(b) What is most needed is an established methodology to determine the efficiency of irrigation systems and projects in physical, economic and social terms. Criteria and priorities for selection of irrigation schemes, the efficiency of which is to be improved, in accordance with their productivity and economic and social significance should be also established.

(c) A comprehensive approach for the improvement of irrigation efficiency should be used and should include engineering, managerial, agricultural, socio-economic and institutional measures.

BIBLIOGRAPHY

Report and materials of the Seminar on Measures to Improve Irrigation Efficiency at the Farm Level in the USSR, 1979, E/ESCAP/NR. 6/27.

Proceedings of the Seminar on the Improvement of Irrigation Performance at the Project Level in the USSR, 1980, Water Resources Series, No. 56.

Report and materials of the Expert Group Meeting on Measures to Improve the Performance of Irrigation Projects, ESCAP, Bangkok, 1981.

Proceedings of the Expert Group Meeting on Water Pricing, ESCAP, Bangkok, 1980, Water Resources Series, No. 55.

International Commission on Irrigation and Drainage, ICID Bulletin (New Delhi), 27 January 1978.

International Institute for Land Reclamation and Improvement, on Irrigation Efficiencies, Wageningen, 1974.

International Rice Research Institute. Report of a Planning Workshop on Irrigation Water Management, The Philippines, 1980.

Food and Agricultural Organization of the United Nations. Report of the Expert Consultation on Farm Water Management. USA, 1980.

Taylor, D.C., and Wickham, T.W., *Irrigation policy and the management of irrigation systems in south-east Asia*. Bangkok, Agricultural Development Council, Inc., 1979.

VI. ASSESSMENT OF IRRIGATION EFFICIENCY – NOTE PREPARED AND PRESENTED BY THE UNITED NATIONS FOOD AND AGRICULTURE ORGANIZATION

Introduction

In the Asia-Pacific region in 1980, about 122 million hectares were being irrigated (28 per cent of the arable land) which forms about 60 per cent of the total area being irrigated in the world. The irrigated area has increased in the seventies at the rate of 1.8 per cent annually (Annex 1). During the same decade, production increase of all cereals and rice were 3.1 per cent respectively (Annex 2). These figures are said to be rather satisfactory as a whole. Yet some reflections have been raised on the necessity to insure higher benefit from irrigation projects developed with a big investment. This calls for a good irrigation water management for improving the efficiency.

Irrigation water management has become a major concern in many countries, coinciding with the awareness that large investments in irrigation development did not pay off in the planned increase of agricultural production under irrigation. It has become clear from a range of studies that to obtain the full benefits of irrigation developments, more attention should be given to irrigation both in the government controlled main system and in the farmer-operated and maintained on farm irrigation system.

In several countries of the region, investigations and studies have been carried out to evaluate the different factors in the operation of an irrigation system. These studies have revealed a better insight into the functioning of an irrigation system, and focussed attention on the shortcomings in the planning and design of such systems. Recent trends to conduct irrigation studies and investigations in actual irrigation system, whereby measurements, surveys, and analyses are carried out under operating conditions in the field, has focussed attention on shortcomings of operation and maintenance. The approach is described under different names and titles such as "action research" (Bottrall), "diagnostic analysis" (Lowdermilk). For a successful evaluation of the shortcomings and improvements, a multi-disciplinary approach is needed, as water management is dependent not only on technical but also on agricultural, socio-economic and institutional factors. This approach has been demonstrated recently in Nong Wai project of Thailand (Kathpalia) assisted by ADB, where increased cropping intensity, higher yields and improved irrigation efficiencies were achieved.

FAO has also been involved in assessing the performance of various irrigation schemes since the mid-sixties covering 90 countries first (1965-67) in a study on irrigation potential and later (1975-77) while planning for agriculture towards the year 2000. As a result of these studies it was felt that greater emphasis should be given to the improvement of irrigation systems. Since then, FAO has been actively involved in assisting member countries through its Technical Co-operative Assistance Programme (TCP), a special international support programme on Farm Water Management and Research Programme in Irrigation.

A. ASSESSMENT

Water utilization efficiency is the main criterion of measuring the performance of an irrigation project. The use of this criterion has the advantage that any physical or socio-organizational feature can be tested against the same yardstick. The criteria of crop yields of financial returns per unit volume of water only partially reflect the effect of irrigation. Moreover, many and wide variations in agronomic and economic conditions do not allow comparisons to be made for the same norms. However, one has to be careful that higher efficiencies are not achieved, with lower yields or much less economic benefits.

1. Standardization

It is now proposed to focus attention on evaluation and monitoring for improving the operation of an irrigation system on a systematic basis through collection of data on Irrigation Efficiency on a standardized basis for all projects irrigating more than 1,000 ha in the Asia and the Pacific region countries. This would enable the member countries to fix priorities for improving the operation and management of irrigation projects for increased production.

In various countries a great deal of work has been done on measuring and calculating irrigation efficiencies but it is difficult to make use of it on a universal basis as the terminology and definitions used vary a great deal. ICID made the first attempt to standardize these for common use and understanding. In 1974, ILRI published the results on the basis of work done by the committee set up by ICID under the chairmanship of Bos. Since then further work has been done by that committee and published in 1978 and 1980. All this work was based on the data supplied for 91 irrigation projects through a questionnaire issued to each country, and collected through specialized agencies of the countries concerned. This gave indication of the effect of various factors on the efficiencies of different parts of the system and their range. However, not much data could be had from the rice growing areas.

The standardization would begin with the use of common concepts, terminology of the system, definitions and terms, as over a period of time various terms and definitions have been used. The information could be collected on the basis of a simple questionnaire by all countries for all projects within a limited time. These are discussed in the following paragraphs.

B. CONCEPTS

The system of water distribution can be split into the following successive stages:

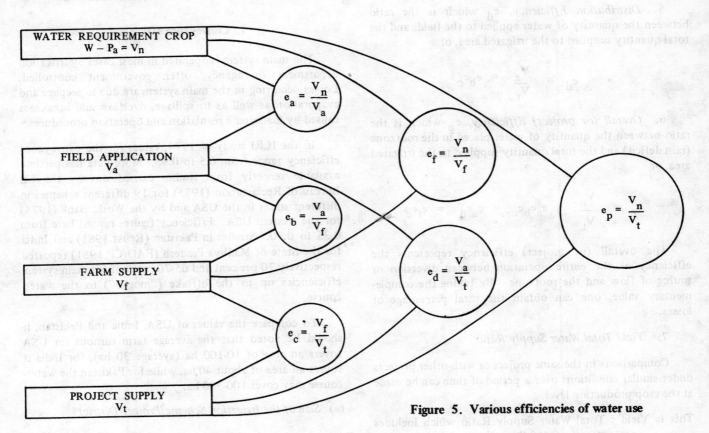

— Conveyance by main, lateral, and sublateral canals to the farm turnout.

— Conveyance by irrigation ditches to the farm/field inlet.

— Application to and distribution over the field from the farm/field inlet onward.

Figure 5. Various efficiencies of water use

1. The efficiency in the first stage is defined as the *Water Conveyance Efficiency*, e_c and can be expressed as

$$e_c = \frac{V_f}{V_t}$$

where V_f is the volume of water delivered to all farms or group inlets through the irrigation ditch or water course in the area and V_t is the total quantity of water supplied to the area.

2. The efficiency in the second stage is defined as the *On Farm Ditch Efficiency*, e_b and can be expressed as

$$e_b = \frac{V_a}{V_f}$$

where V_a is the field application of water to the cropped area and V_f is the volume of water delivered to all farm inlets in the area.

3. The efficiency in the third stage is defined as the *Field Application Efficiency*, e_a and be expressed as

$$e_a = \frac{V_n}{V_a}$$

where V_n is the rainfall deficit (i.e. the difference between the consumptive use and the effective rainfall over the cropped area) and V_a is the field application of water to the cropped area.

4. *Chak or Tertiary Unit Efficiency*, e_f which is the ratio between the quantity of water placed in the rootzone (rainfall deficit) and the total quantity under the farmer's control, or

$$e_f = \frac{V_n}{V_f} = e_a e_b$$

5. *Distribution Efficiency*, e_d which is the ratio between the quantity of water applied to the fields and the total quantity supplied to the irrigated area, or

$$e_d = \frac{V_a}{V_t} = e_b e_c$$

6. *Overall (or project) Efficiency*, e_p which is the ratio between the quantity of water placed in the rootzone (rain deficit) and the total quantity supplied to the irrigated area, or

$$e_p = \frac{V_n}{V_t} = e_a e_b e_c = e_a e_d = e_f e_c$$

The overall (or project) efficiency represents the efficiency of the entire operation between diversion or source of flow and the rootzone. By taking the complementary value, one can obtain the total percentage of losses.

7. *Yield Total Water Supply Ratio*

Comparisons in the same project or with other projects under similar conditions over a period of time can be made at the crop production level.

This is Yield : Total Water Supply Ratio which includes effective rainfall

This is defined as below:

$$R_{yw} = \frac{Y.A.}{W_t + W_{er}}$$

Where,

Y   =   Yield Kg/ha

W_t =   volume of irrigation water furnished to the field

W_{er} =   volume of effective rainfall over the area

A   =   irrigated cropped area

8. *Cost effectiveness*

Increased efficiency at any stage or for the project as a whole needs good management which is cost effective, but sometimes certain physical engineering works have also to be done to improve the efficiency. These have to be carefully evaluated for cost effectiveness before an investment is made. In an operating system such improvements can be decided on the basis of increase in efficiency expected.

C. RANGE OF EFFICIENCIES

1. Conveyance efficiency

The main system is operated in most cases by irrigation department or agency, often government controlled. Losses occurring in the main system are due to seepage and evaporation as well as to spillage, overflow and breakages caused by inadequate regulation and operation procedures.

In the ILRI study of 1974, values for the conveyance efficiency range from 0.5 to 0.95. More data has become available recently from studies carried out by the US Bureau of Reclamation (1975) for 19 different schemes in different states in the USA and by the World Bank (1978) for the western USA. Efficiency figures ranged here from 0.35 to 0.90. Studies in Pakistan (Reuss 1981) and India for the State of Madhya Pradesh (FAO/CP 1981) reported respectively 70 per cent and 65-70 per cent for main system efficiencies up to the offtake ("mogha") to the water-course.

To compare the values of USA, India and Pakistan, it should be noted that the average farm turnout for USA covers an area of 10-100 ha (average 30 ha), for India it covers an area of about 40 ha, while for Pakistan the water-course may cover 100-300 ha.

(a) *Size of the Irrigation Scheme/Project/District*

An evaluation of the effect of size of the irrigation schemes in USA which varied between 1,000 to 200,000 ha, showed no significant correlation with conveyance efficiency but the ILRI study of 1974 showed that for a size of $1,000 - 10,000$ ha an efficiency of 85 per cent was achieved and for larger schemes the value decreased to 70 per cent. The Indian studies in Madhya Pradesh which refer to tank schemes of size 700 to 6,000 ha, reported conveyance efficiencies of 65-70 per cent.

(b) *Operation and Maintenance*

The importance of good operation and maintenance for the performance of an irrigation system has been stressed

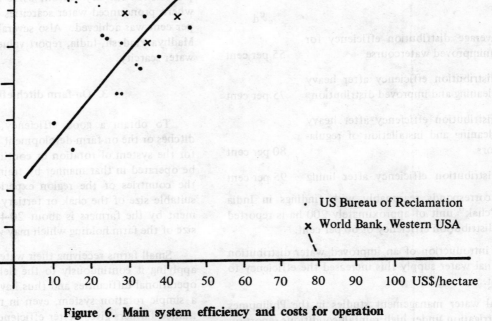

Figure 6. Main system efficiency and costs for operation and maintenance per hectare

in several studies. This is well illustrated in figure 6, which shows that with increasing annual costs of O & M, the irrigation efficiency improves markedly. The low O & M costs reported for many schemes in Asia ($US 5-20/ha) is one of the reasons for low irrigation efficiencies reported from many irrigation schemes.

A good operation of the system and improved efficiency with the help of feedback information and control structures has been reported from Nong Wai project. Intermittent supply during scarcity conditions and weekly adjustment of supplies as per requirements also helped in increasing efficiency.

The conveyance efficiency is generally taken as 85-95 per cent for designing and planning purposes. But actually it varies from 42 to 98 per cent as determined in many

countries depending on local factors. Keeping in view the many factors, including insufficient maintenance due to low budgets it would be good to aim at achieving 80-90 per cent efficiency.

2. Distribution efficiency

The efficiency relates to the water distribution within the tertiary unit or the farmers' controlled irrigation unit.

In most countries, this includes the watercourse and farm ditches after the farm turnout (the "mogha" in Pakistan, the "chak" in India and Thailand). In certain cases, it may include a complete irrigation system, such as the small tank or river pump schemes or tube wells in Bangladesh, Pakistan and India, or the village schemes in

Indonesia. The size of the tertiary farmer controlled unit or small schemes may vary from 10 ha to 250 ha.

The management of the irrigation water in the farmers' controlled system plays, in most irrigation schemes, an important part in the effectiveness of the irrigation system. Technical, organizational and social factors play a crucial role. In particular, good co-operation among farmers will determine in many ways the success of efficient water management. Values for the distribution efficiency accordingly vary greatly from scheme to scheme. A few systematic studies have provided reliable data in this field. The well documented studies carried out in Pakistan (Reuss 1981) for a watercourse area of approximately 150 ha give the following values:

$$e_d$$

— average distribution efficiency for unimproved watercourse   55 per cent

— distribution efficiency after heavy cleaning and improved distribution   75 per cent

— distribution efficiency after heavy cleaning and installation of regulators   80 per cent

— distribution efficiency after lining   95 per cent

This corresponds reasonably with findings in India where a "chak" unit of approximately 200 ha is reported to have a distribution efficiency of 60 per cent.

After introduction of an improved water distribution by rotational water supply this increased the efficiency to 72 per cent.

Several water management studies in the Philippines with rice irrigation under high rainfall conditions report on distribution efficiency (Siy 1982; Levine and Miranda 1978; Early 1978) indicating values varying from as low as 15 per cent for communal schemes in the wet season to 60-70 per cent in the dry season.

The ILRI study of 1974 indicates values for distribution efficiencies varying from 70 to 80 per cent.

Several factors affect the efficiency of the irrigation system controlled by the farmers, which have become apparent in a number of recent studies. They include:

(a) *Rotational supply*

Introduction of rotational supply is reported in several cases to increase efficiency.

Gujurat, India, efficiency increased from 41 to 70 per cent. Taiwan studies indicate an increase of 20-30 per cent, to values as high as 80 per cent.

Lower Talavera River project, Philippines, efficiencies increased from 43 (wet season) and 51 (dry season) to 60 per cent.

(b) *Water scarcity*

There is a pronounced effect of water scarcity on the efficiency confirmed in several studies. This becomes particularly clear in the Philippine studies, where differences vary from 40-50 per cent in the wet to 60-70 per cent in the dry season. The study carried out by Siy (1982) in the Philippines is illustrative, where most communal irrigation schemes do not achieve much higher values than 15 per cent in the wet season; this value increases to 30 per cent in the dry season, while for one of the schemes, where pronounced water scarcities occurred, a value of 80 per cent was achieved. Also several of the tank schemes in Madhya Pradesh, India, report values of 80 per cent under water scarcity.

3. On-farm ditch efficiency

To obtain a good efficiency, the network of farm ditches or the on-farm development should be well designed for the system of rotation or continuous flow adopted and be operated in that manner by trained farmers. In most of the countries of the region experience has shown that a suitable size of the chak or tertiary unit for good management by the farmers is about 20-40 ha depending on the size of the farm holding which may vary from 0.5 to 3 ha.

Small farms receiving their water at a constant rate and applying it continuously to the field (rice basin) have less operational difficulties and thus have a good efficiency but a simple rotation system, even in rice areas, operated by trained farmers gives better efficiency, reliability, if upland crops are also being grown.

4. Field application efficiency

The field application efficiency relates to the ratio between the amount of irrigation water applied to the field and that which is effectively used for crop production. The losses occur through deep percolation, surface runoff or evaporation. The field efficiency depends mainly on the type of irrigation method. Factors influencing the losses include, in the case of surface irrigation, the inadequate levelling of fields, too large or too small flow discharges to the field (see Figure 7); in the case of sprinkler irrigation, wind drift and inadequate coverage. Furthermore the handling of irrigation water by the farmers is an important factor which depends on his knowledge and skill.

Depending on soil conditions, system layout and irrigator's skill, the following values are given by Merriam

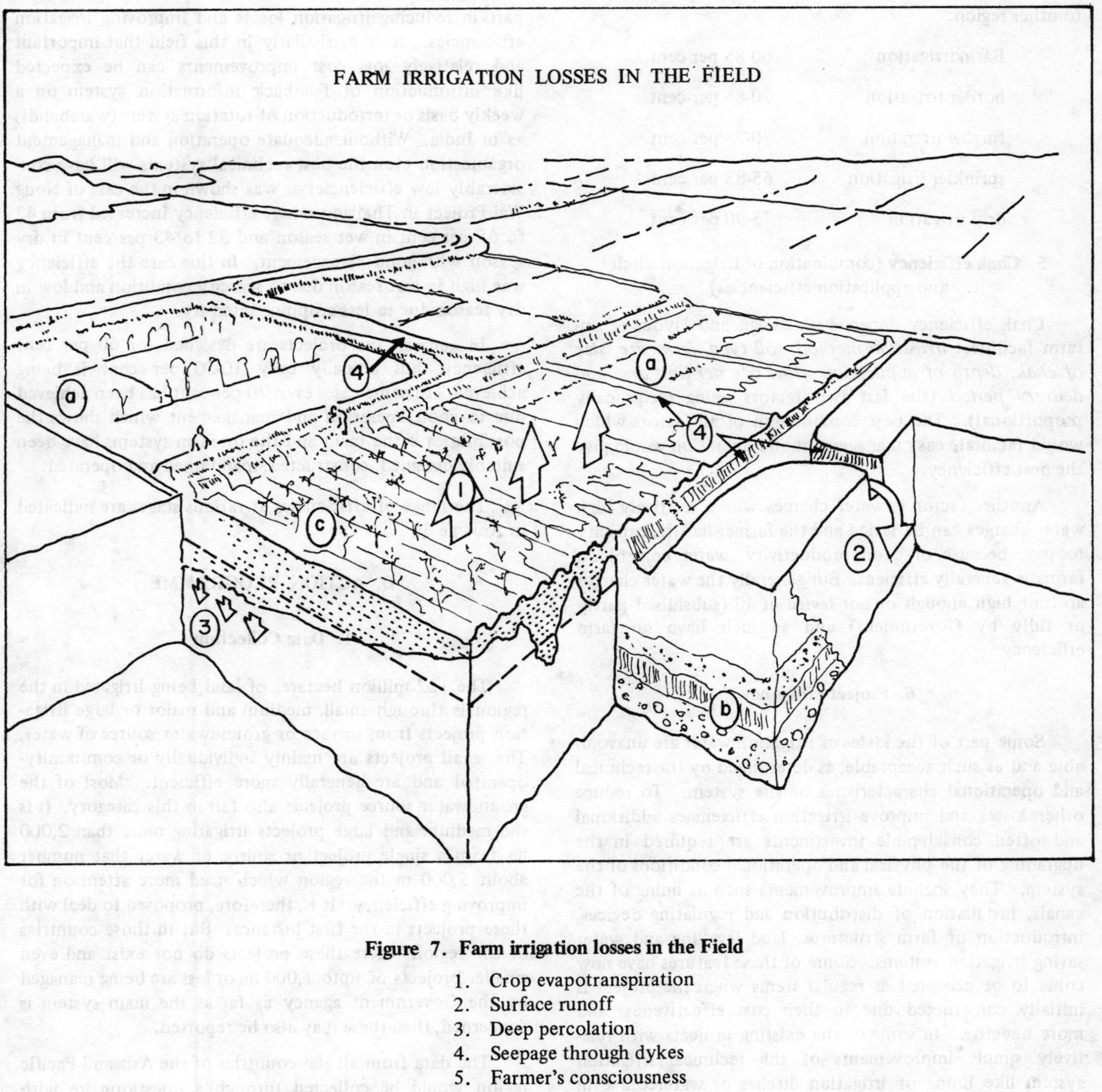

FARM IRRIGATION LOSSES IN THE FIELD

Figure 7. Farm irrigation losses in the Field

1. Crop evapotranspiration
2. Surface runoff
3. Deep percolation
4. Seepage through dykes
5. Farmer's consciousness

depending on:

a. irrigation method
b. soil condition
c. crop characteristics
d. field layout
e. maintenance
f. farmer's training and skill
g. farmer's consciousness

and Keller (1978) for the USA which are equally relevant to other region:

Basin irrigation	60-85 per cent
border irrigation	70-85 per cent
furrow irrigation	70-75 per cent
sprinkler irrigation	65-85 per cent
drip irrigation	75-90 per cent

5. Chak efficiency (combination of irrigation ditch and application efficiencies)

Chak efficiency depends on design and layout of on-farm facilities: *irrigation method, soil type, farm size, size of chak, depth of application, flow size per unit area* and *delivery period* (the last two factors being reciprocally proportional). The best combination of all factors which would facilitate easy management and operation would give the best efficiency.

Another factor is water charges where relatively high water charges can be levied and the farmer has the capacity to pay, because of good productivity, water control on farms is generally efficient. But generally the water charges are not high enough or not levied at all (subsidised partly or fully by Government) and as such have no farm efficiency.

6. Project efficiency

Some part of the losses of irrigation water are unavoidable and as such acceptable, as determined by the technical and operational characteristics of the system. To reduce other losses and improve irrigation efficiencies additional and often considerable investments are required in the upgrading of the physical and operational conditions of the system. They include improvements such as lining of the canals, installation of distribution and regulating devices, introduction of farm structures, land levelling and water saving irrigation systems. Some of these features have now come to be accepted as regular items when the project is initially constructed due to their cost effectiveness and more benefits. In some of the existing projects with relatively simple improvements of the technical irrigation system like lining of irrigation ditches or watercourse in India and Pakistan or construction of on farm facilities as in India, Thailand and Indonesia or rehabilitation of the neglected main system, considerably more water may become available for irrigation of new areas and the additional value in crop production may well pay off the investments.

In addition to the improvement of the technical system, the operation, management and maintenance of the main system as well as of the farm system plays a major part in reducing irrigation losses and improving irrigation efficiencies. It is particularly in this field that important and relatively low cost improvements can be expected like introduction of feedback information system on a weekly basis or introduction of rotation system (warabandi) as in India. Without adequate operation and management organization even the best technical systems will have considerably low efficiencies as was shown in the case of Nong Wai Project in Thailand where efficiency increased from 42 to 65 per cent in wet season and 32 to 43 per cent in dry season with good management. In this case the efficiency was high in wet season due to scarcity condition and low in dry season due to less cropping intensity.

In general, the projects are designed for 60 per cent efficiency, but actually only 10-50 per cent is being achieved. In some cases even 70 per cent has been achieved due to good operation and management which shows the possibilities if the main and the on farm systems have been suitably designed, constructed, maintained and operated.

The range of efficiencies at various stages are indicated in Annexe 3.

D. ACTION PROGRAMME

1. Data Collection

The 122 million hectares of land being irrigated in the region is through small, medium and major or large irrigation projects from surface or groundwater source of water. The small projects are mainly individually or community-operated and are generally more efficient. Most of the groundwater source projects also fall in this category. It is the medium and large projects irrigating more than 2,000 ha from a single project or source of water that number about 5,000 in the region which need more attention for improving efficiency. It is, therefore, proposed to deal with these projects in the first instance. But in those countries of the region where these projects do not exist and even smaller projects of upto 1,000 ha or less are being managed by the Government agency as far as the main system is concerned, then these may also be reported.

The data from all the countries of the Asia and Pacific region would be collected through a questionnaire with common understanding of terminology and definitions based on the suggestion by ICID.

Effort would be made to include only that information which is generally available at the project manager level and is regularly collected for normal monitoring and evaluation, to facilitate early reporting but at the same time sufficient to identify projects on the basis of irrigation efficiency. In most cases, no specialised agency need be employed for collecting the data to answer the questionnaire. If, however, some research or specialised agency has collected additional information and analysed, the same may also be included.

2. Efficiency calculation

The efficiency can be measured at various stages depending on the data collected in the normal course of operation and management of the project in almost all projects, and specialised data collection in a few projects. If very little data is available even then the overall Project Efficiency (e_p) can be calculated. It represents the efficiency of the entire operation between diversion or source of flow and the rootzone. The data on the quantity of water diverted from the source and the rainfall in the project area is generally known. From these two actual data a comparison can be made with the design data and efficiency calculated indirectly provided the design parameters are initially based on actual measurements in similar conditions.

3. Follow-up action

After collection of data and its analysis it would be possible to identify as to which projects in a country need priority attention for improvement of its operation and management. Then a detailed study for identifying the shortcomings and suggestions for remedial measures can be taken up by the countries concerned with the help of FAO if necessary. Even during the reporting of data and filling the questionnaire, some help may have to be given by FAO to countries for getting the correct information and in time.

It is proposed to collect the information in about 6 months, so that it can be reported to the committee next year and detailed studies on identified projects can be started in about a year's time by the countries concerned.

REFERENCES

Apichart A. 1980. Irrigation efficiency. Proceedings of the national workshop on water management and control at the farm level. FAO RAPA, Bangkok.

Bos M.G. 1978. Standards for the calculation of irrigation efficiencies. ICID.

Bos M.G. 1978. Irrigation efficiencies at crop production level. ICID.

Bottrall A.F. 1979. Comparative study of the management organization of irrigation projects. World Bank Research Project No. 671/34.

Bottrall A.F. Action research towards improved water distribution. Proc. Int. Seminar Tamil Nadu Agricultural University.

Chambers R. 1980. In search of a water revolution, questions for managing canal irrigation in the 1980s. Workshop Report IRRI, Los Baños, Laguna.

Early A.C. 1980. An approach to solving irrigation system management problems. Workshop Report, IRRI, Los Baños, Laguna.

FAO/WB Co-operative Programme. 1980. Madhya Pradesh medium irrigation project. Internal Report.

FAO-N.G. Dastane. 1974. Effective rainfall. Irrigation and Drainage Series 25, Rome.

ILRI. 1974. On irrigation efficiencies. Publication No. 19. Wageningen.

Jayaraman T.K. 1981. Water use efficiency and rotational water supply at the farm level in Gujarat state, India. Water Supply and Management 5(6): 391-399.

Kathpalia G.N. 1983. System operation in Nong Wai pioneer agriculture project. Nong Wai Irrigation Management Seminar, Khon Kaen, Thailand.

Kathpalia G.N. 1983. Management of canal supplies and social environment. Utilization of canal waters: A multi-disciplinary perspective on irrigation. Publication No. 164 Central Board of Irrigation Power Madch Marg, New Delhi, India.

Kathpalia G. N. 1981. Water management and command area development programme in India. Pakistan/FAO International Expert Consultation on Farm Water Management, Islamabad.

Merriam and Keller. Farm Irrigation System Evaluation: A Guide for Management.

Miranda S. and Levine G. 1978. Effects on physical water control parameters on lowland irrigation water management. IRRI, Los Baños, Laguna.

Siy R.Y. Jr. 1981. Community Resource Management — Lessons from the Zanjera.

Tabal D. and Wickham T. 1978. Effects of location and water supply on water shortages in an irrigated area. IRRI, Los Baños, Laguna.

World Bank. Operation, Maintenance and Repair of Selected Irrigation Systems.

Annex 1

Table 17. Irrigation in Asia-Pacific Region

Country	Arable Land (AL) (1,000 ha)		Irrigated Land (IL) (1,000 ha)		IL/Al (per cent)		Annual Increase Rate of IL (per cent)
	1969-71	1980	1969-71	1980	1969-71	1980	69-71 – 80
Developing Countries							
Bangladesh	9 089	9 145	1 054	1 620	11.6	17.7	4.4
Bhutan	76	93	–	–	–	–	–
Burma	10 423	10 023	849	999	8.1	10.0	1.6
China, PR	102 233	99 200	41 000	46 000	40.1	46.4	1.2
Fiji	225	236	1	1	0.4	0.4	–
India	164 690	169 130	30 183	39 350	18.3	23.3	2.7
Indonesia	18 047	19 500	4 371	5 418	24.2	27.8	2.2
Kampuchea	3 075	3 046	89	89	2.9	2.9	–
Korea, DPR	2 017	2 240	500	1 050	24.8	46.9	7.7
Korea, Rep.	2 293	2 196	993	1 150	43.3	52.4	1.5
Lao	842	880	18	115	2.1	13.1	20.4
Malaysia	3 950	4 310	243	370	6.2	8.6	4.3
Maldives	3	3	–	–	–	–	–
Mongolia	775	1 182	10	35	1.3	2.0	13.3
Nepal	1 935	2 330	116	230	6.0	9.9	7.1
Pakistan	19 282	20 320	12 904	14 300	66.9	70.4	1.0
Papua New Guinea	347	366	–	–	–	–	–
Philippines	9 557	9 920	830	1 300	8.7	13.1	4.6
Samoa	114	122	–	–	–	–	–
Sri Lanka	1 979	2 147	436	525	22.0	24.5	1.9
Thailand	13 749	17 979	1 965	2 650	14.4	14.7	3.0
Tonga	53	53	–	–	–	–	–
Viet Nam	5 690	6 055	980	1 700	17.2	28.1	5.7
Sub-Total	370 643	380 562	96 542	116 902	26.0	30.7	1.9
Developed Countries							
Australia	41 595	44 400	1 474	1 500	3.5	3.4	0.2
Japan	5 467	4 881	3 312	3 250	60.6	66.6	-0.2
New Zealand	521	453	109	166	2.3	3.4	4.3
Sub-Total	47 583	49 734	4 895	4 916	10.3	9.9	0.04
Region	418 226	430 296	101 437	121 818	24.3	28.3	1.8
Rest of World	995,215	928 135	67 849	89 851	6.8	9.7	2.8
World	1 413 441	1 358 431	169 286	211 669	12.0	15.6	2.3

(Basic Data: FAO Production Year Book)

Annex 2.1

Table 18. Cereal production in countries of the Asia and Pacific Region, 1971-81
(in thousand metric tons)

S.N.	Country	Ann. average for triennium ending 1971	Ann. average for triennium ending 1981	Compound ann. growth rate for 1971-81, per cent
	Developing Countries			
1.	Bangladesh	16 727	20 981	2.3
2.	Bhutan	82	104	2.4
3.	Burma	8 276	12 956	4.6
4.	China	196 474	286 018	3.8
5.	Fiji	23	23	0.0
6.	India	111 146	138 775	2.3
7.	Indonesia	21 711	33 558	4.5
8.	Kampuchea Dem.	3 142	1 093	- 10.9
9.	Korea, DPR	5 147	8 483	5.2
10.	Korea, Rep.	7 508	8 005	0.6
11.	Lao	896	1 056	1.6
12.	Malaysia	1 711	2 146	2.3
13.	Maldives	—	—	—
14.	Mongolia	263	302	1.4
15.	Nepal	3 475	3 575	0.1
16.	Pakistan	11 668	17 138	3.9
17.	Papua New Guinea	3	7	8.8
18.	Philippines	7 141	10 841	4.3
19.	Samoa	—	—	
20.	Sri Lanka	1 495	2 063	3.4
21.	Thailand	15 578	21 092	3.1
22.	Tonga	—	—	
23.	Vietnam	10 198	12 183	1.8
	Sub-Total	422 664	580 399	3.2
	Developed Countries			
24.	Australia	14 039	21 003	4.1
25.	Japan	17 595	14 333	- 2.1
26.	New Zealand	707	821	1.5
	Sub-Total	32 341	36 157	1.1
	RAPA Region	455 005	616 556	3.1
	Rest of World	776 680	976 198	2.3
	World	1 231 685	1 592 754	2.6

Annex 2.2

Table 19. Rice paddy: production and yield

Country	Production (unit 1000 metric tons)			Yield (kg/ha)		
	Annual Ave. Triennium ending 1971	Annual Ave. Triennium ending 1981	Compound Annual Growth Rate	Annual Ave. Triennium ending 1971	Annual Ave. Triennium ending 1981	Compound Annual Growth Rate
Developing Countries						
1. Bangladesh	16 540	20 140	2.0 %	1 681	1 976	1.6 %
2. Bhutan	42	52	2.2 %	1 098	1 103	0.05%
3. Burma	8 107	12 730	4.6 %	1 708	2 538	4.0 %
4. China	109 853	145 128	2.8 %	3 295	4 228	2.5 %
5. Fiji	18	17	- 0.6 %	1 839	1 768	- 0.4 %
6. India	62 861	75 135	1.8 %	1 668	1 890	1.3 %
7. Indonesia	19 136	29 685	4.5 %	2 346	3 317	3.5 %
8. Kampuchea	3 016	1 003	-10.4 %	1 454	932	- 4.4 %
9. Korea, DPR	2 392	4 833	7.3 %	5 371	6 093	1.3 %
10. Korea, Republic of	5 570	6 741	1.9 %	4 628	5 512	1.8 %
11. Lao	870	1 025	1.7 %	1 307	1 420	0.8 %
12. Malaysia	1 696	2 137	2.3 %	2 396	2 833	1.7 %
13. Maldives	–	–	–	–	–	–
14. Mongolia	–	–	–	–	–	–
15. Nepal	2 299	2 310	0.05%	1 937	1 828	- 0.6 %
16. Pakistan	3 431	4 198	2.0 %	2 246	2 450	0.9 %
17. Papua New Guinea	2	2	0.0 %	2 898	2 898	0.0 %
18. Philippines	5 225	7 688	3.9 %	1 655	2 196	2.9 %
19. W. Samoa	–	–	–	–	–	–
20. Sri Lanka	1 463	2 023	3.3 %	2 526	2 514	- 0.05%
21. Thailand	13 475	17 375	2.6 %	1 947	1 933	- 0.07%
22. Tonga	–	–	–	–	–	–
23. Vietnam	9 981	11 668	1.6 %	2 018	2 102	0.4 %
Developing Countries	265 977	343 875	2.6 %	2 270	2 753	1.9 %
Developed Countries						
24. Australia	267	689	9.9 %	7 026	6 207	-1.2 %
25. Japan	16 280	13 320	- 2.0 %	5 485	5 587	0.2 %
26. New Zealand	–	–	–	–	–	–
Developed Countries	16 547	14 009	- 1.7 %	5 505	5 615	0.2 %
Asia-Pacific Region	282 524	357 884	2.4 %	2 350	2 810	1.8 %
Rest of World	27 267	38 375	3.5 %	2 151	2 431	1.2 %
World	309 791	396 259	2.5 %	2 331	2 767	1.7 %

Annex 3

Table 20. Range of efficiencies
(Reference: Apichart)
Average conveyance efficiency

Irrigation method	Method of water delivery	Irrigated area (ha)	Efficiency (per cent)
Basin for rice cultivation	Continuous supply with no substantial charge inflow	–	90
Surface irrigation (Basin, Borders, and Furrow)	Rotational supply based on predetermined schedule with effective management	3000-5000	88
	Rotation supply based on predetermined schedule with less effective management	>1000 <10000	70
	Rotational supply based on advance request	>1000 <10000	65

Table 21. Average farm ditch efficiency

Irrigation method	Method for delivery	Soil type and ditch condition	Block size (ha)	Efficiency (per cent)
Basin for	Continuous	Unlined: Clay to heavy clay		
		lined	up to 3	90
	Rotation or intermittent	Unlined: Clay to heavy clay	<20	80
		lined	>20	
Surface irrigation	Rotation or intermittent	Unlined: Silt clay	<20	60-70
		lined	>20	80
	Rotation or intermittent	Unlined: Sand, loam	<20	55
		lined	>20	65

Table 22. Average distribution efficiency of rotational supply under optimum conditions

Adequate organization and communication	65 per cent
Sufficient organization and communication	55 per cent
Insufficient organization and communication	40 per cent
Poor organization and communication	33 per cent

Table 23. Average application efficiency

Irrigation method	Method of Delivery	Soil Type	Depth of application (mm)	Efficiency (per cent)
Basin	Continuous	Clay Heavy clay	>60	40-50
Furrow	Intermittent	Light soil	>60	60
Border	Intermittent	Light soil	>60	60
Basin	Intermittent	All soil	>60	60
Sprinkler	Intermittent	Sand, loam	>60	70

Table 24. Designed and Actual efficiency ranges

Item	Design/Planned	Actually achieved	Remarks
1. Conveyance efficiency	85 - 95	42 - 98	The higher range is more often for small schemes.
2. On-farm efficiency	80 - 90	68 - 95	
3. Field application efficiency	80 - 85	24 - 88	
4. Project efficiency	50 - 70	10 - 65	

Table 25. Some examples of conveyance loss

Place	Canal type	Area	Quantity	Loss	Loss rate
Aichi Irrigation Project	Concrete open	20 182 ha (10.1 km)	30 m^3/s	5.0 1/s/km	2-20 %
Ajikata Project	Concrete open	275 ha (5.5 km)	1.214 m^3/s	0.103 m^3/s	8.5 %
Kahoku Project	Pipe line	267 ha	0.77 m^3/s	0.021 m^3/s	2.7 %

Table 26. Some examples of distribution loss

Place	Canal type	Area (ha)	Water requirement Plan	Actual	Loss rate[1] (per cent)
Kunigami	Open	106-168	20.0 mm/dy	35-36 mm/dy	42.9-44.4
Aijikata	Open	36.7	0.082 m^3/s	0.220 m^3/s	37.3
Fukushima N.	Open	42.1	0.022 m^3/s	0.041 m^3/s	46.0
Maki	Pipe	22.4	14-18 mm/dy 17-24 mm/dy	20.0 mm/dy 26.0 mm/dy	15-20 10-15
Morowa (Aichi)	Pipe	15.2	9-11 mm/dy	11.5 mm/dy	6.0
Yahagi	O & P	4 367.8	68.0 x 10^6 m^3/yr	(80.1-100.3) x 10^3/yr	15.2-32.2[2]
			(51.9-62.0) x 10^3/yr	(80.1-100.3) x 10^3/yr	38.2-35.2[3]

Note: [1] conveyance loss is included   [2] ignoring effective rainfall   [3] considering effective rainfall

(Source of above two lists: Handbook of Agricultural Engineering, Japan)

Table 27. Loss in early stage of irrigation, Muda project, Malaysia

Time of measurement	Irrigated area[1] ha	Water supply mm	Accumulated w. supply mm	Loss mm	Loss rate[2] per cent	Rate of supplied area per cent
79.3.1	153					20.9
5	252	78.1	78.1	39.0	49.9	34.5
10	374	74.3	152.4	70.5	46.3	51.2
15	470	66.3	218.7	84.4	38.6	64.3
20	492	50.6	269.3	89.5	33.2	67.3
25	549	92.4	361.7	150.6	41.6	75.1
4.2	572	153.8	515.5	294.7	57.1	78.2
7	563	52.1	567.6	247.1	43.5	77.0

Note: [1]   Total irrigable area is 731 ha

   [2] $Accumulated = \dfrac{(supply-balance\ of\ storage-evaporation+storage)}{Accumulated\ Supply}$ per cent

(*Source:* Tropical Agricultural Research Centre)

VII. POLLUTION PROBLEMS RELATED TO THE CURRENT PROGRAMMES OF LOW-COST TECHNOLOGY APPLICATIONS TO WATER SUPPLY AND SANITATION IN THE ESCAP REGION

VII.A. MEASURES TO REDUCE THE COST OF RURAL WATER SUPPLY
(E/ESCAP/NR10/4)

Introduction

Water is essential to life and economic and social development. According to a report by the World Health Organization (WHO), some 1,320 million people, or 57 per cent of the population in the developing countries (excluding China), in 1980 lack safe drinking water. Of that number, 1,128 million people or 85 per cent belong to the ESCAP region. Statistics which were compiled in preparation for the Water Decade indicated that at least 30,000 people in the developing countries died every day because of inadequate water supply and water-borne diseases. A large number of these developing countries are facing difficulties in ensuring the supply of safe·drinking water because of a shortage of not only financial but also technological resources.

In view of the urgent need to provide an adequate supply of drinking water for the world's population, the United Nations designated the period 1980-1990 as the International Drinking Water Supply and Sanitation Decade. Since then, members of the United Nations system have been active in providing various kinds of support to the developing countries in their efforts to achieve the objectives of the Decade.

It is clear, however, that because of the high cost involved the developing countries of the region cannot afford the conventional water supply system used by advanced countries. This high cost is mainly due to refinements in treatment processes and conveyance systems for achieving a very high standard of user convenience. Therefore, in striving to provide water supplies for people of the developing countries, the primary objective should be the improvement of public health, while further refinements to increase user convenience could be made at a later stage if and when the community can afford it. This primary health objective can be achieved fully by the application of technologies which are much simpler and cheaper than the conventional ones. For instance, less sophisticated facilities, such as village wells, public standposts or yard taps, may be used instead of multiple tap in-house connections.

The main purpose of this paper is to examine various options in the provision of a safe and adequate supply of water for rural areas and to identify measures that can be taken to reduce the cost so that safe drinking water can be made available to as many people as possible within the constraints of a relatively short time frame and available financial resources. The provision of safe drinking water does not merely mean improvement of public health; it also means higher living standards and increased economic productivity. The economic benefits come from relieving the people of the delibitating effects of water-related diseases resulting in improved productivity in agriculture and industry, releasing women and children from the burden and drudgery of carrying water and thus making them available to be engaged in more productive occupations, and financial savings on curative medical care as a result of prevention of diseases made possible by the provision of safe drinking water.

The nature of the water supply problem in the ESCAP region is such that the need to provide safe drinking water is more urgent in rural areas than in urban areas. This is supported by the statistical data compiled by WHO indicating that out of the 1,128 million people without safe drinking water in the developing countries of the ESCAP region, 925 million people live in the rural areas, while only 203 million people or 18 per cent are in urban areas. In view of this, the scope of the present paper is limited to the problem of domestic water supply in rural areas.

Measures to reduce the cost of rural water supply facilities are discussed under four sub-headings: measures related to programme aspects, selection of water supply source, cost reduction in lifting of water and cost reduction in treatment and conveyance of water.

A. MEASURES RELATED TO PROGRAMME ASPECTS

1. Planning and design of rural water supply

A reduction in the cost of rural water supply may be achieved if rural water supply is planned within the context of integrated rural development. This is because, while water is a basic need for many aspects of rural development, the development of rural water schemes faces many difficulties characteristic of other activities in the rural area. Imboden[1] pointed out that an integrated approach to rural development did not necessarily mean the provision of all services possible and imaginable but of the critical input at the time needed so as to permit the continuous development of the countryside. By incorporating rural water supply schemes into rural development programmes, duplication of work resulting in wastage can be avoided, better co-ordination can be achieved leading to optimum scale and level of development of water supply service, and reduction in costs through multiple use of the same facility, thereby permitting sharing of costs.

In order to achieve flexibility in the scale of development without affecting economic efficiency, planning should be carried out with standardized small-scale low-cost

modules for water supply packages consisting of treatment plants, distribution systems and pump houses, etc. A cost reduction can be achieved by considering a stage-by-stage development approach in planning, with the first phase to meet immediate demand and with provision for expansion at a later date to meet the future demand. For any project there is an optimal time for implementation; by investing too early for a future demand, costs may be incurred that could have been postponed.

The cost of rural water supply systems can be significantly reduced by the use of standard designs and materials and the selection of an appropriate acale of development to suit the locality. Standardization also shortens the time frame in project preparation and implementation. Therefore, in those developing countries which have not yet developed such standard designs, it may be necessary to start developing standard design manuals based on their own and other countries' experiences. These designs should be as simple as possible, keeping in mind the need for providing ease of operation and maintenance and yet meeting the minimum acceptable level of service. One possible method of acquiring the experience required to produce standard design manuals is intercountry co-operation within the region. It was reported in a bulletin published by the International Reference Centre for Community Water Supply and Sanitation that some countries in the region had already developed similar manuals through bilateral programmes; for instance, the modular water treatment plant in Indonesia. The Philippines also developed rural water supply design manuals for its integrated water supply programme which could serve as a useful guide for other developing countries in the region.

Plans for rural water supply development should consider the use and local manufacture of standard components. The introduction of standard components to rural water supply projects will not only reduce costs but will also facilitate the accelerated completion of these projects. These standardized components can be introduced in equipment for lifting, conveyance and treatment of water. In introducing the use of standardized components, it is advisable to begin with parts standardization for items that are subjected to wear-and-tear and that could be readily manufactured locally. In the beginning, these standard components may be imported from foreign manufacturers and their design should match as much as possible the local capabilities. Then, once, local home industries acquire the necessary technology from foreign manufacturers they start manufacturing those items. Since the components must fulfil their function in the best possible way with the longest possible lifetime, there is a need for establishing standards which must be met by both imported and locally manufactured products. As the variety and quantity of locally manufactured components increase, it may become necessary to establish an agency to enforce specified standards.

Logistically, the standardization of units and equipment is necessary in order to reduce the type and number of different pieces of equipment so that greater efficiency in procurement and storage of spare parts and training of operating staff can be achieved. In addition, in order to ensure the reliability of service, spare parts should be made readily available at convenient points in the logistic system, so that repairs can be carried out as soon as defects occur.

The use of standardized components in water supply systems will reduce the need for highly skilled personnel. However, manpower development will still be necessary for the successful implementation of the programme. With regard to the number of personnel, a standard manpower chart should be defined, which should be related to the size of the water supply system, the capacity of the plant, the population served etc.

Another important step that should be taken towards successful implementation of a programme for the use and manufacture of standard components in the water supply system is the development of local expertise for planning and developing new approaches in standardization with regard to design, manufacturing, construction, operation and maintenance.

Finally, consideration of the social factor is an important element in the planning and design of rural water supply schemes if the practical implementation of cost reduction measures is desired. Quite often, social factors have been almost completely ignored in planning and the main emphasis was on the physical aspects alone. This situation has sometimes lead to failure or high cost of operation and maintenance of the water supply facilities. A high degree of community participation in rural water supply planning is, therefore, necessary. The input from the community at the planning stage should deal mainly with the identification of community needs and priority setting, the choice of suitable technology, the selection of water sources and the siting of the supply points in a way that is acceptable to the community.

The social aspect of rural water supply development calls for a thorough investigation and adequate knowledge of local conditions. Information on problems perceived by the community, community resources, experience and preference are prerequisites for such joint planning of rural water supply programmes. Miller,[2] after synthesizing the major findings of case studies regarding self-help programmes in Senegal and Mexico, concluded that self-help and community participation could bring substantial benefits if they were incorporated into the project from the project planning and design stage. The delay in project implementation, which might sometimes happen in the case of self-help water supply schemes, could also be minimized by allowing a greater role of self-help during the early phases, especially project identification and pre-design. Outside interventions in the form of technical services by either local, regional, national or international organizations could have an important role to play in these early stages. According to these studies, the financial impacts of public participation have not yet been established, but it was said that savings to public funds and efficient collection of water bills were quite evident.

2. Implementation, operation and maintenance

The organization and management of rural water supply schemes are equally important in terms of reducing the cost. Since rural drinking water supply programmes usually consist of a large number of relatively small schemes which are scattered all over a country, co-ordination of these activities is necessary in order to avoid mismanagement and waste. Further, in order to achieve greater efficiency, different activities are best pursued and decisions best taken at different levels in the organization of rural water service. This means that a clear line of authority and responsibility should be established at each level concerning construction work, operation, maintenance and financial operations.

Community participation during the implementation, operation and maintenance phases is an essential element in reducing the cost of rural water supply facilities. Enthusiastic community participation can play a significant role in creating and increasing community awareness, a sense of responsibility and pride of ownership of the village water supply system, resulting in a high level of performance of the system and corresponding cost reduction.

In general terms, community participation implies development to be achieved with and by the people, not just for the people. Community participation can be motivated in order to achieve such objectives as efficient utilization of the available resources by encouraging the community to invest either cash or labour in the construction, operation, and maintenance of water supply projects; success of village water supply systems and reduction of chances of failure of systems as a result of misuse, vandalism or lack of maintenance; and promotion and encouragement of community-operated and initiated self-help water supply schemes. It is important that people should be involved in as many stages as possible in the entire process of a water supply scheme.

During the construction phase, the degree of community participation is generally influenced by the type of technology being used. When sophisticated technology is applied, community participation is generally low. In order to promote community involvement in rural water supply development, it is necessary to adopt simple technology, such as tapping spring water and digging shallow hand-dug wells. However, if motivated effectively, even in schemes requiring sophisticated technology, community participation in the form of free labour can significantly reduce the costs.

Although organization of self-help[1] and public participation schemes with outside technical supervision can reduce the labour costs of a project, Fresson[3] pointed out that there was still a certain tendency to regard development schemes based on local participation as uneconomic. It was contended that such schemes might be cheap in terms of capital costs but they were usually technically inadequate and therefore uneconomic and unprofitable in the long run for the local population. This contention may be true only in cases where sophisticated technology is involved. An analysis of the experiences of self-help and public participation in rural water supply schemes in Mexico by de la Barra-Rowland[4] indicated that user involvement usually lead to better and cheaper maintenance, but was rather inefficient and uneconomical in the implementation phase as a result of poor technical standard of construction and more frequent breakdowns. However, it was observed that self-help or user involvement in water supply projects generally encouraged communtiy motivation and served as a catalyst of other development actions.

In spite of various arguments by some analysts against self-help or public participation, it is receiving increased attention in every aspect of development as a means of achieving decentralized development. The evaluation of self-help programmes in Mexico[4] indicated that such programmes facilitated institutional actions by reducing labour problems, created community development, improved maintenance and preservation of the project by creating a feeling of ownership of the work among the people and generated employment.

The need for training with respect to the operation and maintenance of rural water supply projects is widely accepted, because it is usually the weakest area in such projects. In order to have an efficient operation and maintenance system, it is necessary to decentralize maintenance procedures and training. This requires in-service training which should be carried out by experienced persons in the field. Operation and maintenance training is very important when constant care is necessary to minimize

wear and tear, for example, of handpumps. Often, this maintenance can best be carried out by the local village people. It is important, however, that people have a sense of ownership and responsibility for the pump or rural water supply facility as a whole.

3. Charging a fee for rural water supply

Opinion is divided among water supply experts regarding the question of whether or not rural water supply should be provided free of charge. Advocates for the free supply of water to rural populations argue that the rural peasantry cannot afford to pay tariffs commensurate with the cost of development and maintenance and that they will be forced to resort to their former sources of water if there is a price for getting water. They further believe that the villagers, in most cases, may have contributed much of the labour for the construction and maintenance of the system which gives them every right to think that they have in fact provided a form of payment. Advocates against the free supply of water argue that asking people to pay something for the water will cut down wastage of water and help reimburse some of the operational costs of the system. This is considered necessary because, although donors may contribute funds for capital assistance, they cannot be expected to fund the operation and maintenance costs. It is to be noted, however, that unlike cases of piped water supply in urban areas, metering is either impractical or impossible and that any fee imposed on the supply of water should be done only on an arbitrary basis charged to the community as a whole rather than individually. The question of whether or not to impose a fee on rural water supply will be greatly influenced by the availability of water, the cost of development and maintenance and the socio-economic status of the community which varies widely from place to place.

B. SELECTION OF WATER SUPPLY SOURCE

Selection of a proper water supply source to suit the local conditions of a rural community can contribute to a significant reduction in cost. However, it is very difficult to establish which source is the least expensive to develop, as this depends on the availability of each source at a given place, the quantity of water which can be tapped from each source, climatic and other local conditions. In general, a water supply source requiring the minimum sum of capital, operating and maintenance costs for exploration, tapping, lifting, conveyance, treatment etc. may be regarded as the most economical source.

The sources of water generally considered for rural water supply may be divided into four broad categories: rain-water spring water, ground water and surface water. A

---

[1]   Self-help refers to the most fundamental level of involvement, which may be an individual or a small group. Public participation implies a greater scale in terms of group size.

general approach for selection of the water supply source which takes into account the quality of water and its availability in different forms as suggested by the International Reference Centre for Community Water Supply and Sanitation[5] in the Hague, follows.

When a spring of sufficient capacity is available not very far from the consumers, this source is considered as the most suitable source of supply. Where springs are not available or not suitable for development, the next option suggested is ground water. Again, if ground water is not available or if the cost of digging a well or drilling a tube-well is too high, it is suggested to consider surface water from sources such as rivers, streams or lakes. When springs, ground water and surface water are not available or insufficient or poorly operated and maintained resulting in frequent breakdowns, and when the rainfall pattern in the locality is favourable, then the option of rain-water harvesting is suggested.

Some of the low-cost methods for developing the sources of water mentioned above are discussed in the following paragraphs.

1. Rain-Water

According to history, the use of rain-water for domestic water supply began some 4,000 years ago in the Mediterranean region. About 2,000 years ago Nabateans in Israel collected rainfall from hillsides in the Negev desert for cultivating crops in a region where the average annual rainfall was only about 100 mm. In Jamaica and other parts of the Carribean, artificial hillside catchments paved with concrete have been in use for domestic water supply since the end of nineteenth century.[6] The research and development programmes of the late 1960s and early 1970s demonstrated that rainfall collection was still a practical and viable method for water supply in areas where water was scarce.[7] [8] In many developing countries of the ESCAP region, rain-water harvesting is still being used for the provision of drinking water, particularly in the rural areas and on small islands. In the absence, or due to high cost of development, of other sources of water supply, rain-water is the only source of domestic water supply.

Rain-water is harvested as it runs off roofs, over natural ground or specially prepared catchment areas. Harvesting of rain-water requires adequate provision for the interception, collection and storage of water, and depending on the circumstances at site, collection may take place on the ground or on the roofs.

a. Roof catchments

Rain-water can be collected from house roofs made of tiles, slates, galvanized iron, asbestos cement, thatch etc.

Roof catchments permit collection of reasonably pure rain-water which needs no treatment. A recent study by Hall[6] indicated that thatch was still the most common roofing material in the world, particularly in the developing countries of the region. Thatch, whether grass, palm leaves or some other plant material is most commonly used in rural areas, and it is in these areas that domestic water supplies are usually lacking. Thatched roofs are usually constructed with wide, overhanging eaves. The edge of these eaves becomes ragged within a few years because of the erosive action of wind and rain. Hence, if rain-water is to be collected from thatched eaves without taking measures to protect the edges from becoming ragged, a very wide gutter may be needed which is very expensive.

To simplify and reduce the cost of rain-water collection at eaves level, the first course of thatch can be replaced with a course of tiles or even corrugated roofing sheet (figure 8). Hall designed and tested this method, which he called "tile substitution", to make collection at eaves more efficient. By incorporating a hard, straight eave in an otherwise ragged thatch roof, a light narrow gutter can be used which needs smaller and lighter brackets. Since

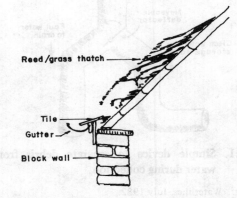

Figure 8. Schematic diagram of water collection off thatch

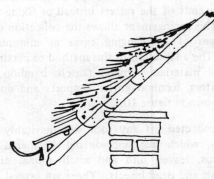

Figure 9. Extending the rafters to produce overhanging eaves

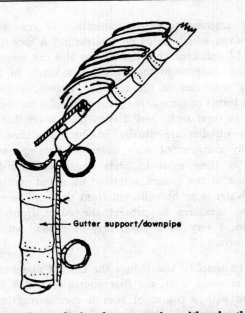

Figure 10. Using split bamboo guttering with palm thatch

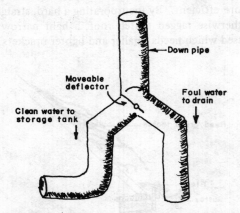

Figure 11. Simple device to separate debris from rain water during collection

Source: Waterlines, July 1982.

the weight is reduced considerably, the brackets can be fixed to the ends of the rafters instead of fixing them to the wall. This arrangement allows the collection of water at the edges of overhanging eaves at minimum cost (figure 9). The adaptation of this method to maximize the use of local materials – palm thatch, bamboo rafters, bamboo gutters, bamboo gutter supports and down-take pipes – is shown in figure 10.

Water collected off any roof will inevitably contain some debris, which may include old weathered roofing material, dust, leaves, bird and small animal droppings and both live and dead insects. There are several ideas or mechanisms to separate rubbish from rain-water, among which the most simple and economical for rural application

is the moveable deflector device shown in figure 11. The moveable deflector is operated manually by a lever, so that clean water is collected after first flushing down the debris laden water.

b. *Ground catchments*

Ground catchments are used for collecting rain-water runoff. The amount of rain-water that can be collected in ground catchments will be dependent on whether the catchment is flat or sloping, and the water tightness of the top layer. Evaporation and infiltration losses can be reduced by preparing the ground surface to have a sufficiently rapid flow and impervious surface. This can be achieved by laying tiles, concrete, asphalt or plastic sheeting. If these methods are found to be expensive, the simplest and cheapest method is to compact the ground. Compacted ground catchments of sufficient size can provide a domestic water supply for a number of families or even a whole village community, but they need proper management and maintenance and protection against damage and contamination. Trees and shrubs surrounding the catchment area can be planted to limit the entry of wind blown materials and dust into the ground catchment area.

c. *Storage*

Storage facilities for collected rain-water can be located either above ground or below ground. In any case, provision of an adequate enclosure is required to prevent possible contamination. The containers should also be covered to ensure dark storage conditions so as to prevent algal growth and mosquito breeding.

Storage containers can be constructed of imported or local materials depending upon their availability. Those constructed of imported materials include tanks using plastic sheeting, polyethylene tubes, metals and reinforced concrete. A brief description of some storage containers that can be constructed of local materials is given below.

(a) *Wooden barrels*

In areas where there is a cheap supply of timber, cylindrical wooden barrels may be used for rain-water storage.

(b) *Underground pits*

For storing larger volumes of water, underground pits may be dug and compacted by hand. The walls may be plastered with cement to make them impervious.

(c) *Bamboo-reinforced concrete*

Reinforced concrete tanks have the advantage of great durability and of being able to form part of the building foundation. Bamboo-reinforced concrete tanks have been successfully used where bamboo is available in suitable length, size and strength (for example, China, Indonesia and Thailand).

(d) *Water jars*

A cement water storage jar technology was first introduced in Thailand and was later introduced to east Africa by UNICEF. There, a local innovation was born from the synthesis of this technology and traditional African basket work, namely, the Ghala basket tank, which is actually a basket with cement plaster on the inside. This facilitates the storage of larger volumes of water than do cement jars. This technique can be adapted in the ESCAP region, particularly in those countries where baskets are produced very cheaply. In areas with shortage of cement, a cement substitute may be used. Such a substitute has been produced in Nepal (see *Nepal News*, 8 July 1977) in 1977 on an experimental basis from the ashes of paddy chaff and lime-sludge, a by-product of limestone used in the sugar-refining process. The cement substitute was found to be 50 per cent cheaper than ordinary cement.

(e) *Clay pots*

Clay, which is available in many countries of the region, can be used to build suitable rain-water storage containers of limited size. Simple glazing techniques, which already exist in most countries, can be used in improving the permeability of the clay pot.

2. Spring water

Springs are usually found on the slopes of hill-sides and river valleys. Spring water is pure and can be used without treatment. There are two types of springs, namely, gravity springs and artesian springs. These two types can be further subdivided into depression and overflow springs.

a *Gravity springs*

Gravity springs are those springs that occur in unconfined aquifers. Gravity depression springs occur in the depression of the ground surface which dips below the water table. Such springs usually have a small yield with a further reduction during the dry season. Owing to their low yields, they should be tapped only in the form of drains and hand-dug shallow wells.

Gravity overflow springs occur where an outcrop of impervious material, such as a solid or clay fault zone, prevents the downward flow of ground water and forces it up to the ground surface. These springs have a larger yield with less fluctuation than gravity depression springs. A low-cost method of tapping these springs is by drains consisting of pipes with open joints placed in a gravel pack.

b. *Artesian springs*

Artesian springs are springs that occur in a confined aquifer overlain by an impervious layer. Artesian depression springs are similar in appearance to gravity depression springs. However, the water is forced out under pressure so that the discharge is higher and shows less fluctuation. To tap water from an artesian depression spring, the seepage area should be surrounded by a wall extending above the maximum level to which the water rises under static conditions, and then convey the collected water to consumers by a pipe line. Artesian depression springs can usually supply enough water for a village community, but in cases where the seepage area is large, catchment works can become expensive.

Artesian overflow springs usually have a large recharge area and a considerably large water discharge under pressure with little or no seasonal fluctuation. These springs have the advantage of the impervious cover protecting the water in the aquifer against contamination. As a result, they are excellent sources for rural water supply. Where the outflow of water from an artesian overflow spring occurs at only one point, it can be tapped in a small catchment construction. For a large lateral spring, a retaining wall should be constructed over its full width with abutments extending into the overlying impervious layers and the base of the wall constructed into the bedrock to prevent leakage, erosion and possible collapse.

3. Ground water

Tapping of ground water resources for drinking water supply dates back to ancient times and is now widely practised. As far as water quality is concerned, ground water is the preferred source because it is less likely to be contaminated than other sources and is subject to less seasonal fluctuation. Ground water, if it is available from hand-dug wells, can be used as a source for rural water supply at a reasonably low cost. However, if tapping of ground water requires sinking of tubewells to great depths, the cost involved and the high technology required may be prohibitive. The costs involved in developing ground water include the cost of tapping for digging wells, the cost of pumps for lifting water and the cost of piping for conveyance (which may be necessary in some cases). Since ground water can be consumed without any treatment, no treatment costs are involved.

Ground water is usually tapped by digging a hole in the ground to a depth below the ground-water table. The amount of water collected in this way is quite limited, and for greater withdrawals the aquifer has to be tapped over a greater area of contact. This may be done by horizontally extending the width of excavation or vertically extending to a greater depth or by increasing both the width and depth depending on the thickness of the aquifer and depth of the ground-water table.

The ground-water catchments formed by horizontal extension into the aquifer are called galleries and are used for withdrawal of water from shallow aquifers (about 5-8 m below ground level) with a small saturated thickness. Galleries may be divided into seepage ditches, infiltration drains and tunnels. Ditches are easy to construct, have a relatively low cost, a large capacity and long useful life but there is a danger of contamination as they are left open. Infiltration drains and tunnels, being buried underground, are protected against contamination but are difficult and costly to construct and hence should not be considered for low-cost rural water supply.

A vertical extension into the aquifer for increased withdrawal of ground water may be achieved by means of large diameter dug-wells or small-diameter tube-wells. The cost of rural water supply may be reduced by resorting to relatively shallow hand-dug wells. These wells usually have a limited capacity and are suitable for individual household or small-scale water supply. Tube-wells have larger yields and are feasible only in aquifers of sufficient thickness. Tube-wells are costly because of the need to use sophisticated technology and equipment. In addition, large withdrawals of ground water from tube-wells may some-times be accompanied by ground subsidence.

In general, using ground water as a source of water supply involves considerable cost except in cases of shallow hand-dug wells. Further, exploration of ground water involves both high technology and cost. The cost of lifting groundwater may be reduced by using appropriate handpumps rather than those driven by electric motors or combustion engines. In cases where ground water needs to be conveyed over a certain distance to reach a consumer point, the cost involved may be reduced by using pipes made of locally available materials. In selecting the sources, it should be noted that potable ground water is not readily available everywhere, and in some cases it may be too salty for human consumption. In addition, in certain cases the recharge rate of wells may be inadequate to meet the demands. In such situations, the groundwater source may have to be supplemented by surface water, and

if communities are remote from permanent streams, rivers or lakes, rainfall collection may possibly be the only option available.

4. Surface water

When a large-scale rural water supply is desired, surface water, such as rivers, streams and lakes, may be used as sources of supply. Rivers and streams, particularly in tropical countries, have a wide seasonal fluctuation in quantity of flow as well as water quality — water having high turbidity during the wet season and low turbidity during the dry season. Lake water is of higher quality than that of rivers and streams due to the self-purification effect through aeration, bio-chemical processes and settling of suspended solids. Hence, artificial lakes or reservoirs are created by impounding water behind dams built across rivers and streams to create the head, to obtain an even distribution of seasonal flow and to improve water quality. However, building of dams involves a large capital investment as well as high technology. Therefore, a certain saving for rural water supply may be achieved by direct withdrawal from rivers, streams and natural lakes. Other costs for surface-water development include pumping for the intake of water, cost for conveyance by a pipeline and treatment cost.

In selecting the most appropriate water supply source for a rural community, the results of a study on the cost of development of various water sources by Grover and Kukielka, quoted in Sternberg,[9] as shown in table 28, give a rough comparison of overall costs. The study was carried out in Thailand and did not consider the cost of water supply from springs, which otherwise would be the cheapest source.

Table 28. Cost data for various sources for water supply

Facility	Population served by one installation	Unit cost (Baht)	Per capita cost (Baht)	(\$US)
Conversion of existing drinking water dug-well into a protected well (Ground-water source)	45	1 100	24	1.20
Small diameter tube-well equipped with a simple handpump (Ground-water source)	200	60 000	300	15.00
Family rain-water storage tank (Rain-water source)	5.57	3 500	628	31.40
Simple piped water supply (Surface-water source)	n.a.	n.a.	700	35.00

The above cost data clearly indicate that in areas where shallow wells exist or a shallow aquifer can be developed, their use is substantially cheaper than rain-water catchment or provision of piped water supply from surface water. It should be noted, however, that the costs will largely vary from place to place and from country to country depending on local conditions. Moreover, the costs indicated are capital costs and do not include operation and maintenance costs.

C. COST REDUCTION IN LIFTING OF WATER

Since water has to be lifted in almost every rural water supply facility, a significant saving in the cost of rural water supply can be achieved by taking measures to reduce the cost component related to the lifting of water. Devices for lifting water can be divided into two broad categories: those that lift water on a small scale, which are suitable for water supply from sources, such as rain water, springs and ground water, and those that lift water on a large scale, which are suitable for supply from surface water sources.

1. Small-scale water lifting devices

The simplest and least costly way of lifting water, other than by using a bucket tied to the end of a rope, is by using hand pumps. As there are many types of hand pumps now in use all over the world, a maximum reduction in cost for lifting water may be achieved by selecting the particular type of hand pump that is most suitable for a given locality. As a general rule, the following points should be considered in the selection and use of hand pumps.

Since hand pumps require a certain amount of maintenance, the expense can be reduced if the pump design is such that parts which wear out quickly are inexpensive and replaceable by the village pump attendant. Worn-out parts should be easily detected and they should cause only less satisfactory operation rather than total pump breakdown. Replacement parts for the pumps should also be easily available from stores nearby. Field assistants should be familiar with simple methods of checking the condition of plungers and foot valves and should replace them if they are not up to a certain minimum standard. Since wells that cannot supply sufficient water cause greater wear and tear of the pump, it is necessary to make sure that the wells have sufficient yields.

A panel of United Nations, World Bank and other experts is now encouraging manufacturers of hand pumps throughout the world to improve their existing designs so they are suitable for operation and maintenance by trained villagers in developing countries. This is because present hand pump designs necessitate high expenditure on repair and maintenance in most developing countries and cause long interruptions of water supply. The panel's suggestion is to simplify the below-ground components of hand pumps in such a way that replacement of worn and broken parts is simple and cheap. Substitution of plastic for conventional galvanized steel is also suggested in order to cut down the weight and cost as well as to permit easier installation and dismantling.

In order to reduce the maintenance costs, it is also suggested that the conventional design criteria of strength and durability, which have led to the predominance of heavy equipment, should be changed over to new village-level operation and maintenance rules of making repairs easy and cheap. The reason behind this change in concept is that, even if the working parts of a hand pump can be completely replaced more frequently, providing these parts are cheap, readily available, locally manufactured, and easily installed, cost savings and improved pump usage would be substantial compared with an expensive, robust, heavy installation, which might require fewer service calls during the same period of time, say about five years. The panel also suggested that the pump manufacturers should carry out fabrication in the developing countries by forming joint ventures with local firms. The panel sees the local manufacture of hand pumps both as a way of overcoming foreign exchange problems for spares and as an incentive through employment for governments to assure ready availability of replacement parts.

Regarding the testing and evaluation of existing hand pump designs, the Consumers' Association Testing and Research (CATR) in the United Kingdom carried out laboratory tests on 12 hand pumps which were chosen to represent as many design types as possible. These pumps, the brand names of which were not made known, were put through rigorous trials, including a 4,000-hour endurance test. According to the results, reported in October 1980, CATR concluded that, of the 12 pumps tested, only four were worthy of consideration for general use in developing countries, namely, the United Kingdom Consallen pump, the India Mark II pump, the British Monolift pump and the French Vergnet footpump. Of these four types, the Consallen pump was supposed to be closest to the concept of villagelevel operation and maintenance. The Consallen achieved an excellent rating in CATR's tests for overall design, frequency of maintenance and breakdown, corrosion resistance and safety, and high ratings for ease of manufacture, efficiency, resistance to abuse or neglect and well head sealing. It also had the advantage of using a plastic drop-pipe, which makes repair and maintenance operations cheap and simple.

Another pump, which was rated as second only to the Consallen pump according to CATR tests, was the India

Mark II pump. This pump was specifically designed for heavy-duty applications on rural water supply schemes in India and was found to be extremely popular both in the Indian subcontinent and quite recently in some parts of Africa. The pump is said to be capable of operating without servicing for at least 12 months continuously even when lifting from depths of 60 m. The only problems that occur when using this pump are inefficient downstroke when used on shallow wells (below 20 m) and difficulty in servicing and removing due to its heavy galvanized steel drop-pipe. The first problem arises from the use of a chain and quadrant system to link the pump handle to the pump-rod which makes the system dependent on the weight of the pump-rod to return the plunger on the downstroke. Modifications of the pump design are now in progress which include using plastic components below ground level.

Mark II's biggest manufacturer, Inalsa of India, has introduced a modified version to meet the recommendations of the UNDP/World Bank global research project for a simple village pump. It has a cylinder design which allows easy withdrawal of the pump-rod and piston assembly, the option of PVC or ABS pipe as an alternative to the standard galvanized iron riser pipe and a solid link in place of the standard chain connection between the handle and the pump-rod, thus making it possible to be used on shallow wells.

The other two pumps, which CATR thought could be suitable for use in developing countries after certain modifications, are the British Monolift pump and the French Vergnet footpump. The main disadvantage of the Vergnet pump, according to CATR, is its complexity which makes it difficult to be manufactured and maintained in developing countries. This pump design is said to have been simplified by the manufacturers, who are also working on the hand-operated version of the pump.

The British Monolift pump was said to be the least satisfactory among the four types recommended by CATR because of high leakage between the rotor and stator, which made it difficult to achieve any flow once the head exceeded about 20 m. The manufacturers identified the problem as differential expansion between the rubber stator and metal rotor and corrected it by using cylinders designed for specific water temperature ranges. The salient feature of this pump is that it is particularly suitable for application where the water is likely to contain sand.

According to Mammo,[10] the imported cost of the Consallen and Monolift pumps in Ethiopia, excluding transportation and other costs, are $US 432 and $US 1,190 respectively. According to information obtained from UNICEF, the cost of the India Mark II pumps is

approximately $US 2,000, which is inclusive of two years' maintenance, while another version modified by UNICEF and manufactured and introduced in Bangladesh under the brand name of Mark I, but which did not appear to be among the pumps tested by CATR, is said to cost about $US 300. Cost information on the French Vergnet foot-pump is not available at present for comparison. It appears that the costs of the pumps recommended by CATR are rather high for rural application in developing countries of the region.

The cost of the pump is an important factor in determining its accessibility to the rural population. In this connection, a revolutionary pump developed in Zimbabwe,[11] although not listed among the pumps recommended by CATR, could play a vital role in providing low-cost water supply in the rural areas of the region. The pump, which was initially conceived as a shallow-well hand pump, could operate at depths of up to 15 m and could be cheaply installed at wells operated with simple rope and bucket arrangements. The pump was designed by Blair research laboratory, Zimbabwe, and developed and manufactured by Prodorits, a local company which specialized in plastics extrusion. The pumps have a low cost — $US 72 for a 6 m pump, and have proved to be extremely robust and virtually maintenance free.

A distinguishing feature of the Blair/Prodorite pump is its compactness and simplicity. Above ground, the galvanized iron handle, which also serves as the water spout, protrudes only about one foot in its resting position. Below ground, the pump is basically two plastic cylinders one inside the other each fitted with identical valves at the base. The inner pipe, which is attached to the galvanized iron handle, serves as a moving piston. To pump water, the user moves the piston up and down. On the upstroke, water is drawn into the cylinder through the lower fixed foot valve. When the piston is pushed down, the foot valve closes and water is forced up the hollow piston through the upper moving valve to the surface. The pump can lift water at the rate of 20 litres per minute. The Blair/Prodorite pump design carries no patents and therefore can be manufactured in the developing countries of the region.

In Bangladesh,[12] the UNICEF-promoted new No. 6 cast iron handpump has a PVC plastic version, called the Rower suction handpump, which is suitable for use on shallow wells. It has a 2-inch diameter, 4-foot long PVC pipe attached above ground to the vertical rising main at an angle of 30 degrees to the horizontal. The pump has a very low cost — $US 9.5 (the cast iron version costs $US 15) and is said to be easy to install, operate and maintain.

Local manufacture of similar shallow well pumps also takes place in Thailand[13] under four brand names: MRD (Mineral Resources Department) hand-pump and PWD (Public Works Department) handpump which cost $US 92, Korat handpump which costs $US 109, and ARD (Accelerated Rural Development) handpump which costs $US 131. These handpumps are suitable for depths of up to 8 m.

At an FAO/UNDP/China workshop on water lifting devices and water management, which was held in China from 2 to 26 November 1981, it was noted that while there was a tendency to replace some of the traditional devices with modern pump equipment, the majority of FAO member countries feel that the improvement of traditional facilities which were locally produced, repaired and used by farmers must receive due attention.

2. Large-scale water lifting devices

In view of the increasing shortage and rising cost of energy, any effort to reduce the cost of rural water supply should necessarily involve the use of energy-saving or energy-conserving water lifting devices. In view of this, the traditional means of lifting water by human, animal and wind, as well as water power should be considered wherever possible. In this regard, China was said to have ample experience which many developing countries of the region could take advantage of.

a. Man and/or wind-powered dragon-bone water lift

The dragon-bone water lift has been used in China, Thailand and Viet Nam. It is cheap, because it can be made of locally available materials. This device permits water to be lifted continuously for a head of 2 m or less and can be powered by man or wind.

The dragon-bone water lift mostly used over a long period of time in China is that of the foot-stamping one, as shown in figure 12. It is made of moving-chained blocks named dragon-bones mounted within a wooden trough and connected with a horizontal shaft on the bank. It can deliver more water from the river or ditch to the field because of continuous turning, and it is easy to transport.

b. Wind-powered water pumps

In some developing countries of the region, such as Indonesia, Sri Lanka and Thailand, efforts are being made for the development and application of wind power for pumping water. The type of system recommended by the 1981 workshop in China[14] is the multi-bladed low-speed windmill rotor coupled to a surface-mounted single or double-acting piston pump. Systems with a sail-type rotor coupled to a piston pump were also recommended.

Although wind is freely available, the low density of air compared to water requires construction of large, expensive windmills. In general, windpump size requirements and the need for water storage make wind-powered water supply capital-intensive. Therefore, wind-powered water lifting is favourable only when low lift is involved and double-acting pumps are used when high wind speeds are available.

c. Waterwheels

Waterwheels are highly practicable for use on rivers and streams, provided favourable site conditions, materials and skills exist. They are also reliable, easily manufactured locally, easily installed and repaired. However, they are liable to damage when floods occur. The bamboo-made waterwheel, which was said to be originated in northern Thailand, has been successfully introduced in Sri Lanka. It should find successful application in other developing countries as well.

d. Water-turbine pump

The water-turbine pump, which is widely used in south China, was identified by the 1981 workshop as one of the most promising devices for immediate applicability to other developing countries. The water-turbine pump consists of two major components — the water turbine, which acts as the prime mover, and the pump. The turbine is usually an axial-flow propeller type which is co-axially connected to a centrifugal pump. The water-turbine pump can be used when the stream or river can provide sufficient hydraulic head and water flow. The minimum head required is 0.5 m but the most commonly used head averages between 3 and 4 m. The quantity of flow needed for the turbine to operate averages about 10 times the quantity of water to be lifted. The water-turbine pump has a high efficiency as the water energy is directly utilized by the pump for lifting water. The only problem is said to be the relatively short life of bearings when water contains a large amount of silt. According to China's experience, the introduction of plastic bearings has led to a much longer life compared to roller or ball bearings.

Most of the water-turbine pumps in China are said to be operated as part of the integrated rural development schemes, thereby reducing the cost component allocated to the domestic water supply sector. For example, the water turbines are put to multipurpose use, such as lifting water for both domestic consumption and irrigation, hydropower generation and providing mechanical power in the form of rotating shafts for agricultural processing.

The workshop noted, however, that although there are many opportunities for application of this technology in the developing countries of the region. any attempt at replication should begin with modest pilot projects aimed at verifying the feasibility for local conditions while building up their local skills and expertise.

D. COST REDUCTION IN TREATMENT AND CONVEYANCE OF WATER

In general, treatment of water for rural water supply is required only when surface water is selected as a source, because rain water, spring water and ground water can usually be consumed without treatment. Hence, measures to reduce treatment costs discussed in this section are concerned with treatment methods for surface water tapped directly from streams and rivers. In order to keep the costs low, the treatment methods should necessarily be small in scale, require little or no maintenance, be simple and not involve the use of sophisticated technology and equipment and be able to be manufactured or constructed, operated and maintained with local materials and local expertise.

Conveyance of water is necessary in order to improve user convenience. In the absence of conveyance facilities, quite often villagers have to carry water over long distances when the source is very far from consumers, thus causing much inconvenience as well as waste of time and labour. The cost of conveyance of water can be avoided totally if a source of supply is available at the consumer point; this is usually possible with such sources of supply as ground-water and rain water. For sources, such as surface water and spring water, conveyance facilities are usually necessary in order to provide a certain level of user convenience. The cost of conveyance increases as the level of service is raised, namely, from public standposts to yard taps or from yard taps to house connections. Conveyance of water is achieved by using pipes or drains depending upon topography and other local conditions. When conveying water through pipes, it is more economical to depend on gravity flow rather than on pumps for creating delivery head. It is also important to use local materials and labour to reduce the cost.

1. Measures to reduce water treatment costs

The cost of water treatment for rural water supply can be eliminated if a source of supply of potable water which does not need any treatment, such as a natural pond or lake, is readily available. However, in cases, such as rural water supply from streams or rivers where some treatment will be necassary in order to maintain minimum health standards, the cost involved can be reduced by using simple water treatment methods.

First, the agency responsible for controlling water quality should not set unnecessarily high standards. It is

enough to purify water to a stage where it is safe for human consumption. Secondly, the agency should avoid the use of treatment processes which the community concerned cannot afford to procure, operate and maintain with its financial resources. When considering treatment systems, it is useful to keep in mind that one treatment may be able to perform various functions, namely, removal of suspended matter, removal of iron and pathogenic organisms, control of tastes and odours etc. Finally, it is necessary to give due consideration to the cost effectiveness of various alternatives under different local conditions, because a less costly variant may need constant maintenance and repair and result in frequent interruptions of service.

Quite often, alternatives that help to minimize initial costs lead to early failure in service and a loss of supply for protracted periods while replacements are obtained and installed. According to Gecaga,[15] field investigations in Kenya showed that out of more than 20 slow filters constructed, none of them were functioning properly. This indicates that a careful study based on engineering and economic analyses is necessary to determine, in doubtful cases, whether to install long pipelines bringing in clean water from distant springs or to use sand filters to purify the water available locally.

The three simple water treatment methods which can be used in any rural community are plain sedimentation, aeration and slow-sand filtration. Plain sedimentation in natural or impounded reservoirs is useful for the removal of gross turbidity and for a reduction in bacteria, particularly pathogenic bacteria. It can be effective either alone or in combination with slow-sand filtration. Aeration is used only in cases where it is necessary to control tastes and odours, to precipitate iron and manganeese and to expel carbon dioxide from water. Slow-sand filtration has a high degree of efficiency in the removal of turbidity, tastes and odours without the use of chemicals. Its other advantages are low cost of construction, simplicity of design and operation, possibility of using local materials and equipment, and longer life as no moving parts are involved. However, slow-sand filters are suitable for treatment of water with turbidity below 50 mg/litre. When purification is required for water with higher turbidity, slow-sand filtration should be preceded by some type of pretreatment such as plain sedimentation.

A simple innovative method of purifying surface water at low cost, which can be found applicable in developing countries, was presented by the SWS Filtration Ltd. of the United Kingdom. The firm devised a system which allows a river, canal or stream bad to be used as a water filter. Since beds of water courses seldom dry out, their filter efficiency is constant. Moreover, self-cleaning of the filter is achieved to a certain extent by the flow of water over the surface of the filter bed which washes away dirt.

The unit consists of two portions — filter and pump. Generally, a river bed system is used as an induced gravity filter by placing the pump on the suction side of the filter. The filter unit consists of a bucket shaped glass-reinforced plastic container (or stainless steel container) and a stainless steel abstraction screen as shown in figures 13 and 14. It is buried in the stream or river bed in an inverted position in order to protect the intake, maximize water flow and allow water to be abstracted until the bed is almost dry. The pump is usually a hand pump with a sturdy diaphragm, since petrol or diesel fuel supplies cannot be guaranteed in most developing countries. The pump is generally mounted on the bank. In an ideal bed, 50 per cent of the material is between 1 mm and 5 mm diameter. In such a bed the unit with a cross-section of 30 cm x 60 cm has a capacity of up to 22 cu m an hour and draws from a zone of about 5 metres radius.[6] If the river bed is laid with excessively fine dust and found to be unsuitable in terms of particle size, it can be excavated and back-filled with selected material. The SWS pumps used in the test area near Abu Usher in the Sudan was reported to cost $US 180 each.[6]

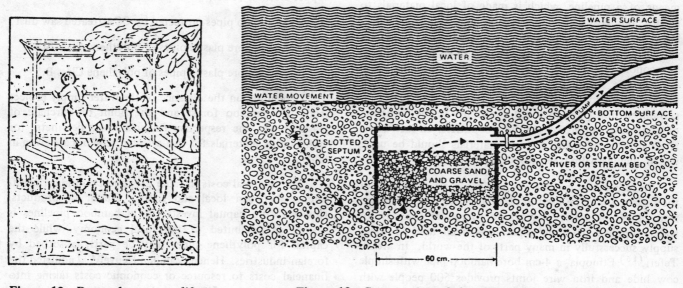

Figure 12. Dragon-bone water lift

Figure 13. Cross-section of glass fibre SWS "Camp" filtration unit in sand bed.

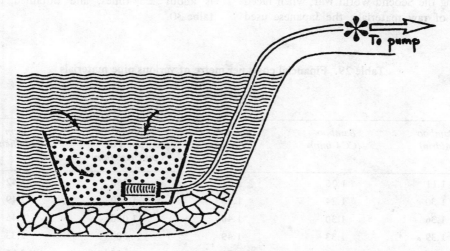

Figure 14. Stainless steel mini-filtration unit buried in a sand bed. Dotted line shows extent of excavation.

2. Measures to reduce water conveyance costs

If topography and site conditions permit, the cheapest way of conveying water is by constructing drains of appropriate capacity lined with locally available impervious material. This method of conveyance has the risk of contamination by human beings and animals unless the drains are provided with covers. Thus, drains are suitable for carrying spring water in mountainous areas where there is no danger of pollution by human or animal habitation.

In areas where topography and site conditions do not permit construction of a drain, water can be conveyed by means of a pipeline, which is made of local materials to reduce the cost. In some developing countries which have an industrial base for manufacturing plastic or galvanized iron pipes, the use of such pipes may found to be economical. However, a majority of developing countries in the region have to import such pipes for their urban water supply. In view of this, the use of plastic or galvanized iron pipes may not contribute to the reduction of rural water supply cost in those countries. In such cases, alternative pipes made of local materials should be used, which, include palm trees, wood and bamboo.

Since bamboo is quite abundant in most rural areas of the region it may be used in place of plastic and galvanized iron pipes for water conveyance to reduce the cost of water supply. Bamboo pipes have been used in water supply successfully in many parts of the world. In Mezan Teferi,[16] Ethiopia, a 4-cm bore bamboo pipe with simple cow hide and iron wire joints provides 500 people with clean water. Bamboo pipes are used traditionally in the hilly villages of Indonesia and the Philippines to transport water under gravity. During the Seocnd World War, when faced with acute shortage of raw materials, the Japanese used

them in their cities. Tanzania[17] is also using bamboo for water conveyance in villages and conducted research work in 1978-1979 to determine the technical and economical feasibility of using bamboo pipes for rural drinking water supply.

The Tanzanian research work considered the following alternative pipes for comparative studies of cost:

(a) Bamboo pipes protected by a 0.5 per cent Aldrin soil treatment (treatment of soil around pipe to protect it from termites);

(b) Bamboo pipes impregnated with chromated copper arsenate (CCA) wood preservative;

(c) Bamboo pipes protected by CCA-treated saw dust;

(d) 4-cm bore plastic pipes of polythene Class B;

(e) 5-cm bore plastic pipes of polythene Class B.

Depending on the distance of the water supply project from the bamboo forest and the point of purchase of plastic pipes, the respective financial costs per metre for various pipe materials for five selected schemes are given in table 29.

The financial costs in table 29 do not consider the difference between local and foreign labour or products. However, the capital investment in bamboo pipelines is mainly re-distributed in the local economy, while the capital for polythene pipes may be partly absorbed by foreign industries. Hence, Van den Heuvel[17] adjusted the financial costs to resource or economic costs taking into consideration the difference between the official and higher free market prices of the imported materials, which is about 2.5 times, and obtained the costs shown in talbe 30.

Table 29. Financial costs per metre of various pipe materials

(in US dollars)

Distance from forest (km)	Bamboo (Aldrin)	Bamboo (CCA imp)	Bamboo (Sawdust)	Distance from point of purchase (km)	4-cm polythene	5-cm polythene
100	1.11	1.06	1.21	950	2.42	3.32
400	1.30	1.24	1.40	1 150	2.49	3.40
500	1.36	1.30	1.46	1 050	2.45	3.36
550	1.39	1.33	1.49	300	2.33	3.09
900	1.60	1.54	1.70	50	2.15	3.00

Source: Reference 13.

Table 30. Economic costs per metre of various pipe materials

(in US dollars)

Distance from forest (km)	Bamboo (Aldrin)	Bamboo (CCA imp)	Bamboo (Sawdust)	Distance from point of purchase (km)	4-cm polythene	5-cm polythene
100	1.70	1.54	1.81	950	4.00	6.63
400	2.09	1.93	2.20	1 150	4.13	6.95
500	2.21	2.08	2.33	1 050	4.07	6.80
550	2.27	2.12	2.39	300	3.59	5.64
900	2.73	2.57	2.84	50	3.43	5.25

Source: Reference 17.

Table 31. Economical lifetime of bamboo pipes for different methods of protection and different project locations

Location of project		Economical lifetime of bamboo pipe in years					
		Aldrin treatment		CCA impregnation treatment		Sawdust treatment	
Distance from forest (km)	Distance from point of purchase (km)	Equivalent to 4-cm polythene	Equivalent to 5-cm polythene	Equivalent to 4-cm polythene	Equivalent to 5-cm polythene	Equivalent to 4-cm polythene	Equivalent to 5-cm polythene
50	680	4-7	2-3	3-4	2	4	3
300	700	4-5	3	4	2	5	3
375	850	5	3	4-5	2-3	5-6	3-4
400	550	5-6	3-4	5	2-3	6	3-4
550	1 050	5-6	3-4	5	2-3	6	3-4
575	400	6-7	3-4	6	3	7	4
650	1 250	5-6	3-4	5-6	3	6	3-4
900	50	9-10	5	9	4-5	10	5-6
930	689	8	4-5	7-8	4	6-7	5

It will be observed from table 30 that bamboo pipes are always cheaper than polythene pipes at any location in the country. However, these figures are based on the assumption that both bamboo and plastic have equal lifetimes of 15 years, which may not be true. The useful life of bamboo pipe depends on the type of treatment or protection to which it is subjected, which in turn determines its cost. The expected lifetime of preserved bamboos in contact with the soil is 10-15 years.[18] In deciding the level of protection to be given to bamboo pipes, it is necessary to determine their economical lifetime, that is, how long they should be able to operate in order to become competitive with plastic. The economical lifetime indicates the number of years after which a bamboo pipe will be economical compared to an equivalent polythene pipe. This economical lifetime is dependent on the location of the water supply scheme, the method of protection of the pipes and the size of the pipes. For the use of bamboo pipes to be feasible, it is necessary that the actual useful life is equal to or greater than their economical lifetime. According to a study by Van den Heuvel,[17] under Tanzanian conditions the economical lifetime of bamboo pipes compared with 4-cm and 5-cm bore polythene pipes is presented in table 31.

From table 31, it will be observed that:

(a) CCA-impregnated bamboo pipes have the shortest economical lifetime, that is, lowest cost compared to polythene pipes of equivalent capacity;

(b) The economical lifetime of bamboo pipes generally decreases as the water supply scheme is nearer to the forest from which bamboo is extracted;

(c) Bamboo pipes of size equivalent to 5-cm polythene pipes have shorter economical lifetime than those of size equivalent to 4-cm polythene pipes.

The research in Tanzania showed that the use of bamboo becomes more economical as its size or water-carrying capacity increases. The water discharge through bamboo pipes can be increased without using a larger diameter by improving the boring techniques for the removal of the partition walls to reduce frictional losses. As bamboo of size larger than 5 cm is quite abundant in countries of the ESCAP region, greater attention should be given to selecting large-bore bamboo for water supply. Regarding the location of the rural water supply scheme, it is advisable to use bamboo pipes only in those areas which are close to the bamboo forest, because if far from the source of bamboo supply the cost will increase due to transportation as well as wastage through damage.

Bamboo pipes need protection against termites and other insects, because unprotected pipes may be damaged by termites within a week. Among the three types of treatment considered in the study, impregnation with CCA is the most economical type for Tanzanian conditions. When similar studies are carried out in the developing countries of the ESCAP region, it is possible that other types of treatment may prove to be more economical. One major disadvantage with using treated bamboo pipes is that these toxic preservatives may be harmful to human beings. However, a test of water samples from treated bamboo pipes for toxicity of CCA components was said to show lower than allowable concentrations of the toxic elements.

A selection of an appropriate lifetime for bamboo pipelines is necessary so that it is cheaper than an equivalent alternative pipeline of other materials and at the same time provides regular and reliable water supply. If the lifetime selected is too short, the supply will not be regular because of the necessity to renew the pipeline frequently. As protection of the bamboo for a period of 10 years makes it 10 to 60 per cent cheaper than plastic,[17] it is suggested that a lifetime of about 10 years should be selected for a rural water supply scheme.

In spite of the various advantages and opportunities associated with the use of bamboo for conveyance of water in rural areas, the following statements in a 1977 report by WHO should be given due consideration:

(a) Bamboo, being vegetable matter, is very susceptible to decay, and once this sets in and is accelerated by moisture, the compression strength is rapidly reduced; with intermittent flow, bacterial growth develops and this pollutes the water and gives it an unpleasant taste;

(b) With material of varying diameter and uneven cross section, it is virtually impossible to make a lasting and watertight joint, especially where pressures are high;

(c) It will be found that except in a few cases bamboo has little advantage, if any, over well-proven conventional materials.

E. CONCLUSIONS AND RECOMMENDATIONS

The following conclusions and recommendations may be drawn from the discussions carried out in previous sections:

1. The cost of rural water supply facilities can be reduced by incorporating them into an integrated rural development programme;

2. Standardization is suggested to a certain extent with respect to designs, components and manuals for rural water supply and urban sanitation facilities to improve efficiency in construction, operation and maintenance;

3. Local manufacture of equipment and parts, such as handpumps and pipes using local materials, is recommended not only to reduce costs but also to increase self-reliance;

4. Social factors should be given due consideration in all phases of rural water supply programmes in order to achieve effective public or community participation and cost reduction;

5. Just as there are strong reasons for charging a fee to consumers for rural water supply, there are also sound reasons for not imposing any charge for water supply in rural areas. Irrespective of which policy is adopted by decision makers, an important fact to keep in mind is that appropriate and adequate arrangements should be made in order to ensure that the water supply system are operated and maintained on a sound basis in the long run;

6. Spring water, if available, is the best and cheapest source of water for rural areas. The remaining sources in ascending order of cost of development are non-artesian ground water, rain water and surface water;

7. Hand or manually operated pumps are the cheapest and most appropriate water lifting devices for rural water supply. There is also a general trend of changing over from the concept of using a durable but expensive type to that of using a substantially cheaper

type that can be locally manufactured, installed and re-paired. Therefore, each country should select a suitable type of pump that can be manufactured locally with the assistance of international organizations, if necessary;

8. Costs related to treatment of water can be avoided by selecting sources that provide clean potable water. In cases where treatment becomes necessary, cost reduction may be achieved by using simple treatment methods that do not involve the use of chemicals. These methods are plain sedimentation, aeration and slow-sand filtration;

9. Costs related to conveyance of water can be avoided by developing the source at consumer point. In cases where water has to be conveyed from supply source to consumer point, the cost involved can be reduced by a gravity flow system using locally produced pipes. If plastic and galvanized iron pipes are found to be expensive, bamboo pipes can be a good substitute in areas with bamboo forests;

10. International agencies should provide greater assistance in training to develop local expertise for planning and in developing new approaches to standardization with regard to design, manufacturing, construction, operation and maintenance of rural water supply systems.

REFERENCES

1. Imboden, N., "Planning and design of rural drinking water projects", *Studies on Rural Development,* vol. II, Development Centre of the Organisation for Economic Co-operation and Development, Paris, 1980, pp. 1-61.

2. Miller, D., "A self-help paradigm for rural water systems", *Studies on Rural Development,* vol. II, Paris, 1980, pp. 213-271.

3. Fresson, S., "Public participation on village level irrigation perimeters in the Mantam region of Senegal", *Studies on Rural Development,* vol. II, Paris, 1980, pp. 96-160.

4. De la, Barra-Rowland, F., "Analysis of experiences of self-help and public participation in rural water supplies: The case of Mexico", *Studies on Rural Development,* vol. II, Paris, 1980, pp. 162-209.

5. "Technology of small water supply systems in developing countries", *Technical Paper Series,* International Reference Centre for Community Water Supply and Sanitation, The Hague, Netherlands, August 1981.

6. Hall, Nick, "Water collection from thatch", *Waterlines,* The Journal of Appropriate Water Supply and Sanitation Technologies, vol. 1, No. 1, July 1982; p.23.

7. Lauritzen, C.W., "Collecting desert rainfall", *Crops and Soils,* August-September 1961.

8. Intermediate Technology Development Group Ltd., The introduction of rainwater catchment tanks and micro-irrigation to Botswana", *ITDG,* London, September 1969.

9. Sternberg, Yaron M., "Report on mission to the Kingdom of Thailand", *Demonstration Projects in Low-Cost Water Supply and Sanitation,* UNDP project No. GLO/78/006, 4-11 July, 1981.

10. Mammo, A., "Shallow wells and hand pumps", *Rural Water Supply in Developing Countries,* Proceedings of a workshop on training held in Zomba, Malawi, 5-12 August 1980, pp. 18-25.

11. *World Water,* May 1982, p. 8, p. 16, pp. 22-25, p. 36.

12. *Waterfront,* UNICEF Publication No. 22, 26 November 1979, New York.

13. *Improvement of Handpump Design in Thailand,* UNICEF, Bangkok 1979.

14. FAO/UNDP/China Workshop on Water Lifting Devices and Water Management, China, 2-26 November 1981, Draft report.

15. Gecaga, J., "Simple water treatment methods", *Rural Water Supply in Developing Countries,* Proceedings of a workshop on training held in Zomba, Malawi, 5-12 August 1980, pp. 53-58.

16. Morgan, J., "Water pipes from bamboo in Meza Tefari, Ethiopia", In *Appropriate Technology,* vol. 1, No. 2, ITP, London, 1974.

17. Van den Heuvel, K., *Wood and Bamboo for Rural Water Supply, a Tanzanian Initiative for Self-Reliance,* Delft University Press, Delft, Netherlands, 1981.

18. Purushotham, A.S. et. al., "Preservation treatment of green bamboos", *Journal of the Timber Development Association,* vol. 11(4), 1965, pp. 8-11.

19. "Report of a regional seminar on a modular approach in small water supply systems design", Bulletin Series 17, International Reference Centre for Community Water Supply and Sanitation, The Hague, Netherlands, January 1981.

VII.B. MEASURES TO REDUCE THE COST OF URBAN WASTE-DISPOSAL FACILITIES
(E/ESCAP/NR. 10/5)

Introduction

Because excreta-related diseases increase the rates of morbidity and mortality, the provision of sanitary waste-disposal systems is basic to ensuring a safe environment and improvement of public health in the developing countries of the region. Water is the breeding place for insect and snail vactors which cause different kinds of diseases and sicknesses which result quite often in disability or death. Statistics invariably indicate that in developing countries, the provision of sanitary waste-disposal systems lags even further behind than that of water supply. This calls for greater national and international attention in order to provide adequate sanitation facilities in those countries.

A review of the history of the development of waste-disposal facilities in industrialized countries reveals that the current high standard of sanitation has been achieved in stages. In the initial stages, the main objective was to achieve basic public health standards. Further refinements were made at substantial cost in order to attain higher public health standards as well as to maximize users' convenience. In striving to provide waste-disposal facilities for people in the developing countries the primary aim should be to achieve basic public health standards. Refinements can be made at a later stage as and when the community can afford them. This primary health objective can be fully achieved by technologies which are much simpler and cheaper than conventional ones. For example, non-conventional on-site and off-site waste-disposal systems are more readily accessible to the poor than conventional sewerage.

The main purposes of this paper are to examine options for the provision of sanitary waste-disposal facilities for the developing countries in the region, to provide useful information regarding low-cost technology and cost-reduction techniques in sewage disposal through reuse of waste materials, and to discuss some practical approaches in selecting the type of facilities and levels of service which are most suitable under various socio-economic conditions in the developing countries, so that basic health objectives can be achieved at minimum cost.

The nature of sanitation problems in the ESCAP region is such that the need to provide waste-disposal facilities is more urgent in urban than in rural areas, because comparatively lower population densities in rural areas permit natural assimilation of human wastes, while in urban areas there is no room for such natural assimilation to take place with the result that the risk of major epidemics is greater in the absence of adequate sanitation facilities. Recent studies by the World Bank also indicate that urban sanitation has improved very slowly even in many of the largest cities in developing countries although water-supply facilities are constantly being upgraded. Owing to the rapid and often unplanned growth of cities in the developing countries, the situation can become critical unless urgent attention is directed to it. In view of the foregoing, the scope of the present paper is limited to the provision of domestic waste-disposal facilities in urban areas.

The availability and form of water supply in an urban area has a profound influence on the sanitation system possible. For example, a house connection will provide a wider choice of sanitation systems than will a public standpipe or yard tap. An intermittent form of water supply will produce its own constraints on system design. It is, therefore, necessary to select a sanitation system that can be maintained by the level of water-supply service in the area. Thus, for example, selection of a septic tank system or a conventional sewerage system in an area serviced by a standpipe water-supply system is not practical.

When discussing the subject of urban waste disposal, there is a general tendency to think of it only in terms of conventional sewerage, which is a high-cost, high-convenience sanitation technology. In this system, human waste is deposited in a cistern-flush water-seal toilet from where it is flushed by clean, potable water into a network of underground sewers, in which is also discharged all domestic sullage. These pipes transport the wastewater to a treatment plant, where the solid and liquid fractions of the wastewater are separated and treated to remove most of the organic pollutants present in the wastewater. Generally, 30 to 40 per cent of the domestic water consumption is used for toilet flushing. Conventional sewerage, which is generally considered to be the best system for urban areas, is not suitable for low-income urban communities in developing countries because of its very high cost and the requirement for a multiple-tap, in-house level of water-supply service. Therefore, in low-income urban areas, non-conventional or rural sanitation technology is often more appropriate than an extension of urban sewerage technology.

The ultimate goal of developing countries in urban waste disposal will undoubtedly be conventional sewerage as used in developed countries. Thus, urban sanitation development programmes may start with one of the baseline low-cost technologies, which is suitable for local conditions, and then as the socio-economic status rises and sullage flows increase, it can be upgraded in a planned sequence of incremental improvements to the desired level of users' convenience. It should be recalled again that although conventional sewerage provides the highest level of users' convenience, it is not the only system which provides an acceptable standard of sanitation. Non-conventional waste disposal systems can also provide an equally high standard of sanitation with a substantially lower cost than that of conventional sewerage.

The major constraints to successful provision of sanitation facilities in developing countries are shortage of financial resources and lack of knowledge about non-conventional sanitation technologies. It should also be noted that most engineers received formal training in sophisticated advanced technology which deals with conventional sewerage only and therefore are not usually aware of non-conventional sanitation technologies. In view of this, it is necessary to identify those alternative sanitation technologies which are appropriate to local conditions in the developing countries are to disseminate information about them.

The use of excreta and wastewater to provide fertilizer, nutrients for fish, or a gaseous fuel can have substantial benefits which could offset a certain portion of waste-disposal costs. The economic benefits from using excreta in these ways are often more tangible than the benefits to public health. Therefore, the re-use of excreta is expected to provide stronger motivation for better sanitation. However, in view of possible health hazards involved in the re-use of waste material, it is desirable that the waste materials should be subjected to a treatment process such as composting or oxidation ponds in order to reduce health risks. It should also be kept in mind that although waste material is a valuable commodity for some developing countries, its re-use should not be regarded as an economic activity but only as a means of offsetting sanitation costs.

A. NON-CONVENTIONAL SANITATION TECHNOLOGY FOR URBAN WASTE DISPOSAL

The following are some of the non-conventional waste-disposal options which may be applied to urban areas with varying degrees of socio-economic development. They can be classified into two broad categories: on-site disposal systems and off-site disposal systems. Generally, the on-site systems require greater space and are, therefore, unsuitable for densely populated urban communities. On-site disposal systems comprise dry pit latrines, ventilated improved pit latrines with or without pour-flush, pour-flush septic tanks, aquaprivies and composting toilets.

Those belonging to the off-site disposal systems are small-bore sewers, bucket latrines and vault toilets. There is a wide range of choice for urban waste disposal between simple techniques used by remote rural communities and the most specialized of recent innovations. The options discussed below are devoted to the first of these, that is, simple techniques.

1. On-site disposal systems

a. *Dry pit latrines*

A dry-pit-latrine, human-waste-disposal system is an effective method of controlling faecal-borne diseases and is cheap to build, easy to maintain, and within the reach of all people. Therefore, it may be considered as a starting point in introducing a waste-disposal system to the poorest urban communities without any kind of sanitation.

The pit latrine consists of three main parts: the dug pit, the superstructure, and the squatting plate, which may be made of timber or concrete. A pit measuring 1 m x 1 m x 4 m deep can usually accommodate the wastes from a family of five people during a three-four year period. The pit is usually dug by the householder himself, and does not involve any special problems or costs if it is sited at an adequate distance downhill from any water source. Superstructures can be made from local materials.

According to studies by WHO, some of the barriers to the success of pit latrines in towns are:

(i) Poor town planning and plot allocation, which makes emptying of a filled-up pit latrine by a vacuum tanker difficult;

(ii) Lack of space to construct pit latrines;

(iii) Landlord-tenant conflicts in cases of rented houses;

(iv) Diversified social and economic nature of the town resulting in certain socio-cultural groups objecting to the use of pit latrines;

(v) The user is exposed to contaminated water when the groundwater level is high or the pit is open to rain;

(vi) Opposite sexes and/or different religious groups sometimes do not like to share the same facility;

(vii) The faecal material is visible;

(viii) In some places, rocky soil formations and high water levels may not allow the construction of pit latrines;

(ix) The latrine has a bad odour when it is constructed close to a dwelling;

(x) Flies usually gather about the latrine.

The two major disadvantages of dry pit latrines, namely, the smell and serious fly nuisance, can be overcome by providing ventilation to the pit. Such latrines are called ventilated improved pit (VIP) latrines and a typical example of these is as shown in figure 15.

b. *Ventilated improved pit latrines*

Ventilated improved pit latrines are suitable for urban communities which are without readily available water. They are proved to be effective in preventing the development of fly populations and to control odour, and they can be used for family ownership as they are cheap to install.

The VIP latrine as shown in figure 15 consists of a pit, preferably deep and wide so that it has a long life, on which is placed a concrete slab containing two holes — one the squatting hole and the other for fitting a vent pipe. The vent pipe is painted black and located on the sunny side of the superstructure. Under the influence of solar radiation the air inside it heats up, causing an up-draught thereby removing obnoxious gases from the pit. This causes a down-draught of fresh air through the toilet and the squatting hole into the pit resulting in the circulation of air and removal of odours from the pit.

The vent pipe also plays an important role in fly control. Few flies enter the pit as they are attracted to the top of the vent by the odours coming therefrom. As the vent pipe is provided with a fly screen, flies cannot enter the pit through it. The superstructure of the latrine is deliberately kept dark with only sufficient light for the user to see. As a result, the strongest light reaching the pit comes from the vent pipe and thus, during the day, flies in the pit are attracted to the top of the vent pipe, where they stay until they die and drop back into the pit.

The single pit VIP latrine can be designed for a life of up to 10 years or more and with appropriate access to permit it to be desludged so that it can be constructed as a permanent structure. However, it is more convenient and less expensive to install a twin-pit VIP latrine as shown in figure 16. Here, one pit is used for a given period, say one year, until it is full and then the second pit is put into use. When the second pit is full, the first is emptied and used again. Thus, the excreta are never handled until they are at least one year old, when only a few *Ascaris* ova at most will be viable.

The use of twin-pit VIP latrines in urban areas presupposes the existence of a pit-emptying programme. It may be done by the householder if he is able to use the humus-like material on his plot, but usually this function is the task of a municipality. An alternative design to a VIP latrine is the Reed Odourless Earth Closet (ROEC), in which a chute is used to completely offset the pit.

c. *Pour-flush toilets for displaced pits*

A further refinement to the VIP latrine for complete odour elimination is to introduce a water-seal toilet pan or pedestal in place of the usual squatting plate separating the pit and the latrine compartment as shown in figure 17. This allows the toilet to be placed inside the house for increased user convenience. Since flushing is done manually, water requirements are low — 1 to 3 litres per flush as compared to 9 to 20 litres per flush for cistern-flush toilets. Such toilets do not require a multiple-tap, in-house water supply and they can be used with a yard tap or public standpipe if the user can carry enough water home for their operation.

d. *Septic-tank systems with pour-flush toilets*

The septic tank consists of a compartmentalized vault, within which settlement and some liquefaction of solids take place, and a subterranean tile or leaching field where most of the biological treatment of the septic tank effluent occurs. A two-compartment septic tank as shown in figure 18 is now generally preferred to one with a single compartment because the suspended solids concentration in its effluent is considerably lower. The first compartment receives only the pour-flush wastewater; after settlement, this passes into the second compartment which also directly receives all sullage. The effluent is then discharged into a soakaway pit or drainfield. In areas where stormsewers already exist, it may be discharged into a small-bore sewer or a covered stormwater drain.

The costs of septic tank installation, as well as periodic desludging, make it inappropriate for use in poor urban areas. The extensive area required also precludes its application in densely populated areas although it can be designed for use in moderately densely populated areas by adding one more compartment and discharging the effluent into a drainfield, which is two to three times smaller than the usual size. Various studies have indicated that in urban areas, septic tanks could cost more on a per-household basis than conventional sewerage. Since the manual pour-flush system can be replaced by a cistern-flush unit, pour-flush toilets can be fully upgraded to a sewered cistern-flush toilets.

e. *Aquaprivies*

The aquaprivy is essentially a modified septic tank located directly below a squatting plate with an integral vertical drop pipe, which extends just below the water surface within the tank. The tank is charged with water at the outset and water is added in sufficient quantities to maintain this water seal. Household wastewater is not usually disposed off in the aquaprivy. Solids sink to the bottom, and the effluent is carried to a soakaway field for

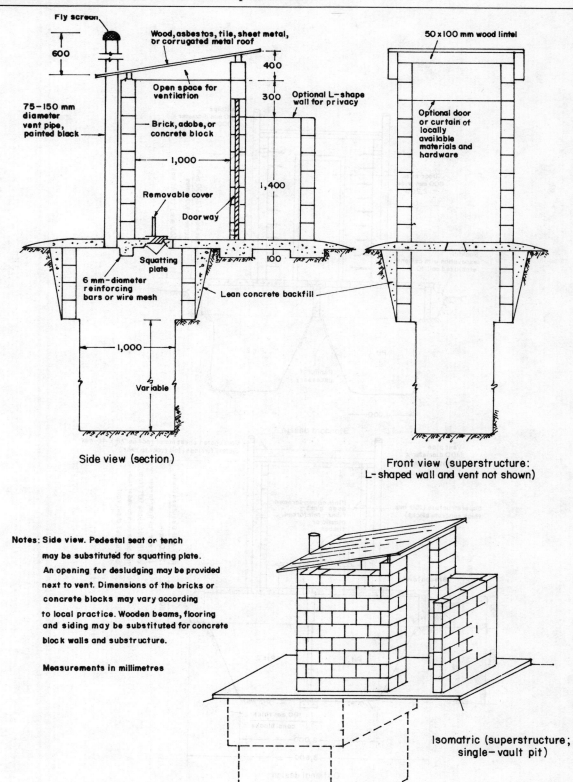

Notes: Side view. Pedestal seat or tench
may be substituted for squatting plate.
An opening for desludging may be provided
next to vent. Dimensions of the bricks or
concrete blocks may vary according
to local practice. Wooden beams, flooring
and siding may be substituted for concrete
block walls and substructure.

Measurements in millimetres

**Figure 15. Ventilated improved pit latrine (measurements
in millimeters)** [1]

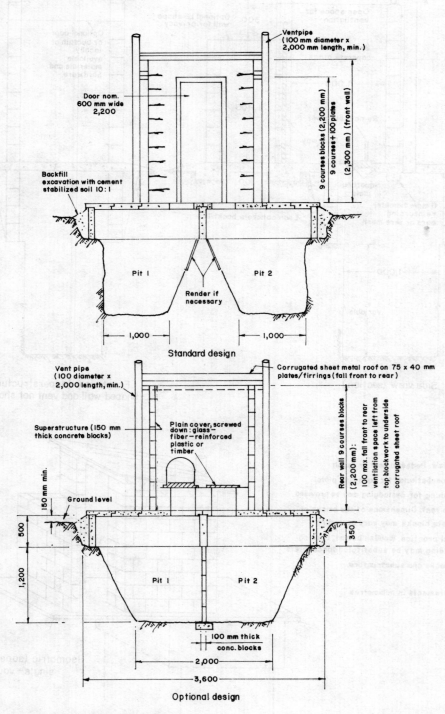

**Figure 16. Ventilated improved double-pit latrine [1]
(millimeters)**

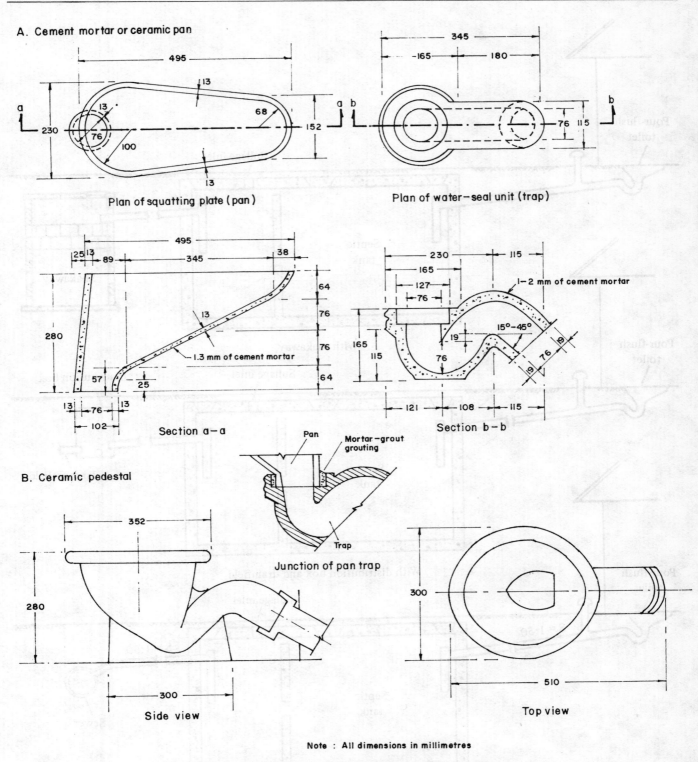

A. Cement mortar or ceramic pan

Plan of squatting plate (pan)

Plan of water-seal unit (trap)

Section a–a

Section b–b

B. Ceramic pedestal

Junction of pan trap

Side view

Top view

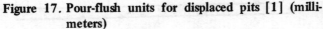

Note : All dimensions in millimetres

**Figure 17. Pour-flush units for displaced pits [1] (milli-
meters)**

Source: A. adapted from Wagner and Lanoix (1958); B. soapted
from CIMDER Colombia.

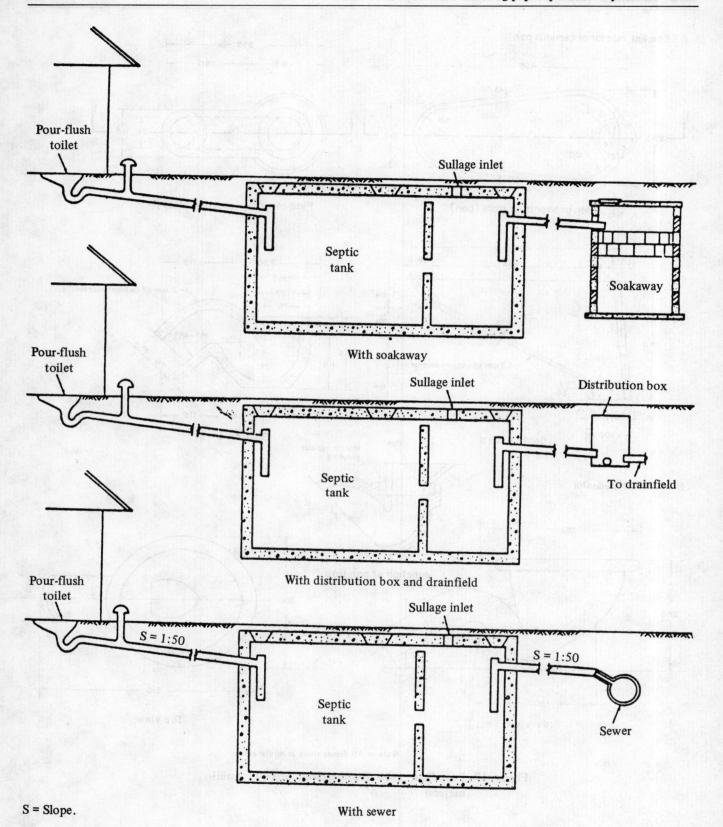

Pour-flush
toilet

Sullage inlet

Septic
tank

Soakaway

With soakaway

Pour-flush
toilet

Sullage inlet

Distribution box

Septic
tank

To drainfield

With distribution box and drainfield

Pour-flush
toilet

Sullage inlet

S = 1:50

Septic
tank

S = 1:50

Sewer

S = Slope.

With sewer

Figure 18. Pour-flush toilet – septic-tank systems [1]

infiltration into the soil. The tank has to be desludged periodically and if enough water is not added to the aquaprivy, the water seal ceases to function and flies and odour enter the house. Hence, aquaprivies can be used only with a yard tap or a multiple-tap, in-house water-supply service. The aquaprivy is equivalent to a VIP latrine with a separate soakaway for sullage or a pour-flush VIP latrine the offset soakaway of which can receive sullage. The latter systems are less expensive and less prone to malfunction. For instance, the waterseal of the pour-flush toilet is much superior to that of the aquaprivy and does not require a watertight tank.

An aquaprivy sewerage system has been developed in Zimbabwe for treatment and disposal of sewage from dwelling houses.[2] The ideas behind selecting this system are to discharge all the wastewater from the household into the aquaprivy tank and by this means retain the seal around the chute; to dispense with soakaways by discharging the effluent from the aquaprivy tank through sewers in to stabilization ponds; and to use the aquaprivy as a sedimentation tank for all inorganic solids and to pretreat the organic pollution solids to a more amenable form for transportation in the sewers. The economy in the design of the sewer is achieved by reducing the velocity of flow to 30 cm per sec and making the gradient of the sewer layout very flat. Zimbabwean experience with this type of system has revealed random blockages in the sewer lines owing to the introduction of large-size materials into the manholes.

f. Composting or mouldering toilets

Composting is a relatively fast process of decomposition of organic matter. It achieves a relatively high temperature in the early stages of the process. Mouldering is a slower, mainly aerobic process which takes place at room temperatures. Household systems for composting night soil and other organic materials can be successful in developing countries when a high degree of user care and attention is motivated by an urgent need for fertilizer. In general, tropical climates offer better operating conditions for composting latrines, but local climate has to be taken into account in the design. There are two types of systems, continuous and batch.

(i) Continuous type

Continuous composting toilets are developments of a Swedish design known as a "multrum". They are extremely sensitive to the degree of user care: the humus has to be removed at the correct rate, organic matter has to be added in correct quantities, and only a minimum of liquid can be added. Sometimes even with a high level of user care short circuiting may occur resulting in the wash down of viable excreted pathogens into the humus

chamber. Field trials by various researchers are said to indicate that continuous composting toilets are not suitable for use in developing countries.

(ii) Batch type

Double vault composting (DVC) toilets are the most common type of batch composting toilet. There are two adjacent vaults, one of which is used until it is about three-quarters full. Then it is filled with earth and sealed and the other vault is used. Ash and biodegradable matter are added to the vault to absorb odour and moisture. When the second vault is filled and sealed, the contents of the first vault are removed and it is put into service again. The composting process takes place anaerobically and requires approximately one year to make the compost microbiologically safe for use as a fertilizer.

In densely populated urban areas, batch type composting toilets may be unsuitable because it is highly unlikely that the users will be motivated to produce good humus for agricultural use. Besides, there may not be sufficient biodegradable organic wastes to regulate the moisture and carbon content of the vault contents.

2. Off-site disposal systems

a. Small-bore sewers

The small-bore sewer system is less expensive than conventional sewerage because it carries settled effluent, which requires smaller pipes laid at shallower depths and at flatter slopes, and involves fewer manholes. Septic tanks, soakage pits, vaults or similar units may be used as settling tanks for a small-bore sewer system. Small-bore sewers are, therefore, suitable in areas where on-site disposal has been practised but cannot be continued without modification because infiltration beds are no longer adequate, clogged soakage pits cannot be rehabilitated, or the amount of sullage water has increased to such an extent that on-site disposal is no longer possible. In such situations small-bore sewers can provide relief at a lower cost than conventional sewers while providing the same level of service.

b. Bucket latrines

The traditional bucket latrine consists of a squatting plate and a metal bucket located in a small compartment immediately below the squatting plate. Excreta are deposited into the bucket, which is periodically emptied by a night-soil labourer into a larger collection bucket, which, when full, is carried to a night-soil collection depot. From there the night soil is taken by a tanker to treatment works or a trenching ground for burial. This system is suitable for densely populated urban areas with any level of water-supply service. However, it is an extremely poor form of sanitation which is only better than no sanitation at all.

Although improved bucket systems are said to provide satisfactory service in parts of Australia and Singapore [3], in general, the system is hygienically unsatisfactory because of the high probability of spillage of night soil during removal and transport. It is not a form of sanitation that can be recommended for new communities.

c. *Vault toilets*

The vault toilet is essentially a pour-flush toilet which discharges into a watertight vault that is emptied at regular intervals by a vacuum tanker and the contents taken away for treatment. It is a hygienic form of night-soil removal although it has high operating costs. It is, however, applicable to high-density, low-income urban areas as the vacuum tanker does not have to be a large, expensive vehicle and can be replaced by animal-drawn carts and manually-operated vacuum pumps.

The principal advantages of vault toilets are low initial costs, low risks to health, minimal water requirements and suitability for high-density areas. Vault toilets are said to be popular in Japan and other countries in east Asia.

3. Communal latrines

A greater economy for both conventional and non-conventional waste disposal systems can be achieved by installing communal facilities. Since they serve many people, they are substantially cheaper on a *per capita* basis than individual household facilities. A major problem with a communal facility is that it appears to belong to no one so that there is little commitment by individual users to keeping it clean and operating properly. Other disadvantages of a communal facility are that there is less privacy and less convenience especially when it is needed at night.

B. COST REDUCTION THROUGH REUSE OF WASTE MATERIALS

Farming, fish culture, algae and aquatic plant production and energy production are promising means for reusing waste materials from urban sanitation, particularly for agriculturally oriented, developing countries. Recycling, or reuse, of waste material resources is not new in developing countries. This is not done for reasons of environmental control, as in developed countries, but out of dire necessity. Excreta and sewage contain many essential nutrients for the growth of terrestrial and aquatic plants. Sewage is also a valuable source of water and

energy. The anaerobic digestion of excreta yields biogas (60-70 per cent methane) which can be used for cooking and lighting. There are, then, three principal ways in which waste materials can be reused: agricultural reuse, aquacultural reuse and biogas production.

1. Agricultural reuse

Agricultural reuse is the most common and simple form of excreta reuse. Human waste can be used either for fertilization or irrigation or both. Night soil contains three main plant nutrients: nitrogen (0.6 per cent), phosphorus (0.2 per cent) and potassium (0.3 per cent) [4] and the most widespread reuse of human wastes, now as in the past, is direct fertilization of crops with untreated night soil [5]. This technique is practised by farmers throughout south east and east Asia, particularly in China and the Republic of Korea and to a lesser extent in Indonesia, Japan, Malaysia, the Philippines and Thailand. The use of un-treated night soil can cause health risks. Therefore some form of treatment is necessary to reduce this risk to an economically acceptable minimum. Where sewage effluent is reused, waste stabilization ponds and conventional treatment followed by maturation ponds, land application or sand filtration can effectively remove the pathogens. Where sludge or night soil are reused, batch thermophilic digestion, thermophilic composting or drying for a minimum of two years can remove the pathogens. One method of treatment practised in China is the composting of night soil mixed with animal manure, organic rubbish and soil. In India and Viet Nam, anaerobic composting is said to be practised.

The humus value of night soil is as significant as its nutrient properties, and this may be the reason why it is still used in Japan and the Republic of Korea where chemical fertilizers are abundant [6].

Another aspect of agricultural reuse of wastewater is irrigation. However, in view of the limited access of developing countries to a sewerage system, this aspect of reuse is considered to be of minor importance to these countries. Moreover, there are hazards associated with using untreated sewage directly in irrigation: the danger of transmitting diseases into the food chain; the health hazards of handling untreated sewage in the irrigation process; and the possible damage to the soil through salinity or alkalinity development. Another negative aspect of wastewater reuse in agriculture is that it is produced on a year-round basis, whereas agricultural uses of water are related to specific stages of crop growth. Thus, efficient reuse of wastewater for agricultural production is likely to require costly wastewater storage. Finally, the use of treated sewage in irrigation in developing countries is not advisable because of the considerable cost of sewerage as well as treatment.

2. Aquacultural reuse

Sewage can be used to promote the growth of aquatic plants and animals. There are four main types of aquaculture: freshwater fish farming, mariculture (culture of marine animals, such as fish, shellfish and shrimps), algae production and aquatic macrophyte production.

Freshwater fish farming has found common use in developing countries particularly in Asia. Cultured fish are a major source of animal protein in China, Indonesia, Japan, Malaysia and the Philippines and fish culture is also practised in Bangladesh, India, Pakistan, Sri Lanka and Thailand [6]. A similar practice may be adopted in the remaining countries of the ESCAP region which can substantially offset the cost of waste disposal facilities. This is because fertilization of the fishponds can be achieved through the disposal of wastes into them. The night soil which is introduced into the fish pond provides nutrients for the algae, which in turn are the basic food form for the fish.

Another technique for combining human waste reuse and aquaculture is to introduce fish into the waste stabilization ponds. This serves a dual purpose of breeding fish as well as improving the functioning of the pond with regard to algae removal, reduction of suspended solids and reduction of faecal coliform bacteria in the final effluent. It also provides the possibility of integrating aquaculture with agriculture by introducing fish into stabilization ponds and then using the effluent for irrigation.

The possibility also exists with regard to combining wastewater effluents with marine culture. According to Ryther [7], an attempt to use secondary sewage effluent mixed with sea water as a source of nutrients for marine algae to be consumed by shellfish on a pilot-plant scale at Woods Hole Oceanograph Institution in the United States of America was quite successful. It was said to be observed that phytoplankton remove the nutrients from the sewage effluent and then filter-feeding shellfish remove the phytoplankton from the water. Solid wastes produced by shellfish in turn serve as food for secondary commercial crops of marine animals, such as lobster and flounder. There are possibilities for adapting such a system to coastal locations in tropical regions, where plentiful solar energy and high water temperatures would promote marine food production.

One of the important aspects of aquacultural reuse of human wastes is algae production. Algae need nutrients for growth. Most natural waters do not contain all the required levels of nitrogen, phosphorus, or potassium, while human and animal wastes contain all three elements. Hence, algae can be cultivated in waste stabilization ponds with no supplementary nutrients. Several studies have shown that the nutritive value of algae as food for fish and other animals is very high due to high protein content — usually about 50 per cent. The usefulness of algae as an animal feed substitute attaches a special significance to algae production, particularly in developing countries experiencing food shortage, because it can make more grains available for human consumption. The production of algae can be maximized by reducing the stabilization pond depth to 20-40 centimetres to improve sunlight availability throughout, the resulting pond usually being referred to as a high-rate pond. Conventional algae production is practised on a pilot scale in Japan and Mexico, while production in high-rate ponds is being studied in the Federal Republic of Germany, Israel and Singapore. Algal harvesting is said to be a complex and expensive process in practice and there are doubts that sufficient yields can be achieved from small experimental ponds.

The fertilization of aquatic macrophytes with excreta and sewage, although practised traditionally in certain countries, has not been evaluated technically or economically. Water hyacinths are reported to be used for sewage treatment in the United States [8] where they are harvested for animal feed, and a recent proposal has suggested converting them into fuel using the biogas process. In Viet Nam and throughout south-east Asia, aquatic weeds are said to be grown in ponds to which animal waste and night soil are added, the harvested weeds being used for animal feed.

3. Biogas production

The anaerobic decomposition of sewage produces a combustible gas called biogas. Biogas plants are found in large numbers in China, in significant numbers in India and the Republic of Korea and in smaller numbers in Indonesia, Japan, the Philippines and Thailand. The gas is used primarily for domestic cooking and lighting. Since biogas plants usually cost more than an individual household can afford, its utilization in developing countries depends on the improvement of this technology to reduce the cost.

C. ECONOMIC COMPARISON OF WASTE-DISPOSAL SYSTEMS

A criterion commonly used in evaluating the net economic effect of a given project is the benefit-cost ratio. This criterion, when applied to the economic analysis of waste disposal systems, may not give a true indication of the economic effectiveness of a system, because the benefits of sanitation systems cannot be quantified. There are also unquantifiable costs (cost of advanced technology, failure to make use of local materials etc.) associated with alternative technologies which make it more difficult in determining the benefit-cost ratio. To alleviate this difficulty, a scoring device was introduced for ranking alternatives with unquantifiable costs and benefits. However, this method is also unreliable because there is no completely satisfactory scoring system for comparing alternatives.

In the case of mutually exclusive alternatives with identical benefits a least-cost comparison may be used for ranking purposes. Although alternative sanitation systems can be designed for full health benefits, there still remains a wide range of benefit levels resulting from varying qualities of service. Therefore, a least-cost criterion is also not the best indicator for selecting among sanitation alternatives. Nonetheless, a comparison of costs between various alternatives gives an idea of trade-offs in cost corresponding to different service standards. Once the comparable cost data have been developed, the consumers or community can use these as one of the basic criteria in selecting an appropriate waste-disposal system. Hence, a comparable economic costing is an effective tool in the economic comparison of waste disposal systems.

The following are some of the recent works on the economic comparison of waste disposal systems. Holland[9], Hansen and Therkelsen[10], and McGarry[11] attempted to make economic comparisons between different urban systems. The main objective is to determine the least costly solution based on capital and operating costs while considering certain factors such as population density and interest rates. Morrow[12], in his study on sanitary waste disposal in low-income communities in Jakarta, concluded that a night-soil collection system, utilizing vacuum carts and steam pasteurization and eventual use as fertilizer, is not only the most economic but has the best chance of easy implementation. Pradt[13], after studying recent developments in night-soil treatment, concluded that the night-soil collection and treatment systems as practised in Japan are more practical for most Asian developing countries than a waterborne system. McGarry[11], in his study on waste collection in hot climates — a technical and economic appraisal, concluded that the vacuum truck and vault was found to have the lowest cost when compared with other urban sanitation systems. According to these studies, therefore, the bucket latrines and vault toilets appear to be the least costly system for developing countries. Obviously, this will hold true only in populated urban areas where houses are located close to one another. In cases where housing in widely scattered, on-site disposal technologies, such as ventilated improved pit latrines and pour-flush toilets, may prove to be more economical and practical. Rybczynski, Polprasert and McGarry[16] made a general comparison of the significant characteristics of the on-site and off-site waste disposal systems, which is given in table 32. These characteristics will, of course, vary from country to country, and quantitative data will be required for making final decisions.

As a general rule, the on-site disposal systems involve a much lower cost than the off-site systems, because they provide the opportunity for self-help construction. It is believed that self-help can provide unskilled labour and some of the skilled labour required for the installation of on-site disposal systems. Generally, the off-site disposal systems have less potential for self-help, because they require experienced engineers and skilled builders for their design and construction.

Table 32. A general comparison of on-site and off-site technologies

	Off-site		On-site
	Conventional sewerage and small-borne sewers	Bucket latrines and vault toilets	
Capital cost	High	High/low	Low
Operating cost	Low	High	Low
Offshore cost component	High	High/low	Nil
Water consumption	High	Low/nil	Low/nil
Optimal density (population)	High density (high rise buildings)	High density (low rise buildings)	High and low density (low rise buildings)
Adaptability to incremental implementation	Nil	High	High
Adaptability to self-help	Nil	Low	High
Reuse potential	High	High	High/low

Source: Adapted from [6].

Kalbermatten *et al* [14] carried out a comparative economic costing of various sanitation technologies based on data obtained from countries of the ESCAP region, Africa and Latin America. The authors suggested the total annual cost per household (TACH) as a figure for cost comparison of technologies, which includes both investment and recurrent costs. Since TACH could be misleading when applied to communal facilities where several households share one toilet, it was said to be calculated by scaling up *per capita* costs by the average number of persons in a household which was taken as six. The TACHs obtained for various technologies were arranged in ascending order of annual costs and grouped into three levels — low, medium and high (see table 33). The prices of the three main inputs to sanitation systems (unskilled labour, water and land), which were used to obtain the TACH, are given in table 34. In order to arrive at a meaningful value of TACH for different sanitation technologies, these market prices were said to be modified by applying shadow rates or conversion factors which were obtained from World Bank economists specializing in the countries concerned. The authors also considered the opportunity cost of capital in order to reflect the real cost of capital to the economy. In obtaining the total cost of a sanitation system, the average incremental cost (AIC) approach was used whereby the

sunk costs or those costs which were already incurred were disregarded. The *per capita* AIC of a system is calculated by dividing the sum of the present value of construction and incremental operating and maintenance costs by the sum of the incremental persons served. A breakdown of on-site, collection and treatment costs per household for various technologies is given in table 35. This breakdown is useful in determining as to where the cost reduction efforts can be made most effective.

It will be observed from table 33 that within the low-cost group of technologies there is a fairly large variety of systems ranging from pit latrines and pour-flush toilets to bucket latrines and low-cost septic tanks. Since the costs derived in table 33 were obtained from particular case studies, including those outside the region, these could not be considered as representative of the situation in the region. It is, therefore, advisable to study the overall variation of cost in different countries of the region before making an examination of the cost data for each country. The economic comparison may be refined further by taking into consideration some costs that may be offset by the reuse potential in various technologies if sufficient data can be collected for this purpose.

Table 33. Average annual investment and recurrent cost ($US) per household
for sanitation technologies

Technology	Mean TACH	Investment cost	Recurrent cost	Percentage of total	
				Investment	Recurrent
Low-cost					
PF toilets	18.7	13.2	5.5	71	29
Pit latrine (VIP)	28.5	28.4	0.1	100	...
Communal latrines	34.0	24.2	9.8	71	29
Low-cost septic tank	51.6	40.9	10.7	79	21
Composting toilet	55.0	50.9	4.8	92	8
Bucket cartage[a]	64.9	36.9	28.0	57	43
Medium-cost					
Sewered aquaprivy[a]	159.2	124.6	34.6	78	22
Aquaprivy	168.0	161.7	6.3	96	4
Japanese vacuum-truck cartage	187.7	127.7	60.0	68	32
High-cost					
Septic tank	369.2	227.3	141.9	62	38
Sewerage	400.3	269.9	130.4	67	33

Source: Appropriate technology for water supply and sanitation, vol. 1, Technical and economic options (Washington, D.C., World Bank, 1980), p. 54.

a Per capita costs were used and scaled up by the cross-country average of six persons per household to account for large differences in the number of users.

Table 34. Selected input costs ($US) and conversion factors for sanitation

Country	Unskilled labour (daily)[a]	Water[a] (per cubic metre)	Land[b] (per hectare)	Capital (percentage)	Conversion factors Unskilled labour	Conversion factors Foreign exchange
Indonesia	1.80	0.11[c]	n.a.	20	1.0	1.0
Japan	10.50	0.85[c]	n.a.	10	1.0	1.0
Malaysia	3.40	0.35	200	12	1.0	1.0
Republic of Korea	4.00	n.a.	n.a.	14	0.8	1.12
Botswana	1.80	0.38	100	10	0.7	1.0
Ghana	5.50	n.a.	65	12	0.8	1.75
Nigeria	3.40	1.60	n.a.	12	0.8	1.15
Sudan	1.90	0.39[c]	100	16	1.0	1.25
Zambia	4.00	0.70	65	12	0.6	1.25
Colombia	3.20	0.30	n.a.	12	0.3	1.0
Nicaragua	2.10	0.13	n.a.	20	0.5[d]	1.1
Mean	3.78	0.53	106			

Source: World Bank country economists and field consultants reporting on case studies. For more detail, see Richard Kuhlthau (ed.), *Appropriate Technology for Water Supply and Sanitation,* vol. 6, Country studies in sanitation alternatives (Washington, D.C.: The World Bank, Transportation, Water, and Telecommunications Department, 1980).

Notes:

a   Market price in studied communities including benefit package where applicable.

b   Average incremental cost (AIC).

c   Average of several community studies.

d   Unskilled rural labour only; for urban unskilled labour, conversion factor is 1.

Table 35. Average annual on-site, collection, and treatment costs ($US) per household

Technology	Mean TACH	On-site	Collection	Treatment	Percentage of total On-site	Percentage of total Collection	Percentage of total Treatment
Low-cost							
PF toilets	18.7	18.7	...	...	100	...	...
Pit latrine (VIP)	28.5	28.5	...	...	100	...	...
Communal latrines	34.0	34.0	...	...	100	...	...
Low-cost septic tanks	51.6	51.6	...	...	100	...	...
Composting toilets	55.0	47.0	...	8.0	85	...	15
Bucket cartage[a]	64.9	32.9	26.0	6.0	51	40	9
Medium-cost							
Sewered aquaprivy[a]	159.2	89.3	39.2	30.2	56	25	19
Aquaprivy	168.0	168.0	...	...	100	...	...
Japanese vacuum truck	187.7	128.0	34.0	26.0	68	18	14
High-cost							
Septic tanks	369.2	332.3	25.6	11.3	90	7	3
Sewerage	400.3	201.6	82.8	115.9	50	21	29

Source: [14]

a   Per capita costs were used and scaled up by the cross-country average of six persons per household to account for large differences in the number of users.

D. CHOICE OF SANITATION SYSTEM

A selection of the least costly waste-disposal system should take place bearing in mind the socially and environmentally acceptable options for each country or society, because the least costly system may fail technically if the users' social preferences militate against its use and proper maintenance. In the selection process, it will be necessary to take into consideration population density, water availability, climate, topography, soil conditions, availability of construction materials and labourers, and the urgency for improved health through effective waste disposal. Some of the salient features that should be borne in mind in selecting an appropriate system in addition to economic considerations are:

(a) For a number of developing countries one particular scarce resource is clean water — many developing countries, particularly those in the tropical and subtropical regions, usually have periodic or permanent shortages of water which act as a constraint to the adoption of any sanitation system that tends to increase water demand;

(b) According to previous studies, the waterborne waste-disposal option is generally associated with increased water consumption;

(c) The tropical and subtropical climate in most developing countries create ideal conditions for pathogen survival which means that pathogen destruction rather than biochemical oxygen demand (BOD) reduction should be the first priority in selecting a waste disposal system;

(d) Most developing countries have a shortage of financial resources and trained personnel at various levels which means that simple and less capital intensive systems are more practical and feasible for development than the sophisticated systems;

(e) The limited availability and high cost of chemical fertilizers mean that human waste has its value as a fertilizing material.

The following are some of the physical and environmental factors that should be considered in selecting an appropriate low-cost waste disposal system in developing countries: climate and site conditions, levels of water supply service, housing density and space limitations.

1. Climatic and site conditions

Climatic conditions may affect the choice of sanitation systems, because low temperatures in regions with a cold climate can affect the performance of waste-treatment ponds, digesters and biogas units.

Selection of the least costly option for waste disposal also depends to a certain extent on site conditions, because adverse site conditions may sometimes prohibit the use of the most economical sanitation system. For instance, soil stability is important for VIP latrines and PF toilets. In unstable soils pits must be lined thus increasing their cost. Also, if the groundwater table is high, that is, about one metre or less below the ground level, the VIP latrines and PF toilets may not be feasible options. Similarly, the presence of rock near the ground surface may create difficulties and make this technology more expensive. In the case of septic tanks, the use of soak away trenches may not be feasible in impermeable soils.

2. Levels of water-supply service

A public water hydrant supply service may prohibit the use of any system that requires water to transport the excreta. A yard tap or household pump may permit PF and vault toilets but not conventional sewerage. A house-connection service will make any system of waste disposal technically feasible.

3. Housing density

In densely populated areas, VIP latrines, PF toilets, composting toilets, aquaprivies and septic tanks with soakaways may not be feasible. It is difficult to define up to what population density these on-site disposal systems will be feasible. According to Kalbermatten[14], the figure suggested is around 250-300 persons per hectare for single storey homes and up to double that figure for two-storey houses. Vip latrines, however, are said to provide satisfactory service at much higher population densities. They are feasible if there is enough space for two alternating pit sites that have a minimum lifetime of two years, or if the pit can be easily emptied in case there is no space for alternating pit sites.

4. Individual versus collective system

An individual sanitation system is essentially an on-site sewage disposal system which does not require the installation of drainage or a sewerage network. A collective sanitation system is an off-site sewage disposal system which generally, but not always, require a sewerage network. In this connection, it is necessary to differentiate between a collective system and a communal system. In a collective system, sewage at different locations in an urban area is collected and transported by means of a sewerage network or tankers to a treatment plant, while in a communal system, all the people of a certain group or community share the same toilet facilities irrespective of the way in which sewage from such facilities are disposed of or treated. Thus, a communal system can be on-site or off-site, while a collective system should necessarily be an off-site disposal system.

The main advantages of individual sanitation are its high degree of autonomy, that is, it can be installed and operated individually without relying on the municipality; the high standard of environmental protection; and its low cost compared with collective sanitation systems particularly in areas where dwellings are scattered. It can also be adapted to achieve modern convenience standards comparable with that from a collective network. In areas where general public opinion is inclined towards conventional sewerage as an objective, an individual system may be used as a provisional arrangement while awaiting the installation of the main drainage network. In newly expanded urban areas which cannot be served by the existing conventional sewerage operating at maximum capacity, an individual sanitation system is very effective as a complement to the collective system. The disadvantages of an individual system are that it requires an appropriate subsoil for infiltration and purification of wastewater and a minimum site area for each installation which means a larger overall space when compared with a collective system.

A collective system, particularly a conventional sewerage system, is generally recognized as capable of providing maximum users' convenience and hence is the ultimate objective of most urban areas. While collective sanitation is efficient in densely populated areas, its cost becomes prohititive wherever dwellings are scattered.

Kalbermatten and others ([14]) carried out a descriptive comparison of sanitation technologies which is given in table 36. Factors that were considered in the comparison were population density, construction cost, operating cost, ease of construction, potential for self-help and use of local materials, water requirement, required soil conditions, complementary off-site investments, reuse potential, health benefits and institutional requirements. The comparison is purely descriptive and no overall ranking or conclusions were attempted. It is useful for excluding certain technologies that are not suitable for a given locality. A list of technically and institutionally feasible alternatives may be prepared from such a comparison. Then, from this list certain socially unacceptable alternatives may be excluded and a short list of financially feasible alternatives will be obtained after identifying a community's level of affordability. Final designs of and cost estimates of this short list of feasible alternatives may then be prepared resulting in a comparative economic costing of feasible sanitation technologies for that locality. The community will then select the best or the most appropriate technology from the comparison of costs.

E. CONCLUSIONS AND RECOMMENDATIONS

The following conclusions and recommendations may be drawn from the discussions in the preceding sections:

(1) A reduction in cost of urban waste disposal facilities can be achieved if greater importance is attached to improving public health rather than maximizing users' convenience.

(2) One possible way of achieving this primary health objective in the urban context is to apply non-conventional or rural sanitation technology, particularly for low-income areas.

(3) The use of simple low-cost technology is to be preferred to sophisticated technology because advanced technology is not the only means of achieving economy and, besides, it may not be appropriate for rural application.

(4) The use of local technology and local materials is an important factor in reducing the cost of sanitation. This means that pit latrines, composting toilets, pour-flush toilets, bucket latrines etc. should be used more to minimize costs, particularly during the initial stages.

(5) The cost of sanitation can be reduced by offsetting it with the benefits gained through the reuse of waste materials. The areas suggested for reuse are agriculture, aquaculture and biogas production.

(6) Analysis of previous studies on the economics of waste-disposal systems indicates that if local conditions permit, the on-site disposal systems generally have a lower cost than off-site disposal systems.

(7) Most of the studies on the economics of waste-disposal systems were carried out in countries outside the ESCAP region and cost data pertaining to countries in the region are almost non-existent. A cost survey of different sanitation systems in the countries of the region should, therefore, be carried out in order to ascertain which system can achieve a maximum reduction in cost.

(8) The least-cost factor should not be the only consideration in selecting an appropriate sanitation system for an urban community. Other factors that should be considered are social acceptance, climate and site conditions, levels of water-supply service, housing density and space limitations.

(9) A least-cost waste-disposal system that can achieve substantial reduction in costs may not be applicable to a certain area or community owing to social prejudice as a result of lack of education on the part of users. In such cases, a public educational programme on sanitation should be initiated by the countries concerned.

Table 36. Descriptive comparison of urban sanitation technologies for developing countries[14]

Sanitation technology	Population density	Construction cost	Operating cost	Ease of construction	Potential for and use of local materials	Water requirement	Required soil conditions	Complementary off-site investments[a]	Reuse potential	Health benefits	Institutional requirements
On-site disposal systems											
1. Ventilated improved pit (VIP) latrines	Suitable in low/medium-density areas	L	L	Very easy except in wet or rocky ground	H	None	Stable permeable soil; groundwater at least 1 metre below surface[b]	None	L	Good	L
2. Pour-flush (PF) toilets	Suitable in low/medium-density areas	L	L	Easy	H	Water near toilet	Stable permeable soil; groundwater at least 1 metre below surface[b]	None	L	Very good	L
3. Septic tanks	Suitable in low/medium-density areas	H	H	Requires some skilled labor	L	Water piped to house and toilet	Permeable soil; groundwater at least 1 metre below ground surface[b]	Off-site treatment facilities for sludge	H	Very good	L
4. Aquaprivies	Suitable in low/medium-density areas	M	L	Requires some skilled labor	H	Water near toilet	Permeable soil; groundwater at least 1 metre below ground surface[b]	Treatment facilities for sludge	M	Very good	L
5. Composting toilets	Suitable in very low-density areas	M	L	Requires some skilled labor	H	None	None (can be built above ground)	None	H	Good	L
Off-site disposal systems											
6. Small-bore sewers	Suitable	H	H	Requires skilled engineer/builder		Water piped to house	None	Sewers and treatment facilities	H	Very good	H
7. Vault toilets and bucket latrines (cartage)	Suitable	M	H	Requires some skilled labor	(for vault construction)	Water near toilet	None (can be built above ground)	Treatment facilities for night soil	H	Very good	H
8. Conventional sewerage	Suitable	VH	M	Requires skilled engineer/builder		Water piped to house and toilet	None	Sewers and treatment facilities	H	Very good	H

a On or off site sludge disposal facilities are required for non sewered technologies.
b If groundwater is less than 1 metre below ground, a plinth can be built.
L = low; M = medium; H = high; VH = very high.

REFERENCES

(1) Mara, D., "Sanitation alternative for low-income communities — a brief introduction", *Appropriate Technology for Water Supply and Sanitation,* vol. 16, The World Bank, Feb. 1982.

(2) Vincent, L.J., and others., "A system of sanitation for low cost high density housing", *Symposium on Hygiene and Sanitation in Relation to Housing,* CCTA/WHO, Nigeria, Pub. No. 84, pp. 135-137, 1961.

(3) Kalbermatten, J.M., and others, "Appropriate technology for water supply and sanitation", *A Planner's Guide,* volume 2, The World Bank, Dec. 1980.

(4) McGarry, M.G., "The taboo resource . . . the use of human excreta in Chinese agriculture", *The Ecologist,* vol. 6(4), pp. 150-154, June 1976.

(5) Williams, G.B., *Sewage Disposal in India and the Far East,* Thacker, Spink & Co., India, 1924.

(6) Rybczynski, W., and others, *Low Cost Technology Options for Sanitation — A State-of-the-Art Review and Annotated Bibliography, Ottawa,* IDRC, 1978.

(7) Ryther, J.H., "Preliminary results with a pilot plant water recycling marine aquacultural system", *Wastewater Renovation and Reuse,* Marcel Dekker Inc. Institute of Water Research, Michigan State Univ., 1977.

(8) National Academy of Sciences, *Making Aquatic Weeds Useful: Some Perspectives for Developing Countries,* Washington D.C., 1976. pp. 115-126.

(9) Holland, R.J., *Unit Costs of Domestic Sewage Disposal in Kenya,* Univ. of Nairobi, Kenya, 1978.

(10) Hansen, J.A., Therkelsen, H., *Alternative Sanitary Waste Removal Systems for Low-income Urban Areas in Developing Countries,* Polyteknisk Forlag Publishers, Denmark, 1977.

(11) McGarry, M.G., "The choice between technology", *Developing Country Sanitation,* International Development Research Centre, Ottawa, 1972.

(12) Morrow, D., *"Sanitary Waste Disposal in Low-income Communities in Jakarta",* Unpublished report, Workshop II, Public Policy Programme, 1975.

(13) Pradt, L.A., "Some recent developments in night soil treatment", *Water Research,* vol. 5, 1971.

(14) Kalbermatten, J.M., and others., "Technical and economic options", *Appropriate Technology for Water Supply and Sanitation,* vol. 1, The World Bank, Dec. 1980.

(15) King P.E., "Vacuum sewers — the future for sewage collection?", *Civil Engineering ASCE,* December 1981, pp. 54-55.

(16) *Water Services,* the Journal for Water, Sewage and Industrial Effluent Treatment, Feb. 1982, p. 79.

(17) Golucke, C.G., "Using plants for wastewater treatment", *Water Resources Journal,* ESCAP, Dec. 1981, pp. 77-81.

(18) Szives, L., and others., "Treatment of municipal liquid wastes in areas without sewerage", *Seminar on Drinking Water Supply and Effluent Disposal Systems,* Albufeira, Portugal, Oct. 1982.

(19) Pacey, A., *Sanitation in Developing Countries,* New York, John Wiley and Sons. 1978.

VII.C. WATER QUALITY MANAGEMENT IN THE ESCAP REGION
(E/ESCAP/NR.10/7)

Introduction

1. Need for the study

Of the many environmental problems faced by developing countries, protection and conservation of water quality is one of the most serious. Whereas this was a relatively minor problem in many countries up to about the time of the Second World War, since that time many developing countries have undergone a syndrome of accelerating growth of population, urbanization and industrialization. This, together with the advent of modern agricultural technology with its heavy dependence on agricultural chemicals, has already led to a serious depreciation in water quality in congested urban zones and to initial stages of pollution in many other areas.

Because of the importance of water as a vital resource for continuing development for a wide array of beneficial uses, including community and industrial water supply, fisheries, irrigation, recreation, navigation and wildlife,

ESCAP has recognized it is timely now to promote effective national water pollution and quality control programmes in the developing countries in order to help these countries control the problem before it gets out of hand. This is especially important for those developing countries with relatively limited economic resources as compared to the industrialized countries, in as much as after-the-fact correction of pollution is generally much more costly than planned prevention. As shown by many studies over the past several decades, virtually all countries can afford the costs of planned prevention, whereas correction after-the-fact may be beyond the resources of many developing countries.

2. Approach to the study

On the recommendation of the Committee of Natural Resources at its seventh session in 1980, the ESCAP secretariat undertook a preliminary investigation on water quality management in the region based primarily on the use of a mailed questionnaire. The objective was to assess the current situation in the region and to develop recommendations for practicable measures which could be undertaken to help bring the problem under control. Replies to the questionnaire were received from 14 countries, namely Afghanistan, Australia, Bangladesh, China, Hong Kong, Indonesia, Iran, the Republic of Korea, Pakistan, Papua New Guinea, the Philippines, Singapore, Sri Lanka and Thailand.

In addition to the questionnaire survey, considerable additional information was obtained from a review of reports relating to water quality investigations in the region over the past decade, particulary studies sponsored by the World Bank, the Asian Development Bank, WHO and UNEP as well as other United Nations agencies.

Most of the reports dealt with water quality problems in Thailand, the Philippines and Indonesia. They were chosen for the present review because of their ready availability and because these three countries are considered representative of the developing countries in the ESCAP region and thus are more in need of the assistance which may be furnished by the international agencies concerned.

The present paper presents the results of the survey, augmented by the review of available reports, considering both those countries where considerable progress has already been made in water quality management and those countries where such programmes are in earlier stages of development.

3. Adequacy of survey data

As is the case with most data collected by mail by use of questionnaires, the amount and quality of the data sup-

plied varied widely from country to country. As was expected, in all 14 countries a number of national agencies are involved with water quality considerations, including the national resource development, the public health and the environmental protection agencies. In nine of the 14 cases, the national agency completing the questionnaire was the national water resource development agency, which in most cases is generally concerned primarily with hydropower and irrigation rather than with urban problems. Hence the responses cover effects of pollution on irrigation more so than effects on beneficial uses in urban areas. Of these nine water agencies, there are only three (Australia, Indonesia and the Philippines) where the agency's interests are comprehensive with respect to beneficial uses, including urban, industrial, fishery and recreational uses of water as well as hydropower and irrigation. While practically all of the countries have national environmental protection agencies, there was only one case (Thailand) where the environmental agency took the lead responsibility for completing the questionnaire.

Because of the complexity of collecting the data, considering the multiple agencies involved, the quality of the data (amount and reliability) depended especially upon the individual who completed the questionnaire, on his background of experience, his level of interest, and especially on his ability to obtain information from the agencies involved other than his own. Considering that the selected individual may not have been especially experienced in water quality technology and that proper completion of forms of this type is not easy even for experts, it would have been helpful if examples had been distributed illustrating how the form could have been completed, both for countries known to have made significant progress in water quality management and those known to be in earlier stages of progress.

Despite the problems noted above, the collected data nevertheless have significant value when reviewed by a water quality expert with sufficient experience in the subject and in the region to enable him to interpret the data. This is the approach used in preparing the present paper.

4. Organization of the report

The results of the study are presented in four parts (sections 2 to 5). The first section gives a general picture of the current situation regarding water quality problems in the countries of the region. The second section contains information on the national policy pursued by these countries and measures to achieve the objectives of water quality management. The third section outlines the major problems and constraints encountered in the field of water quality management. The last section comprises recommendations for national and international action. To facilitate review of the survey data, the data have been organized into a series of 11 tables.

A. GENERAL SITUATION REGARDING WATER QUALITY IN THE REGION

1. Severity and extent of problem

The responses are summarized in table 37. As expected, the data indicate that severe pollution is limited to congested urban/industrialized areas. Water pollution from human and industrial wastes is a function of the extent of urbanization/industrialization, hence in most cases it is severe only in the vicinity of large communities or industries, moderate in the vicinity of smaller communities, and elsewhere tends to be negligible except for pollution of waterways from runoff containing agricultural chemicals, especially pesticides. Examples of severe pollution in the dry season include conditions in the Chao Phya river in and below Bangkok (1, 2), in the river/drainage channels of metropolitan Jakarta (3) and in Laguna lake and the Pasig river at Manila (4). In all these situations the degree of pollution is comparatively so severe during the dry season that the rainy season conditions hardly qualify as a problem (unlike the situation in the industrialized countries, the United States, for example, where a great deal of effort over

the past decade has focused on control of pollution from combined sewer overflows during the rainy season).

Examples of moderate and incipient pollution in urban zones are (a) the Musi river at Palembang in south Sumatra (5), where the huge flow in the river tends to mask all pollution except for oil discharges in the harbour areas, ammonia discharges from the urea factory (which have caused a number of serious fish kills) and oil discharges below the city from a major oil refinery, (b) Songkhla lake in southern Thailand (6), which is still in reasonably good condition as regards water quality but which faces an uncertain future due to anticipated rapid development in the lake basin and (c) the Han river at Seoul in the Republic of Korea (7).

2. Major contributors to degradation

As shown in table 38, the bulk of pollution affecting waterways stems from urban sources, with significant contributions also in rural areas from runoff of agricultural chemicals and discharges from non-urban-sited industries, including mining operations and agro-industrial processing. Another significant problem is salt water intrusion into both surface and ground waters. The primary source of severe natural organic pollution (commonly measured as BOD) is human wastes (which are generally uncontrolled),

Table 37. Severity and extent of water quality problem in some ESCAP regional countries

	Severe in widespread areas	Severe in certain limited areas	Moderate	Negligible	Unknown
Afghanistan	x	–	–	–	–
Australia	–	–	x	–	–
Bangladesh	–	x	–	–	–
China	–	x	x	–	–
Hong Kong	–	x	–	–	–
Indonesia	–	x	x	–	–
Iran	–	x	x	–	–
Pakistan	–	x	–	–	–
Papua New Guinea	–	–	x	–	–
Philippines	–	x	–	–	–
Republic of Korea	–	x	–	–	–
Singapore	–	x	–	–	–
Sri Lanka	–	–	x	–	–
Thailand	–	x	–	–	–

Notes: The classification used here is based on the assessment of each country and not on any defined standard criteria.

x: Applicable
– : Not applicable

Table 38. Major contributors to degradation of water quality in some ESCAP regional countries

	Urban development			Agriculture	Silviculture	Mining	Recreation	Others
	Domestic wastes	Industrial wastes	Thermal wastes					
Afghanistan	x	x	x	–	–	–	–	–
Australia	–	–	–	x	–	x	–	–
Bangladesh	–	–	–	x	–	–	–	Sea water intrusion
China	x	x	–	–	–	–	–	–
Hong Kong	x	x	–	x	–	–	–	–
Indonesia	x	x	–	x	–	x	–	–
Iran	x	–	–	–	–	–	–	–
Pakistan	x	x	–	x	–	–	–	–
Papua New Guinea	x	x	–	–	–	–	–	Coffee/oil palm waste disposal
Philippines	x	x	–	x	x	x	–	–
Republic of Korea	x	x	–	–	–	–	–	–
Singapore	x	x	–	–	–	–	–	–
Sri Lanka	x	–	x	–	–	–	–	Solid waste used for land filling
Thailand	x	–	–	x	–	x	–	–

Notes: x: Applicable

      –: Not applicable

including both liquid wastes (sewage and sullage) and solid wastes (which are commonly deposited in waterways). Industrial natural organic pollution is sometimes severe in the vicinity of factories, for example, from cassava and palm oil processing plants, but the more important impact of industrial wastes is from discharges of oily substances (especially from refineries), of toxic heavy metals and of toxic synthetic organics. However, whereas in industrialized countries about half of the total pollution loading may come from industries, in the developing countries the proportion from industries in still relatively small. Nevertheless, where the governments have initiated pollution control regulatory programmes, these have tended to focus on industrial polluters rather than on people.

Illustrations of the above include (a) Laguna lake in the Philippines (4), where both sanitary and industrial waste loadings are severe, but where the industrial wastes pose the greater long-term hazards because of the effects on aquatic ecology (especially the lake fishery) of accumulated toxicity in bottom sediments, (b) the Inner Gulf region of the Gulf of Thailand (2), where the major problem is the impact on fishery reproduction from oxygen depletion due to heavy organic waste discharges (from both people and industries, especially cane sugar processing), but where bottom sediment toxicity is beginning to be significant, and (c) the Banjir canal at Jakarta (8), the raw water supply source for the municipal water supply system, which is heavily polluted by both sanitary and industrial wastes to

the extent the existing filter plants can scarcely cope with the problem.

Examples of severe pollution due to mining are the extensive damage in Thailand (9) to mangrove ecology and to recreational beaches due to silt discharges from tin mining, and extensive damage to agricultural operations in the Philippines from tailings discharges from mining operations at Baguio (especially during storms when the stored tailings are generally released to the waterways) (10).

The problems from runoff of agricultural chemicals include both fertilizers and pesticides and other toxic agricultural chemicals such as herbicides. An example is the situation in Indonesia where "hard" pesticides were widely used in the early 1970s. While these have since been replaced with degradable compounds, significant residuals of the hard pesticides accumulated and remain in the soils (11, 50).

Examples of salinity intrusion problems include (a) deltaic river systems used for municipal water supply, where abstractions of river water for irrigation or other uses have induced seawater intrusion, as at Calcutta and Bangkok, so that water supply intakes must be located far upstream, and (b) local salt water intrusion into fresh water aquifers due to overpumping, as at Bangkok.

Another important source of organic pollution is from livestock farms, especially piggeries. In some provinces of the Philippines, for example, the total organic waste discharge from piggeries equals that from people (12). This poses major problems not only in terms of BOD or oxygen depleting capacity but for pathogen content.

B. IMPACTS OF WATER QUALITY DEGRADATION

1. Disease hazards

The pollution discharges noted above result in damage or impairments to virtually every beneficial water use (table 39). Of these, the most important is the hazard of disease contamination. Community sewerage systems are mostly non-existent in the developing countries in the region. Hence excreta disposal is through individual subsurface disposal units, such as at Jakarta (3, 13), where most of the excreta go into individual leaching pits (and in the more affluent areas, into individual septic tank/leaching

systems). While the bulk of the pits function effectively, under present conditions a significant percentage do not, especially in the rainy season, owing to high ground water tables and/or impermeable soils. As a result, the local shallow ground waters and the community environment in general, especially in slum or poor-people areas, are heavily contaminated. The previously mentioned Banjir canal, the major raw water supply source for the Jakarta municipal water system, is believed to be one of the most contaminated water supply sources in use by a major city anywhere. A "saving factor" at Jakarta is that virtually every family boils its drinking water, whether taken from local shallow wells or from the municipal system. Even so, such boiling is not effective for reducing other contamination hazards, including insect vectors circulating between faecal materials and foods.

Another problem stems from direct discharge of faecal waste into waterways which are also used directly for drink-

Table 39. Problems relating to or induced by degradation of water quality in some ESCAP regional countries

	Water-related diseases	Unidentified local diseases	Loss of fish and related resources	Damage to agricultural crops	Shortage of municipal and industrial water supplies	Increased cost of industrial production	Eutrophication	Damage to recreational areas	Others
Afghanistan	b	–	–	–	a	–	–	b	–
Australia	f	f	f	e	f	f	f	f	–
Bangladesh	d	–	d	d	e	d	unknown	unknown	–
China	–	–	–	–	–	–	–	–	–
Hong Kong	f	f	f	f	e	e	e	e	–
Indonesia	d	–	e	d	d	e	e	e	–
Iran	b	unknown	d	unknown	a	unknown	unknown	e	–
Pakistan	unknown	unknown	unknown	e	unknown	unknown	unknown	f	Saline ground water intrusion (from irrigated lands)
Papua New Guinea	a	e	f	f	f	f	f	f	–
Philippines	e	unknown	e	e	e	f	f	e	–
Republic of Korea	e	f	f	e	e	e	e	e	–
Singapore	f	f	f	f	f	f	f	f	Increased cost of water treatment
Sri Lanka	moderate throughout the country	f	e	e	e	e	e	f	–
Thailand	d	f	e	e	e	unknown	e	d	–

Notes: a: Widespread areas, serious, throughout the year
b: Widespread areas, serious, certain seasons only
c: Limited areas, serious, throughout the year

d: Limited areas, serious, certain seasons only
e: Limited areas, moderate or negligible
f: Almost none
–: Not indicated

ing water. The situation in Lake Lanao in Mindanao in the Philippines is a typical example (14).

In general, excreta disposal is only partially managed in most developing countries and as a result rates of enteric communicable disease are high everywhere.

An interesting example of an extreme sanitation problem due to excreta discharge is at Chonburi municipality in Thailand. The homes in a portion of the city are located in a coastal zone where they are elevated over marshy areas which are no longer flushed by the sea. A recent WHO/ GTZ* study proposed to solve this problem by filling in these areas under the homes with refuse (15).

Some countries in the ESCAP region do utilize public sewerage systems to varying degrees, but most urban areas are not sewered and will so remain for the foreseeable future. At Manila, for example, the first stages of construction of a comprehensive metropolitan sewerage system are underway, and when implemented this system will do much to "clean up" community sanitation hazards in the "core" area of the city where the sewers are located. At Seoul, planning is underway (7) for sewerage improvements which will reduce contamination hazards in the Han river, perhaps sufficiently to permit safe recreational use of the river.

2. Recreation, aesthetics and eutrophication

Recreational uses are closely related to the disease contamination hazard noted above. Existing contamination in congested urban zones has virtually eliminated safe recreational use of many waterways, for example, the Chao Phya river below Bangkok, Laguna lake in the Philippines and the rivers in Jakarta and Surabaya. Other examples of pollution events affecting recreational uses in the region include (a) several instances of oil pollution (presumably from ship discharges) at Pattaya and other beaches along the Eastern Seaboard zone of the Gulf of Thailand (17), (b) sewage pollution of the main recreational beach at Songkhla in southern Thailand (18) and (c) degradation of beaches along the southern coast of Phuket island in Thailand by silt discharges from tin mining (9). The Phuket pollution is especially serious as it has effectively lowering the quality of the best beaches of Phuket, along the southern coast, from "international standards class" to "ordinary class".

While recreational use has not received much attention in governmental priorities, such attention is beginning with the recognition that this potential can be of real significance to the tourist industry and to the "poor-people sector" of the total community population.

---

* Deutsche Gesellschaft fur Technische Zusammenarkeit (German Agency for Technical Co-operation)

Closely related to recreational use is the problem of eutrophication due to discharge of nutrients, mostly from sanitary wastes. This commonly results in prolific growth of water hyacinths and other vegetation which has literally blocked numerous waterways from further use for navigation. At Laguna lake in the Philippines eutrophication has also been judged responsible for massive fish kills of *bangus,* which represents a large-scale lake squaculture industry. This problem seems destined to become increasingly more serious in the future.

3. Fisheries and wildlife

Fishery values are, of course, seriously affected in heavily polluted zones. In the Upper Gulf of Thailand, for example, a rich fishery reproduction zone, especially for shellfish, it has been estimated that perhaps half of this resource has been lost owing mainly to pollution over the past four decades (1, 19). Another example of loss in fishery reproduction resources is that of Segara Anakan, a large estuarine mangrove swamp complex on the south coast of Java, where silt discharges from upstream watershed development have filled up much of the lagoon in only a few decades (20).

The hazards to fishery reproduction zones include oxygen depletion due to natural organic wastes and, perhaps even more serious, the accumulation of toxic substances in bottom sediments. For this reason, the solution to the pollution in Laguna lake in the Philippines appears to depend upon the use of interceptors to collect industrial waste discharges to permit export of these to the sea via the metropolitan Manila sewerage system (4). The comprehensive plan to create a major new urban/industrial complex, recently completed by the National Economic and Social Development Board in Thailand for the Eastern Seabroad zone along the Gulf of Thailand, includes special attention to the use of marine waste disposal technology which will not impare the offshore fishery reproduction areas (21).

In the public mind, it is the fish kills that occur periodically, such as those at Palembang mentioned above, which are spectacular and seemingly most damaging. Actually, damage to the reproduction zones represents a much more serious hazard in the long run. Massive fish kills of note in the ESCAP region in recent years include those at several locations in Indonesia in the early 1970s due to pesticide runoff and periodic kills of cultivated *bangus* in Laguna lake as well as mercury-induced kills in Japan. Even Tonga experienced a serious kill of marine species at the capital of Nuku'alofa in 1979 due to an oil spill from a pipeline transferring oil from ship to shore (22).

In addition to natural fisheries and aquatic ecology, terrestial wildlife can be adversely affected by degradation in water quality (25). Generally, however, these effects have received little attention.

4. Municipal and industrial water supplies

This is another important aspect of pollution. The situation at Jakarta has already been mentioned. Another serious problem in Indonesia is at Surabaya, where the main water supply source, the local river, is heavily contaminated with industrial wastes (23). Pollution of Laguna lake near Manila has led to virtual abandonment of earlier plans to use this water as a supplemental water supply for Manila (4). Continuing salinity intrusion at Bangkok has led to progressive abandonment of wells previously serving good quality water (24).

It is generally possible to remove pollutants from water supply sources, using conventional treatment methods (usually rapid sand filtration), to a considerable degree, but when the loadings become excessive the result is water which may contain disease organisms or toxic chemicals. Even when the pollutants can be removed, this is accomplished at considerable extra treatment plant costs involved in the use of increased coagulant dosages, increased turbidity loadings onto filters and increased chlorination.

5. Irrigation

Pollutants in some cases have seriously impaired the usefulness of irrigation water supplies. A common problem

is oil pollution from refineries or other petroleum operations, such as have occurred in Indonesia (23). Another common problem is discharge of mine tailings into waterways, as at Baguio as noted above.

C. NATIONAL WATER QUALITY MANAGEMENT POLICY

1. Awareness of need for water quality management

The current state of awareness of the need for water quality management can be rated as moderate in most countries which replied to the questionnaire. In almost all the countries the basis for such a rating included the number and extent of newspaper reports, the coverage of the problem by the mass media and the number of complaints by those affected. As noted in table 40, common water quality management activities in the countries of the region include public and educational campaigns and agitating for the passage of appropriate legislation. Eleven countries have undertaken a wide range of activities in this respect, while three countries are still in earlier stages of planning.

In most countries in the region, as elsewhere, recognition or awareness of the need for water quality management has been associated with the establishment and implementation of national environmental protection

Table 40. Action being taken for water quality management in some ESCAP regional countries

	Agitating for passage of legislation (a)	Legal proceedings for damages (b)	Court injunction (c)	Public and educational campaign (d)	Others (e)	Which of the actions have been successful? (a, b, c, d, e)
Afghanistan	–	–	–	x	–	d
Australia	x	–	–	x	–	–
Bangladesh	x	–	–	x	Augmentation of major river flows	a, d, e
China	x	x	x	x	–	a, b, c, d
Hong Kong	x	–	–	x	Potable water quality legislation	a, d, e
Indonesia	x	–	–	x	Development of appropriate technology	a, d, e
Iran	–	–	–	–	–	a
Pakistan	–	–	–	–	Improvement of poor ground water quality	e
Papua New Guinea	x	–	–	x	–	a
Philippines	x	x	x	x	–	–
Republic of Korea	–	x	–	x	–	d
Singapore	–	x	–	x	Legislative enforcement control of land use	e
Sri Lanka	–	–	–	x	–	–
Thailand	x	–	–	x	–	none

Notes: x: Applicable
       –: Not applicable or not indicated

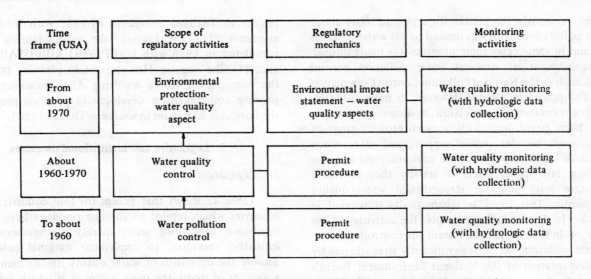

Figure 19. Evolution of governmental programmes in water quality control

Source: Reference 43.

Table 41. Availability and general objectives of national policy for water quality management and its consistency with national water policy in some ESCAP regional countries

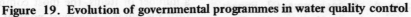

	Avail-ability of QMP	Plan to establish QMP available	QMP stated by highest legislative body	QMP implied in legislative documents	QMP is an integral part of NWP	QMP independent but consistent to NWP	General objectives of QMP		
							Improve water quality	Maintain present conditions	Prevent further degradation of water quality
Afghanistan	–	x	–	–	–	–	–	–	–
Australia	x	–	–	–	–	–	–	–	–
Bangladesh	x	–	–	x	–	–	–	–	–
China	x	–	–	x	–	–	–	–	–
Hong Kong	x	–	–	x	–	–	–	–	–
Indonesia	x	–	x	–	x	–	x	x	x
Iran	x	–	–	x	–	–	x	x	x
Pakistan		x (at least for irrigated agriculture)	–	–	–	–	–	–	–
Papua New Guinea	x	–	–	x	x	–	x	–	x
Philippines	x	–	–	x	–	partly consistent but there are plans to remedy inconsistency	x	–	x
Republic of Korea	x	–	x	x	–	partly consistent but there are plans to remedy inconsistency	–	–	x
Singapore	x	–	x	–	x	–	x	–	–
Sri Lanka	x	–	–	x	–	–	x	–	–
Thailand	x	–	–	x	x	–	x	x	x

Notes: QMP: national policy for water quality management.
NWP: national water policy.
x : Applicable
– : Not applicable or not indicated

agencies. Previously the burden for trying to move ahead in water pollution control was limited to the water agencies *per se,* and in some cases some progress was made through the establishment of national water pollution control agencies, such as the National Pollution Control Commission of the Philippines in 1964. However, in most countries national environmental protection agencies have subsequently been established, with a much broader range of interest, much broader public support and often much more "clout", and now that these environmental agencies are shifting into higher levels of activity they provide a much more solid base for strengthened water quality management. This trend is schematically illustrated in figure 19. In Thailand, for example, the activities of the Ministry of Industry's permit system for controling industrial waste pollution has been significantly strengthened by the implementation of the National Environment Board's requirements for preparation of environmental impact assessments for all new major projects including industries.

2. Policy objectives and relationship to water resource development

Almost all the countries which replied to the questionnaire have national policies for water quality management except for two countries which plan to establish such a policy in the near future (table 41). In all countries, the policy is either stated by the highest legislative body or implied in certain legislative documents. The main objectives of the national policy in 11 countries are to improve water quality. Of the 11, seven incorporate the objective of preventing further deterioration of water quality, while four of these seven also include the objective of maintenance of present conditions.

In nine countries, the national policy for water quality management is an integral part of a national water resources development policy. Only in two countries is the national policy for water quality management independent from, but partly consistent with, the national water resources development policy. These countries have plans to remedy the inconsistencies.

All the countries indicate awareness of the necessity of a national policy for water quality management which is co-ordinated with policies for water resources development. In Thailand, for example, the joint policy is spelled out in a policy document prepared jointly by the National Economic and Social Development Board and the National Environment Board (26) and in a recently issued comprehensive policy document issued by the National Environment Board (27). Only in the past few years, however, has this joint development-cum-environmental protection policy been reflected in major comprehensive land use planning projects. These include the eastern seaboard

project in Thailand completed in 1982 with World Bank assistance (21), the Laguna lake basin planning project completed in 1978 with UNDP/WHO/ADB/USAID assistance (4), the ongoing Han river basin planning project in the Republic of Korea involving ADB assistance, and a pending comprehensive development planning project for the Songkhla lake basin in southern Thailand (28).

3. Legislative and institutional measures

a. *Legislation*

Table 42 shows that except for four countries all the countries which replied to the questionnaire have specific legislation concerning water quality management. The legislative measures, to implement national policy and achieve the objectives of water quality management, cover a number of items, the most common of which are regulatory measures. The most popular regulatory measures are those for the establishment of water quality standards, the issuance of permits and licenses, land-use control and growth management.

Planning and management measures are included in the legislation of eight countries. The legislation of five countries covers almost all the items listed in the questionnaire, namely institution building and financial, planning, management and regulatory measures. In one country water quality management legislation is limited only to regulatory measures. Most of the agencies responsible for water quality management are of the planning, management, monitoring and surveillance type. Some of them are also responsible for construction and operation and maintenance. Only in three countries are these agencies in charge of financing.

A common problem in the region is the lack of enforcement mechanisms for making the legislation truly effective. In a number of the countries the existing legislation is excellent, comparable to that used in industrialized countries, but enforcement is often lacking because the governments have not yet been willing to make the necessary commitments in financing and controls. Thus, much of the legislation represents ideals to be aimed at rather than realistic objectives. In general the primary problem is the limited budgets made available to the water quality management agencies.

It is of interest to note that, while the international agencies have conducted a number of surveys on existing water quality management legislation (50), there has been no known evaluation of the extent of enforcement.

b. *Institutions*

Table 42 also presents the situation regarding institutional measures. All the countries have agencies or similar

Table 42. Legislative and institutional measures to implement national policy and achieve objectives of water quality management in some ESCAP regional countries

	Availability of specific legislation concerning WQM	Availability of agencies responsible for WQM		Number of agencies involved	Type of co-ordination among various agencies	Availability of adequate legal authority	Availability of adequate financial capacity
		At national level	At local level				
Afghanistan	–	–	x	1			
Australia	x	at state level		17	(1) Co-ordinating Committee (2) Voluntary consultations	x	x
Bangladesh	x	x	x	5	Voluntary consultations	x	x
China	x	x	x	2	Voluntary consultations	x	x
Hong Kong	–	–	–	6	Co-ordinating agency specially established for this purpose	x	x
Indonesia	–	x	x	5	(1) Co-ordinating agency (2) Co-ordinating Committee (3) Voluntary consultations	x	
Iran	x	x	x	2	Voluntary consultations		
Pakistan	–	x	x	7 Six of them are irrigation agencies	(1) Co-ordinating Committee (2) Voluntary consultations		
Papua New Guinea	x	x	x	2	Voluntary consultations		
Philippines	x	x	x	2	Voluntary consultations		
Republic of Korea	x	x	x	4	(1) Co-ordinating Committee (2) Voluntary consultations	x	
Singapore	x	x	x	2	(1) Co-ordinating agency (2) Voluntary consultations	x	x
Sri Lanka	–	x	x	2	Voluntary consultations	–	–
Thailand	x	x	–	4	Co-ordinating Committee	–	–

Notes: WQM: Water quality management.
 x: Applicable
 –: Not applicable or not indicated

bodies responsible for water quality management either at the national or at the local levels or both. They range from one to 17 in number with co-ordination among these agencies generally carried out by a co-ordinating body or through voluntary consultations or both. Only three countries have established special agencies for co-ordination purposes. Generally, however, much has to be done to improve co-ordination among the various agencies interested or engaged in water quality management. The lack of a single agency responsible for water quality management at the national level is a problem faced by most countries everywhere.

The primary reason for the multiplicity of agencies is the fact that water resources development has been historically compartmentalized among various single-purpose development agencies, such as hydropower, irrigation,

water supply and fishery agencies. While the term "multipurpose" is now commonly used for describing water resource development projects, such projects would better be described as "partial multipurpose". The lead implementing agency is usually single-purpose and a much lesser level of attention is usually given to the other purposes, and co-ordination, to try to change the behavioral patterns of the existing agencies, is not easy. For example, in Thailand, co-ordination is managed through a national committee which operates under the auspices of the National Economic and Social Development Board, and through this mechanism some real measure of co-ordination is obtained. In the Philippines, the National Water Resources Council has the legal basis for co-ordination, but the numerous other agencies involved have their own legal bases for continuing pretty much to operate on their own. Only Indonesia has a single water resource development agency, the Directorate

General of Water Resources Development, but even this agency is only partially comprehensive; for example, it is hardly involved in urban water supply projects.

Looking to the future, it seems that the best hope for achieving true multipurpose water resources development, including comprehensive attention to water quality, lies with the national economic planning agency and the national environmental agency. The role of the national environmental agency, including participation and leadership in comprehensive regional development planning and including judicious use of the environmental impact report requirement, seems to offer a great deal of promise toward achieving this goal.

4. Technical strategies and measures

a. *Pollution control facilities*

Table 43 shows that the primary approach used for water quality control in most countries is the requirement of facilities for treating wastes including sanitary and industrial wastes. However, as previously noted, in most of the developing countries, excluding those which are relatively advanced, there are few public sewerage systems, hence few sewage treatment plants, and dependence for excreta disposal is placed largely on use of individual subsurface dis-

posal systems which are only partially satisfactory. This commonly results in gross contamination of the community environment. This problem is assessed by the recent World Bank series of manuals on "Appropriate Technology for Water Supply and Sanitation" (29), which have already had a remarkable impact on development of country planning (30). The answer is not in building of comprehensive sewerage systems, which will hardly be affordable in the foreseeable future, but in limited use of sewerage systems to serve community "core" areas, together with much more careful use of appropriate subsurface disposal units so that virtually all of these systems can function effectively. A pioneer project of this type is the ongoing Jakarta sewerage and sanitation project (31), and the methodology used in planning the project, including the field survey technology, was recently presented as another manual in the World Bank series (32).

With respect to wastes management of industrial, as previously noted, industrial and commercial establishments, are generally more subject to management than are communities in the developing countries. Most point-source treatment systems which have been installed over the past decade in the region have been for either industrial or commercial establishments, especially in the less advanced developing countries. This is the case, for example, in Thailand, in Indonesia and in the Philippines (36).

Table 43. Technical strategies for implementation of national policy and achievement of objectives of water quality management in some ESCAP countries

	Municipal waste water treatment	Industrial waste water treatment	Residual water management	Urban storm water management	Non-point source management	Water quality modelling
Afghanistan	–	–	–	–	–	–
Australia	x	x	x	x	x	x
Bangladesh	x	x	–	x	–	–
China	x	x	x	–	x	–
Hong Kong	x	x	x	x	x	x
Indonesia	x	x	–	x	–	–
Iran	x	x	–	x	–	–
Pakistan	x	x	–	x	–	–
Papua New Guinea	x	x	–	x	–	–
Philippines	–	x	–	x	–	–
Republic of Korea	x	x	x	x	x	x
Singapore	x	x	–	x	x	–
Sri Lanka	x	x	–	x	–	–
Thailand	x	x	x	x	x	x

Notes: x: Applicable
      –: Not applicable or not indicated

As noted earlier, water pollution problems are generally much more intense in the dry than in the rainy season, so much so that little priority can be expected to be given to rainy reason problems in the foreseeable future. This means that sewerage systems which are built will generally be of the combined sewer type, that is, a single system of sewers will be used both for storm drainage and waste disposal. Examples are given in recently completed feasibility reports for Chonburi municipality in Thailand (15) and Magalang municipality in the Philippines (33).

Reclamation or reuse of treated wastes as a supplemental water supply is an alternative strategy which has thus far been used only rarely in the region but which seems promising for the future. The existing installations mostly involve reuse of waste waters for irrigation, including one case in Thailand where treated pulp and paper mill waste is used for irrigation of sugar cane.

Additional control measures have been used in limited instances. These include in-stream aeration by mechanical means, land disposal, dredging to remove contaminated sediments from waterways and low flow augmentation.

b. *Elements of water quality management programmes*

The survey data indicate the following to be the most commonly used measures for assessing water quality problems and evaluating needs for control:

(i) Monitoring and surveillance of water quality, including:

(1) Status of quality of waterways, including water column and bottom sediments;

(2) Information on amounts and characteristics of pollutants (communities, industries, and commercial establishments);

(3) Information on amounts and characteristics of pollutants from non-point sources (including agricultural runoff and erosion);

(4) Hydrology of affected waterways;

(5) Beneficial uses of affected waterways;

(ii) Establishment of water quality standards;

(iii) Regulatory programmes;

(iv) Public information and education programmes;

(v) Establishment of appropriate data banks (storage and retrieval systems for water quality-cum-hydrology data) and use of these data in mathematical modelling;

(vi) Strengthening of institutions;

(vii) Planning of pollution abatement measures and programmes, including inventories and analysis of waste loadings, preparation of appropriate landuse policies, assignment of priorities by geographical region for needs for abatement measures, establishment of goals and setting of target abatement dates.

The listing above, which is illustrated in figure 20, represents measures which generally are being used only in beginning stages, especially in the less advanced developing countries in the region, but which are intended to be progressively more utilized. Examples are cited below.

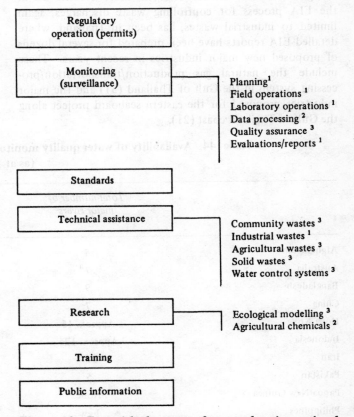

Elements of comprehensive water quality control programme — **Components of elements**

- Regulatory operation (permits)
- Monitoring (surveillance)
  - Planning[1]
  - Field operations[1]
  - Laboratory operations[1]
  - Data processing[2]
  - Quality assurance[3]
  - Evaluations/reports[1]
- Standards
- Technical assistance
  - Community wastes[3]
  - Industrial wastes[1]
  - Agricultural wastes[3]
  - Solid wastes[3]
  - Water control systems[3]
- Research
  - Ecological modelling[3]
  - Agricultural chemicals[2]
- Training
- Public information

Figure 20. Essential elements of comprehensive national water quality control programme

[1] Existing
[2] Beginning activity
[3] Planned for next phase

Source: Reference 43.

c. *Regulatory measures*

These include both (i) use of waste discharge permit systems for communities, industries and other establishments, and (ii) use of the environmental impact assessment report requirement (co-ordinated with item (i)). Permit systems have been utilized in the Philippines for two decades by the National Pollution Control Commission (36) and over the past decade in Thailand by the Ministry of Industry (35), but thus far their use has been limited essentially to control of industrial wastes. A similar system is being considered by the Ministry of Population and Environment of Indonesia.

The advent of the environmental impact assessment (EIA) or statement has served to strengthen permit control systems because the EIA requirement itself is a kind of permit mechanics which includes water quality as well as other environmental parameters. The relationship is shown in figure 19. In south-east Asia, the most effective use of the EIA process for controlling waste discharges, again limited to industrial wastes, has been in Thailand, where detailed EIA reports have been prepared for several dozens of proposed new major industries in recent years. These include the natural gas production/transportation/processing system in the Gulf of Thailand (51) and the major industries proposed for the eastern seaboard project along the Gulf of Thailand coast (21).

A common and complex problem is how to accept and regulate industrial waste effluents to be discharged into public sewerage systems. Reference 34 is a manual prepared for such use in Indonesia and is considered appropriate for most developing countries. This includes guidelines for use by the municipal sewerage authority for determining the extent of pretreatment which may be needed before an industry discharges its wastes into the public sewer, and on fixing reasonable tariffs or charges to be paid by the industry.

d. *Monitoring/data banks/modelling*

The present status of water quality monitoring in the ESCAP region is summarized in tables 44 and 45. It is noted that, while most of these programmes in their early stages tend to be limited to use of physical and chemical parameters and to sampling of the water column, there is increasing recognition that to get a competent assessment the programme must also include biological parameters and sampling of bottom sediments. This recognizes that, whereas the water column samples usually represent transitory events, the bottom sediment samples generally show the accumulated or chronic effects of pollution in the

Table 44. Availability of water quality monitoring systems in some ESCAP regional countries (as at 1981)

	Total number of major rivers	Number of major rivers with permanent monitoring systems installed	Total number of permanent monitoring systems regularly operated on major rivers
Afghanistan	4	None	None
Australia	7[a]	7	7
Bangladesh	9	6	80
China	7	7	
Hong Kong	Approx. 15	None[b]	None
Indonesia	Approx. 125	79	132
Iran	11	3	27
Pakistan	5	2	1
Papua New Guinea	None	None	None
Philippines	Few	Few	Few
Republic of Korea	6	6(5)[c]	205(23)
Singapore	7	7	30
Sri Lanka	—	1	—
Thailand	4	3[d]	3

[a]   Rivers with a catchment area exceeding 100,000 km^2 or with annual discharge exceeding 10^{10} cu m/year.

[b]   No permanent systems exist currently but several planned and budgeted.

[c]   In parenthesis — automatic monitoring systems.

[d]   Monitoring systems with manual operation.

—:   Not indicated

Table 45. Stream-water quality parameters usually monitored in some ESCAP regional countries

	Water temperature	PH	BOD	COD	TDC	SS	EC	Coliform count	DO	Others	Availability of correlation of monitoring and hydrometeorological data
Afghanistan	–	–	–	–	–	–	–	–	–		
Australia	x	x	x	x	x	x	x	–	x	–	At some stations
Bangladesh	x	x	x	x	x	x	x	x	x	Note 1	At some stations
China	x	–	x	–	x	x	–	x	x	–	At some stations
Hong Kong	x	x	x	x	x	x	x	Somewhat	x	Note 2	–
Indonesia	x	x	x	x	x	x	x	x	x	Note 3	At most stations
Iran	x	x	x	x	x	x	x	x	x	Note 4	At some stations
Pakistan	x	x	x	x	x	x	x	x	x	–	At some stations
Papua New Guinea	x	x	–	x	x	x	x	x	x	Note 5	No co-ordination
Philippines	x	x	x	x	x	x	x	x	x	–	No co-ordination
Republic of Korea	x	x	x	x	–	x	x	x	x	Turbidity	At some stations
Singapore	x	x	x	x	x	x	x	x	x	–	At some stations
Sri Lanka	x	x	x	x	x	x	x	x	x	–	At some stations
Thailand	x	x	x	x	x	x	x	xx	x	Note 6	At some stations

x: Parameters monitored
– : Not monitored

Note 1: Chloride, ammonia, nitrite, nitrate, orthophosphate and alkalinity.
Note 2: Flow rates are measured in a few streams.
Note 3: Major cations and anions, heavy metals, synthetic organics, biologic prarameters for bottom sediments.
Note 4: Nitrate, phosphate, turbidity and heavy metals.
Note 5: Only limited samples taken over several years plus some chemical constituents.
Note 6: Salinity, total solid, nitrogen, phosphorus, heavy metals and pesticides.

water column much better than water column measurements *per se*. There is also increasing recognition of the need for bioassays for measuring toxicity, both gross toxicity and specific toxicities.

Systematic water quality monitoring, as practiced in the industrialized countries, has not yet been possible in most developing countries, including those in the ESCAP region, owing to lack of budgetary support. However, a number of special monitoring programmes have been carried out in the region extending over periods of from one to ten years. In Thailand, these include (a) a monitoring programme for evaluating marine water quality and ecology in the Gulf of Thailand as related to a proposed nuclear power plant, believed to be the first such comprehensive study in south-east Asia (39), (b) extensive water quality monitoring of Songkhla lake in southern Thailand over a 10-year period by the Department of Fisheries (52), (c) periodic monitoring of marine water quality, including toxic substances accumulations in bottom sediments, in the Inner Gulf of Thailand, under the auspices of the National Research Council (55) and (d) a one-year detailed water quality monitoring programme of beach waters at Pattaya (41). A comprehensive regional environmental monitoring programme, with emphasis on water quality, is proposed for the eastern seaboard region, to be carried out by the National Environment Board with World Bank sponsorship. This will be part of the implementation of the recently completed Eastern Seaboard Regional Planning Project conducted by the National Economic and Social Development Board, which represents Thailand's first effort on comprehensive development planning for an entire region (21).

In the Philippines the National Pollution Control Commission has carried out limited continuing water quality monitoring in major rivers and other waterways for many years (36), but the only comprehensive water quality monitoring was the extensive programme of detailed limnological monitory included in the UNDP/WHO sponsored project completed in 1978 for preparing a comprehensive development plan for the Laguna lake basin near Manila (4). In connection with the new metropolitan sewerage system now under construction, continuing detailed water quality monitoring will be carried out in Manila Bay by the Metropolitan Water and Sewerage System together with the National Pollution Control System (6, 36).

The most systematic approach to continuing water quality monitoring on a national scale is in Indonesia, where the Directorate General of Water Resources Development, through its Division of Environmental Quality in the Institute of Hydraulic Engineering, has made excellent progress over the past decade (42). This programme includes periodic monitoring of selected major rivers throughout the country plus numerous special studies (43, 44). Of these, the ongoing programme at Segara Anakan, which is a large mangrove swamp complex on the south coast of Java, is the most comprehensive (20) and includes detailed use of physical, chemical, biological, and hydrological parameters.

None of the less advanced developing countries has as yet established an effective data bank programme but all are considering this step. A beginning effort has been made in the Philippines as part of the Laguna lake basin planning project (4), which utilized the Canadian/GEMS* Naquadat system for collating the detailed monitoring data and adapting it for use for ecological monitoring. A major problem is that water quality data banks, to be meaningful, must be co-ordinated with water quantity/hydrology data banks, and often the two systems develop independently and are not compatible. In addition, there is little agreement on which data bank systems are most appropriate. In the Philippines, for example, the Naquadat system is not compatible with the hydrological data bank system established by the National Water Resources Council (36).

With reference to modelling of water quality data, which amounts to modelling of aquatic ecology, the Laguna lake basin planning project made a pioneering effort (4), with assistance from the Corvallis Laboratory of the United States Environmental Protection Agency (EPA), but the model was not completed when the project finished and little has been done since. The Asian Institute of Technology at Bangkok and the Institute of Hydraulic Engineering at Bandung are now working with the Athens Laboratory of EPA to explore use of the Athens technology in southeast Asia.

One of the most common problems hampering development of analytical technology for water quality in many countries in the region is lack of attention to the quality of the data. There is little interest in reviewing laboratory reports to check the validity/consistancy of the data, although the reports are often "certified correct" by high-ranking officials with advanced degrees and are signed by laboratory staff. This is true even of the best laboratories

* Global Environmental Monitoring System.

with ample staff and excellent facilities. Very few of their reports which have been reviewed are found to be acceptable by international standards. For mineral analyses of water, for example, (a) the decimal points on the concentrations are often incorrect (especially in using sopisticated equipment where one reads the answer on a dial), (b) the total cations and total anions do not reasonably balance in terms of equivalent units, (c) the total dissolved solids values are inconsistent with the total magnitude indicated by the individual consistent analyses, (d) carbonate alkalinity values are reported at pH levels below 8.3, and (e) the significance of the precision of the analysis is ignored, thus a constituent is reported at 112.67 mg/1 when the analytical method when duplicated varies in the range of several per cent, etc.

e.   *Water quality standards*

This is the most difficult problem facing most of the national water pollution control regulatory agencies in their present stage of development in the ESCAP region. The problem involves very complex technology, involving setting effluent standards or criteria both for waste discharges and for the receiving waters, and involving the complex relationships between them. While a great deal of work has been done on the subject by EPA (involving costs of hundreds of millions of dollars), the resulting standards which have been set are hardly appropriate for most developing countries. However, EPA publications represent the only detailed data base available, hence they tend to be copied. The result is that many of the existing standards in the less advanced developing countries in the ESCAP region are idealistic rather than realistic, i.e., are not achievable, hence they are of little value for furthering regulatory programmes and often are of negative value.

An AIT study of 1973 (45) recognized this problem, and the Ministry of Industry of Thailand in 1980 updated its set of standards to be more realistic (35). In general, however, the situation is very confused. The urgent need is recognition that the EPA effort has produced virtually the entire data base needed to set appropriate standards in developing countries, so the problem is to make appropriate use of the data. The need is for a co-ordinated regional approach to the problem in order to develop appropriate guidelines. Such a step should greatly strengthen the programmes of the national regulatory agencies.

f.   *Regional planning*

National water quality regulatory agencies have done much to promote incorporation of the water quality parameter into regional planning in the industrialised countries, and in some cases have taken the lead in formulating regional economic development plans in the interest of protecting water quality. The Laguna lake basin planning project in the Philippines is an example in the ESCAP region.

The advent of national environmental protection agencies in virtually all countries has markedly changed the picture and has led to increasing recognition of the need for preparing regional development plans making use of both economic and environmental parameters. This policy is spelled out for Thailand in the paper prepared for ESCAP in 1980 jointly by the National Economic and Social Development Board and the National Environment Board (26). This policy has since been implemented in the Eastern Seaboard Planning Project conducted by NESDB with World Bank assistance (21), which represent's Thailand's first effort at comprehensive regional development planning. A second such project is now being implemented for the Songkhla lake basin in southern Thailand with ADB assistance.

The most impressive of this new type of project is that underway in the Han river basin of the Republic of Korea with ADB assistance. Another pioneering project is that at Segara Anakan in Java, which has the objective of preparing an optimal plan for utilizing the existing Segara Anakan estuarine mangrove swamp complex considering both aquatic and land cropping potentials (20). In both these projects water quality parameters are of paramount importance.

g. *Strengthening of institutions*

Table 46 summarizes activities in the 14 countries in education and training, including ongoing water quality management projects which represent "on-the-job" case studies by which local professional personnel can gain expertise in applying their academic knowledge. As known by the table, Indonesia has taken the lead with the largest number of projects, in most cases with support from international assistance agencies. Experience has shown the need, in practically all these cases, for participation of an outside expert for guiding the project so it will achieve its desired results including maximum technology transfer.

It is also being recognized that, in addition to working on local projects, the local professionals would benefit greatly from on-the-job apprentice type experience working in an agency doing similar work in an industrialized

Table 46. *Education, training and research activities* to implement national policy and achieve objectives of water quality management in some ESCAP countries

	Formal education	Non-formal education	Training	Research	Water quality management projects
Afghanistan	–	–	–	–	–
Australia	x	–	x	x	–
Bangladesh	x	x	x	x	–
China	x	–	x	x	–
Hong Kong	x	–	x	x	–
Indonesia	x	x	x	x	Five projects involving water quality management aspects with support of UNDP, ADB and World Bank by providing experts, training and equipment
Iran	x	–	x	x	–
Pakistan	x	–	x	x	–
Papua New Guinea	x	–	x	–	Two projects involving monitoring and water quality management standards with full support of private companies
Philippines	x	–	x	x	One water quality management project supported partly by World Bank
Republic of Korea	x	x	x	x	–
Singapore	x	x	x	x	One water quality management project financed partly by ADB
Sri Lanka	x	x	x	x	–
Thailand	x	x	x	x	–

x: Applicable
– : Not applicable or not indicated

country, under the supervision of experts engaged in successful water quality programmes. This means, not making a trip as an "observer", but serving as an actual working member of the agency's staff. The underlying principle is that it is very difficult to acquire expertise without working under the supervision of experts with experience in successful management of programmes in the subject areas of concern.

One illustration of this problem is in the monitoring programmes described above. Review of these shows that, while the agencies involved have excellent physical facilities, including sophisticated equipment for sampling and analysis, plus staff with good academic credentials (including certificates of attendence at seminars/workshops/conferences), they do not have staff experienced in checking to ensure the reliability of the data, or in the need to obtain comparable data on hydrology parameters, or in collating and interpreting the data so it will be meaningful for development planning. Often the project reports tend to be little more than compilations or tabulations of the data.

Another point is the need for the professional individual to invest some of his time in keeping aware of international developments in his field, most of which are in the industrialized countries. This means establishing effective communication with international counterparts, obtaining key publications, learning to be fluent in English and building up meaningful reference libraries. All of these are more or less alien concepts, not part of their local educational backgrounds, but they are essential where dependence on technology developed in the industrialized countries is critical for success.

The planning of local research programmes is also an area of concern. Too often these programmes attempt research, with very small budgets, on subjects where large research projects on the same subject have already been carried out elsewhere. The need is to find out first what has been done already and then to plan an appropriate programme suited to the local needs. For illustration, some investigators evaluating the effects of silt on aquatic ecology in the region seem unaware of the major contribution in acquiring basic data on the subject made by the United States Corps of Engineers (46). The "rationale" is that the conditions are different in the local country, which of course is correct. The problem is lack of recognition that the studies done elsewhere furnish data bases which can be very valuable, properly interpreted, for evaluating the local situation, and which in no way can be reproduced locally because of the costs involved, and lack of recognition of the complexities involved and of the very limited work that can be done, as compared to expectations, with the budget proposed. Very few of the research proposals which were

examined have included either a competent review of the work already done elsewhere or a competent description of the various work tasks making up the research study.

Still another need is for training of professional staff in the spectrum of international assistance agencies interested in helping promote water quality management in developing countries, including the types and amounts of assistance available, how to keep up to date on this, how to prepare competent proposals, and the need in preparing project reports to include summaries of them in English in order to build up a reservoir of information on studies done for use in supporting future research proposal applications. An assessment of this problem was made by WHO for the Ministry of Human Settlements of the Philippines in 1980 (37), and some guidelines on preparing proposals were prepared for use by the Institute of Hydraulic Engineering at Bandung (38).

h. *Economics and financing*

Table 47 summarizes the data obtained on the financing of pollution control facilities and systems. As indicated, this field is in its beginning stages in the less advanced developing countries. Of the lessons learned over the past two decades, the most important is that self-financing is essential for successful replication, even for slum areas. The pioneering Jakarta Sewerage and Sanitation Project (31) illustrates this approach. However, in many cases subsidization in slum areas is needed in the initial stages of development for demonstrating the feasibility of the proposed infrastructure improvements. Public facilities generally will be financed by a combination of taxes and rental charges.

D. SUMMARY OF MAJOR PROBLEMS AND CONSTRAINTS

More than 80 per cent of the replies indicated that the most common problems faced by the countries in the field of water quality management are the lack of funds for water quality management activities and the lack of coordination among various agencies involved in water quality management. A problem of almost equal importance is the lack of qualified experienced personnel and lack of knowledge on appropriate technology in the water quality management field.

Associated with these problems are the lack of institutions, technical facilities including laboratories and expert advisers for conducting water quality studies including training of local staff.

The third group of problems and constraints identified were the following:

Table 47. Economic and financial instruments for implementing national policy and achieving objectives of water quality management in some ESCAP regional countries

	Economic				Taxes	Financial				Bonuses
	Pricing policies	Effluent charges	Fines and penalties	Compensation by pollutor		Grants and subsidies by government	Loans for treatment technology	Tax concessions for treatment plants	Financial assistance for technology	
Afghanistan	–	–	–	–	–	–	–	–	–	–
Australia	x	x	x	x	–	x	x	x	–	–
Bangladesh	not yet applied although legal proposal exists									
China	–	–	x	x	–	–	–	–	–	–
Hong Kong	–	planned	x	–	–	x	–	–	–	–
Indonesia	–	–	–	–	–	–	–	–	–	–
Iran	–	–	–	–	–	–	–	–	–	–
Pakistan	–	–	–	–	–	–	–	–	–	–
Papua New Guinea	–	x	x	x	–	–	–	–	–	–
Philippines	–	–	x	x	–	–	–	–	–	–
Republic of Korea	–	x	x	x	x	–	x	x	–	–
Singapore	–	x	x	–	–	–	–	–	–	–
Sri Lanka	–	–	–	–	–	–	–	–	–	–
Thailand	–	–	–	–	x	x	–	–	x	–

x: Applicable
– : Not applicable or not indicated

1. Lack of awareness of the need for water quality management;

2. Lack of sufficient information on the existing status of degradation in water quality and on projections for the future;

3. No single body responsible for water quality management at the national level, hence lack of co-ordinated strategy for planning and achieving national water quality goals.

E. CONCLUSIONS AND RECOMMENDATIONS

1. Water quality management related to environmental protection and economic development planning

Based on the information and discussion presented above, it is concluded that, even though water quality management (which is closely related to management of wastes) has not in itself commanded a high priority in national development planning in most developing countries in the region, considerable progress has nevertheless been made in gaining public acceptance of the need for protecting water quality as an essential element in national development planning. Of major importance in this respect has been the establishment in virtually all countries over the past decade of national environmental protection agencies with levels of authority and with scope of interest much above the typical water pollution/quality control agency (see figure 19). Generally, the new environmental protection agencies represent "environmental planning counterparts" to the national economic/social development planning agencies which were established in most developing countries some two decades earlier. A primary objective of the environmental agency has been to gain due recognition for the environmental parameter in national development planning, that is, for the two agencies to work together to achieve economic-cum-environmental planning.

The environmental agencies have made good progress in a number of approaches, all of which have been and can be very helpful in advancing and strengthening national water quality management programmes simply because water quality is generally recognized to be one of the most important of all environmental quality parameters. The efforts of the environmental agencies which have been helpful include (a) promotion and sponsoring of economic-cum-environmental developing planning, with appropriate attention to water pollution/quality control, (b) use of the environmental impact assessment mechanics to strengthen the waste disposal regulatory programmes, including permit procedures, so that appropriate water quality control systems are built into new facilities at the outset when they are much more affordable, (c) establishment of appropriate water quality standards, including development of staff and facilities with the capabilities for doing this and (d) planning and implementation of public information and education programmes.

There is a need for national governments with the assistance of international agencies to focus attention on the specific problem of how to make optimal use of the national economic and environmental planning agencies for promoting co-operation with the existing national water control pollution/quality control and national water resources agencies in order to realize an effective national water quality management programme. The approach will of course vary from country to country depending on the existing institutional set-up but would require enlisting the assistance of the national economic and environmental planning agencies to help the water quality management agencies obtain governmental support, including funds for implementing the basic elements of an appropriate national water quality management programme as illustrated in figure 20.

The approach suggested above recognizes that achieving co-ordination of the existing national agencies affecting water quality management has proven to be a most difficult problem. Yet the "charters" for the national economic and environmental planning agencies encompass this potential, hence this opportunity should be utilized.

2. Critical needs

At the present stage of development of environmental and water quality management in the region, especially for the developing countries, the most important needs for assistance to these countries for the next decade of effort would seem to be the following.

(a) Provision of training to local personnel, involving working under the supervision of experts who have demonstrated ability for successful management of programmes in the areas of concern. This is believed to be the single most important problem hampering progressive development in the water quality management (and other environmental protection) fields;

(b) Implementation of adequate and properly designed national water quality monitoring programmes, including use of data banks and mathematical modelling

when appropriate, and continuing evaluation of the information to produce the "hard facts" on degradation of benefical water uses and resulting economic and socio-economic losses which are essential for making a convincing case for support from the decision-makers;

(c) Establishment of a flexible system of appropriate water quality standards to be usable throughout the region with suitable modifications for particular countries, including both effluent and receiving water standards. This is a problem which virtually all of the developing countries are now struggling with;

(d) Indentification of important potential water quality management projects, which would be eligible for consideration for external funding, and preparation of appropriate proposals, including making maximum use of local staff, and encouraging joint ventures between groups from different government agencies who can effectively participate on a co-operative basis;

(e) Promotion of new legislation where needed for a strengthening regulatory programmes, with due recognition of the importance of enforcement for making the legislation meaningful.

3. Recommendations

(a) *For national action*

(i)   Countries should consider assigning a high priority to water quality management to ensure that appropriate policies in this area, consistent with national policy, are formulated and that the corresponding legislative, institutional, technical and financial measures are adopted.

(ii)   Consideration should be given to the establishment of a single body at the national level with sufficient authority and resources to be responsible for water quality management. Should this not be practicable, a viable alternative would be to establish a co-ordinating body which should be empowered to harmonize and co-ordinate the policies, programmes and activities of various agencies engaged in some way or other in water quality management.

(iii)   A national assessment of manpower requirements in various aspects of water quality management should be carried out, and training institutions capable of providing training in such aspects should be identified with a view to formulating a short- to medium-term training programme to meet the needs of the countries.

(iv)   Government information agencies should consider stepping up the pace of their campaigns to make the public aware of the need to protect and preserve the quality of national water supplies. Such campaigns need to be organized on a systematic and sustained basis and should not be carried out sporadically.

(v)   The effectiveness of existing monitoring systems should be assessed, and redesigned and revised, if necessary, to ensure that the necessary information is obtained on the current situation concerning water quality in major rivers. Where monitoring systems have not been established, consideration should be given to doing so.

(vi)   Serious consideration should be given to the codification of legislative measures concerning water quality management in order to ensure that there are no conflicting provisions. Similarly, attention should be given to ensuring that technical strategies and measures adopted by various agencies for water quality management in their respective sectors are co-ordinated and not conflicting.

(vii)   The effects of economic and financial instruments to achieve the goals of water quality management should be carefully studied with the end in view of introducing them where necessary.

(b) *For international action*

(i)   Relevant information on the principles, effective practices and techniques concerning water quality management should be compiled and disseminated as widely as possible by the members of the United Nations system.

(ii)   Consideration should be given to the organization of a regional seminar on water quality monitoring for the purpose of exchanging experiences in national water quality monitoring systems as well as in disseminating technical information on network design, equipment, field collection techniques and laboratory and analytical procedures.

(iii)   The concerned participating institutions in the proposed regional network for training in water resources development should include water quality management as one of the major areas of training.

(iv)   Concerned members of the United Nations system should continue to support the efforts of countries in their water quality management efforts through the provision, on request, of advisory services.

REFERENCES

(1)   "Water Pollution Control in Bangkok Metropolitan Region", National Research Council, Bangkok, 5 February 1973.

(2)   "A Proposed Action Programme for Water Pollution Control for the Bangkok/Inner Gulf Megalopolis", Pakit Kiravanich et al, National Environment Board, Bangkok, June 1979.

(3)   *Jakarta Sewerage and Sanitation Project, volume I, Summary Report,* by Nihon Suido for UNDP/WHO, September 1977.

(4)   *Final Report, Comprehensive Water Quality Management Programme, Laguna de Bay,* UNDP/WHO/Laguna Lake Development Authority, May 1978. *Summary Report* (volumes 1, 2, 3), (b) Annex I, *Limnology of Laguna de Bay,* (volumes 4 to 7), (c) Annex 2, *Fisheries of Laguna de Bay,* (d) Annex 3, *Ecological Model,* (e) Annex 4, *Water Quality Data Storage and Retrieval System,* (f) Annex 12, *Environmental Assessment.*

(5)   "Preliminary Evaluation of Water Pollution and Quality in Musi River at Palembang, South Sumatra", Division of Environmental Quality, Institute of Hydraulic Engineering, Directorate General of Water Resources Development (DEQ/WHE/DGWRD), Bandung, Indonesia, 1983.

(6)   "Manila Bay Monitoring Programme", Metropolitan Waterworks and Sewerage System and National Pollution Control Commission, Manila, April 1981.

(7)   "Evaluation of Proposed Seoul Metropolitan Sewerage and Water Pollution Control System", WHO Regional Office, Manila, 1977.

(8)   "A Note on the Quality of Water in Jakarta", Jakarta Water Supply Review, World Bank, 5 July 1982.

(9)   "Environmental Guidelines for Coastal Zone Management in Thailand, Zone of Phuket", National Environment Board, 31 January 1976.

(10)   "Evaluation of Environmental Effects of BM/BX Mining Operations at Baguio", by H. Ludwig for BM/BX Mining Companies, Baguio, Philippines, February 1979.

(11)   "Environmental Analysis of Bali Irrigation Project", ELC/ADC Consulting Consortium for Directorate of Irrigation, 1980.

(12)   "Final Report, Agricultural Waste Recycling Project" (Draft), by the Engineering Consortium for Asian Development Bank, April 1983.

(13)   *Jakarta Sewerage and Sanitation Project, Volume VIII, Immediate Programme for Sanitation,* by Nihon Suido for UNDP/WHO, Geneva, September 1977.

(14)   "Effects of Augus I Hydropower Project on Environmental and Ecological Resources of Lake Lanao", Mindanao, Philippines, Asian Development Bank, 1975.

(15)   "Urban Sewerage and Excreta Disposal, Master Plan for Urban Chonburi, Thailand", by Seatec International for WHO/GTZ, Bangkok, April 1983.

(16)   "Master Plan for Water Supply, Sewerage, and Drainage for Calcutta Metropolitan Region", UNDP/WHO, Geneva, 1965.

(17)   "Environmental Guidelines for Coastal Zone Management in Thailand, Zone of Pattaya", National Environment Board, Bangkok, November 1975.

(18)   "Preliminary Evaluation of Sewage Pollution at Songkhla Beach", National Environment Board, Bangkok, 1978.

(19)   "Environmental Guidelines for Coastal Zone Management in Thailand, Inner Gulf Zone", National Environment Board, Bangkok, June 1976.

(20)   "Environment Assessment of Lower Citanduy Irrigation Project", Asian Development Bank, Manila, 1980.

(21)   "Final Report, Eastern Seaboard Planning Project", for National Economic and Social Development Board (NESDB), (a) "Main Report", and (b) "Environmental Analysis" (by Seatec International).

(22)   "Environmental Analysis of Nuku'alofa Lagoon in Tonga", WHO Regional Office, Manila, 1979.

(23)   "Illustrative Field Surveys for Evaluating Water Quality and Related Environmental Problems for Selected Sensitive Development Areas in Indonesia", UNOTC/DEQ/IHE/DGWRD, Bandung, April 1979.

(24)   "Post Evaluation of Metropolitan Water Supply Improvements at Bangkok", Asian Development Bank, Manila, 1982.

(25)   "Environmental Effects of Pa Mong", by H. Ludwig, Mekong secretariat publication MKG/36, Bangkok, December 1975.

(26)   "Role of Environment in Planning in Thailand", by Kasem Snidvongse and Kosit Panpiemras, ESCAP, February 1980.

(27)   "National Policies and Implementation Measures for Environmental Development", National Environment Board, Bangkok, 1982.

(28)   "Project Outline and Proposal for Resources Development and Management Planning in Songkhla Basin", Annex 2-2 of report, "Environmental Policy and Planning", National Environment Board, Bangkok, August 1981.

(29)   "Appropriate Technology for Water Supply and Sanitation", series of manuals published by World Bank including (a) *A Planner's Guide*, December 1980, and (b) *Health Aspects of Excreta and Sullage Management, A State of-the-Art Review*, Washington, December 1980.

(30)   "More than 35 Developing Countries Adopt World Bank's Low Cost Approaches to Solution of Urban Problems", World Bank, Washington, 13 April 1983.

(31)   "Jakarta Sewerage and Sanitation Project", by Alpinconsult Consortium for Cipta Karya, Ministry of Public Works, Jakarta, May 1982.

(32)   "Appropriate Technology for Water Supply and Sanitation, Urban Sanitation Planning Manual Based on Jakarta Case Study", World Bank, Washington, June 1981 (draft).

(33)   "Feasibility Report, Environmental Analysis, Magalang Water Supply Improvements", by Asiatic Consultants for Ministry of Human Settlements, Manila, 1983.

(34)   "Guidelines for Preparation of Ordinances for Regulating Sanitary and Industrial Waste Discharges to Municipal Sewerage Systems in Indonesia", UNOTC/DEQ/IHE/DGWRD, Bandung, Indonesia, May 1978.

(35)   "Industrial Waste Pollution Control Management", by R. Ludwig for National Environment Board, Bangkok, January 1980.

(36)   "Appropriate Technology for Environmental Protection Planning in Philippines", by H. Ludwig for National Environment Protection Council/WHO-PEPAS, Kuala Lumpur, 1980.

(37)   "Guidelines for Preparation of Technical Reports and Proposals", by H. Ludwig for UNOTC/DEQ/IHE/DGWRD, Bandung, Indonesia, December 1980.

(38) "Example of Marine Ecological Survey in Southeast Asia Tropical Waters", UNOTC/DEQ/IHE/DGWRD, Bandung, Indonesia, May 1978.

(39) "Environmental Review of Water Pollution Control System for Kujang Nitrogen Fertilizer Plant", UNOTC/DEQ/IHE/DGWRD, Bandung, Indonesia, April 1978.

(40) "Report on Pattaya Beach Water Quality Monitoring Programme" (in Thai), National Environment Board, Bangkok, 1978.

(41) "Programme of Division of Environmental Quality, Institute of Hydraulic Engineering, DGWRD", DEQ/IHE/DGWRD, Bandung, Indonesia, 1982.

(42) "Water Quality and Government, the International Scene, the Situation in Indonesia, and the Role of the Institute of Hydraulic Engineering", Badruddin Machbub and H. Ludwig, DEQ/IHE/DGWRD, Bandung, Indonesia, July 1978.

(43) "Water Quality Monitoring Programme of the Institute of Hydraulic Engineering of Indonesia", by Badruddin Machbub and H. Ludwig, DEQ/IHE/DGWRD, Bandung, Indonesia, October 1978.

(44) "Investigation of National Effluent and Stream Standards for Tropical Countries", M. Pescod, Asian Institute of Technology, Bangkok, 1973.

(45) "Synthesis of Research Results, Dredged Material Research Programme, Executive Overview and Detailed Summary", Technical Report DS. 78.22, United States Corps of Engineers, Washington, December 1976.

(46) "Guidelines for Water Quality Monitoring and Surveillance in Indonesia", UNOTC/DEQ/IHE/DGWRD, Bandung, Indonesia, April 1978.

(47) "Final Report of UNOTC Consultant on Water Quality on Activities in Assisting Institute of Hydraulic Engineering, Bandung, during Year 1978", UNOTC/DEQ/IHE/DGWRD, Bandung, Indonesia, December 1978.

(48) "Environmental Protection and the National Environment Board in Thailand", Journal National Environment Board, Bangkok, October 1978.

(49) "Water Pollution from Agrochemicals in Bali", by Badruddin Machbub et al, DEQ/IHE/DGWRD, Bandun, Indonesia, January 1981.

(50) *Environmental Impact Statement for Natural Gas Development* by Fluor Ocena Services International for Petroleum Authority of Thailand, September 1979 (5 volumes):

(a) Volume 1: *Summary Report* (about 25 pages).

(b) Volume 2: *Introduction, Description of Project* (about 50 pages).

(c) Volume 3: *Existing Environment, Physical Resources* (about 100 pages).

(d) Volume 4: *Existing Environment, Ecological Resources, Human and Economic Development, Quality of Life Values* (about 100 pages)

(e) Volume 5: *Possible Environmental Impacts and Plans for Protection, Summary and Conclusion,* Appendices (about 100 pages).

(51) Reports of Thailand Department of Fisheries Songkhla Research Station on water quality monitoring of Songkhla lake (annual monitoring for 10-year period, circa 1960-1970).

(52) *Industrial Process Profiles for Environmental Use* (series of volumes), Industrial Environmental Research laboratory, United States Environmental Protection Agency, Cincinnati, Ohio (1977) including:

(a) Industrial Organics Chemicals Industry (No. EPA-Gov./2-77-023f).

(b) Phosphate Rock and Basic Fertilizer Industry (No. EPA-600/2 77-023v).

(c) Basic Petrochemicals Industry (No. EPA-600/2-77-023e).

(d) *Petroleum Refining Industry* (No. EPA-600/2-77-023c).

(53) Treatability Manual United States Environmental Protection Agency, series of volumes including:

(a) Volume I, *Treatability Data* (EPA-600/8-80-042a).

(b) Volume II, *Industrial Descriptions* (EPA-600/8-80-042b).

(c) Volume III, *Technologies for Control/Removal of Pollutants* (EPA-600/8-80-042c).

(d) Volume IV, *Cost Estimating* (EPA-600/8-80-042d).

(e) Volume V, *Summary* (EPA-600/8-80-042e).

(54) Pollution Surveys in Upper Gulf of Thailand by National Research Council, Subcommittee for Pollution Survey in Gulf of Thailand:

    (a) "First Pollution Survey in Gulf of Thailand, 11-13 April 1973", 1974.

    (b) "Second Pollution Survey in Gulf of Thailand, 20-31 October 1973", 1974.

(55) Initial Environmental Examinations by NEB for Proposed Eastern Seaboard Projects (1979-1980):

    (a) "Initial Environmental Examination, Heavy Industry Projects at Sattaheep, Chonburi", 30 May 1979.

    (b) "Soda Ash Project Summary of Potential Effects", 19 August 1980.

(56) "Criteria for Marine Waste Disposal in Southeast Asia", by H.F. Ludwig, Second International Congress on Mediterranean Marine Pollution, International Association on Water Pollution Research, San Remo, Italy, 1973 (Pergammon Press).

VII.D. LOW COST WATER TREATMENT PROCESSES AND EQUIPMENT
(E/ESCAP/NR. 10/10)

Introduction

In many developing countries people live in areas where readily consumable safe drinking water is scarce. The scarcity of potable water compels people to resort to sources that are contaminated by human or animal faeces. Safe drinking water is important in the control of many diseases. This is particularly well-established for diseases, such as diarrhoea, cholera, typhoid and paratyphoid, infectious hepatitis, amoebic and bacillary dysentery. It has been estimated that as many as 80 per cent of all diseases in the world are associated with unsafe water. There are many situations in which treatment of water is necessary to render it fit for drinking and domestic uses.

The purpose of water treatment is to convert raw water taken from a ground or surface source into potable drinking water. In this regard, the quality of treated water must satisfy two requirements: it must be safe to consume and it should be attractive to use. Most important is the removal of disease-causing pathogenic organisms and poisonous substances. Other substances may also need to be removed or at least considerably reduced. These include suspended matter causing turbidity, iron and manganese compounds imparting a bitter taste or staining laundry, and excessive carbon dioxide corroding concrete and metal parts. For small community water supplies, other water quality characteristics, such as hardness, total dissolved solids and organic content, would generally be less important and may be given only modest consideration in selecting low-cost treatment processes and equipment. Various water treatment processes have been developed. While some may serve just a single purpose, others have multiple applicability. Quite often it is observed that a simple and cheap treatment process like storage or filtration can be effective to a certain extent. For example, storage can remove schistosomiasis cercariae, because they are normally unable to survive 48 hours of storage. The number of faecal coliforms and faecal streptococci will also be considerably reduced when raw water is subjected to storage. Moreover, storage allows sedimentation to take place reducing the settleable solids content of the water.

The provision of any form of treatment in a water supply will require a capital outlay that may be relatively substantial. However, it should be noted that sometimes operational and maintenance requirements are the key factors that influence the cost in the long run. The objective of a study on low-cost water treatment processes and equipment is to contribute towards making safe drinking water available to as many people as possible within the 1980-1990 decade. In view of this, treatment processes and equipment discussed in this paper are concerned only with domestic aspects, industrial and agricultural aspects are not dealt with.

The cost of water treatment for the supply of a given quantity of safe drinking water depends upon the quality of its source, the quality of treated water stipulated by regulation standards and the processes and equipment used for treatment. For example, ground-water and clear surface-water sources may need only one or two simple treatment processes to render them safe for drinking and other domestic use. Slightly polluted surface water can generally be treated to required standards by using just a few more processes, while heavily polluted water requires many treatment processes, including those that are expensive, to render it safe for drinking. Therefore, the quality of the raw water source must be sufficiently high so as to permit the use of simple treatment processes and equipment to meet the regulations.

Imposing very high standards of water quality can unnecessarily increase treatment costs. Therefore, regulations to control the quality of water are divided into two categories: primary and secondary. The primary regulations usually limit the level of contaminants affecting the health of consumers, whereas the secondary regulations deal with those contaminants that affect the aesthetic qualities of drinking water. The cost of water treatment can be reduced significantly by enforcing the primary regulations only and considering the secondary regulations as guidelines.

The cost of treatment can be minimized by the maximum use of local materials, minimum use of mechanical equipment and chemical wherever possible, and simplicity of design, operation and maintenance. Therefore, selection of low-cost water-treatment processes and equipment for developing countries should be based on their feasibility of being constructed, operated and maintained by local materials, technology and labour, which are available at a particular site.

A. PROCESSES AND EQUIPMENT FOR TREATMENT OF GROUND WATER

Ground water originates mainly from infiltration of rainwater which after reaching the aquifer flows through the ground. During infiltration, the water picks up many impurities, such as inorganic and organic soil particles, debris from plants and animals, micro-organisms, natural and man-made fertilizers and pesticides, among others. However, during its flow underground, suspended particles are removed by filtration, organic substances are degraded by oxidation, and micro-organisms die because of lack of nutrients resulting in a great improvement of water quality.

Generally, ground water is free from turbidity, pathogenic organisms and other hazardous or objectionable substances. In such cases, ground water may be used as drinking water without any treatment.

When the ground water comes from an aquifer containing organic matter, it will contain less oxygen than usual (anaerobic) but excess carbon dioxide. Water lacking in oxygen will dissolve iron, manganese and heavy metals in the ground. These substances can be removed from water by a treatment process called aeration. Some type of aerators are capable of reducing excess carbon dioxide which makes the water corrosive.

When the ground water contains excessive amounts of iron, manganese and ammonia, it has to be treated with chemical coagulation, flocculation and filtration to render it suitable for drinking. These processes are expensive and complicated and should be avoided when alternative sources of water are available.

The types of treatment required for different qualities of ground water are indicated in table 48. It should be

noted that disinfection by chlorination is generally not necessary for ground water and is done only as an optional treatment to ensure added safety.

Table 48. Types of low-cost water treatment for different qualities of ground water

Ground water quality	Types of treatment required
1. Aerobic, fairly hard, not corrosive	Nil
2. Aerobic, soft and corrosive	A
3. Anaerobic, fairly hard, not corrosive (no iron and manganese)	A
4. Anaerobic, fairly hard, not corrosive (with iron and manganese)	A, RF
5. Anaerobic, soft, corrosive (no iron and manganese)	A
6. Anaerobic, soft, corrosive (with iron and manganese)	A, RF

Source: Reference (1).

A — Aeration for increasing O_2 and/or reducing CO_2.
RF — Filtration (rapid).

1. Aeration

Aeration is the treatment process whereby water is brought into intimate contact with air in order to increase the oxygen content, reduce the carbon dioxide content, and remove hydrogen sulphide, methane and various volatile organic compounds which give bad taste and odour to the water.

Aeration is also used for the treatment of ground water with high iron and manganese content that impart a bitter taste to water. However, oxidation of these compounds by aeration can be achieved only when there is no organic matter in the water. Otherwise, oxidation can be achieved only by a chemical process which is expensive and complex and therefore is not suitable for rural areas in the developing countries.

Treatment by aeration for drinking water can be achieved either by waterfall aerators or bubble aerators.

a. *Waterfall aerators*

This type of aerator disperses the water through the air in thin sheets or fine droplets. Some of the most common and simple aerators of this type are the multiple-tray aerator (figure 21), the cascade aerator (figure 22) and the multiple-platform aerator (figure 23). The multiple-tray

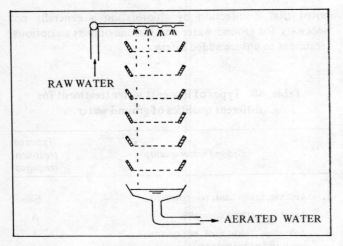

Figure 21. Multiple-tray aerator

Source: Reference (1)

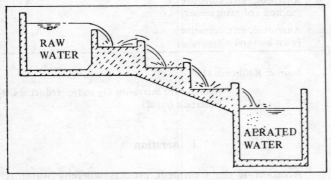

Figure 22. Cascade aerator

Source: Reference (1)

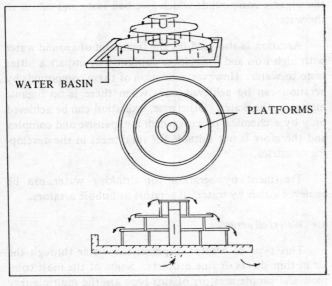

Figure 23. Multiple-platform aerator

Source: Reference (1)

aerator is the simplest and most inexpensive aerator of the three. It occupies little space, can be constructed of local materials, such as wood and bamboo, and can use the skill of local people.

b. *Bubble aerators*

In bubble aerators, aeration is achieved by mixing the water with dispersed air. In general, bubble aerators are a little more complex and expensive than the waterfall aerators. The common types of bubble aerators are the venturi aerator and the submerged cascade aerator.

In venturi aerators, aeration is achieved by the natural sucking of air into the water at the venturi throat. At this point the water velocity is high and pressure drops below the atmospheric pressure. After passing through the venturi throat, the water flows through a larger pipe section where its velocity drops and pressure increases thereby mixing the air bubbles intimately with water.

In submerged cascade aerators, aeration is achieved by entrapping air in the falling sheets of water which carry it deep into the water collected in the troughs.

2. Rapid filtration

Filtration is the process whereby water is treated by passing it through a porous medium. For rapid filtration, coarse sand of grain size from 0.4 to 1.2 mm is used as a medium and the filtration rate is generally maintained from 5 to 15 m^3/m^2/hour. The use of coarse sand permits the effective utilization of the filter bed allowing even very turbid water to be treated by rapid filtration.

In the treatment of groundwater, rapid filtration is used for the removal of iron and manganese. For this purpose, water is first pretreated by aeration to form insoluble compounds of iron and manganese. Some of the important types of rapid filters are gravity filters, pressure filters, upflow filters and multiple media filters.

a. *Gravity filters*

Gravity filters are the simplest form of rapid filters with water passing down the filter bed by gravity as shown in figure 24. The open gravity-type filter is also suitable for treatment of surface water with low turbidity, which is frequently found in lakes and some rivers, in order to produce clear water. These filters, however, cannot remove pathogenic organisms from water.

A schematic diagram of an open gravity-type rapid filter with pretreatment by aeration for the removal of iron and manganese from ground water is presented in figure 25.

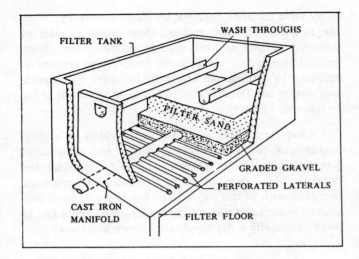

Figure 24. Rapid filter (open, gravity-type)

Source: Reference (1)

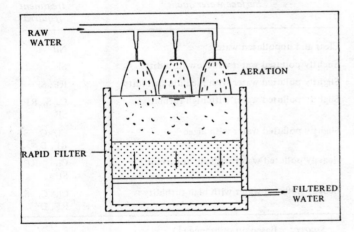

Figure 25. Rapid filtration of pre-treated (aerated) water

Source: Reference (1)

b. *Pressure filters*

These filters work on the same principle as gravity filters, but the filter bed together with the filter bottom is enclosed in a watertight steel pressure vessel. The water pressure on the filter bed is maintained by a high water head so that any desired length of filter run can be obtained. Pressure filters are commercially produced in developed countries as complete units. However, they are not suitable for use in developing countries as they are not easy to install, operate and maintain.

c. *Upflow filters*

These filters have the advantage over the previous types in that they provide for a coarse-to-fine filtration process.

The coarse bottom layer of the filter bed with large pores filters out the major part of suspended impurities, while the overlaying finer layers with smaller pores filter out the remaining particles. The disadvantage is that the filter run and the allowable rate of filtration are very limited as the allowable resistance over the filter is not more than the submerged weight of the filter bed. These filters are suitable for pretreatment before gravity type filtration and slow sand filtration.

d. *Multiple-media filters*

These are gravity type downflow filters using different materials for the filter bed, which are arranged coarse-to-fine in the direction of flow. In most cases only two materials are used in combination: 0.3 to 0.5 m thick layer of anthracite, pumice or crushed coconut husks with an effective size of 1.0 to 1.6 mm at the top. When used as final treatment, these filters can give very clear water and they are suitable for application in areas where suitable materials are available locally.

e. *Horizontal gravity filters*

The rapid filters described above may not find ready application in villages in developing countries because of their complex design and construction; and the need for a certain expertise in operation and maintenance. Therefore, a much simpler type of rapid filtration should be used instead, even if a more limited treatment can be achieved.

The horizontal gravity filter shown in figure 26 is an alternative that will be found useful for village applications.

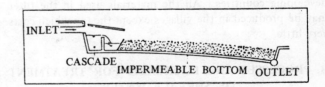

Figure 26. Horizontal gravel filter

Source: Reference (1)

The filter bed has a depth of 1 to 2 m and is subdivided into three zones, each about 5 m long and composed of gravel with sizes of 20 to 30 mm, 15 to 20 mm and 10 to 15 mm. A large area will be required for such a filter, but the advantage is that clogging of the filter will take place only very slowly, so that cleaning will be needed only after a period of years.

3. Charcoal water filter

The charcoal water filter, shown in figure 27, is essentially a rapid sand filter and may be regarded as the

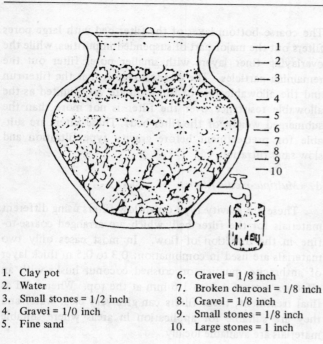

1. Clay pot
2. Water
3. Small stones = 1/2 inch
4. Gravei = 1/0 inch
5. Fine sand
6. Gravel = 1/8 inch
7. Broken charcoal = 1/8 inch
8. Gravel = 1/8 inch
9. Small stones = 1/8 inch
10. Large stones = 1 inch

Figure 27. Charcoal water filter.

Source: Reference (2)

cheapest household water-treatment plant because of its simplicity of construction and its use of local materials. The filter consists primarily of a locally made 20-litre clay pot filled with graded layers of stones, gravel, sand and broken charcoal, which serve as an effective filter for solids and other pollutants. The unit can filter sufficient drinking water for one family and is suitable for use in rural areas in developing countries. All the materials used in the filter may be produced in the villages except the tap which costs very little.

B. PROCESSES AND EQUIPMENT FOR TREATMENT OF SURFACE WATER

Water from surface sources originates partly from ground water and partly from surface runoff. The ground water brings dissolved solids into surface water, whereas surface runoff brings in turbidity, organic matter and parthogenic organisms. However, in lakes and ponds, sedimentation results in the removal of suspended solids, while lack of suitable food results in the elimination of some pathogenic organisms.

Clear water from rivers and lakes in sparsely populated areas is suitable for drinking without any treatment except some chlorination as a safety measure.

Unpolluted surface water of low turbidity may be treated by slow sand filtration as a single treatment process,

or by rapid filtration followed by chlorination only. When the turbidity of water is high, these processes must be preceded by pretreatment, such as sedimentation. When colloidal suspended particles are present, the removal of turbidity by settling can be greatly improved by chemical coagulation and flocculation. When algae is present, it can be removed by pre-chlorination.

Water from rivers and lakes varies widely in quality; heavily polluted water needs expensive and complicated processes in order to make it suitable for drinking and domestic use. Such complicated treatment processes are not dealt with in this paper. The low-cost treatment processes for surface water, which can be found applicable to small community water supplies are shown in table 49.

Table 49. Types of low-cost water treatment for different qualities of surface water

Surface water quality	Types of treatment required
Clear and unpolluted water	Nil
Slightly polluted water with low turbidity	SF
Slightly polluted water with medium turbidity	RF, SF
Slightly polluted water with high turbidity	C, S, RF, SF
Slightly polluted water with algae	Cl, C, S, RF, D
Heavily polluted water with slight turbidity	Cl, RF, SF
Heavily polluted water with high turbidity	Cl, C, S, RF, D

Source: Based on reference (1).

Notes:
C — Chemical coagulation and flocculation.
Cl — Pre-chlorination.
D — Disinfection (Post-chlorination, boiling, etc.).
RF — Rapid filtration.
S — Sedimentation.
SF — Slow sand filtration.

1. Chemical coagulation and flocculation

Coagulation and flocculation is a treatment process by which finely divided suspended and colloidal matter in water is made to agglomerate and form flocs. This enables their removal by sedimentation or filtration. The substances that are to be removed by coagulation and flocculation are those that cause turbidity and colour in surface waters. Coagulation is initiated by adding to the water a chemical, such as alum which induces suspended particles to combine physically and form a floc. It can remove a certain amount of pathogenic organisms from water.

Alum is by far the most widely used coagulant, but iron salts such as ferric chloride and ferric sulphate are also used. Sometimes, iron salts have a significant advantage over alum in having a broader pH range for good coagulation.

Factors which affect coagulation and flocculation rates are the pH and temperature of the water, the size of the particles, the rate at which the coagulant and water are mixed, and the ultimate quantity of coagulant used. When the pH of the water ranges between 6.8 and 7.5, alum is the most suitable coagulant. When the pH range of water is between 5.5 and 8.8, ferric sulphate can be used (3). For good coagulation, the optimum dose of coagulant should be fed into the water and properly mixed with it. The optimum dosage will vary depending on the nature of raw water and its overall composition. It is not possible to compute the optimum coagulant dosage for a particular raw water. A laboratory experiment is generally necessary for the periodic determination of the optimum dosage.

Chemical coagulation and flocculation are not suitable for small community water supplies and they should, therefore, be used only when other treatment processes cannot reduce the turbidity and colour of raw water to acceptable levels without the use of chemicals. However, it is generally possible to reduce the turbidity and colour of raw water to acceptable levels by a slow sand filtration process. Another reason against the use of chemical coagulation is the health hazards involved in newly developed synthetic coagulant aids.

2. Sedimentation

Sedimentation is the settling and removal of suspended particles that takes place when water stands still in, or flows slowly through, a basin. It is also a process by which floc or suspended matter is separated from water by precipitation and deposition.

Sedimentation can be accomplished in a quiescent pond or properly constructed tank or basin. Basically, the process depends on the effect of gravity on particles suspended in a liquid or lesser density. Sedimentation takes place in any basin and its cost is low because it does not require any mechanical equipment or chemicals. However, at least a 24-hour detention time must be allowed in order to achieve a significant reduction in suspended matter.

Sedimentation allows household treatment of turbid water by storing it in large containers for a long duration without any treatment cost. For small water-treatment plants, horizontal-flow, rectangular tanks are usually used for sedimentation which are simple to construct and are cost-effective. Like coagulation and flocculation, sedi-

mentation can also remove a certain amount of pathogenic organisms from water.

3. Slow sand filtration

In slow sand filtration, a bed of fine sand with an effective size of about 0.2 mm and bed thickness of 1 to 1.2 m is used, through which the water slowly percolates downward. Owing to the fine grain size, the pores of the filter bed are small and the suspended particles in raw water are retained in the upper 0.5 to 2 cm of the filter bed. As low rates of filtration, 0.1 to 0.3 m/hour, are used cleanings of the top layer of the filter bed are necessary only after several months of use. Slow sand filtration can have a trouble-free operation only when the turbidity of raw water is low, and therefore in cases where the turbidity is high, some form of pretreatment, such as sedimentation, coagulation and flocculation, or rapid sand filtration, is necessary. Slow sand filters can be designed and constructed for both small-scale community water supply and household water supply.

a. Slow sand filter for community water supply

A simplified version of this type of slow sand filter is presented in figure 28. It consists of a tank, open at the top and containing a 1 to 1.2 m thick bed of sand. The depth of the tank is about 3 m and the area can vary from a few tens to several hundreds of square metres. At the bottom of the tank, an underdrain system is placed to support the filter bed. The bed is usually composed of ungraded fine sand, which should be free from clay, loam and organic matter. The water to be treated usually stands to a depth of 1 to 1.5 m above the filter bed.

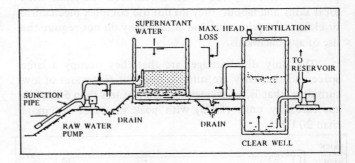

Figure 28. Simplified slow sand filter

Source: Reference (1)

These slow sand filters effect the removal of impurities by a combination of processes, such as sedimentation, absorption, straining and, most importantly, bio-chemical and microbial actions. The major part of these processes takes place in the top layer of the filter bed. Sedimentation removes fine suspended solids as they are deposited on the surface of the sand grains of the filter bed. This takes place in the upper part of the filter bed and only organic matter of low density is carried deeper into the bed. The remaining suspended solids, together with colloidal and dissolved impurities, are removed by absorption either on the sticky gelatinous coating formed around the filter bed grains or through physical mass attraction and electrostatic attraction. Straining removes those suspended particles that are too large to pass through the pores of the filter bed. The matter accumulated on the sand grains is then transformed by bio-chemical and bacterial activity, whereby soluble ferrous and manganous compounds are turned into insoluble ferric and manganic oxide hydrates that become part of the coating around the sand grains. As the water flows deeper through the filter bed, the degradable organic matter is gradually broken down and transformed into inorganic compounds, such as carbon dioxide, nitrates, sulphates and phosphates, which are finally discharged with the filter effluent. Various studies have indicated that the bacterial activity extends over a depth of about 0.6 m of filter bed so that the effective bed thickness should not be less than 0.7 m.

A slow sand filter is capable of removing pathogenic organisms from raw water by absorption and other processes. It has been claimed that slow sand filters are capable of reducing the total bacteria content by a factor of 1,000 to 10,000, and the E. coli content by a factor of 100 to 1,000 (1). Therefore, these filters are supposed to produce a bacteriologically safe water when treating lightly contaminated raw water.

Slow sand filters have many advantages for use in developing countries. They can produce a clear safe potable water; they can be built with local materials using local skills and labour; they do not use complex mechanical or electrical equipment; and finally they do not require the use of any chemicals.

The only disadvantages are that they occupy a large space and that they are suitable only for raw water of low turbidity, that is, an average turbidity of less than Formazin turbidity units (FTU) with peak values of not more than 20 FTU.

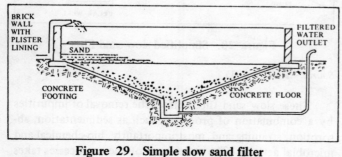

Figure 29. Simple slow sand filter
Source: Reference (1)

An example of a very simple slow sand filter that can be used in villages in developing countries is shown in figure 29. If site conditions permit, slow sand filtration can be designed without the use of pumps or any other mechanical equipment and make maximum use of local materials and labour.

b. *Slow sand filter for household use*

For isolated homes in sparsely populated areas, the use of an individual slow sand filter may prove to be more practical.

A schematic sketch of a slow sand filter suggested by Dhabadgoankar (3) is shown in figure 30. The filter was designed for a family of four consuming water at the rate of 10 litres per capita per day. The main components of the filter consist of a filter box with inlet and outlet control valves, raw water and filtered water containers.

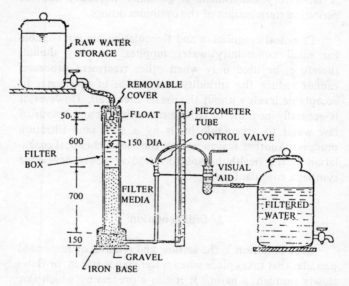

Figure 30. Sketch of a 4-person household slow sand filter

Source: Reference (3)
Note: All dimensions are in mm.

The filter box is of 150 mm dia, 1,500 mm high asbestos cement pipe provided with an end cap at the bottom to which the filter outlet and piezometer tube connections are made. The filter box is also provided with a removable cover, to which is attached a float valve that maintains a raw water level of 50 mm below the top edge of the box. The filter box contains 150 mm of gravel at the base and 700 mm of filter sand at the top. The filtration rate may be adjusted to about 0.1 m/hr by means of the control valve and the development of a negative head can be prevented by adjusting the position of the outlet end of the tube.

Raw water for treatment is stored in an earthen pot of about 50 litres capacity. For efficient operation, the turbility of raw water should not be more than 50 turbidity units (TU) measured by Hilger's colorimeter. Raw water with high turbidity can be pretreated by sedimentation so as to come within acceptable levels of turbidity. The container for filtered water has a capacity of about 80 litres and can be either an earthen pot or a copper pot. The advantage of storing filtered water in copper vessels, according to Dhabadgaonkar, is that the bacterial kill in the water stored in a copper vessel is considerably greater than that for the water stored in a polythene container. The reason for this bacterial kill was stated as being due to the copper ions dissociating from the surface of the vessel into the water. According to his studies, well water with a coliform count of 1,600/100 ml when stored in clean copper vessels for 48 hours had reduced its coliform count to less than 10/100 ml in 90 per cent of samples, or when stored for only 24 hours, the same reduction was achieved in 60 per cent of samples. If the bactericidal action of copper vessels is supported by the results of other studies, it can even replace the use of conventional disinfecting chemicals such as chlorine. However, disinfection by a copper vessel takes a much longer time than chlorine and its effectiveness has not been proved as yet. Besides, the initial cost of a copper vessel may be quite high.

Regarding the pathogens removal efficiency of this filtration unit, Dhabadgoankar has stated that with the initial well water coliform count exceeding 1,600/100 ml, all filtered water samples have a coliform count of less than 10/100 ml, while most filtered water samples showed zero coliform count. The virus removal efficiency was also said to be quite comparable to bacteria removal. According to the Metropolitan Water Board (4), a slow sand filter operating at a standard rate of 0.2 m/hr and a temperature of 11° to 12°C can reduce "Poliovirus 1" by 99.999 per cent, while the same filter at a temperature of 6°C can reduce by 96.8 per cent. This significance of increased virus reduction at higher temperatures should be an advantage for countries with an average water temperature above 20°C.

4. Potential for enhancing the capability of slow sand infiltration

It has already been mentioned that slow sand filters are capable of effectively treating raw water of low turbidity (approximately 5 FTU) only and that pretreatment by a sedimentation process or rapid filtration is necessary if raw water of high turbidity is to be treated by slow sand filtration. This pretreatment is required because high turbidity water has a high solids content, a major portion of which has to be removed by sedimentation or rapid filtration, thus allowing the slow sand filter to be used primarily as a polishing process. In the absence of a pretreatment process,

all solids removed from the water are stored within the filter bed, thus causing not only the rapid clogging of the sand beds and subsequent accumulation of head loss, but also a reduction of effective length of the filter run.

This drawback can be overcome by using the idea borrowed from a research by McCormick and King (5) on factors that influence the effectiveness of direct filtration in large scale water treatment plants. The authors studied the performance of direct filtration using three different types of dual media filters as shown in table 50 with a filtration rate of 3.5 mm/sec and average raw water turbidities ranging from 15 to 24 nephelometric turbidity units (ntu). It was concluded that filter 2 with a 51 cm bed of coal with an effective size of 1.3 mm and a 25 cm bed of sand with an effective size of 0.45 mm is the most effective media among the variables considered, and is capable of producing filtered water with a turbidity of less than 1 ntu for a continuous period of 8 hours.

Table 50. Filter media characteristics

Filter number	Media type	Media depth (cm)	Effective size (mm)	Uniformity coefficient
1	Coal	25	1.0-1.1	<1.7
	Sand	30	0.42-0.49	1.3-1.5
	Garnet	23	0.21-0.25	1.6-2.1
2	Coal	51	1.3	1.35
	Sand	25	0.45	1.4
3	Coal	51	1.7	1.1
	Sand	25	0.45	1.4

This indicates that an additional layer of coal on top of the sand bed will enhance the capability of the slow sand filter to treat raw water with higher turbidities without clogging for long durations. The introduction of the coal layer on top permits the storage of greater amounts of solids removed from the water without excessive head loss and clogging. Hutchison and Foley (6) reported that with a coal size of 1.3 mm, 92 per cent of head loss (and hence the storage of filtrate solids) took place in the coal layer. This supported the study by McCormick and King that 1.3 mm is the most effective size of coal to be used on top of the sand bed. An inference can also be made from the fact that if the dual bed filter media studied by McCormick and King can operate flawlessly for eight continuous hours even at a rapid filtration rate of 3.5 mm/sec for the raw water turbidity of up to 24 ntu, a slow sand filter with a coal layer on top with very slow infiltration rates of less than 0.3 m/hour (0.08 mm/sec) can filter comparable qualities of raw water for longer periods — may be a few months. The optimum depths of coal and sand layers for peak performance has yet to be established by further studies for various conditions.

5. Traditional treatment methods for drinking water

a. *Filtration through cloth*

Traditional filtration through a piece of tightly woven cloth can remove plant debris, insects and coarser suspended materials from water. The degree of removal depends on the fineness of pores of the filter material. In some cases it can even remove large parasites, such as protozoan cysts and eggs. However, it is important to clean the cloth in boiling water after each use.

b. *Filtration through vessels of clay or porous stone*

Jars of burnt clay with a suitable pore size allow slow filtration of the water through the clay. As an improvement the jars are sometimes surrounded by a cubic receptacle fitted with a tap.

In Bali, Indonesia (7), muddy water from irrigation canals is filtered with a Jempeng stone filter as shown in

figure 31. The filter stone is carved from a porous stone material called *cadas*. It has an average height of 60 cm, a diameter of 50 cm and a wall thickness of 10-12 cm. Turbid canal water is allowed to circulate through small shallow artificial ponds into which these filters are inserted. As the receptacle is small and the rate of filtration slow, filtered water can be used only for drinking and cooking.

A modern application of filtration through porous pottery is the ceramic water filters with different pore sizes. Water filtered through porous stone and pottery is free from cysts, ova and cercariae, however some disinfection may still be necessary to destroy bacteria and viruses if the water is contaminated.

Water passing through such filters should have a low content of suspended matter to prevent frequent clogging of the pores. Therefore, pretreatment by sedimentation will be necessary when the raw water to be filtered has a high turbidity.

WATER FILTRATION IN BALI THROUGH JEMPENG STONE FILTERS

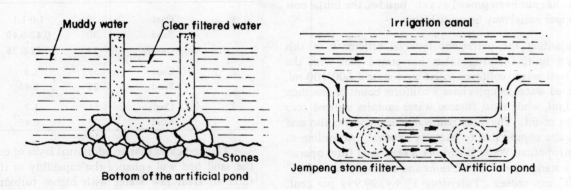

Figure 31. Jempeng stone filter

Source: Reference (7)

c. *Infiltration wells*

When local site conditions are favourable, infiltration wells established at suitable distances from a river bank can provide a relatively clearer water than that in the river. This type of shore filtration is a method which yields varying results depending on the geological conditions of the strata through which the water infiltrates, the flow time and the distance from the river at which percolating water is collected. One major disadvantage of this type of well is that well-water can become contaminated by domestic sewage during the flood season when the flood water overflows the wells. During the dry season, infiltration wells are known to have a high efficiency for the removal of organic

pollutants, virus and pathogenic bacteria. However, additional treatment by disinfection is advisable as a precautionary measure.

d. *Long-term storage in water jars*

Water from a surface source can be stored in clay pots for a few months before use allowing for sedimentation and natural purification. For example, schistosomiasis cercariae are normally unable to survive 48 hours of storage. The number of faecal coliforms and faecal streptococci will also be considerably reduced when raw water is subjected to storage.

6. Disinfection

Treatment processes, such as storage, sedimentation, coagulation and flocculation, and rapid filtration, reduce the content of pathogenic organisms in water to varying degrees, but cannot ensure a completely pathogen-free water. Final disinfection may, therefore, be necessary in order to obtain safe drinking water.

Disinfection of drinking water can be achieved by using physical or chemical means. The requirements of a disinfection system are:

(i) It should be effective against all types of pathogens present in water;

(ii) It should be automatic, that is, not requiring continuous attention;

(iii) It should require only simple maintenance which should be infrequent;

(iv) It should be simple, safe, and inexpensive to set up and use;

(v) It should be as fail-safe as possible;

(vi) It should provide residual protection against possible recontamination;

(vii) It should not make the water unpalatable or non-potable in any other respect.

However, since no single type of disinfectant meets all these requirements, a certain amount of compromise is necessary in making a selection.

a. Physical disinfection

The two principal physical disinfection methods are boiling water and radiation with ultraviolet rays. The latter uses electricity and advanced technology and is, therefore, not suitable for developing countries.

Boiling is a simple and safe method which destroys pathogenic organisms, such as viruses, bacteria, cercariae, cysts and ova. Although it is an effective method for household treatment, it is not a feasible method for community water supplies, as it will be expensive, energy-intensive and confer no residual effect.

Ultraviolet light radiation is an effective disinfection method for clear water but is not effective when the water is turbid. This disinfection method does not produce any residual (as in chemical disinfection) that would protect the water against any new contamination during distribution. Another drawback of ultraviolet irradiation is the uncertainty regarding its effectiveness against viruses (8). There-

fore, it would not be advisable to depend on ultraviolet disinfection without full assurance of its dependability. According to Beauman (9), ultraviolet irradiation is ineffective at killing cysts, which sets a condition that water should be subjected to fine filtration before being subjected to ultraviolet disinfection.

Other physical methods of disinfection, such as ultrasonics and DC electricity, have not been tested with regard to their capability in destroying all the pathogenic organisms which are present in water. Besides, other particulars, such as economics, upkeep and dependability of these methods, have not been adequately studied as yet.

b Chemical disinfection

Chemicals that have been used for disinfection are chlorine and chlorine compounds, iodine, ozone, and other oxidants like potassium permanganate and hydrogen peroxide.

(i) Chlorine and chlorine compounds

Chlorine is the most widely used chemical disinfectant. Its ability to destroy pathogens fairly quickly and its wide availability make it well suited for disinfection. Various experiences in the past have proved that effective chlorination of water supplies can achieve a substantial reduction in enteric diseases. Although recent studies have raised the possibility that organic compounds which are formed when chlorine is added to water might cause certain forms of cancer, the results have not been conclusive so far. The disinfecting properties of chlorine are well established and therefore outweigh the possible side effects when it is used as a disinfectant to safeguard public health. In drinking water, chlorine residuals of 0.2 to 1.0 mg/l after 15 to 30 minutes of contact will generally produce a decontamination factor of 1,000 (99.9 per cent destruction) for E. coli and 37C bacterial counts. A 15-minute residual of 0.5 mg/l appears to be a safe average. It should be noted, however, that chlorine (as with other chemicals) cannot effect the total destruction of viruses and helminths. The cost of chlorination is moderate and for this reason it is widely used.

(ii) Iodine

In spite of its attractive properties as a disinfectant, iodine has serious limitations. First, as in the case of chlorine, viruses are somewhat resistant to iodine while spores and cysts are not affected. Secondly, high doses (10-15 mg/l) are required to achieve satisfactory disinfection. Thirdly, longer contact times and careful pH controls are needed for virus kill, which is a problem for small systems. Fourthly, it is not effective when the water to be disinfected is coloured or turbid. Fifthly, the high volatility of iodine in aqueous solution is not suitable for use as a disinfectant. Finally, its physiological connection with thyroid gland function in human beings is a factor that makes it unsuitable for routine disinfection in community water supplies.

(iii) *Bromine*

In the opinion of many experts, bromine is the ideal disinfectant, but it is expensive and dangerous to use. There are some bromine-based disinfectants which are known to be safe and effective, but they are not available for domestic systems even in developed countries.

(iv) *Ozone*

Ozone is said to be an effective disinfectant by many experts, but it has to be manufactured on site. Besides, ozonators are too complex and undependable for domestic use and hence ozone is not a suitable disinfectant for use in developing countries.

(v) *Potassium permanganate and hydrogen peroxide*

These are excellent chemical oxidizers, but neither is well-regarded for their disinfection capability. For example, potassium permanganate is effective against cholera

vibrio but not for other pathogens. They are, therefore, not satisfactory disinfectants for community water supplies.

C. EFFECTIVENESS OF VARIOUS TREATMENT PROCESSES IN REMOVING CONTAMINANTS

The potential of various treatment processes in removing contaminants from raw water is summarized in table 51. In this table, the maximum contaminant level (MCL) for each contaminant prescribed by United States national primary drinking water regulations of 1976 as well as the highest initial concentration (Ci) of the contaminant that can be reduced to the MCL by a single pass through a particular treatment process are also indicated. The reason for assessing the effectiveness of various treatment processes in terms of meeting United States national primary drinking water regulations instead of the 1973 World Health Organization (WHO) international standards for drinking water is that there is not sufficient information available on the comparable in-depth studies of the effectiveness of these processes in meeting the standards prescribed by WHO. Besides, there is not much difference in the two regulations as far as the requirements concerning major toxic chemicals and disease causing pathogens are concerned.

Table 51. Treatment potential of various processes in removing contaminants from raw water

Contaminant	MCL	C_1^a for treatment shown	Aeration	Coagulation and flocceulation	Plain sedimentation	Filtration Rapid	Filtration Slow sand	Disinfection Physical Boiling	Disinfection Physical Ultraviolet irradiation	Disinfection Chemical Cl_2	Disinfection Chemical O_3	Disinfection Chemical $KMnO_4$
Arsenic — trivalent	0.05 mgr	1.0 mgr	—	—	—	—	—	—	—	x	x	x
		0.33 mgr	—	—	—	—	—	—	—	—	—	—
Arsenic — pentavalent	0.05 mgr	1.0 mgr	—	x	—	—	—	—	—	—	—	—
		0.1 mgr	—	x	—	—	—	—	—	—	—	—
Barium	1.0 mgr	10.0 mgr	—	—	x	—	—	—	—	—	—	—
		45.0 mgr	—	—	—	—	—	—	—	—	—	—
Cadmium	0.01 mgr	0.5 mgr	—	x	—	—	—	—	—	—	—	—
		0.1 mgr	—	x	—	—	—	—	—	—	—	—
		0.1 mgr	—	x	—	—	—	—	—	—	—	—
Chromium — trivalent	0.05 mgr	2.5 mgr	—	x	—	—	—	—	—	—	—	—
		0.5 mgr	—	x	—	—	—	—	—	—	—	—
		0.4 mgr	—	—	—	—	—	—	—	—	—	—
Chromium — hexavalent	0.05 mgr	5.0 mgr	—	x	—	—	—	—	—	—	—	—
		0.4 mgr	—	—	—	—	—	—	—	—	—	—
Coliform organisms	1/100 ml	100/100 ml	—	—	—	—	x	x	—	—	—	—
		<5,000/100 ml	—	—	—	x	x	x	—	—	—	—
		<20,000/100 ml	—	—	—	x	x	x	—	—	—	—
		>20,000/100 ml	—	—	—	—	—	—	—	—	—	—
Fluoride	Varies with air temperature 1.4 to 2.4 mgr		—	x	—	—	—	—	—	—	—	—
			—	x	—	—	—	—	—	—	—	—

Table 51. *(continued)*

Contaminant	MCL	$C_1{}^a$ for treatment shown	Aeration	Coagulation and floceulation	Plain sedimentation	Filtration Rapid	Filtration Slow sand	Disinfection Physical Boiling	Disinfection Physical Ultraviolet irradiation	Disinfection Chemical Cl_2	Disinfection Chemical O_3	Disinfection Chemical $KMnO_4$
Lead	0.05 mgr	1.7 mgr	–	x	–	–	–	–	–	–	–	–
		0.4 mgr										
Manganese – inorganic	0.05 mgr^b		Reduction	–	–	–	–	–	–	x	–	x
– organic	–	–	–	x	–	–	–	–	–	x	–	x
Mercury – inorganic	0.002 mgr	0.007 mgr	–	x	–	–	–	–	–	–	–	–
		0.006 mgr	–	x	–	–	–	–	–	–	–	–
		0.07 mgr	–	x	–	–	–	–	–	–	–	–
		0.01 mgr	–	–	–	–	–	–	–	–	–	–
		0.1 mgr	–	–	–	–	–	–	–	–	–	–
– organic		–	–	x	–	–	–	–	–	–	–	–
		0.1 mgr	–	–	–	–	–	–	–	–	–	–
		0.01 mgr	–	–	–	–	–	–	–	–	–	–
Nitrate – as N	10 mgr	67 mgr	–	–	–	–	–	–	–	–	–	–
		50 mgr	–	–	–	–	–	–	–	–	–	–
Organic chemicals	–	–	x	–	–	–	–	–	–	–	–	–
Radium	5 pcr	30 pcr	–	x	–	–	–	–	–	–	–	–
		70 pcr	–	x	–	–	–	–	–	–	–	–
		165 pcr	–	x	–	–	–	–	–	–	–	–
		100 pcr	–	–	–	–	–	–	–	–	–	–
Selenium – quadravalent	0.01 mgr	0.05 mgr	–	x	–	–	–	–	–	–	–	–
		0.33 mgr	–	–	–	–	–	–	–	–	–	–
Selenium – hexavalent	0.01 mgr	0.33 mgr	–	–	–	–	–	–	–	–	–	–
Silver	0.05 mgr	0.17 mgr	–	x	–	–	–	–	–	–	–	–
		0.5 mgr	–	–	–	–	–	–	–	–	–	–
		0.17 mgr	–	x	–	–	–	–	–	–	–	–
		0.83 mgr	–	–	–	–	–	–	–	–	–	–
Sodium	c	285 mgr	–	–	–	–	–	–	–	–	–	–
		133 mgr	–	–	–	–	–	–	–	–	–	–
Sulphate	250 mgr^b	3570 mgr	–	–	–	–	–	–	–	–	–	–
		8330 mgr	–	–	–	–	–	–	–	–	–	–
Turbidity	1 tu	25 tu	–	–	–	Reduction	Reduction x	–	–	–	–	–
		1000 tu	–	x	x	Reduction	Reduction x	–	–	–	–	–
		>1000 tu	–	x	x	Reduction	Reduction x	–	–	–	–	–

Source: Based on information contained in United States Environmental Protection Agency, *Estimating Water Treatment Costs*, vol. 1, (EPA-600/2-79-162a) (1979), pp. 12-15.

Notes:

a C_1 = Highest initial concentration of the contaminant that could be reduced to MCL by a single pass through the particular treatment technique.

b Secondary drinking water regulation.

c No primary or secondary regulation established.

MCL = Maximum contaminant level according to United States national interim primary drinking water regulations of 1976.

x = Capable of reducing to MCL by a single pass.

– = Not capable or information not available.

It will be observed from table 51 that most treatment processes are applicable to the removal of more than one contaminant, and that among the low-cost processes, sedimentation, slow sand filtration and disinfection by boiling or chlorination are the most simple processes for application in the developing countries.

It follows that the low-cost water treatment processes and equipment that are applicable to the developing countries, if they are to produce drinking water meeting the WHO standards or United States primary drinking water regulations, should treat only fresh water from sources that do not contain high concentrations of toxic chemicals or radio-nuclides.

A more generalized assessment of the effectiveness of water treatment processes in removing various impurities is presented in table 52. It should be noted that slow sand filtration (or any fine filtration including the use of porous clay pot or stone vessel) can remove some of the viruses and bacteria and 100 per cent of the protozoa and helminths. Therefore, effective chlorination after fine filtration will generally render the water safe from bacteriological contamination.

Table 52. Effectiveness of water treatment processes in removing various impurities

Water quality parameter \ Treatment process	Aeration	Chemical coagulation and floceulation	Sedimentation	Rapid filtration	Slow sand filtration	Chlorination
Dissolved oxygen content	+	o	o	+	--	+
Carbon dioxide removal	-	o	o	+	++	+
Turbidity reduction[a]	o	+++	+	+++	++++	o
Colour reduction	o	++	+	+	++	++
Taste and odour removal	++	+	+	++	++	+
Bacteria removal	o	+	++	++	++++	++++
Iron and manganese removal	++	+	+	++++	++++	o
Organic matter removal	+	+	++	+++	++++	+++

Source: Reference (1).

[a] Turbidity of water is caused by the presence of suspended matter scattering and absorbing light rays, and thus giving the water a non-transparant, milky appearance.

++, +++ etc. = Increasing positive effect.
o   = No effect.
            = Negative effect.

D. CONCLUSIONS AND RECOMMENDATIONS

The following conclusions and recommendations may be drawn from the discussions carried out in the previous sections.

(1) The efficiency of low-cost water treatment processes and equipment in meeting the requirements of international standards for drinking water will be greatly enhanced if the source of supply is chosen so that the raw water is free from toxic chemicals and pathogenic organisms.

(2) Information regarding the cost (capital, operation and maintenance) of various water-treatment processes and equipment for different qualities of raw water under varying physical and socio-economic conditions at site are very scarce and so do not allow a comprehensive quantitative analysis of the cost effectiveness of various water treatment processes and equipment.

(3) Among the low-cost water-treatment processes which have been studied, sedimentation, slow sand filtration and disinfection by boiling or chlorination are the most effective processes in producing safe potable water at low cost. These are also the most simple processes that can avoid the use of imported machinery and equipment, and at the same time permit a maximum use of local materials and expertise. Depending on the quality of the raw water source, these processes can be used as a single treatment process or as a combination of two or more processes to provide a safe drinking water supply.

(4) Generally, if ground water is a source which is free from turbidity, disinfection by chlorination may be the only treatment required to obtain safe drinking water. At the other extreme, if a very turbid surface water contaminated by pathogenic organisms happened to be the only available source, presedimentation followed by slow sand filtration and disinfection by chlorination is the least costly and most effective way of providing a safe drinking water supply.

(5) Traditional methods of water treatment are suitable only for household drinking water supply. When turbid and contaminated surface water is a source, the safest and simplest low-cost method for household drinking water supply is to store water in locally made containers for more than two days, filter through a household slow sand filter or porous clay vessels or porous stone filter, and finally disinfect the water by boiling.

(6) Boiling is the simplest and safest method of disinfection, however, it is feasible only on an individual household basis where the product water is used strictly for drinking purposes. When used for community water supply, it is not only very expensive and energy-intensive, but also is not feasible as there is no residual effect to prevent recontamination.

(7) Further studies and research on low-cost water treatment processes and equipment should be carried out with a view to enhancing their performance and further reduction of costs.

(8) A study on methods to protect natural water sources from contamination should be carried out, which should receive wide dissemination among the developing countries, in order to keep the quality of raw water source sufficiently high enough so that low-cost treatment processes and equipment may be applied to provide a safe drinking water supply.

(9) Since natural sources of raw water are not usually contaminated by poisonous chemicals or radionuclides in the absence of agricultural and industrial wastes, formulation of individual primary water quality regulations to suit different local conditions is recommended in order to achieve a wider application of low-cost treatment processes and equipment in developing countries.

VII.E. LOW COST WASTEWATER TREATMENT PROCESSES AND EQUIPMENT
(E/ESCAP/NR 10/14)

Introduction

Lack of treatment of wastewater is one of the major causes of outbreak of diseases. The damage that can be done by untreated wastewater includes contamination of the drinking water supply, destruction of fish and other aquatic life and impairment of water quality for recreation,

REFERENCES

(1) International Reference Centre for Community Water Supply and Sanitation, "Technology of small water supply system in developing countries", *Small Community Water Supplies,* Technical Paper Series No. 18, The Hague, The Netherlands, August 1981.

(2) Centre for Integrated Rural Development for Asia and the Pacific (CIRDAP), Newsletter, December 1981.

(3) Dhabadgaonkar, S.M., "Low cost household water treatment for developing countries", *Water and Waste Engineering in Asia,* Proceedings of the 8th WEDC Conference, Madras, India, February 1982, pp. 47-53.

(4) *Fortyfifth Report of the Director of Water Examination,* Metropolitan Water Board, London, 1971-1973.

(5) McCormick, R.F. and King, P.H., "Factors that affect use of direct filtration in treating surface waters", *Journal of the American Water Works Association (AWWA),* May 1982, pp. 234-242.

(6) Hutchison, W. and Foley, P.D., "Operational and experimental results of direct filtration", *Journal AWWA,* February 1974.

(7) Jahn, S.A., *Traditional Water Purification in Tropical Developing Countries – Existing Methods and Potential Application,* German Agency for Technical Co-operation (GTZ), Federal Republic of Germany, 1981.

(8) Davis, B.D. and others, *Microbiology,* Hagerstown, Maryland, Harper and Row, 1973, p. 1464.

(9) Beauman, W.H., "Disinfection techniques", *Proceedings of the Third Domestic Water Quality Symposium (for individual water systems),* St. Louis, Missouri, 1979, ASAE Publication 1-79, pp. 122-132.

agriculture, commerce or industry. Consequently, wastewater treatment may be regarded as one of the effective means of conserving water resources.

According to a 1980 report (1), there are many conventional sewage treatment works in developing countries, but only a few of them are said to be operating satisfactorily. The three major disadvantages of these conventional sewage treatment works were identified in the report as poor efficiency of pathogen removal, high capital and operating costs and requirement of highly trained personnel for maintenance. Thus, in order to provide safe and affordable wastewater disposal systems for as many people as possible in the developing countries, it may be necessary to use non-conventional lowcost wastewater treatment processes and equipment. It is observed that the high capital and operating cost associated with sewage treatment works in developing countries can be reduced substantially by promoting greater use of local technology, equipment and materials, while reducing the use of imported mechanical equipment as much as possible. The main purpose of a study on low-cost wastewater treatment processes and equipment is to identify those which can have practical application in the developing countries within the constraints of the limited funds available, expertise and available local materials, while at the same time achieving the major objectives of prevention of outbreak of diseases and prevention of injury to the receiving natural water courses by various contaminants present in wastewater.

The cost of a wastewater treatment process depends to a large extent on the quality of the influent and the desired quality of the effluent. The greater the variety of contaminants in the influent and the higher their concentration, the higher is the cost of treatment. Likewise, the higher the desired quality of treated effluent, the higher will be the cost. Treatment processes and equipment discussed in this paper are confined to those that deal with domestic wastes only and do not deal with agricultural and industrial wastes. Generally, treatment of domestic wastewater involves the removal to acceptable levels of particulate solid materials, organic compounds (indicated by biochemical oxygen demand and/or chemical oxygen demand), pathogenic organisms and odour. As regards the quality of the effluent, the standards should not be set unnecessarily high if it is desired to keep the cost of treatment low.

Wastewater treatment is usually carried out by processes, which are different combinations of individual operations or unit processes. Treatment processes and equipment for large communities are expensive, because in addition to handling large quantities of influent at a given time, they have to employ a larger number of unit processes in order to cope with the kind of influent that contains a greater variety of contaminants, the removal of some of which needs sophisticated and expensive processes. Besides, the quality of effluent required of such treatment plants is very high because of the large quantity of effluent discharge.

Treatment processes and equipment for small communities are less costly as they employ only a few simple unit processes. In these small community and household wastewater treatment processes, the cost can be reduced considerably by emphasizing the removal of pathogenic organisms in order to achieve the health objective.

In this paper, low-cost domestic wastewater treatment processes are classified into two broad categories as biological and physical treatment processes. A section on disinfection has been included in order to evaluate the effectiveness of various disinfection options which may be required in the form of tertiary treatment for those low-cost treatment processes that cannot achieve the total removal of disease causing pathogens. An overall evaluation of selected wastewater treatment processes is also carried out in order to identify those processes among the low-cost options which can achieve the effective removal of particulate solid materials and organic compounds as well as the total removal of pathogenic organisms.

A. BIOLOGICAL TREATMENT

Biological treatment processes are effective in removing chemical oxygen demand (COD), biochemical oxygen demand (BOD), suspended solids (SS), pathogens, phosphorus and nitrogen from the wastewater. Biological treatment processes can be generally classified as composting, alternating aerobic/anaerobic, aerobic, anaerobic, and emergent vegetation processes. The cost comparison of biological treatment processes is summarized in table 53

1. Composting processes

Composting can be defined as the biochemical degradation of organic materials to a humus-like substance by natural microbiological processes. Composting can be effected either by anaerobic or aerobic decomposition.

The anaerobic form of composting, as long practised by farmers throughout the world, is often associated with the formation of foulsmelling gases, usually requires a very long time and takes place at a relatively low temperature close to ambient. Aerobic composting requires a sufficient amount of atmospheric oxygen and is said to produce none of the objectionable features associated with anaerobic decomposition. Besides, both mesophilic and thermophilic organisms, which are involved in composting, are said to be widely distributed in nature and are, therefore, present in the sewage to be treated.

A study of the literature on composting processes indicated that the only reliable composting method which will assure effective and total pathogen inactivation, including the most resistant helminths, such as *ascaris* eggs and all other bacterial and viral pathogens, is thermophilic composting with heat treatment to a temperature of $55°$ - $60°C$

for several hours. Extensive modern research in composting has demonstrated that high temperatures required for heat inactivation of pathogens can be obtained during the active decomposition of organic matter by aerobic thermophilic micro-organisms that operate effectively in a temperature range of 45°- 85°C and generate a considerable amount of excess heat required for destroying the more sensitive pathogens.

Temperature and time are the two most important factors in the achievement of low pathogen survival in composting. Efficient composting also requires an appropriate balance between carbon and nitrogen (C/N), favourable moisture content, particle size and pH. According to Feachem and others (2), a C/N ratio of between 20:1 to 30:1 and a moisture content of between 20 to 60 per cent were said to create favourable conditions for composting. The survival conditions of selected pathogens in compost systems which depend upon the composting time and

Table 53. Cost comparison of biological treatment processes (cost of each unit for a household consisting of approximately five persons)

Name of process	Total annual unit cost ($US) representing the sum of annual O & M costs and equivalent annual cost of capital amortized over 20 years at 7 per cent discount rate factor = 0.09439
Composting processes	210-280
Alternating aerobic/anaerobic processes (facultative ponds)	150-300[a]
Aerobic processes:	
Maturation ponds (shallow-not aerated)	150-300
Aerated lagoons	400-550
Oxidation ditches	400-700[a]
Anaerobic processes:	
Septic tank	50-100
Anaerobic pretreatment ponds	200-400[a]
Emergent vegetation or photosynthetic processes	250-500[a]

Source: Adapted from information contained in reference (12).
Notes: Since the costs were estimated based on prices in the United States of America around 1981, the figures presented are rather high for developing countries. For instance, a more realistic cost for composting processes in developing countries should be $US 105 and that for septic tanks should be $US 63 according to information provided in reference (14).

[a] This estimate is based on insufficient on-site data and should be re-evaluated when sufficient data become available.

temperature, are given in figure 32. For each pathogen, time-temperature points above the curve represent its total destruction. From figure 32, it will be noted that even the most hardy of the pathogens, enteric viruses and *ascaris* ova, will be destroyed at the following time-temperature combinations: one hour at 62°C, one day at 50°C, one week at 46°C, and one month at 43°C. Thus, if all parts of a compost pile can be brought to a time-temperature state within the zone of safety on figure 32 it can be assured that complete pathogen destruction has been achieved.

There are two main types composting: continuous and batch. Both types require the addition of a carbon source, such as garbage, vegetable leaves or sawdust, to get a favourable C/N ratio.

a. *Continuous type*

The continuous composting types are based on the Swedish aerobic household composting system called "multrum", which consists of a watertight container with a sloping bottom. Human excreta (not including flushing water) is introduced at the upper and of the container, and mixes with organic kitchen and garden wastes, which are introduced lower down. Air ducts and a vent pipe are provided to promote aeration, evaporation and elimination of odours, and the decomposed material moves towards the lower end, from where it is periodically removed. The decomposition period is quite long, about four years, and hence the size of the container is large (3 m x 1 m x 1 m). The main feature of the "multrum" is its sloping bottom, which permits continuous use of a single container by separating the fresh and the decomposed material. The operation of this type of composting is fairly simple as a single container is used and the fresh excreta is not handled. Rural and urban experiments with multrums in the United Republic of Tanzania (3) were said to indicate that with adequate education, the majority of the users seem to adapt easily to the main requirements of composting, namely, sparing use of water when cleaning, adding sweepings and grass for the composting process, and adding ashes to neutralize acidity. Another similar experiment was said to be carried out in Manila (4) in order to evaluate its effectiveness in providing a low-cost sanitation solution for the Philippines, the result of which has not been available.

In India, anaerobic composting known as the Bangalore process is said to be practised on a communal basis with some success. City refuse is said to be mixed with night soil resulting in C/N ratios of about 6:1 to 8:1 in the compost achieving high levels of pathogen destruction (5).

In China (6), a composting technique is used, which operates on a household basis and consists of anaerobic digestion of night soil with small quantities of water. It

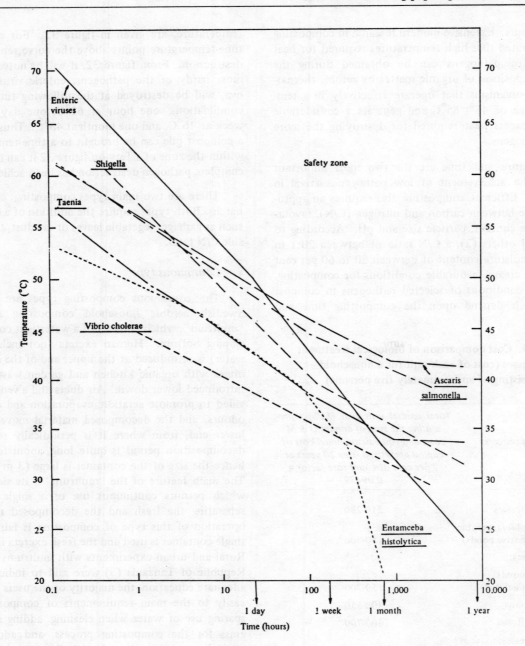

Figure 32. Influence of time and temperature on survival of selected pathogens in composting

Source: Feachem and others, *Sanitation and Disease.*

Note: The line represents conservative upper boundaries for pathogen death — that is, estimates of the time temperature combinations required for pathogen inactivation. A treatment process with time temperature effects falling within the "safety zone" should be lethal to all excreted pathogens (with the possible exception of hepatitis A virus — not included in the enteric viruses in the figure — at short retention times). Indicated time temperature requirements are at least: 1 hour at ≥62°C, 1 day at ≥50°C, and 1 week at ≥46°C.

takes the form of a two-partitioned, three-compartment septic tank, where the biological treatment takes place inside all the three compartments which have retention periods of 10, 10 and 30 days respectively. About 2 litres of water *per capita* are added daily and the liquid effluent is used as a fertilizer. Complete destruction of *ascaris* ova is said to be attained in the third compartment.

Wilson and Walker (7) stated that composting is also carried out in the United States for sewage sludge as well as raw sewage; and quite recently a variety of composting privies because available on the commercial market. The methods used are either the Windrow technique or the forced aeration method. The Windrow method consists of composting digested vacuum filtered sewage sludge with 23 per cent solids together with old well-composted sludge in open Windrows turned at least once a day by mobile mechanical composter-shredder machines. The forced aeration method relies on mechanically induced air movement through the pile; and organic waste, sawdust and wood chips are usually added to the sewage in order to reduce moisture content, provide a carbon source and prevent clogging during the aeration process.

b. *Batch type*

The batch type of composting is most common in China and Viet Nam. The composting of night soil in a systematic way was introduced to China in the 1930s (6) and is still practised. The centralized system of composting as practised in China consists of separating faeces and urine immediately at the squatting plate by means of a "urine drain" and separate collection in pots the contents of which are collected and transported to a centralized composting site on the outskirts of a village. Two kinds of composting are said to be used: pit composting and pile composting, both of which employ the aerobic action. In pit composting, air is channelled through trenches at the bottom of the pit; while in pile composting air is introduced into holes made by the removal of sticks. The ingredients of the compost are human excrement, animal faeces, organic rubbish and soil by approximately equal weights; while the moisture content is reported as between 30 and 50 per cent. The pile is then covered with an earth-mud mixture and left for 20 to 30 days before the composted material is used in agriculture.

The Vietnamese double vault toilet (8) was said to provide on-the-spot composting of excreta. It has two watertight tanks, which alternately serve as receptacles for defecation and composting. An opening is made in the face of each, together with a groove to channel urine into a separate vessel, while apertures are made in the back wall for the collection of the waste for composting. The tanks, which are often paved, are constructed above ground level to keep away surface runoff during the rains. Before using

the tank, its bottom is covered with a layer of powdered earth, while after use the faeces are covered with kitchen ashes to absorb moisture and to deodorize them. The opening is then covered with a lid, which is usually fitted with a long handle. When the tank is two-thirds full, its contents are levelled with a stick before it is filled to the brim with dried powdered earth. Then all the openings are tightly closed to create an anaerobic condition for composting. It was stated that the addition of kitchen wastes to the tank, while it is in use, effectively neutralizes the bad odours normally associated with anaerobic composting, which also effects the destruction of intestinal worm ova. The anaerobic composting was also said to play an important role in converting organic nitrogen into inorganic forms which are more readily available to plants.

2. Alternating aerobic/anaerobic processes

Waste stabilization ponds are the most economical method of sewage treatment if sufficient space is available at a relatively low-cost. They are the best form of treatment in tropical developing countries because they can achieve any desired level of pathogen removal, even complete removal. Generally, three types of ponds are in common use: anaerobic pretreatment ponds which are anaerobic owing to high sewage loads and lack of oxygen; maturation ponds which are aerobic with oxygen provided by algae; and facultative ponds which are alternating aerobic/anaerobic processes.

Facultative ponds do not employ mechanical aeration devices and are generally characterized by an aerobic zone at the surface, a transition aerobic-anaerobic zone at the middle depth and an anaerobic zone at the bottom. The oxygen necessary for bio-oxidation of the organic material is supplied principally by photosynthetic algae. The action of sunlight on algae in the pond enables them to grow and consume the nutrients in the sewage. Also essential to the process are the large numbers of aerobic bacteria in the pond, which break down organic solids in the sewage, making their nutrient content available to the algae. The carbon dioxide released, as the bacteria work on the organic solids, is utilized by the algae in their growth. The algae and the bacteria are interdependent (symbiotic). While the algae use the nutrients and carbon dioxide released by bacterial decomposition, the bacteria make use of and need the oxygen liberated by the algae during photosynthesis.

Facultative ponds usually have retention times of ten to forty days and depths of 1-1.5 metres. Their primary purpose is to reduce the BOD of the effluent. According to studies carried out by the United States Environmental Protection Agency (EPA) in 1974 (9) on the performance of facultative ponds, it was observed that although these systems are subject to seasonal variations, a properly designed, maintained and operated facultative waste stabilization pond system can produce a high quality effluent with a BOD concentration of less than 30 mg/l. The results of the studies also indicated that facultative ponds can produce an effluent that has a low suspended solids concentration composed of algae cells that may not be harmful to receiving streams and faecal coliform reductions that are primarily a function of hydraulic residence time. An effective system of facultative ponds usually consists of two or more ponds connected in series.

3. Aerobic processes

a. Maturation ponds

Maturation ponds generally receive facultative pond effluent and their primary function is to remove the pathogens. Hence they are responsible for the final quality of the effluent. These ponds usually have depths of 1 to 1.5 metres and retention times of 5 to 10 days. They do not employ mechanical aeration devices and are generally aerobic throughout the entire depth. They are feasible when there is sufficient space available. As a result of longer retention times, they achieve better pathogen removal than that obtained in the conventional activated sludge process. A complete removal of excreted protozoa and helmith ova from the effluent may be achieved although there may still be some hookworm larvae, bacterial pathogens and viruses. Schistosome larvae will be eliminated if the snail host is prevented from infesting the pond.

To achieve any desired level of pathogen removal, the effluent can be treated in one or more maturation ponds. According to Feachem and others, if two or more maturation ponds are used, with 5 to 10 days retention in each, a complete removal of cysts and ova will result. Very high levels of viral and bacterial removal are also achieved, and by adding sufficient ponds, a pathogen-free effluent may be produced.

Another variation of maturation ponds, which also operates as an aerobic process, is the wetland system. Wetland is defined as land where the water table is at (or above) the surface long enough each year to maintain saturated soil conditions and growth of related vegetation. Thus, wetlands can be either marshes, swamps, bogs, cypress domes etc. or man-made wetland systems. Routing wastewater flows to wetlands and letting the bacteria there decompose the wastes is an effective method of reducing the treatment cost, because when a natural wetland is already available nearby, wastewater treatment can be obtained with almost zero cost.

Currently, natural wetland systems are said to be limited to further treatment of secondary effluents, while constructed wetland systems are used for further treatment of primary effluents. The removal efficiency of typical pollutants as stated by Reed and others (10) is given in table 54.

Table 54. Performance of wetland processes
(Percentage removal of contaminants)

	Natural wetland secondary effluent	Constructed wetland primary effluent
BOD	70-96	50-90
Suspended solids	60-90	—
Total nitrogen	40-90	30-98
Total phosphorus	10-50	20-90

Bacteria attached to plant stems and humic deposits are assumed to be the major factor for BOD and nitrogen removal when plant harvesting is not practised. According to Reed, the land area required for natural wetland systems ranges from 30 to over 60 acres per million gallons of wastewater applied, while the surface area for constructed marshes ranges from 23 to 37 acres per million gallons of wastewater. Wetland processes are said to achieve high removal efficiencies for BOD, suspended solids, trace organics and heavy metals. They have considerable potential as a low-cost, low-energy technique for upgrading wastewater effluents, particularly in areas where natural wetlands exist.

b. Aerated lagoons

Aerated lagoons are wastewater stabilization ponds that employ some type of mechanical aeration devices. These may be regarded as one of the modifications of activated sludge process in order to make it suitable for application in developing countries. They are aerobic throughout the entire depth, but depending on the degree of mixing and the type of aerator employed, they may have an anaerobic bottom layer. According to studies by EPA (9), aerated lagoons can produce an effluent BOD concentration of less than 30 mg/l, which can be satisfactorily disinfected with chlorination. However, since they employ mechanical devices they are not simple enough and their cost may not be low enough for use in the developing countries.

c. Oxidation ditches

Oxidation ditches are another modification of the activated sludge process. Screened sewage is aerated in and circulated around a continuous oval ditch by one or more special aerators called rotors, which are placed across the ditch. The ditch effluent is settled in a conventional secondary sedimentation tank and almost all the sludge (95 per cent) is returned to the ditch, while only a small quantity of excess sludge is placed directly on sludge drying beds. The hydraulic retention times are one to three days in the ditch and two hours minimum in the sedimentation tank. The mean solids retention time, however, is 20-30 days because of recycling. As a result, only a small quantity of excess sludge is produced, which is highly mineralized and requires only dewatering on drying beds.

The removal of pathogens in oxidation ditches is comparable to that of the conventional activated sludge process or slightly higher as a result of a longer retention time. The main advantages of oxidation ditches are that primary sedimentation is not required and that sludge production and treatment are minimal. However, they are not suitable for use in developing countries for the reasons stated for aerated lagoons.

d. *Trickling filter*

A trickling filter is a treatment unit in which biological contact is made independent of filtration and is used where intermittent sand filtration is not feasible owing to a lack of natural sandy soil and large space. The purification effected by trickling filters is not due to filtration but contact.

Crushed rock is the most common filter or contact medium, but large gravel, anthracite coal, coke, cinders, blast-furnace slag, broken bricks, clinkers, wooden laths, brushwood, ceramic and other materials can also be employed depending on local availability. Wastewater or sewage is sprayed onto the surface of these beds from fixed or movable nozzles. The sewage then trickles over the contact media downward through the beds. Currents of air, induced mainly by differences in the temperature of the atmosphere and the sewage, sweep through the beds and keep them aerobic. The distribution of sewage may be intermittent or almost continuous.

Low-rate operation at rates of 1 to 4 million gallons per acre per day (mgad) preceded and followed by settling tanks are said to remove from 80 to 95 per cent of the BOD, from 70 to 92 per cent of the suspended solids, and from 90 to 95 per cent of the bacteria (11). High-rate operation at rates of 10 to 30 mgad are said to have lower values of removal, unless the sewage or wastewater is recirculated. Trickling filters are said to produce an effluent that will meet almost any specified degree of treatment at comparatively low-cost. However, Feachem and others gave the removal of various types of pathogens by trickling filters as follows, which indicates that they cannot achieve complete removal of pathogens.

Pathogen	Log_{10} unit reduction
Viruses	0-1
Bacteria	0-2
Protozoa	0-2
Helminths	0-1

4. Anaerobic processes

a. *Septic tank*

Anaerobic septic tanks have been widely used in most on-site wastewater treatment systems to remove settleable and floatable solids. They have liquid retention times of the order of one to three days, and the effluent is normally discharged to a soakaway. There are two ways by which pathogens are removed from effluent in septic tanks. First, solids settle to the sludge layer at the bottom, taking along with them, any bacteria or viruses that are absorbed onto them and also any ova or cysts that are sufficiently dense to settle. Secondly, pathogens that do not settle with the solids remain in the liquid layers but will eventually die out before the effluent is discharged to the soakaway. The degree to which the pathogens are removed depends on retention times and on their reaction to the rich anaerobic liquor. According to Bauer and others (12), BOD and SS concentrations of a septic tank effluent varies from 120 to 150 mg/l and from 40 to 70 mg/l respectively or even over a wider range depending on tank size, configuration, number of compartments and influent water characteristics.

b. *Anaerobic pretreatment pond*

Anaerobic pretreatment ponds function much like open septic tanks. They have retention times of one to five days and depths of 2 to 4 metres. When using facultative ponds and maturation ponds for stabilization of wastewater with BOD concentration of more than 400 mg/l, the use of anaerobic lagoons as pretreatment units ahead of facultative ponds is advantageous, because they minimize the land requirements of the whole waste stabilization pond system.

Anaerobic ponds are generally deeper than aerated and facultative ponds and are devoid of oxygen throughout the entire depth. However, under specific limited conditions, anaerobic lagoons may exhibit a very thin aerobic surface layer. The removal of pathogens, particularly *Escherichia coli*, in anaerobic lagoons has been reported by Feachem and others as 70-85 per cent at 20°C in 3.5 days and 46-65 per cent at 9°C in 3.5 days.

5. Emergent vegetation processes

The basic goal in wastewater treatment is either to remove the objectionable waste substances and organisms from water, or to convert the former into non-objectionable forms. In emergent vegetation processes, plants serve as scavengers and thereby carry out two functions of treatment — conversion and removal. In making use of this process, plants are inserted at any point in the treatment flow. Thus, raw sewage is treated by exposure to plants; however, oversize particles should be removed from raw sewage before processing. Insertion of plants further down the line removes the stabilized or oxidized materials in the preceding treatment steps. Heavy metal removal is accomplished through direct assimilation by the plants or indirectly through the formation of insoluble complexes brought about by a change in pH level due to plant growth. Harvesting of plant material produced in the treatment process constitutes the final removal.

The cost effectiveness of this process as compared with other treatment processes has not yet been studied, but judging from the fact that subtropical and tropical regions are favourable to plant growth, the harvested plant material from treatment process can be used as fertilizer or feedstuff and that a considerable amount of manual labour rather than expensive equipment is required in harvesting and periodical removal of dead and decaying vegetative matter, this system may have a lower cost than other processes of comparable capacity in the developing countries of the region.

According to Golueke (13), the emergent vegetation processes can be divided into two categories: the algal and vascular plant systems.

a. *Algal systems*

The algae used in algal systems can be subdivided into single cell and filamentous types. Examples of single cell algae are *Chlorella* and *Euglena* and various species of *Scenedesmus,* while those of filamentous types are *Spirulina* and *Spirogyra.*

A characteristic of algal systems is the fact that photosynthetic organisms are distributed throughout the body of wastewater, although they may be more numerous in the zone of light penetration; and treatment of wastewater is achieved through a loose symbiosis between algae and bacteria. The removal of waste nutrients by algae is not limited to nitrogen alone. It also includes others that can be assimilated by the plants. Thus, a certain amount of phosphorus, magnesium and other metallic compounds are converted to algal protoplasm. The conversion is accelerated by certain changes in the physical-chemical conditions that result from algal growth. Since algae have the capacity to concentrate DDT, its derivatives, radio-active strontium and an assortment of heavy metals, it is essential that such substances are excluded from wastewaters if harvested algae are to be used as a feedstuff. It is also

essential that the algae be removed from the reclaimed water to prevent them from recontaminating it when they eventually die and decompose.

b. *Aquatic plant systems*

Aquatic plant treatment systems are generally similar in concept to that of waste stabilization ponds. Some of the aquatic plants that grow well on sewage are the common reed *Phragmites communis,* the bulrush *Scirpus lacustris,* water hyacinths, duckweeds, forms of elodea, *Egeria densa,* hydrilla, and *Cerato-phyllum demersum.* Among these plants, water hyacinth is receiving most attention, because the extremely vigorous growth of the plant appears to offer the potential of effectively removing the nutrients from wastewaters. According to the United States National Academy report, the amounts of nutrients removed under ideal conditions are as indicated in table 31. In addition to the nutrients listed in table 55, water hyacinth systems are also capable of removing high levels of BOD and suspended solids.

Table 55. Nutrient removal by water hyacinths

Element	Amount recovered (kg/ha/day)
Nitrogen	22 to 24
Phosphorus	8 to 17
Postassium	22 to 24
Calcium	11 to 22
Magnesium	2 to 4
Sodium	18 to 34

One disadvantage of using water hyacinths is that the weed can cause damage to waterways if allowed to escape the treatment ponds. The aquatic system is suitable for countries in subtropical and tropical regions where the climate is warm and land and manpower resources are abundant. Cheap labour is required, because harvesting of water hyacinths may be essential to maintain high levels of system performance.

According to Reed (10), a pond surface area of approximately 15 acres (61,000 m^2) per million gallons of wastewater is required for treating primary effluent to secondary effluent quality or better. For systems treating secondary effluents to achieve higher levels of BOD and SS removal, an area of about 5 acres (20,000 m^2) per million gallons of wastewater is said to be required.

Based on his studies, Reed concluded that aquatic plant systems using water hyacinths can achieve high removal efficiencies for BOD, SS, trace organics, heavy metals and nitrogen; that the potential can equal or even exceed that achieved in mechanical treatment systems; that the effluent from the water hyacinth system can be much better in quality than that from a waste stabilization pond, particularly with respect to removal of SS, metals, trace organics and nutrients; and that duckweeds are a more cold-tolerant plant than water hyacinths, which paves the way for application of such system in colder climates.

Although the aquatic plant systems have been identified by many authors as a low-cost process, it has not yet been established that the costs of plant harvesting and processing will be completely offset by the value of useful products, such as animal feeds, compost, biogas etc. A survey and evaluation of costs and benefits to reflect local conditions in different countries may be necessary before suggesting an extensive application of this system. Additional study may also be needed to establish optimum plant harvesting and utilization techniques.

B. PHYSICAL TREATMENT

Physical treatment processes may be used for on-site wastewater treatment in conjunction with, or independent of, biological treatment processes. When used in conjunction with biological treatment processes they can reduce COD, BOD and SS concentrations to levels much lower than those which can be achieved by biological processes and/or remove wastewater constituents, such as phosphorus and dissolved inorganic salts which do not respond readily to biological treatment processes. When used independently of other treatment processes, they can remove waste-

water constituents, such as COD, BOD, SS, ammonia, nitrates and phosphates to acceptable levels. Physical treatment processes may be generally divided into separation and filtration processes. The performance of physical processes is summarized in table 56.

1. Separation

The separation process may be subdivided into screening and sedimentation, both of which may be used in low-cost wastewater treatment systems.

The main purpose of screening is to remove coarse suspended and floating matters of substantial size from the wastewater, for which either racks or bar screens may be used.

Sedimentation is a process in which settleable solids are separated from wastewater by gravitation and by natural flocculation or aggregation of particles, and is usually employed before wastewater is discharged into receiving waters or in advance of biological treatment.

2. Filtration

Household wastewaters are not amenable to treatment in conventional slow or rapid sand filtration plants as they are putrescible and clog filters rapidly. However, treated effluents can be filtered to provide improved protection to receiving water courses. There are two types of filtration, namely, pressure and gravity. Pressure filtration cannot be regarded as a low-cost process as it usually requires surge tank, pressurization pump, tank, filter media or membrane bypass piping, strainer backwash water supply, distribution, collection, and holding or disposal system.

Gravity filtration of wastewater is generally accomplished through three types of systems, namely, buried sand filter, single stage or series type intermittent sand filter and recirculating sand filter. Among these three types, the intermittent sand filter is the most commonly used type and is simple enough for use in developing countries. The main features of intermittent sand filtration are as follows.

When there are natural, sandy areas and agricultural utilization of sewage is dispensed with, intermittent sand filters can be developed at reasonably low cost. Although a high degree of treatment of wastewater can be achieved by filtration, it is advantageous to have a pretreatment by plain sedimentation. Sand filtration following biological treatment usually results in an effluent, which is hardly distinguishable in appearance from drinking water. However, attempts to use sand filters in the absence of natural, sandy areas should be avoided as they will incur high costs.

Table 56. Performance of physical treatment processes

	Selected contaminants removed	Range of total annual cost ($ US)[a]
Separation:		
Screening	SS	100-300
Sedimentation	SS, BOD	N.A.
Filtration:		
Pressure filtration:		
Sand media	SS, BOD, P	150-300
Membrane	SS, BOD, COD, microbiological	400-600
Gravity filtration	SS, BOD, NH$_4$, NO$_3$	100-300

Source: Based on reference (12).

[a] The total annual cost represents the annual operation and maintenance cost plus the equivalent annual cost of the capital investment amortized over 20 years at 7 per cent discount rate (factor = 0.09439).

Intermittent sand filters contain drainage pipes that are laid in the sand bed with open joints at depths of 3 to 4 ft (approx. 1 m) and surrounded with layers of coarse stone and gravel graded from coarse to fine to keep the sand out. These sand filters can reduce BOD and SS levels of wastewater to less than 10 mg/l and reduce coliform levels by 90 to 99.9 per cent (12). Operation and maintenance of intermittent sand filters are simple, and the process is well suited for treatment of wastewater from small communities and isolated institutions.

C. DISINFECTION

Pathogens of all kinds are destroyed or removed from wastewater in varying degrees by most treatment processes. Some treatment processes can achieve the total destruction or removal of pathogens, while others can effect only their partial elimination. In the latter case, some pathogens may still remain in the effluent and pose the danger of spreading and transmitting diseases. Therefore, wastewater effluents from such treatment processes may require disinfection prior to their disposal into natural water courses by direct discharge, irrigation, or non-potable reuse to meet environmental and/or public health requirements. Disinfection is the selective destruction of disease-causing organisms and can be effected by both physical and chemical agents.

1. Pathogens in wastewater

Pathogens that may be present in wastewater are classified into four groups of microbes — viruses, bacteria, leptospires, and protozoa — and worms parasitic to man which are referred to as helminths. All these pathogens are found to cause one kind of disease or another and should be eliminated to avoid health problems.

In conventional water bacteriology there are three main groups of bacteria which are used as faecal indicators. These are: the coliform bacteria; the faecal streptococci; and the anaerobe, *Clostridium perfringens* (2). These indicators, however, are useful in assessing the safety of drinking water supplies only but not in assessing the effectiveness of pathogen removal in wastewater treatment processes, because their presence is related to the presence of bacterial pathogens only and not to other pathogens, namely, viruses, leptospires, protozoa and helminths. Therefore, in order to make a reliable assessment of the health risk posed by the treated wastewater effluent, it is necessary to use a pathogen indicator organism instead of faecal indicator organism. A survey of recent literature on water bacteriology indicates that such pathogen indicators have not yet been discovered.

2. Disinfection options

Disinfection options can generally be divided into three major categories: chemical agents, physical agents, and combined chemical — physical agents. Wastewater disinfection options, their performance, environmental acceptability and costs are summarized in table 57. From this table, it will be observed that options represented by the use of chlorine, iodine, ultraviolet irradiation and ozone combined with ultraviolet irradiation have the least costs among several alternatives, which are discussed in the following sub-sections.

a. *Chemical agents*

(i) *Chlorine*

Earlier authors on wastewater treatment (11) described the addition of chlorine to sewage as capable of serving such purposes as disinfection, destruction or control of undesirable algae and aquatic growth in receiving waters, prevention of anaerobic conditions giving undesirable odours, increased removal of grease etc. Chlorine is applied to wastewater either as a gas through a submerged diffuser or as a solution of chlorine gas in water. For temporary or emergency chlorination, bleaching powder or calcium hypochlorite can be used.

Imhoff and Fair (11) defined satisfactory disinfection as 99.9 per cent of E. Coli destruction and 37C bacterial count. This condition is said to be attained when the chlorine residual after 15 to 30 minutes of contact lies between 0.2 and 1.0 mg/1. The authors, therefore, prescribe a residual of 2 mg/l after 15 minutes of contact as a condition for attaining safe disinfection. Based on this definition of safe disinfection, the amounts of chlorine required for satisfactory disinfection of wastewater effluent are suggested in table 58.

A study of the time-concentration-temperature relationship of disinfection by chlorine indicated that the concentration is somewhat more important than the time of exposure. Therefore, for improved chlorination, it is better to increase the dose rather than the detention time.

Currently, chlorination of sewage effluents is practised in only a few countries (notably in North America and Israel) for reducing the pathogen content. Recent studies by Feachem and others on effluent chlorination, however, indicated that it has serious limitations with regard to pathogen removal in order to ensure safe disposal into natural receiving waters. Some of the major reasons for such limitations are given as follows.

First, to achieve a coliform effluent concentrations of less than 100/100 millilitres, chlorine has to be applied in

Table 57. Disinfection options

Generic type	Performance	O & M requirements			Environmental acceptability (potential hazards and nuisances)	Range of annual cost ($US)[a]
		Frequency of sheduled maintenance (number per year)	Hardware complexity	Equipment failure (requiring) unscheduled service		
Chemical agents:						
Halogens:						
Chlorine	Consistent	2-4	Simple	Frequent	Toxicity (chlorinated organics)	150-250
Iodine	Consistent	2-4	Simple	Infrequent	Toxicity uncertain	150-250
Bromine	Potentially consistent	Unknown	Unknown	Unknown	Unknown	250-350
Halogen Mixtures	Potentially consistent	2-4	Simple-moderate	Frequent	Toxicity (halogenated organics)	250-350
Ozone	Consistent	2-4	Complex	Frequent	Toxicity unknown; safety (for pure oxygen feed)	450-600
Halogen plus Ozone	Potentially consistent	2-4	Complex	Frequent	Toxicity uncertain	500-650
Acids and Bases	Potentially consistent	Unknown	Moderate	Unknown	Neutralization required	450-600
Alcohols	Potentially consistent	Unknown	Moderate	Unknown	Increases effluent BOD	250-450
Dyes	Ineffective	–	–	–	–	–
Heavy Metals	Potentially consistent	Unknown	Unknown	Unknown	Toxicity, residuals disposal	450-600
Hydrogen Peroxide	Ineffective	–	–	–	–	–
Permanganage	Potentially consistent	Unknown	Unknown	Unknown	Residuals disposal	450-600
Phenols	Potentially consistent	Unknown	Moderate	Unknown	Effluent toxicity	250-450
Quaternary Ammonia	Potentially consistent	Unknown	Unknown	Unknown	Toxicity	450-600
Surfactants	Ineffective	–	–	–	–	–
Physical agents:						
Irradiation:						
Ultraviolet	Consistent	2-4	Moderate	Infrequent	Toxicity unknown	150-250
Gamma ray	Appears consistent	2-4	Complex	Infrequent	Safety	500-700
X-ray	Potentially consistent	Unknown	Moderate	Unknown	Safety	400-600
Electrochemical	Unknown	–	–	–	–	–
Thermal:						
Heating	Potentially consistent	–	Moderate	Frequent	High effluent temperature	1500+
Freezing	Potentially consistent	–	–	–	–	–
Ultrafiltration	Potentially consistent	2-4	Moderate	Frequent	Concentrate disposal	250-400
Ultrasonics	Unknown	–	–	–	–	–
Physical plus chemical agents						
Ultraviolet plus ozone[b]	Appears consistent	2-4	Moderate	Infrequent	Toxicity unknown	150-250
Ultraviolet plus halogens	Potentially consistent	2-4	Moderate	Frequent	Toxicity (halogenated organics)	300-600

Source: Reference (12)

Notes: a Amortized capital cost plus annual operation and maintenance cost (1981) per household consisting of 4-5 persons.
       b Ozone generated by specialized ultra violet (UV) lamp.

Table 58. Amounts of chlorine required for disinfection of sewage and sewage effluents

(chlorine residual = 2 mg/l; contact period = 15 min)

Type of sewage or effluent	Probable chlorine requirements	
	mg/l	lb/day per 1,000 persons[a]
Raw sewage, depending on strength and staleness	6 to 25	5 to 21
Settled sewage	5 to 20	4 to 17
Chemically precipitated sewage	3 to 20	3 to 17
Trickling-filter effluent	3 to 20	3 to 17
Activated-sludge plant effluent	2 to 20	2 to 17
Intermittent sand-filter effluent	1 to 10	1 to 3

Source: Reference[11]

a For sewage flow of 100 gallons per capita per day.

heavy doses (10-30 mg/l). These levels of chlorine will kill pathogenic bacteria, but there is evidence of their regrowth after chlorination. Secondly, such high levels of chlorine also destroy some other bacteria that are essential for the natural self-purification of the effluent and thus adversely affect the ecology of the receiving waters. Thirdly, viruses are much more resistant to chlorination than bacteria with the result that complete viral removal may not be achieved even with a chlorine concentration of 30 mg/l. Finally, it is unlikely that chlorination of effluents will be effective in eliminating protozoan cysts, because these are more resistant than either bacteria or viruses. Most helminth ova are said to be totally unharmed by effluent chlorination. In view of the foregoing, it may be concluded that chlorination cannot effect total removal of pathogens from wastewater.

(ii) Iodine

Iodine is less widely used than chlorine for wastewater disinfection. As in the case of chlorine, bacteria are readily killed by iodine disinfection while viruses are somewhat resistant and spores and cysts are not affected. Bauer and others (12) stated that an analysis of effluents from iodine contact chambers providing approximately 20 minutes detention time revealed only trace faecal coliform counts. It should be noted that information on iodine disinfection of wastewater are very scarce and only very limited data indicate that iodine provides effective disinfection. Hence, it may be concluded that the effectiveness of iodine in the complete removal of pathogens for wastewater has not yet been confirmed.

b. Physical agents

According to Bauer and others, currently available ultraviolet (UV) disinfection units appear to be capable of providing consitently high levels of disinfection provided that routine maintenance is performed. The UV units are said to be capable of destroying bacteria and viruses, while higher levels of UV energy and detention times are required for destroying spores and cysts. However, since UV irradiation does not produce a residual, which is capable of providing long-term disinfection, there is a possibility of pathogenic regrowth or recontamination of UV disinfected wastewater. The technology involved in UV irradiation is not simple and information regarding the application of UV disinfection are scarce. For these reasons, it is not regarded as a suitable method for application in developing countries.

c. Combined physical-chemical agents

Ultraviolet radiation plus ozone-disinfection also involves the use of advanced technology and complex equipment. Besides, performance information on this disinfection technique is not available and since it has not been tested yet, its application in developing countries is not appropriate.

D. EFFECTIVENESS OF VARIOUS LOW COST WASTEWATER TREATMENT PROCESSES

As mentioned earlier, the major contaminants in wastewater that tend to pollute receiving waters are particulate solid materials, organic compounds and pathogenic organisms. The presence of particulate solid materials in the form of suspended solids (SS) makes the water turbid and unsuitable for domestic and other uses, while the presence of organic compounds affect the existence of fish and other aquatic life. In assessing the quality of wastewater, the concentration of SS is used as a measure of contamination by solid particles and the biochemical oxygen demand (BOD) and/or chemical oxygen demand (COD) are used as a measure of the presence of organic compounds. To be more precise, BOD is an indirect measure of the amount of decomposable matter (significant organic matter) present and a direct measure of the respiratory oxygen requirements of the living organisms that are responsible for decomposition, while COD is a measure of the amount of carbon in many types of organic matter. COD is useful in identifying the performance of various steps of treatment and it is of considerable value as an estimate of the strength of those wastewaters for which BOD cannot be determined owing to the presence of certain substances that are toxic to the organisms activating the BOD test.

The potential presence of disease-causing organisms in wastewaters poses a health hazard for people using the receiving natural waters downstream. In evaluating the effectiveness of wastewater treatment with respect to health aspects, the removal of five types of pathogens is considered, namely, viruses, bacteria, leptospires, protozoa and helminths. In the virus group, only enteric viruses are considered and non-enteric viruses are not considered. Pathogens considered in the bacteria group are salmonellae, shingellae, E. coli, and cholera vibrio, whereas only the entamoeba histolytica cysts are considered in the protozoa group. The helminth group consists of hookworm ova, ascaris ova, shistosome ova, and taenia ova.

The performance of selected wastewater treatment processes in the removal of particulate solid materials and organic compounds is presented in table 59. It will be observed that some of the treatment processes listed in this table are combinations of two or more individual processes discussed in previous sections. It was also assumed that processes, such as lagoons, gravity slow sand filtration and disinfection by chlorination, are being used as tertiary treatment for wastewater effluent already treated by other treatment processes. As the values indicated in table 59 are based on information contained in different sources, it will be observed that the performance is indicated as the minimum level (mg/l) to which the concentration of contaminants can be reduced in some cases and as the percentage removal of these contaminants in others.

The performance of treatment processes in pathogen removal is presented in table 60. It will be observed from tables 59 and 60 that four low-cost treatment processes, namely, thermophilic composting, waste stabilization

ponds, lagoons and gravity slow sand filtration have the highest efficiency in the removal and major contaminants, particularly with regard to waste stabilization and the complete removal of the pathogens. It should be noted that not even disinfection by chlorination as tertiary treatment can completely remove the helminths and viruses. The total annual costs indicated in table 59 are based on the prices in the United States and therefore do not reflect the local market in developing countries. However, these figures are useful in giving a rough comparison of the costs of these treatment processes.

Table 59. Performance of selected wastewater treatment processes in removing particulate solid materials and organic compounds

	Type of treatment	BOD	COD	SS	Approximate total annual cost ($US)
1.	Composting (aerobic, anaerobic and thermophilic digestion)	...[a]	...	N.A.[b]	210-230
2.	Waste stabilization ponds (anaerobic pretreatment pond, aerobic/anaerobic facultative pond, and aerobic maturation pond) 3 cells with 25 days retention	30 mg/l[c]	...	...	500-1000
3.	Lagoons (aerated aerobic or anaerobic) as tertiary treatment	33 mg/l[c]	308 mg/l[c]	60 mg/l[c]	400-550
4.	Oxidation ditch with sedimentation and sludge drying	...	...	...	400-700
5.	Trickling filter with primary and secondary sedimentation	80-95[d]	–	70-92[d]	...
6.	Activated sludge process with primary and secondary sedimentation (generally used as part of conventional treatment processes)	75-95[d]	–	85-95[d]	...
7.	Septic tanks	138 mg/l[c]	327 mg/l[c]	49 mg/l[c]	50-100
8.	Primary sedimentation (a) Plain sedimentation (b) Chemical coagulation	25-40[d] 50-85[d]	– –	40-70[d] 70-90[d]	... ...
9.	Gravity slow sand filtration as tertiary treatment	90-95[d]	–	85-95[d]	100-300
10.	Disinfection by chlorine as tertiary treatment	...	...	...	150-250

Source: Based on references (11) and (12).

Notes: The total annual cost represent the annual operation and maintenance cost plus the equivalent annual cost of the capital investment amortized over 20 years at 7 per cent discount rate (factor = 0.09439) for a household consisting of approximately 5 persons.

[a] ... – Data not available.

[b] N.A. – Not applicable.

[c] Minimum level to which contaminants in wastewater can be reduced by a treatment process.

[d] Percentage removal of various contaminants.

Table 60. Performance of selected wastewater treatment
processes in pathogen removal

Type of treatment	Type of pathogens				
	Viruses	Bacteria	Leptospires	Protozoa	Helminths
1. Composting (aerobic with three months minimum retention)	B	B	A	A	B
2. Unheated anaerobic digestion or composting	B	B	A	B	C
3. Thermophilic digestion or composting	A	A	A	A	A
4. Waste stabilization ponds-aerobic, anaerobic, aerobic/anaerobic (3 cells with minimum retention of 25 days)	A	A	A	A	A
5. Lagoons (aerated aerobic or anaerobic) as tertiary treatment	A	A	A	A	A
6. Oxidation ditch with sedimentation and sludge drying	B	B	C	B	B
7. Trickling filter with primary and secondary sedimentation, sludge digestion and sludge drying	B	B	C	B	B
8. Activated sludge process with primary and secondary sedimentation, digestion, and sludge drying (generally used as part of conventional treatment processes)	B	B	C	B	B
9. Septic tanks	B	B	A	C	B
10. Primary sedimentation (with or without chemical coagulation)	C	B	C	B	B
11. Gravity slow sand filtration as tertiary treatment	A	A	A	A	A
12. Disinfection by chlorination as tertiary treatment	B	A	A	A	B

Source: Based on information contained in reference[12]

Note: A – Complete removal or removal to safe levels.
       B – Partial removal
       C – Negligible or zero removal

E. CONCLUSIONS AND RECOMMENDATIONS

The following conclusions and recommendations can be drawn based on the discussions in the previous sections.

(1) The purpose of most low-cost wastewater treatment processes and equipment is only to prevent injury to the receiving natural water courses, with particular emphasis on the prevention of outbreak of diseases. Direct reuse of the effluent as a raw water supply source is not advisable as it would require raising the quality of the treated effluent which would inevitably involve higher costs.

(2) Among the low-cost wastewater treatment processes that have been evaluated, thermophilic digestion/ composting, waste stabilization ponds, aerated lagoons and gravity slow sand filtration are the most effective processes with regard to their overall performance in the removal of particulate solid materials and organic compounds as well

as in the complete elimination of pathogenic organisms. These processes, with the exception of aerated lagoons, are suitable for application in developing countries as they are comparatively simple and can make maximum use of local materials and labour.

(3) Emergent vegetation processes, particularly those involving the use of water hyacinths, are low-cost processes that can be found applicable in the developing countries of the region. However, their effectiveness in the complete elimination of pathogens has not been established as yet.

(4) Disinfection of wastewater by chemical agents can achieve only partial elimination of pathogenic organisms. Besides, the extensive use of chemical disinfectants poses the danger of damaging the ecological balance of natural water courses. Chemical disinfection is complicated and needs trained personnel as the dosage has to be varied according to the strength and quantity of wastewater.

These facts together with the need for importation of chemicals from abroad make chemical disinfection not practical in the developing countries.

(5) Physical disinfection, that is, ultraviolet irradiation, although capable of destroying all pathogens, involves the use of electrical energy, advanced technology and complicated equipment. Besides, it cannot ensure the prevention of pathogenic regrowth and recontamination because of the lack of a residual effect capable of providing long term disinfection.

(6) Selection of an appropriate wastewater treatment process for use in developing countries should be made from those options that are capable of eliminating all the disease causing pathogens and which do not require additional disinfection.

(7) The faecal indicators used in current practice to monitor the concentration of disease causing pathogenic organisms are not reliable. Further research on the identification of a pathogen indicator organism would be useful in making a reliable estimate of the pathogen concentration in the treated effluent from low cost treatment processes and equipment.

(8) More studies and research should be carried out for low-cost wastewater treatment processes with a view to enhancing their performance and further reduction of costs. The results of these studies should be disseminated among the countries of the region.

(9) A field survey should be conducted on the cost and performance of existing wastewater treatment processes and equipment in the countries of the region, so that a comparative analysis of the cost effectiveness of various processes and equipment can be made. Such an analysis can be expected to identify treatment processes and equipment appropriate for various site specific conditions so as to achieve maximum efficiency at minimum cost.

REFERENCES

1. UNICEF Waterfront No. 27, WS/399/81, 5 June 1981, p. 21.

2. Feachem, R.G., Bradley D.J., Garelick, H., Mara, D.D., *Health Aspects of Excreta and Sullage Management — A State of the Art Review,* Appropriate Technology for Water Supply and Sanitation, Vol. 3., World Bank, Dec. 1980.

3. Eygelaar, J., "Composting toilets", *Report of a Visit to the Alternative Waste Disposal Project, Dar-es Salaam, Tanzania,* University of Nairobi, Kenya, 1977.

4. Rybezynski, W., "The Minimus composting toilet — an inexpensive sanitation solution for the Philippines", *Report to the UNEP, Philippines,* 1976.

5. Bhaskaran, T.R., and others, "Studies on the survival of pathogens in nightsoil compost", *Indian Journal of Agricultural Science,* vol. 27, part I, 1957, pp. 91-102.

6. Rybczynski W., and others, "Low-cost technology options for sanitation: A-state-of-the-art review and annotated bibliography", *Appropriate Technology for Water Supply and Sanitation,* International Development Research Centre, World Bank, Feb. 1982.

7. Wilson, G.B., Walker, J.M., "Composting sewage sludge: how?, *Compost Science,* vol. 14(5), Sep-Oct 1973, pp. 30-32.

8. McMichael, J.K., *Health in the Third World — Studies from Vietnam,* London Spokesman Books, 1976.

9. McClelland, N.I., ed., "Individual on-site wastewater system", *Proceedings of the Fifth National Conference on Wastewater Treatment Alternatives for Rural and Semirural Areas,* 1978, Ann Arbor Science Publishers Inc., pp. 155-184.

10. Reed, S.C., and others, "Engineers assess aquaculture systems for wastewater treatment", *Civil Engineering ASCE,* July 1981, pp. 64-67, November 1982, pp. 51-53.

11. Imhoff, K., Fair, G.M., *Sewage Treatment,* New York, John Wiley and Sons Inc., 1956.

12. Bauer, D.H., Conrad, E.T., and Sherman, D.G., *Evaluation of On-site Wastewater Treatment and Disposal Options,* Springfield, VA 22161, National Technical Information Service, United States Department of Commerce.

13. Golueke, C.G., "Using plants for wastewater treatment", *Water Resources Journal,* December 1981, pp. 77-81.

14. Kalbermatten, J.M., and others, "Technical and economic options", *Appropriate Technology for Water Supply and Sanitation,* Vol. 1, World Bank, Dec. 1980.

VII.F. LOW-COST TECHNOLOGY FOR WATER SUPPLY AND SANITATION: POLLUTION AND HEALTH PROBLEMS RELATED TO INCORRECT APPLICATIONS
(E/ESCAP/NR. 10/15)

Note by the secretariat

The attached paper was prepared by the South-East Asia Regional Office of the World Health Organization at the request of the ESCAP secretariat.

It has been recognized that low-cost technology for water supply and sanitation is one of the most effective means of providing safe drinking water and hygienic waste disposal facilities to as many people as possible in developing countries within the constraints of limited financial resources and the relatively short time frame set by the targets of the International Drinking Water Supply and Sanitation Decade (IDWSSD).

However, like any technology, low-cost technology for water supply and sanitation can be applied successfully to achieve the basic health objectives only if great care and attention are paid to pollution and health hazards during its use. Even conventional technology, which uses modern, expensive equipment and processes in order to achieve basic health objectives and ensure a high standard of user's convenience, may not provide the protection against environmental health problems caused by human abuse and adverse climatic conditions, if the technology is inappropriate or improperly executed. Examples of this abound in developing countries.

The main objective of this paper is to create an awareness among national governments and various international agencies involved in the implementation of the IDWSSD programmes of certain pollution and health problems that can arise as a result of the incorrect application of low-cost technology to water supply and sanitation and to suggest practical solutions to these problems. In addition to improper application of low-cost technologies, other causes of possible health problems are unfavourable site conditions and adverse climatic conditions, which need careful consideration in the planning of low-cost water supply and sanitation projects.

The strategy recommended to overcome such pollution and health problems includes, among others, highlighting and disseminating information regarding pollution and health hazards arising from faulty design and incorrect application of low-cost technologies and preventive measures necessary to forestall such hazards, systematic monitoring and evaluation of the systems to assess the performance and utilization of the facilities by the community and initiating training programmes for the staff involved in implementation at all levels as well as educational prog-

rammes for the public to achieve social acceptance and proper operation and maintenance of the system.

On the basis of the information provided in the paper the Committee may wish to recommend appropriate precautionary measures required to be taken by governments as well as supportive regional and international action to prevent, minimize or solve pollution and health problems related to the incorrect application of low-cost technology for water supply and sanitation.

Introduction

Simple, low-cost technologies have been used in the ESCAP Region for a long time, particularly in the provision of water supplies to rural communities. Several applications have also been made for excreta disposal. However, over the last few years governments and public authorities have begun to give increased consideration to their use not only in rural but also in urban areas to be able to accelerate the coverage of unserved and underserved populations.

Thanks to the efforts of various governments with the assistance of the World Bank, UNICEF, WHO and other international as well as bilateral agencies, several demonstrations and field studies have been made, guidelines for design and operation developed, and actual schemes prepared for implementation. In India alone, schemes for covering nearly 200 towns with low-cost sanitation facilities are under preparation. In Indonesia and Thailand, projects are under way for providing hundreds of rainwater storage systems. Over three million handpumps are estimated to be in use in the countries of the ESCAP Region. In China, over seven million bio-gas digestors, and in India over 70,000 such units are estimated to be in operation.

Low *per capita* cost and simplicity in operation have made these technologies irresistible. Many have proved socially acceptable and economically viable and, therefore, have come to be called "appropriate technologies".

As with all technologies, however, their health implications must be given careful consideration. Being simple, and generally implemented on an individual basis, they are apt to be poorly conceived, constructed and maintained. Simplicity can breed complacency, with the result that the full health benefit of a wider coverage of rural and urban populations may not be obtained. After all, the provision of water and sanitation has a dual purpose — improved environmental health and public convenience — and equal attention should be paid to both aspects.

This paper discusses some of the pollution and health problems related to the current programme of low-cost technology applications to water supply and sanitation in the ESCAP Region.*

A. THE GENERAL SITUATION

The low-cost technologies commonly used in water supply and sanitation and the health problems which may arise out of their improper use are indicated in Table 61. Human excreta being the source of nearly 50 infections which are transmitted through various direct and indirect routes, the list of diseases includes water-borne and water-

* ESCAP Region includes:
  EMR – Afghanistan, Iran, Pakistan
  WPR – Fiji, Republic of Korea, Malaysia, Papua New Guinea, Philippines, Samoa, Singapore, Soloman Islands, Tonga and Vietnam
  SEAR – Bangladesh, Bhutan, Burma, Demo. People's Republic of Korea, India, Indonesia, Maldives, Mongolia, Nepal, Sri Lanka and Thailand.

related ones as well as others resulting from soil pollution and food contamination. Their incidence is quite high in the developing countries of Asia where the major health problems are diarrhoeal diseases, nematode infections, filariasis, malaria and other mosquito and fly-borne infections.

Infant mortality rates of some South-East Asian countries have been shown in Fig. 33 against the percentage of population without adequate sanitation. Since infant mortality is caused by a number of factors, unsafe water and lack of sanitation being only two amongst them, the graph in Fig. 33 merely indicates the general situation without implying any cause-effect relationship. The larger the percentage of population without sanitation, the greater is the infant mortality rate.

The task of providing water and sanitation to the unserved people is so immense that without resort to low-cost technologies it would be almost impossible to accomplish it. If the Decade targets of the ESCAP countries are to be met, nearly half a million people would have to be covered with new water supply and sanitation facilities every day! For this purpose it would be impossible to consider conventional technologies alone owing to their high cost and the level of skills required.

Table 61. Diseases related to improper use of low cost technologies

Low cost technologies	Water borne: such as diarrhoea dysentry typhoid etc.	Water related: such as malaria, filaria dengue schistosomiasis	Soil pollution: hookworm, round worm and other helminths	Fly and insect borne contamination of food
A. Water supply				
i) Rain water harvesting and supply	✓	✓		
ii) Ground water from wells and springs	✓			
iii) Surface water supplies	✓			
iv) Stand pipes	✓			
v) Storage of water	✓	✓		
B. Sanitation				
i) Pit latrine	✓			
Pour Flush	✓			✓
VIP	✓			
ii) Vault and Cartage	✓	✓		✓
Trenching	✓			
iii) Aqua Privy and Septic tank	✓			
iv) Waste				
Standbilisation				
Pond	✓	✓		✓
v) Refuse disposal				✓

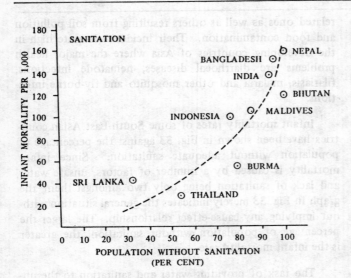

Figure 33. Infant mortality and sanitation coverage in some South-East Asian Countries (Source: Decade Commencement Report, WHO/SEARO, December 1982).

However, the provision of low-cost technology on a wide scale will have a favourable health impact only if due regard is given to a variety of local factors. Unlike conventional technologies, where centralized design, construction and operation are possible, the application of low-cost technologies is by its very nature decentralized and at the peripheral level where construction, operation, maintenance and surveillance could be highly variable from one location to another, and greatly affected by community motivation and participation.

B. TYPICAL SCENARIO

A typical scenario commonly obtaining in many developing countries of Asia is given below to illustrate how the health benefits of low-cost technologies can be frustrated in the rural setting.

The family lives in a mud hut with thatched roof near a coastal belt where the land gets waterlogged during short periods when there is heavy rain. The family depends on seasonal rice cultivation and fishing in sea during other periods. The house is located in a large compound which has a big pond. The pond is used by the family for bathing and for washing clothes and household utensils, and one section of the pond is also used for anal cleansing after defecation. There is a shallow tube-well fitted with a hand-pump and a dilapidated dug-well with little sanitary protection. These wells are used as a source of water supply by the family. The tube-well pump often needs priming water and is also out of order for considerable periods when the family depends entirely on the dug-well

for their water supply. Water is drawn from the dug-well with a bucket and rope that always lie in the compound near the well. When priming of the pump is required, both well and pond water are used.

The family also has a pit latrine with a pour-flush squatting plate with water-seal that is located close to the dug-well. Only the elders use this latrine and the children defecate in the open all over the compound. The water-seal of the squatting plate is not maintained because the trap was broken to remove blockage during use. The kitchen waste and waste food are thrown in the compound without any cover and lead to profuse fly breeding during certain seasons in the year. During rains the latrine gets flooded creating pools of dirty water which harbour plenty of culex mosquitoes.

The family living in the house consists of the parents and four children between the ages of one and ten. Occasionally, the relatives of the family visit them for short periods when they are also exposed to the condition prevalent there.

How the level of environmental sanitation in a scenario of this kind will affect the health of the people living in the house is easy to understand. Although a tube-well with hand-pump and a water-seal latrine have been provided, all members of the family and the occasional guest will suffer from diarrhoeal diseases. Although they may get some relief by visiting the doctor of the health centre of the areas, they will get reinfected. Bacillary dysentery with painful diarrhoea and blood in stool may not be uncommon. The children are prone to infection with hookworm, ascaris and other helminths which will sap away even the little nutrition that they may be getting in the family. They will be anaemic and also manifest other effects of the worm infestation. The elders may also get infected with worms. The environment around the house provides an ideal breeding ground for flies and mosquitoes. The flies will help in transmitting some of the diseases mentioned earlier. The culex mosquito can spread filaria in the family leading to blocking of the lymph circulation culminating in elephantiasis in elders which can seriously reduce their productivity. This is indeed a grim but nonetheless likely scenario.

The low-cost technologies for water supply and sanitation are no longer in an experimental stage but have been sufficiently tested in the field. They can provide a satisfactory solution to the problem from economic, environmental and health considerations, but if this technology is to yield satisfactory results adequate attention should be paid to the proper design, construction and maintenance of the system coupled with community education. An attempt is made in the following sections to discuss these aspects further.

C. LOW-COST TECHNOLOGY APPLICATIONS
IN WATER SUPPLY

For the purpose of highlighting the situation in the ESCAP countries, discussion in regard to the application of low-cost technology in water supply will be restricted to only a few principal ones:

(1) Rainwater harvesting and supply

(2) Ground-water supplies from wells and springs

(3) Surface supplies

In each case, the pollutional effects and health problems due to faulty conception and application of the technology have been described and remedial measures necessary to cope with them indicated.

The problems are mainly due to three reasons: Contamination at sources; contamination in pumping, piping, manual transport, and storage in the home; and fly and mosquito breeding in accumulated water[1].

Faulty conception and design often arise from a lack of understanding of the rural setting. Extrapolation of experiences from the urban to the rural areas is dangerous as the latter involve communities with different behavioural patterns. Lack of adequate operation and maintenance facilities imposes another severe constraint. The designer is thus called upon to simplify further his already simple, low-cost technology, and adapt it to the local situation. Water Supply source and site selection become even more critical.

While a community dug-well may serve a hundred people, a latrine is often meant to serve only a family of 5 or 6 persons. Thus, in a community that is provided with both water supply and sanitation facilities, there may be 15 to 20 latrines (potential sources of pollution) for each drinking water well.

Against this general background we may discuss the following.

(1) Rain-Water Supplies

In some areas rain-water may be the only source of drinking water for a community, and either individual household or community-sized units may be installed. Rain-Water *per se* is safe but its collection, storage use may be fraught with danger (see Annex).

First, if the rain-water storage capacity is not adequate, the people may be forced to use other, probably unsafe, sources of water that may be available in the vicinity to supplement their meagre rain-water supplies. Thus, proper hydrological design is crucial. Secondly, the rain-water collecting surfaces (roof or ground) would in most cases be polluted by dirt, bird droppings, etc. during the dry season and it would be necessary to provide suitable arrangements for by-passing the run-off from the first showers of the rainy season. Access to animals and humans would need to be restricted in case of ground-level collecting surfaces.

Further steps in a proper technological design would be necessary to protect the storage tank from contamination as well as mosquito and insect breeding, as detailed in Annex. Sometimes, a sand filter is provided at the inlet of the storage tank. Facilities are needed for drawing water from the tank either through taps or hand-pumps to avoid entry of contaminants into the stored water. Thus, even a relatively simple system for rainwater supplies must be carefully planned, designed and constructed, if health is to be protected. Consumer education is also essential if their participation is desired in operating and maintaining the system with due care.

Special attention must be drawn to the potential for breeding the Aedes mosquito in the clean water stored in the reservoir unless the latter is closed very tight. The mosquito can readily enter through a mesh or netting. Drinking water stored in household containers can also provide breeding grounds for these mosquitoes. One mode of control in household containers is to make them in a small enough size to require refilling every day or every two days, and educating the people to clean the containers each time before refilling so as to destroy the larvae before they turn into adult mosquitoes.

(2) Ground Water Supplies

Ground water supplies are generally provided through either dug-wells, tubewells or springs, and may be on-site supplies or be piped to community standposts or individual houses. As in the case of rainwater, the ground-water *per se* may be free from pathogenic organisms because of filtration in its passage through soil, but again its abstraction, storage and supply may involve various pollutional and health hazards unless certain precautions are taken, as shown in Annex.

Even in a simple system, such as a covered, dugwell or tubewell with handpump, many things can go wrong. Thousands of handpumps are out of order and await repairs on any given day in the countries of the ESCAP Region, and meanwhile the people use whatever other, mostly unsafe, sources available to them. The choice of pump is important from this viewpoint. Technological improve-

(1) Small Community Water Supplies, Technical Paper Series No. 18, International Reference Centre for Community Water Supply and Sanitation, The Hague, Netherlands, (1981).

ments are necessary and the UNDP is funding a global project with the World Bank as the executing agency to develop a handpump that can be easily operated and maintained at the village level. Even where the pump does work, it may not be adequate for the number of people who have to depend on it as inadequate norms and design criteria might have been used. The same situation may be found with regard to standposts.

The task of keeping handpumps in proper repair has proved a challenge to planners, engineers and operators and various ideas have been tested, some with success, in ESCAP countries.

Many wells now in use do not have the desired degree of sanitary protection through proper choice of site, distance from pollution source, well lining and covering, and the provision of an impervious platform and surface drain around the well. Many technological requirements are, in fact, well known (see Annex) but at times neglected or under-rated or provided but fallen into disuse. Water-borne diseases do occur in such situations but often even rudimentary facilities are not available nor training given to ensure that disinfection either at the source or in the home is done at least during epidemics.

Spring sources, however, pure, may become contaminated unless adequate engineering measures are taken to protect them from surface runoff, humans, animals and insects. These measures are also well known.

The development of low-cost technology has also embraced treatment of water for iron, manganese, fluorides, etc., often found in groundwaters. Their operation generally involves a higher degree of skill and sometimes even the use of a chemical, though the installed plant may be relatively low cost in nature and simpler in conception than conventional ones.

(3) Surface Water Supplies

Surface waters available in rivers, lakes, ponds and canals are invariably polluted and dangerous for human use without purification. The treatment necessary to render these waters safe is often not practicable for small communities because of the high cost of treatment and the need for constant skilled supervision of the treatment plants. Because of this reason surface water is not easily amenable to low-cost technology application and is generally not recommended as a source of water supply for small communities.

A number of simple methods with a few items of mechanical equipment have, however, been devised for the purification of surface water. The slow-sand filter, for example, can be adapted to provide a simple, efficient and reliable method for the filtration of water. The filter can remove 99 per cent of bacteria including all pathogens. Work on standardizing this technology for wide application in the rural areas of developing countries is now in progress.

(4) Piped Supplies

On-site supplies as well as supplies through standposts involve collection of water by the consumers in their own containers, transport to their homes and storage. Here, the general health awareness of the public to the need for protecting their water from contamination determines their behaviour. Health education and promotion of personal hygiene become more important than technological design of the system. Behavioural studies have been, and are being, undertaken to determine community-specific behavioural patterns prior to formulating appropriate community education interventions.

Improper design and installation of pipelines and standposts can also lead to various problems such as; short supply, leakage, wastage, and entry of polluted groundwaters into the piping system during non-supply hours. Use of inappropriate design norms can lead to overcrowding at standposts and hand-pumps which may encourage people to seek other, perhaps unsafe, water sources. Inadequate drainage around standposts and hand-pumps with stagnant pools of water promote mosquito breeding. These aspects have also been listed in Annex.

Various materials have been used for the piping of water supplies. Among the traditional materials, steel, cast-iron, copper, etc. are still in wide use. Lead is generally discontinued from use owing to economic and health implications (plumbo-solvency in soft waters). Use of asbestos cement is declining in some countries owing to the health hazard of asbestos to the workmen engaged in its manufacture. PVC and polyethylene are increasingly being used. Their potential health hazard has been investigated and shown to be negligible. The use of bamboo pipelines is still common in some countries. Pollution by infiltration is probable, especially where make shift arrangements are made for their repair.

(5) Water Quality Surveillance

With low-cost systems as with the more mechanized, urban ones, water quality surveillance is invariably essential to ensure the hygienic safety of the supplies. Low-cost systems, however, pose several problems in surveillance owing to their dispersed nature, lack of skilled manpower and laboratory facilities, logistic difficulties, generally poor quality of construction, operation and maintenance.

Thus, with low-cost technologies greater reliance has to be placed on careful selection of the water source, its continued protection, periodic inspection (sanitary survey) and training of the community health worker. Occasional sampling of the water for its bacterial quality or any suspected changes in chemical quality resulting from changes in land-use patterns in the vicinity, may be necessary. This requires careful attention to the institutional aspects to be built into the programme plan at the initial design stage. All too often, low-cost technology applications have not been backed up by proper surveillance measures required by the very nature of the technology used.

D. LOW-COST TECHNOLOGY APPLICATIONS IN SANITATION

In ESCAP countries, applications of low-cost technology in regard to sanitation are mainly found in the following:

(1) On-site excreta disposal systems consisting of individual or community latrines discharging into pits, tanks, cesspools, digesters or ponds.

(2) Community sewered systems followed by low-cost treatment and disposal methods, such as oxidation ponds and land irrigation.

(3) Drainage of storm and sullage water.

(4) Refuse disposal systems.

The pollutional and health problems arising from poor sanitation are mainly due to (1) fly and mosquito breeding, (2) human contact with faeces, (3) pollution of surface and ground waters by sewage, and (4) food contamination. Furthermore, personal hygiene and health benefits of improved sanitation in a community are difficult to assess and document.

As in the case of water supply technologies, the pollutional effect and health problems of low-cost technology applications in sanitation are due to faulty conception, lack of awareness, incorrect application of technology, poor operation and maintenance and, in some cases, lack of field experience in designing, installing and operating low-cost systems.

Experience in most Asian cities covers the two extremes of sanitation: modern sewered systems for relatively small affluent areas and the filthiest possible manual systems (bucket latrines) for many other areas. To date, very few low-cost technologies have been applied in these cities. In a few cases where enough water supply is available, the undesirable manual scavenging systems have been replaced by septic tanks and soakage pits but, by and large, experience with low-cost, on-site excreta disposal latrines is yet limited and there is a real need for evaluating the few

systems already installed on a large enough scale so as to be able to draw lessons therefrom. Every technological precaution which can be visualized from sound engineering judgement must be incorporated in our designs and implementation programmes. This is discussed further in the following sections.

1. On-site Excreta Disposal Systems

Several studies over the last 30 years have helped determine user acceptance and provide better insights into the design and construction practices, the operational problems and health aspects of various excreta disposal methods in developing countries. Notable among them is the on-going UNDP/World Bank study covering small townships in 14 countries* around the world to help identify appropriate technologies and develop projects and programmes for wide implementation. The results of these and other studies have been reviewed in several publications[2], [3].

As a result of several studies and experiences gained over the years, the older concept of pit and borehole latrines has yielded place to newer ones, such as the ventilated improved pit (VIP) and the Reed Odourless Earth closet, to reduce smell and fly nuisance, and increase acceptance by communities which do not use water for anal cleansing. Pour-flush latrines of improved pan design are being provided where water is available and the people use it for anal cleansing. Similarly, the pits which receive excreta are now provided in duplicate to enable alternate use. Much more attention is now paid to the potential for groundwater pollution by latrines. Aqua-privies have been made safer by making them self-topping. Bio-gas digesters have become more multipurpose. Oxidation ponds have been designed to accept even raw excreta and nightsoil and effluents used for pisciculture. Better engineering concepts have been brought to bear upon the recycle of wastes. However, to promote health benefits and prevent pollution, all these low-cost technologies have to be applied with adequate precautions of an engineering and educational nature. Some of these are detailed in Annex.

---

* These include seven from ESCAP countries: Bangladesh, Bhutan, India, Indonesia, Nepal, Philippines and Thailand.

[2] Health Aspects of Excreta and Sullage Management, R.C. Feecham, D.J. Brodley, H. Garlick and D.D. Mara, World Bank Publication on Appropriate Technology for Water Supply & Sanitation (1980).

[3] Appropriate Technology for Water Supply and Sanitation — A Planner's Guide. By J. Kalbermatten, Richard G. Feachem, David J. Bradley, Hemda Garelick and D. Duncan Mara, World Bank Publication (December 1980).

2. Pit Latrines

Control of fly nuisance is one of the principal objectives of good latrine design. In pour-flush latrines, the water-seal prevents the entry of flies into the pit and of odours from the pit. This water seal must be of adequate depth and must remain intact at all times. In trying to remove chokage the seal may be broken and the whole objective defeated. In the VIP-type latrines, where there are no water seals, odour and fly nuisance is controlled by the use of a vent pipe of sufficient diameter and height to generate an upward draft, and a screen on the top to trap the flies. General cleanliness on the part of the user is, of course, important.

The survival time of pathogens in the pit must also be given due consideration. The provision of two pits for alternate use helps retain the excreta in a pit for a year or two after it is filled up and taken out of use. During this time all viable pathogens and most helminths including the resistant ascaris are destroyed. The public health risk in handling the digested excreta after this long storage underground is minimal and the material can safely be used as manure in agriculture. This safety would not be ensured if only one pit was provided.

3. Groundwater Pollution

This problem has been studied in some detail in many countries and particularly in USA and India. All the data available on the problem have been critically reviewed recently by the WHO International Reference Centre for Waste Disposal[4]. The studies provide valuable conclusions regarding ground-water pollution arising out of on-site disposal of excreta envisaged in the low-cost technologies. The main conclusions were:

(a) The extent of pollution of groundwater arising from pit latrines and other low-cost technologies depends on many factors such as the characteristics of the soil where the pit is located, the groundwater table and the velocity of flow of ground water which determines the residence of the pathogens under the ground. There can be no general or arbitrary limits for distance necessary for safety between latrines and sources of water supply.

(b) The removal of pathogens from the pit is partly through filtration and partly through absorption by the soil. When the pit has been in operation for some time,

---

[4] The Risk of Ground Water Pollution by on-site Sanitation in Developing Countries, W.J. Lewis, Stephen S.D., Foster and Bohumil S. Draser, WHO International Reference Centre for Waste Disposal, Switzerland (1982).

clogging of the soil pores takes place and this provides an effective defense mechanism for filtration and the pollution there is greatly reduced thereafter.

(c) The extent of pollution flow from latrines located in unsaturated zones with at least 2 M soil between the pit and the maximum water table is indeed very limited in soils which are predominantly silt and clay with fine sand and effective size 0.2 mm and less. Under these conditions the latrines can be located as close as 3 M from the well used as water supply. Under saturated soil conditions a distance of 10 M may be necessary between the latrine and water supply.

(d) In coarser soils, an envelope of fine sand (0.2 mm effective size) of suitable thickness (0.5 m) should be provided all around the pit, sealing the bottom of the pit with clay or polythene sheet to give the necessary protection from pollution.

It is evident from the studies already carried out that the pollution of ground-water supply arising out of pit latrines may not pose a serious problem in most soil conditions free from chalk formations, gravel, fissures, root channels and rodent holes provided some precautions are taken in the location and construction of the latrines.

4. Septic Tanks

Many septic tanks are used in Asia without the necessary care and precautions. They are not working satisfactorily and are responsible for soil and water pollution and filthy environmental conditions in the neighbourhood. They are built with no sub-surface *tile* field or with inadequate leaching area for underground disposal of the effluent from the septic tank. The effluent from the tank, which is dangerous, is often let out in open drains with attendant health risks. Regular desludging of the tank which is necessary for the proper functioning of the septic tank is not carried out, with the result that the effective capacity available in the tank for removal of solids by sedimentation is greatly reduced. This results in direct carry-over of fresh solids along with the pathogens in the effluent making it more dangerous.

5. Aqua-privies

Aqua-privies are essentially septic tanks with the toilet mounted directly on the tank. In the aqua-privy proper maintenance of the water seal with periodic addition of water in the tank and its location in soil conditions which can effectively leach out the effluent from the tank are important health aspects. If these two factors are not properly taken care of, the privy will be filthy with bad odours and profuse fly breeding. Flooding of the area with the tank contents will also occur if there is not proper leaching from the tank. The attendant health risk arising out of this situation can be serious.

6. Waste Stabilization Ponds

Although this is a simple technology, some attention is still required if the ponds are to be used without health risk. One of the important health aspects relating to badly maintained stabilization ponds is the breeding of mosquitoes and insects which are vectors of disease. This problem can be well taken care of by preventing the growth of any vegetation in the ponds and on the banks by proper design of the pond and protection of the embankments. If, in spite of this, some vegetation grows in the pond it should be periodically removed to keep the water surface and embankments clear at all times. The design of the ponds should also provide adequate capacity and preferably a cells-in-series arrangement so that there is good pathogen removal in the effluent of the pond. It is desirable to use a final maturation pond in the system if the effluent from the pond is to be used for irrigation or aquaculture.

7. Fish Ponds

Ponds enriched with sewage and nightsoil are often used for fish culture. The sewage is used after some pretreatment or dilution and the nightsoil added to the pond directly in regulated doses. The health problems associated with this practice are (i) the possible passive transmission of pathogens by the contaminated fish to people who handle and prepare the fish and others who eat the fish raw or partially cooked, and (iii) transmission of helminthic diseases, such as fish tapeworm and schistosomiasis, where the required intermediate hosts are present in the pond.

The remedial measures that can be used in this connection are listed in the table in Annex.

8. Bio-gas Digesters

A large number of bio-gas plants using animal and human excreta are in operation in Asia. The main health problem associated with bio-gas plants is the risk involved in using the slurry in agriculture of fish ponds. Since excreta stays in the digestor only for short periods of 5 to 30 days the pathogens present in excreta are not removed from the slurry. The slurry needs further treatment before it can be safely applied on land or fish ponds. Drying and storage for a period of one year or treatment in stabilization ponds can be used for this purpose. The slurry can also be composted along with refuse to obtain compost manure which is safe for use on land. However, if human excreta is excluded from the bio-gas plant the slurry obtained would not pose this problem.

9. Nightsoil Disposal Systems

In these methods, nightsoil is periodically removed and carted away from bucket or vault privies. The bucket system is the oldest methods, and is odourous, most unhygienic and not at all desirable from the public health point of view. This technology has, therefore, *not* been recommended for adoption as low-cost technology.

On the other hand, the vault privy, with a water-seal squatting pan and vent pipe with fly screen on top, can be a hygienic latrine free from bad odours and flies. It is suitable for use in certain conditions, such as rocky soil, high-density habitation, and flooding conditions. However, adequate care is necessary in the collection and transport of excreta from the vaults to the treatment site to minimize health risks. This can be achieved by using good equipment and well trained personnel for operating the trucks used for the purpose. The outlet pipe in the vault and the suction pump and fittings on the trucks should always be maintained in good repair.

After collection the excreta has to be properly treated before disposal. Sometimes the excreta is buried in trenching ground without any attempt to re-use it. These trenching grounds are often a major health risk to the community because of bad operation. A badly operated trenching ground without adequate supervision will not only be a serious health hazard for those who work in the trenching ground but also others, particularly the children who come in contact with the trench. People thus exposed may also transmit the disease to others in the family and the community. Adequate precautions are necessary to make this technology safe. The trenches should be located far away from residential areas and in soils which will not lead to ground-water pollution. The trenches should be at least 0.6 M deep and filled with nightsoil only up to half their depth. Then they should be covered by filling the pits with tampered earth with a mound over the pit and left undisturbed for a period of at least two years before it is dug out.

The re-use of nightsoil in agriculture is often practised. Untreated night soil should not be directly applied on land because there is conclusive evidence that this practice can lead to serious health hazards. This practice should be condemned and discarded. The most appropriate technology for re-use of nightsoil in agriculture is to mix it with suitable proportions of domestic refuse and compost it. The compost manure can safely be used in agriculture.

10. Land Irrigation Systems

Direct application of sewage on land without any treatment is not safe from the health point of view. The effluent from the waste stabilization pond, which is a recommended low-cost sewage treatment method, is generally satisfactory from the point of view of pathogen load for use as irrigation water in agriculture. Pathogen removal, including helminths, is invariably very satisfactory when the pond is provided in two or three cells in series with an adequate retention period.

11. Refuse Disposal

The low-cost technologies used for the disposal of garbage, refuse and other household wastes are (1) manure pits for the rural areas and (ii) sanitary landfill for urban settlements.

The health problems with these technologies are associated with the exposure of the material during collection and transport and breeding of flies, cockroaches and rodents at the disposal sites. These hazards can be avoided by providing properly covered bins for the collection of refuse, their transport in fully covered containers and by covering each day's deposit of refuse at the disposal site with kitchen ash or earth so that the dumpings are not directly exposed to vermins. The location of the sanitary fill should not allow the leachates from the fill to endanger the groundwater.

E. CONCLUSIONS AND RECOMMENDATIONS

The task of providing water supply and sanitation to all people in the ESCAP Region within the Decade is a great challenge. It is fortunate that low-cost technologies do exist which work and are satisfactory from health aspects and are also within the economic resources of communities.

Faulty application of the technologies, however, can lead to health risks. The pollution and health hazards arising from faulty design and use of the technologies and the preventive measures necessary to forestall them are well understood, although not generally known. There is an urgent need for the proper highlighting and dissemination of this information at all levels in the various agencies concerned with the implementation of water supply and sanitation programmes. Planners, administrators and the health and engineering staff executing the programmes should be covered in this education with inter-sectoral co-operation and integration. If this is not done, the technologies may not be applied properly resulting in their failure

and the technology itself falling into disrepute. In consequence, the entire programme may be adversely affected. This is crucial at this time when governments are beginning to allocate more funds for sanitation and apply low-cost technologies in preference to traditional ones.

Two of the important requirements for the success of low-cost technologies are social acceptance by the user and proper operation and maintenance of the systems. An educational programme for the users on the health and maintenance aspects will provide the necessary motivation for demanding the technology and for satisfactory maintenance of the system by the users.

Local governments are often weak and need support if they are to function well as a framework for organizing community participation in the implementation and maintenance of these technologies. Carefully planned training programmes for trainers will be needed to cover the operational staff at all levels and carry the message down to the village-level health workers and volunteers, and the public.

Along with the implementation of the technologies systematic monitoring and evaluation of the systems are necessary to assess performance and the utilization of the facilities by the community. Such monitoring will provide the necessary security and confidence to the users as the programmes move on, and will also indicate the areas where improvements and research are necessary.

Research and development in the field can greatly benefit from the inclusion of socio-behavioural scientists and health educators in the study teams. Technical co-operation among the ESCAP countries themselves would be advantageous as much field experience has already been gained in some of these countries.

National and international agencies funding water supply and sanitation projects involving the application of low-cost technologies should ensure that proper support programmes for community education and follow-up monitoring form an integral part of the project.

ESCAP can play an important role in highlighting the technology and the measures necessary for the success of the programme. It can also initiate action for educational programmes for the implementing agencies and users in the ESCAP Region.

VII.F. Low cost technology for water supply and sanitation: Pollution and health problems related to incorrect applications

187

Annex

Table 62. Pollution and health problems related to use of simple, appropriate and low cost technologies in WSS

System component	Likely nature of related pollution and/or health problems	Precautions/remedial measures
WATER SUPPLIES		
1. Rain water collection from roofs and ground surfaces followed by storage in tanks/reservoirs.	Wash down of dirt and bird-droppings, etc. from roof and ground surfaces.	— Provide bypass arrangements for initial run-off of the season. — Train/educate the householders.
	Contamination of stored water.	— Provide cover on storage tank. — Provide taps for tanks above ground and handpumps for underground tanks. — Provide cleaning/emptying arrangement. — Avoid bituminous paints on inside surface of tanks. — Educate to avoid dipping buckets/hands in stored water, and use of unclean utensils in home. — Provide Slow-Sand Filters.
	Mosquito nuisance.	— Provide drainage around tank and netting on any overflow pipe (Aedes mosquito known to breed even in covered tanks).
	Use of other water sources of unsafe quality to supplement meagre rain-water supplies.	— Provide adequate capacity of rain-water collection systems based on hydrological data. — Educate the householders.
2. Shallow or deep wells with handpumps	Entry of pollution from nearby pollution sources through sub-strata.	— Precautions on construction of latrines (thicker unsaturated zone, impervious materials on pit bottom, etc.) — Tap the water from deeper and more favourable water aquifers. — Generally wells to be lined & located at least 10 m away and on upstream of pollution sources. — Need to raise latrine platform if water table high.
	Pollution from surface run-offs.	— Proper drainage and protection from surface runoffs. Construction of water-tight platforms & well casings (3.00 m. deep)
	Entry of contaminants (example: dirt, etc.), thru handling water.	— Provision of tight lid/cover. No handling by rope and bucket should be possible. — Provision of handpumps (self-priming or with pump cylinder to be under water) avoiding use of contaminated water for pump priming.
	Contamination of water during collection, transport and storage.	— Health education of community. — Clean container & utensils (provide tap on water storage basins). — Practice of personal hygiene. — Disinfection in the home.
	Poor drainage and resulting mosquito nuisance.	— Provide an impervious platform around well and proper drainage to carry away spillage & clothes-washing water.
	Use of unsafe water supplies available more conveniently in vicinity.	— Ensure depth of well is adequate to have water throughout the year. — Provide adequate number of wells and at convenient locations (as per accepted norms in the area). — Check for taste and odour problems in wells. — Educate the community.

Table 62. *(continued)*

System component	*Likely nature of related pollution and/or health problems*	*Precautions/remedial measures*
3. Water supply from surface water sources generally un-protected (village ponds, water holes, rivers, etc.)	Contamination from surface run off and through improper han-dling.	– Select point of collection in the river (i.e. to be as distant as possible and upstream from pollution sources. – Collection container to be clean and protected during transport. – Simple water treatment may be essential (sand filtration and/or chlorination on individual or community basis). – Train community leaders in periodic surveillance of water source through sanitary inspection. – Remove any pollution sources located within the catchment area. – Educate the community.
4. Spring water sources.	Contamination of spring sources by surface run-offs. Entry of contaminents & insects.	– Spring outlet to be located & encased by concrete spring box. – Diversion channel around spring site to be provided. – All opening (overflow pipe, etc.) in the spring box should be pro-vided with nettings.
5. Water supplies from public taps (standposts)	Improper design and installation of pipe-line and standposts, lead-ing to short supply, overcrowding, and contamination and possible use of unsafe water supplies avail-able more conveniently in the vicinity. Contamination of water during collection, transport and storage. Poor drainage and resulting mos-quito nuisance.	– Ensure water-tightness to prevent leakage/wastage and possible entry of polluted groundwaters during non-supply be hours. – Provide adequate size of pipeline and intermediate storage, and sufficient number of conveniently located taps (as per accepted norms in the area) to serve community all through the year. – Health education; promotion of personal hygiene. – Use of clean containers and utensils. – Disinfection of drinking water stored in the home. – Provide impervious platform around standposts and proper – Provide impervious platform around standposts and proper drain-age to carry away spillage and clothes-washing water.
SANITATION (1) **Pit Latrine** Pour-flush with water seal, or Ventilated Improved Pit (VIP) type.	Odour; Fly borne diseases Pollution of groundwater Health hazards in handling and use of pit contents/worm disease	– Keep latrine pan clean and free from sticking excreta. Ensure adequate water seal. – Prevent blockage of pan by proper flushing, Avoid extraneous materials going into the pan. – To prevent mosquito breeding drums used for storing water out-side the latrine should not be left open. – For VIP latrines use vent pipe of 100-150 mm diameter with fly screen on top. Locate vent pipe on the sunny side of the latrines, and paint it black. – Sites for pit should be free from chalk formation, gravel, fissures, root channels and rodent holes. – Locate latrine pit at safe distance from well depending on soil and groundwater (see text). – Provide sand envelope for pits in coarse soils. – Allow contents to remain at least 2 years before removal.

Table 62. *(continued)*

System component	*Likely nature of related; pollution and/or health problems*	*Precautions/remedial measures*
(2) **Vault toilet and cartage**	Odour; Fly borne diseases Spillage during transport	– Keep latrine clean – Provide vent pipe with fly screen. – Empty vault at regular intervals without spillage. – Maintain vault outlet pipe and fittings in truck and pump in good repair.
(3) **Burial of nightsoil in trenches**	Exposure of excreta to flies/human contact.	– Locate trenches away from residential areas. – Trenches should be at least 0.6 M deep. – Provide adequate soil cover (half the trench depth). – Leave the trenches undisturbed for at least 2 years before removal.
(4) **Aqua Privy**	Odour; Fly borne diseases	– Keep squating pan clean and free from sticking excreta. – Ensure adequate water seal in drop pipe; – Avoid flooding of tank by providing adequate soakage area for effluent.
(5) **Septic tank**	Fresh solids carry over; Ponding of effluent; Soil and ground water pollution.	– Desludge the tank regularly. – Provide adequate sub-surface tile field area for soakage. – Do not discharge effluent in open drain or water bodies without further treatment.
(6) **Waste stabilisation ponds**	Mosquito breeding;	– Keep the pond and embankments free from vegetation. – Clear floating vegetation from water surface periodically. – Examine pond water for mosquito larve and use larvicides, if necessary).
(7) **Bio-gas**	Presence of pathogens in slurry	– Dry and store slurry for one year before use. – Treat slurry in stabilisation ponds/composting before use.
(8) **Fish Ponds**	Pathogen transfer by contaminated fish to fish handlers and others who eat raw and partially cooked fish.	– Use stabilization pond effluent. – Allow fish to stay in clean water for some days before harvesting. – Discourage consumption of uncooked fish.
(9) **Refuse**	Nuisance; Fly, cockroach and rodent borne diseases.	– Use covered bins for collection and covered container for transport. – Provide adequate earth cover after each day's dumping. – Locate disposal site suitably to prevent ground water pollution from leachate.

Part Three

COUNTRY INFORMATION PAPERS SUBMITTED BY GOVERNMENT REPRESENTATIVES

I. AUSTRALIA

Overview

Water is vital to Australia. The continent has a harsh environment with low and extremely variable rainfall. Permanent streams exist only in a relatively small area and much surface runoff occurs in areas remote from centres of population and development.

Irrigation developments have contributed significantly to the economic progress of the nation and provide the economic base for a large number of communities in semi-arid inland areas. The provision of reliable reticulated water and wastewater systems to most urban dwellers allows water use per capita for domestic and industrial purposes to be comparable to that of other developed countries and contributes to the high standard of living enjoyed by most Australians.

Development, however, has not been without costs. Significant environmental degradation and deterioration in water quality are becoming evident. Some early constructions are in need of replacement or major maintenance works.

These factors, together with changing community aspirations and demographic, social and economic conditions, contribute to the dramatic shift in emphasis — from development to management — in the Australian water industry in the past 3 years.

Planners are increasingly aware of the need to take account of a wide range of objectives beyond those traditionally recognised by the water industry in order to find the most effective solutions to problems now being faced. Important contributions to these solutions are being made by increasing emphasis on data and information, research and on co-operation between all governments in Australia. In addition, greater accountability and responsiveness to changing community aspirations are being demanded of water management agencies.

In recognition of the need for forward planning in the management of natural resources, and in response to concern that water resource problems could constrain national development, the Australian Government recently conducted a wide-ranging study to identify water issues, needs and problems to the year 2000. The Perspective on Water Resources (POWR) Study's report, *Water 2000,* canvasses the range of issues discussed in paragraph 41 of the Mar del Plata Action Plan dealing with policy, planning and management.

The Study's Steering Committee began from the premise that water is a scarce resource which must be used wisely and not wasted. It identified eight major issues facing the water industry in the next two decades. These are:

. protection and improvement of water quality

. the more efficient use of currently available water supplies

. the conservation of existing water supplies by more appropriate allocation and financial policies

. co-ordinated management and use of water and land resources

. adequate provision for instream uses, which include recreation, ecological, scientific, cultural and commercial purposes

. improvements in data collection and analysis and information dissemination

. provision of adequate funding for water resource purposes, including research

. continuing Australian Government involvement.

The report indicates that in general terms, Australia has sufficient supplies of surface and underground water to meet anticipated demands to the year 2000 at reasonable costs. However, local or regional shortages of water already occur and they will continue, because of the uneven distribution of resources and population.

Water conservation through increased efficiency of water use is, in many cases, the best method of meeting demands. This approach takes account of many of the issues raised in Section B of the Mar del Plata Action Plan, in particular paragraph 6 which states that since water is a limited and valuable resource and its development requires high investment, its use must be efficient and must secure the highest possible level of national welfare. In an era with many competing demands being made on limited public funds and with high interest rates, agencies are paying increased attention to all means of improving efficiency, and in particular to pricing and financial policies which also permit costly capital works to be deferred, and might allow greater internal financing of capital works. Greater efficiency of use also avoids environmental problems associated, for example, with the construction of new headworks or with overwatering of crops.

At the State level, this emphasis on planning, flexibility and accountability is reflected in greater emphasis on corporate planning in major water authorities and in the initiation, in several States, of activities to develop State-wide water plans.

Adequate information, so vital to any planning activity, is not available in a number of key areas despite the extent of development of Australia's water resources. Recognition of the importance of data and information is reflected in:

.   the recent establishment of STREAMLINE, a computerised water information network containing details of research in progress and bibliographic material

.   review of arrangements for water research

.   developments towards the implementation of a new national water resources assessment programme in 1984/85

    publication of *Water News,* a quarterly newsletter circulated widely throughout the water industry.

"Streamline" was established following an expert working group's report on the information needs of the water industry in Australia. The inquiry provided a valuable basis for assessing the need for water information dissemination and for determining the approach most suitable to Australia.

Australians are increasingly concerned with the quality of their environment – of which aquatic ecosystems are a key component. Increasing recognition is being given to the need to consider instream uses in water management decisions, as an extension of the concern about water pollution that emerged in the early 1970s, but this is one objective which has been hampered by inadequate information concerning resource requirements.

Water pollution now derives principally from non-point sources as the major instances of point source pollution have been controlled. Non-point sources are more difficult to contain, as they have their origin in the use and management of land. Salinity and turbidity are major causes of concern, especially in the River Murray system which is extensively used for irrigated agriculture and provides the major part of Adelaide's water supply from offtakes along the lower river. Eutrophication of water bodies because of enrichment by nutrients derived from fertilisers and sewage is another significant water management problem. The need for co-ordinated land and water management is widely recognised, but in most cases institutional arrangements do not reflect this interdependence.

Water resources management in Australia is primarily undertaken by the seven State Governments which have principal responsibility for the implementation of the Mar

del Plata Action Plan. The Australian Government's interests in water resources are furthered through the range of instruments available to it, including financial assistance, taxation incentives, consultation with the States, research, and information dissemination. Co-ordination and consultation between all governments are furthered in the Australian Water Resources Council (AWRC).

Major developments in the water industry in Australia since 1980 are presented in the Attachment, under the headings of the Mar del Plata Action Plan, to show the continuing evolution of water management in Australia.

A. ASSESSMENT OF WATER RESOURCES

In general, waters in the south-east and south-west of Australia are adequately described in terms of quantity, while the arid, semi-arid and northern areas are less well investigated. Indeed, a recent national assessment estimated that the total runoff from the continent is 30 per cent higher than previously thought, principally due to a large rise in a recent estimate for the streams draining into the Gulf of Carpentaria.

Since 1964, the Australian Government has provided assistance to the States for water resources assessment. In 1981, a working group of the AWRC recommended that the programme be restructured, and a new water resources assessment programme which takes account of the recommendations of paragraphs 2 and 3 of the Mar del Plata Action Plan will be implemented by the Australian Government in 1984/85. In most States, networks are being reviewed to permit regional assessments to be made and to bring them to WMO standards. The new arrangements are intended to provide greater flexibility to meet national and State objectives; strengthen national co-ordination; improve the quality of data collected; move to intensive catchment studies rather than fixed networks for water quality data; increase emphasis on data analysis, publication and information dissemination; and overcome backlogs of unprocessed data.

The next major national assessment of water resources is scheduled for 1985.

A number of investigations have shown promising applications of remote sensing to water resources assessment, particularly to the detection of irrigation area salinity, mapping of salinised land, and the estimation of area, turbidity and phytoproductivity of water storages.

B. WATER USE AND EFFICIENCY

1. Water Use

The first national survey of water use was published in 1981. It estimated the total gross applied water in Australia in 1977 to be 17,800 million cubic metres. A second national survey was conducted by the AWRC in 1983/84. It included instream uses of water, which were not covered by the first national survey. A recent Australia-wide study highlighted the paucity of information concerning instream uses, other than for electricity generation.

The first national projections of water use indicate that by the year 2,000, agricultural water use could be 12,600 million cubic metres and urban and industrial water requirements between 5,500 and 6,200 million cubic metres.

2. Water Supply

Water supplies to country towns are generally less adequate than those in the capital cities, in terms of both quality and quantity. The Australian Government has recently initiated a programme, aimed primarily at employment creation, to improve these supplies.

A number of initiatives have been taken for Aboriginal communities, in accordance with the objectives of the International Drinking Water Supply and Sanitation Decade. A survey of needs was undertaken in Western Australia in 1982, and in 1981/82, A$50 million five-year Aboriginal Public Health Improvement Programme commenced to upgrade water supplies and sewerage disposal systems — primarily through providing storages and increasing levels of reticulation.

3. Reuse

Only 5 per cent of treated wastewater is reused and it has been restricted to non-potable purposes, although opportunities exist in 100 towns to reuse up to 40 per cent of treated wastewater or about 50,000 ML annually. This potential is relatively low because many Australian sewerage schemes were designed with ocean outfalls, creating severe physical obstacles to its diversion for reuse. The potential for reuse is increasingly being considered as an alternative to new supplies and is now mandatory prior to supply augmentation in Western Australia.

4. Efficiency of use

It has been estimated that only half the water applied to irrigated crops is used by the plants, and a good deal of water currently applied to crops could be saved by more efficient irrigation methods.

A promising area of research is in the field of irrigation scheduling, which uses advanced technology to determine accurately the most efficient time and quantity for applying irrigation water. SIROTAC, a management plan for cotton is now in use in the Namoi Valley, New South Wales, and SIRAGCROP is being developed for other broad-acre crops. Other topics which are yielding practical results in the field include the use of more efficient sprinklers, drip irrigation, cropping patterns, laser levelling of fields and mixing of fresh and drainage waters to permit reuse. Taxation incentives and State government financial assistance are used to encourage the introduction of efficient on-farm water management techniques.

Water authorities in Australia issue licenses to irrigators which confer rights to use water for irrigation from regulated streams. By making them transferable, the more efficient users of water could have access to larger quantities of irrigation water in addition to their existing entitlements, thus permitting greater flexibility in on-farm water management. In South Australia, water rights have recently been made transferable in private irrigation areas, and in New South Wales a one-year trial water allocation transfer scheme will operate in 1983/84.

In most areas, water prices have not reflected the true cost of supply, although there is now a general trend to increase real prices and to introduce pay-for-use pricing systems (where additional water use directly incurs additional costs) mainly in urban areas.

One side-effect of pay-for-use pricing in Perth has been a large increase in private pumping from groundwater, which has made forecasting and management difficult, and has potential health implications because much of the city relies on septic tanks for sewage disposal. The Perth Metropolitan Water Authority is now undertaking a major survey of water use to permit more effective demand management. A number of other water authorities have introduced pay-for-use pricing, and are promoting efficient use through water conservation education campaigns and technical conservation measures such as reducing leakages by controlling water pressure, piping and lining of channels, and promoting the use of dual flush toilets.

Traditionally, water managers have aimed to provide reliable supplies through even the worst of droughts. Two consequences are the construction of larger and more expensive storages and the irrigation of smaller areas than would have been possible if a greater degree of supply uncertainty were accepted.

C. ENVIRONMENT, HEALTH AND POLLUTION CONTROL

1. Salinity

Agricultural development has been the major activity leading to the man-induced salinisation of 4,260 km² of dryland agricultural areas and 1,230 km² of irrigated land, with consequent effects on stream and groundwater quality.

It has been estimated that average annual economic cost of salinity damage and abatement is A$93 million.

The Australian Government provided A$28 million from 1978/79 to 1982/83 towards half the cost of salinity reduction projects in irrigation areas. A$1 million has been allocated for a national soil conservation programme in 1983/84, to supplement State funds used for this purpose.

In the Murray Valley, action has been based on a comprehensive plan which includes works to intercept saline inflows, reduce waterlogging and improve drainage. Improved on-farm irrigation practices are being encouraged, and a supporting programme of research, monitoring and investigation is underway.

In the south-west of Western Australia, the causes of catchment salinity are being controlled through purchase and reafforestation of selected properties, and bans on further clearing of vegetation in salinity sensitive catchments.

Despite this action, control measures taken to date address only urgent short-term problems and are unlikely to deal with problems arising from any further agricultural developments. There are no established methods for the prevention of saline seepages or reclamation of areas of dryland salinity.

2. Aquatic Weeds

A national committee was established in 1981 to be a clearing house for aquatic weed problems.

Comprehensive guidelines for the use of herbicides are being finalised to assist users to select the most suitable herbicide and to encourage responsible use. The guidelines will cover herbicides registered for use in or near water, with information on toxicity, permitted residue levels, legislation affecting users in each State, compulsory notification requirements and plant identification services.

Commonwealth Scientific and Industrial Research Organisation researchers have been successful in achieving biological control of *Salvinia molesta* in north Queensland. Other biological control agents are now being used with varying degrees of success on different aquatic weeds.

3. Aquatic Environments

A major factor in past neglect for protecting aquatic and riparian environments has been the lack of information concerning their resource requirements. The Thomson River Dam, Victoria, is the first major development for which the downstream flow requirements for fish and aquatic invertebrates have been investigated and quanti-

tative recommendations made concerning downstream river management.

Two Australian sites with significant aquatic features have been listed as World Heritage. The Western Tasmanian Wilderness National Parks contain a number of rivers, including the Franklin and the Gordon, within the last great temperate wilderness remaining in Australia, and one of the last remaining in the world. Plans to dam the Franklin River for hydroelectricity generation have recently been halted by the Australian Government. Kakadu National Park contains wetlands of world significance as habitat for numerous species of birds, many of which are winter migrants from the sub-arctic making their first contact with the Australian continent.

Within Australia, sites with aquatic features have been listed on the Register of the National Estate. In some States, inventories of wild and scenic rivers have been compiled and consideration is being given to the adoption of policies for their protection.

Following the launching of World Conservation Strategy by the International Union for the Conservation of Nature and Natural Resources in 1980, Australia embarked on a process of consultation between government, industry, conservation and other interested groups and the general public to produce a National Conservation Strategy. Consensus was reached on a strategy which has recently been published. It contains sections dealing with the protection and preservation of land and water resources. It is now before the various governments for their consideration.

4. Water-Related Health Issues

Drinking water quality guidelines for Australia were published jointly by the AWRC and the National Health and Medical Research Council in 1980. These guidelines were reviewed, updated and revised during 1983/84 by the two Councils.

Nitrate levels in groundwater are higher than desirable for potable water in many areas of Australia. Its use can cause a blood disorder in babies, methaemglobinaemia, and has been linked with birth abnormalities. In some cases the risk is managed by provision of low nitrate waters for mothers.

In 1982, dengue fever became established in Queensland, affecting approximately 2000 people. The disease is transmitted by a species of mosquito which only breeds in small artificial water bodies and is thus restricted to areas of human settlement. The disease has now disappeared, although the mosquito is still found.

Inadequate quantities of water cause continuing trachoma problems in small remote communities of the arid regions, principally among Aboriginals. The problem is being reduced by progressive improvement of water supplies.

Trihalomethane levels in water in Australia are generally low compared to levels reported from major cities overseas. The levels in South Australian water supplies, however, are often very high due to the high chlorine demands for disinfecting the very turbid waters of the River Murray. Filtration plants are being installed to reduce turbidity levels and hence the potential for trihalomethane formation.

In discussion of the suspected link between sodium intake and cardio-vascular diseases, attention has focused on the levels of sodium in water supplies, although drinking water provides only a minor source of dietary sodium.

Although microbiological counts in water supplies often exceed criteria for drinking water and blue/green algae which can form toxic blooms are common, diseases caused by water-dwelling bacteria, viruses or other organisms are rarely recorded.

A rare event which illustrates the potential for health problems in uncontrolled catchments occurred recently in a small New South Wales town. Its water supply was poisoned when 1080, an arsenic-based pesticide used for rabbit control, was washed into the local reservoir during a severe thunderstorm.

D. POLICY, PLANNING AND MANAGEMENT

1. Australian Government Activities

Following the change in the Australian Government in March 1983, a new national water policy was developed using the report of the Perspective on Water Resources Study, *Water 2000*, as an important input.

A major benefit from the Study is the extensive range of information collected on a national basis, which is used throughout this report.

Under the National Water Resources Programme, the Australian Government provides funds to the States for water activities, including water resources assessment, irrigation projects, urban and industrial water supply and treatment, floodplain management and research. In most cases this assistance is on a dollar for dollar grant basis, but for floodplain management works local government contributions are also required. Expenditure by the Australian Government has been A\$29.2 million in 1980/81, A\$32.7 million in 1981/82 and A\$38.7 million in 1982/83. A new programme commenced in 1984/85.

In addition to this expenditure, the Australian Government has undertaken to fund completely Stage 1 the Burdekin Dam in north Queensland. It is estimated to cost A\$115 million and will be able to supply water to 660 new farms. Later stages could greatly increase the storage capacity and support a hydro-electric station.

2. State Government Activities

At the State level, the trend towards broad-scale planning, accountability and flexibility is reflected in greater emphasis on corporate planning in major water authorities and in the initiation, in several States, of activities to generate State-wide water plans.

Although each State has taken a different approach to the development of its water plan, in general the aims have been to generate informed public discussion of the goals and objectives of water planning, and to establish a flexible framework for examining management options and resolving conflicts in the future. The Australian Government is providing some financial assistance for these activities.

The need for institutional reform has been highlighted by a major parliamentary inquiry into the water industry in Victoria. The Public Bodies Review Committee has reported on a range of issues including central management structure, rural water pricing, financial accountability, and the multitude of very small unco-ordinated local government agencies controlling aspects of water supply and sewerage.

Dramatic changes in water management have been made by the Hunter District Water Board in the past 2 years. The top management structure has been substantially altered and active steps taken to promote water conservation, which has permitted the construction of costly new headworks to be deferred. This in turn will allow those works, when needed, to be financed substantially from internally generated funds. This strategy for coping with an environment of limited public financial resources and high interest rates has also emerged from urban water services financing studies in Western Australia and Victoria.

Looking to the future, a number of investigations have been carried out into the potential for diverting coastal rivers on the east coast into the inland rivers of New South Wales and Queensland. In all cases, however, the schemes are uneconomic for the foreseeable future, and their environmental costs have not been adequately addressed.

3. Australian Water Resources Council (AWRC)

The AWRC is the prime forum for dealing with water resource matters of mutual concern to the national and State governments of Australia. It comprises the Australian and State Ministers responsible for water resource matters, and is advised by a Standing Committee which is supported by a range of specialist committees. The Council has an extensive conference, workshop and publication programme which disseminates information in the water industry.

At its twenty-fifth meeting on 1 July 1983, the Council agreed that 'Water 2000' would provide a sound basis for the future development of water policy throughout Australia. It also decided to review its objectives, functions and structure to ensure that it has sufficient flexibility to concentrate on important policy issues. Other matters which the Council has discussed recently include water resources assessment, the funding of water resources projects in the States, and water research.

4. River Murray Waters Agreement

The River Murray Waters Agreement was first signed in 1914 between the Australian, New South Wales, Victorian and South Australian Governments. The formal signing of a new Agreement by the Prime Minister and each of the three State Premiers was completed on 1 October 1982. The new Agreement allows the River Murray Commission to take account of water quality in its investigations and operations, to formulate water quality objectives for selected locations on the River and to make representations to the States on all matters which could affect the quality of River Murray water in addition to its previous powers over works and water sharing between the States.

E. NATURAL HAZARDS

1. Floods

Floodplains are recognised as an important environmental resource. While floods cannot be controlled, the severity of their impact can be considerably reduced by discouraging activities for which the potential flood damage would be unacceptable. Over the last 5 years, the Australian and State Governments have funded comprehensive catchment-wide studies and mapping programmes. Strategies involving both structural and non-structural management measures have been implemented in many of the most seriously flood-affected river valleys in Australia.

Nevertheless, it is estimated that there are still 185 cities and towns throughout Australia which are liable to flooding with some 61,000 buildings in the 100-year floodplain, representing average annual direct flood damage of approximately A$19 million.

2. Droughts

In the major drought which occurred in eastern Australia in 1982/83 when many farms were already weakened

from the effects of drought in previous years, agricultural output dropped by nearly 20 per cent and it is estimated that overall economic growth was reduced by 1-1.5 per cent. The impacts of drought can be as damaging for irrigated agriculture as for dryland enterprises, and the regional effects are more severe than indicated by national figures. In Melbourne, Australia's second largest city, severe restrictions were placed on water use.

F. PUBLIC INFORMATION, EDUCATION, TRAINING AND RESEARCH

1. Research

As recognised in paragraph 80 of the Mar del Plata Action Plan, research results are a vital input to water management. Since 1980, arrangements for water research in Australia have been reviewed and revised, in accord with the recommendation of paragraph 81 of the Plan.

In January 1982, an AWRC working group reported that water research in Australia was poorly funded, ill-co-ordinated and at a low level. The working group's recommendations for a higher priority for water research; substantially increased funding; establishment of a National Water Research Council; improved co-ordination of water research undertaken by Australian Government agencies; and development and support for a wider range of research and research-related activities. These recommendations were accepted by the AWRC.

In addition, the new Labour Government has recently established an Interim Council to investigate the need for a national Institute of Freshwater Studies.

2. Information Dissemination

Activities associated with the "Streamline" data base are undertaken co-operatively by national and State government agencies. In addition to its on-line availability through computer terminals, two publications are produced: the annual *Water Research in Australia: Current Projects* and a regular current awareness bulletin, *Streamline Update*. The first (1982) edition of the former has just been published and the first issue of the latter is about to be published.

In addition, the Department of Resources and Energy publishes *Water News* on behalf of the AWRC. Its primary aim is to provide its readers with accurate, up-to-date and comprehensive information on water matters, and is thus the Australian equivalent of ESCAP's *Confluence* publication. Its frequency is to be increased to six issues per year in 1984.

G. INTERNATIONAL CO-OPERATION

1. Development Assistance

The Australian Government operates an official development assistance programme that aims to contribute to the social and economic advancement of the peoples of developing countries by financing self-sustaining development. The programme is developed mainly in response to requests from participating countries and is formulated to reflect each country's policies and priorities, and to utilise special Australian skills. A feature of the Australian programme is the emphasis given to water resources investigations and project preparation — 16 per cent of the 1982/83 contribution to bilateral water projects. The majority of feasibility studies for large projects are for use by recipient governments in approaching international financing agencies. A summary of recent Australian contributions to water resources development in the ESCAP region is in Table 63.

Table 63. Summary of recent Australian contributions to water resources development in the ESCAP Region

Projects current in 1982/83	Expenditure to 30.6.82 A$000	Estimates 1982/83 A$000	Total Cost (1982 $) A$000
Water supply	31 532	15 206	89 018
Hydro-electric	8 987	5 003	14 824
Irrigation/flood control	12 557	5 798	22 381
Sewerage/sanitation	5 786	1 960	8 040
Sub total	58 862	27 967	134 263
Integrated rural development (having irrigation and water supply components)	42 377	11 712	78 773
Total	101 239	39 679	213 036

Projects approved during 1982/83	Est. Total Cost A$000
Bilateral Projects	A$49 740
Multilateral Projects* (UNSO, UNICEF)	US$1 640

* End use of most funds provided to international institutions is not distinguishable by sector.

2. Other International Activities

During the second phase of the International Hydrological Programme, Australia is making direct contributions to three areas.

- the importance of water resources in socio-economic development
- evaluation of experiences in hydrological and operational research applied to water resources
- mathematical modelling of surface and groundwaters.

Within the region, Australia provided lecturers for a technician's training course in Singapore in October 1982. Follow-up visits to participants in their own work environments were scheduled for November 1983.

Australian papers were presented at the workshop in Manila, on estimation of sediment supply and transport capacity of rivers November 1982, and at the ESCAP meeting on water resources development in the South Pacific, April 1983, which was supported by the Australian Government. Australia was also represented at the Workshop on the Hydrology of Large Flat Lands, Buenos Aires, April 1983, and has shown an interest in the activities of the Asian Regional Co-ordinating Committee on Hydrology.

The Australia-UNESCO Committee for the IHP has submitted a proposal for a regional workshop to be held in late 1984 or early 1985 on appropriate techniques for assessing the effects of land use changes on water resources, using data from experimental basins.

Australia is participating in the ESCAP water information exchange service.

Papers on demand and supply forecasting and the role of water pricing in demand management are being prepared by the Department of Resources and Energy for the OECD Environment Committee's project on the Economics of Water Conservation.

There are four contributions from Australia in the World Meteorological Organisation's Hydrological Operational Multipurpose Subprogramme (HOMS) Reference Manual, and several others are currently being prepared.

The International Executive of the International Commission on Irrigation and Drainage met in Melbourne, Victoria, in September 1983, and a major international conference, Groundwater and Man, was held in Sydney, in December 1983.

II. PEOPLE'S REPUBLIC OF CHINA

THE WORK OF RIVER HARNESSING AND PLANNING

A. GENERAL CONDITIONS

The territory of China is 9,600,000 Km^2 in total with high altitude in the west and low altitude in the east. From Qinghai — Tibet plateau at the height over 4,000 metres above sea level the land slopes towards north and east and lowers down to the east plain by the sea. There are many more mountains than plains in the national territory, about two-thirds being plateaus, mountains, and hills. At present the cultivated land is about 100,000,000 hectares, with a number of rivers and streams, each with river basin over 1,000 Km^2. Among them are large rivers such as: the Yangtze River, the Huai River, the Hai — Luan River, the Pearl River, the Liao River, the Songhua River, etc. The total river basins of the seven river systems are 4,470,000 Km^2, about 47 per cent of the national territory.

The annual total runoff of all the streams and rivers in the country is about 2,660 Km^3, i.e., 5.7 per cent of the annual total surface runoff of the whole earth, less than that of Brazil, U.S.S.R., Canada or U.S.A. The average supply of water per capita is about 2,700 m^3, less than those in many other countries.

The main peculiarities of the water resources are:

(1) *Extremely uneven distribution in various districts:* As a whole, there is abundant rainfall along the east sea-shore and scanty in north — west inland possibly varying from over 1,700 mm to less than 200 mm. According to the quantity of rainfall the whole country may be divided into the following: regions rich in water (over 1,700 mm), regions of much water (800-1,700 mm), regions in transition (400-800 mm), regions lacking water (200-400 mm) and regions of drought. The Yangtze River, the Pearl River and rivers in the south-east and south-west are in the regions rich in water and those of much water and there the annual runoff is about 82 per cent of that in the whole country, while the area and the cultivated land of these regions are all only 36 per cent of the respective sum total of the country.

(2) *Seasonal and Annual variations of precipitation and runoff.* The precipitation in the *four* months of highest rainfall is often up to 50-60 per cent of that of the whole year in the South, while it is often up to 70-80 per cent or more in the North. Besides, these quantities of rainfall occur mainly as torrents or storms, and thence, though there is not enough rainfall in the North, yet people have to make greatest efforts to divert the flood and the logged water to the sea during the flood period. Since the rainfall of the most part of the districts is mainly influenced by monsoon, the yearly variation of rainfall is great, espe-

cially in the northern district where the maximum quantity may be several times or even over ten times the minimum quantity. Besides, the more awful condition is due to years of drought and then followed by many years of abundant water such as in the district of the Yellow River, where the average runoff of the years, 1922-1932, is 24 per cent less than those in normal years, while the average runoff of the years from 1943-1951 is 19 per cent more than those of normal years. The average annual runoff of Songhua River in 1916-1928 is 40 per cent less than those of the normal years, while in the years 1960-1966, it is 32 per cent more than those of the normal one. The above pecularities of water resources make special conditions on the development and utilization of our national water resources, mainly as the followings:

(a) Because of the unbalanced combinations of soil and water resources, population concentrates in certain parts of the districts, hence, there must be higher demands for the utilization of soil and water resources. At the same time over population within the district usually evolved overconsumption and unreasonable usages of the soil and water resources, and hence resulted in some problems harmful to the ecological balance.

(b) The River basins of the middle and lower reaches of the seven main large rivers of our country is about 1,000,000 Km^2 in total, containing many large cities and inhabited by more than half of our national population. These are the districts of political, economical and cultural centres of our country. However, the elevations of these districts are mostly below the flood levels of the rivers and consequently involve the extraordinary flood control problems of our country.

(c) Because of the conspicuous seasonal types of runoff distribution, difficulties in river harnessing and river development are increased to certain degree. For the purpose of efficiently regulating runoff, large scale and difficult engineering measures for flood control are usually indispensable. Moreover dominant problems of sediments in most of the rivers also greatly increase the complexity in the work of river harnessing and river development.

B. THE PRESENT STATE OF RIVER PLANNING AND RIVER HARNESSING

In order to achieve the construction works of water conservancy according to the scheme, our government and our Party have been paying much attention to the planning of it. River planning has been treated as the important basis for developing national construction programme of water conservancy. Various kinds of plannings we have worked out in recent years are mainly as follows:

(1) The planning of large river basins, e.g. the Yangtze River, the Yellow River, the Huai River, etc, each with its river basin as an unit of plan;

(2) The planning of water conservancy works in important districts, such as those in the commercial grain base and those in the base of commercial economical crops set by the government and those water conservancy plans in the districts of low yield and grain shortage, where supports are needed;

(3) The planning of middle and small river basins, and planning of counties and communes. The former are supplements to the plannings of large rivers, thus they should always embody the intentions of the large river plans. The latter are for engineering works of mainly popular small scale type, including small scale agricultural water conservancy works, small size hydro-electric power stations and water and soil conservation structures, etc, for which the planning is commonly worked out by respective administrative organizations.

(4) Cross river basins planning for river flow regulation. The present example is the planning to divert river flow from the South to the North to supply necessary water for industrial and agricultural uses in the district of drought.

Organizations for the seven large river basins of our country have been established and are responsible for preparing respective plans. Since the planning of the districts is in close relation to the planning of the river basins, the organizations of river basins are duly responsible for directing the planning of relative districts for better co-ordination of the two. In recent years, the organizations of some river basins have also been entrusted by the Ministry of Water Resources and Electric Power undertaking the tasks of the planning of cross river basins.

We realize that there were many shortcomings in our work of planning due to lack of experience. However the river basin planning and the district planning of water conservancy, as a whole, have functioned as they should have. Many large scale hydraulic engineering structures have been built mostly having been selected and built on the basis of the planning. After over thirty years of development and management, the benefits acquired are mainly:

(a) The preliminary promotion of the ability of flood control on various large rivers. Among the main rivers, flood of 1958 type on the Yellow River, about once in a hundred years, can be controlled. The flood once in 40-50 years in Huai River and Luan River can be controlled. In the main stretches of the Pearl River, Songhua River and Liao River, flood once in 10-20 years can be controlled. Because of the large volumes of flood in the Yangtze River, there should be planned flood diversion for the middle and lower stretches. Under the conditions of no flood diversion, flood once in a decade may be controlled.

(b) For the purpose of increasing agricultural products, facilities of water conservancy have been provided and thus about 380 Km^3/year to 400 Km^3/year of water have been used in agriculture.

(c) For the purpose of promoting industrial development and city construction, about 49 Km^3/year-57 Km^3/year of water have been supplied. Up to 1982, the installation capacities of various scales of hydro-power stations have reached over 21,000,000 Kw. In 1982 the output of hydroelectric power was 65,500,000,000 Kwhr (including nearly 16,000,000,000 Kwhr of rural small scale water power output). Through river regulation, navigation has also been partly improved. The river traffic for both travellers and goods in the inner rivers has been 11-13 times increased compared to that at the beginning of Liberation of China. Besides, nearly 1.3 million hectares of water surface have been increased.

C. THE WORK OF PLANNING ONWARD

At present, the problems confronted are numerous. There is much work to be done, no matter what it is for, e.g. flood control, irrigation, water logging diversion, saline-alkalinity management, power generation, navigation, water supply for industrial and domestic use, aquatic products, soil and water conservation, environmental water conservancy, or others. However, for the present and in the long run, we consider the main problems concerning our national overall arrangement are the problems in four aspects, i.e., the flood control work for the main rivers, water supply to the northern district, the multiple further utilization of water resources and the protection of water resources to promote the environmental qualities.

The present problems of flood-control on the main rivers have been described above and they may possibly cause more loss with the later development of national economy, so, it is necessary to study further to increase necessary engineering structures, to raise continually the standards of flood control and at the same time to study how to take non-engineering measures to strive for reducing loss from flooding. It has been long for China taking emergent measures, such as: flood diversion, flood detention district on some rivers to prevent extraordinary large flood, which are in essence non-engineering flood-control measures. Nevertheless, in recent past, there has been no flooding for years in certain districts of flood diversion or flood detention. And there the economic development has hastened up, so, in case flooding occurs, loss and damage in the district would certainly be more serious. Hence, how to practice and manage by necessary and better measures of intervention from administrative, economic sides, etc. in these districts seems also to be one of the important subjects to be studied.

As to the problem of water supply, according to the results from the present analysis, it is predicted that until the beginning of the 21st century, the total water consumption will be increased from the present 450 Km^3 to about 670 Km^3. While, in the same period the annual supply would be only 600 Km^3, and the shortage would be about 70 Km^3. The districts in short of water concentrate mainly in the four river basins, i.e., those districts of the Yellow River, the Huai River, the Hai River and the Liao River, where the conspicuous contradiction between supply and demand of water resources, having become the largest restraint factor at present in the economic development must be intensively studied in the work of planning. To solve these problems, two approaches — development of water resources and saving of water must be put into consideration. Thus, on the one hand, possible measures to develop water resources must be put into consideration. On the other reducing the water consumption must be emphasized so that, either in industry or in agriculture, techniques for saving of water should be studied, and in some districts rational adjustment in the arrangement for optimum productivity should be undertaken.

The multiple uses of water resources must be in close combination to the national requirements in different periods. From now on it has been considered that intensive development of hydro-power to solve the problem of power source and the extensive development of inland river navigation to meet the needs of transportation are all important subjects of China's national economy. These two strategic tasks should be better combined with the necessities of the development and management of water resources which must be considered in an integrated and overall way and must be unified in planning in order to achieve the optimum economic benefits.

As to the protection of water resources and the quality of environment, we have not yet paid adequate attention. Though we have taken some measures since the seventies, there are lots of problems to be solved. At present, many rivers in China have been polluted in different degree, with some reaches even more seriously polluted; in many mountainous districts the conditions of soil erosion and water loss have not been radically changed; in some places, forests and vegetations having been seriously damaged, soil erosion and water loss are going on worse; in many places, the grasslands have been either over pastured or aimlessly

cultivated, hence become sandy, deteriorated and alkalized and in other places, especially where consumptive use of water for industry was concentrated, underground water has been over pumped thus causing the settlement of ground surface. Besides, among the constructed hydraulic engineering works, to some reservoirs, there are problems of emigrant settlement still left to be solved; to some places, there are problems of secondary saline — alkalinity caused by the improper disposition between irrigation and drainage; and to some dams, there are problems of navigation, timber passing and fish migration due to lack of integrated consideration. All these have brought unfavourable consequences to the environmental ecology. For the effective protection of water resources and the improvement of the environmental quality; measures in different aspects should be taken, including making comprehensive and complete rules and laws for water resources. In the research work of river planning the emphatic points are on the investigation of the quality of water and on the analysis of the environmental influence on the whole scheme of the planning of multiple uses of water resources. At the same time, tentative plan on the quality protection of river should also be proposed.

To improve the present unfavourable condition of water resources new research and investigations on the above problems and others involved in the river basins are being made for different large rivers. With much more scientific information, and experience and teachings of success and failure for over thirty years, the new work of planning will certainly be much more progressive than before, both in its depth and extent.

D. THE APPLICATION OF MULTI-DISCIPLINARY SYSTEMATIC ANALYSIS IN PLANNING

Through long experience it is now recognized that planning of water conservancy is related to other activities. They all must be the composite parts of the synthetic planning for the development and management of national territorial resources. In order to integrate the construction works of water conservancy into the overall planning for the development and management of the national territorial resources; avoiding discrepencies with others; to build water conservancy works according to the national requirements in different periods; and to bring forth their greatest economic profits, social profits and the profits of environmental ecology, multi-disciplinary co-ordination must be stressed. All planning must be studied, under the leadership of the organization in charge of the development and management of the national territory, while in the process of planning, all relative departments, colleges, institutes and scientific research units should take part, each with certain emphasis on the respective phase. In this way not only the specialized contents can be further and deeply investigated but also problems may be discovered from different points of view and thence the quality and level of planning may be promoted and raised. On the other hand method of synthetic analysis should be stressed on, i.e., considering the phenomena studied as an integrated system, in order to search for an overall plan, pertinent to the optimum principle of systematic integrated arrangement.

In these two respects more experience is required. As to the former it is mainly co-ordinated through the "Planning Guide", that is, the organization that works out the plan is asked to put all the main things, such as: its objectives, purposes, principles, subjects necessary to be studied, etc., into the guide clearly to be examined and approved by the authoritative organizations. According to present national regulations, with the exception that the water conservancy plans within the scope of a province or a county may be examined and approved by the respective organizations of the province or the county, all those plans concerning more than two main parts or branches of large rivers, plans of cross river basins, as well as the strategic regional plan concerning the overall arrangement should all be examined finally and approved by the national authorities. As to the latter more experience is required. Considerable experience has been acquired in the following:

(1) *Optimization of the operations of hydropower stations and reservoirs.* It has been adopted in several cases, such as the cascade power stations on Longxi River, the power station of Zhexi, that of Feng-shu ba, etc., According to the analysis, since the adoption of optimization regulation and operation, the annual output of the whole country in 1981 did increase about 1,700,000,000 Kwhr, equivalent to 3 per cent of the annual power output;

(2) *Optimization in the design of hydro-power station group.* In the plan for the development of Ta — tu River, we have considered the requirements of multipurpose, such as: power generation, timber transport, irrigation, etc., and established a mathematical model, to make combined and integrated operation of 15 cascade power stations, with the aim at the optimum guaranteed output, and the restraint on water balance and monthly output. Having been treated by linearization and reduction, the optimum regulated reservoir capacity of the different cascade reservoirs and the optimum combinations between different reservoirs have been attained;

(3) *The optimum selection of the hydro-electric power resources of the power system.* For example: in the development plan of the electric power system of Beijing — Tianjin — Tangshan, optimum selected mathematical model for the power resources of the system has been studied, and has been utilized to verify the economic rationality of constructing the Shi-sanling (the Ming Tomb) pumping and storage power station. On the basis of presently available facilities for research, the principle of large system differentiated co-ordination has been adopted to divide problems into two parts — integer programming and linear programming to study investment policy with the former and operational analogy with the latter and to realize final calculation by the iterative method.

From the above, it can be seen that progress in these respects, especially on the application of the methods of systematic analysis are far from enough. Comparing the requirements of planning at present stage, there is a considerable gap. China is now preparing to enlarge the field of application in this respect for different work being carried on. In planning of hydro-power, research shall continue on the mathematical model for the development of systematic power resources and also study for the optimum development programme of electric power station, and the optimum parameter selection. It is also planned to study the water resources planning of some river basins, the optimum way of the utilization of water for various purposes. On the environmental problems China will investigate the influences from engineering structures on different environmental systems (system of physics, system of biology, system of sociology) and also the techniques for their synthetic evaluation. All of these, it is believed, will help planning work to achieve better results.

III. INDONESIA

III. A. IRRIGATION EFFICIENCY

Introduction

The agriculture sector is the largest single sector in the Indonesian economy, it contributes about 55 per cent of the national total output and provides livelihood to about 75 per cent of the population.

To meet the growing demand for rice, the staple food of the country, Government of Indonesia imported large quantities of rice in the 1960's. Food crop policy is an important issue for the Government of Indonesia because these crops account for about 18 per cent of total GDP (60 per cent of agriculture GDP); supply most of the country's food; and constitute important sources of employment and income.

The Government of Indonesia's consistent policy throughout their Five Years Development Plans has been to try to make Indonesia independent of food imports. To this end, the Government has invested heavily in irrigation, furtilizer production and distribution support services for food crop farmers, and credit and price support programmes.

A. IRRIGATION DEVELOPMENT

1. Gravitational Irrigation

The total population of Indonesia in 1980 was about 147 million people. About 62 per cent of the population of Indonesia lives on the island of Java and Madura which has less than 6.6 per cent of the land area. About 59 per cent of the total irrigated area of 5.3 million ha is on Java and Madura.

Land Area (km²)	Agricultural Land (km²)	Per cent of land area	Population 1980 (person)	Population density (person/km²)
1,919,443	13,728.9	7%	147,490,298	77

Approximately 57 per cent of the working population works directly in the agricultural sector as farmers and farm labour, and 13 per cent provides small-scale rural, agro-support goods and services.

Since Indonesia is astride the Equator, has a tropical monsoon climate and the difference between the longest and shortest day is very small throughout the islands, hence the duration of sun's radiation is quite uniform.

The temperature varies between 20°C and 33°C with an averange of about 25°C. At low altitudes there is little variation throughout the year and the daily temperature changes are also small. The average humidity varies from 75 to 85 per cent. Due to tropical monsoon climate, soils in Indonesia tend to be highly laterized. There are 2 types of soil which are very important to water resources development, i.e. alluvial soils cover about 16.8 million ha, or nearly 4 per cent of the total land area and the second, swamps about 38 million ha or 9 per cent of the total land area.

Irrigation has been practised in Indonesia for centuries. Early systems were premitive, usually involving the diversion of streams into rice fields. Later, more sophisticated systems were constructed by the Dutch, originally for sugar

cane plantation. Since 1848 when the lowland in East Semarang, North coast of Central Java was attacked by heavy flood resulting in famine, rice crop irrigation has been regarded to be very important. So in 1852 the Government begun with the construction of the weir Glapan and its systems for serving 12,000 ha.

Irrigation in Indonesia is classified as "technical", "semitechnical" and "simple" irrigation, this classification is usually according to the type and quality of irrigation facilities. These types of systems are under the control by of the Government, i.e. Ministry of Public Works, and are usually called "Public Works" irrigation systems, and those which are called "village" irrigation are controlled by the farmers.

In 1915 it was recorded that about 2.4 million ha were irrigated, in 1940 the area increased to about 3,4 million ha and then in 1960 as per figure recorded by the Ministry of Public Works, the total irrigated areas both for "Public Works" and "village" irrigation systems reached 5.0 million ha.

However during this period of irrigation development the activities of operation and maintenance were neglected thus putting both the "Public Works" and "Village" systems in serious problem and resulting in the deterioration of the systems and reduced productivity.

The Post World War II population growth has created an ever increasing need for infrastructural services. Contrary to the increasing requirement for the infrastructure, investment in the rehabilitation and extention of this and related facilities has not been carried out. As a result, deterioration in almost all infra-structure facilities is evident. Because of this situation, out of 7 million ha irrigable area in the country, 3.8 million ha were under irrigation, the remaining being dependent upon rainfall or used for dry land cultivation. Out of 3.8 million ha, only 1.7 million could be classified technical irrigation, and of this 60 per cent was in bad need of reconstruction and improvement. Annual flood areas accounted for 250,000 Ha, especially in the rice bowl of Java.

The Five Year Development Plans beginning 1969 for the agricultural sector aim at increasing food production by providing better irrigation facilities such as rehabilitation, extension and — proper operation and maintenance of the systems. The Plans also improved the use of irrigation water, protected agriculture lands from floods, alleviating population problems by improving drainage facilities which will simultaneously create imployment opportunities especially in rural areas.

In three Five Years Development Plan 1969-1984, the achievement in Irrigation Development Programmes (ha) is as follows:

Irrigation Programmes	Repelita I	Repelita II	Repelita III	Total
Rehabilitation	936,073	527,890	388,637 (x)	1,853,550
New Developing Irrigation Networks	191,246	325,942	405,440 (x)	922,628
Tertiary Development	–	324,769	839,132 (xx)	1,163,901

Repelita : Five Years Development Plan.
(x) Estimated figures, (xx) Data in March 1982.

2. Groundwater

Starting early 1970 the Government, i.e. Directorate General of Water Resources Development, Ministry of Public Works carried out several activities in groundwater development for the purpose of irrigation in the frame of increasing food production.

Surveys, investigation and exploration in the field of geology, geophysics, geohydrology, hydrology, irrigation, agriculture, socioeconomics etc. were carried out. Based on such investigation it was found, that in certain areas of the island the groundwater potential exists and could be utilized for irrigation purpose.

The use of groundwater for irrigation by using deep-well pumps is still rather new, because various consideration should be taken into account technically, economically as well as socially. Therefore the development is carried out first in the stage of Pilot Project, before the large scale development could be implemented.

The presently used criteria for selecting possible groundwater irrigation schemes and further investigation are:

a.   There should be intensive cultivation and dense population locally.

b.   There should be a tendency for water shortage which can not be met from surface sources.

c.   There should be a good response from local farmers and local officials to the need for careful operation and maintenance.

d.   Preliminary reconnaisance should have indicated good hydro-geological potential.

At the early stage of the Project, the groundwater development was primarily intended for irrigation purpose, but later it was considered that groundwater potential should also be utilized for drinking water supply.

In line with the Government policy at the present time, the operation and maintenance of tubewell and other equipment should be taken over by Water Users Association after an initial period managed directly by Project.

There are some constraints in implementing this policy:

(i)   Most of the existing pumps originally come from technical foreign assistance, which are not available easily in local market. Consequently the spareparts can only be obtained from the Sole Agents located in the main cities.

(ii)   Workshop near the project area does not exist at present time, which makes the maintenance costs beyond the farmers capacity.

(iii)   The wells have to be cleaned up periodically which is also beyond the farmers technical ability.

(iv)   The cost for pumps replacement is far from the farmers' capacity.

To overcome the above situation the Project has made its proposal:

(1)   Operation and Maintenance cost for canalization and pump houses will have to be born by the farmers. Which is usually done under "Gotong Royong" system (Mutual Help).

(2)   Operation and Maintenance cost for tubewells borne by the farmers are limited only to operation cost, such as fuel consumption, grease, operator salary and minor repair or routine maintenance.

(3)   Major repairs and well maintenance remain under Government responsibilities which cannot be done by the farmers.

(4)   Replacement of pumps and engines remain under Government responsibility.

The present groundwater developments are located in Java, Bali, and Islands in east part of the country. See table 64.

Table 64. Wells already commissioned and those handed over to farmers

| No. | Sub Project/Location | Pumps in Operation | | | | Handed over to local Government/Water User Association |
| | | No. of Wells | Irrig. Areas (ha) | Domestic Water Supply | | |
				No. of Wells	Inhabitants	
1.	Madiun – Solo	44	3 500	19	7 500	9 Nos. for water supply
2.	Kediri – Nganjuk	129	5 550	7	8 550	71 Nos. for irrigation 2 Nos. for water supply
3.	Madura	36	1 089	12	10 106	14 Nos. for irrigation 1 For water supply
4.	Other East Java	22	827	5	1 825	4 Nos. for irrigation 3 Nos. for water supply
5.	Gunung Kidul/D.I. Yogyakarta	36	1 150	6	6 100	28 Nos. for irrigation 4 Nos. for water supply
6.	Central Java	–	–	5	6 100	5 Nos. for water supply
7.	Bali	3	91	1	3 700	1 For water supply
8.	Lombok/Western Lesser Island	7	120	1	1 000	–
9.	Timor/Eastern Lesser Island	–	–	10	500	–
10.	West Java	–	–	7	1 350	5 Nos. for water supply
	Total	227	12 327	73	47 131	117 Nos. for irrigation 30 Nos. for water supply

3. Swampy Area

The Government of Indonesia considers swamp land reclamation an important issue in their development programmes, and can expect that more than two million hectares of new arable land will be reclaimed in the coastal swampy areas at the end of this century.

Actual and planned development of tidal lands (extensification) during 25 years (ha).

Five Years Development	Area opened[x]	Area planned to be opened[x]	Comulative total area (rounded)
I. (1969-70/1973-74)	33 000	–	33 000
II. (1974-75/1978-79)	248 722	–	282 000
III. (1979-80/1983/84)	–	400 000	682 000
IV. (1984-85/1988-89)	–	500 000	1 182 000
V. (1989-90/1993-94)	–	600 000	1 782 000
	Total (rounded)	282 000	1 500 000	

x) Not including areas already opened or to be opened by spontaneous settlers.
Source: DPU/Dit. Rawa/P4S, 1979.

Potential arable areas, though of lower fertility are utilized or underutilized in the other islands, Sumatera, Kalimantan, Sulawesi and Irian Jaya. In these islands there is an estimated 35 million hectares of swampy area. The coastal swamps have agricultural potential, especially for rice production, though concentration of primary and mangrove forest, soil constraints and land rights may reduce the area which can be developed.

Coastal swamps occupy broad, flat and drained zones that are partially inundated during rainy seasons by high tides of floods in adjacent rivers.

Recent marine or fluvio-marine clays are dominant soil types overlaid by peat layers of various depths and at various stages of decomposition. At, or near the mangrove belts, pyrite layers are common which should be considered dangerous upon drying and have to be treated very carefully.

Since 1969 until present, about 700,000 hectares of swampy area has been reclaimed by the Government, including, about 600,000 hectares, coastal swamps where more than half a million people have been settled (see Table 65).

In addition an estimated 300,000 hectares have been reclaimed and settled by approximately 200,000 Banjarese and Buginese.

The Government has adopted a multistage implementation strategy for swamp development : the first low-cost stage comprises basic, minimal infrastructure and land

Table 65. Reclaimed and settled swamps, sumatera and kalimantan

Provinces	Repelita I 1969-1973		Repelita II 1974-1978		Repelita III (Target) 1979-1983	
	Reclaimed area (gross) ha	Settled families No	Reclaimed area (gross) ha	Settled families No	Reclaimed area (gross) ha	Settled families No
Sumatera:						
Riau	900	355	70 372	700	23 388	10 948
Jambi	6 800	2 584	27 164	500	28 222	7 055
South Sumatera	9 830	2 103	78 280	4 810	213 140	43 666
Subtotal	17 530	5 042	175 816	6 000	264 750	61 669
Kalimantan:						
West	2 730	500	35 964	2 600	34 655	5 250
South	8 178	1 536	17 898	750	17 029	2 500
Central	4 652	1 673	12 506	250	79 569	17 040
Subtotal	15 560	3 709	66 368	3 600	131 253	24 790
Total	33 090	8 751	242 184	9 610	396 003	86 459

Source: P4S progress Report, 12/81 and MOT records.

clearing for subsistence rice based agriculture. In the second stage, the infrastructure is upgraded to enable the introduction of higher level agriculture to increase farm production, to be followed by a third stage of final and ultimate development, based on a modern community structure.

Reclaimed swamp land is subdivided into individual holdings of about 2.25 hectares per family of which 0.25 hectares is designated as houselot. The hydraulic infrastructure includes the building of navigation canals and open surface drainage system. Water control structures and flood dikes are built only if necessary in the first stage.

B. IRRIGATION WATER MANAGEMENT

There are three Ministries involved in controlling the irrigation water management, i.e. Ministry of Public Works, Agriculture and Home Affairs.

Ministry of Public Works through the Provincial Public Works has a responsibility to operate and maintain the system down to the tertiary outlet. Beyond that point, i.e. at farm level the responsibility is on the beneficieries to manage through their various village organizations. It became apparent, however, that the farmers were incapable of executing the construction, due to their limitation on technical knowledge and also on their financing, so since 1976 the Government provides its assistance with preparation of plans on design and also the construction. However

for the operation and maintenance of the systems the responsibility is on the farmers.

The Ministry of Home Affairs, through the local Administration (Governors, District, Sub District, Chief and Village Head), provides the formation of farmers organization of water management at tertiary systems.

The Ministry of Agriculture is responsible for research, extension and other agriculture technics.

To ensure that management would be done intensively, the Government has issued a Presidential Instruction No. 1/1969 to 3 Ministers (Minister of Home Affairs, Minister of Public Works and Minister of Agriculture) to intensity the supervision and guidance of implementation of operation and maintenance activities. Approved budget for routine activities will be delivered from Central Government i.e. the National Development Planning Agency (BAPPENAS) to each Provincial Public Works Office through the Ministry of Home Affairs and the Provincial Government.

According to Presidential Instruction No. 1/1969, the Directorate General of Water Resources Development, Ministry of Public Works has been appointed as the agency responsible for water management from the resources down to the farm level. The Government through the "law no. 11, 1974 on Water Resources Management" regulates and controls the development and management of water resources.

In Indonesia, there is no formal water charge, since water is considered to have a social function and should be used for the people's welfare. But farmers are requested to maintain tertiary systems facilities. By the Presidential Instruction No. 1/1969. all farmers and water users are encouraged to develop water user association amongst themselves in order to solve disputes concerning water distribution at the farm level and to have good maintenance activities.

The main feature of the water user associations is that they provide an administrative structure designed to ensure the efficient and equitable supply, management and distribution of water to farmer's fields.

An important semi official body in irrigation service is the Irrigation Committee which has been set at Kabupaten (Administrative District) level to co-ordinate the Agriculture, Irrigation and other local Government bodies involved in irrigation activities. Each body has its relevant role in the irrigation activities : the Agricultural office in the supplying seeds of high yielding crops, fertilizer, pesticide etc., and the Irrigation office in distributing water, preparing flood control co-operation with the Irrigation and Agricultural office. The Irrigation Committee meets at least twice a year before the planting periods.

This Committees should announce the decision taken concerning planting dates, irrigation schedule, rotation and other decision which should be followed by all water users.

C. IRRIGATION EFFICIENCY

Application of efficient irrigation water is an effort to achieve maximum use of the water resource. The amount of efficiency can be measured by various criteria and concepts.

The factors which influence irrigation efficiency can be stated as follows:

(i) Variety and stage of crops growth: In this case, change in physiology causes differences in photo synthesis and transpiration. Consequently water requirements will vary.

(ii) Types of soil: Soil types possessing different physical characteristics produce different relationships among soil particles, plants and water. These relationships influence either conveyance systems or water stored for plants needs in the soil.

(iii) Climate: Temperature, sunshine, humidity influence amount of epavoration and transpiration.

These factors, consequently, influence irrigation water requirements-for crops. Besides, rainfall in natural water source which supplies additional inflow for crops, hence, it will reduce irrigation water requirements.

(iv) Water conveyance systems. Various systems of water conveyance influence irrigation water efficiency. Particularly in Indonesia, low application efficiency cannot be avoided, in view of utilization of *ponding system* as a higher component of water requirement during the crop growth.

(v) Distribution system. Water losses from the irrigation systems is an effect of seepage and evaporation and are commonly negligible. Nevertheless, these particular water losses should be reduced as far as possible. Particularly in Indonesia existence of seepage in considerable amount causes low irrigation efficiency.

Based on the above aspects, this paper makes the efforts to discuss irrigation water efficiency, especially its relation to conveyance system which represents irrigation efficiency in Indonesia.

1. Conveyance Efficiency at the Main System

In calculating water conveyance efficiency, it is necessary to differentiate between earth canals which have considerable losses from those which are covered by impervious material (lined canals) where losses are considered negligible.

Water losses from the earth canal during conveyance occur through seepage, leakage, evaporation and evapotranspiration from "agneticweed" which exist along the canals.

Water losses from the lined canal occur through evaporation process which is relatively small, except if cracks take place and the possibility of water losses through seepage or leakage occurs.

For observation of irrigation efficiency in the field it is necessary to differentiate and categorize primary and secondary canals whether those are excavation canals or embankment canals because water losses or water conveyance efficiency for the excavation canal and embankment canals can vary.

The assumption is based on difference in topography and degree of soil compaction, where level of excavation canal is generally lower than level of existing land and possesses higher degree of compaction compared to the embankment canal.

Measurement of water losses at the irrigation canal can be conducted in quantitative, qualitative and indicative manners. By qualitative manner it is meant testing parts of the particular canal where its degree of water losses is relatively high and when necessary observations can be made.

Measurement of water losses in quantative manner could be : ponding method, inflow-outflow method and by using seepage meter.

Ponding method is conducted by closing the flowing water at the particular length of canal and lowering of water level can be observed to evaluate water losses in particular length of time. This method is relatively accurate to know the total and percentage of water losses of short reaches of canal.

Practically, this method is not suitable, because water conveyance will be disturbed.

For measuring the total and percentage of overall water losses at the irrigation canal *inflow-outflow* method can be used closing a distance of measurement between 500-1,000 meter. Measurement structures likes Cippoletti, Thompson and Parshall Flume can be utilized. Although this method is not as accurate as *Ponding Method*, but this method can be conducted without stopping or disturbing irrigation water conveyance.

Application of *seepage meter* is not suitable because of several weaknesses i.e. placement of seepage meter in a particular location for a length of the canal is unrepresentative, besides, problem is in the erection of seepage meter for the whole envelop part of the canal section, considering that the seepage of water through the bed and either side of the canal is not uniform.

2. Conveyance Efficiency at the Tertiary System.

Different from the primary and secondary canals which are designed with the canal width between 5-20 meter, tertiary, sub-tertiary and quartenary are designed with a width of 1-3 meter.

In the main system excavation or embankment canals can easily be distinguished according to the conditions of the existing topography along with planning and location of the system. Whereas the tertiary, sub-tertiary and quartenary canals do not indicate extreme difference either excavation canal or — embankment canal.

Calculation of water losses and irrigation water efficiency by inflow-outflow method for tertiary, sub-teriary and quartenary canal can be observed by several measurement structures i.e. Current Meter, Cip poletti, Thompson or Parshall flume.

Measurement distance of inflow — outflow method ranging between 25 to 100 meter, depend on field condition of the canal system on the tertiary block concerned.

Considering that tertiary block is located at the relatively even to gently sloping field with a slope of 0-5 per cent; utilization of measurement structure is not easy to get

condition of *free flow*. Application of standard meter and parshall flume can be accounted for accurate measurement point of view.

3. Application Efficiency at the Tertiary Block.

Calculation of water application efficiency at the tertiary block is to know the total or percentage of water which is really required for plants growth, especially for paddy crop, in relation to available water at the particular area of tertiary block.

Available water at the tertiary block consists of *rainfall* and irrigation water from *tertiary off take,* reduced by drained water through drainage canal.

In this case, climate factors, types of soil topography condition, total area along with canal intensity at the tertiary concerned are the main factors in determining water application efficiency.

Calculation of water application efficiency at the tertiary block covers the works of observation and measurement of climate, soil physics characteristics, level of ground water, inflow-outflow, evapotranspiration and percolation, total area and canal intensity of tertiary concerned.

4. Water Losses

There is a pressing need to conserve water resources in Indonesia to meet increasing demands in coming years. It is to this end that intensive upgrading is proposed to devise and evaluate advanced systems that can be introduced by major users to conserve this valuable asset.

There are two major demands on water availability:

a.   Increased rice production.

b.   Domestic and industrial requirements compounded by improved living standards.

Water availability is limited by.

a.   Environmental and social constraints to development of storage reservoirs.

b.   Considerable deforestation affecting yields and soil — conservation (Forest cover in East Java is already below minimum standards).

c.   High cost and technical problems related to alternative sources such as groundwater, storage, desalination etc.

Low irrigation efficiency is particularly caused by large amount of water losses at the farm level, as an effect of the habit of farmers in application of excessive irrigation water.

Irrigation efficiency can be increased by reducing water losses at the conveyance system by improved operation, and by reducing field losses.

The improvements that can be practically implemented on operation and maintenance at the present time do not address the problem of conserving water as a scarce resource. A higher degree of control and distribution is envisaged but this would nevertheless accept the use of about 10,000 m^3 per crop of rice and associated conveyance and other losses.

It is difficult to estimate losses at the present time because of the anomolies in discharge data. However some calculations ware recently carried out on the basis of flow data available in two Ranting Dinas in Jember, and Rawatamtu.

The estimated losses in two Rantings Dinas from head of the system to the tertiary head are as follows:

Ranting Dinas Irrigation Unit		Losses	
		Wet Season (Feb. 1983)	Dry Season (Oct. 1983)
Janggawah	Mayang	18 %	52 %
Glundengan	Begadung II	38 %	55 %

Both systems are large with about 5 to 6,000 ha, and lie in the southern sandy areas.

The high losses especially in the dry season are indicative of the order of water abstractions for the dry season rice crop. Some of these losses can be reduced by tightening up operation procedures within the presently envisaged ideal staffing levels but net losses could probably not be reduced to less than about 30 per cent as a lower limit.

With main system, losses tend to increase with dryness because of increased seepage, infiltration and other losses associated with filling/wetting time during rotation. But at farm level farmers resort to rotation and increase the efficiency of application when dry conditions are encountered. The main system in this context comprises primary and secondary channels as well as the main tertiary channel.

The losses from main system are not necessarily recouped for use in lower system. Firstly deep infiltration is often lost irretrievably to groundwater reservoir. Secondly even through flow to shallow drains may not emerge as usable flow within a short time. Thirdly, when water is spread out on large areas and conveyed through a number of seepage prone channels, evaporation, and percolation losses increase manyfold.

Diversion losses may include a structure leakage, operational waste and sometimes over delivery to the irrigation area. An accurate prediction of the losses is extremely difficult to make and the result are at best uncertain. The prediction of the losses is therefore based on management within the limits of existing data and natural factors.

The following rough loss rates are conveniently used for preliminary studies in Indonesia i.e.

No.	Description	Losses
1.	Main canal	5 – 7 %
2.	Secondary canal	7 – 12 %
3.	Tertiary canal	30 – 60 %
4.	Diversion structure	15 – 45 %

Water losses will occur due to:

a. Farmers being unable to prevent spillage from area fields entering drains or running off into waste land.

b. The irrigation managers being unable to ballance supply exactly with demand and so causing water to escape from the tail end of canals.

c. Prevention of illegal turnout and check structures.

Conveyance and distributional losses due to seepage and leakages through crab holes and gates, or illegal diversion, may be minimized by observing the following.

a. Proper maintenance of canal and their embankment.

b. Control of legal turnout.

c. Prevention of illegal turnout and check structures.

d. Control of weed growth.

e. Proper operation and maintenance of irrigation structures.

Field application losses caused by seepage and leakages of the paddy dikes, over application of irrigation water, improper or unscheduled drainage and spillage may be minimized by observing the following:

a. Proper maintenance of paddy dikes and spillways.

b. Better co-operation of the Water Users.

c. Strict supervision of water distribution.

5. Practical Values of Irrigation Efficiency

For calculation of irrigation efficiency on the field in implementation of operation and maintenance of irrigation systems in Indonesia, particulary in Java island with total area ranging between 5,000 up to 20,000 ha the following percentage values can be used.

No.	Canals	Losses
1.	Primary	5 – 10 %
2.	Secondary	10 – 15 %
3.	Tertiary	15 – 30 %
	Total	30 – 50 %

This is the reason why expert in irrigation engineering say that efficiency of irrigation in Indonesia is approximately 60 per cent.

D. CONCLUSION AND ACTIONS TO BE TAKEN IN INCREASING IRRIGATION EFFICIENCY

1. Conclusion

a. Water is lifeblood for mankind, the quantity of water is fixed, whereas total requirements increase with increase in population, so it is necessary to make every effort for application of water effectively and efficiently.

b. To make sure that application of water is efficient, it is necessary that distribution and management of irriga-tion be put into order, especially concerning infrastructure i.e. control structures and measuring devices.

c. Up to the present time, farmers in Indonesia feel that crop will successfully yield if water is over applied. Consequently, they are not interested in following any regulation about application of water and they tend to run against the regulation.

2. Actions to be taken in increasing irrigation efficiency

a. During national development plan (Pelita III), with reference to increment of food production, especially rice, implementation of irrigation intensification is started i.e. development of tertiary system and operation and maintenance of main system.

b. Increasing the operation and maintenance cost of main system besides the cost of maintenance of infrastructure and also for completion of needed quantity, qualification of personnel is necessary.

c. Considering that water requirements are progressively increasing, whereas the quantity of available water is basically fixed, hence to succeed in the effort to increase food production, it is necessary to implement discipline in cropping pattern.

d. Farmers are needed to be trained in extension service programme to convince them that to increase food production (rice) it is not necessary to overapply irrigation water to the field.

III. B. SYSTEM APPROACH IN INTEGRATED RIVER BASIN DEVELOPMENT IN THE CIBEET-JAKARTA-CISADANE (CJC) BASIN.

Introduction

Since the end of the second world war, Jakarta has been under-going a rapid and steady population growth. This gorwth has occured simultaneously with the expansion of political, administrative and economic activities within the capital city since the country became independent. As a result, the Indonesian nation is faced with increasingly delicate urban management problem: transportation, housing, water supply networks, sewerage networks, garbage collection and other public utilities. In these various fields of activity, large-scale works have been carried out or are planned.

The expansion has not been limited to Jakarta Cities area but also along major thoroughfares, following a process that is more or less under control : eastwards (towards Bekasi and Karawang), westwards (towards Tangerang) and southwards (towards Bogor). Some farmland is no longer used for agricultural purposes, but for the erection of buildings and the establishment of industrial zones. Life in the agricultural areas is also subject to profound changes as a result of the job opportunities offered by nearby cities (temporary and permanent immigration) and the proximity of these large markets for agricultural products. At an early stage, it became clear that town planning of Jakarta could not be understood and developed separately from that of the surrounding greater metropolitan areas.

Water management should be understood within this metropolitan context. Certainly, schemes — some on a large scale — have been studied and implemented in the past. However, the rapid development and far reaching transformations of the metropolitan area have gradually raised more serious, diverse and interdependent issues. Solutions to these problems increase in complexity, cost and increasingly serve multiple purposes. The investigation of efficient and economically justified solutions calls for a system approach.

A. BRIEF DESCRIPTION OF THE STUDY AREA

The study area of the so-called Cibeet — Jakarta — Cisadane area (CJC area) has been defined so as to constitute at the same time the hydrological, geographical and human entity.

It stretches over an area of approximately 750,000 ha in the north-western region of Java surrounding Jakarta.

Its boundaries are : to the north, the sea of Java; to the east, the Cibeet watershed, north of the Cibeet — Citarum confluence, the Citarum itself; to the west, the boundaries of the Cidurian watershed, contained in the area; and the south, the crest line dividing the watersheds of the CJC area rivers and the watersheds of the rivers flowing soutwards.

The average monthly temperature fluctuates little throughout the year. In Jakarta this is approximately 25°C.

Climatically, there are two distinct seasons resulting from the monsoon system in this part of the world : the dry season, which lasts approximately five months from June to October inclusive, and the wet season, which lasts seven month from November to March inclusive. Winds blow from the east and the north-east.

During the wet season, relative moisture content in Jakarta averages 80 per cent and 85 per cent, and average sunshine drops to between 40 per cent and 70 per cent.

Rainfall varies according to season and elevation, the yearly average ranging from 1,500 mm on the sea front to 5,500 mm on the most exposed uplands.

Rivers of the study area flow from south to north. Main rivers are from east to west:

. the Cibeet, a tributary of the Citarum,

. the Cikarang,

. the Bekasi made up of the Cikeas and the Cileungsi

. the Ciliwung crossing Jakarta,

. the Cisadane crossing Bogor and Tangerang,

. the Cidurian.

Figure 34 is a location map of the project.

Situation map of the study area is shown on figure 35.

Nowadays, the population of Jakarta is more than 6 million. Average density is therefore close to 100 inhabitants per ha, with much higher figures in some districts. Approximately 4 million inhabitants live in the remaining part of the CJC area. The central area, undergoing uncontrolled urban development, shows the highest densities (over 10 inhabitants per ha), while the eastern and western regions have retained their agricultural features (less than 10 inhabitants per ha). Population growth is particularly rapid in the urban area.

B. PROBLEM STATEMENTS

Problems pertaining to water management issues in the study area can be briefly summarised as follows:

1. Water requirements

Jakarta draws its supplies partially from the city network which serve ¼ of the population, while the rest of the population taps groundwater. Given the growth rate of the population and of activities on the one hand the planned network development on the other hand, foreseeable raw water requirements stand at a much higher level than present dry season resources. Increased water pollution could preclude the future use of some resources which are presently tapped (river Ciliwung).

At present, an attempt is made to organise urban development outside Jakarta, around a number of growth poles. Water distribution in the urban centres will lead to a high consumption levels of raw water which nobody knows where to tap, since nearby existing resources are entirely consumed by irrigation.

Rice represents the main crop in the area. Rice production is an important activity from the point of view of the volume of rice produced and the number of people earn their living in this way.

It consumes large quantities of water, which is plentiful in the wet season, but inadequate in the dry season. Thus, double (or even triple) cropping is only feasible on some of the rice fields. The possibility to develop irrigation and how to overcome the competition between agricultural and urban requirements are still in question.

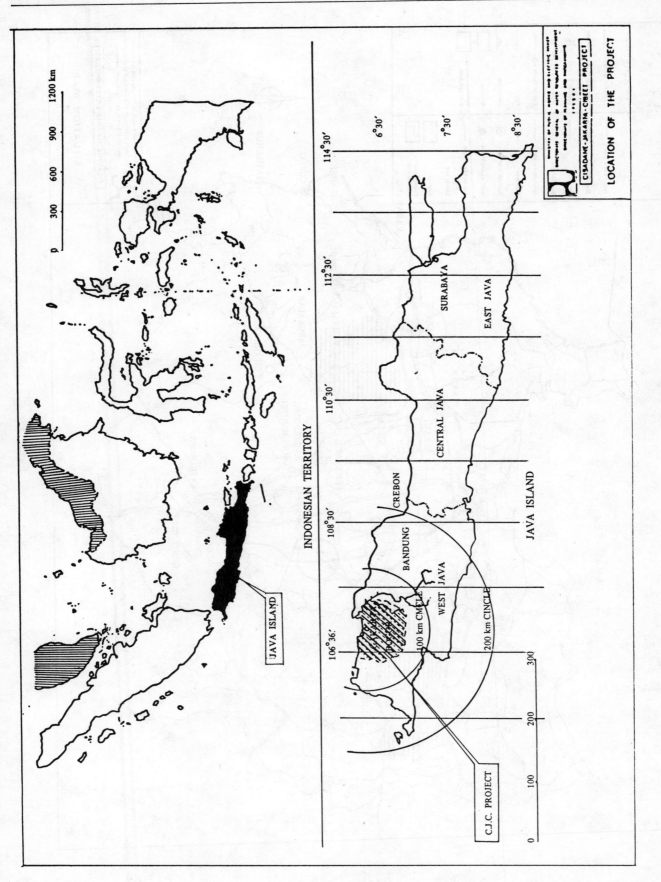

CISADANE-JAKARTA-CIBEET PROJECT

LOCATION OF THE PROJECT

Figure 34.

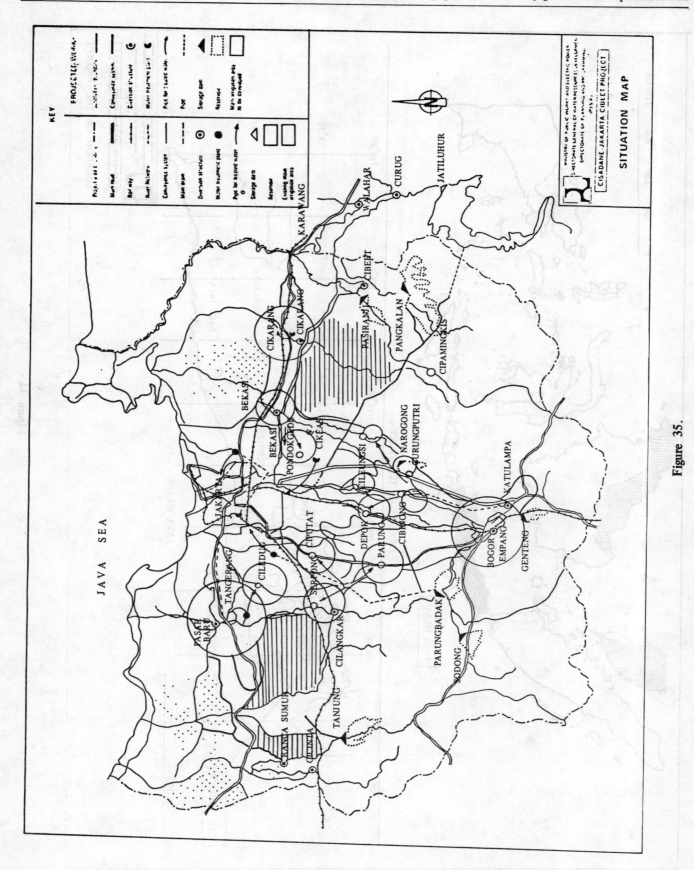

Figure 35.

2. Water quality

On the whole, rivers in the Jakarta area carry large quantities of sediments. This is a problem as these sediments deposit in canals, weirs and dams, necessitating costly dredging operations. Sediments come from extensively eroded areas in the upper basins. These are a threat to water and soil resources at the same time. However, water pollution caused by waste water from industries as well as from dwelling areas is even more serious. Occasionally it already hampers the smooth operation of the Jakarta water treatment plant and it has transformed the open air canals of Jakarta into sewers. This is also a serious threat to public health.

3. Floods

Floods have been experienced in Jakarta for a long time. They are caused by heavy rainfall and also by the overflow of rivers crossing the city. The former Banjir Canal (flood way) accommodated and rerouted river floods. However, urban development extended beyond the boundaries of the area formerly protected. The extension of Banjir Canal eastwards and westwards should offer a long-lasting solution.

4. Hydropower generation

Hydropower consumption in Indonesia is rapidly increasing. Hydroelectric power plays an important part within the framework of efforts undertaken world-wide to reduce oil consumption. Hence, this concern should not be overlooked each time dams are planned, though other needs are more important.

Structures have been built in the past. The most important is the Jatiluhur dam on the Citarum, with which a capacity of 2,900 hm^3 generates hydropower (installed capacity : 150 MW) and by means of three canals and diversion weirs, supplies irrigation water to more than 200,000 ha of rice fields and to Jakarta (10 m^3/sec). Weirs built on the main rivers (Pasar Baru and Empang on the Cisadane, Katulampa on the Ciliwung, Ranca Sumur on the Cidurian) or on secondary rivers (Cibeureum, Cikeas and Cipamingkis) serve large rice-plant areas.

Water distribution networks in Jakarta, Bogor and Tangerang at present only serve a small percentage of the population of these cities.

Recently management schemes are being studied or are already planned. They concern the water distribution networks of Jakarta, Tangerang and Bogor, the sewerage network of Jakarta and the extension of Banjir Canal, storm water drainage in Jakarta. West Tarum Canal and the irrigation networks area are in the process of rehabilitation. A dam upstream of Jatiluhur on the Citarum (Saguling dam) is supposed to be commissioned in 1984. It will mainly be used for hydropower generation.

Existing or planned structures are inadequate to meet future needs and even present-day needs. Competition between water users already exists. Solutions that can be envisaged in principle under the conditions prevailing in the region, are more intricate because they are nearly always "interbasin" and "multipurpose". The general need for advanced techniques to facilitate water resource planning especially of an unusually complex system such as that of Jakarta area calls for the application of system approach identified by simulation modelling, data management and optimisation technique.

Aware of these difficulties, The Directorate General of Water Resources Development in 1973 ordered a presentation of issues and terms in respect to what should become the overall study of water resources development in the Jakarta area. This study, to which two French consulting firms SOGREAH and COYNE & GELIIER were appointed by contract in September 1976, has been conducted in close co-operation with the Division of River Basin Planning (P2WS) of the Directorate of Planning and Programming and more particularly with its branch responsible for project co-ordination and study of the "Cisadane — Jakarta — Cibeet Project".

C. POSSIBLE DEVELOPMENT

Given the natural resources and the existing water development structure, new development can be envisaged to satisfy future requirement at the optimum economic result. There is obviously an infinite number of schemes including slight variation on basic schemes.

Therefore a number of schemes could be deliminated at the outset : those which are predicated to be more costly for the same result or those which will involve excessive risks or complication for the same cost at the same result.

Systematic investigation of the water management works are carried out i.e. dam, main and secondary water conveyance works, urban water supply works. (including the water treatment plant and distribution networks).

D. SELECTION OF DEVELOPMENT SCHEMES

To determine how far the available water resources and planned structures could meet requirements and subsequently determine the optimum scheme to be recommended for implementation, a selection of development schemes was carried out.

Prior to this a preliminary selection was made in the course of possible alternatives, where a number of possible schemes were systematically discarded, because they were clearly more expensive than others at the same efficiency.

In this study the principles of economic optimization geared to the selection are:

.   The cheapest schemes allowing satisfaction of urban consumption demands,

.   The most profitable schemes for irrigation purpose.

In line with those principles, several situations were examined: one is characterized by the implementation of works required to meet urban demand only and the other alternatives are being characterized by the coverage of urban water demand in parallel with the extensive development of irrigation.

The optimum development scheme for the "reference" situation was then investigated, followed by investigation of the development of scheme which allows the extensive development of irrigation.

A number of processes of the selection schemes are explained in brief i.e. : the simulation process with the aim to see the water availability of the river basin system, the optimum calculation to reduce alternatives to which costs are minimized, water management alternatives to include scheduling of each structure, and finally the multicriteria analysis to involve other aspects such as social aspects as well as economical aspect.

1. The Simulation Model

The purpose of the hydrological simulation was to examine how some system of structures and some of their operational rules could contribute to satisfaction of demand, provided that hydrological resources correspond to the observed or reconstituted monthly flow rate.

A simulation of this type is based first of all on a hydraulic diagram. The basic hydraulic diagram used is shown on Figure 36. For some specific studies a few changes were made to this basic diagram.

A given requirement may sometime be satisfied from two or more different sources. In this case operation is designed so as to minimize the risk of shortfalls and supply costs.

It was essential to define the conditions in which demand is assumed to be met. It is generally considered if urban requirement (domestic and industrial) need to be met with a low deficiency risk (in general, one year out of 50), standards are not so stringent for agricultural requirement.

Therefore it was considered that the system could satisfy demand if during the simulation using observed (or estimated) monthly flow rates over 50 years, the following condition could be met:

.   Industrial and urban requirement were met without deficiency.

.   A minimum firm flow of the flushing of open drains of Jakarta was also supplied without deficiency.

.   At least 80 per cent of dry season irrigation requirements could be met.

Certainly these standards are only approximate, but they are well adapted to the type of consumers concerned, in particular since they apply to monthly flow rates. Provision of an adequate monthly flow rates does not rule out the possibility of flow being inadequate for half of the month, but for the purpose of this study this approach appears to be reasonable. Procedure taken for the simulation model is shown on Attachment A on page 227.

The main simulation results are summarized on Table 66. It is interesting to determine whether the potential resources of the planned storage dams can meet the maximum requirements of the year 2000.

Table 66 is based on the most critical dry season of the 50 year of simulation, 80 per cent of nominal irrigation requirements and 100 per cent of urban water requirements.

Maximum flow available for flushing = Resources − Requirements + Other natural or return flows into the Banjir Canal (Flood way) = 3728 − 3425 + 176 = 479 hm³ (= 46 m³/sec). Result shows that total demand can be met by the total potential resources with an additional supply of 46 m³/s for flushing, which corresponds to the upper limit of reasonable flushing requirements i.e. 25 to 40 m³/sec.

It would probably not be reasonable to build all these structures between now and the year 2000. Selection of water management schemes is then carried out to guide the Administration's choise of the most advantageous management scheme from the economic and social point of view.

2. The Optimization Calculation

It was necessary to reduce the number of alternatives to be compared in detail, in view of their large number. To this end, an optimization mathematical calculation was made in respect to all possible development schemes, taking into account that only the requirement by the year 2000 were constant.

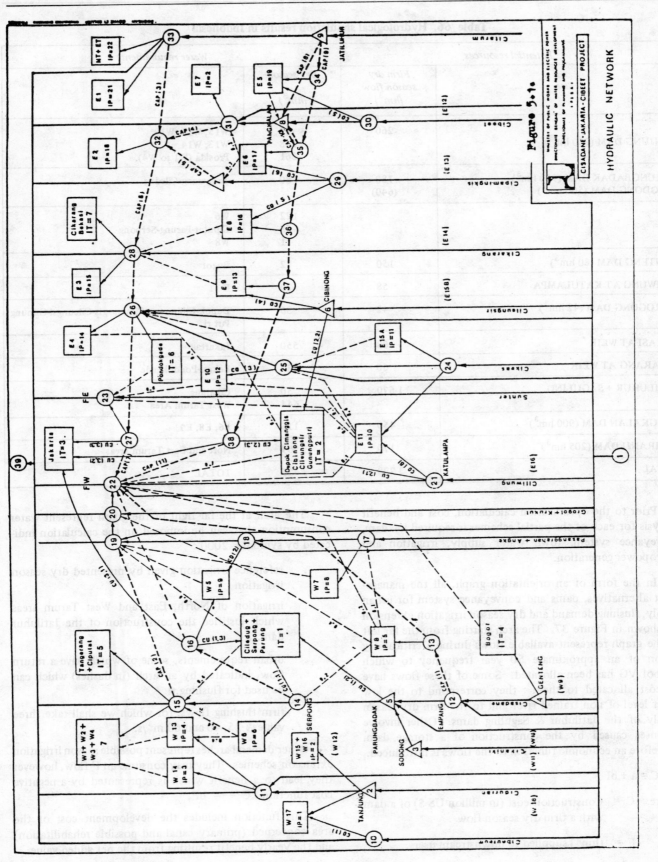

Figure 36.

Table 66. Hydrological simulation results in Indonesia

Potential resources		Water requirements	
Site	Firm dry season flow (hm^3)	Dry season (hm^3)	
TANJUNG DAM (280 hm^3)	260	92 148 361	W15, W16, W19 W13, W14 Prosida (W1 to W4).
PARUNGBADAK DAM (950 hm^3) or SODONG DAM (500 hm^3)	780 (640)	89	Tangerang-Ciledug
		122 58 71	W6 Ciputat-Parung-Serpong W8
GENTENG DAM (80 hm^3)	150	72	Bogor
CILIWUNG AT KATULAMPA	58	20	E 11
NAROGONG DAM (42 hm^3)	42	36	Depok-Cibinnong-Cimang-gis-Cileungsi-Gunung Put ri.
BEKASI AT WEIR	88	550	Jakarta.
CIKARANG AT WEIR	60	37	Bekasi-Pondokgede
JATILUHUR + SAGULING	1 670	50 644	Cikarang West Tarum Area
PANGKALAN DAM (900 hm^3)	450	116	E6, E8, E9
PASIRANJI DAM (205 hm^3)	170	969	Nort and East Tarum areas
TOTAL	3 728	3 425	TOTAL

Prior to the optimization calculation, cost and benefit analysis for each of the partial schemes is required i.e. dam, conveyance system, town water supply, irrigation and hydropower generation.

In the form of an orientation graph, all the management alternatives, dams and conveyance system for urban supply, flushing demand and dry season irrigation extension are shown in Figure 37. The arch starting from the far left of the graph represent available flows during a critical dry season of an approximate 50 year frequency to which symbol VG has been allocated. Some of these flows have no cost allocated to them : they correspond to the low water level of non trained river and to the firm dry season supply of the Jatiluhur & Saguling dams. Other involve expenses caused by the construction of a storage dam. Therefore an economic function to the flows is introduced.

$$C = a + bF$$

Where : C = Construction cost (in million US $) of a dam with a firm dry season flow

F = (hm^3) supplied to downstream users.

The arch at the far right of the graph represent water consumption that can be imposed on the calculation indicated by symbol F 2000 :

.   reference irrigation given by presented dry season irrigation

.   irrigation of North, East and West Tarum areas which justified the construction of the Jatiluhur dam.

.   urban requirements, some of which have a return flow, indicated by an arch (in dashes) which can be used for flushing.

.   firm flushing flows, for which we shall take three values : 25, 40 and 60 m^3/s.

Other demand arches represent possible season irrigation extension schemes. They may consume an F flow, however they lead to a benefit which is represented by a negative cost function : $C = - bF$.

This function includes the development cost of the area concerned (primary canal and possible rehabilitation) and the yearly benefit resulting from the net added value.

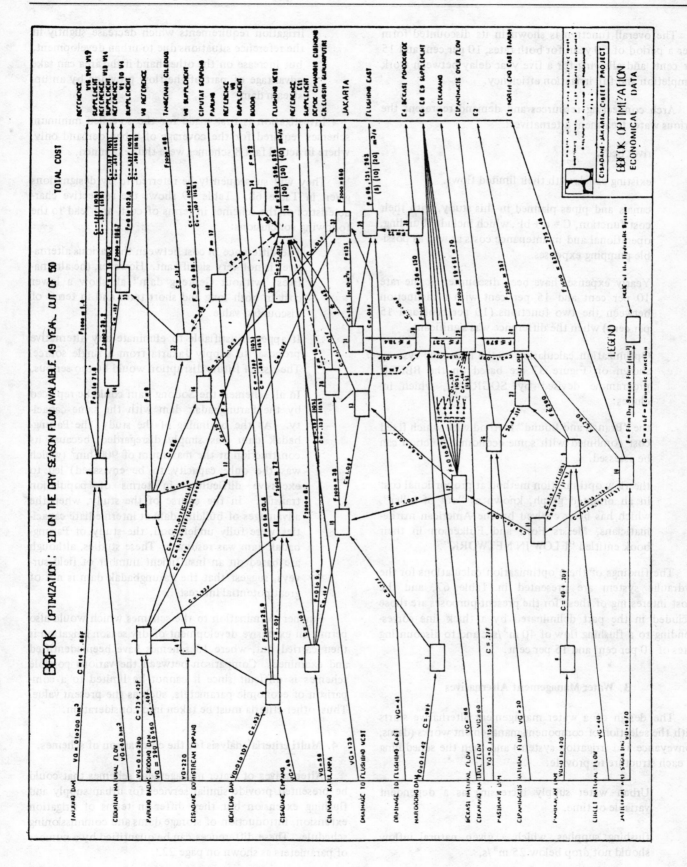

Figure 37.

The overall function is shown in its discounted form over a period of 50 year, for both rates, 10 per cent and 15 per cent, and allowing for a five year delay between work completion and full irrigation efficiency.

Arch connecting resources and demand represent the various water treatment alternatives:

. river beds.

. existing canals with their limited flows.

. canals and pipes planned in this study, with their cost function, $C = a + bF$, which includes building, operational and maintenance costs as well as possible pumping expenses.

Yearly expenses have been discounted at the rate 10 per cent and 15 per cent with a distinction between the two functions (10 per cent and 15 per cent) when the difference was significant.

Optimization calculation of the hydraulic system, shown on Figure 37 are based on the BBFOK programme devised by SOGREAH, which includes:

. the "Branch and Bound" method with which fixed cost combined with some economic function can be assessed.

. the flow optimization method at proportional cost in an oriented graph, known as "out of killer", which has been evolved by the American mathematicians, Messrs Ford and Fulkerson in their book entitled "FLOW IN NETWORK".

The findings of these optimization calculations for the hydraulic system are presented in Table 67, and the most interesting of these for the present purposes are those included in the part deliminated by a thick line corresponding to a flushing flow of 40 m³/sec and to discounting rates of 10 per cent and 15 per cent.

3. Water Management Alternatives

The design of a water management alternative starts with the selection of component management works (dams, conveyance and irrigation system) and then the scheduling of each structure to provide:

. Urban water supply increasing as a dependent variable of time.

. flushing supplies, which a given natural inflow should not drop below 25 m³/s.

. irrigation requirements which decrease slightly in the reference situations due to urban development, but increase on the other hand if the area can take advantage of part of the flow provided by an upstream dam.

Investigation is first made for the so-called minimum schemes required for the coverage of urban demand only, where in actual fact 8 schemes were thus examined.

They will subsequently be referred to by designations given in Table 68. Table 69 shows the respective characteristics of the schemes in terms of cost, and lead to the following conclusions:

. The difference in cost between the various alternatives is not very significant. However, the alternatives "without Genteng dam" all show a lower cost in both long and short term and in terms of discounted value.

. It appears justifiable to eliminate any alternative proposal to supply Jakarta from a single source. The risk of future disruption would be too serious.

. In all schemes, the Sodong dam could be replaced by the Parungbadak dam with the same capacity. At the beginning of the study, the Parungbadak dam was simply disregarded, because its construction at the maximum of 900 hm³ (which was the only capacity to be envisaged) led to excessive difficulties in terms of population transfer. In the course of the study, when the advantages of building dam at intermediate capacities were fully understood, the study of Parungbadak dam was resumed. These studies, although are based on an insufficient number of field surveys, suggest that the Parungbadak dam is not of great potential interest.

Further examination to the schemes which would also permit an extensive development of dry season irrigation is then carried out, where 15 schemes have been identified and examined. Comparison between the various possible schemes is difficult since it cannot be limited to a comparison of economic parameters, such as the present value. Thus, other criteria must be taken into consideration.

4. Multi criteria analysis for the comparison of schemes.

Alternatives of water management schemes that could be presented provide similar services for urban supply and flushing extension but they differ in terms of irrigation extension, introduction of storage dams and commissioning schedule. These differences can be quantified by a number of parameters as shown on page 222.

Table 67. OPTIMISATION RESULTS GIVEN BY THE "BBFOK" PROGRAMME
(Urban water supply — year 2000)

Flushing		$25 \ m^3/sec$	$40 \ m^3/sec$	$60 \ m^3/sec$
REFERENCE SITUATION	Dams	Genteng Pangkalan	Genteng Sodong* Pangkalan	Genteng Sodong* Pangkalan Pasiranji
	Convey	Cibeet C. W.T.C. 2,3	Flushing Via K. Grogol Cibeet Canal W.T.C. 2,3,4	Flushing via K. Grogol Cibeet Canal W.T.C. 2,3,4
		Total Cost 366 10⁶ $	497 10⁶ $	641 10⁶ $
EXTENSION OF IRRIGATION WITH a-15 per cent	Dams	Sodong Pangkalan	Genteng Sodong* Pangkalan	Genteng Parungbadak Pangkalan
	Convey	W.T.C. 2,3 pump St. 2B Canal 20	Flushing via Cibeet Canal W.T.C. 2,3,4	Flushing via Cibeet Canal W.T.C. 2,3,4
	Irrigation	Prosida E6, 8, 9	Prosida	Prosida
	Balance	320 10⁶ $	443 10⁶ $	587 10⁶ $
EXTENSION OF IRRIGATION WITH a-10 per cent	Dams	Tanjung Genteng Sodong* Pangkalan	Tanjung Genteng Sodong* Pangkalan	Tanjung Genteng Parungbadak Pangkalan
	Convey	W.T.C. 2,3 Pump St. 3B Canal 2C	Flushing via K. Grogol Cibeet Canal W.T.C. 2,3,4 Pump St. 2B Canal 2C	Flushing via K. Grogol Cibeet Canal W.T.C. 2,3,4 Pump St. 2B Canal 2C
		W13, 14 W15, 16, 19 Prosida W8 E6, 8, 9	W13, 14 W15, 16, 19 Prosida W8 E6, 8, 9	W13, 14 W15, 16, 19 Prosida W8 E6, 8, 9
	Balance	152 10⁶ $	249 10⁶ $	390 10⁶ $

* Or Parungbadak (small capacity).

Table 68.

DESIGNATION OF SCHEME SUBJECT TO EXAMINATION		
Supply of Jakarta with drinking water	With Genteng	Without Genteng Dam
West Tarum Canal only	R 11	R 21
West Tarum Canal and Cisadane (Canal 3)	R 12	R 22
West Tarum Canal and Canal 2 (Pangkalan – Jakarta)	R 13	R 23
West Tarum Canal, Canal 2 and Cisadane (Canal 3)	R 14	R 24

Table 69.

CHARACTERISTICS OF ALTERNATIVES Value in 10^6 US $		With Genteng Dam				Without Genteng Dam			
		R11	R 12	R 13	R 14	R 21	R 22	R 23	R 24
Discounted cost (I = 10 %)	Without urban supply	181	186	192	191	131	141	137	144
	Without urban supply	481	486	492	491	431	441	437	444
Investment cost (until 2,000)*	Without urban supply	585	639	623	677	513	577	504	565
	With urban supply	1 142	1 196	1 180	1 234	1 070	1 134	1 061	1 122
Investment cost (until 1,990)*	Without urban supply	446	487	446	487	327	376	327	376
	With urban supply	783	824	723	824	664	723	664	723
Population to be transferred		47 300	58 900	47 300	58 900	53 900	65 500	45 900	57 500
Safety for supply of Botabek growth poles **		+	+	+	+	–	–	–	–
Percentage of Jakarta water supply from Cisadane (per cent)		0	20	0	20	0	20	0	20

*   1978 US $

**   (+ With Genteng – Without Genteng)

(a) *From the economic point of view*

(i) The discounted cost-benefit balance sheet over a period extending from 1981 to 2005.

(ii) The total investment required.

(iii) The amount of investment expenditure to be incurred between 1981 to 1990.

(b) *From the economic and social point of view*

(i) Annual added value from agriculture in year 2000.

(ii) The additional dry season irrigated area.

(c) *From the social point of view*

(i) Total population effected by flooding under each alternative.

(ii) Safety for water supply to Botabek growth poles between 1979 and 1989.

(iii) Percentage of Jakarta water supply from the Cisadane Basin by the year 2000.

Values of these parameters in respect to each alternative are shown on Table 70.

Table 70. Characteristics of alternatives

	ALTERNATIVE GENTENG						ALTERNATIVE WITHOUT GENTENG								
	Sodong				Parungbadak		Sodong					Parungbadak			
	2	4	2A	4A	3	3A	6	8	9	8A	9A	7	10	7A	10A
Discounted (i = 10 per cent) Cost – Benefit (10⁶ US $)	411 (86)	432 (82)	404 (88)	419 (85)	421 (84)	411 (86)	383 (93)	405 (88)	416 (85)	393 (90)	400 (89)	381 (93)	368 (96)	370 (96)	335 (100)
Net present value of the programme compared with the related ref. programme	+75	+54	+82	+67	+65	+75	–54	+32	+21	+44	+37	+56	+69	+67	+82
Investment cost for dams, conveyance works, 10⁶ US $ Irrigation	646 (80)	851 (60)	658 (78)	866 (59)	855 (60)	871 (59)	514 (100)	863 (60)	860 (60)	862 (60)	874 (59)	743 (69)	632 (81)	747 (69)	636 (81)
Investment cost from 1979 to 1990 for same 10⁶ items US $	452 (72)	502 (65)	442 (74)	484 (67)	454 (72)	391 (83)	325 (98)	515 (63)	355 (92)	495 (66)	406 (80)	335 (97)	428 (76)	318 (100)	411 (77)
Annual added value from agriculture in year 2000, 10⁶ US $/year	40 (46)	56 (64)	63 (72)	79 (91)	59 (68)	82 (94)	30 (34)	65 (75)	65 (75)	87 (100)	87 (100)	49 (56)	49 (56)	72 (83)	72 (83)
Supplement of dry season irrigated area (ha) (–unundated rice fields)	11 800 (45)	18 000 (60)	24 600 (77)	30 900 (92)	17 100 (58)	30 000 (90)	6 400 (32)	21 100 (68)	21 100 (68)	34 000 (100)	34 000 (100)	11 700 (45)	12 500 (47)	24 500 (76)	25 300 (78)
Population living in the reservoir areas	58 000 (86)	82 000 (61)	50 000 (100)	74 000 (68)	120 000 (42)	117 000 (43)	56 000 (89)	87 000 (57)	87 000 (57)	79 000 (63)	79 000 (63)	118 000 (42)	99 000 (51)	110 000 (45)	91 000 (55)
Safety for water supply to Botabek growth poles between 1979 and 1989 (+with Genteng, – without Genteng)	+ (100)	+ (100)	+ (100)	+ (100)	+ (100)	+ (100)	– (0)	– (0)	– (0)	– (0)	– (0)	– (0)	– (0)	– (0)	
Percentage of Jakarta water supply from Cisadane	20 % (0)	20 % (57)	20 % (57)	20 % (57)	35 % (100)	35 % (100)	– (0)	30 % (86)	30 % (86)	30 % (86)	30 % (86)	33 % (94)	30 % (86)	33 % (94)	30 % (86)
Cost of compensation for land acquisition at dams sites (10⁶ US $)	101	132	83	132	152	134	85	145	145	116	166	136	121	118	103

N.B. – Investment costs without urban water supply (pipes, pumping station and treatment plants).

Marking were given to each parameter ranging from 0 to 100, to which the best value for each parameter is set to "100".

For example : for parameter (1) alternative (2).

$$\text{mark } 86 = \frac{355}{411} \times 100 = \frac{\text{actual max. cost (alt. 10A)}}{\text{actual cost of alt. 2}}$$

This mark shows that in respect to the above parameter, alternative 2 only represent 80 per cent of the best alternative (10A). Parameter 1 to 7 is then merged into two main criteria : economic & social criteria. In order to allocate to each alternative:

. an overall "economic" mark,

    Ec. = 0.25 (1) + 0.25 (2) + 0.25 (3) + 0.15 (4) + 0.10 (5).

. and two "social" marks

    — one including problems resulting from the non construction of Genteng (parameter 7):
       Soc. 1 = 0.1 (4) + 0.3 (5) + 0.5 (6) + 0.1 (7).

    — The other excluding this parameter:
       Soc. 2 = 0.2 (4) + 0.3 (5) + 0.5 (6).

Results of this final analysis is shown in table 71.

Table 71.

MULTICRITERIA ANALYSIS COMPARISON OF ALTERNATIVES			
Alternative	Economic Criteria	Social Criteria I	Social Criteria 2
2	71	71	66
4	67	65	61
2A	79	90	88
4A	76	81	80
3	70	55	52
3A	80	68	67
6	81	56	61
8	71	56	64
9	77	56	64
8A	79	72	82
9A	82	72	82
7	78	40	46
10	76	45	51
7A	86	54	62
10A	85	59	68

E. WATER RESOURCES DEVELOPMENT PROGRAMME

From this study it was clear that the research into optimum development programme followed two basic directions:

— Firstly, economic efficiency which was attempted to identify the cheapest development programme that would satisfy urban requirements at all times, combined with the development of such irrigation as water resources will allow and ensuring the highest possible net present benefit.

— secondly, the consideration of non-economic selection criteria, in recognition of the fact that non-economic (or not exclusively economic) factors must be taken into account in the choice of the final programme, e.g. the difficulty of reinserting displaced populations in the economic and social life of the country, the security of water supply, the development of rice production, etc.

This is why this study is presenting not one but several possible programmes, with the most important characteristic of each, to assist in making the choices. They should finally be based on a multi-criteria analysis scheme, as presented in the previous discussion.

Clearly there can be no objective selection process. Any choice is arbitrary, and will reflect the relative importance attributed by the decision-maker to one of the previous-mentioned features. Consequently, the multi-criteria analysis does not aim at making an objective choice, but merely at providing a synthetic and coherent view of the issues that the Indonesian Government will have to tackle when making its final choice.

In conclusion to the multi-criteria analysis and subject to the findings of the above-metioned studies, alternative 9A should be adopted as the ideal solution, if necessary, replacing Sodong by Parungbadak. Should it appear necessary to built Genteng dam, this would then correspond to alternative 2A.

The diagrammatic map on Figure 38 illustrates the recommended alternative, the main features of which are presented in Table 72.

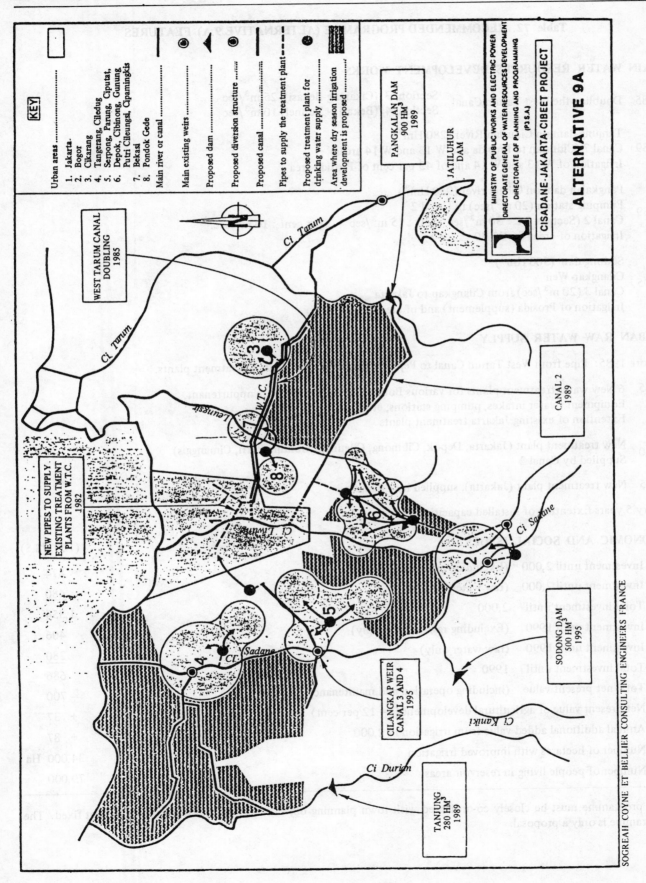

Figure 38.

Table 72. RECOMMENDED PROGRAMME (ALTERNATIVE 9.A) FEATURES

1. MAIN WATER RESOURCES DEVELOPMENT WORKS

1985   Doubling the West Tarum Canal   Section 3 (Cikarang-Bekasi) 25 m³/sec
                                        Section 4 (Bekasi – Tunnel) 10 m³/sec

1989   Tanjung dam on Cidurian River (280 Hm³)
      Canal 7 (Cidurian to Prosida and W 13 and W 14 areas)
      Irrigation of W 13 and W 14 and of 43 per cent of Prosida area

1989   Pangkalan dam on Cibeet river (950 Hm³)
      Pumping station (20 m³/sec) to Canal 2
      Canal 2 (Section 2 C : 30 m³/sec – 2D : 15 m³/sec – 2 per cent : 10 m³/sec.
      Irrigation of areas E6 E8 E9

1995   Sodong dam (500 Hm³)
      Cilangkap Weir
      Canal 3 (20 m³/sec) from Cilangkap to Jakarta
      Irrigation of Prosida (supplement) and of area W6

2. URBAN RAW WATER SUPPLY

Before 1985: Pipe from West Tarum Canal to Pejompongan and Pulo Gadung treatment plants.

1985   6 New water treatment plants for various Botabek growth poles, with appurtenant.
      Equipment (water intakes, pumping stations, etc)
      Extention of existing Jakarta treatment plants

1990   New treatment plant (Jakarta, Depok, Cibinong, Cileungsi, Gunung Putri, Cimanggis)
      Supplied by Canal 2

1995   New treatment plant (Jakarta), supplied by Cisadane

Every 5 years Extention of installed capacities.

3. ECONOMIC AND SOCIAL ISSUES

(10⁶ US.$)

- Investment until 2,000   (Excluding raw water supply)   874
- Investment until 2,000   (raw water supply)   480
- Total investment until   2,000   1,354
- Investment until 1990   (Excluding raw water supply)   406
- Investment until 1990   (raw water only)   280
- Total investment until   1990   686
- Total net present value   (including operation and maintenance I = 12 per cent)   − 700
- Net present value of agricultural development (I = 12 per cent)   + 37
- Annual additional added value from irrigation in 2,000   + 87
- Number of hectares with improved irrigation   34,000 Ha
- Number of people living in reservoir areas   79,000

― This programme must be closely co-ordinated with town planning objectives. Since these objectives are not fixed. The programme is only a proposal.

ATTACHMENT "A"

DESCRIPTION OF THE SIMULATION MODEL

The simulation model programme for the whole hydraulic system comprises the following stages:

. Readings of the monthly discharge rates at the hydrological station.

Q (I, N, M)   I = 1 Cidurian at Kopomaja,
                  2 Cisadane at Masing,
                  3 Cisadane at Serpong,
                  4 Ciliwung at Rawajati,
                  5 Cileungsir at Bekasi Weir,
                  6 Cikarang at W. T. C. Weir,
                  7 Cibeet at Cibeet Weir,
                  8 Citarum at the Jatiluhur inlet.

. Readings of monthly discharge rates at Saguling, Q (9,N,M), and calculation of incoming flow at Jatiluhur Q (8,N,M), taking into account regulation by Saguling.

. Flow rate calculation Q (10,N,M) : catchment area of the river Cisadane between Empang and Serpong.

. Flow rate calculation Q (11,N,M) : catchment area of the Ciliwung between Katulampa and Rawajati.

Transformation of all discharge rates (M3/s) into monthly inflow, (hm^3).

. Readings of the table of irrigation per unit requirements (1/s/ha).

B (JC, IR, M)   M = month
                IR = rainfall index
                JC = cropping pattern index (see report on agriculture).

. Readings of the IRT (IP) table showing the rainfall index of the irrigated area No. IP.

. Readings to the table S (IP, JC) of cultivated acreages (ha) according to the JC cropping pattern on the No. IP irrigated area.

. Readings of the table UR (IT) of the monthly urban water requirements (hm^3) for the IT urban centre.

. Readings of the minimum supply for:

  — Flushing West : FW (hm^3)
  — Flushing East : FE (hm^3)

and the monthly minimum quantities of water to be turbined at Jatiluhur : QG.

. Readings of the table VU (IRV) of the dam and reservoir usable storage capacities,

  — IRV = 2 Tanjung
            3 Sodong
            4 Genteng
            5 Parung Badak
            6 Cibinong
            7 Pasiranji
            8 Pangkalan
            9 Jatiluhur.

and of the table STIN (IRV) of initial reserves at the onset of the simulation operation.

. Readings of the table CAP (K) of the canals' maximum capacities (see graph on F 1).

. Readings of the table CO (I) of the distribution coefficients of supply to the areas that can be irrigated from two river network points (see graph F 1).

. Readings of the table CU (IT, J) of the distribution coefficient of supply to the IT urban centres that can draw on several network points (see graph F 1).

Calculation of the table RI (IP, M) of irrigation water requirements (hm^3) for each area IP, and for each month M.

Calculation of table TNR (IRV, M) of total net requirements of the IRV point, during month M,

TNR (IRV, M) = total of planned diversions at the IRV point — total of return flow at IRV.

This equation refers to the graph F 1, which indicates diversions and return flows.

. Flow calculation in each arc A (i, j) joining two points i and j of the river network, using subroutine DIV (DI, SU, DE, OU) for the points with a regulation dam.

In subroutine DIV (DI, SU, DE, OU) the data is the following:

  — DI = incoming flow from upstream,
  — SU = flow to be diverted at the point.

the calculation shows:

— DE = possible deficit if Su > DI
— OU = outgoing flow at downstream point.

In subroutine DAM (V, DI, SU, QS, DE, OU, ST) the data is the following:

— V = dam usable storage capacity,
— DI = incoming flow from upstream,
— SU = flow to be diverted at the dam site,
— QS = flow to be released to meet downstream requirements.

the calculation shows:

— DE = SU supply deficit,
— OU = Outgoing flow at the dam
       > QS if there is overflow
     = QS when the dam is not empty at the end of the month < QS when the dam empties itself in the course of the month

ST = end of the month reserves

The management rules applied to the dam are given in the QS value that is calculated before using the subroutine.

. Supply deficits DEF (IRV) that appear at the IRV point, to supply TNR (IRV, M) are distributed over the various consumption poles (urban centres and irrigated areas) according to the order of priorities.

. Calculation of tables TUD (IT, M, N) and TD (IP, M, N) of deficits allocated to urban centres IT and irrigated areas IP based on the deficits DEF (IRV), with a view to supplying urban centres first, then the minimum imposed flushing level, and lastly the irrigated areas. Excess water is only allocated to flushing above the imposed minimum, when irrigation water requirements are met.

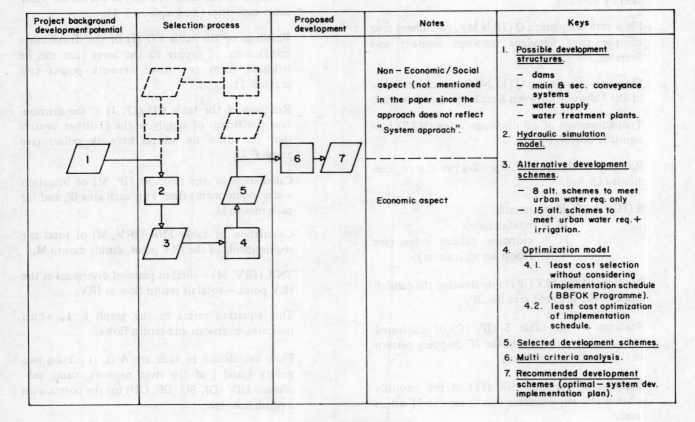

Project background development potential	Selection process	Proposed development	Notes	Keys
1	2, 3, 4, 5	6, 7	Non – Economic / Social aspect (not mentioned in the paper since the approach does not reflect "System approach". —————— Economic aspect	1. **Possible development structures.** – dams – main & sec. conveyance systems – water supply – water treatment plants. 2. **Hydraulic simulation model.** 3. **Alternative development schemes.** – 8 alt. schemes to meet urban water req. only – 15 alt. schemes to meet urban water req. + irrigation. 4. **Optimization model** 4.1. least cost selection without considering implementation schedule (BBFOK Programme). 4.2. least cost optimization of implementation schedule. 5. **Selected development schemes.** 6. **Multi criteria analysis.** 7. **Recommended development schemes (optimal – system dev. implementation plan).**

ATTACHMENT "B"

Figure 38A. Flow Diagram of the System Approach

IV. THE ISLAMIC REPUBLIC OF IRAN

AVAILABILITY OF WATER RESOURCES

Introduction

The Iranian territory which lies between 25 and 40 degrees north latitude and 44 and 64 degrees east longitude has a total area of about 1,650,000 square kilometers. Over 50 per cent of the total land surface of Iran is mountainous and rough with different climatic characteristics. The Caspian Sea and the Caucasus ranges of the northern border, the Persian Gulf and the Sea of Oman at the southern border distinguish its orography and geographical position.

The total annual precipitation in Iran averages about 440 billion cubic meters (440 BCM) of water. Due to uneven areal distribution of the precipitation, most of the precipitated water is used where it falls and vanishes through the hydrological processes of evaporation, percolation and evapotranspiration, so that about 91 BCM of it reaches the nation's water courses. The portion of the surface water resources that is available to meet the nation's requirements is the total runoff which amounts to 116 BCM. This volume of water which is partly controlled and regulated consists of the following proportions:

— about 39 per cent (45 BCM) of it is diverted from the water courses for various uses including those of agriculture, municipal, mining, industrial and rural domestic supply.

— about 9 per cent (11 BCM) of it is used in the water courses themselves for hydro-electric power generation, navigation, and fish and wildlife, and

— the remaining 52 per cent (60 BCM) flows into seas, gulfs, lakes, sinks, marshes and across international borders.

The annual precipitation which mostly occurs during spring and winter with the exception of the Caspian Sea littoral which has occasional summer rainfall, averages from 250 to 300 millimeters (10 to 12 inches) of rain and snow. The averages vary from less than 50 millimeters in the desert interior to more than 2000 millimeters in the south-western Caspian region.

Consequently, the country is now and will continue to be faced with the dilemma of how best to control, protect, conserve, manage, and develop her water resources. Therefore, the water affairs of the Ministry of Energy in collaboration with other relevant institutions and authorities challenges the problem of water and does its best to acquire an overall enhancement of the water resources of the country.

A. REPORT ON WATER RESOURCES STUDY IN IRAN

The study of water resources in Iran from management point of view is divided into 11 regions which are in affiliation with the regional water authorities of each province. For a better and comprehensive study of water resources, about 42 study centres have been established throughout the country. The Bureau of Water Resources Study, as a planner and co-ordinator, is acting to supervise and direct the studies by giving all technical assistance to these study centres. The investigation here is composed of two main parts.

1. *Groundwater investigation*

2. *Surface water*

1. Groundwater investigation

The objectives of groundwater studies are as follows.

a. Investigation of water resources potential from quality and quantity point of view, determination of groundwater potential in each water basin for agricultural development, drinking water to cities, villages and Industries.

b. Discovery of new groundwater aquifer in both alluvium and Karstic reservoirs of the country.

c. Collection, preparation, and analysis of all water resources data collected from Qanats, springs, wells, and rivers for establishing the basic water resources data which plays an important role in most of the country's development plans.

d. Performance of artificial recharging for a better yield and protection of groundwater resources, and also study of methods of preventing the saline water advancement.

e. Investigation and study of Karstic resources and method of its production.

f. Preparation and production of groundwater maps showing all physical features, the quality and quantity.

g.   Planning and programming of the regulation policy for producing from water resources in order to achieve a proper and logical method of production and development of the country's water resources.

In general, the programme which has so far been investigated for the study of the country's groundwater resources are as follows:—

(i)   Programme of study of reconnaissance survey of alluvium plains.

(ii)   Programme of semi-detailed study of alluvium plains.

(iii)   Programme of study and continuous control of groundwater.

(iv)   Programme of reconnaissance study of Karstic region.

(i) *Programme of study of Reconnaisance Survey of Alluvium Plain includes:*

(1)   Collection of water resources data and estimation of its withdrawal.

(2)   Investigation of the general condition of hydrology of the region.

(3)   Investigation of the groundwater resources from quality and quantity point of view.

(4)   Preparation of future programme of groundwater study — so far on more than 200 alluvium plains, totally of about 440,000 square kilometers reconnaissance study was performed for groundwater study and for each a separate report was printed.

(ii) *Programme of Semi-detailed Study of Alluvium Plain*

Under this programme the duration of study of each region with an area of 1,000 square kilometers is from 18 months to 3 years. It includes the following:—

(1)   Investigation and study of groundwater quantity and quality characteristics.

(2)   Estimation of hydrological parameters of aquifer.

(3)   Study of method of developing the groundwater resources.

Based on the programmes until 1982 a total of 89 alluvial plains with an area of 280,000 square kilometers were studied.

(iii) *Programme of Study and Continuous Control of Groundwater*

In this programme the activities of drilling, and control of the routine data collection of water level by the help of piezometric wells network, particularly the production from groundwater and groundwater balance, are reviewed. This is particularly important since from the year 1978 there has been a great tendency for increase of production from non-permitted wells drilled in many parts of the country. Therefore, the compilation of data and its review was of great importance for the Bureau of Water Resources. Our recent studies show a great withdrawal from alluvial plains. The number of our water point resources have been increased from 85,635 to 138,771 and the amount of discharges from the groundwater resources have been increased from 23 billion cubic feet in the year 1976 to 37.6 billion cubic feet by now. The Bureau of Water Resources finds it an obligation to keep a continuous study of these water data in order to control the groundwater balance in the country.

(iv) *Programme of Reconnaissance Study of the Karstic Region*

After studying the potentials of groundwater from alluvium plain it became clear that in some of the country's plains expansion and production is not possible. Therefore, the study of Karstic reservoir came to our attention. Considering the geological features of Iran, the following programme of study was planned.

(1)   Study and re-organization of Karstic resources of the country and the method of production for these resources,

(2)   Preparation of water resources data

(3)   Location, study, and distribution of these resources

(4)   Estimation of Karstic resources balance. It must be mentioned that the study and planning of Karstic resources started in 1971 by the Bureau of Water Resources, and also considering the giant exposure of these Karstic reservoirs in the country, we hope to estimate the actual potential reservoirs in the near future. Upto 1982 about 65 per cent of programme of Karstic study have been completed.

2. Surface water management

Iran is divided into six water management areas, based on major: river basins, hydrological and geographical conditions.

These are the Caspian Sea, the Persian Gulf, the Sea of Oman, Rezaieh (Oroomieh), the Central Plateau and the eastern boundry of Hamoon and Kara-kum basins. Figure 39 shows these basins.

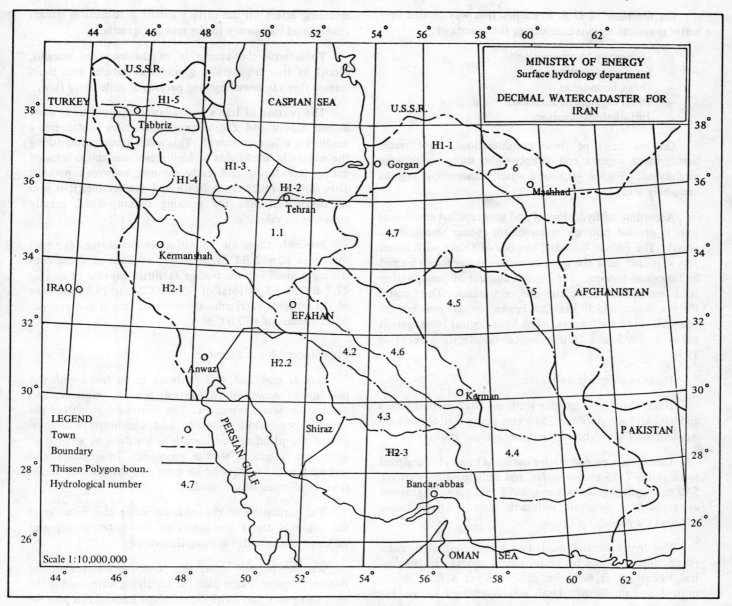

Figure 39.

On the basis of D & R studies Iran was divided into water resources regions considering the criteria of:

— Distinctive hydrologic units
— Economic significance
— Ostan boundaries
— Other regional delineations
— Jurisdictional territory

On the basis of these considerations, eight water management regions and twenty-eight study areas were established. Figure 40 shows water management regions and study areas.

According to hydrological and geographical conditions Iran is divided into six major basins (water management areas). The Persian Gulf and the Sea of Oman with about $136 \times 10^9 \text{m}^3$ have the most important water resources and hydrological regions. The highest amount of precipitation is in the Caspian Sea plains and mountains. The Central Plateau basin which has the largest desert area has inadequate supply of water. The hydrological investigation began in 1945 and meteorological investigation began in 1958.

These two departments have:

1005 water level gauging stations, 1012 evaporimeters and climatology stations, 2549 rain gauge stations and 60 Agroclimatologic, synoptic, and radio sound stations.

There are 4 representative basins in Iran. It is designed to establish 7515 evaporimeter, and climatological stations, 540 new hydrological stations, 8495 rain gage, 320 marine meteorological, synoptic and radio sound stations during the next 20 years.

The hydroclimatological data will be collected, computed, and produced by 15 provincial offices. In the central hydrology section the data will get a final check, printed and published. Until now hydrology section has published 63 year-books of hydrology data. The availability of water in use in Iran is not high. Figure No. 41A and Table No. 74A show the water cycle and water resources available in Iran respectively. Figure 41 shows locations of existing major dams in Iran.

a) *Run Off*

Runoff in Iran drains to 4 principal areas — the Caspian Sea, Lake Rezaieh (Oroomieh), the Persian Gulf, and the Central Plateau. Most of the rivers and streams flow not just into one of the three large bodies of water, but, also into the vast deserts of the interior plateau.

Runoff in Iran is seasonal as is the precipitation. The steep slopes, shallow soil mantle, and relatively sparse vegetative cover in many of the watersheds have little retarding effect on the surface runoff it collects in stream channels on its journey to the seas and deserts.

Thus, with the exception of the snow-fed streams, runoff in Iran is generally sporadic in nature, with short intense flows followed by long periods of little or no flow.

The portion of Iran's precipitation that occurs as snow in the Alborz and Zagros mountain ranges contributes a modifying effect on runoff. This water accumulates during the winter in snowfields at high elevations and is released during late spring and early summer snowmelt periods. This flow is relatively uniform and predictable, it is also sustained well into the growing season, which greatly enhances its value.

Presently there are 15 surface water storage facilities that store 10.682 B.C.M. of water. Planned or under construction are 75 more storage facilities capable of storing 27.7 B.C.M. This total of 38.4 B.C.M. is 29.54 per cent of the nation's total annual combined runoff and groundwater volume of 130 B.C.M.

b) *National Water Planning*

Iran is now and will continue to be faced with the problem of how best to control, protect, conserve, and develop her water resources. The continued growth of the nation's population, industry, and agriculture will compound the planning considerations involved in arriving at acceptable solutions to the problem. Imagination and foresight will be required to meet the diverse and sometimes conflicting future needs.

The formation of the national water plan in national and regional terms has identified the water supply and various requirements for using that supply.

At the present time, the National Water Planning Bureau prepared a new plan for supplying water during the next five years (i.e. 1983-87). On the basis of this plan we must supply 20763 M.C.M. per five years for agriculture, industry, and municipality from surface and groundwater resources (1818 M.C.M. for industry and municipality and 18945 M.C.M. for agriculture). The source of supply for industry and municipality from G.W. and S.W. are 973 M.C.M., 845 M.C.M. respectively, for agricultural use 7745 M.C.M. for improvement, and 11200 M.C.M. for development.

Presently, the National Water Planning Bureau prepared a plan for completion of Iran's national water plan in the next five years (i.e. 1983-1987). The following factors must be studied.

— Defining the existing national water resource policies.

Map No. 2

Figure 40. Water Management and Study Areas of Iran.

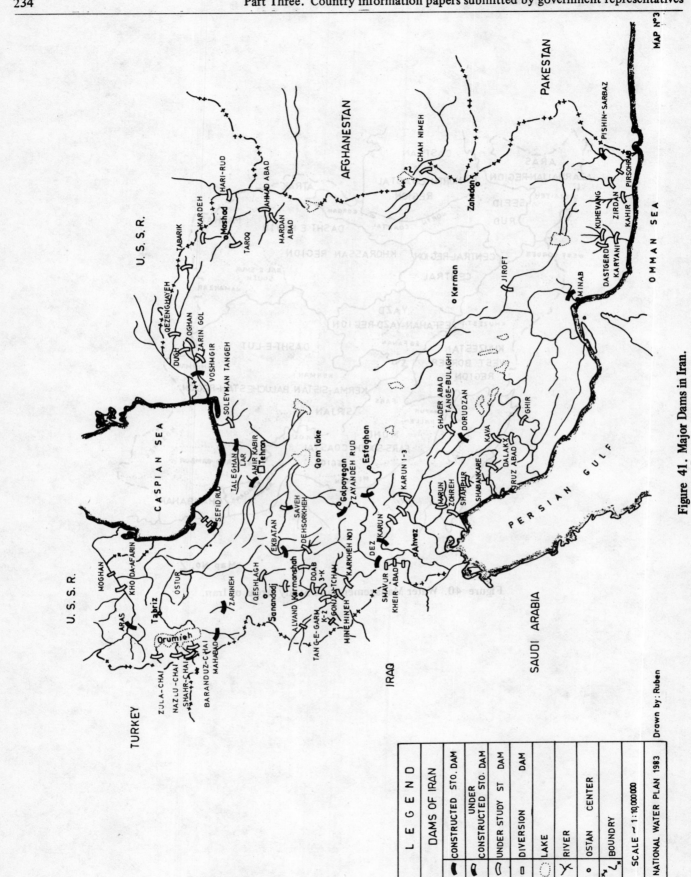

Figure 41. Major Dams in Iran.

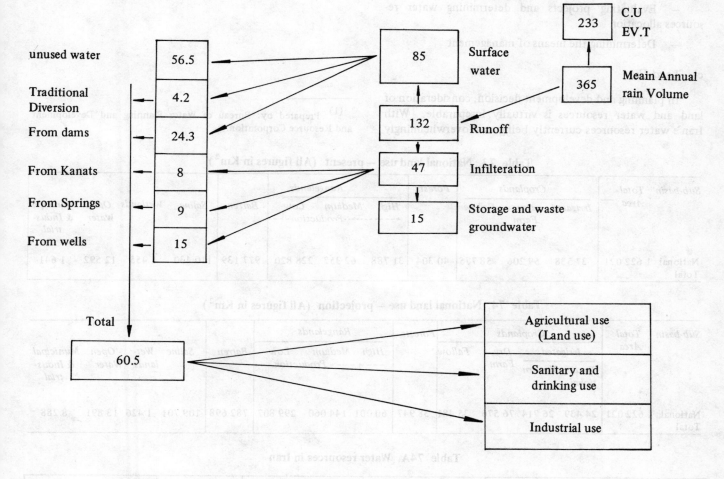

Figure 41 A. Water cycle in Iran

— Defining the plan concept

— Determining the national water plan goals

— Performing socio-economic base studies, make projections

— Determining environmental quality objectives

— Determining objectives by water use categories

— Determining plan formulation procedures

— Defining decision criteria

— Defining alternative projects

— Evaluating projects and determining water resources allocation

— Determining the means of management

c) *Land Use*

In planning and development decision, consideration of land and water resources is virtually inseparable. With Iran's water resources currently being used overwhelmingly for agricultural purposes, and with future agricultural development and use of the water resources expected to be no less than 95 per cent of the total water supply diverted from the nation's water-courses and extracted from groundwater basins, an understanding of existing and planned improvements and development of the land resources is essential. To contribute further to this understanding two summarized statistical tables follow. Table 73 contains data about present uses of the nation's land, and table 74 contains in a comparable format data about projected uses of the nation's land during the years 1984-2005.[1]

---

[1] Prepared by: Bureau of Water Planning and Development and Resource Corporation.

Table 73. National land use — present (All figures in Km²)

Sub-basin	Total Area	Croplands			Forests	Rangelands			Barren	Saline	Wetlands	Open Water	Municipal & Industrial
		Irrigated	Dry Farm	Fallow		High	Medium Low ----------Production----						
National Total	1 622 021	37 538	59 206	58 775	40 304	31 788	62 353	228 820	977 139	110 430	1 455	12 592	1 641

Table 74. National land use — projection (All figures in Km²)

Sub-basin	Total Area	Croplands				Forests	Rangelands			Barren	Saline	Wetlands	Open Water	Municipal & Industrial
		Irrigated		Dry Farm	Fallow		High	Medium Low -------- Production --						
		Traditional	Modern											
National Total	1 622 021	24 439	26 714	76 576	35 481	38 947	60 001	144 060	299 807	782 698	109 701	1 426	13 891	8 288

Table 74A. Water resources in Iran

| Available water | | Volume of precipitation 10⁹ m/year | Aver. annual Precipitation (mm) | Area (Km²) | Basin |
Groundwater	Surfacewater				
2.5	21.	77.4	437	177 000	Caspian Sea
5.6	43.6	136.1	314	433 000	Persian Gulf & Sea of Oman
3.3	7.7	20.6	306	52 000	Rezaieh
20.4	12.6	130.8	135.8	963 000	Central Plateau Karakum & Hamun
31.8	84.4	364.9	224.5	1 625 000	Total

References

1. Draft Final Report Prepared by Bureau of Water Planning and Development and Resources Corporation, Volume X Mehr 1957.

2. Country Report Prepared by Dr. H. Arfa for submission to the IHP Paris UNESCO August 28-29, 1981.

3. Report on Water Resources Study in Iran by Dr. Afrasiabian.

4. Planning for Water Supply in Iran in the next 5 years (1962-1966), prepared by the Bureau of Water Planning — Azar 1961.

5. Report on Hydrology in Iran by Eng. Ghotbi — 1982.

V. JAPAN

HYDRO RESOURCES IN JAPAN

A. GENERAL DESCRIPTION

1. Hydro Resources in Japan

Japan has its total population of some 115 million (1978) with a gross national land of about 378 thousand km.[2] Annual precipitation from rainfall throughout the country is averaged at 1,788 mm and reaches 674.9 billion cubic m in total volume.

Such precipitation tends to vary seasonally. It is concentrated in the rainy season of early summer (June — July) and also in the typhoon season during the summer — autumn period (August — October), while in the northern and central regions on the Japan Sea side it mostly comes from snowfall during the winter season. In addition to such seasonal characteristics of the precipitation, Japan is extremely handicapped in utilizing the river water by rapid outflow of rainfall or snowfall precipitation into the sea because of its terrain feature with short length and steep grades of rivers.

The maximum available water resources is the balance after deducting the evapo-transpiration from the total precipitation, that is to say, the potential net reserve of available resources. In Japan, it amounts to some 450 billion cubic m in a normal year and some 330 billion cubic m in a dry year (Table 75).

When distributed by regions, the available water resources is varied largely by regions because of climatic difference, particularly large in winter, between the Japan Sea side and the Ocean side, being divided by the mountain ranges through the islands of Japan stretching long from North to South. When compared by indexes on a per-capita basis, the indexed figures in the Tokyo-centered Kanto provinces and in the Osaka-centered Kinki provinces appear to be extremely small, less than half of the nation-wide average index. Excessive concentration of population and industrial facilities into such provincial areas presents a problem of hydro resources with which Japan is confronted now.

2. Administrative Organizations Involved in Water Resources

The administrative organizations of the Japanese Government are diversified into various ministries and agencies.

Table 75. Precipitation and Available Water Resources in Japan

	Annual rainfall height	Annual precipitation	Net available resources (After deducting evapo-transpiration from annual precipitation)
	mm/year	100 million m³/year	100 million m³/year
Dry year	1 480	5 587	3 338
Normal year	1 788	6 749	4 494
Wet year	2 131	8 044	5 791

Note: The normal year is set at an average of annual precipitation recorded in the past 18 years, the dry year is set at the second least precipitation and the wet year is set at the second largest precipitation.

Among them the ministries and agencies involved directly in the water resources development are the National Land Agency (planning and co-ordination), the Ministry of Construction (river control and multi-purpose dam), the Ministry of Health and Welfare (public water service), the Ministry of International Trade and Industry (industrial water supply and power generation) and the Ministry of Agriculture, Forestry and Fishery (irrigation, drainage and forestry maintenance). Under the joint supervision of those four (4) ministries and one (1) agency, the government-financed Water Resources Development Corporation is established.

The following are the executing organizations for the projects on water resources development and water utilization by purposes.

a. *Water resources development project*

Construction and maintenance of water resources development facilities, such as dams, headwater channels and estuary weirs, are under the jurisdiction of different organizations depending upon the purpose of each project. For instance, the flood control and its related multi-purpose development projects are undertaken by the Ministry of Construction, the irrigation projects are by the Ministry of Agriculture, Forestry and Fishery and the power development projects are by electric power companies or the Electric Power Development Company. All development projects in those river systems designated specifically under the Water Resources Development Promotion Act are mainly executed by the Water Resources Development Corporation. The direct governmental involvement is limited to those projects planned on a relatively large scale. All other projects on a medium or small scale are assigned to each prefectural government or public body concerned with water utilization.

b. *Waterworks*

As a rule, the waterwork is operated by each local municipality and its authorized co-operative under the authorization of the Ministry of Health and Welfare. In many instances, those municipal enterprisers depend on the available water sources from the multipurpose dams constructed and operated by the Water Resources Development Corporation, the Ministry of Construction and the Prefectural Government involved, except some special cases where the waterwork enterpriser provides construction of the dam to be exclusively used for his own water supply.

c. *Industrial water supply projects*

Each prefectural government operates industrial water supply nearly in all instances by permission of (or by application to) the Ministry of International Trade and Industry.

The source of water supply is made available in the same way as mentioned in the preceding case of municipal water supply.

d. *Irrigation and drainage projects*

The projects are normally undertaken by the regional office for land improvement, except that the project on a large scale is carried out by either the Ministry of Agriculture, Forestry and Fishery or each prefectural government concerned after receipt of application from the regional office for land improvement. Although the available source of water is very often exploited by the enterpriser himself, he sometimes depends upon the multipurpose dam built by the Ministry of Construction or the Water Resources Development Corporation.

e. *Hydro power generation projects*

The projects are generally undertaken by nine (9) electric power companies, each serving one of nine (9) divided block of this country and the Electric Power Development Company as the nationwide electric wholesaler and, in some instances, by prefectural governments or local municipalities. In case of power generation from the facility of large dam reservoir the enterpriser provides construction of the dam solely for this purpose by himself or often depends upon the multi-purpose dam constructed by others. River control in this connection is under the jurisdiction of the Ministry of Construction or each prefectural government concerned. Especially, control relevant to preservation of water quality and overall co-ordination with other ministries and agencies are assigned to the Environmental Agency.

Surveillance and monitoring for water quality preservation are carried out mainly by prefectural governments. However, such monitoring service is also performed by the river administration authorities and by the river water users.

Besides these projects, there are forestry improvement projects intended for enhancement of the multiple function potentially possessed by the forestry, such as recharging of water resources. Such improvement projects are carried out by the Ministry of Agriculture, Forestry and Fishery (the Forestry Agency), the Forestry Development Corporation and the forestry owners.

3. Present Status of Water Utilization

Trend of water demand in Japan is as shown in Table 76, accounting for about 26 per cent of the maximum available water resources in a dry year.

According to the 10-year trend of demand for the 1965-1975 period, it is noted that domestic water demand reaches about two folds and industrial water demand increases up to about 1.4 times. After 1975 domestic water demand has continued its further increase while industrial water demand (fresh water supply basis) has decreased in some degree, reflecting slowdown of production activities and rationalization of water use after the shock from oil crisis in 1973.

Table 76. Trend on Water Demand

Unit: 100 million m³/year

Purpose		1965	1970	1975	1980
Municipal use	Domestic use	63	94	123	137
	Industrial use	126	180	183	165
Agricultural use		–	–	570	580
Total		–	–	876	882

Source: 'Water Resources of Japan in August 1983' by the National Land Agency.

Note 1: Each figure is totalized on an intake withdrawal basis. Industrial water is based upon fresh water make-up supplies.

2: Agricultural water is calculated from general observation of farm land preparation and cropping status.

3: Domestic water excludes consumption for industrial plant use in total supply available from the city water supply system.

In the analysis of water utilization by water sources available, the river water ranks the top overwhelmingly with consumption to the volume of 64.9 billion cubic m, or 74 per cent of 87.6 billion cubic m annual total supplies, followed by the ground water being utilized to 13.8 billion cubic m, or 16 per cent of the annual total, and then by the spring water or the pond storage being used to 10 per cent. In particular, as far as the municipal water (general term combining both domestic and industrial water) is concerned, it is showing greater dependence upon the river water and the dam reservoir.

4. Development of Water Resources

In Japan, traditionally there have been lots of reservoir ponds developed for agricultural use, which now totals about 180,000 ponds. Development of water resources by dam construction, as is seen today, can be traced back to 1930s. Specially, in the post-war period, the multi-purpose dam has been taken as the main object for development. As of 1980, the total number of dams in excess of 15 m height with reservoir capacity for water utilization (not including reservoir for power generation) reaches about 1,800 across the country.

Besides dam construction, some other construction projects have been under way for development of estuary weirs, lakes and ponds and also for establishment of the flow regime adjusting river course by interconnection of rivers. In utilizing the river water the water utilization plan is formulated generally on the basis of the flow discharge estimated for the dry year ranking the top place during the 10-year period.

With start in 1960s toward high economic growth and urban concentration of population, the 'The Water Resources Development Promotion Act' was enforced in 1961 thereby to meet the need to establish the ways and means for water utilization especially in large city areas. Since that time, in an effort to cope with water demand increase in the area where such emergency measures should be taken for utilization on a wide-co-ordinated basis, various development projects of water resources have been in progress for some specific river systems designated under the Act.

To this date, six (6) large river systems including Tonegawa and Arakawa running through the Tokyo Metropolitan Area have been designated for development.

Established is the 'Basic Plan for Water Resources Development' envisaging future water demand, target supply and construction of required facilities. Pursuant to this Plan, the development projects are carried out mainly by the Water Resources Development Public Corporation under the governmental supervision and guidance.

As of this date, dams, weirs and channels at 28 sites have been completed with development of additional water resources for 5 billion cubic m in municipal water and 1.3 billion cubic m in agricultural water respectively each year.

In addition to the cost problem, there is another difficulty involved in obtaining full consent from the local community people concerned prior to start of the dam construction project, because they are forced to transfer from their own land proposed for submergence by dam construction to the new but strange land where they have to enter into different life style. To help resolve this new problem, in addition to the compensation for land submergence to each owner, the Act on Special Measures for the Reservoir Area Development was put into enforcement in 1973 with a view to executing implementation of various necessary measures for economic promotion of the reservoir area and for re-settlement of the inhabitants in the area.

Groundwater has been of wide use for various purposes because of its good quality and cheap price. Because of this, the problem of ground sinkage is still provoked, though at a slow pace recently, in connection with ground water utilization in every part of this country. To cope with this situation, study is now being made for legislation relevant to proper utilization of the ground water including its conversion into the river water. The total ground water consumption in 1975 reached 13.8 billion cubic m across the country, which is broken down into 52 per cent for industrial use, 27 per cent for agricultural use and 21 per cent for domestic use.

As one of new approaches to the water resources exploitation, the desalination project of sea water is under way with 60 unit plants installed in 1982, whose total production capacity is planned for 83,529 cubic m per day. Among them, 24 units are being operated for domestic use on some isolated islands to serve water supply of 9,276 cubic m per day. The desalination method is conventionally divided into two different processes: the main one is the evaporation process as applicable to the sea water and the other is the electrolysis or reverse osmosis process as applicable to the brine water. Although the production cost may be variable depending upon raw water quality, productive scale, availability factor and desalination method, it is within the range of 200 to 1,000 yens per cubic m with raw water from the sea and 60 to 860 yens per cubic m from the brine water. But recently in view of the energy-saving, the reverse osmosis process has come to be adopted more for the desalination of sea water.

5. Long-term Projection on Water Demand

In August 1978 the National Land Agency formulated and published its Long-range Water Demand & Supply Plan with the aim to promote effective and efficient development and utilization of the potential water resources on the assumption that the resources would be of finite nature.

This Plan covers the long range projection on future water demand and supply by 1985 and 1990 with the perspective view up to the year 2000, on the basis of integrated residence policy under the 3rd Comprehensive National Development Plan, and includes the matters basically essential to development, preservation and utilization of the water resources over the long term projection. The Plan is therefore expected to take the role as a guideline for promotion of the governmental measures to be taken toward stabilization of the future demand and supply balance. It is further expected that any future projects related to development of water resources by dam construction and expansion of various water supply facilities will be pushed forward along the basic line of this Plan. In this Plan the 1990 forecast on water demand and supply by regions on a nationwide scale is as shown in Table 77. It is estimated that some of the unstabilized condition would still continue in the Tokyo coastal zone and some

others, even with the smooth lauching of the development project of water resources, like dam constructions and others, to meet the future increase in water demand. As stated previously, the water demand since 1975 has been increasing at more gradual pace than initially predicted in this plan.

On the other hand, it is also predictable that the utilization factor of water resources would reach its considerably high level, when projected on the super-long term perspective, with continuing demand increase in Kanto (Tokyo), North Kyushu, Kinki (Osaka) and Okinawa. Since there is increasing difficulty to be anticipated in regard to the development of water resources by dam construction in those industrialized regions every possible effort must be made for (i) rationalization of water utilization, (ii) reduction in water consumption, and (iii) full recognition of the finite nature of water resources, so that the balance of demand and supply can be stabilized on a firm basis.

6. Major Problems in Water Resources Development and Water Utilization

In order to meet future increased water demand as predictable from improvement in the people's living standard and the socio-economic growth, it is necessary that comprehensive, well-planned measures should be pushed forward not to mention of the need to promote development of water resources by every possible effort to reduce and rationalize water consumption and to co-ordinate fully with all the related fields for balancing demand and supply of water. To comply with this need, the National Land Agency prepared its 'Long-term Plan for Water Demand and Supply in August 1978 in co-operation with other ministries and agencies concerned, thereby indicating publicly the basic line toward future stabilization of demand and supply. The overall system chart of stabilization as proposed in the said Plan is shown in Table 78. All those problems noted in the Plan should naturally require joint efforts for solution by the national government, prefectural authorities, local municipalities, water users and the general public. Among them, the problems of particular importance are as follows.

a. *Promotion of water resources development*

In order to meet further increase in water demand and to stabilize water supply, new projects for development of water resources must be executed. To achieve this task further effort must be exerted to promote development of water resources with due consideration to the tapering number of optimum sites for construction projects, the compensation for loss or damage, the incentive measures for reservoir area development and the harmony with environmental preservation.

Table 77. Estimated Water Balance Between Supply and Demand in 1990

Unit: 100 million m³/year

Area		Increase of municipal water demand				Increase of agricultural water demand (1976-1990)	Total	Increase of water developed (1976-1990)	Deficiency in 1990
		Increase 1976-1990	Planned reduction of groundwater	Unstable intake of river water	Sum				
Hokkaido		14.7	0.3	0.1	15.1	6.8	21.9	25.5	–
Tohoku		27.3	1.3	0.5	29.1	17.3	46.4	49.6	–
Kanto	Inland	20.7	1.9	2.8	25.4	12.7	38.1	40.4	–
	Littoral	27.7	6.4	16.3	50.4	2.2	52.6	45.7	6.9
	Total	48.4	8.3	19.1	75.8	14.9	90.7	86.1	
Tokai		32.6	7.5	2.8	42.9	6.5	49.4	52.1	–
Hokuriku		6.6	2.1	0.9	9.6	2.1	11.7	13.4	–
Kinki	Inland	9.6	0.3	0.5	10.4	4.0	14.4	17.3	–
	Littoral	12.8	1.8	7.3	21.9	1.9	23.8	22.7	1.1
	Total	22.4	2.1	7.8	32.3	5.9	38.2	40.0	
Chugoku	San'in	3.2	0.1	0.0	3.3	0.8	4.1	4.6	–
	Sanyo	14.3	0.4	1.2	15.9	0.6	16.5	18.8	–
	Total	17.5	0.5	1.2	19.2	1.4	20.6	23.4	
Shikoku		7.5	0.9	0.0	8.4	3.3	11.7	13.6	–
Kyushu	North	14.0	0.8	0.4	15.2	5.1	20.3	19.3	1.0
	South	9.1	0.2	0.0	9.3	3.9	13.2	14.4	–
	Total	23.1	1.0	0.4	24.5	9.0	33.5	33.7	
Okinawa		1.1	0.0	0.4	1.5	0.6	2.1	2.2	–
Nationwide total		201.2	24.0	33.2	258.4	67.8	326.2	339.6	9.0

Note 1: Figures are on the intake base.

2: Planned reduction of groundwater is the amount for which diversion of source to river water is planned between 1975 and 1990 in such areas as subsidence occurred.

3: Unstable intake of river water is the amount of river water intake such as temporary intake which is likely to be difficult during drought season.

4: Increase in agricultural water demand is the amount which will increase resulting from land improvement works expected to be completed by 1990. This includes the increase in demand due to diversion of ground source or the increase due to stabilization of unstable intake of water resulting from land improvement works.

5: Increase in water developed includes the unused water which had been developed by 1975.

Table 78. Comprehensive Measures Regarding Water Supply and Demand

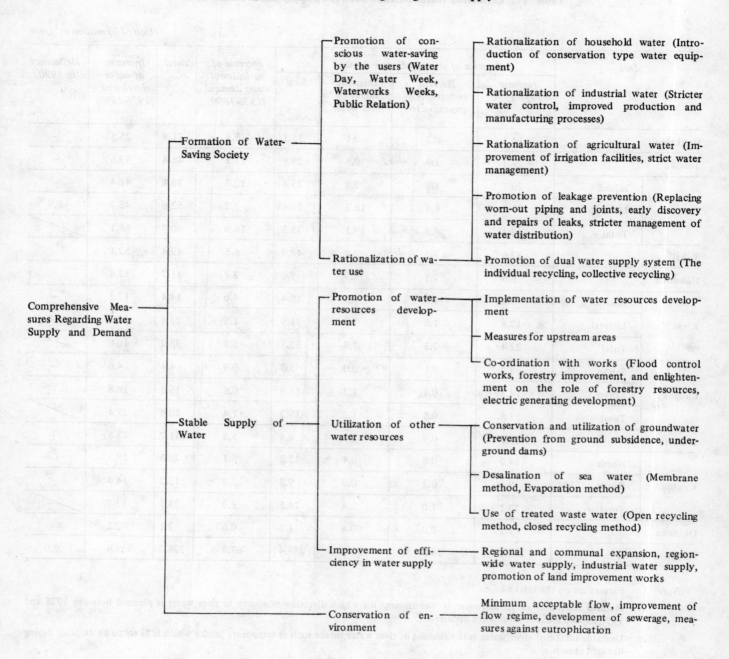

b. *Strengthening of incentive measures for reservoir area development*

To promote development of water resources, it is necessary to expedite construction of the dam and other reservoir structures which may be in many instances confronted with reluctancy or rejection by the local community people concerned. For this reason it becomes necessary that the living environment and the industrial foundation in the reservoir area should be improved for stabilization of the community people's livelihood and improvement of public welfare. To comply with this necessity, consideration must be given to strengthen and expand the scope of application of incentives under the Special Measures for the Reservoir Area Development and the Fund for the Reservoir Area Development. In parallel with those administrative measures, it is also important that the well-planned measures should be taken for improvement of forestry resources near the reservoir area, because of its significance in recharging of water resources into the forestry.

c. Formation of water-saving type society

With deepened recognition that water is a limited resource of high value, by full awareness of difficulty in the water resources development, effort must be exerted to form a community of water saving type for orientation and implementation of the water saving policy. This requires special effort for rationalization of domestic, industrial and agricultural water consumption through propagation of rationalized equipment for water saving and promotion toward recycled use of waste water and also for consolidation of water leak preventive measures to mitigate possible loss in the water supply network system.

B. PRESENT STATUS BY PROJECT SECTORS AND FUTURE PROSPECT

1. Integrated River Development by Construction of Multi-Purpose Dam or Others

a. General outline of river development project

The purpose of the integrated river development project is to construct a dam at the upstream site of the river, thereby to control flood by storing excess flow in the reservoir and releasing stored reservoir water during dry period and supplement high demand for water in the dry season.

With expansion of the project scale, it is now being diversified into construction of flood control dams, development of lakes and ponds and adjustment of river flow regime, and advanced water utilization project in addition to construction of multi-purpose dams. As far as existing dams are concerned, they endeavour to strengthen the operational system by adopting the integrated operational system and to improve the dam environment as well as to promote anti-sedimentation measures or hydraulic power generation. Also, they carry out enlargement or renovation of existing dams as a result of change of purpose.

Those projects under the jurisdiction of the Ministry of Construction may be summarized as stated hereunder.

(i) Multi-purpose dam construction

(1) Specified multi-purpose dam

Notwithstanding the fact that the discharge in the main river in Japan should reach the immense volume of flow because of the nation's climatic and topographic features, the river is affected by large fluctuation of discharge between wet and dry seasons. Such being the circumstances, dams are constructed under the comprehensive develop-

ment plan throughout the whole river system. According to the Specified Multipurpose Dams Act (enforced in 1957), it is provided that planning, construction and maintenance of such dams should be reverted solely to the responsibility of the Minister of Construction.

On the other hand, the right in the terms of 'Right of Dam Use' is created legally for those enterprisers for domestic water supply, industrial water and power generation who share the construction cost. Property right invested to each of them corresponding to their share of cost.

(2) Dam construction by Water Resources Development Corporation

In order to cope with the ever-increasing water demand in Japan's main 6 river systems the Japanese Government draws up the basic plan for water resources development under the provisions of the Water Resources Development Promotion Act and assigns construction of dams and other facilities to the Water Resources Development Corporation pursuant to the basic plan. The Corporation then takes charge of construction and maintenance of dams and water channels in line with principles and basic rules on project work execution and management of facilities as instructed by the governmental authorities concerned.

(3) Dam construction by governmental subsidies

Under the provisions of the River Act (enforced in 1964) the Minister of Construction is authorized legally as the River Administrator and thereby assigns part of his authorization to the Governor of each Prefecture. The Governor then undertakes, as authorized to do so by the Minister, construction of multi-purpose dams or flood control dams by grant of the governmental subsidies.

(ii) Flood control dam construction

The dam exclusively for flood control is constructed so as to maintain the regular function of the river discharge and used solely for this purpose by preclusion of any other specific joint users.

(iii) Development of lakes and ponds

The purpose of this development project is to develop new potential water resources available by enlarging the fluctuation between high and low levels of water in lakes and ponds. To meet the fluctuation on an increased scale, it becomes necessary that the embankment should be raised to a higher elevation and any other structural facilities existing over the water surface, such as the platform of landing from boats and the fishery facilities, should be remodeled.

(iv) *Channel for adjustment of different river flow regime*

The purpose of this project is to construct a water channel to interconnect more than one river, each of different flow regime and thereby to develop new potential water resources available by adjusting a different phase of such flow regime between the rivers.

Total number of dams completed and the outline of dams under construction as of 1983 and the economic effect from those completed dams are shown respectively in Tables 79, 80 and 81.

(v) *Advanced water utilization project*

Coupled with river improvement project like dam construction or others, this project aims at maintaining normal function of the river flow by returning highly processed sewage into the river, thus making it possible to develop new municipal water resources in certain areas where the demand and supply is not balanced.

(vi) *Enlargement and renovation of existing dam*

The purpose of this project is to develop the flood control capacity and water supply function of existing dams by enlarging the dams and renovating the intake and outlet facilities.

Table 79. List of Dams
(Ministerial jurisdictional and subsidized)

Classification	Dam sites completed by 1982		Project sites in 1983					
	No. of projects	No. of dams	Construction work		Feasibility study		Total	
			No. of projects	No. of dams	No. of projects	No. of dams	No. of projects	No. of dams
Dam in jurisdiction	54	59	49	51	23	23	72	74
Dam constructed by Corporation	13	13	14	14	4	4	18	18
Dam subsidized	171	171	122	127	81	84	203	211
Multi-purpose	132	132	86	87	56	59	142	146
Flood control	39	39	36	40	25	25	61	65
Total	238	243	185	192	108	111	293	303

Note: No. of dams include estuary weir, lake, retarding basin, flow adjusting river and higher water utilization work.

Table 80. List of Dams under Construction in 1983

Classification	Purpose	No. of projects	Effective storage (1,000 m³)	Project cost (million yen)		Project cost in 1983 (Joint share)
				Joint share	Public spending	
Ministerial jurisdiction	Specified multi-purpose	72	3 701 056	3 948 700	1 931 444	207 200
Water Resources Corporation		18	3 476 630	1 572 700	578 683	76 870
Government subsidized	Multi-purpose	142	1 976 890	1 456 578	1 100 511	115 262
	Flood control	61	246 371	475 580	475 580	27 544
	Total	203	2 223 261	1 932 158	1 576 091	142 806
Grand total		293	9 400 947	7 453 558	4 086 218	426 896

Note: Neither public spending for dams under ministerial jurisdiction nor joint share for government subsidized dams include feasibility study expenses.

Table 81. List of Economic Benefits from Completed Dams (by 1982)

Classification			Ministerial jurisdiction	Public Corporation	Government–subsidized	Total
No. of dams			59	13	171	245
Project cost (million yen)			(302 723) 466 989	(114 442) 240 621	(335 698) 486 752	(752 863) 1 194 362
Economic effect	Flood control	Flood inflow (1,000 m³/S)	94.6	33.2	120.1	247.9
		Controlled discharge (1,000 m³/S)	45.3	13.4	57.1	115.8
	Power generation	Annual energy production (MWH)	(8 661 193)	1 513 913	4 600 830	14 775 936
	Domestic water	Supply (100 million m³/Y)	9.7	19.8	18.3	47.9
	Industrial water	Supply (100 million m³/Y)	6.7	12.9	14.3	33.9

Note: Figures in (   ) show public spending by Ministry of Construction.

Table 82. Project Work Items under Reservoir Area Development Scheme in Connection with Designated Dam Construction

① Land improvement
② Land slide protection
③ Flood control
④ Road
⑤ Public water supply
⑥ Sewerage system
⑦ Elementary educational facilities
⑧ Clinic
⑨ Housing lot development
⑩ Public housing construction
⑪ Forest walkway improvement
⑫ Silvaculture
⑬ Joint facilities for modernization of agricultural, forestry and fishery managements
⑭ Protection facilities for natural park and utilization
⑮ Public and other social assembly halls or facilities for conservation and utilization of folk art and cultural properties
⑯ Sports or recreational facilities
⑰ Nursery school, child institute and child playground
⑱ Welfare Centre for the Aged
⑲ Wired/wireless radio
⑳ Fire fighting facilities
㉑ Human waste treatment facilities
㉒ Refuse & garbage disposal facilities

b. *Measure for the reservoir area development*

Unlike any other public works of ordinary pattern, the dam construction project exerts, by its nature, grave influence upon the inhabitants in and around the reservoir area and its environs. Therefore, in order to promote execution of the dam construction project, it is essential that in parallel with the construction project any effective measures for easement of the impact from dam construction (called generally 'Measures for Reservoir Area') should be taken in all instances.

Because of this, the enterpriser of the project is required to promote improvements of the living environment and the productive foundation for the inhabitants in the reservoir area, in addition to his obligation to fulfil with regard to compensation to cover loss or damage, under the Act on Special Measures for the Reservoir Area Development (enforced in 1973) in the event that construction of the dam requires a large scope of submergence in the reservoir area. The area development project actually contains 22 items (Table 82). Dams designated under this Act total to 53 now under construction. The plan for reservoir area development with regard to those designated dams is prepared by the National Land Agency in coordination with other ministries and agencies concerned. Those specific projects included in that plan are entitled to governmental subsidies at preferential priorities or subsidies at an increased rate of grants-in-aid, if the dam construction project requires an extraordinarily large scale reservoir. The same can also apply to the development project of lake or pond on a large scale. At present, one (1) lake development project is included in the scope of application under the Act.

To further complement the compensation or the special measures for the area development as aforestated, the Fund for Reservoir Area Development is set up in some areas by joint investment of national government, prefectural authorities concerned and local municipalities and is being utilized for re-settlement of the inhabitants in the reservoir area.

c. *Recent trend of activities*

(i) *Dam as countermeasures for extraordinary drought*

The purpose of this project is to store water to supply minimum necessary water for domestic and industrial functions during extraordinary drought in the area where the tight balance of demand and supply is experienced. A survey for execution of the project started in 1983.

(ii) *Dam for local flood control and water supply*

The purpose of this project is to construct a mini dam in the upstream of existing dam for local flood control and water supply.

(iii) *Water quality conservation Project*

The purpose of this project is to install aeration apparatus or artificial convection system to cope with the deterioration of water quality, resulted from the eutrophication of reservoirs of existing dams. A pilot project started in 1982.

(iv) *Japan Dam Engineering Centre*

This centre was established to excute the subsidized dam project. The centre pools the specialists and technical information on dam in order to serve local government and to carry out investigation on dam.

2. Agricultural Water Resources

a. *Introduction to land improvement and its present status in Japan*

(i) *Purpose of land improvement project*

The land improvement project is executed in accordance with the provisions under the Land Improvement Act for improvement, development, preservation and collective control of farm land aiming at improvement of water and land conditions to be better suited for agricultural production.

(ii) *Content of land improvement project*

The content of the project includes irrigation, drainage, farm land improvement, land disaster prevention, road expansion, arable site formation and reclamation by drainage. The project has been in progress under the Land Improvement Long-term Plan updated every 10 years. The total budgetary fund of 32.8 trillion yens will be invested for execution of this project under the long-term plan of 1983 to 1992.

(iii) *Mechanism of land improvement project*

The project is undertaken by national government, prefectural authorities or local municipalities according to the scale of the project. It is executed with due reference to the application submitted to either the governmental or prefectural authority concerned jointly by more than 15 persons who are actually engaged in farming of the land. The total project cost is principally borne by either national government as prefectural authority but partially shared by those applicants as beneficiaries. In any event, the rate of grant-in-aid is stipulated legally according to the scale of the project. Financing for the beneficiaries' share of the total expenses is arranged by the government. With regard to the share of responsibility for maintenance of the facilities after completion of the project, either the national government or the prefectural authority assumes responsibility for the facilities of high public interest and the private beneficiaries take charge of others.

(iv) *Present status of land improvement*

As of 1982, the land improvement project is being executed in 358 areas under governmental management, 7,729 areas under prefectural management and 9,310 areas under municipal management. Total annual spending for execution of the project reaches 1,300 billion yens, ranking the second highest to the road improvement project in its share of the nation's total expenditure for the public work.

In the meantime, the main object of this undertaking has been shifted from increased production of foods to improved productivity of agriculture, as emphasis is being placed upon the farm rather than the paddy field. In particular, the improvement of living environment in rural areas is taken up as a part of the land improvement project in recent years.

b. *Present status and future prospect of agricultural water utilization in Japan*

As of 1982, the nationwide total area of farm land accounts for about 15 per cent, or 5,430,000 ha, of the total national land. The irrigation area covers about 55 per cent of the total arable land, or 3,010,000 ha in paddy field and 250,000 ha in farm (Table 83).

As noted from the Table, irrigation covers the whole area of 3,010,000 ha paddy field while it covers a very minor portion, or only 10 per cent, of the total 2,420,000 ha farm land. This is evidently because the greater majority of agriculture depends upon the paddy field, which has conventionally been the main object of the agricultural water utilization project, and also because the introduction of the full-scale irrigation system into the dry farm land has been far behind until the recent years.

Table 83. Projected Arable Area Versus Irrigable Area

Unit: 10,000 ha

		1982	1992
(1)	Arable area	543	550
	Paddy field	301	281
	Dry field	242	269
(2)	Irrigable area	326	347
	Paddy field	301	281
	Dry field	25	66

Note: Estimate by Ministry of Agriculture, Forestry and Fishery

To secure stabilized and efficient supply of farm crops in response to escalating demand, there still remain much to be done to help further expansion of the irrigation system over the farm land.

Meanwhile, turning eyes to the recent trend of water utilization in paddy fields it comes to notice that as a general tendency, changes are being made to the period, timing and quantity of irrigation to paddy fields as a result of change in the cultivating pattern of paddy by mechanization and progress in the farm land improvement.

In 1982, the mechanized harvesting area has reached 97 per cent of the total harvesting area. The transplanting area by machine use accounts for 94 per cent of the total rice cropping area. For transplantation by machine, earlier or medium rice sprouts are used instead of late sprouts as used conventionally before mechanization. As a result, the retention period of rice plantation in the field is prolonged and the time allowance as timing for transplantation from nursery to field is narrowed within the very limited period, which requires large quantity of irrigable water all at a time with resultant shortage of water supply beyond normal capacity in some areas.

In the event that the drainage condition will be improved under the sophisticated irrigation control system as the improvement project will progress further on the farm land to such an extent that the field soil foundation can be strengthened for operation by machine, rotation of farm crops to rice crop and introduction of second crop, it is observed that future water consumption in rice fields will be increased by 20 per cent or so at average.

Although it may be difficult to measure future demand for irrigation water indiscriminately on a nationwide basis, since the irrigation pattern is varied by regions because of difference in both natural condition and agricultural management pattern, future demand may be estimated as shown in Table 84 by trial calculation on the following basis:

Table 84. Water Demand for Agricultural Use

Unit: 100 million m³/year

Purpose	1975	1980	1990
Irrigation for paddy fields	560	565	
Irrigation for dry fields	7	11	
Stock-farming water	3	4	
Total	570	580	638*

Note: Figures indicated above are results of calculations by due reference of farm land preparation and cropping condition.

* Figures as to 1990 denote estimated water demand resulting from the land improvement projects which have already started, are planned and under survey with target completion by 1990. (Refer to Table 77)

i) With regard to paddy field irrigation demand, calculation is made by analysis of the negative factor reflecting the possible decrease of demand due to the tapering trend of paddy field area to result from continuing urbanization and the positive factor reflecting the possible demand increase as the result of farm land improvement.

ii) Large increase is allowed for irrigation to the farm land in line with future expansion of the irrigation system to the dry farm land.

iii) Incremental demand is estimated for livestock use.

3. Municipal Water Supply

a. *Present status and future prospect of waterworks*

The water supply system in Japan has been spreading at a rapid tempo since 1955. As a result, the total population served as of March 1982 has reached 108,000,000 with a high rate of 91.9 per cent of the nation's total population. The total water supply has reached 14.1 billion cubic m per annum. In anticipation of the continuing increase in both population served and annual water supply, it is estimated that by 1990 the total population served will amount to 118,000,000 with the rate of 96 per cent and the annual water supply will increase to 18.1 billion cubic m. At present, the daily water requirement on a per-capita basis remains at 366 liters in 1981.

It is estimated, however, that such per-capita demand will stretch to 426 liters per day in 1990, mainly because of demand increase for domestic use to result from higher living standard and further spread of water-related home appliances and also increase for commercial and industrial uses keeping paces with brisk economic activities.

As of March 1982, the total number of water supply systems serving the population over and including 101 persons, the lowest limit of application by the Water Works Law, amounts to 18,086 across the country, which may be broken down into 1,097 public water supply systems with a population served over and including 5,001 persons, 11,936 public water supply systems on a reduced scale to serve a population up to and including 5,000 persons, 83 bulk water supply system supplying purified water to the public supply system and 4,160 private supply systems to their own dormitories, residences and sanatoriums.

In spite of the ever-increasing water demand, as stated earlier, the whole country was troubled by scanty rainfall in 1978. Especially, in the western part of this country about 11 million people were forced to hard time during suspension or restriction of water supply for a long period.

To avoid re-occurrence of such distress, it is necessary that the balance between demand and supply of water should be improved on the comprehensive basis by effective measures for saving of water consumption as well as by promotion of dam construction for development of water resources.

b. *Available water sources for public supply*

Available supply sources in 1981 may be broken down into 38.6 per cent from river discharge (run-of-river), 28.7 per cent from reservoir (dam), 1.4 per cent from lake, 6.3 per cent from river-bed water, 21.6 per cent from ground water through both shallow and deep wells and 3.4 per cent from any other sources available. Although ground water may be generally well-fitted for city water supply in its quality, excessive use of ground water would become a cause of ground subsidence. Therefore, the future prospect is that any future increment of demand will have to be covered mainly by surface water available from the large reservoir with the dam.

c. *Waterworks expenditure and water rate*

Total investment on the public water supply system for 1982 fiscal year amounts to 935.8 billion yen, the greater majority of which is financed by municipal bonds (loan financing from government or financing corporations) and by governmental subsidies. In 1982, such financing fund amounts to 709 billion yen by bond issue and 130.7 billion yen by governmental grant-in-aid including 68.5 billion yen granted for development of water sources related to the public water service system.

The water rate is averaged generally at 110 yen per cubic m though varied more or less depending upon the supply system. The average spending for water consumption is 1,977 yen for each household family per month, which corresponds to 0.8 per cent of the monthly total expenses for household.

d. *Region-wide water supply system*

Conventionally in Japan, the water supply network has been spread and improved for each unit of city, town or village independently. At present, however, with further increase of water demand the selected side for the new water supply source tends to be more and more remote from the consuming terminal. Under such situation, a small body of waterwork enterprise, such as local municipalities, finds it difficult to develop a new source at its own financial and technical capability. It is for this reason that each individual unit of water supply system existing today on a limited scale will have to be reorganized and merged into the region-wide integrated supply system with plenty of financial background and technical capacity for promotion of new supply source development projects.

By integration into the wide service network, it is expected that the unbalanced situation of water demand and supply by service areas will be ironed out and the facilities will be utilized more effectively and efficiently.

To promote amalgamation of local supply systems into the region-wide co-ordination system on a well-planned basis, the provisions relevant to the region-wide water supply plan were added in 1977 to the Water Works Law.

Today, this plan is being formulated for implementation at about 35 local areas and the region-wide supply system is expected to spread with increasing number of projects.

e.   *Water saving and leakage prevention*

To cope with rapid increase of water demand, the continuing effort, to try to curb future demand increase of water, has become essential, in increasing recognition that water resources is of finite nature.   The Ministry of Health and Welfare conducts its survey for cost-benefit analysis on leakage prevention and provides administrative guidance to all the nationwide supply systems for strengthening of the preventive measures against possible leakage, setting the target rate of availability at 90 per cent.   It also appeals to the people the necessity of water saving, taking the advantage of the Waterwork Week starting annualy from June 1.

4. Industrial Water

a.   *Present situation of demand and supply*

(i)   *Trend of industrial water demand*

Today, the Japanese industry is making its structural change by switching-over from the heavy chemical industry conventionally as a core to machinery and its associated assembling industry.   In line with such change, the demand structure of industrial water shows a gradual change, as the result of which the increase rate of water demand has been slowed down as compared with that in the high economic period.

As shown in Table 85, the recent trend of industrial water consumption is featured as follows:

①   Industrial water has been consumed increasingly year after year.

②   Since increase of returned water is well matched with increase of industrial water consumption, the additional make-up supplies remain at a nearly same level for recent years.

③   Ground water available from wells is being less consumed with expansion of the industrial water supply network.

(ii)   *Present status of industrial water supply system*

The purpose of the industrial water supply system in Japan is to prevent settlement of ground due to excessive use of ground water and also to help development of basic industrial activities.

At present, there exist nearly 170 water supply systems across the country, the greater majority of which are operated by local municipalities.

As noted from Table 85, supplies through the industrial water supply systems reach as much as 12 million cubic m per day, which is nearly equivalent to one-third of the total daily water supplies to the industrial plants.

As the result of recent system expansion, such ground sinking as observed with grave concern so far on the highly industrialized coastal zone of Tokyo and Osaka, has come nearly to cease its movement.

b.   *Rationalization in use of industrial water*

Rationalized use of industrial water can be witnessed from the rate of return water for recycling use.

The recycling use of industrial water by industrial sectors in 1980 is as shown in Table 86.   A large quantity of water is consumed in the sectors of chemical and steel industries, but the greater part is recycled water consumption.   Among those most modernized steel manufacturing plants, there exist some advanced plants whose recycling use of water exceeds 95 per cent.

The rate of recycling use is averaged at more than 70 per cent throughout all industrial sectors.   Rationalized use of water at such high rate of recycling has produced favorable result in easement of tight balance between demand and supply and preservation of environmental quality.

c.   *Technical research and development on hydro resources*

(i)   *Desalination of sea water*

Desalination of sea water is expected greatly as the most encouraging means to solve the problem of water shortage.

The desalination technology by evaporation has been developed successfully by the National Institute of Industrial Technology and exported to the Middle East countries as a part of overseas technical co-operation.

Table 85. Trend on Industrial Water Consumption by Available Supply Sources

(Unit: 1,000 m³/day)

Year	Public water service		Surface Water	River-bed Water	Well	Others	Make-up Water	Return Water (per cent)	Total
	Industrial Water	City Water							
1965	4 444 (14.2)	2 780 (8.9)	7 281 (23.2)	3 554 (11.3)	12 679 (40.5)	598 (1.9)	31 336 (100.0)	17 826 (36.3)	49 162
1966	5 138 (16.0)	2 899 (9.1)	7 831 (24.5)	3 329 (10.4)	12 594 (39.3)	224 (0.7)	32 015 (100.0)	21 092 (39.7)	53 107
1967	6 622 (19.8)	2 945 (8.8)	7 496 (22.4)	3 227 (9.6)	12 937 (38.5)	291 (0.9)	33 518 (100.0)	24 180 (41.9)	57 698
1968	7 500 (20.8)	3 206 (8.9)	7 753 (21.5)	3 016 (8.4)	13 944 (38.6)	644 (1.8)	36 063 (100.0)	28 907 (44.5)	64 970
1969	8 729 (22.6)	3 271 (8.5)	8 019 (20.8)	3 207 (8.3)	14 473 (37.4)	916 (2.4)	38 615 (100.0)	35 790 (48.1)	74 405
1970	9 801 (23.9)	3 491 (8.5)	8 286 (20.2)	3 247 (7.9)	15 360 (37.4)	871 (2.1)	41 056 (100.0)	43 986 (51.7)	85 042
1971	10 395 (24.8)	3 876 (9.2)	8 292 (19.8)	3 188 (7.6)	14 915 (35.6)	1 271 (3.0)	41 937 (100.0)	53 310 (56.0)	95 247
1972	11 491 (27.0)	3 530 (8.3)	8 257 (19.4)	3 163 (7.4)	15 243 (35.8)	884 (2.1)	42 568 (100.0)	58 889 (56.1)	101 457
1973	11 437 (26.5)	3 880 (9.0)	8 397 (19.4)	3 131 (7.2)	15 326 (35.4)	1 086 (2.5)	43 257 (100.0)	70 658 (62.0)	113 915
1974	11 995 (28.4)	3 351 (7.9)	8 192 (19.4)	3 066 (7.2)	14 646 (34.7)	1 000 (2.4)	42 250 (100.0)	77 790 (64.8)	120 040
1975	11 945 (29.7)	3 152 (7.8)	7 921 (19.7)	2 925 (7.3)	13 622 (33.9)	628 (1.6)	40 193 (100.0)	81 432 (67.0)	121 625
1976	12 237 (30.7)	2 888 (7.3)	10 842 (27.2)		13 336 (33.5)	528 (1.3)	39 831 (100.0)	88 030 (68.8)	127 861
1977	11 966 (30.7)	2 727 (7.0)	10 653 (27.4)		13 062 (33.5)	549 (1.4)	38 957 (100.0)	92 747 (70.4)	131 704
1978	11 752 (31.3)	2 608 (6.9)	10 333 (27.5)		12 344 (32.9)	523 (1.4)	37 560 (100.0)	95 434 (71.8)	132 994
1979	12 052 (32.5)	2 501 (6.8)	10 109 (27.3)		11 884 (32.1)	478 (1.3)	37 024 (100.0)	100 792 (73.1)	137 816
1980	12 015 (32.7)	2 517 (6.9)	9 955 (27.1)		11 775 (32.1)	441 (1.2)	36 702 (100.0)	102 225 (73.6)	138 927
1981	11 759 (32.9)	2 486 (7.0)	9 724 (27.2)		11 300 (31.7)	436 (1.2)	35 705 (100.0)	101 441 (74.0)	137 146

Source: Industrial Statistics

Note: Plant with employment of 30 persons or more
         Number inside ( ) indicates the rate toward make-up water amount

Table 86. Industrial Water Consumption by Sectors (1980)

Source: Industrial Statistics   Unit: 1,000 m^3/day, (per cent)

Type of Industry	Non-Salt Water						Purposes	
	Total		Make-up Water		Return Water		Return Rate	Product Processing, Washing Water	Cooling, Air Conditioning Water
Chemical	46 041	(33.1)	8 552	(23.3)	37 489	(36.7)	81.4%	4.8%	92.2%
Steel	35 530	(25.6)	3 931	(10.7)	31 599	(30.9)	88.9	8.4	87.2
Paper & Pulp	16 135	(11.6)	9 505	(25.9)	6 630	(6.5)	41.1	80.9	13.3
Transport Equipment	8 163	(5.9)	909	(2.5)	7 254	(7.1)	88.9	41.8	54.4
Oil-Coal	6 416	(4.6)	926	(2.5)	5 490	(5.4)	85.6	1.2	93.8
Foods	6 099	(4.4)	3 790	(10.3)	2 309	(2.3)	37.9	30.7	55.2
Non-ferrous	5 348	(3.8)	1 333	(3.6)	4 015	(3.9)	75.1	17.2	78.1
Textile	3 955	(2.8)	3 064	(8.3)	891	(0.9)	22.5	31.1	58.2
Pottery & Masonry	2 798	(2.0)	1 027	(2.8)	1 771	(1.7)	63.3	20.6	69.9
Others	8 442	(6.1)	3 665	(10.0)	4 777	(4.7)	56.6	13.5	73.1
Total	138 947	(100.0)	36 702	(100.0)	102 225	(100.0)	73.6	19.8	74.9

Note: Enterprise with employment of 30 persons or more.

The other approach is being made by the Ministry of International Trade and Industry to develop the new desalination technology by the reverse osmosis process which could reduce the energy cost to minimum. At present, experimental test is going on by use of the model plant on practical scale with a daily production capacity of 800 cubic m and the test results are really encouraging.

Request has been made from the Middle East & Latin American countries for technical co-operation on the reverse osmosis process as well. The government takes positive attitude toward accepting any such request from the countries abroad now facing water shortage.

(ii) *Recycling of sewage water*

Sewage discharge is certainly a potential source of supply.

In fact, there exist some industrial water supply systems which serve industrial plants with highly processed effluent once processed at the sewage treatment plant. Especially, at the Kohoku Purification Plant of Johoku Industrial Water Supply System in the Tokyo Metropolitan Area, the processed effluent is fed back into the industrial plant after purified to the equal quality level to the river water by the activated carbon process.

(iii) *Recycling of industrial waste discharge*

Industrial waste discharge is now abandoned as refuse of no recycling potentiality. However, research is being done for recycling of such industrial waste as potential water resources by clarifying the question how and in what fields of industrial engineering process the waste could be reused and how much influence would be exerted upon the equipment and the product by recycling of such waste and then by full grasp of water quality acceptable to each engineering process.

5. Hydro Power Generation

a. *Basic policy for hydro power development in Japan*

(i) In view of importance that domestic energy resources should be utilized most effectively, power generating sources should be diversified into various patterns and energy supply should be secured on a stabilized basis, every effort is being exerted for development of conventional hydro power generating sources.

In reality, however, with regard to the selection of exploitable sites there remain a reduced number of prospective sites with favorable conditions for hydro power development. Although there may be difficulty in execution of the development project, there still remain some potential hydro power resources as itemized hereunder.

(1) Exploitation of sites on medium or small scale

(2) Participation in the integrated river development scheme (multi-purpose dam) for power generation as a part thereof

(3) Abolition of existing power generating facilities with low utilization factor of river discharge or re-development by improvement of flow regime

(4) Exploitation of sites with low effective head

(ii) With the highly improved living standard of people in recent years, it is the general tendency that the peak load shows a very acute rise with a declining trend of load factor in a long run.

As the regulating capacity to cope with such peak demand, the development projects for pumped-storage power generation will be further promoted.

b. *Present status of power development*

Because of steep landscape and rainfall in abundance, Japan is favored with suitable site conditions for hydro power generation. Over a century to this date, concentrated effort has continued for development of hydro power generating sources. As of this date, hydro power stations are in operation at 1,666 sites with maximum generating capacity of about 33,000 MW. At 67 sites with total capacity of about 9,000 MW are now under construction (Tables 87-90).

c. *Future projection on hydro power development scheme*

By reference to the "Summary report of Japan's long-term energy supply and demand outlook and future energy policy" published by the General Energy Survey Committee in August 1983, the future hydro power development plan is as shown in Table 91.

6. Water Quality Conservation

a. *Water pollution problems at present*

By reference to the result of measurement of the water quality in the nationwide public water area in 1981, it is reported that with regard to specific items of pollutants such as cadmium and cyanogen toxic to human health the quantity of tested matters in excess of the environmental standard is contained at a rate of 0.05 per cent in the total quantity as tested. When compared with 1.4 per cent in 1970 and 0.17 per cent in 1975, the latest figure implies remarkable improvement of water quality with declining tendency year after year.

With regard to those items, such as BOD and COD, related to conservation of the living environment, the requirement of the environmental standard for BOD (or COD) has been satisfied to 63.3 per cent in the river, 42.7 per cent in the lake and 81.6 per cent in the sea. As a whole, the requirement is not as yet accomplished in the water area of 34.0 per cent. Especially no improvement is observed in the lake, inland sea and inner bay. Rather, in those water areas rapid progress is being made toward eutrophication which is regarded as being a cause of inadequate filtration or nasty smell in the city water supply system and red tide in the sea (Table 92).

b. *Intensified effluent control*

The effluent control standard as provided in 1958 under the 'Water Quality Conservation Law' and the

Table 87. Existing Hydro Power Generating Facilities

As of March end 1983

	Conventional hydro power		Mixed-type pumped-storage		Pure pumped-storage		Total	
	No. of stations	Max. output (10^4 kW)	No. of stations	Max. output (10^4 kW)	No. of stations	Max. output (10^4 kW)	No. of stations	Max. output (10^4 kW)
9 power companies	1 109	1 292	15	381	11	650	1 135	2 323
E.P.D.C.	43	310	4	171	2	168	49	649
Municipal	198	194	–	–	1	25	199	219
Others	62	28	–	–			62	28
Total	1 412	1 824	19	552	14	843	1 445	3 219
Private	221	114	–	–			221	114
Grand total	1 633	1 938	19	552	14	843	1 666	3 333

Table 88. Hydro Power Generating Facilities under Construction

As of March end 1983

	Conventional hydro power		Mixed-type pumped-storage		Pure pumped-storage		Total	
	No. of stations	Max. output (MW)	No. of stations	Max. output (MW)	No. of stations	Max. output (MW)	No. of stations	Max. output (MW)
9 power companies	24	602.8	1	200.0	8	6 930.0	33	7 732.8
E.P.D.C.	2	16.3	1	400.0	1	1 000.0	4	1 416.3
Municipal	19	77.9	–	–	–	–	19	77.9
Others	2	6.3	–	–	–	–	2	6.3
Total	47	703.3	2	600.0	9	7 930.0	58	9 233.3
Private	9	30.7	–	–	–	–	9	30.7
Grand total	56	734.0	2	600.0	9	7 930.0	67	9 264.0

Table 89. Trend of Hydro Power Generating Capacity in Total Generating Capacity

Unit: 10 MW

Year / Source / Item	Hydro		Fossil-fueled		Nuclear		Total	
	Max. output	Ratio per cent	Max. output	Ratio per cent	Max. output	Ratio per cent	Max. output	Ratio per cent
1955	891	61.4	560	39.6	–	–	1 451	100.0
1960	1 268	53.6	1 098	46.4	–	–	2 366	100.0
1965	1 628	39.7	2 472	60.3	1	0.0	4 101	100.0
1970	1 999	29.3	4 693	68.8	134	1.9	6 826	100.0
1975	2 485	22.1	8 082	72.0	662	5.9	11 229	100.0
1980	2 978	20.7	9 823	68.4	1 569	10.9	14 370	100.0
1981	3 160	21.1	10 219	68.1	1 626	10.8	15 004	100.0

Table 90. Trend of Hydro Energy Production in Total Electric Energy

Unit: 100 million kWHs

Year / Source / Item	Hydro		Fossil-fueled		Nuclear		Total	
	kWH	Ratio per cent	kWH	Ratio per cent	kWH	Ratio per cent	kWH	Ratio per cent
1955	485	74.4	167	25.6	–	–	652	100.0
1960	585	50.6	570	49.4	–	–	1 155	100.0
1965	752	39.5	1 150	60.5	0	0.0	1 902	100.0
1970	801	22.3	2 749	76.4	46	1.3	3 596	100.0
1975	859	18.1	3 648	76.7	251	5.2	4 758	100.0
1980	921	15.9	4 028	69.8	826	14.3	5 775	100.0
1981	906	15.5	4 049	69.4	878	15.1	5 832	100.0

Table 91. Share of Hydro Power Energy in Primary Energy Supply

(Oil Equivalent)

	1982 Actual	1990 Estimated	1995 Estimated
Alternative Energy (Unit: 10^8 Kl)	1.49	about 2.2 ~about 2.3	about 2.7 ~about 3.0
(10^6 Kl)			
Coal	72	81~86	86~102
Nuclear	27	48~51	74~ 79
Natural Gas	27	56~60	65~ 69
Hydro Power	22	26~27	about 28
Geothermal	0.4	1.5~ 2	3.5~ 4
Others	0.9	7~12	15~ 26
Oil (10^8 Kl)	2.4	about 2.4 ~about 2.5	about 2.4 ~about 2.5
Total (10^8 Kl)	3.89	4.5~4.8	5.0~5.5

'Factory Effluents Control Law' posed such problems that it did not act effectively as the preventive measure in all instances because the control standard was set up separately for each designated water area and no penalty clause applied to any violation against the standard. For this reason, those two Laws were replaced in 1970 by the Water Pollution Control Law newly enacted, under which the nationwide uniform effluent standard could be put into enforcement and, if necessary under the local regulations, each prefectural governor was authorized to set up a more intensified control standard for the specified water area.

In 1973, for improvement of the water quality in the Seto Inland Sea severely affected by pollution, the Seto Inland Sea Environmental Conservation Law (revised in 1978 as the permanent law) was enacted with provisions of water quality control which requires the official permission for any effluent discharge into the Sea and also provides implementation of environmental assessment.

Later, in 1978 in order to intensify control over water pollution in the wide semi-closed water area, the Water Pollution Control Law and the Seto Inland Sea Environmental Conservation Law were revised so as to enforce, in 1980, regulation on total emission of COD, as one of organic polluting indexes, in the Tokyo Bay, the Ise Bay and the Seto Inland Sea.

In recent years it has been drawn to attention that pollution of water quality is being shared increasingly by organic matters related to livelihood load and this tendency becomes conspicuous especially in the semi-closed water area. Besides, the impact from non-point polluting sources flown out by rainfall from the urban, forest and arable areas are significant. Since those recent problems are shared increasingly by such polluting sources as are not familiar to the items stipulated by the control standard, necessary measures must be taken for legislation of survey, estimation and assessment on environmental impacts from the development project and also for consolidation of the social capital related to water pollution control.

Furthermore, with a view to preventing any inadequately filtered and nasty smelly city water supply system and any damage from red tide to arise from enriched-nourishment in the lake, inland sea and inner bay, the comprehensive measures must be taken as the pressing task to reduce such pollutants as phosphorus and nitrogen leading to enriched nourishment of water quality.

Table 92. Accomplishment Rate on Water Quality Criteria

(i) Toxic matters
Ratio of tested quantity in excess of criteria in total tested quantity.

Year \ Item	Item-1*	Total mercury
1970	1.4 %	%
1971	0.6	
1972	0.3	
1973	0.23	
1974	0.20	0
1975	0.17 **	0
1976	0.09 **	0
1977	0.08 **	0
1978	0.07 **	0
1979	0.06 **	0
1980	0.05 **	0
1981	0.05 **	0

Note: *: Including cadmium, cyanogen, organic phosphorus, lead, chrome (hexad), arsenic, alkyl mercury, total mercury and PCB (to be included in and after 1975).
**: Excluding total mercury

(ii) BOD or COD
Ratio of number of water areas satisfying the pollution control standard in total water areas in application is shown in the following table.

Water area Year	River	Lake	Sea
1977	58.5%	35.2%	76.9%
1978	59.5	37.6	75.3
1979	65.0	41.8	78.2
1980	67.2	41.6	79.8
1981	63.3	42.7	81.6

7. Forestry Improvement

In order to secure the potential water resources, it is necessary to enhance the recharging function of water resources which the forestry contains by improving the forestry resources near the reservoir area, besides construction of dams and improvement of river systems. For this purpose, the 5.66 million forest area of particular importance is designated as the forest reserve district for recharging of water resources (as of March 1983).

To further enhance the function, measures are being taken for safety control against natural disasters of the mountain near the reservoir area and integrated model project for strengthening water and soil conservation function.

8. Research and Public Relations

a. Research

A research study concerning the development and utilization of water resources is conducted at related public offices and affiliated organs to meet each of the administrative requirements. We will introduce several examples here of researches in the field of water resources.

(i) The Science and Technology Agency

(1) National Institute of Resources

(a) Achievements since 1980

Researches were carried out on various problems, related to the development of water resources, and studies were made on how to cope with the problems or about the prospects of controlling water resources.

Researches were carried out on the observation and survey methods of rheological system of ground water, to help in the preparation of plans for rational utilization of ground water. Also, in order to seek appropriate methods for future control of ground water various studies were made with the use of simulation models, to find out problems expected at the time of actual use or to clarify usage conditions as well as merits and demerits.

Inquiries were made on future subjects concerning the use and preservation of ground water by analyzing various problems which may occur along with an increase in the demand of ground water.

(b) Surveys Currently Undertaken

A survey of a possibility to dispose household waste water through a full utilization of natural purifying functions possessed by the mountains, agricultural land or the water area.

A survey of the rainwater storage system which would raise the function of water conservation in city area while diminishing the danger of flood damage in urban lowlands.

(2) National Research Centre for Disaster Prevention

In order to prevent flood disaster and to evaluate water resources, researches are conducted on the development of runoff models and observations are made on varying characteristics of flood and the runoff in urban areas.

Also in order to help preventing disasters to be caused by localized torrential downpour, studies are carried out with the use of meteorological radar on the short-term prediction method of rainfall. And experimental studies are made on the runoff, infiltration and breakdown by utilizing a large scale rainfall simulator.

Furthermore, a field investigation is conducted on major flood disasters and reports are compiled through collection of necessary data.

(ii) Ministry of Construction (Public Works Research Institute)

The Public Works Research Institute is an integrated research organ in the field of civil engineering technology. For the prevention of disasters or for the development of water resources or the preservation of rivers, it conducts various surveys and experiments concerning the design of engineering construction or the related technical standards. Among such study results, some achievements which are worthy to be introduced to overseas are published in the form of 'Journal of Research — Public Works Research Institute'.

Concerning the prevention of disasters, the institute tries to grasp the runoff phenomenon and improve the precision in flood forecasting. Also it studies the influence the transforming basins have on the runoff and the necessary countermeasures. It carries out a large-scale model experiment for studying the design and construction of river channels and dykes. And researches are made to know the mechanism of debris flow and landslide, and to prepare measures to prevent them.

Concerning the development of water resources, it makes fundamental studies about water circulation, the development of water resources and its effective use. Also, it studies the possibility to construct a solid dam in the area which has insufficient base rock. Other studies are made about the flood-emitting facilities which match the environment, or about the cultivation technology of ground water.

Also, concerning the preservation of river environment, it carries out conservation studies of water quality, such as analyzing the pollution mechanism or water purification method in sewage disposal. And a study is conducted on creating good environment for the conservation of rivers.

(iii) *Ministry of Agriculture, Forestry and Fisheries (National Research Institute of Agricultural Engineering)*

The demand for agricultural water is growing in recent years in Japan along with a big transition in water utilization forms as a result of farm land consolidation and the advancement of agricultural technology. Therefore, it would be necessary to promote new development plans of water resources and to plan for efficient utilization through the systematization of water usage in broad-ranging areas.

In coping with problems of development and rational distribution of water resources the institute studies the relationship between meteorological and geographical features and the runoff mechanism of low water from the hydrological viewpoint. Also it launches an analysis of water balance in wide areas, and investigates measures to enhance water resources.

Also, for conducting the most appropriate utilization of limited water resources, it carries out studies on the systematization of the development, utilization or supervision of water resources in a wide area, with the use of mathematical models and computer simulation.

In the study of ground water, a ground water probing method has been established, with the use of natural radioactivity, for investigating undeveloped regions. And, for enhancing wide-ranging water supply, it launches a technological study concerning the artificial cultivation of ground water or the possibility of underground dams, and at the same time makes a survey of the quantitative proof method for the flow and storage structure of ground water, as well as of the control method of ground water.

Meanwhile, concerning the water balance in agricultural regions, it makes a survey in the point of water pollution and studies about conserving good water quality in irrigation canals and rivers, as well as of underground water.

b. *P.R. Activities*

Some examples of the P.R. activities, concerning water resources are specified below.

(i) The 'River Beautification Month' is set for April, and the 'River Conservation Month' for July, and during those periods, enlightenment campaigns are carried out effectively for letting the public acquire the idea of river conservation and for promoting proper and safe utilization of rivers, while preserving them in good condition.

(ii) Waterworks Week

The 'Waterworks Week' has been enforced since 1959. Under a different theme, each year, the importance of the waterworks and the significance of such campaign week have been publicized to the public. In 1983, a campaign was conducted under the following targets.

(1) To seek understanding and co-operation in advancing and improving waterworks facilities.

(2) To seek understanding on the importance of prevention of pollution in water resources, as well as on the importance of development of water resources to cope with the increasing demand for water; and seek co-operation for the solution of the difficulties.

(3) To seek co-operation for the effective utilization of water supply.

(4) To spread the knowledge on the management situation of waterworks, as well as on water charges; and seek understanding.

(iii) Beginning 1977, August 1 of every year was designated as the 'Water Day', in order to raise the public interest on the situations of water, as to its limited nature; and about the preciousness of water, as well as the importance of development of water resources. During the week, starting on August, various events are conducted to meet the theme of the 'Water Week'.

In August, 1982, research papers on various problems, concerning water resources were presented and discussions ensued. Then, for the purpose of contributing to the future studies and helping in the administrative measures, the 2nd 'Symposium on Water Resources' was held, with the presence of many researchers from various fields.

(iv) Japan decided to participate in the International River Exposition, to be held in New Orleans, the U.S.A., on May 12 – Nov. 11, 1984, under the theme of 'The World of Rivers – Fresh Water as a Source of Life'.

c. *Present Status of International Co-operation*

As a part of international co-operation toward developing countries, the Government has actively been promoting both loan and grant aids in the field of water resources, as well as carrying out technical co-operation through the acceptance of trainees from those nations or sending the

Japanese specialists to overseas. The Government intends to continue such international co-operation further in the field of water resources in meeting the needs of developing countries.

The summary of Japan's co-operation results, from 1980 to 1982, is as follows.

(i) Loan Assistance

The number of loan assistance schemes concluded between Japan and other nations concerning water resources during 1980-1982 rose to 49, and the total amount exceeds ¥200 billion. (Among them, 42 schemes are for the ESCAP regions, with the total amount exceeding ¥150 billion). The schemes cover such divisions as specified below. Development of water resources in rivers – 5; irrigation – 16; water supply and sewerage – 8; dam – 2; flood control – 1; and hydropower generation – 17. (see table 93)

(ii) Grant-Aid

During 1980-1982, the number of grant aids which Japan provided in the field of water resources, rose to 49 schemes in total, which amounted to about ¥39 billion. (Among them, 28 schemes are for the ESCAP regions, with the total amount reaching to about ¥29 billion)

The schemes are specified as follows: Household water – 25; agricultural water – 12; ground water resources development – 5; dam construction – 4; flood forecast – 2; and hydropower generation – 1.

(iii) Acceptance of Trainees:

Japan provides various training courses in the field of water resources, and receives a number of trainees every year from developing countries. The following are several examples of group training courses. Tap water facilities; sewerage technology; river engineering; flood control; irrigation; drainage; development of water resources in farmland; development of groundwater resources; hydropower generation; and meteorology. During 1980-1982, total 284 trainees were accepted. Also, 208 trainees were accepted in various individual training courses such as that of waterworks. (see table 93)

(iv) Dispatch of Specialists:

Specialists are dispatched under three forms – individual unit, project type, and survey team. During 1980-1982, 85 people were dispatched in individual unit; 39 in project type; and total 1,391 in survey team. The scopes, those specialists engaged in, include waterworks; environ-

Table 93. Training Courses & Dispatch of experts on Water Resources

(1980-1982)

a. Training Courses

Year	Group	Individual
80	92	75
81	91	62
82	101	71
Total	284	208

b. Dispatch of experts

| year | individual | | project-type | | survey-team |
	short-term	long-term	short-term	long-term	persons
80	16	11		10	311
81	18	27	2	5	503
82	6	7	11	11	577
Total	85		39		1 391

mental sanitation; flood forecast; irrigation; river development and others. (see table 93)

(v) *Project-Type Technical Co-operation*

Three forms of technical co-operation, such as the dispatch of specialists; acceptance of trainees and the granting of mechanical equipment are consolidated as a single project. Co-operation forms, which comprehensively handle, and enforce the process of making plans and carrying them out are called the 'technical co-operation under the project system'. Such project-system technical co-operation, Japan conducted during 1980-1982 in the field of water resources, amounts to 13 schemes. (Among them, 7 schemes are for the ESCAP regions). Specifically, 10 schemes are for the agricultural water and 3 schemes for household water.

(vi) *Development Survey*

The development survey, conducted by Japan in the field of water resources, amounted to 98 schemes during 1980-1982 (62 schemes in the ESCAP regions). It is divided into feasibility studies, master-plan surveys, basic design surveys, a survey for detailed designs and others. Those schemes are specified as — 17 in hydropower generation; 17 in the development of water resources in river; 20 in water supply and drainage; 38 in agricultural water; 2 in ground water resources development; 3 in desalination; and 1 in purification of lake.

International Organizations

Besides those introduced above, Japan has been carrying out co-operation toward the water resources activities, launched by the ESCAP and other international organizations. For instance, Japan helped in opening seminars by the TOPEX — the ESCAP's typhoon committee, and sent specialists to the ESCAP's MEKHONG committee.

VI. NEW ZEALAND

VI. A. ACTIVITIES IN WATER RESOURCES DEVELOPMENT AND MANAGEMENT

Introduction

During the last three years, progress in the management of water resources has been achieved through legislation and in the collection and presentation of data associated with water resources planning and landuse capability mapping. Management plans are taking note of an increasing public awareness of "natural" resources, and the need for conservation of wildlife habitats and enhanced recreational opportunities.

As in the past, New Zealand has continued to develop its water resources for use in agriculture, hydro-electric generation, water supplies and waste disposal, but greater emphasis is being placed on multi-purpose uses of water, and the amelioration of some of the harsher aspects of development through landscaping.

A significant recent development in the use of water resources has been the growth of horticultural irrigation.

Measures Taken Specifically in Response to the Action Plan

New Zealand was in the fortunate position of already having started thinking along the lines of water resource management before the Mar.del Plata water conference, so it is difficult to isolate any particular policy or project

which New Zealand initiated specifically in response to the action plan.

However, undoubtedly the action plan has had indirect influence on the development of water resource management plans in this country, and New Zealand is interested to keep abreast with developments in other countries.

1. Legislation

The major changes to water resource legislation over the last three years are as follows:

a. *National Development Act 1979*

When it became apparent that for large development projects it was taking a considerable time to go through the various statutory procedures, government decided that this process should be speeded up. The National Development Act provides for the prompt consideration of proposed works of national importance by the direct referral of the proposals to the Planning Tribunal, a judicial body, for an inquiry and report and recommendation to government and by providing for such works to receive the necessary statutory approvals.

The body which would normally grant the consent for a water right, the local regional water board, or the

National Water and Soil Conservation Authority, gives a recommendation to the Planning Tribunal which, after hearing evidence, makes a recommendation on the consents to be granted. This "fast track" planning process usually takes no more than 12 months.

The two projects which have so far been implemented through this act both convert natural gas to liquid fuels (methanol and synthetic petrol).

A recent amendment to the NDA made provision for the recovery of costs incurred by regional water boards on essential investigatory activities leading up to the processing of applications under the act.

b. *Water and Soil Conservation Amendment Act 1981*

The object of this legislation is to recognise and sustain the amenity afforded by waters in their natural state. Applications may be made to have a river, stream or lake preserved in its natural state, or to the degree necessary to maintain its wild, scenic, recreational, fisheries, wildlife habitat, scientific or other natural characteristics. The needs of primary and secondary industry and the community must be taken into account as well as the natural values when considering an application.

The Motu River is currently under consideration. As a result of an initial investigation a draft national water conservation order has been prepared and is the subject of a further public inquiry. Three other applications are at earlier stages of consideration. Of these, the application for the Rakaia River is creating considerable interest; there is an apparent conflict between allocating the water resource to satisfy irrigation demand and the maintenance of instream values particularly relating to the salmon fishery.

c. Amendments to the Water and Soil Conservation Act 1967 and Town and Country Planning Act 1977 provided for the joint hearing of applications and appeals.

d. An amendment to Soil Conservation and Rivers Control Act 1941 included protection of lakes and the sea from erosion and detritus.

e. The Harbours Amendment Act included provision to delegate powers of control over sand and gravel extraction to catchment authorities.

f. *Other Progress Relating to Legislation*

Some consideration has been given to possible revision of the Water and Soil Conservation Act, but this work has not received a high priority in the legislative programme.

A review of the structure, functions and role of NWASCO and catchment authorities has been conducted and attention drawn to areas where changes in legislation would be desirable.

2. Irrigation and stock water supply

Much of New Zealand receives sufficient rainfall to sustain a moderate level of farming activity, but agricultural output in many areas is limited by the availability of water. Considerable increases in production can be expected as a result of the extension of irrigation practices.

Currently only 187,000 ha or 0.7 per cent of the total land area (1.9 per cent of all "improved" farm land) is irrigated, but this will increase by some 40 per cent as a result of schemes currently under construction. A further 312,000 ha are included in projects currently being considered (see Table 94). In addition, 36 stock water supplies servicing an area of 484,800 ha are currently under construction, and 27 more schemes are being planned.

While most of the irrigation schemes are for pastoral farming, there is a substantial growth in horticultural irrigation; the area under trickle irrigation for citrus and other subtropical fruit being likely to increase by 500 per cent over the next 3-5 years.

3. Hydro-electric power generation

Hydro-electric power generation has increased from 18,700 Gwh/yr (1980) to 20,000 Gwh/yr (72 PJ/yr), 1983. By the late 1990s the existing planned hydro stations will have the capacity to generate 26,300 Gwh/yr (95 PJ). In addition, there is potential to generate a further 37,000 Gwh/yr (133 PJ), however, adverse environmental, technical and economic factors will considerably limit prospects for development.

Currently hydro-electricity provides 84 per cent of the total generation in a mean year, but this is expected to drop to 74 per cent by 1986 reflecting the gradual transition to a system based more on thermal fuel.

a. *Small Hydro*

Small hydro-electric schemes built by local power boards receive grant assistance for investigation and design, and loan assistance for construction.

Grants for the investigation and design of schemes are current for 12 schemes with a total power output of 90 MW and a total estimated cost of $126 million.

When construction proceeds, the grants are included in the provision of loan finance for up to 90 per cent of the

Table 94.

		July 1980			July 1983		
		Pastoral	Horticultural	Total	Pastoral	Horticultural	Total
Area under irrigation (ha)		166 400	Nil	166 400	183 770	3 230	187 000
Schemes under construction at	No	13	2	15	13	7	20
	Area	62 660	2 840	65 500	69 250	4 850	74 100
Schemes approved during last three years (to start construction)	No	2	2	4	1	4	5
	Area	18 510	2 840	21 350	5 500	3 150	8 650
Schemes planned (with AIP* and progressing towards approval)	No				1	3	4
	Area				2 740	3 390	6 140
Schemes under investigation (proceeding towards AIP)	No				26	21	47
	Area				270 000	36 000	306 000

* AIP: Approval in Principle

Stock Water Supplies

		July 1980	July 1983
Area under RWS			
Schemes under construction at	No	45	36
	Area	541 300	484 800
Schemes approved during last three years (to start construction)	No	23	
	Area	260 400	
Schemes planned (with AIP)	No		27
	Area		
Schemes under investigation (proceeding towards AIP)	No		
	Area		

cost of the station. Loans have been made for 13 schemes presently under construction or recently completed. Their installed capacity totals 157 MW and the total estimated cost of the schemes is $229 million.

b. *Other Energy Requirements and Development Policies*

At present, geothermal energy provide 1000 Gwh/yr or 4 per cent of the total electricity generation, but output will increase to 1600 Gwh/yr or 6 per cent by 1988.

Coal, gas and oil fired thermal power stations currently supply 12 per cent of the power requirements in a mean year (25 per cent in a dry year), but this is expected to increase to 20 per cent within the next 3-5 years.

Government is also deeply committed to a programme of conversion of natural gas to liquid fuels, and expansion of the country's steel, aluminium, fertiliser and pulp and paper production, and oil refining capability. Some of these developments have attracted considerable attention in relation to effects on water quality.

4. Water supply and wastewater disposal

a. *Policy*

The major changes in this area are those that have resulted from a review of the Health Department's subsidy scheme for capital works. Changes include:

(i) a phasing out of the 1:2 subsidy on initial sewerage reticulation. No new applications for this subsidy were accepted from 1 April 1982;

(ii) a revision of the rates of subsidy payable on main water supply and sewage treatment and disposal. Previously this subsidy was 1:2. As from 24 May 1982 it is on a sliding scale varying from 40 per cent for schemes serving communities up to 1,000 down to 10 per cent for communities of 100,000 and over.

The intention of these changes is to reduce government expenditure and to redirect government support to those areas where it can achieve the best results. Now that virtually all large urban areas are reticulated with water and sewerage, the need is to encourage those smaller communities, which often face relatively high per capita costs, to provide services.

Steady, if unspectacular, progress has been made on the upgrading of facilities where this has been required. In addition, local authorities with the encouragement of central government are showing increased interest in leakage control, inflow and infiltration reduction, and sewer repairs and renovation. With the aging of New Zealand sewers, this last matter is going to be the focus of increased attention in future.

b. *Public Water Supplies*

The last grading of public water supplies conducted in 1980 indicated that 87 per cent of the total population was served by public water supplies. Of this number 93 per cent were served by supplies classed as satisfactory or better.

156,000 people living in 383 communities of more than 200 people and representing 5 per cent of the population were without public water supplies. The remaining 8 per cent of the population without public water supplies live either on unreticulated outskirts of towns, or rural areas.

In the period 1980-1983, it is estimated that the population served by public water supplies has increased from 87 per cent to 88 per cent.

All people not connected to a public water supply do however, have access to water, e.g., roof rainwater collection systems, springs and private bores.

c. *Sewage Disposal*

The 1981 survey of local authority sewage disposal statistics indicated that 79 per cent of the population was connected to a public sewerage system, the remainder being mostly served by individual household septic tanks.

Of the population sewered, 75 per cent are connected to a sewage treatment plant, 23 per cent to untreated marine outfalls, and 2 per cent untreated discharges to inland receiving waters.

Of the population connected to a sewage treatment plant, 17 per cent receives primary treatment only, 12 per cent receives primary and secondary treatment only, while 71 per cent receives full tertiary treatment. See figure 42.

5. Water quality control

Effluent control is achieved by a system of water rights. Conditions placed on water rights for discharges are designed to meet the receiving water quality standards set by the classification. Where the receiving water is not classified the water right conditions for discharge are designed to meet regional water boards' desired standards of water quality.

Water Resources Council policy is to classify receiving waters where there is a conflict in the use of the waters. This is done following a request for such action and is undertaken if the local regional water board is agreeable.

Two reclassifications and one preliminary classification for stretches of water have been completed in the period.

6. Protection schemes

Flood control, river control, soil conservation, drainage, and coastal erosion protection.

In 1982/83 schemes with a total estimated cost of $180 million were under construction. There were 164 schemes each costing more than $80,000. The annual budget for grants for these schemes in 1983/84 is $35 million and the average duration of a scheme is five years. Thirty-eight of the schemes cost over $1 million each.

Government assistance is by way of a grant ranging from 70 per cent of the cost for comprehensive schemes down to 40 per cent for isolated works and 30 per cent for coastal and urban works. The remaining cost is raised by a rate on the scheme beneficiaries graduated according to the degree of benefit.

The works are promoted and carried out by catchment authorities which are locally elected bodies.

7. Water management planning

Regional water boards are the local authorities responsible for managing water use, that is, the balancing and integration of water use with the conservation of soil and water.

Most boards now have, at least for one waterway, an operative water allocation plan, that is, a policy on the taking or damming of water while ensuring sufficient water is left instream for ecological and cultural uses.

Finance for water allocation plans is provided by local sources and government assistance.

Two notable examples of regional water and soil management plans prepared to date are plans for the Waitaki River and the Upper Waitemata Harbour of Auckland. The responsibilities, functions, works and advisory roles which the regional water boards and associated catchment autho-

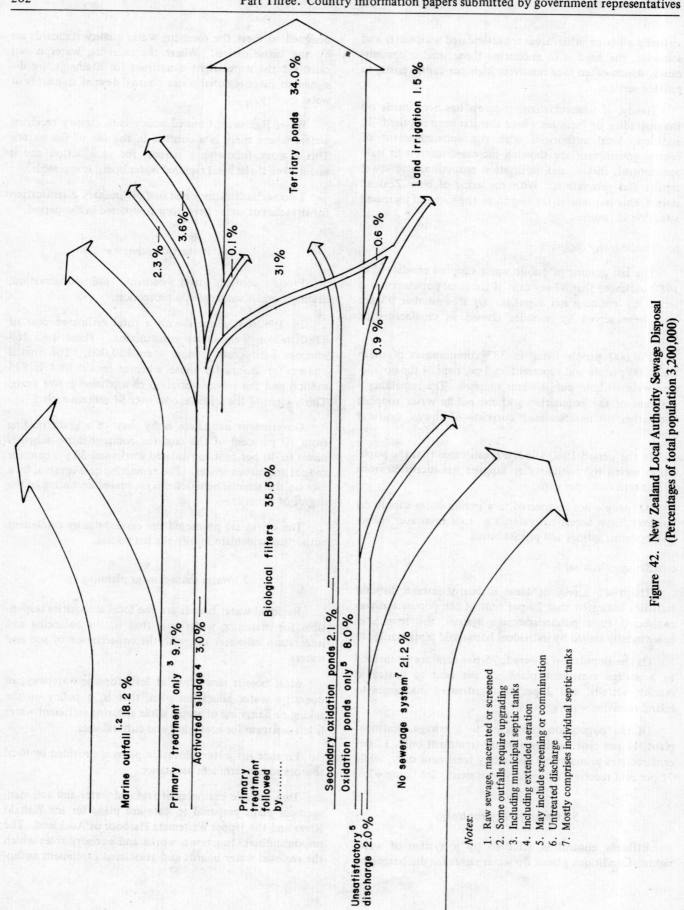

Notes:
1. Raw sewage, macerated or screened
2. Some outfalls require upgrading
3. Including municipal septic tanks
4. Including extended aeration
5. May include screening or commination
6. Untreated discharge
7. Mostly comprises individual septic tanks

Figure 42. New Zealand Local Authority Sewage Disposal
(Percentages of total population 3,200,000)

rities have under various legislation are discussed in the plan and the above examples include published objectives, policies and methods of implementing the policies. The policies were prepared on a basis of local and national public participation in both research and formulation, and policy implementation will depend on public co-operation as well as statutory controls.

Water management research and planning is also being undertaken with co-operation between regional water boards and national technical agencies, for specific instances of large scale government development. One experience has highlighted the necessity for such planning to take account of the different cultural attitudes of the Maori groups affected. In this particular instance, local Maori people objected to aspects of one industry's permitted water use, which, they believed, did not take account of the cultural and economic importance to Maori people of seafood reefs in the vicinity of the industrial effluent discharge point. The agencies involved are now reviewing water use policies and researching water quality parameters in relation to the discharge of industrial waste.

The planning of water use and soil conservation is encouraged by NWASCO through the publication of detailed technical guidelines listing the impacts and hazards of unwise development, and the statutory controls and remedial measures available to local agencies. Particularly important are those involving mining (including open cast coal mining and gold dredging), coastal development, aggregate extraction, forestry harvesting and timber processing.

Protection of rivers with outstanding natural and scenic qualities has been facilitated by recent changes to legislation, as described previously.

8. Technical Support

a. *Telemetry*

A completely automated, hydrological data acquisition/flood warning/data based management system has been developed which will be installed in a number of New Zealand rivers over the next few years. The system which was demonstrated and publicised at the 1983 WMO conference on the use of hydrological data for mitigating natural disasters, could well have application in ESCAP countries.

The system includes control functions which can be used for operating flood gates, for example, and a further step will be to add in a soil moisture content monitoring system to assist with irrigation.

An objective is to build a national hydrological network involving both Ministry of Works and Development,

and catchment authorities. All systems will incorporate similar base stations and use the same computer language. Systems will be linked to mini and micro-computers for data storage and to enable flood forecasting procedures to be performed.

The data is transmitted directly from the field to the computer, thus minimizing labour costs and human error.

b. *Assessment of Water Resources*

A national hydrological data bank has now been constructed, enabling

(i) regional hydrological data to be available to regional water boards operating hydrological statistics computer programmes;

(ii) development of a regional flood frequency determination method;

(iii) access by development agencies to knowledge of water resources;

(iv) planning of water resources;

(v) estimation of minimum flows necessary for the survival of wildlife and fisheries;

(vi) flood flow estimation.

A second development is that data processing is now becoming the responsibility of those involved in data collection — the hydrological field parties.

c. *Land Resource Inventory*

Regional subsets of our national land resource inventory, as they become available, will be distributed to catchment boards.

9. International Co-operation

Assistance has been given to a number of countries in the South Pacific region for the financing, design and construction of water supply and sanitation schemes. In addition, training has been given for water supply and sewage treatment operations where operator training facilities have been established. Training has also been provided within New Zealand for personnel from other countries.

The Indonesian Government has been assisted in providing an improved city water supply system for Bengkulu (population 600,000) in Sumatra.

In Thailand, New Zealand has provided 6½ man years of professional engineering services and finance to design and supervise very small scale water storage projects in villages of Khon Kaen — a province of the semi-arid north-east Thailand. The project team has produced Thai language manuals on weir construction and ferro cement water tank construction. (See reference 1)

A similar project, concentrating on village scale projects of storing water for farming and general village purposes, was recently commenced in the adjoining province of Chaiyaphum. This project, of at least three years' duration, will involve three New Zealand engineers in conjunction with a similar number of Thai professional staff. The team is set up in the provincial government and will be funded by both Thai and New Zealand money (see reference 1).

In Western Samoa, New Zealand has been involved in the feasibility of a major improvement to the present Apia town water supply, following several years of providing specialist engineering and financial aid to the Western Samoan Government to help operate, maintain and carry out minor improvements to the existing system. New Zealand has also been assisting with, extending and improving rural water supply systems.

In the Cook Islands, New Zealand has provided engineering expertise, finance and construction management assistance with the installation of an improved water supply to the perimeter coastal strip of Rarotonga.

In Tonga, engineering advice and finance has been provided for the erection of village roof catchments and ferro cement tanks.

In the Solomon Islands, New Zealand is currently assisting in a water resources evaluation.

For the Solomon Islands and other Pacific islands, a ferro cement tank manual has been developed, giving guidance on the construction of tanks using local materials.

In Papua New Guinea, New Zealand has helped develop a school of training for operators of water treatment and wastewater treatment plants. This school is successfully in operation.

In Fiji, New Zealand has run training courses on water treatment.

In the area of exchange of technical information New Zealand has provided lecturers for WHO organised seminars in Malaysia (PEPAS: industrial and hazardous waste control), and New Zealand has hosted the 1982 ESCAP seminar on catchment management for optimum use of land and water resources, and also the 1981 International Association of Scientific Hydrology conference on steepland erosion.

New Zealand is also a participant in GEMS (water — two rivers and one groundwater site are being monitored) and SCOPE (carbon — one New Zealand river is being monitored).

There has also been contact with OECD water management group, involving urban runoff problems, eutrophication problems, and recently, biological monitoring methods.

Under the auspices of the Environment Committee of OECD, a group of experts from a number of countries conducted an examination of New Zealand's environmental stewardship, and presented an assessment report in November 1980.

Reference

1.   UNESCO: Proposed Regional Project: South East Asia and Pacific: rational use and conservation of water resources. Report from MWD to NZ Commission for UNESCO. 31 August 1983.

VI. B. MULTI-DISCIPLINARY AND SYSTEMS APPROACH TO INTEGRATED RIVER BASIN DEVELOPMENT

The National Water and Soil Conservation Organisation (NWASCO), the national agency for water use management, considers that proper planning of water resources use should also involve planning for soil conservation, if development is to be beneficial. For this purpose NWASCO promotes the use of water and soil resource management planning (WASRMP) through catchment authorities at the local level, by assistance with financial and technical support. WASRMP integrates all developments in a catchment, and in order to achieve this, a large multi-disciplinary staff is required — planners, engineers, scientists, lawyers, landscape architects, sociologists, farmers, industrialists; and comment is sought from ratepayers, recreational users, ethnic groups and the general public.

Integrated WASRMPs are drawn up within a statutory framework involving a number of pieces of legislation, notably the Town and Country Planning Act 1977 (providing for the preparation of district schemes, regional schemes and maritime plans), and both the Water and Soil Conservation Act 1967 and the Soil Conservation and Rivers Control Act 1941, which together provide powers and responsibilities to catchment authorities for integrated water use planning.

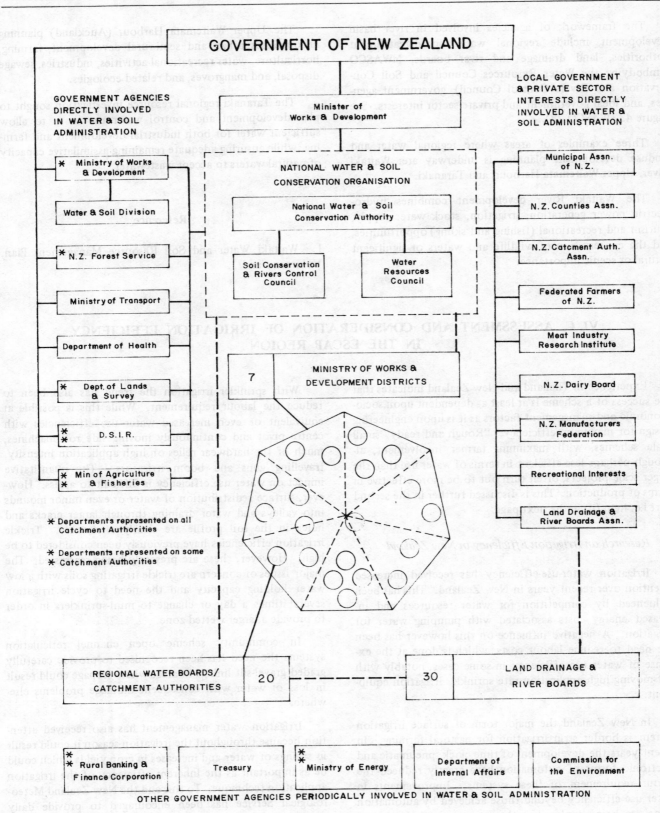

**Figure 43. Water And Soil Conservation Administration
In New Zealand**

The framework of agencies involved in river basin development include regional water boards/catchment authorities, land drainage and river boards, NWASCO (embodying the Water Resources Council and Soil Conservation and Rivers Control Council), government agencies, and local government and private sector interests. See Figure 43 (WASCO 28).

Three examples of areas where regional water and landuse development planning is underway are: Waitaki River, Upper Waitemata Harbour, and Taranaki.

The Waitaki River development combines hydroelectric power generation, irrigation, stock water supply, tourism and recreational (fishing and skiing) opportunities, and the conservation of wildlife and waters of significant natural or scenic importance.

The Upper Waitemata Harbour (Auckland) planning encompasses urban and semi-rural development, farming, horticulture, water recreational activities, industries, sewage disposal, and mangroves, and related ecologies.

The Taranaki regional resource investigation sought to plan development and control water use so as to allow sufficient water for both industrial development and farming, while ensuring adequate remaining assimilative capacity of natural waters to accept wastewater.

Reference

1. Waitaki Water and Soil Resource Management Plan. Volumes 1 and 2.

VI. C. ASSESSMENT AND CONSIDERATION OF IRRIGATION EFFICIENCY IN THE ESCAP REGION

Experience in Thailand and New Zealand indicates that the success of a scheme is at least as dependent upon socio-economic and management factors as it is upon engineering design for maximum efficiency. "Rough and ready" small scale schemes, with maximum farmer involvement, although perhaps less efficient in terms of water use than the larger scale projects, often turn out to be more effective in terms of production. This is discussed further in the second part i.e. item (ii) in the next page.

(i) *Research on Irrigation Efficiency in New Zealand*

Irrigation water-use-efficiency has received increased attention over recent years in New Zealand. This has been influenced by competition for water resources and increased energy costs associated with pumping water for irrigation. A negative influence on this however has been the need to reduce labour costs, which is done at the expense of water use efficiency in some cases, notably with self-moving high application rate sprinkler irrigation equipment.

In New Zealand the major form of surface irrigation system is border strip irrigation for pastoral farming. In recent years the development of time clock, pneumatic and electronic forms of automation have greatly reduced the labour requirement of these systems. Improvements in water use efficiency beyond those achieved by automation alone are being explored, such as matching flow rates in each trip to the soil intake rate and providing a more constant flow rate to each farmer.

With sprinkler irrigation the trend has also been to reduce the labour requirement. While this is possible at equivalent or even increased water use efficiencies with centre pivot and continuously moving side roll machines, much of the hardwear relies on high application intensity, travelling guns and boom irrigators. The quantitative impact on water use efficiency is difficult to assess. However, surface redistribution of water or even minor mounds into valleys and water draining through larger cracks and holes in the soil profile are clearly observable. Trickle irrigation efficiencies have previously been considered to be high. However, these are presently being reassessed. The major issues of concern are trickle irrigating soils with a low water holding capacity and the need to cycle irrigation several times a day or change to mini-sprinklers in order to provide a larger wetted zone.

In community scheme open channel reticulation systems the need has been recognised to provide carefully graded gravel-silt linings in areas where seepage could result in loss of water with consequent drainage problems elsewhere.

Irrigation water management has also received attention because throughout the irrigation season it could result in savings of water and increases in crop yields which could be as important as the inherent efficiency of the irrigation application technique. To this end the New Zealand Meteorological Service has been encouraged to provide daily estimates of potential evapotranspiration in the newspapers from which manual or computer-aided irrigation scheduling systems are being developed.

(a) *Measures to Improve Efficiency*

(1) *General*

Design standards improvement.

Advisory services through Ministry of Agriculture and Fisheries.

Design services by private consultants.

(2) *Surface Systems*

Automation of water strip systems.

Matching flow rates and soil types.

Monitoring existing systems.

(3) *Sprinkler Systems*

Improving uniformities with computer estimates of sprinkler overlap patterns.

Use of some low intensity moving sprinkler systems (not the high intensity systems).

(4) *Trickle Irrigation*

Varying wetting patterns to suit soil types, either by changing to mini-sprinklers or by intermittent application of water.

(5) *Community Systems*

Lining open canals.

Providing a more constant supply to farmers.

(6) *Management*

Evapotranspiration estimates in newspapers.

Irrigation scheduling systems.

(ii) *Improving Effectiveness Through Greater Farmer Involvement*

The following two examples, one in Thailand (involving a New Zealand aid project) and the other in New Zealand, are illustrations of how irrigation developments are more likely to be successful if farmers are actively involved in the promotion and implementation of the schemes, compared with schemes which are imposed on farmers from outside.

The New Zealand-Thailand bilateral aid programme has helped to establish that small scale schemes built according to village needs and by village teams are very effective. They seem to be more beneficial than the large scale water distribution project with its attendant management, maintenance and social complications that often inhibit effective water use and add other disadvantages to displaced people.

The absence of water management problems on these small schemes and the high motivation of the farmers ensures a good rate of return on investment. Normally the material and plant costs can be recovered within two years of operation (reference 1).

In New Zealand, irrigation development is an activity which has grown into a partnership between government and the farmers. It has not always been so — early developments were still treated as essentially a public work with little reference at the time to farmers' needs and expectations. The combination of farmers having limited knowledge of irrigation, a natural conservation, and a lack of prior commitment to take advantage of the scheme, resulted in slow utilisation of irrigation facilities and inefficient operation.

Now, however, there is a changed approach to irrigation development. Farmers are actively involved in the promotion and implementation of a scheme, and farm advisory services are increasing farmers' awareness and knowledge of the changes in farm management which will be possible and necessary with irrigation. Schemes are also subject to majority (at least 60 per cent) approval by the farmers concerned prior to construction. If approved, all farmers within the boundary of the scheme are required by law to pay annual charges for their share of the off-farm works, whether they use water or not, and those who do irrigate are required to pay charges to offset the full cost of operation and maintenance (reference 2).

References

1. UNESCO: Proposed Regional Project: Southeast Asia and Pacific: Rational Use and Conservation of Water Resources. Report from MWD to NZ Commission for UNESCO. 31 August 1983.

2. Improvement of Irrigation System Engineering and Management — New Zealand Country Paper. Agenda item no 4, ESCAP meeting on measures to improve the performance of irrigation projects. 26 May — 2 June 1981, Bangkok.

VII. PHILIPPINES

VII. A. MULTI-DISCIPLINARY AND SYSTEM APPROACH TO INTEGRATED RIVER BASIN DEVELOPMENT

This concept has been applied in some of the major river basin development projects in Bicol Area and Cotabato-Agusan, large scale multi-purpose water resources development projects, like Magat and Pantabangan and in the Water Supply and Flood Control Masterplans in Metro Manila. The techniques applied in these projects and their degree of sophistication vary with the scope, the objective and complexity of the problem. More often sophisticated techniques like computers and physical modelling are hampered by data constraints and costs.

Other limitations are due to expertise, institutional and/or social problems.

Almost all of the projects were undertaken or assisted by foreign experts or foreign consultancy firms and were partly financed by foreign institutions and/or UN bodies. Local technical expertise have been enhanced through the experience from working closely with consultants and from the training programmes/fellowships usually obtained with the technical assistance.

One of the essential elements of the approach is co-ordination. Integrated planning precludes interlinking water sector with other sectors in the economy and involved various disciplines and organizational structures. Linkages with other sectors are effected through several ways; legislations, interlocking Board of Directors or councils of government agencies, collaborative arrangements through the conduct of interagency work, multipartite meetings, public hearings and other modes of forum for thrashing out issues of immediate concern.

Some examples of institutional mechanisms instituted to effect co-ordination in the water sector are as follows:

1. the establishment of the National Water Resources Council, which is the body responsible for integrating and co-ordinating all water resources development activities in the country.

2. the creation of Task Forces special types of bodies formed to lay the groundwork for the implementation of special projects.

3. For major multi-purpose projects, a technical review or steering committee is formed to monitor progress of the project, review and evaluate the work done, provide advisory services and facilitate co-ordination among project proponents.

4. the adoption of a "lead" agency concept wherein the agency with most influence in the project is tasked with spearheading project development and implementation.

With regards to the problem on data availability — the government is stepping up rehabilitation and development of hydrologic and groundwater observation networks to improve data collection efficiency. Anticipating the bulk of data to be stored once the network becomes fully operational, a system of storage and retrieval of data has been developed. This computer-based system known as PAWIS (Philippine Automated Water Information System) is under the auspices of the Council.

Resource assessment studies are likewise instituted to ascertain the magnitude of water resources available for future developments. Extensive studies on groundwater availability is emphasized because it is an area where data is scarce and because it is an essential factor in rural water supply planning.

VII. B. ASSESSMENT AND CONSIDERATION OF IRRIGATION EFFICIENCY IN THE IRRIGATED AREAS OF THE ESCAP REGION

In the Philippine setting, the overall assessment of irrigation efficiency of the national systems was about 65 per cent as of 1982.

1. Problems/causes

a. One of the major problems in these systems is siltation. The two main sources of silt are soil erosion and mine tailings. Soil erosion is accelerated by improper land

use such as the extensive practice of "Kaingin"* agriculture, unsound logging, illegal cuttings, improper road construction, uncontrolled grazing and forest fires. On the other hand, silt materials from mining operation may result as a consequence of surface excavation which includes ore

---

* Kaingin is a form of shifting cultivation through indiscriminate clearing of vegetation from hillsides by cutting and/or by burning.

extraction, road construction and sites for project facilities and mill tailings. Mine wastes even adds to the deterioration of the quality of irrigation water thereby causing reductions in yield.

Damages caused by siltation in the irrigation systems are classified into: losses due to silting of canals, reduction in crop yields and service areas, and losses in irrigation fee collection which is very much tied up to yields.

Silt deposited in irrigation canals requires removal several times during the irrigation season. The silt is mainly deposited near the main points of delivery, thus building up ground surfaces until releveling of the field becomes necessary. The silt in the paddies caused cementing action on the soil as well, resulting in the stunted growth of crops.

Wastes produced by mining operations produce a slight toxicity to plant and animal life and inhibit normal plant growth and yield.

The reduction in yields results in a significant direct loss not only to the farmers in affected areas but also to NIA due to the difficulty in collecting irrigation fees.

b. The mismatch of design and operation criteria also was found to impede efficiency in the management of water in the field.

Design and operation of the irrigation systems in the Philippines refer to either an *intensive* or an *extensive* model. In the intensive design and operation concept, the system is provided with complete structures and facilities to allow full control of water from source down to the last land unit receiving a measured flow, which is about 10 hectares in size and is commonly called the rotation unit. This method requires that water delivery in the required amount will be made continuously to the turnout and that farmers will be organized to effectively share the water following the rotation method of water distribution. For the extensive concept, the water control is in the main system only meaning it stops at the turnout. Water allocation from the main canal to the different lateral canals, or allocation within the different sections of a lateral canal, may be made in turn or by rotation. The farmers shall follow a simultaneous or a demand method of water distribution.

The intensive concept of irrigation systems design, and operation was adopted in most of the large national system (about 68 per cent of the total systems followed this concept). However, it was observed that rotational irrigation method as conceived originally was hardly practiced by the farmer beneficiaries (only 13 per cent of the farms used the rotational method). Consequently a number of operational problems surfaced i.e. problems of canal capacity and adequate head for all turnouts. Also it resulted in inefficient

and highly inequitable water use. Some farmers closer to the supply canal exploit their locational advantage by constructing illegal turnouts at the expense of downstream farmers.

c. Another common problem of systems is the high level of water losses i.e. farm waste, farm ditch and conveyance losses, due to seepage, percolation and leakage in the paddy dikes, canals and laterals. Farm losses are high due to the poor maintenance of the paddy dikes and spillways and the non-co-operation of farmers in maintaining the systems. The farm ditch and conveyance losses are affected by the poor maintenance of the control gates and illegal diversions. This also results in an uneven water distribution with a shortage of water realized at the tail section.

d. Efficiency is also hampered by inaccurate and inadequate hydro-meteorological data, rainfall forecasting difficulty and lack of trained and skilled manpower.

2. Mitigating measures/solutions

In general, the programmes/measures being pursued by the Philippines to improve efficiency of irrigation systems are:

a. *On Sedimentation Problems*

(i) Desilting of canals and rehabilitation of existing facilities.

(ii) The development of control structures at farm level i.e. settling basin, turnout regulation and a combination of both.

(iii) The development of more tailing control measures i.e. river rerouting, retaining dam, impounding basin. This problem is also given due consideration at the feasibility stage of project development and incorporated in recent irrigation plans.

(iv) Reforestation of watersheds is being implemented extensively.

b. *On Design*

(i) The design criteria for farm level facilities are being revised to consider acceptability to the farmers, durability as well as economics, facility in management, efficiency in water distribution and application and flexibility to different irrigation schemes and farming practices.

(ii) Development of irrigation service improvement programmes which specify among others, the strengthening of viable irrigator groups for the O & M responsibilities of the systems.

c. *On water losses*

   (i) Lining of canals and laterals

   (ii) Proper maintenance of systems and paddy dikes

   (iii) Close supervision and patrolling of canals and control gates

   (iv) Campaign for the co-operation of the farmer/irrigators/water users.

VII. C. ACTIVITIES RELATED TO THE IMPLEMENTATION OF THE MAR DE PLATA ACTION PLAN

1. Policy and Planning

a. *Shared Water Resources Development*

   (i) The State requires that all water resources development projects be undertaken on a multi-purpose concept using the river basin or closely related basin's approach. Single-purpose projects shall only be implemented when they are compatible with the multi-purpose concept and can be incorporated into the contemplated basin-wide development programme.

   (ii) In the selection of water resources programmes, considerations are given to the depressed and deprived regions/areas which have lagged behind in development compared to other regions/areas. Thus, multi-purpose projects on an integrated area development concept are preferred. This consists of providing a package of complementary projects. Since implementation of individual projects are undertaken by different agencies, co-ordination for the delivery of the package of projects is entrusted to a lead agency chosen from among the various implementing agencies.

b. *National Water Resources Planning*

Recently; there has been a shift in the national policy of the government towards the following: i) accelerated development of indigeneous hydro and geothermal resources to significantly reduce the country's reliance on fuel-oil in power production; and ii) increased emphasis on the provision of water supply and sanitation services to rural communities (where the need is particularly extensive) in conjunction with the resolution of the "International Drinking Water Supply and Sanitation Decade."

2. Water Resources Development Activities in the 1980's

a. *Framework Planning*

On the basis of the policy of the State to conduct water resources development projects on a multi-purpose

d. *Others*

   (i) A current programme on the installation of additional hydrometeorological stations which is being co-ordinated with the existing weather forecasting agency.

   (ii) Acceleration of training programmes for irrigation personnel and farmer-clientele.

   (iii) Strengthening the institutional mechanism i.e. the irrigators associations, to cope with problems in the farm level, e.g. collection of irrigation fees and resolution of conflicts.

concept using the river basin or closely related basin's approach, the NWRC as a co-ordinating agency for water resources development activities undertook the preparation of reconnaissance type of framework planning studies on a regional and basin-wide development from 1979-1980. This project received funding support from UNDP. The studies were intended to provide an assessment of the existing water resources in the region/basin to determine its capacity to meet projected demand requirements of the area up to year 2000. On the whole, there were 41 basins and 12 water resources regional framework studies that were prepared corresponding to the 41 basins in 12 water resources regions that were identified.

b. *Sectoral Water Resources Development Activities*

   (i) *Water Supply and Rural Sanitation*

As of May 1980, the population served by water supply systems comprised 53 per cent of the country's total population: 36 per cent in the rural areas and 64 per cent for Metro Manila and other urban areas. The level of public investment expenditures on water supply averaged at about ₱801 million annually in 1980-1981, a marked improvement from the average annual investment levels of ₱139 million in 1975-1979. However, 80 per cent of these investments in the sector still went to urban centres particularly in Metro Manila.

In the field of rural sanitation, of the 7 million households, only 52.9 per cent were equipped with sanitary toilets, 27.3 per cent were with unsanitary toilets and 19.3 per cent with no toilets at all.

Following the formulation of the integrated Water Supply Programme (1980-2000) in July 1980, a more detailed planning document was prepared for the rural water sector known as the *Rural Water Supply and Sanitation Masterplan*. The Plan focuses on specific policies, targets and action programmes related to the provision of water supply and sanitation services to rural communities.

(ii) Power

Hydro and geothermal power component of the power industry currently account for only about 41 per cent with 59 per cent of the annual power demand met from oil based power generation. Since some hydropower projects are so capital-intensive with long gestation period, mini-hydropower plants are being developed. So far, NEA has installed 3 power stations through 1981. At the end of 1982, there are 12 power plants nearing completion.

(iii) Irrigation

NIA undertook the repair and rehabilitation of 53,918 hectares of areas already covered by existing systems, and generated some 72,426 hectares of new areas, bringing to about 1,400,000 hectares the total area with irrigation facilities in the country as of December 1982. It has completed the ₱3.3 B Magat Dam, the biggest single infrastructure project in the Philippines and in Southeast Asia. About 80,000 hectares of the targeted irrigation component of 100,000 ha under the Magat River Multi-purpose Project are now being served. Likewise several irrigation projects were constructed in Mindanao, namely: the Davao Irrigation Projects II and III, the Agusan Irrigation Projects I and II, Pulangui River Irrigation Project, Tago River Irrigation Project, Bukidnon Irrigation and Allah River Irrigation Project. These projects have a total irrigable area of 98,754 hectares when completed. NIA also has improved the facilities and expanded the irrigable areas of the existing systems under the National Irrigation System Improvement (NISIP I and II), as well as the reforestation of 5,120 hectares of the land at the Pantabangan and Magat Watershed Areas.

Under the FSDC, 15 projects were completed servicing 8,388.2 hectares tilled by farmers nationwide. Furthermore, in terms of Small Irrigation Systems, 7 projects were completed servicing a total of 1,999.7 hectares of farm lands.

(iv) Flood Control

The major flood prone areas in the country consists of about 1.3 M hectares where 10.3 M people live. A study made in 1977 indicates an average annual loss of about ₱98.4 M. The bulk of the flood control activities is concentrated in Metro Manila. About 20 per cent of the total area susceptible to flooding nationwide has been afforded flood protection measures. All of the Flood Protection measures employ structural devices such as dikes, channel improvements and detention reservoirs. In the countryside, the MPWH has completed a total of 469 protective structures.

As of the end of 1982, the MPWH has completed a total of 216 projects while 86 projects are on-going. The newly completed ₱370.70 M Napindan Hydraulic Control

Structure in Pasig is expected to minimize flooding in the Metro Manila area. Similarly for, the on-going Mangahan Floodway Projects slated for completion on early 1984.

There are at present 10 major flood control schemes nationwide under implementation, foremost of these are the Metro Manila Flood Control and drainage plan, the Agno and the Pampanga Flood Control System. For the Agno River Control System, 8 projects were practically completed, under the Pampanga River Control System 56 projects were completed and 18 are partially completed.

Complementing the flood control measures is the extensive implementation of the SWIM projects which aims to avert destructive floods upstream as well as to utilize the reservoirs for various uses such as irrigation, fisheries, power generation and soil erosion control. As of December 1982, some 456 projects had been identified. The status of the projects is as follows:

a) Completed/under construction — 53
b) Scheduled for construction — 137
c) Under Investigation and Study — 70
d) Identified for future Investigation and Study — 196

Total — 456

c. Sectoral Water Resources Development Activity Targets

(i) Water Supply and Rural Sanitation

The target set for the rural water supply sector includes the attainment of 85 per cent service coverage in year 2000 through the provision of some 210,900 water supply systems (Levels I to III), equivalent to an investment of about ₱12,300 M. As for rural sanitation, the target involves the installation of 371,000 units of sanitary toilets and the rehabilitation of about 3.4 M existing units up to year 1990. The corresponding investment for the programme will amount to about $216 M at the end of 1990.

(ii) Power

With the continuing oil crisis, the national power programme calls for the acceleration of the development of indigenous hydro and geothermal resources for power production. The NPC programme complemented by the NEA, NIA and FSDC mini-hydro programmes aims to increase the share of hydro and geothermal power generation to 31 per cent and 21 per cent respectively or a total of 52 per cent by 1987. The total investment requirement for the programme would consists of about ₱26.9 B for the large hydro-power plants, ₱3.2 B for mini-hydro, and ₱16.1 B for geothermal plants.

(iii) *Irrigation*

The irrigation development thrust of NIA for this year aims to generate an additional area of about 110,000 hectares, including 25,000 hectares under the communal systems with an appropriated 85,000 hectares under the national systems. Among the major irrigation projects are the Magat, Cagayan Integrated and the Chico Projects in the Cagayan Valley; Palsiguan Irrigation Project in Ilocos Norte; Tarlac system improvement and groundwater development in Central Luzon, Laguna de Bay development and Mindoro/Palawan Medium-Scale projects in Southern Tagalog; Bicol River Basin Development; Jalaur River Project in Panay; Agusan, Bukidnon, Davao, Surigao, Zamboanga and Allah Valley Projects in Mindanao; and the Nationwide Irrigation Systems improvement Project. Complementing the NIA projects is the FSDC irrigation programme which aims to cover about 40,000 hectares.

(iv) *Flood Control*

Efforts to minimize loss of lives, damages to crops and property due to yearly floodings necessitate the construction of various protection structures. For these, the MPWH will continue with the completion of the Mangahan Floodway. This will include the completion of drainage mains, outfalls and laterals to service critical areas and complemented by dredging of rivers, esteros and other waterways in Metro Manila Area. In the countryside, flood control activities will centre on major river basins which consist of downstream projects — extensive dredging of critical rivers, construction of levees, channels and drainage facilities. A back-up support will be the upstream works to include some 35 small impounding water reservoirs all over the country and 7 sabo (erosion) dams in the Mayon Volcano area and the Zambales mountains. Likewise, drainage of schistosomiasis — endemic areas will also be undertaken.

3. Assessment of Water Resources

a. *Rapid Assessment of Water Supply Sources*

From June to August 1981, the NWRC in co-ordination with NHRC prepared a rapid assessment of Philippine groundwater resources based on readily available data. The report which came in 73 volumes, one for each of the 73 provinces of the Philippines contained information like the groundwater map showing the areal extent of groundwater areas for shallow well and deep well developments and delineation of difficult areas for groundwater development. Based on the safe yield concept an assessment was made of the carrying capacities of resources in terms of well development as well as the well requirements based on the demand considerations. The study indicated that the country has more than enough groundwater resources to

meet demand for year 2000 and that aereal extent suitable for tubewell development is about 50 per cent of the total area.

b. *National Survey of Existing Water Supply Sources and Facilities*

The project was commissioned by MPWH to MLG in August to September 1981 for the purpose of establishing base information necessary in determining the quantity and type of water supply facilities in every barangay.

c. *Nationwide Groundwater Resources Investigation Survey*

Providing further refinements to existing information on groundwater availability, a geo-resistivity survey was undertaken by NWRC in co-operation with NHRC from September 1981 to December 1982. Unlike in the rapid assessment, the results of the resistivity survey indicate the approximate areas of high yielding and low-yielding aquifers as well as the areal extent of salt-water encroachment. It also provides contours of water depth below the natural ground surface.

4. Emerging Water Problems

In spite of the significant headway in water resources development in terms of physical facilities as well as informational and technological gains, brought about by the remarkable support extended by the government, there persists a number of water related problems. Among these are:

a. Expanding economic activities increasingly strain available water supplies in some regions.

b. Some natural resources lie untapped, and opportunities for employment and economic expansion are unrealized because of deficient or uncontrolled water resources.

c. Floods still plague many watersheds and developed downstream areas in the country.

d. Erosion from rural and developing urban areas continues to wash away our lands and choke streams and lakes with sediments.

e. Organic and chemical wastes from our industrialized society threaten the usefulness of streams, lakes and estuaries.

f. Overpumping in some highly developed areas shortens the useful life of the groundwater reservoir due to rapid decline of groundwater level and salt water intrusion and causes land subsidence.

g. Conflicts are widening between the need to develop water resources and to preserve the natural quality of water-related environment.

5. Policy Study Areas

In terms of the country's major functional needs, the above water related problems and issues could very well be considered priority areas for policy studies. These are as follows:

a. *Municipal and Industrial Water Supply*

Planning and implementation of water supply facilities to accomodate future growth and critical water-shortage periods.

Efficient operation and maintenance of water supply facilities.

Identification of alternative means of developing various water supply.

b. *Irrigation*

Reducing irrigation water losses through improved water management.

Maximization of water use and rainfall through improved cultural practices.

Reducing the adverse impact of irrigation water use on competing or conflicting water use.

c. *Hydroelectric Power*

Optimization of hydroelectric power production while accomodating competing water uses.

Minimization of adverse impact of streamflow and stream level fluctuation on other water use.

Development and utilization of mini-hydro projects.

d. *Flood Control*

Identification and characterization of flood prone and drainage problem areas.

Reducing susceptibility to flood loss and damage through both structural and non-structural measures.

6. In the context of the rural water Supply programme of the government, inasmuch as it is a major undertaking for this present decade, several research and development activities have been identified wherein opportunities for technical co-operation among countries can be tapped.

a. *Technical Research*

(i) *Selection of appropriate drilling equipment*

The intention is to be able to choose the type of drilling rig which is best suited to the needs of the provinces, which can be easily manufactured locally and which is easy and less costly to operate and maintain.

(ii) *The evaluation of the PVC screens and casings*

The use of PVC screens and casings for wells is a relatively new development in this area and in this country. There is a felt need to evaluate its performance in the field and its safety.

(iii) *The use of ferro-cement water tanks*

This is a low cost technology which is already adopted in countries like Thailand, Indonesia and some of the Pacific Islands. Its prospects for introduction in this country can be explored.

b. *Socio-economic research*

(i) *Structural Model to predict Household capacity to pay*

The intention is to be able to come up with a predictive model for determining the capacity to pay, of the rural communities which is less cumbersome and time consuming. Determining real incomes of rural families can be difficult considering that most of the basic needs are not obtained from the markets. Studies in the correlation of incomes to parameters which are easily recognizable like housing structures is desired in this regard.

(ii) *Institutional Research*

The performance of RWSA's have yet to be evaluated. So far observations of their effectiveness in operating systems varied from good to bad. It is best to learn at this early stage the reasons for their successes and failures. A study on the strengths of the RWSA concept and its weaknesses will help in strengthening the water supply programme.

VIII. SRI LANKA

A. ACTIVITIES RELATED TO IMPLEMENTATION OF MARDEL PLATA ACTION PLAN

1. Proposed Water Management Programme in Major Irrigation Schemes

The study on the proposed Water Management programme in major irrigation Schemes in Sri Lanka was undertaken by CH 2M HILL, a U.S. Consulting firm under contract to the USAID. The purpose of the study was to define the details of a programme of assistance to the Government of Sri Lanka to improve water management in major irrigation and settlement schemes in the dry zone. The team pointed out that almost all the schemes operate much below their designated capacities due to poor water control and concluded that the potential economic and social benefits to be reaped from improved water management are immense. The following unfavourable aspects have been identified in the report as leading to the prevailing situation.

a) Scarce resources are diverted to the completion of new construction projects rather than to proper operation and maintenance of existing schemes;

b) Low priority given to operation and maintenance;

c) Lack of training in water management for officials;

d) Inadequate attention given to operational requirements at the designs stage;

e) Extravagant use of water by farmer and lack of effective farmer organisation;

The following needs have been recommended by the report for the improvement of Water Management in irrigation schemes;

a) Physical rehabilitation and improvement, including the installation of control and measurement devices;

b) Increased attention to Operation and Management responsibility for the system;

c) Master planning for the recycle of return flows and cost benefit analysis;

d) Plan for domestic water;

e) Up-grading Galgamuwa Irrigation Training Institute to become the premier institution for training learners and other staff for irrigation management in combination with foreign training;

f) Improved central support from the Department of Irrigation in Colombo;

g) A research development process for institutional development.

It was estimated that the proposed programme would have an economic rate of return of 11.2 to 20.6 per cent.

2. Irrigation Department Options and Investment Strategies for the 1980s

This study was conducted as a part of the Water Management Synthesis project. The team consisted of a multi-disciplinary group of foreign and local personnel and the study was conducted during the period June 6-26, 1982.

Summary and Recommendations

The substantive end of the engineering phase of Sri Lanka's development programme is in sight. But the need to make these massive investments useful and productive in the future will not be met automatically.

Problems in the Irrigation sector will be magnified as irrigation expansion proceeds.

Role of irrigation in the agricultural sector, the weakness of institutional and legal base for management and effective farmer participation and the focus on inputs rather than on outputs may combine to lower the utility of this enterprise of the Government. Substantive changes in Government policy may be necessary along with significant changes in the Ministry or department perspectives and organisations.

The financial costs associated with this phase will be small. The need for political commitment, for intellectual openness, and for bureaucratic flexibility will be high.

a) The implication of major government agricultural policies must be evaluated in terms of their impact on the utility of the current and planned irrigation development;

b) Alternative policies need to be evaluated in relation to the balance between paddy and other crops through crop diversification and options for reducing high fertilizer consumption;

c) During the past ten years, approximately half of the increased production in irrigated area has come from increased yields per ha. (per acre) and half from expanded areas. Implication of agricultural support systems, bias towards paddy mono-crop and the possible changes should be evaluated;

d) Farmers are not only a part of the irrigation problem, but an essential part of the solutions as well. Institutions should be researched and formulated to foster their participation in groups and facilitate conflict resolutions; farmer participation should involve both responsibility and authority;

e) To make land and water resources more productive irrigation capability should turn towards operation, maintenance, rehabilitation, greater recognition of agricultural factors in the engineering process and evolving a more pragmatic approach for structural repair and improvement;

f) Multi-disciplinary approaches and organisation should be developed within the agencies responsible for design, rehabilitation and operation of the project;

g) An output oriented management approach should receive greater emphasis as opposed to administration.

3. Investment Programme — 1983-87

The investment programme of the Ministry, proposes an investment of Rs. 4,594 million in the irrigation sector and Rs. 1,513 million in the forestry and land section for the period 1983-87.

Table 95 shows the details of the investment as accepted by National Planning Division of the Ministry of Finance and Planning. In addition to the on-going projects and annual works, three new projects, namely, Nilwala Ganga Flood Protection Project, the Forestry Resources Development Project and the Nelu Oya Diversion Scheme, have been identified in the investment programme for implementation in 1983. A total of Rs. 979 million and Rs. 214 million have been set aside for other new projects in the irrigation and forestry and land sectors respectively.

Table 95. Medium term investment programme 1983-87: Ministry of Lands & Land Development

	Donor Agency	1983	1984	1985	1986	1987	Total
1. Other Irrigation (Rs. million)							
On-Going							
1. Five Tank Rehabilitation	IDA	45	–	–	–	–	45
2. Village Tanks Rehabilitation	IDA	75	150	175	200	150	750
3. Kirindi Oya Res.	ADB/IFAD/KFW	200	350	350	340	40	1 280
4. Inginimitiya Res.	OECD	80	80	70	16	–	246
5. Gal Oya W.M.	USAID	61	80	80	44	–	265
6. Gin Ganga FPS	CHINA	10	–	–	–	–	10
7. Medium Size Works	–	60	36	–	–	–	96
New							
1. Nelu Oya Diversion	EEC	7	6	–	–	–	13
2. Nilwala Ganga FPS	FRANCE	5	25	75	150	250	505
Annual							
1. Flood Damage		25	12	14	16	18	85
2. Water Managements		8	5	4	3	2	22
3. Investigations		2	2	2	3	4	13
4. Imp. to Major Works		16	10	4	4	6	40
5. Lower Uva Dev.		8	8	6	6	6	34
6. Maintenance of Vehicles		2	2	3	3	3	13
7. Vehicles		4	–	2	–	2	8
8. Buildings		10	10	10	10	10	50
9. RVDB		–	35	35	35	35	140
10. New Projects		–	20	75	289	595	979
TOTAL		618	831	907	1 119	1 119	4 594

Table 95 *(continued)*

Donor Agency	1983	1984	1985	1986	1987	Total
1. Forestry & Lands (Rs. million)						
On-Going						
1. N.W. Region Ground Water UK.ODA	2	7	–	–		9
2. Agricultural Base Mapping USAID	5	5	5	5	5	25
3. SL/Swiss Satellite Imagery SWITZERLAND	1	2	2	2	2	9
4. Land & Water Conservation Fuel-Wood & Forestry Extension USAID	68	70	60	13	3	214
5. Sinha Raja & M & B etc. –	1	2	2	3	3	11
6. Forestry Inventory UNDP	6	5	2	2	2	17
7. Community Forestry ADB	35	46	46	56	65	248
New						
1. Forest Resources Development IDA/FINLAND	5	30	58	72	71	236
Annual						
1. Land Reclamation Board	38	11	12	13	14	88
2. Water Resource Board	3	5	5	6	6	25
3. Acquisition of Lands	30	30	25	20	20	125
4. Land Development Department	3	3	3	3	3	15
5. Land Commissioner's Department	32	35	40	41	41	189
6. Government Factory	1	1	1	1	1	5
7. Dept. of Machinery & Equipment	1	2	2	2	2	9
8. Survey Department	1	2	2	2	2	9
9. Forest Department		1	1	1	1	4
10. Reforestation of Neglected Tea, etc.	2	3	4	4	5	18
11. Reforestation & Development	3	10	10	10	10	ʾ43
12. Provision for New Projects			20	90	104	214
TOTAL	237	270	300	346	360	1 513

Table 96 shows the details of the investment and phasing of 24 additional new projects identified for implementation by the Ministry over the next five year period. Of these projects, the Land Use Planning and the Settlement Training Projects funded by the UNDP are also expected to commence in 1983. The majority of the other projects are scheduled for commencement in 1985.

The Colombo City Drainage Project costing Rs. 300 million will be undertaken with the resources generated by the Sri Lanka Land Reclamation and Development Corporation. The Puttalam City Drainage Project will be undertaken with funds provided under the Puttalam District Integrated Rural Development Project. The investments for these projects are, therefore, not reflected in the Investment Programme of the Ministry of Lands & Land Development (Table 96). The total Estimated Cost of the 8 Projects identified in the Irrigation Sector is Rs. 3,000 million approximately. Fifteen projects identified in the Forestry and Land Sector are estimated to cost Rs. 1,800 million approximately. This includes an investment of Rs. 1,200 million for the Lower Uva Development Projects for Forestry and Settlement and Plan Management.

A brief description of the new projects identified by the Ministry is provided below. Detailed project reports will be prepared by each of the concerned agencies and submitted for approval by government before they are formally included in the Investment Programme. Government will also make an effort to obtain foreign assistance for projects acceptable to donors.

a.   *Irrigation and Drainage Projects*

(i)   *Major Irrigation Rehabilitation Project (Irrigation Department)*

The project envisages the physical rehabilitation of 9 major irrigation schemes in the Northern and Eastern

Regions of the Country. The objective of the rehabilitation will be to improve Water Management and increase productivity and farmer incomes in the schemes. Investigations have been undertaken in the following 9 schemes of which at least 8 are expected to be selected for rehabilitation: Giants Tank, Iranamadu, Nachchaduwa, Rajangana, Huruluwewa, Kantalai, Mora Wewa, Parakrama Samudra and Thannimurippu.

The total cost of the project will be in the region of Rs. 840 million ($ US 40 million), of which Rs. 630 million ($ US 30 million) is expected as a loan fom the IDA. The project will benefit about 40,500 ha. (100,000 ac) of irrigated lands and 40,000 farm families. As a result of improved water management, the cropping intensity in these schemes is expected to increase by about 15-25 per cent. The project is expected to commence in 1984 and will be phased out over a five-year period. The project is under preparation by a FAO/World Bank Co-operative Programme Mission. Appraisal and final negotiations are expected to be completed by mid 1984.

(ii) *Water Management Project II (Irrigation Department)*

This will be a sequel to the Gal Oya Water Management Project. This will be phase II of the above project which is expected to take up about 5 to 6 major irrigation works in the east and south east parts of Sri Lanka, for rehabilitation and water management. The project is expected to commence in 1986 and will stress the institutional build-up and farmer participation in rehabilitation and water management.

The total cost of the project is expected to be in the region of Rs. 650 million of which Rs. 500 million will be funded as loan by USAID. The Project will be phased over a 5 to 6 year period.

(iii) *Kirindi Oya Phase II (Irrigation Department)*

The second phase of Kirindi Oya, to take up balance of the revised programme will commence at the end of Phase I in 1985. Phase II will be for down-stream development of 4,200 ha. and the settlement of 4,200 farm families, the development of 15 hamlets and 2 village centres. The total cost of Phase II is expected to be in the region of Rs. 500 million.

(iv) *Nilwala Ganga Project (Irrigation Department)*

The Nilwala Ganga Flood Protection Project will provide protection to 9,786 acres of agricultural and flood prone lands in the Kiralakele basin of the Nilwala Ganga. The total cost of the project is Rs. 1,114 million. A Phase I

Table 96. Ministry of Lands and Land Development, proposed new projects 1983-87, phasing of investments

Project	T.E.C.#	Possible Funding Agency	Implementing Agency	1984		1985		1986		1987		Total	
				T†	FA¶	T	FA	T	FA	T	FA	T	FA
1. Irrigation Sector (Rs. million)													
1. Major Irrigation Rehabilitation Project	840	IDA	ID	20	15	50	30	140	100	220	160	430	305
2. Water Management Proj. Phase II	650	USAID	ID	–	–	–	–	40	30	70	50	110	80
3. Medium Scale Irrigation Rehabilitation	400	IFAD	ID	–	–	15	10	43	30	120	80	178	120
4. Lower Uva Irrigation Devp't Projects	600	CIDA	ID	–	–	–	–	50	35	104	65	154	100
5. Kirindi Oya Phase II	500	ADB	ID	–	–	–	–	–	–	60	40	60	40
6. Water Resources Planning Project	20	UNDP	M/L&LD	–	–	3	2	5	4	7	6	15	12
7. Ground Water Exploration	20	Not Identified	WRB	–	–	3	2	5	3	6	4	14	9
8. Expansion of Facilities of Training Inst. Galgamuwa	25	UNDP	ID	–	–	4	3	6	5	8	6	18	14
TOTAL				20	15	75	47	289	207	595	411	978	680

#, †, ¶: See footnote at end of Table.

Table 96 *(continued)*

Project	T.E.C.#	Possible Funding Agency	Implementing Agency	1983 T†	1983 FA¶	1984 T	1984 FA	1985 T	1985 FA	1986 T	1986 FA	1987 T	1987 FA	Total T	Total FA
2. Forestry & Land Sector (Rs. million)															
1. Land Use Planning	4.7	UNDP	M/L&LD	3.7	3.3	1	0.6	—	—	—	—	—	—	4.7	3.9
2. Settlement Training	6.6	UNDP	"	3.7	2.3	2.9	1.5	—	—	—	—	—	—	6.6	—
3. Dry Farming Settlements	42.0	Not identified	LCD	—	—	—	—	10	—	10	—	12	—	32	—
4. Upgrading Agricultural Roads	30.0	"	LCD	—	—	—	—	6	—	6	—	6	—	18	—
5. Lower Uva Development															
a. Forestry	246.0	"	LUFDC	—	—	—	—	—	—	30	20	30	20		
b. Rainfed Settlements	810.0	"	LCD	—	—	—	—	—	—	25	15	25	15		
c. Plan Management	113.0	"	M/L&LD	—	—	—	—	—	—	5	—	10	—	15	—
6. Watershed Management	25.0	"	WRB/FD	—	—	—	—	5	2	5	2	5	2	15	6
7. Forest Protection and Enforcement	6.4	"	FD	—	—	—	—	2.5	2	2.5	2	1.4	—	6.4	4
8. Forest Education and Training	21.4	"	FD	—	—	—	—	6	4	6	2	4	1	16	7
9. Coastal Shelterbelts and Sand dune affores.	28.0	"	FD	—	—	—	—	4	—	6	—	6	—	16	—
10. Colombo City Drainage	300.0 ☆	Corporation's own resources	SLLR & DC	—	—	75	—	75	—	75	—	75	—	300	—
11. Puttalam City Drainage	50.0 ☆	IDA & Puttalam IRDP	SLLR & DC	—	—	10	—	10	—	10	—	10	—	40	—
12. Muthurajawela Reclamation	50.0	Not identified	SLLR & DC	—	—	—	—	10	—	10	—	10	—	30	—
13. Expansion of the ISM	20.0	Not identified	SD	—	—	5	—	6	1.5	9	1.5	—	—	20	3
14. Expansion of the Map printing Division	5.0	"	SD	—	—	—	—	1.5	1.5	2	2	1	1	4.5	4.5
15. Expansion of the Investment Division		"	SD	—	—	—	—	2	2	2	2	1	1	5	5
16. Remote Sensing Programme	14.0	Switzerland	SD	—	—	—	—	3	2	4	2	6	4	3	8
TOTAL				7.4	5.6	93.9	2.1	141	15	152.5	13.5	202.4	44	597.2	80.2

#	Total Estimated Cost
†	Total
¶	Foreign Aid
☆	Funding by Corporation's own resources or from Projects complemented by other Ministries
LCD	Land Commissioner's Department
WRB	Water Resources Board
SD	Survey Department
LUFDC	Lower Uva Forestry Development Company
ID	Irrigation Department
M/L&LD	Ministry of Lands & Land Development
SLLRDC	Sri Lanka Land Reclamation & Development Corporation
ISM	Institute of Surveying and Mapping

costing Rs. 450 million, and protecting 4,918 acres, has been proposed initially to be undertaken with a loan of French Franc 100 million (Rs. 300 million) from the French Government.

(v) *Medium Scale Irrigation Project (Irrigation Department)*

This is a programme for the restoration and rehabilitation of Medium Scale Irrigation Projects. The project proposal has been submitted to IFAD requesting assistance for the project. The total cost is in the region of Rs. 400 million phased over a 5 year period.

(vi) *Ground Water Exploration (Water Resources Board)*

The Project is for the extension of Ground Water Investigations and Development throughout Sri Lanka. The total cost of the project is Rs. 20 million.

(vii) *Lower Uva Irrigation & Water Storage Project (Irrigation Department)*

The project envisages the construction of 5 medium scale irrigation reservoir projects in the southern part of the Lower Uva Region and the settlement of 12,300 farm families in the schemes. The new area irrigated under these 5 schemes will be 9,900 ha., while 1,800 ha., will be provided with additional water for yala. The total cost of the project is estimated at Rs. 1,400 million, at 1981 prices.

(viii) *Expansion of the Facilities at the Irrigation Training Institute Galgamuwa (Irrigation Department)*

The Project proposes to expand and improve the facilities at the Training Institute, in order to increase the intake and improve the quality of training at the Institute.

The total cost of the project is estimated at Rs. 25 million and is phased over a 5 year period. UNDP assistance has been requested for the project.

(ix) *Water Resources Planning Project (Ministry of Lands & Land Development)*

The project is for the establishment of a Secretariat for the proposed Water Resources Council, to be established under the Water Resources Act. The project envisages obtaining technical assistance, equipment, and funds for training of counterpart staff, for the proposed Secretariat, which will be involved in the preparation of comprehensive and integrated plans for the conservation, allocation, distribution, utilisation, control and development of all surface and ground water resources of the country.

The total cost of the project is estimated at Rs. 20 million and is phased over a 4 to 5 year period. UNDP assistance has been sought for the project.

4. Water Resources Planning and Watershed Management

The need for Water Resources Planning has been appreciated for sometime and was emphasized at the Land and Water Resources Development Conference of 1979. Although a great deal of useful work has been done by different agencies, the need to co-ordinate them statutorily was spelled out in the draft Water Resources Act. With the eanactment of the Act, the Water Resources Council comprising of Secretaries to the relevant Ministries and a Secretariat to service the Council will be established.

A Water Resources Planning project has been identified within the UNDP 3rd Country Programme to commence in 1984. The planning project will assist the Secretariat to develop methodology for setting up of systems of scientific analysis of data and policy relating to Water Resources.

Few initiatives in watershed management have been made so far although the need to stabilise the critical areas exposed to negative forms of land use have been identified for sometime.

The dilemma facing every administration to identify methodologies which could improve the carrying capacity of the resource base with the minimum disturbance to the communities making a living on it. In a country where the population is converged in ecologically sensitive areas, a successful watershed management programme would be one which could accommodate the needs of both nature and man and strike a happy balance. Such programmes and projects will be identified for early implementation.

5. Conclusion

Sri Lanka has an Irrigation Rate (ie. the Irrigated Paddy Area out of the total Paddy Area) — the highest in South Asia next to Pakistan. Out of 1.5 million acres of paddy land, over 500,000 acres is under major irrigation. This is the result of several decades of investment in irrigation as a conscious policy of Government. Rendering land irrigable is a costly investment. Nevertheless, with the wealth of experience available in this country and the available labour, it is more economical to do it today rather than tomorrow. Irrigation ensures stability in crop yields and farm incomes. It has been estimated, however, that with good water management coupled with supply of inputs, crop yields on irrigable lands could be doubled. Inspite of a high irrigation rate, our rice yields are nowhere near desired levels. Increased emphasis is, therefore, being placed on water management in the ensuing years, backed by a strong extension programme. USAID has agreed to assist us in this project. A Water Management Training Centre and an Educational Programme is an urgently felt need.

Rational exploitation and allocation of the potential water resources is another factor which should engage the attention of several Ministries. Water resources (both underground and surface) are now utilised for irrigation, power generation, community needs, inland fisheries and for industrial uses. Their proper allocation and quality control has to be monitored.

The need for a Water Resources Act to regulate and co-ordinate their allocation and water Courts to swiftly deal with offences relating to water, be it for irrigation or for community purposes, has been appreciated. The draft legis-

lation for this purpose will be presented by the government very soon.

Investigation, design and construction of irrigation works by their very nature takes time, require adequate technical resources, equipment, and adequate financing. If rapid development is to be achieved in minor and medium irrigation works, alongside the massive Mahaweli project, a massive mobilisation of resources, not only in the public sector as hitherto done, but in the private sector, both local and foreign, is necessary.

IX. THAILAND

IX. A. REVIEW OF IMPLEMENTATION OF THE MAR DEL PLATA ACTION PLAN

1. Water Resources Development Activities in Thailand

Introduction

Thailand lies in the tropical zone within the latitudes 6° and 21° N and longtitudes 98° and 106° E. The mainland lies within the central interior of the Indo-China Peninsula. The country is bounded in the north, west and east by several major mountain ranges of neighbouring countries, and in the south by the Gulf of Thailand. The Malay Peninsula, which separates the Gulf of Thailand from the Indian Ocean, forms the southern part of the country.

Thailand is a country of mild rivers, vast plains and mosly forest-covered mountains. The total land area is 514,000 square kilometers. The population at present is estimated at 50 millions, with its growth rate of 2.1 per cent the population of Thailand would reach 61 millions by the end of the next decade.

The climate of Thailand is governed by two monsoons, the northeast and southwest. The southwest monsoon or the rainy season, normally affecting the country from mid-May through early October, is predominant when atmospheric pressures are comparative low over Asia. The northeast monsoon, lasts from early November to mid-March, is predominant when pressures are comparatively high. These two monsoon currents are closely associated with atmospheric pressure conditions over the whole Asia and to a lesser degree with pressure conditions over Australia and the neighbouring oceans. The boundary zone between these flows is called the Equatorial Trough Zone (ETZ). The zone passes back and forth over the country several times during lulls and surges of the monsoon and passes over the area of low pressure systems. The extent of the weather depends upon the degree of convergence occur-

ring along the zone. The southwest is a period of heavy and frequent rainfall. Heavy rainfall is also expected from tropical storms originating in the South Pacific Ocean or the South China Sea.

The mean annual rainfall ranges from about 1,000 mm near Khon Kaen in the northeast to 4,000 mm on the windward slope near the gulf.

Generally, the flows of most rivers are highly concentrated during the southwest monsoon period, which contribute about 80 to 90 per cent of the annual flows. For a smaller stream, the flow during the southwest monsoon season may be as high as 95 per cent. The maximum annual flow of major river varies from 3 to 8 times greater than the minimum annual flow. Runoff yields in selected river basins are used in the estimation of mean annual supply of each water management division. Basic information of irrigated area in each water management division is shown in Table 97.

a. *Irrigation*

Irrigation, drainage, water conservation, flood control by embankment and land reclamation has been carried out over an area of 3,339,717 hectares in 1982. Work in progress covers an area of 480,222 hectares. Reservoirs already completed to the end of 1982 and operated by RID and EGAT are capable of storing 52,705 million m^3. This will help minimize floods over the cultivated areas downstream of the reservoirs, including highways, railways and towns located within the project area. Projects under construction are expected to store 14,684 million m^3 of water.

Pumping irrigation projects have been carried out over an area of 244,392 hectares by the Royal Irrigation Department and the National Energy Administration. There are

Table 97. Basic Information of an Irrigated Area in Each Water Management Division in 1981-1982

Water Management Division	Area (Km^2)	Length of Main Stream (km)	Rainfall (mm) Annual Total	Rainfall (mm) Monsoon Season	Population at end of 1982 (1)	Land Use (ha) (2) Farm Holding	Land Use (ha) (2) Planted	Land Use (ha) (2) Harvested	Irrigation (ha) (3) Irrigable	Irrigation (ha) (3) Irrigated	Storage ($10^6 m^3$) (4)	Estimated Annual Supply ($10^6 m^3$)	Estimated Irrigation Requirement ($10^6 m^3$)
Country	514 000		1 400	1 250	48 684 440	11 717 139	9 025 747	8 484 386	3 952 197	3 339 717	52 705.31	110 000	31 632
1. Chao Phya	177 500				18 392 286	3 615 495	2 712 388	2 606 593	1 982 103	1 749 205	23 047.35	43 450	
Ping	47 760	590	1 220	1 075	2 438 256	433 354	333 707	328 639	247 988	201 648	13 615.21	7 450	3 286
Wang	11 970	335	1 220	1 075	670 247	86 449	80 361	80 021	25 872	24 800	125.74	1 480	433
Yom	20 460	555	1 220	1 075	1 000 064	259 573	165 441	149 679	59 872	54 048	0.38	4 070	800
Nan	35 060	627	1 220	1 075	2 074 381	724 669	493 386	489 358	361 712	246 416	9 039.21	5 760	4 280
Mainstem	62 330	365	1 360	1 140	12 209 338	2 111 450	1 639 493	1 558 896	1 286 659	1 222 293	266.81	12 890	17 753
2. Chi-Mun	125 200		1 000-1 600	950-1 400	12 404 511	4 472 351	3 432 573	3 213 791	328 232	233 186	7 777.86	19 400	5 080
Chi	55 100	442			5 425 268	1 871 565	1 408 647	1 291 113	168 510	123 854	4 376.92	8 300	2 955
Mun	70 100	673			6 979 243	2 600 786	2 023 926	1 922 678	159 722	109 332	3 400.94	11 100	2 125
3. Mekhong	45 000		1 650	1 450	5 719 632	1 668 614	1 368 923	1 281 336	151 041	131 096	1 051.09	–	2 829
North					1 418 188	351 760	321 391	318 621	59 184	47 952	63.33	919	
Northeast					4 301 444	1 316 854	1 047 532	962 715	91 857	83 144	987.76	13 800	1 910
4. Bang Pakong	17 660	294	1 250	1 500	1 414 270	596 576	498 361	480 800	215 978	202 368 (5)	140.80	9 700	3 050
5. Mae Klong	32 600	140		1 100	2 316 003	324 773	206 769	203 236	444 880 (5)	269 595 (5)	17 801.30	15 250	5 042
Kwae Yai	14 630	450									(5)	5 400	
Kwae Noi	10 960	403									(5)	9 900	
6. Peninsula*			1 800-2 500		6 814 087	901 659	708 383	607 160	326 342	253 246	2 610.934		6 212
7. East Coast			1 300-2 900		1 623 651	137 671	98 350	91 470	36 872	34 272	275.98		

Remarks (1) Source : The National Economic and Social Development Board.
(2) Source : Agricultural statistics of Thailand, crop year 1981/82, Office of Agricultural Economics, Ministry of Agriculture and Co-operatives.
(3) Source : Water resources development in Thailand 1982-83, RID. Figures for country are large, medium and small scale irrigation projects, while figures in each water management division the small scale irrigation projects are excluded.
(4) Storage by reservoirs operated by RID and EGAT inclusive.
(5) Including irrigation area outside Mae Klong river basin.

178 pumping stations under construction and expected to complete in 1984 which can be used to irrigate an area of about 85,440 hectares. Most of the projects utilize surface water except an area of 1,024 hectares in Sukhothai province where ground water is utilized.

Dike and ditch project and land consolidation project completed in 1982 cover an area of 1,206,932 hectares and 104,791 hectares while 48,947 hectares and 13,978 hectares respectively are under construction.

The government agencies and their water resources development activities relating to irrigation are as follows:

The Royal Irrigation Department as shown in Table 98.

The National Energy Administration as shown in Table 99.

Accelerated Rural Development Office as shown in Table 100, Table 101 and Table 102.

b. *Hydroelectric power*

Hydroelectric power potential in Thailand has been continuously explored. The large size projects are mostly located in the mountainous regions of the north and western part of the central region. Up to date, one hundred project sites are identified with the estimated total potential of about 6,562 MW and 16,835 GWh of average annual electric energy.

At the present time, thirteen stations totalling 1,514.7 MW with the average annual energy of 4,232.1 GWh are in operation. The total catchment area of these hydroelectric dams is 70,459 km² and the average annual inflow of the dams is estimated at about 23,135 MCM.

Six projects totalling 741.8 MW with average annual energy of 1,456.3 GWh are under construction. Two projects are the generating units addition at the existing dams, Sirindhorn unit #3 12 MW and Srinagarind unit #4 reversible pumped turbine 180 MW. Three projects are the multi-purpose project dams, Khao Laem 300 MW, Chiew Larn 240 MW and Mae Ngat 9 MW. The other one is the mini hydro project, Ban Khun Klang 0.18 MW. The total catchment area is 6,450 km² with the estimated annual inflow of 8,616 MCM.

Two projects of 596.8 MW with average annual energy of 1,276.8 GWh are proposed to the government for construction. The first one is the turbine installation of 16.8 MW at the existing irrigation dam, Chao Phraya dam. The other one is the Nam Chon dam of 580 MW which has the catchment area of 4,908 km² with the estimated average annual inflow of 2,975 MCM. The dam site is proposed to be located at approximately 135 km upstream of Srinagarind dam.

At the present time, the projects which are in operation and under construction shall represent about 34 per cent of the total energy potential availability. By the year 1993, about 53 per cent of the nation's hydro potential will be exploited.

The inventory of international boundary rivers, namely Mekong and Salawin, shows that Thailand can share several hydro power projects of about 14,045 MW with neighbouring countries, particularly with Laos and Burma. Concerning Mekong river, several studies have been made by the Mekong Committee but no plan for implementation has been set yet. Concerning Salawin river, the desk studies of some projects have been prepared and they show very promising results. Future developments of international boundary river projects are of great interest. Thailand is willing to co-operate in such development and expects to see a successful international hydroelectric project in the south-east Asia Region.

Detail information of hydroelectric power in Thailand is presented in Appendix A.

c. *Domestic water supply*

Several Government Departments are responsible for the provision of domestic water systems to urban and rural areas. The Department of Health, Ministry of Public Health, constructs water systems in sanitary districts and village with population of up to 5,000. The Department of Public Works, Ministry of Interior, through its provincial Water Supply Division, is responsible for construction and controlling treatment plant of domestic water supply for provincial municipality, sanitary district and town with population over 5,000. The Metropolitan Water Works Authority (MWWA) is responsible for municipal water supply for Bangkok metropolitan areas which include Bangkok, Thonburi, Nonthaburi and Samut Prakan provinces.

The water supply systems obtain raw water from natural streams, irrigation canals, small reservoirs as well as from ground water. About 84 per cent of water supply, excluding Bangkok Metropolitan areas, utilizes surface water and 16 per cent from ground water.

Wells are drilled by the Department of Mineral Resources and the Department of Public Works. Extensive technological studies have also been undertaken.

Data for well drilling by the Department of Mineral Resources in years 1981 up to 1983 is shown in Table 103. Wells drilled by the Department of Public Works in year 1980 up to 1983 are shown in Table 104. Data for water supply concession is shown in Table 105.

2. Information and experience on measures taken specifically in response to the Mar del Plata Action Plan and the problems encountered in carrying out the recommendations of the United Nations Water Conference

a. *Assessment of water resources*

Hydrologic activities are the pre-requisites for water resources development and, in general, they are classified in three categories: Basic hydrologic data collection and processing are those which belong to the first category. The second includes the qualitative and quantitative analyses of data using scientific methods and engineering judgements to assess the water balance of hydrologic cycle. The third category involves the application of the basic data to water resources development and management.

The hydrologic investigation in Thailand had been started 152 years ago since 1831. A Royal staff gauge was installed at Ayutthaya City by King Nang Kao, Rama III to measure the maximum water level of the Chao Phraya River, the main source of water supply to the nation's largest plain, particularly for agriculture development purpose.

Later in 1950, the systematic hydrologic investigations were started to provide basic data needed for water resources development. At present, the networks for hydrological, meteorological and related data collection are operated by many government agencies in Thailand, such as the Royal Irrigation Department, the National Energy Administration, the Meteorological Department, the Electricity Generating Authority of Thailand, the Land Development Department, the Harbour Department, the Port Authority of Thailand, the Hydrographic Department, the Forestry Department, the Department of Health and the Industrial Works Department. The over-all hydrologic and meteorologic network in 1983 is shown in Table 106. For comparison, the network of hydro-meteorological and hydrological stations in 1976 is shown in Table 107.

Data banks for systematic collection, processing, storage and dissemination of data had been established temporarily at EGAT which are still in the stage of limited dissemination and general use. It is expected to increase ability and capability of the staff and to establish a national body as the centre of water resources data in the near future.

b. *Water use and efficiency*

It is the government's policy to follow-up and make the best use of the existing projects to achieve the water resources development target both in socio-economy and basic water demands. Financial resources are provided for operation, maintenance and improvement of existing irriga-

tion projects to increase project efficiency. Related health and environmental aspects are taken into account in the planning and management of agricultural water use.

c. *Environment, health and pollution control*

The government realizes the importance of this aspect. There is an office of the National Environment Committee to carry out the policy (by working) in the form of the committee.

d. *Policy, planning and management*

National Water Resources Committee had been established to carry out the policy and co-ordinate water resources development plans of the country so as to achieve the target of water resources development according to the national development plan as follows:

— To prevent the problems of difference in socio-economy

— To increase agricultural production

— To supply basic water demands for the people

— To prevent shortage of energy within the country for development of populated area and industry

e. *Natural hazards*

The government pays attention to prevent natural hazards, especially flood hazard in all regions. There are accelerated plans to reduce flood loss in the cultivated area of the central plain and metropolitan areas.

f. *Public information, education, training and research*

There have been many studies relating to water, such as:

(i)   Study project to identify the level of quality of major river basins in Thailand

(ii)   Water quality development project

(iii)   Land subsidence in Bangkok metropolitan areas

(iv)   Flood problem study downstream of Chao Phraya Dam

(v)   Study and report for master plan in obtaining domestic water supply for rural areas of the whole kingdom

(vi)   Study and report for Thai-Australia co-operation project to provide domestic water supply for village

(vii)   Study and report on condition, location and difference of water resources in the north-east region by remote sensing

(viii)   Water resources development study for populated area and industry, especially in the East Coast areas

g.   *Information on opportunities for mutual support in implementing the Mar del Plata Action Plan, with particular reference to technical co-operation among developing countries*

There is close technical co-operation between Thai and Malaysia on the Golok river basin development project under guidance and assistance from Australian government. Water resources development projects in Salawin river basin which is shared water resources of Thailand and Burma, and Mekong river basin which is shared water resources among Thailand, Laos, Cambodia and Vietnam had been studied but no plan for implementation has been set.

Table 98. Summary of Water Resources Development Completed to the end of 1980-1982 and under construction in 1983 undertaken by Royal Irrigation Department

	Unit	Completed to the end of			Under Construction in 1983
		1980	1981	1982	
Storage of Water	Mill. m³.	(1) 50 847.47	(1) 52 327.95	(1) 52 705.31	(1) 14 684.05
Irrigation					
Drainage					
Conservation	Hectare	(2) 3 015 115	(2) 3 189 604	(2) 3 339 717	480 222
Flood protection					
Reclaimation					
Dike and ditch project	Hectare	1 158 735	1 197 456	1 206 932	48 947
Pumping irrigation for rice cultivation					
Rice	Hectare	193 047	116 634	110 472	
Second rice	Hectare	100 033	79 358	104 160	
River training	Km.	539	543	543	
Land consolidation project	Hectare	60 913	75 060	104 791	13 978

Note: (1) From reservoirs operated by RID and EGAT inclusive
(2) Area of large, medium, and small scale irrigation projects.

Table 99. Water resources development activities since 1980 up to 1983 undertaken by the National Energy Administration

No.	Activities	Description
1	Completed project	Mae Kum Luang hydroelectric power, Chiang Mai
2	Project under Construction	2.1 Huai Mong irrigation project, Nong Khai
		2.2 Huai Saphan Hin hydroelectric power, Chanthaburi
		2.3 Mae Phong hydroelectric power, Phayao
		2.4 Mae Sariang hydroelectric power, Mae Hongson
3	Feasibility study completed, seeking finance for construction	3.1 Nam San hydroelectric power, Loei
		3.2 Pak Mun hydroelectric power, Ubon Ratchathani
		3.3 Mae Kok hydroelectric power, Chiang Rai
		3.4 Mae Lao hydroelectric power, Chiang Rai
		3.5 Lower Chi-Mun irrigation project, Ubon Ratchathani
		3.6 Huai Nam Suai irrigation project, Nong Khai
		3.7 Nam Songkhram irrigation project, Nakhon Phanom
		3.8 Mae Salong hydroelectric power, Chiang Rai
		3.9 Prong Nam Ron hydroelectric power, Chiang Rai
		3.10 Nam Mae Khom hydroelectric power, Chiang Rai

Table 99. *(continued)*

No.	Activites		Description
4	Projects under feasibility study	4.1	Lower Nam Phrom irrigation project, Chaiyaphum
		4.2	Lam Nam Yang irrigation project, Kalasin
		4.3	Nam Chi Noi irrigation project, Surin
		4.4	Upper Huai Sam Ran irrigation project, Sisaket
		4.5	Huai Tuk Chu irrigation project, Sisaket
		4.6	Lower Huai Sam Ran irrigation project, Sisaket
		4.7	Satung Sala irrigation project, Sisaket
		4.8	Huai Khayung irrigation project, Sisaket
		4.9	Lam Dom Yai irrigation project, Ubon Ratchathani
		4.10	Huai Chalat irrigation project, Surin
		4.11	Huai Bang Sai hydroelectric, Mukdahan
5	Pumping installation using electric motor		Pumping installation using electric motor for irrigation, from surface water sources, originated in 1967. The size of pump is 12 in. diameter with approximated capacity 0.5 m³/sec. Each station composes of stilling well, main canal about 3 km long, lateral about 6 km long, ditch and drainage canal about 20 km long and can irrigate an area of about 480 hectares.

At present 457 pumping stations have been installed, 279 stations were completed and ready for water diversion, the rest 178 stations are under construction and expected to be completed in 1984 which will cover the total irrigation area about 21 936 hectares.

Table 100. Construction and maintenance of water resources projects (Normal Plan) undertaken by Accelerated Rural Development Office

Fiscal Year	Reservoir/Weir		Dredging Swamp/Pond		Pond Excavation		Diversion System		Total	
	No. of Project	Cost (Baht)	No. of Project	Cost (Baht)	No. of Project	Cost (Baht)	No. of Project	Cost (Baht)	No. of Project	Cost (Baht)
Beginning–										
1976	191	107 393 196	56	7 252 596	450	13 390 005	–	–	697	128 035 797
1977	43	33 854 389	45	10 407 695	77	4 806 704	–	–	165	49 068 788
1978	21	26 674 625	20	5 813 274	–	–	–	–	41	32 487 899
1979	11	27 420 259	24	7 293 306			–	–	35	34 713 565
1980	15	33 825 197	25	15 436 026	14	1 413 320	2	1 360 150	56	52 034 693
1981	20	54 559 571	25	13 720 973	–	–	–	–	45	68 280 544
1982	20	78 377 707	31	15 731 463	–	–	3	1 834 000	54	95 943 170
1983	20	53 943 763	43	24 047 122	18	5 512 208	–	–	81	83 503 093
Total	341	416 048 707	269	99 702 455	559	25 122 237	5	3 194 150	1 174	544 067 549
Draft Plan										
1984	14	64 000 000	20	18 000 000	21	6 300 000	–	–	55	88 300 000

Table 101. Rural community development (6 centres) undertaken by Accelerated Rural Development Office

Fiscal Year	Reservoir/Weir		Dredging Swamp/Pond		Pond Excavation		Diversion System		Total	
	No. of Project	Cost (Baht)	No. of Project	Cost (Baht)	No. of Project	Cost (Baht)	No. of Project	Cost (Baht)	No. of Project	Cost (Baht)
Beginning –										
1980	47	38 363 299	19	5 607 698	186	9 801 172	2	206 060	254	53 978 219
1981	10	27 897 440	1	350 908	21	5 272 950	14	7 706 362	46	41 227 660
1982	13	25 247 725	4	1 357 468	29	7 315 716	7	5 503 982	53	39 424 891
1983	11	27 186 898	3	988 303	21	5 848 731	10	9 911 235	45	43 935 167
Total	81	118 695 352	27	8 304 377	257	28 243 569	33	23 327 639	398	178 565 937
Draft Plan										
1984	7	27 382 000	4	3 600 000	29	8 700 000	3	2 000 000	43	41 682 000

Table 102. Construction of water resources projects for poor villages undertaken by Accelerated Rural Development Office

Fiscal Year	Reservoir/Weir		Pond Excavation		Dredging Swamp/Pond		Total	
	No. of Project	Cost (Baht)	No. of Project	Cost (Baht)	No. of Project	Cost (Baht)	No. of Project	Cost (Baht)
1982	10	34 341 760	19	5 295 577	15	8 465 321	44	48 102 658
1983	11	36 660 966	31	9 332 405	20	13 461 428	62	59 444 799
Total	21	70 992 726	50	14 627 982	35	21 926 749	106	107 547 457
Draft Plan								
1984	17	67 103 000	101	30 300 000	51	43 350 000	169	140 753 000
1985	17	74 800 000	102	37 030 000	51	50 490 000	170	162 320 000
1986	17	86 470 000	102	42 580 000	51	58 370 000	170	187 420 000

Table 103. Data for well drilling years 1981-1983 undertaken by the Department of Mineral Resources

Year	Number of wells	Total depth (ft)	Usable wells	well quality				installed pump			
				fresh	brackish	salty	waste	hand pump	motor pump	wind turbine	spring
1981	1 955	278 104	1 749	1 737	12	34	172	1 741	8	–	–
1982	2 339	328 293	2 161	2 150	11	23	155	2 150	11	–	–
1983	1 721	235 403	1 600	1 598	9	20	113	1 600	–	–	–

Remark : Data in 1983 presents the work up to June, 1983

Table 104. Ground water wells drilling undertaken by Public Works Department

Year	No. of wells	Total depth (m)	Water production m³/hr.	Community served	
				persons	families
1980	350	20 813.31	5 074.1	176 150	35 230
1981	450	22 655.40	5 909.5	220 350	44 070
1982	695	33 578.79	7 886.5	360 750	72 150
1983	774	37 300.52	9 000.0	376 350	75 270

Table 105. Water supply concession year 1982

Number of water supply system classified according to community	Water production m³/day	Number of water users	Population in service area	Remarks
17 provincial municipalities	180 960	91 364	776 377	
9 district municipalities	20 880	12 811	126 572	
12 sanitary districts	18 862	8 308	118 340	
12 public	16 680	4 112	104 135	
Total 50 w.s. systems	237 382	116 595	1 125 424	

Source: The Department of Public Works

Table 106. Hydrologic investigation in Thailand 1983

No.	Description	Operating agency											Total
		RID	NEA	MET	EGAT	HYD	PA	HD	FD	LDD	IWD	DOH	
1	Water level in operation												
	Staff gauge	305	250	19	35	–	–	–	1	165	–	–	775
	Automatic recorder	98	11	11	11	–	–	–	1	–	–	–	132
	Tide gauge	24	–	–	3	6	8	22	–	–	–	–	63
2	Discharge measurement												
	In operation	223	166	11	13	–	–	–	1	165	–	–	579
	Data available	396	226	11	33	–	–	–	1	165	–	–	832
3	Precipitation	639	184	853	41	–	–	–	88	35	–	–	1 840
4	Evaporation	85	131	122	28	–	–	–	9	30	–	–	405
5	Air temperature	79	64	372	24	–	–	–	88	30	–	–	657
6	Water temperature	57	52	–	–	–	–	–	–	–	–	–	109
7	Wind velocity	81	36	97	3	–	–	–	5	–	–	–	222
8	Humidity	73	70	164	23	–	–	–	7	–	–	–	337
9	Sediment	61	187	–	15	–	–	–	–	165	–	–	428
10	Water quality	68	108	–	–	–	–	–	–	165	33	213	587

Remarks:
RID	=	Royal Irrigation Department	NEA	=	National Energy Administration
MET	=	Meteorological Department	EGAT	=	Electricity Generating Authority of Thailand
HYD	=	Hydrographic Department	HD	=	Harbour Department
PA	=	Port Authority of Thailand	LDD	=	Land Development Department
FD	=	Forestry Department	DOH	=	Department of Health
IWD	=	Industrial Works Department			

Table 107. Network of Hydro-meteorological and Hydrological Stations in 1976

| Description | Water Management Division | | | | | | Country |
	1 Chao Phraya	2 Chi-Mun	3 Mekong	4 Bang Pakong	5 Mae Klong	6 Peninsula	
1. Rainfall Station	578	284	166	81	55	261	1 444
2. Streamflow Gauging Station	141	95	49	35	26	78	428
3. Evaporation Station	60	40	61	9	15	46	237
4. Streamflow Sampling Station	19	26	34	13	6	23	122
5. Agro-meteorological Station	9	4	2	2	–	3	20
6. Synoptic Stations	14	6	7	3	1	14	49
7. Sediment Sampling Station	33	27	34	8	12	26	141

APPENDIX A

HYDROELECTRIC DEVELOPMENT

Hydroelectric power potential in Thailand has been continuously explored. The large size projects are mostly located in the mountainous regions of the north and western part of the central region. Up to date, one hundred project sites are indentified with the estimated total potential of about 6,562 MW and 16,835 GWh of average annual electric energy. Some details of power potential and development are shown in Table 108.

At the present time, thirteen stations totalling 1,514.7 MW with the average annual energy of 4,232.1 GWh are in operation. The total catchment area of these hydroelectric dams is 70,459 km² and the average annual inflow of the dams is estimated at about 23,135 MCM.

There are six projects, totalling 741.8 MW with average annual energy of 1,456.3 GWh under construction. Two projects are the generating units addition at the existing dams, Sirindhorn unit #3 12 MW and Srinagarind unit #4 reversible pumped turbine 180 MW. Three projects are the multipurpose project dams, Khao Laem 300 MW, Chiew Larn 240 MW and Mae Ngat 9 MW. The other one is the mini hydro project, Ban Khun Klang 0.18 MW. The total catchment area is 6,450 km² with the estimated annual inflow of 8,616 MCM.

Two projects of 596.8 MW with average annual energy of 1,276.8 GWh are proposed to the government for construction. The first one is the turbine installation of 16.8 MW at the existing irrigation dam, Chao Phraya dam. The other one is the Nam Chon dam of 580 MW which has the catchment area of 4,908 km² with the estimated average annual inflow of 2,975 MCM. The dam site is proposed to be located at approximately 135 km upstream of Srinagarind dam. All the projects as mentioned previously are listed in Table 109.

Several hydro power potential sites have been studied for future development. For the next decade, up to the year 1993, it is anticipated that another fourteen hydroelectric dams with the combined capacity of 705 MW and average annual energy of 1,918 GWh shall be developed. These project dams are listed in Table 110.

At the present time, the projects which are in operation and under construction shall represent about 34 per cent of the total energy potential availability. By the year 1993, about 53 per cent of the nation's hydro potential will be exploited.

The inventory of international boundary rivers namely, Mekong and Salawin shows that Thailand can share several hydro power projects of about 14,045 MW with neighbouring countries particular with Laos and Burma. Concerning Mekong river, several studies have been made by the Mekong Committee but no plan for implementation has been set yet. Concerning Salawin river, the desk studies of some projects have been prepared and they show very promising results. These potential projects are listed in Table 111. Future developments of international boundary river projects are of great interest. Thailand is willing to co-operate in such developments and expects to see a successful international hydroelectric project in the Southeast Asia Region.

Table 108. Summary of hydro potential

Region	Existing		Under Construction		Proposed to Gov.		Remaining Potential Prefeasibility or higher		Desk Study or higher	
	Installed MW	Avg. Energy GWh	Installed MW	Avg. Energy GWh	Installed MW	Avg. Energy GWh	Installed MW	Avg. Energy GWh	Installed MW	Avg. Energy GWh
Northern	929.4	2 422.7	9.18	29 713	–	–	944.9	2 899.2	773.9	1 708.2
Northeastern	95.0	206.9	12.00	5 500	–	–	237.0	686.4	132.9	296.1
Central	417.0	1 387.6	480.00	867 400	596.8	1 276.8	259.5	570.3	872.6	2 584.7
Southern	73.3	214.9	240.00	553 700	–	–	371.0	869.3	117.8	255.4
Total	1 514.7	4 232.1	741.18	1 456 313	596.8	1 276.8	1 812.4	5 025.2	1 897.2	4 844.4
* Total Potential in Thailand	6 562.28	16 834 813								

* *Note:* Excluding pumped storage, small hydro, international scheme and potential at the existing irrigation dams except the existing small hydro projects : Ban Yang 0.1 MW, Huai Kum 1.3 MW, Ban Khun Klang 0.18 MW, Ban Santi 1.3 MW and Mae Ngat 9.0 MW.

Table 109. List of hydroelectric projects

	Project Name	Region	No. of Units	Installed (MW)	Average Energy GWh	Completion Date	
	Existing Plants						
1	Bhumibol	N	7	553.0	1 414.1	May	1964
2	Nam Pung	NE	2	6.0	15.1	Oct	1965
3	Ubolratana	NE	3	25.0	56.1	Mar	1966
4	Sirindhorn	NE	2	24.0	593.0	Oct	1971
5	Chulabhorn	NE	2	40.0	76.4	Oct	1972
6	Ban Yang	N	3	0.1	0.3	Feb	1974
7	Sirikit	N	3	375.0	1 005.3	Jun	1974
8	Kang Krachan	C	1	19.0	77.2	Aug	1974
9	Srinagarind	C	3	360.0	1 143.8	Feb	1980
10	Bang Lang (Pattani)	S	3	72.0	208.8	Jun	1981
11	Tha Thung Na	C	2	38.0	166.6	Dec	1981
12	Huai Kum	NE	1	1.3	3.0	Feb	1982
13	Ban Santi	S	1	1.3	6.1	Oct	1982
	TOTAL		33	1 514.7	4 232.1		
	Under Construction						
1	Ban Khun Klang	N	1	0.18	0.713	Nov	1983
2	Sirindhorn unit 3	NE	1	12.0	5.5	Apr	1984
3	Khao Laem unit 1-3	C	3	300.0	756.0	Oct	1984
4	Srinagarind unit 4	C	1	180.0	111.4	Sep	1985
5	Mae Ngat unit 1-2	N	2	9.0	29.0	Nov	1985
6	Chiew Larn unit 1-3	S	3	240.0	553.7	Jul	1987
	TOTAL		11	741.18	1 456.313		
	Proposed for Government Approval						
1	Chao Phraya Power Plant	C	1	16.8	94.8		
2	Nam Chon	C	4	580.0	1 182.0		
	TOTAL		5	596.8	1 276.8		

Table 110. List of hydroelectric projects up to the year 1993

No.	Project Name	Region	Installed (MW)	Annual Energy (GWh)	Present Status
1	Thikhong	C	87.0	154.0	Completed design
2	Khlong Yan				
	– Kaeng Krung	S	68.0	165.0	Finished feasibility study
	– Kaeng Leh	S	6.0	30.0	
3	Nam Man	NE	26.0	58.0	Under feasibility study
4	Upper Nam Pong				
	– Nam Choen	NE	15.0	44.0	Under pre-feasibility study
	– Nam Su	NE	8.0	29.0	
5	Nam Khek				
	– Huai Ngad	N	58.0	141.0	Preparing for feasibility in the year 1983
	– Pong Bon	N	32.0	88.0	
6	Kaeng Sua Ten	N	65.0	143.0	Under feasibility study
7	Lower Mae Ping & Wang	N	24.4	183.0	Under feasibility study
8	Pak Mun	NE	135.0	462.0	Plan to review feasibility in the year 1984
9	Nam San	NE	58.0	127.0	Plan to study feasibility in the year 1984
10	Upper Pasak	NE	24.0	69.0	Plan to study feasibility in the year 1984
11	Sai Buri	S	99.0	225.0	Plan to review feasibility in the year 1984
	TOTAL		705.4	1 918.0	

Table 111. List of potential international projects

No.	Name of Project	Province	Reservoir (km²)	Installed Capacity MW	Annual Energy Production GWh
1	Salawin	Mae Hong Son	–	3 000	26 280
2	Nam Moei (1)	Mae Hong Son	7 800	1 490	3 263
3	Nam Moei (2)	Mae Hong Son	7 300	414	906.7
4	Nam Moei (3)	Mae Hong Son	5 500	489	1 071
5	Pak Sae	Ubol	538 000	1 120	9 811
6	Khem Maret	Ubol	417 000	1 080	9 461
7	Pa Mong	Knong Khai	299 000	4 800	24 500
8	Bung Karn	Knong Khai	328 000	446	3 907
9	Upper Tha Khek	Nakhon Phanom	357 000	730	6 395
10	Lower Tha Khek	Nakhon Phanom	373 000	476	4 170
	TOTAL			14 045	89 764.70

Sources: NEA

Table 112. Basic data of dam and hydro power plants — existing

		Bhumibol #1-7	Sirikit	Ubolratana	Sirindhorn	Chulabhorn	Kang Krachan	Nam Pung
Location		Tak	Uttaradit	Khon Kaen	Ubol-ratchathani	Chaiya-phum	Phetchaburi	Sakon Nakhon
Dam								
Type		Conc. Arch Gravity	Earthfill	Rockfill	Rockfill	Rockfill	Earthfill	Rockfill
Hight	m	154	113.6	32.0	42.0	70.0	58.0	41.0
Crest Length	m	486	800.0	800.0	940.0	700.0	760.0	1 720.0
Crest Elevation	m(MSL)	261	169.0	185.0	145.0	763.0	106.0	286.5
Total Volume	MCM	0.97	11.0	0.165	0.623	1.64.0	3.425	0.73
Reservoir								
Catchment Area	km^2	26 386	13 130.0	12 000.0	2 097.0	545.0	2 210.0	291.0
Avg. Annual Inflow	MCM	6 392	5 845.0	2 271.0	1 413.0	138.0	917.0	103.0
Normal High Water Level	m(MSL)	260	162.0	182.0	142.2	759.0	99.0	284.0
Minimum High Water Level	m(MSL)	213	128.0	175.5	137.2	739.0	75.0	270.0
Surface Area at NHWL	km^2	300	259.6	412.0	288.0	12.0	46.5	21.6
Storage at NHWL	MCM	13 462	9 510.0	2 559.0	1 966.0	188.0	710.0	165.0
Storage at min. HWL	MCM	3 800	2 850.0	725.0	831.0	43.5	67.0	10.0
Power Generating Facilities								
Rated head	m	100 & 105 *	75.4	16.0	30.3	366.0	43.0	85.0
No. of Unit Installed		6 + 1*	3	3	2	2	1	1
Installed Capacity	MW	420 + 133 *	375.0	25.0	24.0	40.0	19.0	6.0
Avg. Annual Energy	GWh	1 414.1	1 005.3	56.1	59.3	76.4	77.2	15.1
Spillway Capacity	cms	6 000	3 250.0	2 500.0	1 300.0	1 000.0	1 308.0	300.0
Irrigation Area	rai				150 000.0			
Project Cost	M฿	2 545 + 410 *	2 534	557	340	379	289	110
Construction Years		1958-64 79-82	1968-74	1964-66	1968-71	1970-72	1961-66	1964-65

Note: * Bhumibol Unit 7

Table 112. Basic data of dam and hydro power plants — existing

		Srinagarind #1-3	Bang Lang	Tha Thung Na	Huai Kum	Ban Yang	Ban Santi
Location		Kanchanaburi	Yala	Kanchanaburi	Chaiyaphum	Chiang Mai	Yala
Dam							
Type		Rockfill	Rockfill	Concrete & Rockfill	Rockfill	Concrete	Concrete Gravity
Height	m	140.0	85.0	30.0	35.5	1.6	9.5
Crest Length	m	610.0	422.0	860.0	282.0	668.3	
Crest Elevation	m(MSL)	185.0	120.0	63.0	316.5	669.2	
Total Volume	MCM	120.6	2.9	Conc. 0.0496 Rock 0.314	0.34	0.00018	
Reservoir							
Catchment Area	km^2	10 880.0	2 080.0	11 428.0	262.0		30.0
Avg. Annual Inflow	MCM	4 432.0	1 460.0	4 520.0	55.0		20.8
Normal High Water Level	m(MSL)	180.0	115.0	58.8	312.0	669.2	332.0
Minimum High Water Level	m(MSL)	168.0	83.0	55.5	298.0		328.0
Surface Area at NHWL	km^2	419.0	45.0		2.4		
Storage at NHWL	MCM	17 745.0	1 404.0	56.3	22.0		0.124
Storage at min. HWL	MCM	10 275.0	260.0	28.6	2.75		0.0185

Table 112. *(continued)*

Location		*Srinagarind #1-3* Kanchanaburi	*Bang Lang* Yala	*Tha Thung Na* Kanchanaburi	*Huai Kum* Chaiyaphum	*Ban Yang* Chiang Mai	*Ban Santi* Yala
Power Generating Facilities							
Rated Head	m	105.0	62.0	15.1	23.0	70.0	196.0
No. of Unit Installed		3	3	3	1	1	1
Installed Capacity	MW	360.0	72.0	38.0	1.2	0.123	1.3
Avg. Annual Energy	GWh	1 162.0	208.8	166.6	3.0	0.3	3.14
Spillway Capacity	cms	2 420.0	4 500.0	3 000.0	1 480.0		43.0
Irrigation Area	rai						
Project Cost	MB	4 769	2 737.1	1 060.0	177	1.88	40.0
Construction Years		1974-80	1976-81	1977-82	1978-81	1973-74	1981-83

Table 113. Basic data – under construction in 1983

Location		*Extention Sirindhorn #3*	*Kao Laem* Kanchanaburi	*Extention Srinagarind #4* Kanchanaburi	*Mae Ngat Power Plant* Chiang Mai	*Chiew Larn* Surathani	*Ban Khun Klang* Chiang Mai
Dam							
Type			Rockfill		Earthfill	Rockfill	Conc. Weir
Height	m		113		59	90	2
Crest Length	m		980		1 950	680	12.6
Crest Elevation	m(MSL)		163			99.5	1 389.0
Total Volume	MCM		8.0		6 607	6.4	
Reservoir							
Catchment Area	km²		3 720.0		1 280	1 450.0	7
Avg. Annual Inflow	MCM		5 156.0		401.8	3 058.0	4.4
Normal High Water Level	m(MSL)		155.0		396.0	95.0	
Minimum High Water Level	m(MSL)		135.0			61.8	
Surface Area at NHWL	km²				16.0	165.0	
Storage at NHWL	MCM		7 450.0		265.0	5 600.0	
Storage at mim. HWL	MCM		4 800.0		10.0	550.0	
Power Generating Facilities					(max. gross head)		
Rated Head	m	30.3	56.0	105.0	40.0	84.0	100
No. of Unit Installed		1	3	1	2	3	2
Installed Capacity	MW	12.0	300.0	180.0	9.0	240.0	0.18
Avg. Annual Energy	GWh	5.5	756.0	111.4	29.0	553.7	0.713
Spillway Capacity	cms		3 200.0		1 035.0	3 300.0	16.0
Irrigation Area	rai	–		–	188 000	14 700.0	
Project Cost	MB	150.0	9 000	973.0	296	6 970.0	6.5
Construction Years		1982-84	1979-84	1982-85	1982-86	1982-87	1982-83

Table 114. Basic data-proposed for government approval

Location		Chao Phraya Power Plant Chainat	Nam Chon Kanchanaburi
Dam			
Type		*Concrete*	*Rockfill*
Height	m		185
Crest Length	m		450
Crest Elevation	m(MSL)		376.5
Total Volume	MCM		12.7
Reservoir			
Catchment Area	km^2	119 000	4 908.0
Avg. Annual Inflow	MCM	23 600	2 975.0
Normal High Water Level	m(MSL)		370.0
Minimum High Water Level	m(MSL)		331.0
Surface Area at NHWL	km^2		137.0
Storage at NHWL	MCM		5 975.0
Storage at min. HWL	MCM		1 875.0
Power Generating Facilities			
Rated Head	m	6.33	146.5
No. of Unit Installed		1	4
Installed Capacity	MW	16.8	580.0
Avg. Annual Energy	GWh	94.8	1 182.0
Spillway Capacity	cms		2 500.0
Irrigation Area	rai		
Estimated cost (Year)	MB		

IX.B. POLLUTION PROBLEMS RELATED TO THE CURRENT PROGRAMMES OF LOW-COST TECHNOLOGY APPLICATIONS TO WATER SUPPLY AND SANITATION IN THAILAND

Introduction

Thailand, as in the case of other developing countries, suffers from environmental problems concerning with inadequate water supply and poor sanitation. The government has realized and tries to support the current programmes which will provide clean water and better sanitation to its people nation-wide especially in rural areas.

As indicated in the Fifth National Economic and Social Development Plan (1982-1986), the target related to the above policy is to provide adequate clean water and toilets for 95 per cent and 70 per cent of the people respectively within the year 1986. For the Sixth Plan, these figures will go up to 100 per cent of both items within the year 1990.

To meet the water supply provision, several government agencies work for the plan, such as;

1. Royal Irrigation Department
2. Department of Local Administration
3. Department of Mineral Resources
4. Department of Public Works
5. Department of Health
6. Department of Community Development
7. Accelerated Rural Development Office
8. Metropolitan Water Works Authority
9. Provincial Water Works Authority

The tasks which are done by these related agencies are as follows:

a. Shallow dug wells
b. Drilled wells (shallow and deep)
c. Hand-pumps installation and maintenance

d.   Water supply for communities, schools, temples

e.   Reservoir

In case of environmental sanitation, the mainly involved government agency in rural area is the Department of Health, while in the municipal area, it is direct responsibility of the municipolity. The main environmental sanitation services are solid waste disposal and health promotion.

For the fiscal year 1984, it is estimated that the budget used for water supply provision in the rural area is about 1,060 million bahts and if it includes other water resource development, the figure will go up to 3,883 million bahts. On the other hand, the amount of money for environmental sanitation development programme of the Department of Health is only 15 million bahts in the fiscal year 1984.

1. Low-cost Technology Applications and the Related Pollution Problems

The followings are some of the current programmes of low-cost technology applications to water supply and waste disposal in Thailand and the related pollution problems:

a.   *Waste disposal*

Waste disposal can be divided into:

  (i)   excreta disposal

  (ii) refuse disposal

  (iii) sewage disposal

(i)   *Excreta disposal*

In Thailand, nowadays there is no sewerage system, therefore, the excreta disposal will be the on-site disposal system. Generally, the type of low-cost and practically excreta disposal includes pit privy and cesspool latrine.

The pit privy is the local type of human excreta disposal in the rural area of Thailand. It can cause pollution problem because there is no protection of excreta from insects and animals. Therefore, it is the breeding place for flies and it can contaminate the ground water or surface water. However, the present pit privy is developed to control faecal-borne diseases and it is recommended that the pit privy should not be used in the area where the water table is high because it can contaminate the ground water.

At present, the cesspool latrine is the conventional type used in every part of the country. As there is no sealing between casings, the inside liquid will leak to the outside soil and contaminate the ground water or the nearby canals and rivers.

(ii) *Refuse disposal*

In rural area, refuse disposal is done individually mostly by open dumping or burning. Some type of refuse, such as garbage, is used for hog feed so the refuse disposal is not the problem in rural area.

In the dense community such as district or province, the local government agencies (sanitary district and municipality) take care of refuse disposal. The types of low-cost technology application for refuse disposal are:

1.   Open dumping and open burning (very common)

2.   Open composting and open dumping (Bangkok area)

3.   Sanitary Landfill (Haad Yai, Pattaya only)

In case of open composting and open dumping, it causes air pollution problem due to bad odour from refuse fermentation and sometimes it burns itself and produce smoke which is similar to the case of open burning. In rainy season, the wastewater from the refuse dump will contaminate the water nearby. The low efficiency of refuse collection system in big cities is another problem, for example, the amount of refuse collected in Bangkok area is 60 per cent of the daily produced volume and the remaining refuse dumps will cause bad odour and some of them will clog the public sewers. Refuse dumped in canals or rivers causes water pollution problems.

(iii) *Sewage disposal*

In rural area, the wastewater from households is usually disposed to the ground or directly discharged to the natural receiving water. Also, in the dense community, such as municipality area, the wastewater will flow to public sewers, canals or rivers and these will cause water pollution problems due to the large amount of volume and organic loading. Now, there is no wastewater treatment plant for any communities in Thailand, so, the water pollution is the most important problem. So far, the low-cost technology applications, such as stabilization pond system, are widely used for wastewater from agro-industries, such as sugar cane factories, tapioca starch factories, etc.

b.   *Water supply*

Major sources of water supply in Thailand can be divided into the following categories:

  (i)   rain water

  (ii) ground water

  (iii) surface water

(i)   *Rain water*

Rain water is collected as runoff from the house roof. Most of Thai house roofs in rural area are made of galvanized iron or thatch. Rain water runoff is collected by the gutter and flows into the storage which may be the water-jar or reinforced concrete tank.

(ii) Ground water

Ground water is another source of water supply in Thailand. The low-cost technology application for ground water may be divided into:—

1. shallow hand-dug well
2. drilled wells both deep and shallow wells

In using shallow hand-dug well, the weak point is the limited amount of water and the water quality may be unsatisfactory. The contamination might occur from the nearby surroundings, such as toilet or wastewater and it may spread the water-borne diseases.

The drilled well may cost more because of the need of sophisticated equipments and some technology but the limited sources of water supply make this source of water to be necessary. The depth of the drilled well can be as much as 100 ft. or more and the adequate amount can be piped for the commmunity. Generally, the water quality is good and need no or little treatment only.

In case of the large-scale water supply, the bigger size and the greater number of drill wells are desired and the motor pump will be used instead of handpump. If the rate of withdrawal is too high, it may cause land subsidense, such as the case of land subsidence in Bangkok area.

(iii) Surface water

Surface water sources, such as ponds, lakes, canals, and reservoirs, are generally used for water supply in Thailand. When large scale water supply is needed, it requires high cost technology applications, i.e. high power pumps, rapid sand or multi-media filter, elevated storage tank etc., and these factors need experience and sophisticated design. For small scale water supply, the low-cost technology can be applied. In rural area, Thai people always use alum to coagulate the turbidity of surface water and after settling, the clear water is collected in water jar for domestic uses.

Currently, the low-cost technology filter for a family is introduced by the Department of Health. It is a cast cement filter having capacity of 50 litres. The sand and charcoal are used as filter media. The upper part of water which flows through sand and upflow passing charcoal can be used as drinking water, while the lower faucet passing

sand filter only will be used for other domestic supply. It is observed by the Department of Health that the filtered water is free from water-borne diseases, such as cholera and dysentery, so this type of filter will be promoted for use in rural area of Thailand.

2. Conclusions and Recommended Measures

a. The use of simple low-cost technology is appropriate for rural application.

b. Local resources, especially construction materials, must be considered as an important factor to reduce the cost of sanitation.

c. Avoid the uses of treatment processes which the community concerned could not afford to procure, operate and maintain the system.

d. Public education programmes on water supply and sanitation should be provided for the community concerned to make the public understand how to protect and preserve the quality of water supply and sanitation.

e. In case of excreta disposal, the cesspool latrine is an environmental problem especially in the area where the water table is high. The researches of low-cost technology to improve or look for other systems should be envisaged.

f. The refuse collection and disposal are another environmental problem which should be improved. The suitable site for disposal needs careful investigations. To make the collection system more efficient, it is suggested that the funds to cover cost of collection should be increased.

g. The wastewater treatment for the dense community by using stabilization ponds or other suitable process is the necessary means to prevent water pollution in natural waterway. The municipalities themselves must pay strong attention to this problem and look for technical and financial support from other agencies concerned.

h. In case of water supply, hand or manually operated pumps are the cheapest and most appropriate water lifting devices for rural water supply. The water from reservoirs and shallow hand-dug wells should be filtered before using.

i. Integration of the capability of the local technician is necessary.

j. Water Supply and Sanitation Board with representatives from agencies concerned should be established in order to solve problems together closely.

X. U.S.S.R

X.A. STATE WATER CADASTRE AS UNIFIED DATABASE FOR PLANNING OF MULTIPURPOSE WATER USE AND CONSERVATION*

Abstract. The methodology and principles for conducting the USSR State Water Cadastre as Nationwide Database for planning and management of multipurpose water use and conservation are described. The composition of the Cadastre and data allotment are oriented on the information retrieval system providing computer data processing and output for users while solving water-related problems.

To provide Unified Nationwide Database for multipurpose water resources use in the USSR, the State Water Cadastre (SWC) is established. SWC provides a systematic, currently replenished and updated stock of data on water resources, their regimen and quality and on water use. SWC is considered as the unified system and its information is the sole official data necessarily applicable for resolving all problems concerning planning, design, operation and management of the country's water economy.

Stucturally, SWC is composed of three parts, i.e., "Surface Water", "Groundwater" and "Water Use".

Noticeably, systems incorporating similar basic principles and practical methodology are planned in many countries in the world (Czechoslovakia, Bulgaria, USA, France). Some distinctions in water use data acquisition and systematization are stipulated by approaches to national economy planning.

Since 1978, in accordance with the Decree of the USSR Council of Ministers, the State Water Cadastre has been prepared by the USSR State Committee on Hydrometeorology and Environmental Control (general co-ordination and activities on "Surface Water"), USSR Ministry of Geology ("Groundwater") and USSR Ministry of Land Reclamation and Water Management ("Water Use").

By each part, the major activities of the SWC are:

1. analysis, systematization and storing data on water bodies, water resources, their regimen and quality, as well as on water use and users;

2. current evaluation and assessment for:
    a. surface water resources and quality due to water budgets by river and sea basins and

their distinctive subareas, by economical regions, USSR republics and the country as a whole;

   b. groundwater resources and quality by hydrogeological regions, economical regions, USSR republics and the country as a whole;

   c. water use by water use functions, national economy branches, by river and sea basins and their distinctive subareas (for groundwater — by hydrogeological regions), by economical regions, USSR republics and the country as a whole;

3. loading and maintaining the SWC databank;

4. the SWC data publication;

5. the SWC information service for enterprises, organizations and offices concerned.

The informational composition of the SWC is displayed on figures 44 and 45.

The SWC Part "Water Use" (SWC – WU) represents a stock of data in the following sections:

   a. water use catalogs (specification data periodically updated);

   b. water use annual data (including water use budgets in the period reported);

   c. water use historical data.

Water use mapping, developed within the SWC framework, represents territorial fundamentals for acquisition and processing of water use data. The taxonomy of regions and water use subareas encompasses hydrological, administrative, territorial and water economy aspects. Totally, part "Water Use" incorporates over 1,500 water use subareas by 75 major rivers of the USSR. The mapping is compulsory while compiling general, basin and territorial schemes for multipurpose water use and conservation.

The Primary information on water use comprises water users' statistical reports, water project operation reports, irrigation district and regional water management offices' accomplishments as well as operational hydrometric data from the network supervised by the USSR Ministry of Land Reclamation and Water Management.

---

*   By V.A. Vladimirov, Chief Hydraulic Engineer, Department of Multipurpose Water Use and Conservation, V/O "SOYUZVOD-PROEKT", USSR Ministry of Land Reclamation and Water Management, Moscow, USSR.

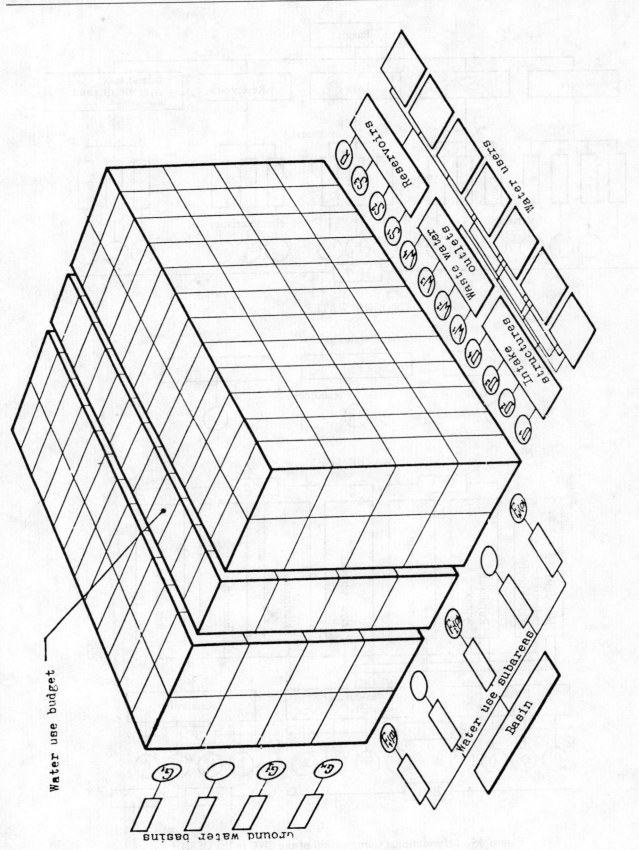

Figure 44. Information composition of the SWC Parts in the USSR.

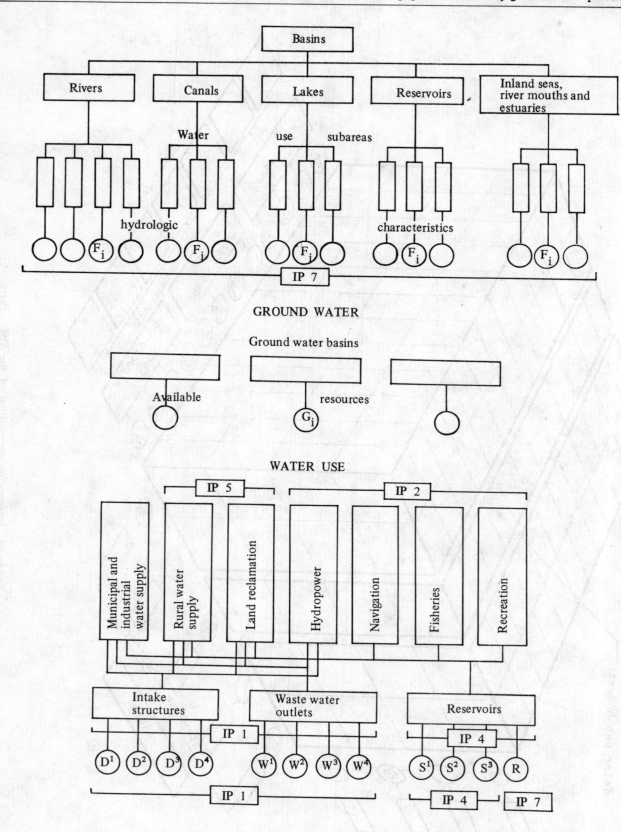

Figure 45. Informational Composition of the SWC in the USSR.

Water Use Catalogs characterize particular water projects and units (intakes, waste water outlets, reservoirs, ponds, water treatment facilities); in-channel water use; areas of irrigated, watered and drained lands. The catalogs are outlined with water use budgets calculated for control points of water use subareas and for entire river basins. The structural pattern of water use catalogs is described on Fig. 46.

Water Use Annual Data encompass current information on volume of water withdrawn, consumed or returned for the year of report; on wastewater quality parameters; on operation of major intakes and reservoirs; on irrigation, watering and drainage; on water flows in main canals and drains. Data are also outlined with water use budgets calculated for control points of water use subareas and for entire river basins.

Water Use Historical Data are compiled on base of Water Use Catalogs and Water Use Annual Data. The section contains information summarized for all preceeding years — on water use dynamics by river basins and their subareas, national economy branches, administrative and territorial units and by the country as a whole.

The water use summary data on each section are published in All-Union and republic's series of the SWC.

Taking into account the great volume of information intended for acquisition, processing and distribution among users, the development of the SWC information retreival system (SWC IRS) is carried out in the USSR at present.

The SWC IRS structurally encompasses three subsystems, i.e.:

a.   "Surface water" subsystem;

b.   "Groundwater" subsystem;

c.   "Water use" subsystem.

The "Water Use" subsystem (SWC WU) is developed for providing management and planning agencies, designing, scientific, research institutions and national economy enterprises with relevant information on water resources use.

The high relevance is attained by means of input data check system, regular replenishment and correction of stored files by current data on water use and reducing time between registration and application of data.

The high-speed information output is provided by SWC IRS access to all elements of water resources data and

SWC IRS WU digital communication with the subsystems "Surface Water" and "Groundwater".

The SWC IRS WU organizational and functional structure comprises three levels, i.e.:

a.   All-Union SWC WU centre;

b.   republic (regional) SWC WU centres;

c.   primary cadastre offices, conducting collection, checking and systematization of initial data with furnishing of primary documents.

The SWC IRS WU information base represents a databank with permanent memory on unified information carriers functioning under programme management system stipulating operative information exchange with the databanks of "Surface Water" and "Ground-water" subsystems.

The SWC IRS WU information service flowchart is displayed on Fig. 47. The first stage of the SWC IRS WU is planned to operate in the standard retrieval mode, the second stage — in a random request mode.

The SWC information is intended for use in the following water-related activities:

a.   current and prospective planning of water use and water conservation measures;

b.   planning of national productive forces allocation;

c.   working out schemes for multipurpose water use and conservation;

d.   planning of measures on water use in various branches of national economy;

e.   development of measures on improvement of water system operation;

f.   conducting Government supervision over water use and conservation;

f.   regulation of interrelations among water users;

h.   elaboration standards for water consumption and waste water effluents including water quality parameters.

Taking into account the multidisciplinary application of the SWC data, their pertinence was defined by the technical and economical analysis. Primarily, the data structure of the SWC part "Water Use" is developed to be homomorphious to river basin simulation models as important tools for prospective planning of multipurpose water use.

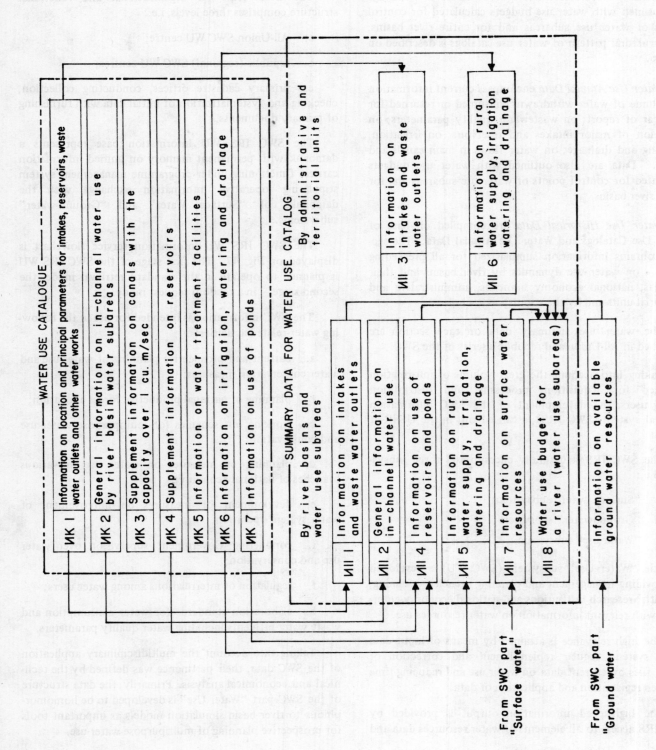

Figure 46. Structural Pattern of Water Use in the USSR.

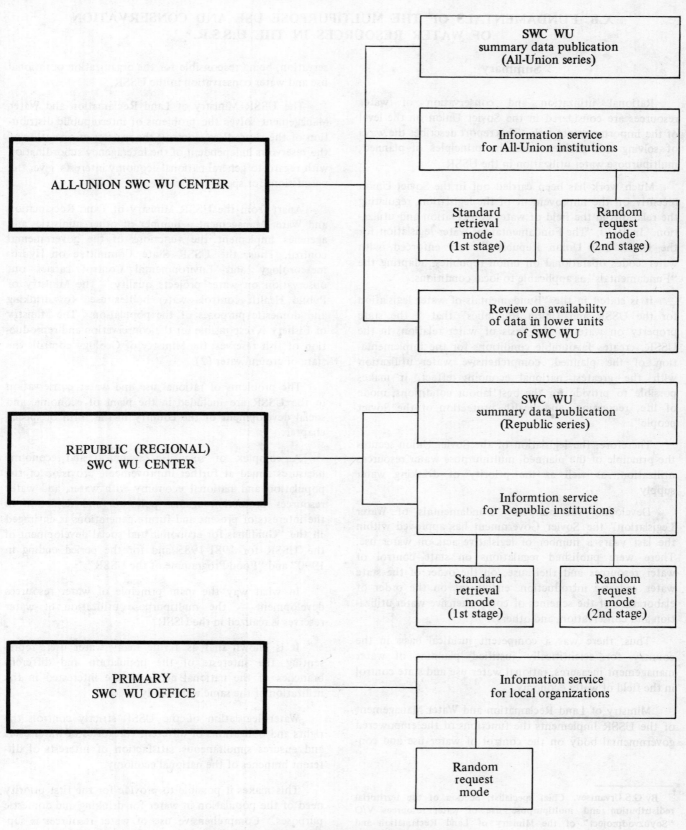

Figure 47. SWC-IRS-WU information flow Chart.

X.B. FUNDAMENTALS OF THE MULTIPURPOSE USE AND CONSERVATION OF WATER RESOURCES IN THE U.S.S.R.*

Summary

Rational utilization and conservation of water resources are considered in the Soviet Union on the level of the important state task. This report describes the ways of solving this problem and the principles of planned, multipurpose water utilization in the USSR.

Much work has been carried out in the Soviet Union recently on the improvement of the legislation, regulating the relations in the field of water conservation and utilization. In 1970, "The Fundamentals of Water legislation for the USSR and Union Republics" were enforced, with water codes operational on union republics, adapting the "Fundamentals" as applicable to local conditions.

It is stated in the "Fundamentals of water legislation for the USSR and Union Republics" that " the state property on water is the basis of water relations in the USSR, creates favourable conditions for the implementation of the planned, comprehensive water utilization with the greatest national economy effect. It makes possible to provide for the best labour conditions, mode of life, recreation, and health protection of the Soviet people".

Therefore, the legislation of the Soviet Union secures the principle of the planned, multipurpose water resources utilization, as well as the priority of drinking water supply.

Developing the adopted "Fundamentals of Water Legislation" the Soviet Government has approved within the last years a number of legislative acts on water use. There were published regulations on state control of water resources and their use, on the order of the state water cadastre introduction, enactment on the order of elaboration of the schemes of comprehensive water utilization and conservation, and others.

Thus, there was a competent juridical basis in the country for scientifically justified planning of water management measures, rational water use and state control in the field of water economy.

Ministry of Land Reclamation and Water Management of the USSR implements the functions of the empowered governmental body on the control of water use and conservation, being responsible for the organization of rational use and water conservation in the USSR.

The USSR Ministry of Land Reclamation and Water Management solves the problems of interrepublic distribution of the rivers flow, controls the regimes of operation of the reservoirs independent of the interagency subordination with regard to general national economy interests, gives the permissions for specific water use.

Apart from the USSR Ministry of Land Reclamation and Water Management a number of other ministries and agencies implement the functions of the governmental control. Thus, the USSR State Committee on Hydrometeorology and Environmental Control carries out observation on water projects quality. The Ministry of Public Health controls water bodies used for drinking and domestic purposes of the population. The Ministry of Fishery is responsible for the conservation and reproduction of fish reserves; the Ministry of Geology controls the state of groundwater (2).

The problems of rational use and water conservation in the USSR are included in the plans of economic and social development of the country in the form of special chapter.

A complex of scientific, technical and economic measures aimed at further improvement, provision of the population and national economy with water, and water resources protection against pollution and depletion in the interests of present and future generations is envisaged in the "Guidlines for economic and social development of the USSR for 1981-1985 and for the peried ending in 1990" and "Food Programme of the USSR".

In what way the main principle of water resources development — the multipurpose utilization of water reserves is realized in the USSR?

It is known that as a rule many water users representing the interests of the population and different branches of the national economy are interested in the utilization of the same water body.

Water legislation of the USSR strictly controls the rights and obligations of different categories of water users and ensures simultaneous satisfaction of interests of different branches of the national economy.

This makes it possible to provide for the first priority need of the population in water for drinking and domestic purposes. Comprehensive use of water resources is supposed to be in close interconnection with the utilization

---

* By G.S.Urvantsev, Chief specialist, Section of the territorial redistribution and multipurpose use of water resources V/O "Soyuzvodproject" of the Ministry of Land Reclamation and Water Management of the USSR.

X. U.S.S.R.

and conservation of other natural resources (land, forests, fishery, etc.).

For optimum development of water economy and determination of components, composition of water management projects, the schemes of multipurpose utilization and water conservation are being prepared for each river basin; special scientific studies of the river basins are carried out.

General (for the whole country) scheme of multipurpose utilization and water conservation is the basis for future planning of water economy development. At present, the elaboration of the general scheme for the perspective up to 25-30 years is under preparation. There are basin schemes for the largest rivers of the country, including such river basins as the Volga, Dnieper, Amu Darya, Syr Darya, West Dvina, Kuban, Ural, Terek, Desna and others.

The USSR possesses considerable water resources and takes second place in the world (4.7 thou. km^3) on the availability of the surface runoff. However, the water resources on the territory of the country are distributed very unevenly. This predetermines the scale of water economy development. Besides, water withdrawal from natural water bodies is increasing. In 1975 the total withdrawal of water in the USSR was up 294 km^3/year. By 1982 it increased up to 344 km^3, including consumptive use of water up to 200 km^3. From the total water withdrawal 30 km^3 was groundwater (1).

The main water consumers are: agriculture with irrigation farming (195 km^3/year), industry, and water supply for domestic use (125 km^3/year).

The main water users are: hydropower, water transport, fishery farming, recreation.

Rational consumption of water resources is of great importance in the USSR. For this purpose a number of measures are taken (rating of water consumption, creation of the recycling and recirculated water systems, introduction of partially or completely wasteless technology, measures of economic stimulation etc.), allowing to reduce essentially water consumption per unit of production.

Unequality of the surface water distribution and the growth of water consumption require the implementation of great water economy programmes.

By present time there are over 2.2 thousand water reservoirs under operation in the country with the total volume of water about 870 km^3 (2).

The volume of the territorial redistribution of flow reaches 60 km^3/year in the USSR. For this aim there

were and are under construction the canals of long run and large carrying capacity. Among them there are such water ways as the Karakum canal, the Amu-Bukhara canal, the Karshi canal, the Large Fergana canal, the Nevinnomysk canal, the Stavropol canal, the Irtysh-Karaganda canal, the Dnieper-Donbass canal, the North Crimean canal and others.

Southern region of the country feels the deficit of water. Replenishment of water resources in the basins of the Caspian Sea and Aral Sea will be made at the expense of water resources of the Pechora, Onega, Sukhona and Onega lake. Basins of the Dnieper and Dniester will be replenished by the flow of the Danube.

The Ob river will be used in future for the replenishment of water resources in Central Asia and Kazakhstan.

Preparatory work is started to transfer a part of the northern rivers flow into the basins of the Volga and Don. The work is also continued on scientific and design studies for water transfer from the Siberian rivers into Central Asia and Kazakhstan.

To increase available water resources within the current Five-Year period the construction of large hydraulic works, canals and water reservoirs is being carried out.

The work proceeded in Central Asia on the Rogun and Kzyl-Ayak headworks, the Zeyda water reservoir on the Karakum canal.

The construction of the Large Stavropol canal is continued in the Northern Caucasus. Construction of the Saratov and Kuibyshev canals is carried out in Povolzhye! The work is in progress in the south of the Ukraine on the construction of the Kakhovka and Danube-Dniester irrigation systems, the Dnieper-Donbass and the North-Crimean canals.

Constructions of the large hydroelectric stations are being carried out on the rivers of Siberia, Far East and Central Asia.

It should be noted that among the measures aimed at further improvement of water resources use there are those which were adopted within the last years in the USSR, such as rating of water consumption and diversion, and introduction of payment for water by the industrial enterprises. Water tariffs for industrial water consumers are higher than for the budgetary organizations and population, who pay for water at reduced tariffs.

1. I.I.Borodavchenko et al. "Multipurpose use and conservation of water resources", Moskva, Kolos, 1983.

2. I.I.Borodavchenko, V.I.Mikhura "The experience of water resources use and conservation in the USSR". M., CBNTI Minvodkhoza SSSR, 1981.

3. N.F.Vasiliev "Food programme of the USSR and the tasks of irrigators", zh. "Gidrotekhnika i melioratsiya", No8, 1982.

4. Certain problems of land improvement in the USSR, Moskva, Kolos, 1975.

5. I.I.Borodavchenko "Main trends of the USSR engineering policy in the field of multipurpose use and conservation of water resources (Report on the UN Conference on water resources). Argentine, March 1977, Moskva, 1977, prospekt VDNH.

X.C. IRRIGATION FARMING IN CENTRAL ASIA AND IT'S EFFECTIVENESS*

Since the ancient times human history has been closely connected with the development of water resources and irrigation. Egypt, Mesopotamia, India, Central Asia, China, the Middle East, Maya and Inca states in America — all centres of ancient civilizations were located in the zones of the irrigation development. The necessity of construction and maintenance of irrigation systems and canals promoted scientific, social and economic development and formation of statehood.

At present irrigation in the world is reviving to its second life, which is supported by the mere fact that during the last 50 years (a very short period in human history) the world irrigation areas increased more than twice. This trend is also true for our country. Irrigation development now takes place not only in the traditional arid zone, but also in some areas of humid zone. Peculiarities of modern environmental and economic conditions in arid zones considerably complicate irrigation development due to the growing water deficit, soaring cost of water supply and also due to the decrease of the potential land capability. In this connection efficiency of the irrigation farming and related water management system in arid zones becomes the top priority problem.

High socio-economic effectiveness of the water management system (WMS) development on the basis of the irrigation farming and its role as a regional economy development factor can be traced well in Central Asia and especially in Uzbekistan.

The most important factors of the irrigation development are: favourable climatic and soil conditions, good hydrogeological conditions (until recently) for agricultural development, considerable rates of growth of labour resources, low migration capability and considerable stability of rural population. Another important development factor is the traditional experience of the rural

population in the irrigation farming which has a record of many centuries. One should also add here available power generation potential of water streams and considerable prospected and partially used oil resources, natural gas, brown coal etc. The Central Asian hydropower potential is reaching 110 billion kwh (generation capacity) and 27 mill. kwh (power capacity), which make correspondingly 13.2 and 13.5 per cent of the national resources. The current use of these potentials is 27 per cent.

Apart from considerable resources of carbonate and hydrocarbon raw materials in the Central Asia there is excellent condition for the development of processing industry on the basis of irrigation farming and the whole WMS (cotton processing, light industry, textiles, cannery, food), agricultural machine building (machinery for cotton growing, irrigation farming, hydraulic engineering, cotton processing, etc.), chemical industry on the basis of oil and gas and also different kinds of vegetable raw materials, including cotton and rice production wastes, etc. Considerable labour resources as well as resources of oil and gas promote development of high power consuming industries with the full scope of production stages.

Availability of cotton fibre and its derivatives in combination with the development of synthetic fibre will promote production of knitted fabric, mixed fabric, mixed rubber, etc. At the same time intensive agriculture, gas and mineral raw materials promote the development of fertilizer production. The only limiting factor for the development of chemical and several other industries is their high water consumption.

Tables 115 and 116 show the increase in the irrigation areas and agricultural production in the republics of the arid zone compared to the average values on the national basis.

This comparison shows that in terms of specific growth rates gross agricultural production on the basis of irrigation in arid zone outnumbers more than twice the average national values, which in general corresponds to and is

---

* By V.A. Dukhovny SANIIRI (Central Asian Research Institute of Irrigation).

Table 115. Increase in the irrigation areas in the republics of Central Asia and Kazakhstan,* (thou. ha) per cent of the background level of 1913

No	Republic	Years							
		1913	1940	1950	1960	1965	1970	1975	1980
1.	Uzbekistan	1 339	2 008	2 122	2 665	2 575	2 751	3 006	3 407
		100	150	161	199	192	205	220	254
2.	Tadjikistan	211	325	336	391	468	518	567	605
		100	154	159	185	228	245	269	288
3.	Turkmenia	307	373	385	434	514	643	855	942
		100	121	116	141	167	209	279	307
4.	Kirgiziya	425	794	797	834	861	883	911	975
		100	175	175	183	189	194	200	214
5.	Kazakhstan	696	994	1 194	1 482	1 368	1 451	1 630	1 930
		100	143	172	213	197	208	234	277
	Total	2 978	4 494	4 864	5 806	5 786	6 246	6 959	7 861
		100	151	163	195	194	210	234	264
	Total for the USSR	3 973	6 087	7 382	9 843	9 897	11 100	14 486	17 487
		100	153	197	247	249	279	365	440

* Before 1960-data from "Water Management Manual" Moscow, GIPROVODKHOZ, 1962, the rest – from "National Economy of the USSR" (reference book), 1980, Moscow, USSR Central Statistical Department. (in Russian).

Table 116. Increase in gross agricultural production in mill. roubles/per cent of the background level of 1913, prices of 1955

No	Republic	Years							
		1913	1940	1950	1960	1965	1970**)	1975	1980
1.	Uzbekistan	636	1 145	1 551	2 238	2 754	3 472	4 062	5 277
		100	180	244	352	433	546	637	830
2.	Tadjikistan	105	260	271	438	623	771	928	1 107
		100	248	258	417	593	735	883	1 054
3.	Turkmenia	141	209	296	398	499	691	845	1 005
		100	148	210	282	354	490	599	712
4.	Kirgiziya	161	316	353	576	742	911	1 094	1 194
		100	196	220	358	461	566	680	742
5.	Kazakhstan	893	928	1 402	3 955	3 652	5 670	5 199	7 204
		100	104	157	443	409	635	582	813
	Total:	1 936	2 858	3 873	7 605	8 270	11 515	12 128	15 787
		100	148	200	393	427	594	626	815
	Total for the USSR	28 182	39 737	39 455	63 128	71 019	87 082	90 675	98 070
		100	141	140	224	252	309	321	348

** before 1970 – data from "National Economy of the USSR" (Russ.) 1922-1972, Moscow Statistics, 1972.

after 1980 – data from "National Economy of USSR" (Russ.) 1980.

determined by the increase in the irrigation areas. From the other side this growth is followed by the increase in water intake from all sources (Table 117), though they do not correspond in rates.

The sharp increase in total and specific water consumption between 1960-1970 can be explained on one side by the considerable increase in non-irrigation water uses and on the other side by the increase in water consumption for each irrigated hectare. The latter is explained by the development of new lands with less favourable properties and also by the construction of major drainage network during this decade (Kara Kalpak ASSR, Tedjen and Murgab systems, Bukhara, Arys-Turkestan and Kyzylkum systems) which intensified the leaching irrigation practice. However, the increase in gross agricultural production due to the increase of the irrigation areas, productivity in this zone outnumbered the increase in total water consumption in the arid zone by 1.5-2 times, which in the final account raised the use efficiency not only of land but also of water resources in the republics of Central Asia and Kazakhstan.

Irrigation efficiency is expressed in terms of social and economic progress not only in the irrigation farming itself, but also in the progress of the whole WMS where irrigation is playing the leading role.

The example of Uzbekistan clearly shows how development of WMS promotes development of new economy branches. WMS and irrigation farming are connected with nearly all economy branches. Some branches are classified as water consumers (metallurgy, chemistry, etc.), the others are classified as water users (fishery, hydropower and thermal power production), the third group includes industries serving water management (water resources engineering, hydraulic engineering), and irrigation farming (production of agricultural machinery, mineral fertilizers part of the chemical industry); finally considerable number of industries are involved in processing the products of irrigation farming, both primary and secondary processing (cotton processing, majority of branches of the light and food industries), thus creating possibilities for further processing of the irrigation farming products, for example: processing of cotton and rice stems in the branches of chemical and microbiological industries (production of furan resin, phenylic acid, olefin and other valuable products).

Table 118 shows that general specific share of the branches based on and connected with WMS makes in agriculture 95-96.7 per cent, in industry 47.3-77.8 per cent, in construction 36.1-48.2 per cent, and in general is at the level of 50 per cent of the whole gross product in the republic. The agricultural share remains stable and seems to remain at the level of 95 per cent in future, in construction — one can expect it at the level of 40-44 per cent,

and in industry, taking into consideration development of chemical industry, oil production, mining, and planned low water-consuming precision machine-building, the share will decrease to 40 per cent.

These examples show considerable impact caused by the development of WMS on the progress of all the regions and the republic in general.

One should also mention great actual effectiveness of WMS development both in social and economic aspects, which can be illustrated by the experience of Uzbekistan.

Here calculations are based on the formula of T.S. Khatchaturov

$$\frac{1}{T_{ok}} = \frac{m + \overline{m} + V}{\varphi + K}$$

where

T_{ok}	—	payback period
m	—	income
$\overline{m}$	—	turnover tax share
V	—	salary
K	—	investments

or in our modification, value V is replaced with social effect in the form of the increment of per capita consumption share of the total national income.

$$\frac{1}{T_{ok}} = \frac{m + \overline{m} + \Delta \ni o}{\varphi + K} \qquad (1^1)$$

where

$\Delta \ni o$	—	social effect;
φ	—	capital reimbursement funds.

Capital funds include reimbursement funds of WMS, including irrigation farming, water management and engineering, hydropower production. Attended capital funds, as well as the incomes of the branches connected with WMS, considered on a share basis, determined by the matrix coefficient of the interbranch connections: for light industry K = 0.41, for food industry — 0.32, for others — 0.16.

We have proposed to consider social effect in terms of the increase in population welfare, determined as a change of per capita consumption share of the national income multiplied by the quantity of population in the zone influenced by WMS. Here the change of specific national

Table 117. Increase in water intake in the republics of Central Asia and Kazakhstan, cu. km

No	Republic	Years				
		1940	1960	1970	1975	1980
1.	Uzbekistan	26.2	30.78	53.2	46.3	58.3
2.	Tad/jikis/tan	7.3	10.08	14.4	14.1	15.5
3.	Turkmenia	6.2	8.07	17.27	22.84	23.0
4.	Kirgiziya	4.8	5.21	9.59	10.17	10.7
5.	Kazakhstan	7.8	9.75	37.85	33.21	39.2
	Total	52.3	63.89	132.3	126.62	146.7
	in per cent	100	122.1	253	241	280
	Growth of irrigation areas	100	129.2	139	155	175
	Growth of gross agricultural prod/uction		266	402	424	552

Table 118. Economic development of Uzbekistan compared to the branches connected with WMS
(comparable prices, 1955)

No	Industry	Unit	Years				
			1940	1960	1970	1975	1980
1.	Industry, total incl. connected with WMS	bill. roubl.	3.6	13.8	30.6	46.21	58.75
	a) Power generation	roubl.	0.03	0.41	1.04	1.88	1.98
	b) Chemical Industry	roubl.	0.02	0.21	0.70	1.32	1.74
	c) Agr.machinery building	roubl.	0.01	0.18	0.54	0.95	1.04
	d) Constr. materials production*	roubl.	0.05	0.11	0.280	0.44	0.52
	e) Light industry	roubl.	1.97	4.61	9.36	12.26	14.13
	f) Food production	roubl.	0.74	2.02	4.28	6.46	8.38
	Total, connected with WMS	roubl.	2.8	7.93	16.2	23.31	27.79
		per cent	77.8	57.6	52.9	50.4	47.3
	Growth rate by 1940			283	578	832	992
2.	Agriculture, total	mill. roubl.	1 145	2 238	3 472	4 062	5 277
	incl. connected with WMS	roubl.	1 090	2 166	3 354	3 910	5 026
		per cent	95	96.7	96.6	96.2	95.2
	Growth rate by 1940		100	198	307	358	460
3.	Construction, total investments	mill. roubl.	202	934	3 085	4 629	5 461
	incl. connected with WMS	roubl.	73	432	1 260	2 060	2 435
		per cent	36.1	46.2	4 038	4 832	44.5
	Growth rate by 1940		100	591	1 726	2 822	3 336

* The figure is only for that part of industry connected with WMS.

Sources: National Economy of the USSR, 1972. National Economy of the USSR, 1980. National Economy of Uzbek SSR, 1975-1980 (in Russian).

income ($H \bar{\Delta}$) goes on proportionally to the change of labour efficiency per 1 man (Πpt).

$$\frac{H\bar{\Delta}t}{H\Delta t-1} = \frac{\Pi p t}{\Pi p t - 1} \quad (2)$$

In this case social effect for the whole population in the region, changing from lt_{t-1} to lt with consumption share "d" will make:

$$\Delta \ni o = H\bar{\Delta}_{t-1} \frac{(Vt.lt_1 - Vt - 1.lt)\, d.\,(lt - lt - 1)}{2V_{t-1}.lt}$$

here V_t and V_{t-1} — corresponding to gross annual production "t", "t−1".

Considering all these factors, effectiveness of the development of WMS on the basis of irrigation farming and

related branches (see Table 119) is expressed in 5 year pay back period (IX five year plan) and 6 year pay back period (X five year plan).

The efficiency of the irrigation development in arid zone can be illustrated by the example of irrigation development in Golodnaya steppe (Hungry desert), started 27 years ago.

Firstly, about pure economic efficiency. By 1.1.1981 all investments into the new zone of Golodnaya steppe (developed area is 326 thou.ha) made 2639 mill. roubles or 8095 roubles/ha. Reimbursement funds made 1970 mill. roubles or 6035 roubles/ha. Total income received in construction, agriculture, industry and other branches was at such level that investments into Golodnaya steppe development were returned back already in 1972. It should be mentioned that the greater effectiveness was reached in 1970-1972, when pure annual income was 66-68 million

Table 119. Effectiveness of the functioning of economy branches connected with WMS in Uzbekistan

No	Items	Units	Years		
			1970	1975	1980
1.	Capital funds of the branches connected with or included into WMS	mill. roubl.	7 370.9	12 747.9	18 547.8
	industry	roubl.	2 240.1	3 638.9	4 605.1
	construction	roubl.	402.8	787	1 078.1
	agriculture	roubl.	4 728	8 322	12 864
2.	Total annual income irrigation	roubl.	195.7	81.0	90.2
	hydropower production	roubl.	33.0	42	40
	income share of branches connected with WMS	roubl.	95.4	207.7	134.9
	light industry	roubl.	57.6	160.0	97.4
	food industry	roubl.	29.5	36.2	36.0
	other branches K = 0.16	roubl.	8.92	11.5	7.52
4.	Total income during design period	roubl.	1 449.5		1 284.5
5.	Turnover tax share	roubl.	9 983.6		11 977.1
6.	Reimbursement funds for period	roubl.	6 991.2		7 540
7.	Salary in WMS branches during the period	roubl.	108.5		106.0
7.[a]	National income* in consumption share by the beginning of period	roubl.	2 427.8	2 763	3 141.5
7.[I]	Increment of social effect	mill. roubl.	1 432		1 879
8.	Effect by formula 1			0.181	0.134
8.[I]	Ditto, formula 1.7	roubl.		0.202	0.163

* Per able-bodied man

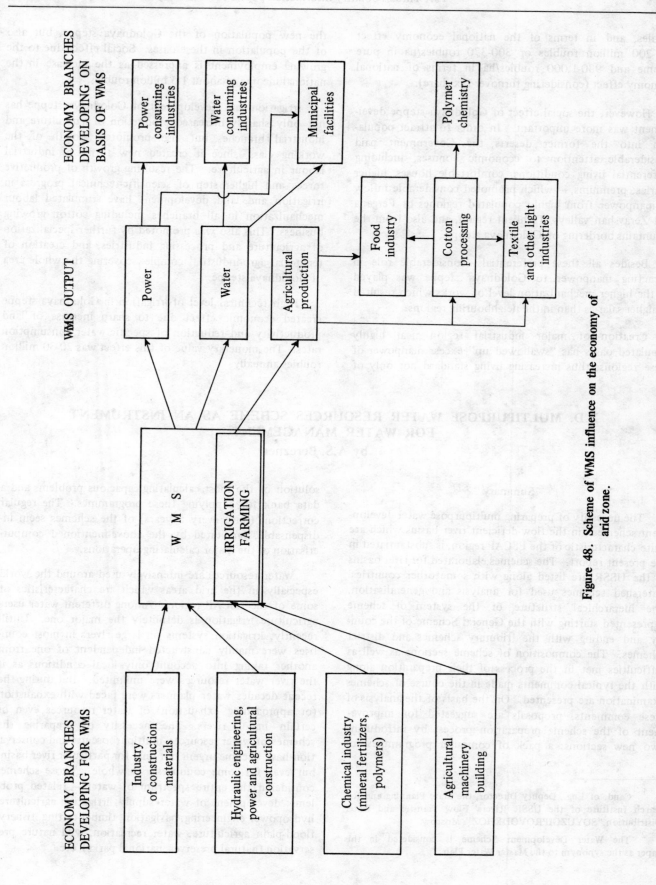

Figure 48. Scheme of WMS influence on the economy of arid zone.

roubles, and in terms of the national economy effect 170-200 million roubles or 300-370 roubles/ha in pure income and 930-1,000 roubles/ha in terms of national economy effect (considering turnover tax share).

However, the social effect of Golodnaya steppe development was more important. In order to attract population into the former deserts, the Government paid considerable attention to economic bonuses, including preferential living conditions, comfortable houses, higher salaries; premiums, — which promoted considerable inflow of manpower from highly populated regiones of Fergana and Zeravshan valleys, Tashkent region, and also from the mountains bordering on Golodnaya steppe.

Besides all these preferentials, considerable role in attracting manpower to Golodnaya steppe was played by the higher mechanization level of works which resulted in higher salaries than in the neighbouring regions.

Creation of major industrial region near highly populated oases has "swallowed up" excess manpower of these regions, thus increasing living standard not only of

the new population of the Golodnaya steppe, but also of the population in these oases. Social effect due to the growing employment is expressed as the increase in the national income of about 1.5 billion roubles.

Irrigation and development of Golodnaya steppe has not only sharply increased production of agriculture and industrial branches but also promoted growth of the working class, since it created new forms of industrial labour in agriculture. The resulting growth of productive forces and higher step of scientific-technical progress in irrigation and land development have stimulated labour mechanization in all branches including cotton growing business. This also was promoted by further specialization of agriculture and processing industries, and creation of territorial agro-industrial complex covering the whole area of Golodnaya steppe.

High technical level of irrigation in Golodnaya steppe created economic effect due to sharp increase of land productivity and reduction of specific water consumption rates. The monetary value of this effect was 20-30 million roubles annually.

X.D. MULTIPURPOSE WATER RESOURCES SCHEME AS AN INSTRUMENT FOR WATER MANAGEMENT
by A.S. Berezner[1]

Summary

The necessity of preparing multipurpose water development schemes[2] in the flow-deficient river basins which are quite characteristic of the ESCAP region, is substantiated in the present report. The schemes elaborated for river basins in the USSR are listed along with some other countries' watershed schemes used for analysis and generalisation. The hierarchical structure of the system of scheme is presented starting with the General Scheme of the country and ending with the tributary schemes and district schemes. The composition of scheme sections as well as difficulties met in the process of their preparation along with the typical comments made in the course of schemes examination are presented. On the basis of the analysis of these comments, proposals are suggested for improvement of the scheme preparation process by introducing two new sections: a pack of computer programmes for

solution of the most calculating-capacious problems and a data bank for supplying these programmes. The regular corrections (once every 5 years) of the schemes seem indispensable, facilitated by the above-mentioned computerisation of the major calculating operations.

Water resources are intensively used around the world especially in the arid areas which are characteristics of some of the ESCAP region. Among different water users agriculture irrigation is definitely the major one. Untill recently, irrigation systems on large rivers in most countries were mainly constructed independent of one from another taking into account only local conditions as if the river water resources were unlimited. But during the recent decades water planners were faced with exhaustion (or approaching exhaustion) of water resources even of certain major rivers. The necessity of preparing the schemes of water resources, multipurpose use and conservation have become urgent not only for particular river basins but even for some countries as a whole. Those schemes considered the entire spectrum of water — related problems: development of water supply, irrigation agriculture, hydropower engineering, navigation, timber-rafting, fishery, flood-plain agriculture, water recreation, wild nature preservation (natural preserves, national parks), etc.

---

[1] Cand. of Eng., Deputy Director, the State Planning and Research Institute of the USSR Rivers' Flow Transfer and Water Distribution "SOYUZGIPROVODKHOZ", Moscow.

[2] The Water Development Scheme is considered in this paper as the synonym to the Master Water Plan.

Though the appearance of the first water resources schemes dates back to 1950's-1960's, the process of their elaboration followed its own evolutionary way during the fairly short period of time. The most important point of this evolution was the transfer from *schemes of use to schemes of use and conservation* of water resources.

A number of multipurpose water development and conservation schemes were prepared in the Soviet Union during the last decades for the river basins which are known as watersheds already suffering from or being on the verge of water deficient and therefore urgent reservoir creation or water transfer are a must in these river basins. Among the most significant basin development schemes already prepared, mention should be made of those for the Volga, Don, Dnieper, Zapadnaya Dvina, Kuban, Terek, Sulak, Ural, Kura, Ob, Irtysh, Syrdarya, Amudarya, Amur river basins, as well as schemes for their major tributaries such as Oka, Desna, Chusovaya. The regional natural resources development and conservation schemes (including water resources studies) were elaborated for coastal areas of the Azov, Baltic and Black seas (within the USSR territory), of the Baikal, Sevan and Issyk-Kul lakes. In 1967 the first version of the USSR Water Resources Development and Conservation General Scheme was prepared and since then it has been subject to regular up-dating every 5 to 10 years. The river basin schemes for Sri Lanka were worked out with the participation of Soviet experts on the basis of economic, scientific and technological co-operation.

In the present paper some recommendations are discussed derived from USSR experience in the field of preparation of water resources schemes. These recommendations are considered suitable for the conditions in many other regions in the world. Thus, the ideas presented in the paper could be to some extent efficiently used in the practical activity of water resources authorities of the ESCAP countries.

Schemes of multipurpose water resources use and conservation are an important element of the Integrated System of water use planning in the USSR. The varieties of the schemes are specified in the "Fundamentals of Water Legislation of the USSR and Union Republics" approved by the USSR Supreme Soviet in 1971. The Legislation envisages working out general, basin and regional schemes of multipurpose water resources use and conservation which are necessary to determine water resources developments and accompanying measures aimed at meeting water requirements of the population and branches of the national economy, conservation of water and related ecological systems and prevention of harmful effects of water.

Irrigation agriculture is a major water consumer in water resources schemes prepared for the river basins of the arid zones. The development scale of this water consumer depends not only on the water resources but on land conditions, availability of lands suitable for irrigation, etc. In context, land and water resources are considered to be organically interrelated.

Elaborating the water resources scheme is mainly aimed at preparing the basis for planning the development of the "water management" branch of national economy for future 5-10-15 year periods, closely connected with the dynamics of the branch for the remote horizon. This basic objective is achieved through realization of a number of objectives of the lower level which are: determination of the proportions for developing major water consumers and the constraints for spatial distribution of water-intensive branches of the economy or for use of different technologies of water consumption or water disposal proposals for construction of new water resource systems and projects needed to ensure the estimated water consumption providing the sufficient period for design, research and construction jobs; planning the measures to prevent water quality deterioration below the admissible levels; determination of capital investments necessary for fulfilling the proposed water resources management and conservation, as well as of sectoral capital investments to develop major water consumers, including the share in water management costs, substantiation of effeciency of these capital investments.

Water resources schemes are one of the vital elements governing technological progress in the sphere of water use and conservation. Thus, when developing the schemes, provision is being steadily made for implementing the basic principles to ensure:

1. constant reduction of specific water consumption rates per unit of produce;

2. introduction of waterless and low-water technologies;

3. reduction of water disposal and wastewater discharge to water bodies; maximum use of recycling systems, closed industrial cycles, wastewater re-use;

4. multipurpose water resources use;

5. localization and compensation of harmful effects of water (i.e. erosion, floods, mudflows);

6. water quality control in water sources;

7. improvement of efficiency of capital investments in water management;

8. improvement of the structure, forms and techniques of water management.

Long-term experience gained in working out water resource schemes permitted the establishment of the most favourable succession of sections of the scheme which are as under:

a. the forecast of the national economy development in a basin (only major water-intensive branches being included);

b. water consumption and water disposal by the national economy branches; integrated water use; requirements placed by the branches upon river discharges;

c. assesment of water resources;

d. water budgets;

e. proposals for water developments to eliminate water shortages (flow regulation by reservoirs and water transfers);

f. the problem of inland seas and lakes;

g. control of harmful effects of water;

h. water quality: present state and forecasts; measures to maintain water quality at the required level;

i. capital investments in water developments and their efficiency;

j. programme of research, design and surveying activities necessary for accomplishing the proposed measures.

Let us dwell upon the peculiar features of each of the above sections and the main difficulties to be encountered by authors of the schemes.

Generally speaking, the forecast of national economy development should not be elaborated as a section of the scheme since it should be considered as a basis for compiling the water resources scheme. As far as the countries with centrally planned economy are concerned this forecast rests upon five-year plans of economic and social development of the country and upon proposals for the productive forces development for the remote future prepared by various design and research institutions. The elements of planning based on the five-year principle are being introduced in many countries with market economies. In such countries water resources use and conservation occupy one of the leading places among the spheres of economy controlled by the State.

Basin schemes require that detailed elaboration be made of the development indices which are usually available for the whole country and large regions, dis-

integrating them to district or even lower level. This work is in the line of special planning institutions. The major difficulty is that detailed forecasts are usually available for a period not longer than 15-20 years. It is obvious that such horizons are insufficient for water management planning since water resources systems should be designed to serve in the remote future. This implies knowledge of the parameters to be attained as a result of extending the structures. In this case of special importance is forecasting the development of the most water-intensive branch, i.e. irrigation agriculture which comprises nearly 70-75 per cent of consumptive use increments in the USSR.

Of all the indices of the productive forces development, the size of population is best forecasted. The theory of this problem is elaborated thoroughly enough. That is why a 20-year forecast with accuracy up to 5-10 per cent can be made for the countries known to have low population growth rates. Greater deviations are possible while forecasting the development of the economy branches.

Water consumption forecasting is a function of the national economic development indices (discussed earlier) and of specific rates of water consumption and disposal, i.e., per unit of produce; per unit of area, etc. Water consumption rates should consider and they do consider technological progress including the one for a remote period when there appear technologies even not known at present. There exist different methods of forecasting the technology changes, the most popular of which are extrapolation — especially for a short period of 10-15 years, the method of expertise, of patent analysis, etc.

Serious difficulty arises when establishing consumptive use rates in municipal services and in industry. It is to be pointed out that as far as these branches are concerned the volume of water with-drawal is normally measured by pump capacity, while the volume of water wastes is not always measured. This results in the fact that in the schemes, the industrial and public consumptive use is determined by means of calculations while assessment values made by various authors differ sometimes significantly. As for irrigation agriculture, account of water withdrawal and discharge — though imperfect — has found wide application.

The elements of water disposals to be calculated in the scheme comprise both volume of wastes and quantities of major pollutants.

Available water resources assessment requires that rather long hydrometric observations be carried out. While preparing the schemes, use is made of series of river flows records for a period not shorter than 25-30 years — sometimes up to 100 years — averaged by one month intervals with the exception of a flood period when an interval is accepted to equal 10 days. Flow series are calculated for major design river sections selected for the scheme, usually for mouths of tributaries and sites of major reservoirs. Additionally, water resources involve ground water which is not connected with the surface flow. When ground water of all horizons is hydraulically interconnected, its resources, independent of the surface flow, are formed resulting from the lowering of water table. This allows for temporarily obtaining an additional water flow. This portion of ground water resources is generally insignificant. One of the principal objectives of water resources schemes is verification of this share.

Water resources comprise water importation from adjacent basin to the given one while water consumption accounts for water transfer from the given river beyond its basin.

In basin schemes, water budgets are prepared with regard for selected sections on the major river and its tributaries. As for main river sections, water budgets are made using many-year series of both inflow and water consumption. Public and industrial water consumption is usually accepted as being the same from year to year, within a design series, while that of irrigation agriculture and evaporation from reservoirs are assumed to change depending on weather conditions of the particular years within a design series with yearly variations similar to river flow variations. As for certain sites of lesser importance for the scheme for which water budgets are made only to control water quality, they are computed for a critical month of the typical year of 95 per cent probability (p = 95 per cent). The results of budget calculations for a long series are represented as yearly summaries for an average, low-water (p = 75 per cent) and extremely low-water (p = 95 per cent) years.

Water budgets in the schemes are made in two stages. At first water resources deficits are revealed in the absence of the measures proposed by the scheme. Then calculations are repeated for cases when the appropriate measures are provided, i.e., additional regulating reservoirs, water transfers. If water resources are limited, the priority of water consumption by different branches given below is usually accepted. The figures in brackets show the guaranteed degree of:

1. public water supply   (97-100%)
2. industrial water supply   (95-97%)
3. sanitary releases   (95%)
4. guaranteed hydropower station
   parameters   (95%)
5. pond fishery   (95%)
6. navigation releases   (85-95%)

7. irrigation   (75-90%)
8. spawning releases for different
   fish species   (50-90%)
9. releases to seas and lakes   (50-75%)

The major kinds of water developments proposed in the schemes are divided into:

a. refusing allocation of some proposed water intensive enterprises, refinement (decreasing) of the capacities of others;

b. employment of more economical water consumption technologies;

c. improvement of wastewater treatment;

d. flow regulation by reservoirs;

e. water transfers.

Problems of inland seas and lakes arise when water abstraction from rivers is responsible for the decrease of water levels or the increase of water salinity in water bodies which these rivers enter. These problems are specific for each particular case and are to be specially considered.

The section dealing with harmful effects of water has no close connection with other materials of the scheme. This makes it easier to prepare the section. The problem of erosion being typical of most basins, destructive floods and mudflows occur only on some rivers.

Water quality is one of the key problems in each scheme, requiring, as a rule, nearly 1/3 of intellectual resources for its preparation. The data for this section are also employed in the sections "Water Budgets", "Water Consumption", and even "Forecasts of National Economic Development" where water quality calculations permit the improvement of allocating the promising industries which discharge wastewater (even somewhat treated) and consequently the refinement of the volumes of water consumption and sanitary releases. When working out the water quality forecast, provision is made for a series of alternative calculations to get satisfactory results with the admissible capital investments.

The section dealing with capital investments and their efficiency is the most important one for applying the results of the scheme for water management planning.

The technology of preparation of schemes of all categories has a number of common features which are as under:

i) Iterativity of scheme preparation process when upon obtaining the results of water budgets and water quality forecast they refine the national economic development indices in a basin or region (country); technology of water consumption and water disposal; composition of water projects. With new data available, budget calculations and water quality forecasts are repeated.

ii) Consideration of alternatives for solving the schemes concerning both development rates of productive forces and water consumption technology, as well as composition of water resources management and conservation projects.

iii) Examination of the present and future water management conditions with reference to fixed time horizons: the present level corresponds to the final year of the previous five-year plan period prior to issuing the scheme; the design perspective – every 5 years within the 15-20 year period; the remote future – every 10 years for the next 20-year period. The studies meant for the distant future are made as very rough estimates.

The standards established in the USSR contemplate examination of the schemes by groups of experts formed at various levels, from the republican ministry of land reclamation and water management to the USSR State Planning Committee. Conclusions of these groups are of great importance for analysing the major disadvantages of compiling the schemes and preparing the suggestions to improve the technologies of this important job.

Omitting some special problems, some typical experts' comments can be offered.

Most comments indicate that the forecasts of the national economic development inherent in the studies are getting sometimes out-of-date in the process of elaboration, co-ordination and examination of schemes, while development indices may be overestimated. The latter is explained by the fact that forecasts for a distant future are often prepared by generalizing the studies submitted by different sectoral ministries and district planning authorities which do not always consider availability of resources for the entire country. Adjusting these suggestions to the growth rates attained in the past, authors of the schemes introduce – at their own risk – reduction coefficients, but sometimes these are insufficient. Accuracy of forecasts decreases sharply when overestimating the development rates of such a water-intensive branch as irrigation agriculture.

The experts' comments on water consumption calculations often pertain to inadequate consideration of technological progress while establishing water rates per unit of produce for the future. As far as irrigation agriculture is concerned, the experts group wishes to hasten the transition to more economical – from the viewpoint of water consumption – irrigation systems and techniques, i.e. drip, subsurface and mist irrigation.

Concerning the section "Water Resources", lack of classification was sometimes pointed out between ground water resources connected with the surface flow and those not connected. As for the section "Water Budgets", comments occur on non-representativeness of calculations with the use of the so-called "typical years" (instead of calculations, using a rather long series of years), lack of justification for design probability of water application rates (i.e., drought frequency for which irrigation canals, pipelines and pumping stations are designed), insufficient number of examined alternatives of water resources management and distribution of water among the branches of the national economy.

Many comments are often received for the section dealing with water quality. The most typical of them are: incompleteness of water pollution assessment and forecast frequently accounting for only pollutants resulting from industry and municipal services, omitting such polluters as agriculture (washing away fertilizers and chemicals from fields, drainage water), urban stormwater, navigation. Some comments refer to underestimation of capital investments in treatment facilities, lack of alternative comparison of capital investments and water purity under different degrees of water treatment. No assessment is sometimes given of the content of pollutants after implementation of water conservation measures envisaged by the Governmental Acts already approved.

As for the economic sections of the schemes, insufficient justification of adopted solutions is sometimes pointed out. While assessing various alternatives of water developments, not all consequences of the proposed construction are represented in economic terms, even if it is possible. This makes the comparison of alternatives incomplete.

Of the above disadvantages of the schemes frequently emphasized by the experts, the most serious are: discrepancy between the applied national economic development forecasts and modern notings of insufficient alternative studies pertaining ot both water budgets and water quality forecasts. Very urgent is, therefore, the requirement for renewal of the major indices for the schemes after the completion of each five-year plan period and verification of plans for the next five-year period.

To overcome the above main disadvantages it is necessary to radically cut down the time of scheme preparation, on the one hand, and to increase the volume of calculations, on the other. The requirements are incompatible, at first glance. Thus, to meet both categories of the requirements, there is only one way out: to revise the technology of working out the schemes, changing – to a maximum – manual operations for computer calculations. Such technology of scheme elaboration is being partially introduced at the Soyuzgiprovodkhoz Institute.

The main idea of the technology suggested is to include two new sections, making them an integral part of the scheme, namely: (1) system of mathematical models with computer programmes to calculate all labour-consuming sections of the scheme and (2) data bank to be approved to make calculations in the present stage of consideration. The introduction of these sections does not increase the total volume of the scheme. On the contrary, it permits the reduction of the volume of other sections.

Mathematical models are developed for types of calculations which require much time if the scheme is prepared manually. These calculations comprise water budget studies, optimization calculations and estimations in the sphere of mathematical statistics and the probability theory.

The following models have been worked out and are being employed in the schemes at the Soyuzgiprovodkhoz:

(1) Optimization of allocating agricultural production on irrigated, drained and rain-fed lands in the regions within the given requirements of production.

(2) Optimization of allocating the increments of reclaimed lands with the fixed levels of capital investments in reclamation.

(3) Processing the results of hydrometric observations.

(4) Calculating water consumption series of irrigation agriculture with reference to river sections with variations depending on meteorological conditions (similar to series of hydrometric observations).

(5) River water budget at selected sections when calculating for a series of years (employing individual models for each basin).

(6) Forecasts of salinity and water levels of inland seas (the Caspian and Azov Seas).

(7) Calculating fish productivity of an inland sea depending on outer factors.

(8) Forecasting the water quality in the river, considering the entry of pollutants and self-purification processes.

(9) Forecasting rise in the groundwater table in the zone of proposed canals and reservoirs.

(10) Search for optimal canal route with the given map of locality and boundary conditions.

(11) Optimization of the canal discharge and operation regime with due regard for proposed reservoirs along the canal route.

(12) Optimization of canal elevations along the chosen route.

(13) Calculating earthwork volumes for canals, slope stability and other engineering calculations.

(14) Economic assessment of alternatives with regard for discount factor.

Long-term experience gained in employing mathematical models in water developments allows stating that elaboration of mathematical models and computer programmes requires usually 10 times less intellectual resources than the data collection. That is why the formation of data bank in the schemes worked out in compliance with the new technology, should receive top priority.

The data bank should be used in the form of a volume containing the input data tables used in the schemes for the models employed. These tables should be thoroughly examined by the experts to approve some of the data, to change the other and to verify the third ones.

Summarizing the information actively used in the scheme, in a single volume, will permit to diminish the other volumes of the schemes through the exclusion from them of the data not used in the computer process.

Owing to the availability to the data bank, preparation and correction of the schemes can be compared with accounting statistical operations, thus promoting the creation of the Integrated System of the National Economy Management.

Conclusions

1. Under the present conditions when fresh water, in general, and especially clean water becomes practically a scarce resource everywhere, preparation of schemes of multipurpose use and conservation of water resources is a must for almost all countries. Such schemes are gaining importance in view of the necessity to take active steps for the environmental protection both at a national and global level. As far as the countries with the arid climate are concerned, water resources use and conservation are becoming a nation-wide problem. The water resources scheme should be considered as one of the main tools permitting the solution of the problem.

2. The principle of hierarchy forms the basis for working out such schemes. The country's General Scheme heads the hierarchical structure to be followed by basin schemes of major rivers, then by basin schemes of tributaries and, finally, by district schemes.

3. Working out the schemes is closely connected with plans (or forecasts) of the national economic development since practically all branches of industry and agriculture are water consumers and water users. On the other hand, the results obtained in the schemes can cause serious changes in the plans or forecasts.

4. It is essential that the schemes be reviewed every 5 years, after verification of accomplishment of a current five-year plan and determination of development indices for the next five-year pariod (for the countries with centrally planned or partially planned economy). To

ensure regular adjustment of the schemes, of great importance is elaboration of mathematical models for solving the most labour-consuming problems of the schemes (models of hydrological calculations, optimization of allocating water-intensive industries, water consumption of irrigation agriculture, water budget calculations, water quality models).

5. The experience of the USSR gained in working-out general, basin and territorial schemes of multipurpose water resources use and conservation can be employed to advantage in the countries of ESCAP region.